KNOWLEDGE AND VALUE

A Project of the
Department of Philosophy
BROOKLYN COLLEGE

Howard W. Hintz

CHAIRMAN AND CO-ORDINATING ADVISER

Walter Cerf

William A. Gerhard

John Hospers

Philip M. Kretschmann

Martin E. Lean

Julius Portnoy

Elmer Sprague

Paul W. Taylor

H. Van Rensselaer Wilson

Knowledge and Value

Introductory Readings in Philosophy

EDITED BY

Elmer Sprague

Paul W. Taylor

BROOKLYN COLLEGE

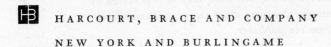 HARCOURT, BRACE AND COMPANY

NEW YORK AND BURLINGAME

Library of Congress Catalog Card Number: 59-6091

God offers to every mind its choice between truth and repose. Take which you please—you can never have both. Between these, as a pendulum, man oscillates. He in whom the love of repose predominates will accept the first creed, the first philosophy, the first political party he meets—most likely his father's. He gets rest, commodity and reputation; but he shuts the door of truth. He in whom the love of truth predominates will keep himself aloof from all moorings, and afloat. He will abstain from dogmatism, and recognize all the opposite negations between which, as walls, his being is swung. He submits to the inconvenience of suspense and imperfect opinion, but he is a candidate for truth, as the other is not, and respects the highest law of his being.

—RALPH WALDO EMERSON

Preface

The purpose of this book is twofold. First, it is designed to enable the reader to come to understand what philosophical problems are and how philosophers have thought about them. Second, it is intended to stimulate the reader himself to think philosophically about these problems. Each of the eight chapters in the book presents one of the great philosophical problems which have perplexed thoughtful people in the past and continue to perplex them today. In the reading selections will be found various ways in which philosophers have approached these problems and different attempts they have made to solve them. The idea behind this book is not to give the reader final solutions to these problems, but to acquaint him with some of the best philosophical thinking which has been done on them and to start him thinking on his own.

Since it is the purpose of this book to get the reader to think philosophically, he must not expect to find a ready-made world view or philosophy of life offered to him here. Everyone has some kind of world view or philosophy of life, some kinds of beliefs about the nature of the world and of one's place in it, about what is morally right and wrong, about political principles and social ideals. But many people's beliefs about these things are not clear or precise, their ideas are sometimes confused or inconsistent, and they are often unable to give good reasons to justify their beliefs. Philosophical thinking helps us correct all three of these shortcomings. It brings to focus in our own minds just what it is we believe about the world around us, about God, about the meaning of life and death. It helps to make our world view more coherent so that we can arrange our beliefs in some kind of orderly system in which they do not contradict one another. And most important of all, philosophical thinking enables us to examine our beliefs critically, to see on what grounds they rest, and to see whether we are willing to accept those grounds after careful reflection. The working out of a clear, coherent, and rational philosophy of life is a lifetime process. It is the primary aim of this book to help the reader make a good beginning in this life work.

The book is organized in the following way. After a general introduction concerning the nature of philosophy there are eight chapters, each of which is devoted to a basic philosophical problem. One of the chapters (Chapter 4) has been broken down into subsections since it deals with a complex problem which may be analyzed conveniently as a set of subordinate problems.

There is an introduction to each chapter whose sole purpose is to present the problem, but not to solve it. The reading selections in a given chapter are attempts either to solve the problem or at least to throw light on its nature. By comparing selections in each chapter the reader will gain some insight into how a problem may best be solved or will come to understand those aspects of the problem which make it difficult to solve.

Immediately preceding each reading selection is a headnote which includes, first, a brief biographical note about the philosopher and, second, a statement indicating how the philosopher approaches the central problem of the chapter. The purpose of these headnotes is to help the reader see the connection between the reading selection and the problem.

At the end of each selection are several questions which the reader may use to test his own comprehension of the reading and which may stimulate his own philosophical thinking about the problem dealt with. The editors have tried to formulate these questions in such a way that they demand the reader's careful reflection.

It will be noticed that both in the headnote to a reading selection and in the questions on it, cross-references are sometimes made to other reading selections. These cross-references are intended to bring out comparisons among readings and to show how various readings may be seen to constitute a philosophical argument or discussion. Thus in one reading a philosopher will make a point to which another objects in another reading, and still another will reply to that objection or will make a new point on the basis of what has been said by someone else, and so on. It is hoped that the reader will not come away with the impression that philosophy consists of scattered fragments of thought about unrelated problems. At the end of each chapter there is a short bibliography especially selected for the use of beginners in philosophy who wish to study a given problem further.

The book has been so arranged that a person can begin his study of philosophical problems with any chapter and then follow with any ordering of the chapters he prefers. No chapter is so written that the reader is assumed to have read any preceding one in the book. On the other hand, the order of readings within a chapter is meant to reveal progressive stages of discussion of a problem, each later stage clarifying, building on, reacting against, or somehow modifying an earlier stage. (Very often these stages occur chronologically and the reader may then gain a sense of the historical development of philosophical thinking on a given problem.) Even here, however, the reader (or his instructor) might find other ways of ordering the selections which better suit his purposes.

When a selection is read whose introduction or questions make cross-references to other selections not yet read, it is suggested that the reader simply disregard these cross-references or make a note of them and return to them when he has read the other selections referred to.

Most of the readings in this book are somewhat longer than those usually offered in books of this kind. The reason for this is the editors' belief that a person cannot adequately come to understand what a philosopher is saying unless he is able to probe deeply into the philosopher's writing and, as it were, immerse himself in the philosopher's point of view. Sometimes this can be done without great difficulty even with a rather short selection from an article or book. But in many cases, and particularly in cases of the works of the classic philosophers in Western history, substantial amounts of their writing must be read before genuine insight into what they are saying is possible. The reader must be sufficiently patient and diligent to read and reread these longer selections if he really wishes to begin his own philosophical thinking on a sound basis.

ELMER SPRAGUE
PAUL W. TAYLOR

January, 1959
Brooklyn, New York

Acknowledgments

The editors are deeply indebted to all the authors, editors, and publishers who have kindly granted permission for the reprinting of their material in this book. The source of each reading selection is stated at the end of its headnote, and specific indebtedness to author, editor, or publisher is given in a footnote at the beginning of each selection. Grateful acknowledgment is due the staff of the Brooklyn College Library, and especially Mr. M. A. Fox, for their co-operation and assistance. This book owes much to the free use which the editors have been able to make of the philosophy collections of the Brooklyn College Library and the Brooklyn Public Library.

The editors are indebted beyond repayment to their colleagues in the Department of Philosophy at Brooklyn College, without whose conscientious efforts this book would not have come into being. The contents of this book have been developed from the syllabus and readings for an introductory course in philosophy required of all students who are candidates for the A.B. and B.S. degrees at Brooklyn College. The choice of readings has resulted from certain modifications in previous sets of readings used in the introductory course, and all members of the department had participated in the selection of those previous sets of readings. Special acknowledgment is due Professor Howard W. Hintz, Chairman of the Department, who has given unfailing support and encouragement to the editors. His indefatigable efforts have in no small measure made possible the publication of this book. We also wish to acknowledge that Professor Elizabeth Lane Beardsley of Lincoln University, Professor Monroe C. Beardsley of Swarthmore College, Professor Joseph L. Blau of Columbia University, and Professor Fadlou Shehadi of Douglass College commented helpfully on early versions of the manuscript.

The editors would like to add that this book is in a very real sense a joint enterprise. They have worked closely together on all the chapters, and they, rather than their advisers, bear mutual responsibility for whatever shortcomings the book may have.

E. S.

P. W. T.

Contents

Chapter Six

The Problem of Moral Knowledge 483

Chapter Seven

The Problem of Political Principles 597

Chapter Eight

KNOWLEDGE AND VALUE

| Philosophy and the
Problems of Philosophy

THE TWO TASKS OF PHILOSOPHY

The word "philosophy" comes from the Greek words *philein,* to love, and *sophia,* wisdom. If we look at the earliest philosophy in Western history, that of the Greeks of the fifth and sixth centuries B.C., we see that "the love of wisdom" meant the pursuit of knowledge and the endeavor to live the good life. The knowledge which philosophers sought included both knowledge of the world around us (knowledge of what *is*) and knowledge of the good life (knowledge of what *ought* to be). Knowledge of the world around us consisted at least in part of what we now call science, and consequently the first philosophers were also the first scientists. In addition to seeking knowledge of the world around us and knowledge of the good life, philosophers reflected about what they were doing and made a critical examination of the foundations of knowledge. The Greek philosopher Socrates (469-399 B.C.), for example, was not only interested in discovering what kind of life is most worth living, he was also interested in examining the grounds on which we claim that one way of life is more worth living than another. Plato (427?-347 B.C.), another Greek philosopher, wrote about an ideal society in which there was perfect justice, but he also made a careful inquiry into the meaning of the word "justice" and into the different ways of determining whether a society is just or unjust. Similarly, Aristotle (384-322 B.C.), who was taught by Plato, not only wrote books in physics, biology, and psychology, but also in logic and theory of knowledge, in which he examined various methods for obtaining truth about the world around us.

The difference between making statements about what exists or what ought to exist on the one hand and on the other examining the reasons we have for making those statements is a difference of great importance for understanding what philosophy is. To be aware of this difference helps us see why philosophy today does not include the sciences and is not included among them.

Before the time of Galileo (1564-1642) philosophers who investigated nature did not agree about what problems they were trying to solve or what methods were to be used to solve them. With Galileo physics passed from a philosophical to a scientific state; for it was he who formulated the principles which define both the subject matter of physics (what can be observed and represented in mathematical terms) and the way in which it is to be studied (by observation and measurement). Galileo's success in advancing the science assured the acceptance of these principles by those who wanted to do physics.

Since that time philosophers have ceased to do what physicists do, although, as we shall see below, physicists sometimes continue to do philosophy.

What happened in the case of physics also happened in the case of astronomy, geology, biology, and all the other natural sciences. Each was originally included in philosophy and each broke away from philosophy as procedures of observation and measurement were applied to clearly defined problems in its own area. More recently a similar process has occurred in the social sciences and psychology. At the present time, it is true, some philosophers still make assertions about "the nature of man" which are meant to describe or explain something about human beings. But there are many philosophers who would say that such talk is merely psychological and sociological guesswork and that it would be better to leave man's nature for psychologists and sociologists to investigate.

If philosophers no longer claim to be doing the kind of thing that scientists do, what do they claim to be doing? There are two sorts of activity which at present are still called philosophy, and these two sorts of activity define the two tasks of philosophy today. The first is concerned with those problems about which there is as yet no universal agreement either with regard to the precise nature of the problems or with regard to correct methods for solving them. Among such problems are *metaphysical and theological problems* (Is the universe blind matter, indifferent to man's fate, or is there a purpose behind things? Does everything exist in our minds, or are there things outside our minds? Did the universe have a beginning, or was it always here? Is there a God, and if so, what is his nature?), *ethical problems* (What is man's supreme moral duty? Can what is morally wrong in one society be morally right in another? If a moral rule tells us it is wrong to kill, can an exception to the rule ever be justified?), *problems concerning political principles and ideals* (Is there some higher standard by which the laws of the state can be judged? Do human beings have natural rights, and if so, from what are they derived? Can a democratic society really be shown to be better than a totalitarian society if there is some dissatisfaction and suffering in the democratic society, while the totalitarian society conditions everyone in it to be perfectly satisfied with his lot?), and *problems of the interpretation of history* (Is there a pattern in the rise and fall of civilizations, and if so, can we predict about the future on the basis of it? Is a classless society inevitable? By what standards can the progress of mankind be measured?). Metaphysics and theology, ethics, political (or social) philosophy, and the philosophy of history are not sciences because there is so much dispute about what their subject matter really is and about the correct way to deal with their subject matter. Some philosophers think that because these fields are concerned with matters which go beyond what we can directly observe by our senses or what we can infer from such observations, they are essentially different from the sciences and consequently will never become sciences. Thus it is said that philosophy need not apologize because it is not scientific. It will always have a task of its own, different from and independent of scientific knowledge, namely, the task of trying to answer the kinds of questions listed above.

The second kind of activity which remains for philosophy now that the sciences have become separate branches of knowledge is the examination of the grounds on which all statements rest, including the grounds of scientific statements. The grounds on which a statement rests are the reasons which would be given to justify the statement if it were challenged. It is always possible to ask three basic questions regarding any statement: What is the statement about? What are the grounds of the statement? Are they good grounds? When our friend comes up to us and says, "I have just returned from a trip to Europe," we know that his statement is about a trip to Europe which has happened in the immediate past. What our friend is talking about is something that actually occurred. But if we ask ourselves, "On what grounds is our friend's statement based?" we are not asking about the trip to Europe. We are asking about the statement itself. To answer such a question by saying, for example, "His statement is based on the grounds of his memory, the public evidence of letters he has written from Europe, and the testimony of those who saw him in Europe," is to make a statement about a statement. It is not to make a statement about a trip to Europe.

①Statements about what is and what ought to be are sometimes called first-order statements, while ②statements about statements are called second-order statements. The second task of philosophy may then be defined as the making of second-order statements about the grounds of first-order statements. Of course it is always possible to inquire into the grounds of those second-order (philosophical) statements, and we can thus make third-order statements about second-order statements. Such third-order statements are also philosophical, as are any statements of a higher order.

The second sort of activity which is philosophical thinking, then, seeks to determine the grounds of any first-order statement and to decide whether they are good grounds. Let us analyze this kind of philosophical thinking a bit further. It is important to notice that the first-order statements whose grounds are examined include the statements of the various sciences as well as the statements of metaphysics, theology, ethics, and the other fields of philosophy (where "philosophy" is understood in terms of its first task). The study of the grounds of scientific statements is known as the philosophy of science. Although philosophers no longer make scientific statements, they do make statements about scientific statements. In the following passage, for example, a philosopher talks about the science of physics but does not say anything about the physical world:

> Let us first try to define what we are to mean by the hypothesis that physics is true. . . .
>
> Every physical theory which survives goes through three stages. In the first stage, it is a matter of controversy among specialists; in the second stage, the specialists are agreed that it is the theory which best fits the available evidence, though it may well hereafter be found incompatible with new evidence; in

the third stage, it is thought very unlikely that any new evidence will do more than somewhat modify it.

When I say that I shall assume physics to be true, I mean that I shall accept those parts of physics which have reached the third stage. . . .[1]

Sometimes scientists themselves make (second-order) statements about their (first-order) statements, and when they do this they enter the domain of the philosophy of science. It is in this sense that physicists sometimes do philosophy. Consider the following two statements made by the physicist, Max Planck (1858-1947). In the first statement he is speaking as a physicist, since he is making a first-order statement about the physical world. In the second statement he is speaking as a philosopher of science, since he is making a second-order statement about the grounds of first-order statements in physics.

Every chemical atom that is electrically neutral consists of a number of protons cohering with one another, and of a similar number of electrons, some of which are firmly fixed to the protons, together with which they form the nucleus of the atom, while the rest revolve around the nucleus.[2]

. . . We cannot but be struck by the fact that the natural phenomena which we can investigate and measure can never be expressed by absolutely accurate numbers; for they inevitably contain a certain inaccuracy introduced by the unavoidable defects of measurement itself. Hence it follows that we shall never succeed in determining by measurement whether a natural law is absolutely valid.[3]

The second task of philosophy consists not only in coming to understand the nature of the grounds of first-order statements. It also attempts to *compare* the grounds of various types of first-order statements, such as scientific statements, moral statements, political statements, and theological statements. Finally, it attempts to *evaluate* the grounds of any given statement. Philosophy investigates the reasons for our beliefs in order to see whether they are acceptable to us as thinking beings.

Comparison of the Two Tasks of Philosophy

We shall now inquire more closely into the differences between the two tasks of philosophy. Historically the two tasks have always gone together, but this does not mean that there is no important difference between them, nor does it mean that it is impossible to carry on one without the other.

The first aim of philosophy, we said, is to answer metaphysical and theological questions, moral and political questions, questions concerning the interpretation of history, and other nonscientific questions about existence and values. Here the activity of philosophizing results in first-order statements about what

[1] Bertrand Russell, *Human Knowledge: Its Scope and Limits,* Simon and Schuster, N. Y., 1948, p. 198.

[2] Max Planck, *The Universe in the Light of Modern Physics,* translated by W. H. Johnston, Allen and Unwin, London, 1931; 2nd. ed., 1937, p. 16.

[3] *Ibid.,* pp. 81-82.

is or what ought to be. These first-order statements are similar to scientific statements (which originally were included among them as part of philosophy) in
that they are all intended to convey information. They are supposed to tell us
something about the nature of the world, about duties and ideals, and about
society and history. The purpose of philosophy in this sense is to discover truth.
Like scientific thinking, philosophical thinking yields knowledge, although the
knowledge it yields is about a different subject matter from that of the sciences.

When this kind of philosophizing is done in a systematic way, it results
in the constructing and expounding of a total "world view" or "philosophy of
life." A world view is a set of fundamental beliefs about the whole of existence
and of man's place in it. Every world view includes three aspects, a *metaphysical*
viewpoint (a conception of the ultimate nature of reality) a *view of man's*
metaphysical and moral place in the universe (a conception of man, for example,
as a helpless creature caught in circumstances beyond his control, or as a being
free to choose his own destiny; as a creature made in the image of God, or as an
animal whose existence on earth has no moral significance; as a being loved
and cared for by God, or as a homeless wanderer in the universe), and *a set of*
ultimate values (those things worth sacrificing all other things for, but not
worth being sacrificed for the sake of anything else, and those ends which are
not means to any further ends but are ends-in-themselves). Two familiar
examples of world views that have been adopted by large numbers of people
are Marxism or dialectical materialism, and supernaturalism or theism (the
world view of the religions of Judaism, Christianity, and Islam).

From a person's world view is derived his "philosophy of life." A philosophy of life may be thought of as the set of values or principles which guide
a person's conduct in his everyday life. Such values would include one's personal
life-goals and one's conception of happiness, one's beliefs about what is morally
right and wrong, and one's political and social ideals. They are the values, based
on a person's world view, which most directly motivate and inspire him.

Throughout the history of philosophy many world views and philosophies
of life have been constructed and expounded by philosophers. Some of these
have had no social influence, having remained the private outlooks of their
originators; others have become the philosophical creeds accepted by large
groups of people. There are other world views which have not been originated
by a single thinker, but have gradually developed as a basic set of values and
an outlook on life which are embodied in the structure and functioning of a
whole society. Thus anthropologists and historians have revealed to us the
underlying world views of different cultures and civilizations.

Every person has a world view and a philosophy of life, whether they have
been accepted by him unconsciously through the process of acculturation or
have been fully thought out and deliberately adopted on the basis of his own
thinking. In general, world views and philosophies of life may conveniently be
classified in three ways: as implicit or explicit, as conventional or unconventional, and as critical or uncritical. All three of these classifications are matters
of degree. That is, there is a whole range of world views and philosophies of life

going from the completely implicit to the completely explicit, a whole range from the completely conventional to the completely unconventional, and a whole range from the completely critical to the completely uncritical. A person's world view (and philosophy of life—whatever is said about world views in this paragraph and the next can also be said about philosophies of life) is *implicit* to the extent that the person has (never thought about his fundamental values and beliefs and to the extent that he would be unable to state what they are if he were asked about them.) On the other hand a person has an *explicit* world view when he is (fully conscious of it and is able to state exactly what it is.) A person has a *conventional* world view to the extent that it is similar to the world view of his parents, friends, teachers, his socioeconomic group, and those who practice the religion in which he was brought up. To the extent that one's world view differs from that of one's family and one's socioeconomic, religious, and cultural groups, it is *unconventional*. It should be remarked that although most unconventional world views would be explicit, not all those which are explicit need be unconventional. A person might well be able to give clear expression to the most conventional beliefs and values.

Finally, there is the distinction between critical and uncritical world views, and this is the classification most important for our present purposes. A *critical* world view is one which a person accepts only after thinking it out for himself. He is able to give reasons for his beliefs and values, reasons which he may or may not have originated himself but which he finds to be acceptable upon calm reflection and after careful examination. If a person has committed himself to a world view and is unable to give good reasons for accepting it, and if he has not even examined the grounds on which it rests, we say that he has an *uncritical* world view. It is important not to confuse the conventional-unconventional dimension with the critical-uncritical dimension. It is true that most uncritical world views are conventional. A typical case is that of a person who believes that God exists and that certain things are right and other things are wrong simply because those around him have always told him so. But it is perfectly possible to have an uncritical world view which is unconventional. This would occur when a person lives what is ordinarily called an "unconventional" life or adopts an outlook on life which is the extreme opposite of his society's as an emotional rebellion against that society. Instead of thinking out what is wrong with his society and how it can be improved, he blindly protests against it by grasping a totally different world view just because it is different. Finally, although once a person begins to think about his world view he may end by accepting beliefs and values which are quite different from those of people around him, this result is not a necessary consequence of his thinking. Critical world views do not always have to be unconventional. A person might be brought up with certain religious, moral, and political beliefs which he finds he can still accept as an adult after having critically examined the grounds on which they rest.

Now it can easily be seen that the first task of philosophy, the constructing and expounding of (explicit) world views, can be pursued without involving

the second task of philosophy. The second task, we said, is the critical examination and evaluation of the grounds of our beliefs, including not only the
beliefs which make up our world views, but also ordinary common sense beliefs
and scientific beliefs. When a person constructs and expounds an explicit world
view he is making first-order statements about the nature of reality, about man's
place in the universe, and about what is ultimately right and good. He can make
such statements without examining and evaluating their grounds, and this indeed is what happens whenever anyone constructs and expounds an explicit but
uncritical world view. Thus not all constructing and expounding of world views
(philosophizing in the first sense) is the result of careful, systematic reflection
(philosophizing in the second sense). A person who seeks a critical world view
has a double task in his philosophical thinking. Not only must he think out an
explicit world view, he must also be able to give reasons for committing himself to that world view and show that they are good reasons.

It is possible, then, to carry on the first task of philosophy without the
second. Let us now see how it is possible to carry on the second without the
first. In the first place, as we have seen, with regard to any scientific subject
matter the philosopher has only the second task to perform. His job is to examine and evaluate the grounds of the statements made by scientists, not to make
such statements himself. For if he were to do the latter he would no longer be
a philosopher but a scientist. Similarly, as soon as the scientist begins to make
statements about the foundations of the branch of knowledge in which he does
his work, he takes on the role of the philosopher. Questions about the foundations of knowledge are second-order questions. They cannot be answered within
the framework of any branch of first-order knowledge. They can only be answered within a second-order (philosophical) framework.

But suppose we consider areas outside the sciences, where people make
metaphysical, moral, political, and other types of first-order statements, whether
in expounding their world views or in carrying on ordinary conversations in
daily life. Is it possible here to philosophize in the second sense without philosophizing in the first sense? Many philosophers of the present day not only believe
this is possible, they believe the second task of philosophy is the only one they
should be concerned with. They say that it is not their business as philosophers
to make any first-order statements, not even metaphysical, theological, or moral
ones (although they admit that many of those who are ordinarily called "philosophers" have done so in the past). Their sole function, as they see it, is to
examine the grounds of whatever first-order statements others wish to make
and they themselves wish to make when they are not functioning as philosophers. They maintain that the only proper concern of philosophy is to make
clear and correct second-order statements about the logical basis of first-order
beliefs. Hence they want to define "philosophy" wholly in terms of philosophizing in the second sense and absolutely to exclude from it the constructing and
expounding of world views.

Such philosophers are interested in world views only to examine them, to
analyze their logical foundations, to distinguish the various kinds of statements

involved in them, to determine the relations of these statements to one another, and to investigate the ways of reasoning which are appropriate to their justification. Although they may have an explicit world view of their own and would be perfectly willing to examine it, they may not be as interested in it as they are in those famous and important world views which have had a great influence upon the history of philosophy and upon the outlook of Western man. Of course their philosophizing about these world views may unconsciously affect their own world view. But they do not philosophize in order to arrive at a critical world view of their own. If they were asked for what purpose they philosophized, they would probably give two sorts of answers. As far as their personal interest in philosophizing was concerned, they would say that they do it for its own sake, that is, just because they find it an intellectually fascinating thing to do. As far as the value of their philosophizing to mankind was concerned, they would claim that it contributes to the general enlightenment of us all by helping us to understand the logical basis of our scientific, religious, moral, and political beliefs. These philosophers are especially desirous of clearing away what their philosophizing has led them to see as the confusions of traditional philosophical thinking and the meaningless jargon in which many of the great world views have been expounded and promulgated.

From this point of view, then, we can see how it is possible to do philosophical thinking and at the same time neither attempt to arrive at a world view by means of this philosophical thinking nor even be concerned with one's own world view. Thus the second task of philosophy can be carried on independently of the first task.

PHILOSOPHICAL PROBLEMS

There are two kinds of problems which may be called philosophical, corresponding to the two tasks of philosophy. First-order philosophical problems consist of all those metaphysical, moral, and other nonscientific types of questions which are answered by the systematic construction of a world view and a philosophy of life. Second-order philosophical problems concern the grounds of all statements of science, theology, morals, politics, and other areas of first-order discourse.

In this book the reader is presented with eight *second-order* philosophical problems, stated in the titles of the chapters. Each problem is centered upon one kind of first-order statement, with the exception of Chapter 3, "The Problem of Meaning and Verification," where the problem applies to many different kinds of statements. Chapter 6, "The Problem of Moral Knowledge," for example, is centered upon moral statements and deals with the questions: On what grounds do people justify their moral statements? Is it possible to discover good grounds for making moral statements? If so, what would be such good grounds? What are their logical features in virtue of which they are good grounds?

The reading selections in each chapter are attempts either to clarify the na-

ture of the problem or to solve it. The reader should try to see whether one philosopher's way of handling the problem of a chapter makes an advance over
another's way of handling it. Often the philosophers will be found to argue
directly against one another, each pointing out what he finds to be mistakes
in the other's reasoning. Thus the chapters may be conceived as great discussions centering upon the problems stated in the titles.

It will be noticed, however, that many of the philosophers in this book do
not limit themselves to making second-order statements. They not only examine
the logical foundations of scientific, theological, moral, and other first-order
statements, they also indulge in speculative assertions about the nature of the
world; they promulgate theological doctrines; they give moral advice; they
advocate political principles; and they set forth interpretations of history. Thus
they shift from second-order to first-order philosophizing. When this happens
it is necessary for the reader to take care to distinguish the two kinds of things
the philosopher is doing. It is one thing, for example, to declare that God has
given man certain knowledge through revelation; it is another thing to study
the grounds on which any claim to knowledge through revelation is made.
And telling us what is morally right and wrong is a very different thing from
telling us what the rational basis of morality is. The reader must try to decide
at what points in a philosopher's discourse he is shifting from second-order
statements to first-order statements and vice versa. In this way the reader will
gain a clear recognition of the twofold nature of philosophical thinking.

This book has been arranged on the basis of second-order philosophical
problems rather than first-order philosophical problems for the following
reasons. In the first place, being reasonable about any particular first-order
philosophical question presupposes consideration of second-order philosophical
questions. Before we can reasonably decide whether God exists, for example,
we must first see what sorts of reasons can be given to show that God does or
does not exist. If it is claimed that such a question is a matter of faith and not
reason, then again we must examine the meanings of the terms "faith" and
"reason" and see whether the limitations placed upon reason are justified. Or
to take another example, how can I know what is morally right and wrong
unless I first investigate the different ways of arguing about what is morally
right and wrong, and unless I undertake to discover which of these different
ways of arguing is the most valid? In every case of making up our minds about
a first-order question, it is always necessary to consider the second-order questions which are relevant to it. Assuming that we want to answer a first-order
question rationally, that is, to find an answer which is acceptable to us as
rational beings, then we must enter upon the relevant second-order questions
in order to know what a rational answer would be. The decision to defend
democracy against totalitarianism on the ground that human beings have certain natural rights which democracy recognizes and which totalitarianism violates is not a rational decision unless we can show why human beings have
natural rights. And this requires that we study certain second-order questions

of political philosophy, namely: Are there any reasons which can legitimately be given in support of the doctrine of natural rights? If so, what are they?

In the second place, second-order philosophical thinking is necessary before anyone can make a rational decision to commit himself to a world view or a philosophy of life. If we want to adopt a critical world view and not merely one embodied in the culture into which we happen to be born, then we must carry on second-order philosophizing. For a world view is simply an organized system of certain fundamental first-order beliefs, and these beliefs can be accepted critically only after second-order reflection about their logical basis. And one cannot defend the choice of a philosophy of life unless one can defend the world view which underlies that philosophy of life, so here again we are forced to inquire into the reasons for accepting or rejecting world views.

It would be difficult to think of a more important question that could be asked us than "What do you believe is the meaning of life?" Yet we would be at a loss to answer such a question unless we had either accepted from others or had thought out for ourselves an *explicit* world view. Suppose, however, that we could give an articulate and coherent reply to the question. What would we then do if we were asked, "Why do you believe what you say to be true?" We would again be at a loss unless our world view was a *critical* one, unless, that is to say, we had ourselves examined the reasons for our beliefs and as a consequence of that examination had concluded that they were good reasons. The times when others confront us with such a challenge to defend our way of life intellectually are few indeed. But this kind of challenge need not come from another person. In moments of quiet reflection we might well have presented the question to ourselves any number of times. The question might not always take the same form. It might be phrased in some such way as "What is life all about?" or "What is the purpose of existing at all?" or "What do I really live for?" But in whatever way it is expressed, it is the ultimate question, the question of questions. And only philosophical thinking on the second-order level can provide an answer to it.

Yet we must realize that second-order philosophical thinking is a lifetime activity. Once it begins it never ends. The problems it deals with are so complex and far-reaching that no final, universally acceptable solutions have yet been found. The only thing we can do is to carry on our second-order philosophical thinking as clearly and as carefully as possible, realizing that no final solutions will probably be reached in our lives but hoping that we may advance a little toward more enlightened points of view. Meanwhile we must live our practical lives. How can this be done in a rational way if we cannot arrive at final conclusions concerning a true world view and philosophy of life? We can only live according to tentative conclusions, constantly examining and re-examining them as our philosophical thinking grows and develops. Such a life has been called "the life of reason." To live this kind of life is to live as a thinking being.

Euthyphro

Plato
(427?-347 B.C.)

To illustrate the Introduction to this book we offer a word portrait by Plato of a philosopher at work. Plato, one of the triad of great Greek philosophers, stands between his teacher, Socrates (469-399 B.C.), and his pupil, Aristotle (384-322 B.C.). Socrates wrote nothing; and those of Aristotle's works which have survived are in a state that requires much editorial effort to make them intelligible. It is no wonder then that the twenty-four of Plato's dialogues which have come down to us comparatively intact, and splendid in their range and power of thought, are regarded as one of the great cultural treasures of the world.

The *Euthyphro* belongs to the set of early dialogues in which Plato both illustrates Socrates' method of doing philosophy and endeavors to vindicate the manner of his life to those Athenians who had sought and achieved Socrates' execution by the state. Indeed, the dramatic occasion of this dialogue is a conversation which Socrates is supposed to have had on his way to be tried for his life, one of the charges against him being that of impiety. Although Plato shows Socrates coming to no philosophical conclusion in the *Euthyphro,* he nonetheless has Socrates describe the kind of philosophical knowledge which Plato thought was most valuable: "Remember that I did not ask you to give me two or three examples of piety, but to explain the general form which makes all pious things to be pious." This search for "general forms" was the philosophical mission of Plato's own life. But it is just because the dialogue is inconclusive that *Euthyphro* is an excellent illustration of the philosopher at work. Undistracted by the need to evaluate any conclusion, we may concentrate wholly on watching Socrates do philosophy.

As becomes a philosopher, Socrates' interest in piety is a second-order interest. He has no desire to propose his own theory of piety. He is interested in the notion simply because, as with every other notion, it is worth while being clear about what one has in mind when one talks of it. Euthyphro claims to be an expert on piety and Socrates decides to test this claim. He prods Euthyphro through several different accounts of the meaning of "piety"; and in each instance Socrates succeeds in showing either that what Euthyphro says about piety makes no sense, i.e., is too muddled to be allowed to stand, or is self-contradictory. Thus Socrates' analysis exemplifies the philosopher's two basic tests of the clarity of first-order statements: Do they make sense? Are they self-contradictory? Notice that Socrates makes no suggestions about the nature of piety until Euthyphro feels that he can say no more without assistance. Then, as a philosopher, Socrates scrutinizes the definitions which he offers Euthyphro with the same care that he gave to Euthyphro's own.

In examining this dialogue the reader will do well first to make a note of each definition of "piety" as it is offered, and then to summarize briefly the points Socrates makes against it. Thus he will be better able to judge the effectiveness of Socrates' criticism and determine whether Euthyphro, at some stage of the dialogue, might have made a stronger case for what he says than he is here given credit for. It must be noticed that at least some of Euthyphro's difficulties stem from the peculiarities of Greek religion. Would his task be easier if he were a monotheist? How? Finally the reader should try to decide what definition of "piety" would satisfy himself; and then he should see whether he can defend it successfully against Socrates' kind of criticism. The way to learn philosophy is by doing it.

The entire dialogue is reprinted here. The translation from the Greek is by Benjamin Jowett, as revised in 1953 by order of the Jowett Copyright Trustees.

From *The Dialogues of Plato,* 4th ed., translated by Benjamin Jowett, 1953. Reprinted by permission of Oxford University Press.

PERSONS OF THE DIALOGUE: Socrates, Euthyphro
SCENE: The Porch of the King Archon

EUTHYPHRO. What can have happened, Socrates, to bring you away from the Lyceum? and what are you doing in the Porch of the King Archon? Surely you cannot be concerned in a suit before the King, like myself?

SOCRATES. Not in a suit, Euthyphro; prosecution is the word which the Athenians use.

EUTH. What! I suppose that someone has been prosecuting you, for I cannot believe that you are the prosecutor of another.

Soc. Certainly not.

EUTH. Then someone else has been prosecuting you?

Soc. Yes.

EUTH. And who is he?

Soc. A young man who is little known, Euthyphro; and I hardly know him: his name is Meletus, and he is of the deme of Pitthis. Perhaps you may remember his appearance; he has a beak, and straight hair, and a beard which is ill grown.

EUTH. No, I do not remember him, Socrates. But what is the charge which he brings against you?

Soc. What is the charge? Well, rather a grand one, which implies a degree of discernment far from contemptible in a young man. He says he knows how the youth are corrupted and who are their corruptors. I fancy that he must be a wise man, and seeing that I am the reverse of a wise man, he has found me out, and is going to accuse me of corrupting his generation. And of this our mother the state is to be the judge. Of all our political men he is the only one who seems to me to begin in the right way, with the cultivation of virtue in youth; like a good husbandman, he makes the young shoots his first care, and clears away us whom he accuses of destroying them. This is only the first step; afterwards he will assuredly attend to the elder branches; and if he goes on as he has begun, he will be a very great public benefactor.

EUTH. I hope that he may; but I rather fear, Socrates, that the opposite will turn out to be the truth. My opinion is that in attacking you he is simply aiming a blow at the heart of the state. But in what way does he say that you corrupt the young?

Soc. In a curious way, which at first hearing excites surprise: he says that I am a maker of gods, and that I invent new gods and deny the existence of the old ones; this is the ground of his indictment.

EUTH. I understand, Socrates; he means to attack you about the familiar sign which occasionally, as you say, comes to you. He thinks that you are a neologian, and he is going to have you up before the court for this. He knows that such a charge is readily received by the world, as I myself know too well; for when I speak in the assembly about divine things, and foretell the future to them, they laugh at me and think me a madman. Yet every word that I say is true. But they are jealous of us all; and we must be brave and go at them.

Soc. Their laughter, friend Euthyphro, is not a matter of much consequence. For a man may be thought clever; but the Athenians, I suspect, do not much trouble themselves about him until he begins to impart his wisdom to others; and then for some reason or other, perhaps, as you say, from jealousy, they are angry.

EUTH. I have no great wish to try their temper towards me in this way.

Soc. No doubt they think you are reserved in your behaviour, and unwilling to impart your wisdom. But I have a benevolent habit of pouring out myself to everybody, and would even pay for a listener, and I am afraid that the Athenians may think me too talkative. Now if, as I was saying, they would only laugh at me, as you say that they laugh at you, the time might pass gaily enough with jokes and merriment in the court; but perhaps they may be in earnest, and then what the end will be you soothsayers only can predict.

EUTH. I dare say that the affair will end in nothing, Socrates, and that you will win your cause; and I think that I shall win my own.

Soc. And what is your suit, Euthyphro? are you the pursuer or the defendant?

EUTH. I am the pursuer.

Soc. Of whom?

EUTH. When I tell you, you will perceive another reason why I am thought mad.

Soc. Why, has the fugitive wings?

EUTH. Nay, he is not very volatile at his time of life.

Soc. Who is he?

EUTH. My father.

Soc. My dear Sir! Your own father?

EUTH. Yes.

Soc. And of what is he accused?

EUTH. Of murder, Socrates.

Soc. Good heavens! How little, Euthyphro, does the common herd know of the nature of right and truth! A man must be an extraordinary man, and have made great strides in wisdom, before he could have seen his way to bring such an action.

EUTH. Indeed, Socrates, he must.

Soc. I suppose that the man whom your father murdered was one of your family—clearly he was; for if he had been a stranger you would never have thought of prosecuting him.

EUTH. I am amused, Socrates, at your making a distinction between one who is a member of the family and one who is not; for surely the pollution is the same in either case, if you knowingly associate with the murderer when you ought to clear yourself and him by proceeding against him. The real question is whether the murdered man has been justly slain. If justly, then your duty is to let the matter alone; but if unjustly, then proceed against the murderer, if, that is to say, he lives under the same roof with you and eats at the same table. In fact, the man who is dead was a poor dependant of mine who worked for us as a field labourer on our farm in Naxos, and one day in a fit of drunken passion he got into a quarrel with one of our domestic servants and slew him. My father bound him hand and foot and threw him into a ditch, and then sent to Athens to ask an expositor of religious law what he should do with him. Meanwhile he never attended to him and took no care about him; for he regarded him as a murderer, and thought that no great harm would be done even if he did die. Now this was just what happened. For such was the effect of cold and hunger and chains upon him, that before the messenger returned from the expositor, he was dead. And my father and family are angry with me for taking the part of the murderer and prosecuting my father. They say that he did not kill him, and that if he did, the dead man was but a murderer, and I ought not to take any notice, for that a son is impious who prosecutes a father for murder. Which shows, Socrates, how little they know what the gods think about piety and impiety.

Soc. Good heavens, Euthyphro! and is your knowledge of religion and of things pious and impious so very exact, that, supposing the circumstances to be as you state them, you are not afraid lest you too may be doing an impious thing in bringing an action against your father?

EUTH. The best of Euthyphro, that which distinguishes him, Socrates, from the common herd, is his exact knowledge of all such matters. What should I be good for without it?

SOC. Rare friend! I think that I cannot do better than be your disciple. Then before the trial with Meletus comes on I shall challenge him, and say that I have always had a great interest in religious questions, and now, as he charges me with rash imaginations and innovations in religion, I have become your disciple. You, Meletus, as I shall say to him, acknowledge Euthyphro to be a great theologian, and so you ought to approve of me, and not have me into court; otherwise you should begin by indicting him who is my teacher, and who will be the ruin, not of the young, but of the old; that is to say, of myself whom he instructs, and of his old father whom he admonishes and chastises. And if Meletus refuses to listen to me, but will go on, and will not shift the indictment from me to you, I cannot do better than repeat this challenge in the court.

EUTH. Yes, indeed, Socrates; and if he attempts to indict me I am mistaken if I do not find a flaw in him; the court will be occupied with him long before it comes to me.

SOC. And I, my dear friend, knowing this, am desirous of becoming your disciple. For I observe that no one appears to notice you—not even this Meletus; but his sharp eyes have found me out at once, and he has indicted me for impiety. And therefore, I adjure you to tell me the nature of piety and impiety, which you said that you knew so well, in their bearing on murder and generally on offences against the gods. Is not piety in every action always the same? and impiety, again—is it not always the opposite of piety, and also the same with itself, having, as impiety, one notion or form which includes whatever is impious?

EUTH. To be sure, Socrates.

SOC. And what is piety, and what is impiety?

EUTH. Piety is doing as I am doing; that is to say, prosecuting anyone who is guilty of murder, sacrilege, or of any similar crime—whether he be your father or mother, or whoever he may be—that makes no difference; and not to prosecute them is impiety. And please to consider, Socrates, what a notable proof I will give you that this is the law, a proof which I have already given to others—of the principle, I mean, that the impious, whoever he may be, ought not to go unpunished. For do not men acknowledge Zeus as the best and most righteous of the gods? and yet they admit that he bound his father (Cronos) because he wickedly devoured his sons, and that he too had punished his own father (Uranus) for a similar reason, in a nameless manner. And yet when I proceed against my father, they are angry with me. So inconsistent are they in their way of talking when the gods are concerned, and when I am concerned.

SOC. May not this be the reason, Euthyphro, why I am charged with impiety—that I cannot away with these stories about the gods? that, I suppose is where people think I go wrong. But as you who are well informed about them approve of them, I cannot do better than assent to your superior wisdom. What else can I say, confessing as I do, that I know nothing about them? Tell me, for the love of Zeus, whether you really believe that they are true.

EUTH. Yes, Socrates; and things more wonderful still, of which the world is in ignorance.

Soc. And do you really believe that the gods fought with one another, and had dire quarrels, battles, and the like, as the poets say, and as you see represented in the works of great artists? The temples are full of them; and notably the robe of Athene, which is carried up to the Acropolis at the great Panathenaea, is embroidered with them throughout. Are all these tales of the gods true, Euthyphro?

EUTH. Yes, Socrates; and, as I was saying, I can tell you, if you would like to hear them, many other things about the gods which would quite amaze you.

Soc. I dare say; and you shall tell me them at some other time when I have leisure. But just at present I would rather hear from you a more precise answer, which you have not as yet given, my friend, to the question, "What is 'piety'?" When asked, you only replied, "Doing as you do, charging your father with murder."

EUTH. And what I said was true, Socrates.

Soc. No doubt, Euthyphro; but you would admit that there are many other pious acts?

EUTH. There are.

Soc. Remember that I did not ask you to give me two or three examples of piety, but to explain the general form which makes all pious things to be pious. Do you not recollect saying that one and the same form made the impious impious, and the pious pious?

EUTH. I remember.

Soc. Tell me what is the nature of this form, and then I shall have a standard to which I may look, and by which I may measure actions, whether yours or those of anyone else, and then I shall be able to say that such and such an action is pious, such another impious.

EUTH. I will tell you, if you like.

Soc. I should very much like.

EUTH. Piety, then, is that which is dear to the gods, and impiety is that which is not dear to them.

Soc. Very good, Euthyphro; you have now given me the sort of answer which I wanted. But whether what you say is true or not I cannot as yet tell, although I make no doubt that you will go on to prove the truth of your words.

EUTH. Of course.

Soc. Come, then, and let us examine what we are saying. That thing or person which is dear to the gods is pious, and that thing or person which is hateful to the gods is impious, these two being the extreme opposites of one another. Was not that said?

EUTH. It was.

Soc. And well said?

EUTH. Yes, Socrates, I think so.

Soc. And further, Euthyphro, the gods were admitted to have enmities and hatreds and differences?

EUTH. Yes, that was also said.

Soc. And what sort of difference creates enmity and anger? Suppose for example that you and I, my good friend, differ on the question which of two groups of things is more numerous; do differences of this sort make us enemies and set us at variance with one another? Do we not proceed at once to counting, and put an end to them?

EUTH. True.

Soc. Or suppose that we differ about magnitudes, do we not quickly end the difference by measuring?

EUTH. Very true.

Soc. And we end a controversy about heavy and light by resorting to a weighing machine?

EUTH. To be sure.

Soc. But what are the matters about which differences arise that cannot be thus decided, and therefore make us angry and set us at enmity with one another? I dare say the answer does not occur to you at the moment, and therefore I will suggest that these enmities arise when the matters of difference are the just and unjust, good and evil, honourable and dishonourable. Are not these the subjects about which men differ, and about which when we are unable satisfactorily to decide our differences, you and I and all of us quarrel, when we do quarrel? [1]

EUTH. Yes, Socrates, the nature of the differences about which we quarrel is such as you describe.

Soc. And the quarrels of the gods, noble Euthyphro, when they occur, are of a like nature?

EUTH. Certainly they are.

Soc. They have differences of opinion, as you say, about good and evil, just and unjust, honourable and dishonourable: there would be no quarrels among them, if there were no such differences—would there now?

EUTH. You are quite right.

Soc. Does not each party of them love that which they deem noble and just and good, and hate the opposite?

EUTH. Very true.

Soc. But, as you say, one party regards as just the same things as the other thinks unjust—about these they dispute; and so there arise wars and fightings among them.

EUTH. Very true.

Soc. Then the same things are hated by the gods and loved by the gods, and are both hateful and dear to them?

EUTH. It appears so.

[1] Cf. 1 Alcib. 111 foll.

Soc. And upon this view the same things, Euthyphro, will be pious and also impious?

EUTH. So I should suppose.

Soc. Then, my friend, I remark with surprise that you have not answered the question which I asked. For I certainly did not ask you to tell me what action is both pious and impious; but now it would seem that what is loved by the gods is also hated by them. And therefore, Euthyphro, in thus chastising your father you may very likely be doing what is agreeable to Zeus but disagreeable to Cronos and Uranus, and what is acceptable to Hephaestus but unacceptable to Hera, and there may be other gods who have similar differences of opinion.

EUTH. But I believe, Socrates, that all the gods would be agreed as to the propriety of punishing a murderer: there would be no difference of opinion about that.

Soc. Well, but speaking of men, Euthyphro, did you ever hear anyone arguing that a murderer or any sort of evil-doer ought to be let off?

EUTH. I should rather say that these are the questions which they are always arguing, especially in courts of law: they commit all sorts of crimes, and there is nothing which they will not do or say in their own defence.

Soc. But do they admit their guilt, Euthyphro, and yet say that they ought not to be punished?

EUTH. No; they do not.

Soc. Then there are some things which they do not venture to say and do: for they do not venture to argue that if guilty they are to go unpunished, but they deny their guilt, do they not?

EUTH. Yes.

Soc. Then they do not argue that the evil-doer should not be punished, but they argue about the fact of who the evil-doer is, and what he did and when?

EUTH. True.

Soc. And the gods are in the same case, if as you assert they quarrel about just and unjust, and some of them say while others deny that injustice is done among them. For surely neither god nor man will ever venture to say that the doer of injustice is not to be punished?

EUTH. That is true, Socrates, in the main.

Soc. But they join issue about the particulars—gods and men alike, if indeed the gods dispute at all; they differ about some act which is called in question, and which by some is affirmed to be just, by others to be unjust. Is not that true?

EUTH. Quite true.

Soc. Well then, my dear friend Euthyphro, do tell me, for my better instruction and information, what proof have you that in the opinion of all the gods a servant who is guilty of murder, and is put in chains by the master of the dead man, and dies because he is put in chains before he who bound him can learn from the expositors of religious law what he ought to do with him, is killed unjustly; and that on behalf of such an one a son ought to proceed against his father and accuse him of murder. How would you show that all the gods absolutely agree in approving of his act? Prove to me that they do, and I will applaud your wisdom as long as I live.

EUTH. No doubt it will be a difficult task; though I could make the matter very clear indeed to you.

Soc. I understand; you mean to say that I am not so quick of apprehension as the judges: for to them you will be sure to prove that the act is unjust, and hateful to all the gods.

EUTH. Yes indeed, Socrates; at least if they will listen to me.

Soc. But they will be sure to listen if they find that you are a good speaker. There was a notion that came into my mind while you were speaking; I said to myself: "Well, and what if Euthyphro does prove to me that all the gods regarded the death of the serf as unjust, how do I know anything more of the nature of piety and impiety? For, granting that this action may be hateful to the gods, still piety and impiety are not adequately defined by these distinctions, for that which is hateful to the gods has been shown to be also dear to them." And therefore, Euthyphro, I do not ask you to prove this; I will suppose, if you like, that all the gods condemn and abominate such an action. But I will amend the definition so far as to say that what all the gods hate is impious, and what they love pious or holy; and what some of them love and others hate is both or neither. Shall this be our definition of piety and impiety?

EUTH. Why not, Socrates?

Soc. Why not! certainly, as far as I am concerned, Euthyphro, there is no reason why not. But whether this premise will greatly assist you in the task of instructing me as you promised is a matter for you to consider.

EUTH. Yes, I should say that what all the gods love is pious and holy, and the opposite which they all hate, impious.

Soc. Ought we to inquire into the truth of this, Euthyphro, or simply to accept it on our own authority and that of others—echoing mere assertions? What do you say?

EUTH. We should inquire; and I believe that the statement will stand the test of inquiry.

Soc. We shall soon be better able to say, my good friend. The point which I should first wish to understand is whether the pious or holy is beloved by the gods because it is holy, or holy because it is beloved of the gods.

EUTH. I do not understand your meaning, Socrates.

Soc. I will endeavour to explain: we speak of carrying and we speak of being carried, of leading and being led, seeing and being seen. You know that in all such cases there is a difference, and you know also in what the difference lies?

EUTH. I think that I understand.

Soc. And is not that which is beloved distinct from that which loves?

EUTH. Certainly.

Soc. Well; and now tell me, is that which is carried in this state of carrying because it is carried, or for some other reason?

EUTH. No; that is the reason.

Soc. And the same is true of what is led and of what is seen?

EUTH. True.

Soc. And a thing is not seen because it is visible, but conversely, visible because it is seen; nor is a thing led because it is in the state of being led, or carried because it is in the state of being carried, but the converse of this. And now I think, Euthyphro, that my meaning will be intelligible; and my meaning is that any state of action or passion implies previous action or passion. It does not become because it is becoming, but it is in a state of becoming because it becomes; neither does it suffer because it is in a state of suffering, but it is in a state of suffering because it suffers. Do you not agree?

EUTH. Yes.

Soc. Is not that which is loved in some state either of becoming or suffering?

EUTH. Yes.

Soc. And the same holds as in the previous instances; the state of being loved follows the act of being loved, and not the act the state.

EUTH. Certainly.

Soc. And what do you say of piety, Euthyphro: is not piety, according to your definition, loved by all the gods?

EUTH. Yes.

Soc. Because it is pious or holy, or for some other reason?

EUTH. No, that is the reason.

Soc. It is loved because it is holy, not holy because it is loved?

EUTH. Apparently.

Soc. And it is the object of the gods' love, and is dear to them, because it is loved of them?

EUTH. Certainly.

Soc. Then that which is dear to the gods, Euthyphro, is not holy, nor is that which is holy dear to the gods, as you affirm; but they are two different things.

EUTH. How do you mean, Socrates?

Soc. I mean to say that the holy has been acknowledged by us to be loved because it is holy, not to be holy because it is loved.

EUTH. Yes.

Soc. But that which is dear to the gods is dear to them because it is loved by them, not loved by them because it is dear to them.

EUTH. True.

Soc. But, friend Euthyphro, if that which is holy were the same with that which is dear to the gods, and were loved because it is holy, then that which is dear to the gods would be loved as being dear to them; but if that which is dear to them were dear to them because loved by them, then that which is holy would be holy because loved by them. But now you see that the reverse is the case, and that the two things are quite different from one another. For one (θεοφιλές) is of a kind to be loved because it is loved, and the other (ὅσιον) is loved because it is of a kind to be loved. Thus you appear to me, Euthyphro, when I ask you what is the nature of holiness, to offer an attribute only, and not the essence—the attribute of being loved by all the gods. But you still do not explain to me the nature of holiness. And therefore, if you please, I will ask you not to hide your treasure, but to start again, and tell me frankly what holiness or piety really is, whether dear to the gods or not (for that is a matter about which we will not quarrel); and what is impiety?

EUTH. I really do not know, Socrates, how to express what I mean. For somehow or other the definitions we propound, on whatever bases we rest them, seem always to turn round and walk away from us.

Soc. Your words, Euthyphro, are like the handiwork of my ancestor Daedalus; and if I were the sayer or propounder of them, you might scoffingly reply that the products of my reasoning walk away and will not remain fixed where they are placed because I am a descendant of his. But now, since these propositions are your own, you must find some other gibe, for they certainly, as you yourself allow, show an inclination to be on the move.

EUTH. Nay, Socrates, I think the gibe is much to the point, for you are the Daedalus who sets arguments in motion; not I, certainly, but you make them move or go round, for they would never have stirred, as far as I am concerned.

Soc. Then I must be a greater than Daedalus: for whereas he only made his own inventions to move, I move those of other people as well. And the beauty of it is, that I would rather not: for I would give the wisdom of Daedalus, and the wealth of Tantalus, to be able to detain them and keep them fixed. But enough of this. As I perceive that you are spoilt, I will myself endeavour to show you how you might instruct me in the nature of piety; and I hope that you will not grudge your labour. Tell me, then—Is not all that is pious necessarily just?

EUTH. Yes.

Soc. And is, then, all which is just pious? or, is that which is pious all just, but that which is just is only in part, and not all, pious?

EUTH. I do not understand you, Socrates.

Soc. And yet I know that you are as much wiser than I am, as you are younger. But, as I was saying, revered friend, you are spoilt owing to the abundance of your wisdom. Please to exert yourself, for there is no real difficulty in understanding me. What I mean I may explain by an illustration of what I do not mean. The poet (Stasinus) sings—

"Of Zeus, the author and creator of all these things,
He will not speak reproach: for where there is fear there is also reverence."

Now I disagree with this poet. Shall I tell you in what respect?

EUTH. By all means.

Soc. I should not say that where there is fear there is also reverence; for I am sure that many persons fear poverty and disease, and the like evils, but I do not perceive that they reverence the objects of their fear.

EUTH. Very true.

Soc. But where reverence is, there is fear; for he, who has a feeling of reverence and shame about the commission of any action, fears and is afraid of an ill reputation.

Euth. No doubt.

Soc. Then we are wrong in saying that where there is fear there is also reverence; and we should say, where there is reverence there is also fear. But there is not always reverence where there is fear; for fear is a more extended notion, and reverence is a part of fear, just as the odd is a part of number, and number is a more extended notion than the odd. I suppose that you follow me now?

Euth. Quite well.

Soc. That was the sort of question which I meant to raise when I asked whether the just is always the pious, or whether it is not the case that where there is piety there is always justice, but there may be justice where there is not piety; for justice is the more extended notion of which piety is only a part. Do you dissent?

Euth. No, I think that you are quite right.

Soc. Then, if piety is a part of justice, I suppose that we should inquire what part? If you had pursued the inquiry in the previous cases; for instance, if you had asked me what is an even number, and what part of number the even is, I should have had no difficulty in replying, a number which is not lopsided, so to speak, but represents a figure having two equal sides. Do you not agree?

Euth. Yes, I quite agree.

Soc. In like manner, I want you to tell me what part of justice is piety or holiness, that I may be able to tell Meletus not to do me injustice, or indict me for impiety, as I am now adequately instructed by you in the nature of piety or holiness, and their opposites.

Euth. Piety or holiness, Socrates, appears to me to be that part of justice which attends to the gods, as there is the other part of justice which attends to men.

Soc. That is good, Euthyphro; yet still there is a little point about which I should like to have further information, What is the meaning of "attention"? For attention can hardly be used in the same sense when applied to the gods as when applied to other things. We do so apply it, do we not? For instance, horses are said to require attention, and not every person is able to attend to them, but only a person skilled in horsemanship. Is it not so?

Euth. Certainly.

Soc. I should suppose that the art of horsemanship is the art of attending to horses?

Euth. Yes.

Soc. Nor is everyone qualified to attend to dogs, but only the huntsman?

Euth. True.

Soc. And I should also conceive that the art of the huntsman is the art of attending to dogs?

EUTH. Yes.

Soc. As the art of the oxherd is the art of attending to oxen?

EUTH. Very true.

Soc. In like manner holiness or piety is the art of attending to the gods? that would be your meaning, Euthyphro?

EUTH. Yes.

Soc. And is not attention always designed for the good or benefit of that to which the attention is given? As in the case of horses, you may observe that when attended to by the horseman's art they are benefited and improved, are they not?

EUTH. True.

Soc. As the dogs are benefited by the huntsman's art, and the oxen by the art of the oxherd, and all other things are tended or attended for their good and not for their hurt?

EUTH. Certainly, not for their hurt.

Soc. But for their good?

EUTH. Of course.

Soc. And does piety or holiness, which has been defined to be the art of attending to the gods, benefit or improve them? Would you say that when you do a holy act you make any of the gods better?

EUTH. No, no; that was certainly not what I meant.

Soc. And I, Euthyphro, never supposed that you did. I asked you the question about the nature of the attention, because I thought that you did not.

EUTH. You do me justice, Socrates; that is not the sort of attention which I mean.

Soc. Good: but I must still ask what is this attention to the gods which is called piety?

EUTH. It is such, Socrates, as servants show to their masters.

Soc. I understand—a sort of ministration to the gods.

EUTH. Exactly.

Soc. Medicine is also a sort of ministration or service, having in view the attainment of some object—would you not say of health?

EUTH. I should.

Soc. Again, there is the art which ministers to the shipbuilder with a view to the attainment of some result?

EUTH. Yes, Socrates, with a view to the building of a ship.

Soc. As there is an art which ministers to the housebuilder with a view to the building of a house?

EUTH. Yes.

Soc. And now tell me, my good friend, about the art which ministers to the gods: what work does that help to accomplish? For you must surely know if, as you say, you are of all men living the one who is best instructed in religion.

EUTH. And I speak the truth, Socrates.

Soc. Tell me then, oh tell me—what is that fair work which the gods do by the help of our ministrations?

EUTH. Many and fair, Socrates, are the works which they do.

Soc. Why, my friend, and so are those of a general. But the sum of them is easily told. Would you not say that the sum of his works is victory in war?

EUTH. Certainly.

Soc. Many and fair, too, are the works of the husbandman, if I am not mistaken; but their sum is the production of food from the earth?

EUTH. Exactly.

Soc. And of the many and fair things done by the gods, what is the sum?

EUTH. I have told you already, Socrates, that to learn all these things accurately will be very tiresome. Let me simply say that piety or holiness is learning how to please the gods in word and deed, by prayers and sacrifices. Such piety is the salvation of families and states, just as impiety, which is unpleasing to the gods, is their ruin and destruction.

Soc. I think that you could have answered in much fewer words the substance of my questions if you had chosen. But I see plainly that you are not disposed to instruct me—clearly not: else why, when we reached the point, did you turn aside? Had you only answered me I should have truly learned of you by this time the nature of piety. But I must follow you as a lover must follow the caprice of his beloved, and therefore can only ask again, what is the pious, and what is piety? Do you mean that they are a sort of science of praying and sacrificing?

EUTH. Yes, I do.

Soc. And sacrificing is giving to the gods, and prayer is asking of the gods?

EUTH. Yes, Socrates.

Soc. Upon this view, then, piety is a science of asking and giving?

EUTH. You understand me capitally, Socrates.

Soc. Yes, my friend; the reason is that I am a votary of your science, and give my mind to it, and therefore nothing which you say will be thrown away upon me. Please then to tell me, what is the nature of this service to the gods? Do you mean that we prefer requests and give gifts to them?

EUTH. Yes, I do.

Soc. Is not the right way of asking to ask of them what we want?

EUTH. Certainly.

Soc. And the right way of giving is to give to them in return what they want of us. There would be no meaning in an art which gives to anyone that which he does not want.

EUTH. Very true, Socrates.

Soc. Then piety, Euthyphro, is an art which gods and men have of trafficking with one another?

EUTH. That is an expression which you may use, if you like.

Soc. But I have no particular liking for anything but the truth. I wish, however, that you would tell me what benefit accrues to the gods from our gifts. There is no doubt about what they give to us, for there is no good thing which they do not give; but how they get any benefit from our gifts to them is far from being equally clear. If they give everything and get from us nothing, that must be a traffic in which we have very greatly the advantage of them.

EUTH. And do you imagine, Socrates, that any benefit accrues to the gods from our gifts?

SOC. But if not, Euthyphro, what is the meaning of the gifts we offer to the gods?

EUTH. What else but tributes of honour; and, as I was just now saying, what pleases them?

SOC. Piety, then, is pleasing to the gods, but not beneficial or dear to them?

EUTH. I should say that nothing could be dearer.

SOC. Then once more the assertion is repeated that piety is that which is dear to the gods?

EUTH. Certainly.

SOC. And when you say this, can you wonder at your words not standing firm, but walking away? Will you accuse me of being the Daedalus who makes them walk away, not perceiving that there is another and far greater artist than Daedalus who makes things that go round in a circle, and he is yourself; for the argument, as you will perceive, comes round to the same point. Were we not saying that the holy or pious was not the same with that which is loved of the gods? Have you forgotten?

EUTH. I quite remember.

SOC. And are you not now saying that what is dear to the gods is holy; and is not this the same as what is loved of them—do you see?

EUTH. True.

SOC. Then either we were wrong in our former assertion; or, if we were right then, we are wrong now.

EUTH. It appears so.

SOC. Then we must begin again and ask, What is piety? That is an inquiry which I shall never be weary of pursuing as far as in me lies; and I entreat you not to scorn me, but to apply your mind to the utmost, and tell me the truth. For, if any man knows, you are he; and therefore I must hold you fast, like Proteus, until you tell. If you had not certainly known the nature of piety and impiety, I am confident that you would never, on behalf of a serf, have charged your aged father with murder. You would not have run such a risk of doing wrong in the sight of the gods, and you would have had too much respect for the opinions of men. I am sure, therefore, that you know the nature of piety and impiety. Speak out then, my dear Euthyphro, and do not hide your knowledge.

EUTH. Another time, Socrates; for I am in a hurry, and must go now.

SOC. Alas! my friend, and will you leave me in despair? I was hoping that you would instruct me in the nature of piety and impiety; and then I might have cleared myself of Meletus and his indictment. I would have told him that

I had been enlightened by Euthyphro, and had given up rash innovations and speculations in which I indulged only through ignorance, and that now I am about to lead a better life.

Questions

1. Give the steps of the argument by which Socrates shows that the definition, "Piety is that which is dear to the gods," leads to a self-contradiction. What new definition is offered to escape this self-contradiction?

2. State in your own words what point Socrates is making by means of the discussion about whether piety is loved by the gods because it is holy, or is holy because it is loved by the gods.

3. Through his questioning, Socrates gets Euthyphro to define piety as one part of justice. What part of justice does Euthyphro say it is? Show how Socrates criticizes this definition, and state why you think his criticism is, or is not, valid.

4. Socrates is in quest of a definition of "piety." What kind of definition is he seeking when he says: "Remember that I did not ask you to give me two or three examples of piety, but to explain the general form which makes all pious things to be pious"? After reading the selection by Hospers in Chapter 3 (page 257), what comments would you make about Socrates' view of what a definition is?

5. If we assume that Socrates is doing what Plato thinks a philosopher should do, while Euthyphro is not, what is Plato's conception of the aim of philosophizing? Of the proper method of philosophizing?

Chapter One

THE
PROBLEM
OF

Knowledge of the World

Perceptual and Conceptual Knowledge

When someone claims to have knowledge of the world, what is meant by that claim and under what conditions is the claim justified? This question summarizes the philosophical problem of knowledge of the world. It is not the philosopher's task to study the world in the way that a natural scientist does. Rather it is the philosopher's task to analyze what a scientist, or for that matter, what anyone else, claims to know about the world. His questions are these: What kinds of knowledge can one claim to have about the world? What grounds are there for claiming to have knowledge of the world? Are these good grounds? Since these questions arise only after someone has tried to learn something about the world, they are second-order questions. On first acquaintance they are apt to seem both trivial in themselves and too remote from the task of studying the world to be worthy of serious consideration. But these questions, far from being trivial or remote, are worthy of our serious attention because they concern the assumptions underlying all our claims to know anything about the world.

The importance of the problem of knowledge of the world may be shown by considering one of its aspects, the question of whether we can rely on our senses as a means of learning about the world. Consider the following conversation between Mr. Black and Mr. White, who are looking through a window at their nephew playing in the garden:

Black. What's the child got hold of now?

White. That's his balloon on a string.

B. Are you sure that's what he's got?

W. Of course I am. I can see it, can't I?

B. I don't know. Perhaps you're having an hallucination. You had rather a lot of sherry with lunch.

W. Well, I *think* I'm seeing a balloon on a string.

B. Now you're saying that you think you see. That's one remove from claiming that you see. Besides, for all you know you may be dreaming right now.

W. Oh, but I'm not. Look, I'll let you pinch me to prove it.

B. That will only prove that you

might be dreaming that I am pinching you.

W. Oh, really now! You are making it so I can never prove that I am not dreaming. I'll have to admit that I might be dreaming all the time.

B. Indeed. And unless you can prove that you really are awake, any claim you make about what you see is unreliable. But even if I grant that you aren't dreaming right now, how can you be sure it is a balloon which Nephew has?

W. Well, it looks like the one I saw him running about with in here before lunch.

B. But it won't do to say that, because then you'll have to show that it's the *same* balloon. Not an easy task.

W. Well, it looks like *a* balloon on a string, even if it's not the *same* balloon I saw before lunch.

B. Now I am wondering why you are confident even about calling it *a* balloon. You are assuming, of course, that the object you see (always allowing that you really are seeing something) resembles those things you have called "balloons" in the past. Your assumption that the present resembles the past is extremely difficult to justify, for you are doing two questionable things here. First, you are relying on your memory. And how do you know your memory is not playing tricks on you? Second, you believe that the character of the world now is what it was in the past. But you are faced with the difficulty that there is no natural law which says that the world must always behave as it did when you last observed it.

W. Oh, all right! I can't claim that I see anything. Or, if I do see something in Nephew's hand, it's really a giant lollipop; and in another minute it's going to fly off the stick and whistle "Yankee Doodle Dandy" as it sails into the wide, blue yonder.

B. Well, I really don't know what grounds you have for claiming *that*.

On first consideration Black may seem merely annoying, or at best only amusing, as he crushes White's attempts to make claims about what he sees. Yet this conversation illustrates in small compass many of the critical points which can be made against perceptual knowledge. Philosophers try to answer these criticisms in order to provide us with good reasons for claiming to know the world on the basis of sense experiences. Black's points may be ignored. But if they are, the grounds for knowledge gained by use of the senses remain unexamined; and their being unexamined is in itself a good reason for doubting the reliability of perceptual knowledge. So if perceptual knowledge is to be respected, its grounds must be made secure by meeting the kinds of points Black raises. Although the ordinary man, and even the scientist, may rely on his senses without questioning them, this only shows that they *assume* the trustworthiness of what the philosopher examines and questions.

Thus far we have been discussing the justification of knowledge gained by way of the senses. Such knowledge may be called *perceptual knowledge.* There is another great division of knowledge called *conceptual knowledge,* which is often contrasted with perceptual knowledge. Some examples of conceptual knowledge are the arithmetical equation "$1 + 1 = 2$," the geometrical definition "A square is a parallelogram having four equal sides and four right angles," and the statement "The whole is the sum of its parts." Conceptual knowledge is often defined as knowledge whose truth depends on consistency among our concepts; and it is often distinguished from perceptual knowledge whose truth depends on consistency between our perceptions and what is perceived. Like perceptual knowledge, conceptual knowledge is open to the philosopher's question, "Do we have good reasons for accepting it?"

In this chapter we shall not be interested in the problem of conceptual knowledge for its own sake, but because of its connection with the problem of knowledge of the world. Throughout the history of philosophy there have been many philosophers who have thought that our knowledge of the world is to be accounted for as a kind of conceptual knowledge. Their goal has been to assimilate perceptual knowledge as closely as they could to conceptual knowledge, and they have attempted to achieve this in various ways. Descartes, who is represented in this chapter, is a good example of this kind of philosopher. Put very briefly, Descartes' program is to work out the consequences of his claim that the only things which exist are those things he can conceive clearly and distinctly. Passing over the large question of whether there is a relation between the conceivability of something and its existence, we may notice that because of his criterion of conceivability, it is much easier for Descartes to find a place in the world for his mind (or self) and God, than for so-called material objects. The place he does find for material objects depends on his ability to form concepts of them in his mind (an ability whose origin Descartes leaves unexplained). He believes that these concepts are used by the mind for classifying and guaranteeing what is perceived by the senses. Thus, Descartes makes the

mind the arbiter of what exists. The reliability of the mind itself is guaranteed by God, who made it. Consequently Descartes believes that he has made the statement "This is a piece of wax I hold in my hand" as indubitable as "$1 + 1 = 2$."

So it may be seen that part of the problem of the knowledge of the world has been created by philosophers like Descartes. In their efforts to justify perceptual knowledge by assimilating it to conceptual knowledge, they have generated the question: Is our knowledge of the world a kind of conceptual knowledge? Almost all of the philosophers represented in this chapter are interested in answering this question one way or the other.

Empiricist and Rationalist

Having introduced the terms "perceptual knowledge" and "conceptual knowledge," we are now in a position to introduce two other terms which have a prominent place in discussions of the problem of knowledge of the world. They are "empiricist" and "rationalist." Empiricists and rationalists are proponents of two different theories of knowledge. The empiricist is a proponent of efforts to analyze and justify perceptual knowledge as a way of knowing about the world. The rationalist is a proponent of efforts to explain and justify our knowledge of the world as a kind of conceptual knowledge. As an opponent of rationalists, the empiricist is thought to be a critic of their emphasis on the role of the mind as opposed to the senses, in our knowledge of the world. As an opponent of empiricists, the rationalist is thought of as disparaging, if not denying completely, the possibility of perceptual knowledge, and consequently a rationalist is supposed to exhibit nothing but disdain for empiricist efforts to account for our knowledge of the world.

We must warn the reader, however, that these categories of "empiricist" and "rationalist" are useful only up to a certain point. Sometimes it may be difficult to classify a given philosopher's theory of knowledge as either rationalist or empiricist. The reader will find Berkeley a case in point. What is more, any view of the problem of knowledge as a wrestling match between empiricists and rationalists, no holds barred, overstates the case. A truer view seems to be that both kinds of philosophers have learned much from each other. Progressively they have become more respectful of each other's views and have made efforts at accommodation.

Theories of Knowledge and Metaphysics

We must also say something here about the connection between theories of knowledge and metaphysics. A man's metaphysics is his view of the ultimate nature of the world or of reality. Now it is possible for someone to work out a metaphysics without being interested in the rationalists' and empiricists' problem of analyzing and justifying our knowledge of the world. However, if one is interested in the problem of knowledge of the world, he may find that his view of the kind of knowledge that is possible implies that the world has a certain character. Most of the philosophers represented in this chapter did work out the metaphysical implications of their theories of knowledge, and some metaphysics is included in several of the readings. (Descartes: Whatever can be conceived clearly and distinctly exists. Berkeley: The furniture of the world is

nothing but collections of ideas. Royce: The real world is an outer mind.) A metaphysical statement, like any statement purporting to describe the world, is, of course, subject to the philosopher's second-order question, "Are there good grounds for accepting it?" The reader should not hesitate to ask this question when he encounters metaphysical statements in this chapter.

Survey of the Chapter

This chapter contains selections on the problem of knowledge of the world by Descartes, Locke, Berkeley, Hume, Kant, Royce, James, and Professor G. E. Moore. Traditionally, Descartes, Kant, and Royce are thought of as rationalists; Locke, Berkeley, Hume, and James are thought of as empiricists. Professor Moore appears in this chapter as a critic of James, and his own positive views on knowledge are not presented here. These writings were produced over a period of almost three hundred years, from the seventeenth to the twentieth centuries; each philosopher writes with his predecessors' views of our knowledge of the world in mind; and each one endeavors to improve on the work of his predecessors and sometimes explicitly criticizes it.

In many respects Descartes, the man "in on the ground floor," sets the tone for the whole chapter. So we begin with a prologue that is Descartes' account of his intellectual development, the framework in which the problem of knowledge of the world presented itself to him. Descartes' own contribution to a solution of the problem is twofold: on the critical side is his method of doubt; on the constructive side is his view that whatever can be conceived clearly and distinctly exists. Locke's contribution is an analysis of perceptual knowledge and a defense of the senses as the sole source of our knowledge of the world. The reader should be careful to note that Locke's use of the word "idea" is quite different from Descartes' use of the word as a synonym for "concept." Berkeley's contribution to the solution of the problem of knowledge of the world is usually called "subjective idealism." With Locke, Berkeley believes that our senses are the source of our knowledge of the world. But after pointing out that in order for us to say that something exists we must perceive it, Berkeley goes on to claim that in order for something to be perceivable it must be in some respect mindlike, or an idea, else the mind could never perceive it. This view requires a new warning about the word "idea," since Berkeley's use of it differs from that of both Descartes and Locke. We may add that Berkeley's successor Hume uses "idea" in yet another way.

It should be remarked that almost all of the philosophers represented in this chapter are interested in the *psychology* of our knowledge of the world as well as the *justification* of that knowledge. Indeed, many of them discuss the psychological question, "What goes on inside our heads when we learn about the world?" as a necessary preliminary to answering the philosophical question, "What are the grounds on which our knowledge of the world rests?" It is important to keep these two questions sharply separated in our minds as we read these philosophers. The former question is a first-order question requiring the description and explanation of the process by which we learn about the world. The latter is a second-order question requiring an examination and evaluation of the foundations of knowledge.

The fact that philosophers in the past dealt with both questions should not lead us into confusing philosophy with the science of psychology. Nowadays philosophers no longer try to answer the questions of psychology as they did in the past.

The aspect of the problem of knowledge of the world which interested Hume is the question of whether our generalizations about causal connections are justified. Do we have good reasons for beliefs of the following kind:

When I plant these zinnia seeds, zinnias will come up.
My chair will continue to support me until I finish my studies tonight.
The sun will rise tomorrow.
Bread will nourish me.
My friends love me.

We expect these and millions of other connections to hold in the future, but will they? Hume argues that our *belief* that the future will be like the past explains why we have our expectations about the future, but we can never *know* that the future will resemble the past. Our minds cannot guarantee the future behavior of zinnia seeds, chairs, bread, and other things in the world; so Hume would have us be content with only probable knowledge of the world. Kant was both impressed and perturbed by Hume's analysis of our knowledge of causal connections; and in this chapter he is represented by his proposals for a philosophical investigation which will show that our minds may have more than merely probable knowledge of the world.

With the selections by Royce and James we shift from philosophy in Europe to philosophy in the United

States. Royce's analysis and justification of our knowledge of the world may be regarded as the Americanization of rationalism, and James's pragmatism as the Americanization of empiricism. Royce, owing much to Kant, transmutes Berkeley's subjective idealism into an objective idealism. The selection by James is a reaction against Royce's kind of solution for the problem of knowledge of the world. James first expounds the pragmatic theory of meaning, the view that for a word to have meaning for someone it must designate some aspect of his experience which can be differentiated from all the rest of it. If there is no differentiation the word is meaningless, and no aspect of experience is being talked about when the word is used. Armed with the pragmatic theory of meaning, James both offers a pragmatic account of our knowledge of the world, and criticizes rationalist accounts of that knowledge. The final selection in this chapter is Professor G. E. Moore's criticism of the pragmatic theory of truth. Taken as a set, the selections by Royce, James, and Moore are an example of the development of philosophical insight through progressive criticism.

The problem of knowledge of the world is closely related to the problems treated in the next two chapters: Chapter 2, "The Problem of Scientific Knowledge"; and Chapter 3, "The Problem of Meaning and Verification." In many respects the problem of scientific knowledge is a refinement of the problem of knowledge of the world, and the possibility of scientific knowledge presupposes that we have good grounds for claiming to have knowledge of the world. But because of the abstractness of its concepts, and its transformation of experience into experiment, scientific knowledge deserves a chapter to itself.

When we express our claims to know, we use words formed into statements. The prospect of talking about the world raises two questions: How do our words come to have meaning? and, What are we doing when we count a statement true (or false)? Most of the philosophers represented in this chapter are well aware of the close connection between the kinds of entities which someone claims to know and the words he uses to talk about what he knows; and this connection is examined in its own right in Chapter 3.

Discourse on Method

René Descartes
(1596-1650)

René Descartes was born at La Haye in Touraine, France. He was educated in the Jesuit school at La Flèche and in the university of Poitiers, where he studied law. As a young man he spent several years in soldiering and travel, but his thoughts were never far from mathematics and the sciences, and he finally decided to devote himself to a life of study. He settled first in France, but in 1628 he moved to Holland, where he spent almost all the rest of his life. His great ambition was to work out an entire reconstruction of all knowledge (including religious knowledge) which would provide as much clarity and certainty as mathematics. It was with this goal in mind that he wrote his chief philosophical works: *Rules for the Direction of the Mind* (1628); *Discourse on the Method of Rightly Conducting the Reason and Seeking for Truth in the Sciences* (1637); and *Meditations on the First Philosophy* (1641). Descartes also made an important contribution to mathematics by his discovery of analytic geometry. In addition he wrote on theoretical physics and carried out investigations in physiology, but he made no lasting contribution to these sciences.

For a prologue to this chapter on the problem of knowledge of the world, we have chosen certain of the autobiographical passages from Descartes' *Discourse*. They reveal in a personal way the intellectual character of the man who set the problem of our knowledge of the world for modern philosophy. He was an independent thinker at a time when people were having to learn once again how to be independent thinkers, and his example is still an inspiration for us today. He is determined to accept nothing as proven, which he has not examined for himself. His determination made the problem of knowledge of the world a more open and vital question than it had been at any time since Aristotle. Descartes' questioning of the nature of our knowledge of the world was both so fundamental and so dramatic that philosophers have felt obliged to consider it seriously ever since.

The *Discourse* is Descartes' manifesto of his resolution to think for himself, and his justification of that resolution by exhibiting his method of reasoning. His dissatisfaction with his education may awaken a sympathetic echo in many readers. But this very dissatisfaction is probably evidence that Descartes had an excellent education. For many a teacher might feel that he has done as much as he can for a student, if he has brought that student to the point where he is so dissatisfied with what he thinks he knows, that he is fired to improve and increase his knowledge. Descartes' dissatisfaction was of this constructive kind; for he was determined to improve his and the world's knowledge in several different areas. His most notable success was in mathematics, where he is credited with the discovery of analytic geometry; and his success in philosophy is certainly not unimpressive. If his physics is now a historical curiosity, we must nonetheless agree that it is no mean accomplishment to be remembered in the history, if not in the presently acceptable teachings, of that science.

Descartes' method of conducting the reason is very much the product of a mind accustomed to mathematical thinking. This is at once its virtue and its fault. No mention is made of observation; no place is found for experiment. These omissions make it sound odd to us as a method for seeking truth in the sciences, if what we call the empirical sciences are meant. It is not surprising then that Descartes' great success in the use of his method came in mathematics, above all in his discovery of analytic geometry. Philosophers are chiefly interested in Descartes' method because he used it in working out his answer to the problem of knowledge of the world. His discussion of this problem, taken from his *Meditations,* is the next reading in this chapter. When the reader comes to examine Descartes' solution to the problem of knowledge of the world, it will be more understandable if he remembers its methodological origin.

From *The Philosophical Works of Descartes,* Vol. 1, translated by E. S. Haldane and G. R. T. Ross, Cambridge University Press, Cambridge, Eng., 1931. Reprinted by permission of the publisher.

. . . My design is not here to teach the Method which everyone should follow in order to promote the good conduct of his Reason, but only to show in what manner I have endeavoured to conduct my own. Those who set about giving precepts must esteem themselves more skilful than those to whom they advance them, and if they fall short in the smallest matter they must of course take the blame for it. But regarding this Treatise simply as a history, or, if you prefer it, a fable in which, amongst certain things which may be imitated, there are possibly others also which it would not be right to follow, I hope that it will be of use to some without being hurtful to any, and that all will thank me for my frankness.

I have been nourished on letters since my childhood, and since I was given to believe that by their means a clear and certain knowledge could be obtained of all that is useful in life, I had an extreme desire to acquire instruction. But so soon as I had achieved the entire course of study at the close of which one is usually received into the ranks of the learned, I entirely changed my opinion. For I found myself embarrassed with so many doubts and errors that it seemed to me that the effort to instruct myself had no effect other than the increasing discovery of my own ignorance. And yet I was studying at one of the most celebrated Schools in Europe, where I thought that there must be men of learning if they were to be found anywhere in the world. I learned there all that others learned; and not being satisfied with the sciences that we were taught, I even read through all the books which fell into my hands, treating of what is considered most curious and rare. Along with this I knew the judgments that others had formed of me, and I did not feel that I was esteemed inferior to my fellow-students, although there were amongst them some destined to fill the places of our masters. And finally our century seemed to me as flourishing, and as fertile in great minds, as any which had preceded. And this made me take the liberty of judging all others by myself and of coming to the conclusion that there was no learning in the world such as I was formerly led to believe it to be.

I did not omit, however, always to hold in esteem those exercises which are the occupation of the Schools. I knew that the Languages which one learns there are essential for the understanding of all ancient literature; that fables with their charm stimulate the mind and histories of memorable deeds exalt it; and that, when read with discretion, these books assist in forming a sound judgment. I was aware that the reading of all good books is indeed like a conversation with the noblest men of past centuries who were the authors of them, nay a carefully studied conversation, in which they reveal to us none but the best of their thoughts. I deemed Eloquence to have a power and beauty beyond compare; that Poesy has most ravishing delicacy and sweetness; that in Mathematics there are the subtlest discoveries and inventions which may accomplish much, both in satisfying the curious, and in furthering all the arts, and in diminishing man's labour; that those writings that deal with Morals contain much that is instructive, and many exhortations to virtue which are most useful; that Theology points out the way to Heaven; that Philosophy teaches us to speak with an appearance of truth on all things, and causes us to be admired by the less learned; that Jurisprudence, Medicine and all other sciences bring honour and riches to those who cultivate them; and finally that it is good to have examined all things, even those most full of superstition and falsehood, in order that we may know their just value, and avoid being deceived by them.

But I considered that I had already given sufficient time to languages and likewise even to the reading of the literature of the ancients, both their histories and their fables. For to converse with those of other centuries is almost the same thing as to travel. It is good to know something of the customs of different peoples in order to judge more sanely of our own, and not to think that everything of a fashion not ours is absurd and contrary to reason, as do those who have seen nothing. But when one employs too much time in travelling, one becomes a stranger in one's own country, and when one is too curious about things which were practised in past centuries, one is usually very ignorant about those which are practised in our own time. Besides, fables make one imagine many events possible which in reality are not so, and even the most accurate of histories, if they do not exactly misrepresent or exaggerate the value of things in order to render them more worthy of being read, at least omit in them all the circumstances which are basest and least notable; and from this fact it follows that what is retained is not portrayed as it really is, and that those who regulate their conduct by examples which they derive from such a source are liable to fall into the extravagances of the knights-errant of Romance, and form projects beyond their power of performance.

I esteemed Eloquence most highly and I was enamoured of Poesy, but I thought that both were gifts of the mind rather than fruits of study. Those who have the strongest power of reasoning, and who most skilfully arrange their thoughts in order to render them clear and intelligible, have the best power of persuasion even if they can but speak the language of Lower Brittany and have never learned Rhetoric. And those who have the most delightful original ideas, and who know how to express them with the maximum of style and suavity, would not fail to be the best poets even if the art of Poetry were unknown to them.

Most of all was I delighted with Mathematics because of the certainty of its demonstrations and the evidence of its reasoning; but I did not yet understand its true use, and, believing that it was of service only in the mechanical arts, I was astonished that, seeing how firm and solid was its basis, no loftier edifice had been reared thereupon. On the other hand I compared the works of the ancient pagans which deal with Morals to palaces most superb and magnificent, which are yet built on sand and mud alone. They praise the virtues most highly and show them to be more worthy of being prized than anything else in the world, but they do not sufficiently teach us to become acquainted with them, and often that which is called by a fine name is nothing but insensibility, or pride, or despair, or parricide.

I honoured our Theology and aspired as much as anyone to reach to heaven, but having learned to regard it as a most highly assured fact that the road is not less open to the most ignorant than to the most learned, and that the revealed truths which conduct thither are quite above our intelligence, I should not have dared to submit them to the feebleness of my reasonings; and I thought that, in order to undertake to examine them and succeed in so doing, it was necessary to have some extraordinary assistance from above and to be more than a mere man.

I shall not say anything about Philosophy, but that, seeing that it has been cultivated for many centuries by the best minds that have ever lived, and that nevertheless no single thing is to be found in it which is not subject of dispute, and in consequence which is not dubious, I had not enough presumption to hope to fare better there than other men had done. And also, considering how many conflicting opinions there may be regarding the self-same matter, all supported by learned people, while there can never be more than one which is true, I esteemed as well-nigh false all that only went as far as being probable.

Then as to the other sciences, inasmuch as they derive their principles from Philosophy, I judged that one could have built nothing solid on foundations so far from firm. And neither the honour nor the promised gain was sufficient to persuade me to cultivate them, for, thanks be to God, I did not find myself in a condition which obliged me to make a merchandise of science for the improvement of my fortune; and, although I did not pretend to scorn all glory like the Cynics, I yet had very small esteem for what I could not hope to acquire, excepting through fictitious titles. And, finally, as to false doctrines, I thought that I already knew well enough what they were worth to be subject to deception neither by the promises of an alchemist, the predictions of an astrologer, the impostures of a magician, the artifices or the empty boastings of any of those who make a profession of knowing that of which they are ignorant.

This is why, as soon as age permitted me to emerge from the control of my tutors, I entirely quitted the study of letters. And resolving to seek no other science than that which could be found in myself, or at least in the great book of the world, I employed the rest of my youth in travel, in seeing courts and armies, in intercourse with men of diverse temperaments and conditions, in collecting varied experiences, in proving myself in the various predicaments in which I was placed by fortune, and under all circumstances bringing my mind to bear on the things which came before it, so that I might derive some profit from my experience. For it seemed to me that I might meet with much more truth in the reasonings that each man makes on the matters that specially concern him, and the issue of which would very soon punish him if he made a wrong judgment, than in the case of those made by a man of letters in his study touching speculations which lead to no result, and which bring about no other consequences to himself excepting that he will be all the more vain the more they are removed from common sense, since in this case it proves him to have employed so much the more ingenuity and skill in trying to make them seem probable. And I always had an excessive desire to learn to distinguish the true from the false, in order to see clearly in my actions and to walk with confidence in this life.

It is true that while I only considered the manners of other men I found in them nothing to give me settled convictions; and I remarked in them almost as much diversity as I had formerly seen in the opinions of philosophers. So much was this the case that the greatest profit which I derived from their study was that, in seeing many things which, although they seem to us very extravagant and ridiculous, were yet commonly received and approved by other great nations, I learned to believe nothing too certainly of which I had only been convinced by example and custom. Thus little by little I was delivered from many errors which might have obscured our natural vision and rendered us less capable of listening to Reason. But after I had employed several years in thus studying the book of the world and trying to acquire some experience, I one day formed the resolution of also making myself an object of study and of employing all the strength of my mind in choosing the road I should follow. This succeeded much better, it appeared to me, than if I had never departed either from my country or my books.

I was then in Germany, to which country I had been attracted by the wars which are not yet at an end. And as I was returning from the coronation of the Emperor to join the army, the setting in of winter detained me in a quarter where, since I found no society to divert me, while fortunately I had also no cares or passions to trouble me, I remained the whole day shut up alone in a stove-heated room where I had complete leisure to occupy myself with my own thoughts. One of the first of the considerations that occurred to me was that there is very often less perfection in works composed of several portions, and carried out by the hands of various masters, than in those on which one individual alone has worked. Thus we see that buildings planned and carried out by one architect alone are usually more beautiful and better proportioned than those which many have tried to put in order and improve, making use of old walls which were built with other ends in view. In the same way also, those ancient cities, which, originally mere villages, have become in the process of time great towns, are usually badly constructed in comparison with those which are regularly laid out on a plain by a surveyor who is free to follow his own ideas. Even though, considering their buildings each one apart, there is often as much or more display of skill in the one case than in the other, the former have large buildings and small buildings indiscriminately placed together, thus rendering the streets crooked and irregular, so that it might be said that it was chance rather than the will of men guided by reason that led to such an arrangement. And if we consider that this happens despite the fact that from all time there have been certain officials who have had the special duty of looking after the buildings of private individuals in order that they may be public ornaments, we shall understand how difficult it is to bring about much that is satisfactory in operating only upon the works of others. . . .

It is true that we do not find that all the houses in a town are rased to the ground for the sole reason that the town is to be rebuilt in another fashion, with streets made more beautiful; but at the same time we see that many people cause their own houses to be knocked down in order to rebuild them, and that sometimes they are forced so to do where there is danger of the houses falling of themselves and when the foundations are not secure. From such examples I argued to myself that there was no plausibility in the claim of any private individual to reform a state by altering everything, and by overturning it throughout, in order to set it right again. Nor is it likewise probable that the whole body of the Sciences, or the order of teaching established by the Schools, should be reformed. But as regards all the opinions which up to this time I had embraced, I thought I could not do better than endeavour once for all to sweep them completely away, so that they might later on be replaced, either by others which were better, or by the same, when I had made them conform to the uniformity of a rational scheme. And I firmly believed that by this means I should succeed in directing my life much better than if I had only built on old foundations, and relied on principles of which I allowed myself to be in youth persuaded without having inquired into their truth. For although in so doing I recognised various difficulties, these were at the same time not unsurmountable, nor comparable to those which are found in reformation of the most insignificant kind in matters which concern the public. In the case of great bodies it is too difficult a task to raise them again when they are once thrown down, or even to keep them in their places when once thoroughly shaken; and their fall cannot be otherwise than very violent. Then as to any imperfections that they may possess (and the very diversity that is found between them is sufficient to tell us that these in many cases exist) custom has doubtless greatly mitigated them, while it has also helped us to avoid, or insensibly corrected a number against which mere foresight would have found it difficult to guard. And finally the imperfections are almost always more supportable than would be the process of removing them, just as the great roads which wind about amongst the mountains become, because of being frequented, little by little so well-beaten and easy that it is much better to follow them than to try to go more directly by climbing over rocks and descending to the foot of precipices.

This is the reason why I cannot in any way approve of those turbulent and unrestful spirits who, being called neither by birth nor fortune to the management of public affairs, never fail to have always in their minds some new reforms. And if I thought that in this treatise there was contained the smallest justification for this folly, I should be very sorry to allow it to be published. My design has never extended beyond trying to reform my own opinion and to build on a foundation which is entirely my own. If my work has given me a certain satisfaction, so that I here present to you a draft of it, I do not so do because I wish to advise anybody to imitate it. Those to whom God has been most beneficent in the bestowal of His graces will perhaps form designs which are more elevated; but I fear much that this particular one will seem too venturesome for many. The simple resolve to strip oneself of all opinions and beliefs formerly received is not to be regarded as an example that each man should follow, and the world may be said to be mainly composed of two classes of minds neither of which could prudently adopt it. There are those who, believing themselves to be cleverer than they are, cannot restrain themselves from being precipitate in judgment and have not sufficient patience to arrange their thoughts in proper order; hence, once a man of this description had taken the liberty of doubting the principles he formerly accepted, and had deviated from the beaten track, he would never be able to maintain the path which must be followed to reach the appointed end more quickly, and he would hence remain wandering astray all through his life. Secondly, there are those who, having reason or modesty enough to judge that they are less capable of distinguishing truth from falsehood than some others from whom instruction might be obtained, are right in contenting themselves with following the opinions of these others rather than in searching better ones for themselves.

For myself I should doubtless have been of these last if I had never had more than a single master, or had I never known the diversities which have from all time existed between the opinions of men of the greatest learning. But I had been taught, even in my College days, that there is nothing imaginable so strange or so little credible that it has not been maintained by one philosopher or other, and I further recognised in the course of my travels that all those whose sentiments are very contrary to ours are yet not necessarily barbarians or savages, but may be possessed of reason in as great or even a greater degree than ourselves. I also considered how very different the self-same man, identical in mind and spirit, may become, according as he is brought up from childhood amongst the French or Germans, or has passed his whole life amongst Chinese or cannibals. I likewise noticed how even in the fashions of one's clothing the same thing that pleased us ten years ago, and which will perhaps please us once again before ten years are passed, seems at the present time extravagant and ridiculous. I thus concluded that it is much more custom and example that persuade us than any certain knowledge, and yet in spite of this the voice of the majority does not afford a proof of any value in truths a little difficult to discover, because such truths are much more likely to have been discovered by one man than by a nation. I could not, however, put my finger on a single person whose opinions seemed preferable to those of others, and I found that I was, so to speak, constrained myself to undertake the direction of my procedure.

But like one who walks alone and in the twilight I resolved to go so slowly, and to use so much circumspection in all things, that if my advance was but very small, at least I guarded myself well from falling. I did not wish to set about the final rejection of any single opinion which might formerly have crept into my beliefs without having been introduced there by means of Reason, until I had first of all employed sufficient time in planning out the task which I had undertaken, and in seeking the true Method of arriving at a knowledge of all the things of which my mind was capable.

Among the different branches of Philosophy, I had in my younger days to a certain extent studied Logic; and in those of Mathematics, Geometrical Analysis and Algebra—three arts or sciences which seemed as though they ought to contribute something to the design I had in view. But in examining them I observed in respect to Logic that the syllogisms and the greater part of the other teaching served better in explaining to others those things that one knows (or like the art of Lully, in enabling one to speak without judgment of those things of which one is ignorant) than in learning what is new. And although in reality Logic contains many precepts which are very true and very good, there are at the same time mingled with them so many others which are hurtful or superfluous, that it is almost as difficult to separate the two as to draw a Diana or a Minerva out of a block of marble which is not yet roughly hewn. And as to the Analysis of the ancients and the Algebra of the moderns, besides the fact that they embrace only matters the most abstract, such as appear to have no actual use, the former is always so restricted to the consideration of symbols that it cannot exercise the Understanding without greatly fatiguing the Imagination; and in the latter one is so subjected to certain rules and formulas that the result is the construction of an art which is confused and obscure, and which embarrasses the mind, instead of a science which contributes to its cultivation. This made me feel that some other Method must be found, which, comprising the advantages of the three, is yet exempt from their faults. And as a multiplicity of laws often furnishes excuses for evil-doing, and as a State is hence much better ruled when, having but very few laws, these are most strictly observed; so, instead of the great number of precepts of which Logic is composed, I believed that I should find the four which I shall state quite sufficient, provided that I adhered to a firm and constant resolve never on any single occasion to fail in their observance.

1.   The first of these was to accept nothing as true which I did not clearly recognise to be so: that is to say, carefully to avoid precipitation and prejudice in judgments, and to accept in them nothing more than what was presented to my mind so clearly and distinctly that I could have no occasion to doubt it.

2.   The second was to divide up each of the difficulties which I examined into as many parts as possible, and as seemed requisite in order that it might be resolved in the best manner possible.

3.   The third was to carry on my reflections in due order, commencing with objects that were the most simple and easy to understand, in order to rise little by little, or by degrees, to knowledge of the most complex, assuming an order, even if a fictitious one, among those which do not follow a natural sequence relatively to one another.

4.   The last was in all cases to make enumerations so complete and reviews so general that I should be certain of having omitted nothing.

Those long chains of reasoning, simple and easy as they are, of which geometricians make use in order to arrive at the most difficult demonstrations, had caused me to imagine that all those things which fall under the cognizance of man might very likely be mutually related in the same fashion; and that, provided only that we abstain from receiving anything as true which is not so, and always retain the order which is necessary in order to deduce the one conclusion from the other, there can be nothing so remote that we cannot reach to it, nor so recondite that we cannot discover it. And I had not much trouble in discovering which objects it was necessary to begin with, for I already knew that it was with the most simple and those most easy to apprehend. Considering also that of all those who have hitherto sought for the truth in the Sciences, it has been the mathematicians alone who have been able to succeed in making any demonstrations, that is to say producing reasons which are evident and certain, I did not doubt that it had been by means of a similar kind that they carried on their investigations. . . .

But what pleased me most in this Method was that I was certain by its means of exercising my reason in all things, if not perfectly, at least as well as was in my power. And besides this, I felt in making use of it that my mind gradually accustomed itself to conceive of its objects more accurately and distinctly; and not having restricted this Method to any particular matter, I promised myself to apply it as usefully to the difficulties of other sciences as I had done to those of Algebra.[1] Not that on this account I dared undertake to examine just at once all those that might present themselves; for that would itself have been contrary to the order which the Method prescribes. But having noticed that the knowledge of these difficulties must be dependent on principles derived from Philosophy in which I yet found nothing to be certain, I thought that it was requisite above all to try to establish certainty in it. I considered also that since this endeavour is the most important in all the world, and that in which precipitation and prejudice were most to be feared, I should not try to grapple with it till I had attained to a much riper age than that of three and twenty, which was the age I had reached. I thought, too, that I should first of all employ much time in preparing myself for the work by eradicating from my mind all the wrong opinions which I had up to this time accepted, and accumulating a variety of experiences fitted later on to afford matter for my reasonings, and by ever exercising myself in the Method which I had prescribed, in order more and more to fortify myself in the power of using it.

1

| *Meditations on the First Philosophy* | René Descartes (1596-1650) |

[A general introductory note on Descartes may be found on page 34.]

In the *Meditations* Descartes attempts to show what we can justifiably claim to know without making any assumptions whose grounds have not been thoroughly examined, and without relying on what others have told us. He takes all the knowledge which he has supposed himself to possess and then sees how much of it will stand up under the most searching criticism he can bring to bear upon it. The operating principle of this procedure is this: Whatever beliefs remain that cannot possibly be doubted after this criticism can safely be claimed to constitute genuine knowledge.

For Descartes the mark of genuine knowledge is objective certainty, which is to be distinguished from subjective certainty. A person is subjectively certain of something if he does not doubt it, whatever may

---

[1] [A reference to his discovery of analytic geometry.—Eds.]

be the reasons for which he does not doubt it. Since anything a person is completely convinced of is subjectively certain to him, it is perfectly possible for a false belief (e.g., that the earth is flat) to be subjectively certain to someone. Objective certainty, however, is a belief which cannot possibly be doubted by any rational person, even after he has used every rational argument in his power to destroy it.

In order to discover what it is that we really know, then, we need only discover what beliefs are objectively certain. And the method by which to do this is to try to doubt every *claim* to knowledge. If we find any such claim to be beyond all possible doubt, then we shall know that in this instance we have genuine knowledge. Thus rational doubt is used by Descartes as a method for arriving at objective certainty.

In this reading Descartes applies his method of doubt to the two possible sources of knowledge: sense experience and pure reason. He finds that he is able to doubt everything of which we might claim to be certain through our senses and our reason. He then goes on to argue that nevertheless there are some things which are objectively certain. Here he offers his own answers to three basic questions about knowledge: *Can* I know anything for certain? *What* can I know for certain? and, *How* can I know something for certain? It remains for the reader himself to discover how Descartes arrives at what he believes to be objectively certain, after he has applied his extreme doubt to everything that has been claimed to be known through the senses or through reason.

This reading is from Meditations I, II, III, IV, and VI of *Meditations on the First Philosophy,* translated from the Latin by E. S. Haldane and G. R. T. Ross.

From *The Philosophical Works of Descartes,* Vol. 1, translated by E. S. Haldane and G. R. T. Ross, Cambridge University Press, Cambridge, Eng., 1931. Reprinted by permission of the publisher.

MEDITATION I

Of the Things Which May Be Brought within the Sphere of the Doubtful.

It is now some years since I detected how many were the false beliefs that I had from my earliest youth admitted as true, and how doubtful was everything I had since constructed on this basis; and from that time I was convinced that I must once for all seriously undertake to rid myself of all the opinions which I had formerly accepted, and commence to build anew from the foundation, if I wanted to establish any firm and permanent structure in the sciences. But as this enterprise appeared to be a very great one, I waited until I had attained an age so mature that I could not hope that at any later date I should be better fitted to execute my design. This reason caused me to delay so long that I should feel that I was doing wrong were I to occupy in deliberation the time that yet remains to me for action. Today, then, since very opportunely for the plan I have in view I have delivered my mind from every care and since I have procured for myself an assured leisure in a peaceable retirement, I shall at last seriously and freely address myself to the general upheaval of all my former opinions.

Now for this object it is not necessary that I should show that all of these are false—I shall perhaps never arrive at this end. But inasmuch as reason already persuades me that I ought no less carefully to withhold my assent from matters which are not entirely certain and indubitable than from those which appear to me manifestly to be false, if I am able to find in each one some reason to doubt, this will suffice to justify my rejecting the whole. And for that end it will not be requisite that I should examine each in particular, which would be an endless undertaking; for owing to the fact that the destruction of the foundations of necessity brings with it the downfall of the rest of the edifice, I shall only in the first place attack those principles upon which all my former opinions rested.

All that up to the present time I have accepted as most true and certain I have learned either from the senses or through the senses; but it is sometimes proved to me that these senses are deceptive, and it is wiser not to trust entirely to any thing by which we have once been deceived.

But it may be that although the senses sometimes deceive us concerning things which are hardly perceptible, or very far away, there are yet many others to be met with as to which we cannot reasonably have any doubt, although we recognise them by their means. For example, there is the fact that I am here, seated by the fire, attired in a dressing gown, having this paper in my hands and other similar matters. And how could I deny that these hands and this body are mine, were it not perhaps that I compare myself to certain persons, devoid of sense, whose cerebella are so troubled and clouded by the violent vapours of black bile, that they constantly assure us that they think they are kings when they are really quite poor, or that they are clothed in purple when they are really without covering, or who imagine that they have an earthenware head or are nothing but pumpkins or are made of glass. But they are mad, and I should not be any the less insane were I to follow examples so extravagant.

At the same time I must remember that I am a man, and that consequently I am in the habit of sleeping, and in my dreams representing to myself the same things or sometimes even less probable things, than do those who are insane in their waking moments. How often has it happened to me that in the night I dreamt that I found myself in this particular place, that I was dressed and seated near the fire, whilst in reality I was lying undressed in bed! At this moment it does indeed seem to me that it is with eyes awake that I am looking at this paper; that this head which I move is not asleep, that it is deliberately and of set purpose that I extend my hand and perceive it; what happens in sleep does not appear so clear nor so distinct as does all this. But in thinking over this I remind myself that on many occasions I have in sleep been deceived by similar illusions, and in dwelling carefully on this reflection I see so manifestly that there are no certain indications by which we may clearly distinguish wakefulness from sleep that I am lost in astonishment. And my astonishment is such that it is almost capable of persuading me that I now dream.

Now let us assume that we are asleep and that all these particulars, e.g. that we open our eyes, shake our head, extend our hands, and so on, are but false delusions; and let us reflect that possibly neither our hands nor our whole body are such as they appear to us to be. At the same time we must at least confess that the things which are represented to us in sleep are like painted representations which can only have been formed as the counterparts of something real and true, and that in this way those general things at least, i.e. eyes, a head, hands, and a whole body, are not imaginary things, but things really existent. For, as a matter of fact, painters, even when they study with the greatest skill to represent sirens and satyrs by forms the most strange and extraordinary, cannot give them natures which are entirely new, but merely make a certain medley of the members of different animals; or if their imagination is extravagant enough to invent something so novel that nothing similar has ever before been seen, and that then their work represents a thing purely fictitious and absolutely false, it is certain all the same that the colours of which this is composed are necessarily real. And for the same reason, although these general things, to wit, eyes, a head, hands, and such like, may be imaginary, we are bound at the same time to confess that there are at least some other objects yet more simple and more universal, which are real and true; and of these just in the same way as with certain real colours, all these images of things which dwell in our thoughts, whether true and real or false and fantastic, are formed.

To such a class of things pertains corporeal (material) nature in general, and its extension, the figure of extended things, their quantity or magnitude and number, as also the place in which they are, the time which measures their duration, and so on.

That is possibly why our reasoning is not unjust when we conclude from this that Physics, Astronomy, Medicine, and all other sciences which have as their end the consideration of composite things, are very dubious and uncertain; but that Arithmetic, Geometry and other sciences of that kind which only treat of things that are very simple and very general, without taking great trouble to ascertain whether they are actually existent or not, contain some measure of certainty and an element of the indubitable. For whether I am awake or asleep, two and three together always form five, and the square can never have more than four sides, and it does not seem possible that truths so clear and apparent can be suspected of any falsity.

Nevertheless I have long had fixed in my mind the belief that an all-powerful God existed by whom I have been created such as I am. But how do I know that He has not brought it to pass that there is no earth, no heaven, no extended body, no magnitude, no place, and that nevertheless they seem to me to exist just exactly as I now see them? And, besides, as I sometimes imagine that others deceive themselves in the things which they think they know best, how do I know that I am not deceived every time that I add two and three, or count the sides of a square, or judge of things yet simpler, if anything simpler can be imagined? But possibly God has not desired that I should be thus deceived, for He is said to be supremely good. If, however, it is contrary to His goodness to have made me such that I constantly deceive myself, it would also appear to be contrary to His goodness to permit me to be sometimes deceived, and nevertheless I cannot doubt that He does permit this.

There may indeed be those who would prefer to deny the existence of a God so powerful, rather than believe that all other things are uncertain. But let us not oppose them for the present, and grant that all that is here said of a God is a fable; nevertheless in whatever way they suppose that I have arrived at the state of being that I have reached—whether they attribute it to fate or to accident, or make out that it is by a continual succession of antecedents, or by some other method—since to err and deceive oneself is a defect, it is clear that the greater will be the probability of my being so imperfect as to deceive myself ever, as is the Author to whom they assign my origin the less powerful. To these reasons I have certainly nothing to reply, but at the end I feel constrained to confess that there is nothing in all that I formerly believed to be true, of which I cannot in some measure doubt, and that not merely through want of thought or through levity, but for reasons which are very powerful and maturely considered; so that henceforth I ought not the less carefully to refrain from giving credence to these opinions than to that which is manifestly false, if I desire to arrive at any certainty.

But it is not sufficient to have made these remarks, we must also be careful to keep them in mind. For these ancient and commonly held opinions still revert frequently to my mind, long and familiar custom having given them the right to occupy my mind against my inclination and rendered them almost masters of my belief; nor will I ever lose the habit of deferring to them or of placing my confidence in them, so long as I consider them as they really are, i.e. opinions in some measure doubtful, as I have just shown, and at the same time highly probable, so that there is much more reason to believe in than to deny them. That is why I consider that I shall not be acting amiss, if, taking of set purpose a contrary belief, I allow myself to be deceived, and for a certain time pretend that all these opinions are entirely false and imaginary, until at last, having thus balanced my former prejudices with my latter, my judgment will no longer be dominated by bad usage or turned away from the right knowledge of the truth. For I am assured that there can be neither peril nor error in this course, and that I cannot at present yield too much to distrust, since I am not considering the question of action, but only of knowledge.

I shall then suppose, not that God who is supremely good and the fountain of truth, but some evil genius, not less powerful than deceitful, has employed his whole energies in deceiving me; I shall consider that the heavens, the earth, colours, figures, sound, and all other external things are nought but the illusions and dreams of which this genius has availed himself in order to lay traps for my credulity; I shall consider myself as having no hands, no eyes, no flesh, no blood, nor any senses, yet falsely believing myself to possess all these things; I shall remain obstinately attached to this idea, and if by this means it is not in my power to arrive at the knowledge of any truth, I may at least do what is in my power, and with firm purpose avoid giving credence to any false thing, or being imposed upon by this arch deceiver, however powerful and deceptive he may be. But this task is a laborious one, and insensibly a certain lassitude leads me into the course of my ordinary life. And just as a captive who in sleep enjoys an imaginary liberty, when he begins to suspect that his liberty is but a dream, fears to awaken, and conspires with these agreeable illusions that the deception may be prolonged, so insensibly of my own accord I fall back into my former opinions, and I dread awakening from this slumber, lest the laborious wakefulness which would follow the tranquillity of this repose should have to be spent not in daylight, but in the excessive darkness of the difficulties which have just been discussed.

MEDITATION II

Of the Nature of the Human Mind; and That It Is More Easily Known than the Body.

The Meditation of yesterday filled my mind with so many doubts that it is no longer in my power to forget them. And yet I do not see in what manner I can resolve them; and, just as if I had all of a sudden fallen into very deep water, I am so disconcerted that I can neither make certain of setting my feet on the bottom, nor can I swim and so support myself on the surface. I shall nevertheless make an effort and follow anew the same path as that on which I yesterday entered, i.e. I shall proceed by setting aside all that in which the least doubt could be supposed to exist, just as if I had discovered that it was absolutely false; and I shall ever follow in this road until I have met with something which is certain, or at least, if I can do nothing else, until I have learned for certain that there is nothing in the world that is certain. Archimedes, in order that he might draw the terrestrial globe out of its place, and transport it elsewhere, demanded only that one point should be fixed and immovable; in the same way I shall have the right to conceive high hopes if I am happy enough to discover one thing only which is certain and indubitable.

I suppose, then, that all the things that I see are false; I persuade myself that nothing has ever existed of all that my fallacious memory represents to me. I consider that I possess no senses; I imagine that body, figure, extension, movement and place are but the fictions of my mind. What, then, can be esteemed as true? Perhaps nothing at all, unless that there is nothing in the world that is certain.

But how can I know there is not something different from those things that I have just considered, of which one cannot have the slightest doubt? Is there not some God, or some other being by whatever name we call it, who puts these reflections into my mind? That is not necessary, for is it not possible that I am capable of producing them myself? I myself, am I not at least something? But I have already denied that I had senses and body. Yet I hesitate, for what follows from that? Am I so dependent on body and senses that I cannot exist without these? But I was persuaded that there was nothing in all the world, that there was no heaven, no earth, that there were no minds, nor any bodies: was I not then likewise persuaded that I did not exist? Not at all; of a surety I myself did exist since I persuaded myself of something. But there is some deceiver or other, very powerful and very cunning, who ever employs his ingenuity in deceiving me. Then without doubt I exist also if he deceives me, and let him deceive me as much as he will, he can never cause me to be nothing so long as I think that I am something. So that after having reflected well and carefully examined all things, we must come to the definite conclusion that this proposition: I am, I exist, is necessarily true each time that I pronounce it, or that I mentally conceive it.

But I do not yet know clearly enough what I am, I who am certain that I am; and hence I must be careful to see that I do not imprudently take some other object in place of myself, and thus that I do not go astray in respect of this knowledge that I hold to be the most certain and most evident of all that I have formerly learned. That is why I shall now consider anew what I believed myself to be before I embarked upon these last reflections; and of my former opinions I shall withdraw all that might even in a small degree be invalidated by the reasons which I have just brought forward, in order that there may be nothing at all left beyond what is absolutely certain and indubitable.

What then did I formerly believe myself to be? Undoubtedly I believed myself to be a man. But what is a man? Shall I say a reasonable animal? Certainly not; for then I should have to inquire what an animal is, and what is reasonable; and thus from a single question I should insensibly fall into an infinitude of others more difficult; and I should not wish to waste the little time and leisure remaining to me in trying to unravel subtleties like these. But I shall rather stop here to consider the thoughts which of themselves spring up in my mind, and which were not inspired by anything beyond my own nature alone when I applied myself to the consideration of my being. In the first place, then, I considered myself as having a face, hands, arms, and all that system of members composed of bones and flesh as seen in a corpse which I designated by the name of body. In addition to this I considered that I was nourished, that I walked, that I felt, and that I thought, and I referred all these actions to the soul: but I did not stop to consider what the soul was, or if I did stop, I imagined that it was something extremely rare and subtle like a wind, a flame, or an ether, which was spread throughout my grosser parts. As to body I had no manner of doubt about its nature, but thought I had a very clear knowledge of it; and if I had desired to explain it according to the notions that I had then formed of it, I should have described it thus: By the body I understand all that which can be defined by a certain figure: something which can be confined in a certain place, and which can fill a given space in such a way that every other body will be excluded from it; which can be perceived either by touch, or by sight, or by hearing, or by taste, or by smell: which can be moved in many ways not, in truth, by itself, but by something which is foreign to it, by which it is touched: for to have the power of self-movement, as also of feeling or of thinking, I did not consider to appertain to the nature of body: on the contrary, I was rather astonished to find that faculties similar to them existed in some bodies.

But what am I, now that I suppose that there is a certain genius which is extremely powerful, and, if I may say so, malicious, who employs all his powers in deceiving me? Can I affirm that I possess the least of all those things which I have just said pertain to the nature of body? I pause to consider, I revolve all these things in my mind, and I find none of which I can say that it pertains to me. It would be tedious to stop to enumerate them. Let us pass to the attributes of soul and see if there is any one which is in me. What of nutrition or walking? But if it is so that I have no body it is also true that I can neither walk nor take nourishment. Another attribute is sensation. But one cannot feel without body, and besides I have thought I perceived many things during sleep that I recognised in my waking moments as not having been experienced at all. What of thinking? I find here that thought is an attribute that belongs to me; it alone cannot be separated from me. I am, I exist, that is certain. But how often? Just when I think; for it might possibly be the case if I ceased entirely to think, that I should likewise cease altogether to exist. I do not now admit anything which is not necessarily true: to speak accurately I am not more than a thing which thinks, that is to say a mind or a soul, or an understanding, or a reason, which are terms whose significance was formerly unknown to me. I am, however, a real thing and really exist; but what thing? I have answered: a thing which thinks.

And what more? I shall exercise my imagination. I am not a collection of members which we call the human body: I am not a subtle air distributed through these members, I am not a wind, a fire, a vapour, a breath, nor anything at all which I can imagine or conceive; because I have assumed that all these were nothing. Without changing that supposition I find that I only leave myself certain of the fact that I am somewhat. But perhaps it is true that these same things, which I supposed were nonexistent because they are unknown to me, are really not different from the self which I know. I am not sure about this, I shall not dispute about it now; I can only give judgment on things that are known to me. I know that I exist, and I inquire what I am, I whom I know to exist. But it is very certain that the knowledge of my existence taken in its precise significance does not depend on things whose existence is not yet known to me; consequently it does not depend on those which I can feign in imagination. And indeed the very term feign in imagination proves to me my error, for I really do this if I image myself a something, since to imagine is nothing else than to contemplate the figure or image of a corporeal thing. But I already know for certain that I am, and that it may be that all these images, and, speaking generally, all things that relate to the nature of body are nothing but dreams. For this reason I see clearly that I have as little reason to say, "I shall stimulate my imagination in order to know more distinctly what I am," than if I were to say, "I am now awake, and I perceive somewhat that is real and true: but because I do not yet perceive it distinctly enough, I shall go to sleep of express purpose, so that my dreams may represent the perception with greatest truth and evidence." And, thus, I know for certain that nothing of all that I can understand by means of my imagination belongs to this knowledge which I have of myself, and that it is necessary to recall the mind from this mode of thought with the utmost diligence in order that it may be able to know its own nature with perfect distinctness.

But what then am I? A thing which thinks. What is a thing which thinks? It is a thing which doubts, understands, affirms, denies, wills, refuses, which also imagines and feels.

Certainly it is no small matter if all these things pertain to my nature. But why should they not so pertain? Am I not that being who now doubts nearly everything, who nevertheless understands certain things, who affirms that one only is true, who denies all the others, who desires to know more, is averse from being deceived, who imagines many things, sometimes indeed despite his will, and who perceives many likewise, as by the intervention of the bodily organs? Is there nothing in all this which is as true as it is certain that I exist, even though I should always sleep and though He who has given me being employed all His ingenuity in deceiving me? Is there likewise any one of these attributes which can be distinguished from my thought, or which might be said to be separated from myself? For it is so evident of itself that it is I who doubts, who understands, and who desires, that there is no reason here to add anything to explain it. And I have certainly the power of imagining likewise; for although it may happen (as I formerly supposed) that none of the things which I imagine are true, nevertheless this power of imagining does not cease to be really in use, and it forms part of my thought. Finally, I am the same who feels, that is to say, who perceives certain things, as by the organs of sense, since in truth I see light, I hear noise, I feel heat. But it will be said that these phenomena are false and that I am dreaming. Let it be so; still it is at least quite certain that it seems to me that I see light, that I hear noise and that I feel heat. That cannot be false; properly speaking it is what is in me called feeling; and used in this precise sense that is no other thing than thinking.

From this time I begin to know what I am with a little more clearness and distinction than before; but nevertheless it still seems to me, and I cannot prevent myself from thinking, that corporeal things, whose images are framed by thought, which are tested by the senses, are much more distinctly known than that obscure part of me which does not come under the imagination. Although really it is very strange to say that I know and understand more distinctly these things whose existence seems to me dubious, which are unknown to me, and which do not belong to me, than others of the truth of which I am convinced, which are known to me and which pertain to my real nature, in a word, than myself. But I see clearly how the case stands: my mind loves to wander, and cannot yet suffer itself to be retained within the just limits of truth. Very good, let us once more give it the freest rein, so that, when afterwards we seize the proper occasion for pulling up, it may the more easily be regulated and controlled.

Let us begin by considering the commonest matters, those which we believe to be the most distinctly comprehended, to wit, the bodies which we touch and see; not indeed bodies in general, for these general ideas are usually a little more confused, but let us consider one body in particular. Let us take, for example, this piece of wax: it has been taken quite freshly from the hive, and it has not yet lost the sweetness of the honey which it contains; it still retains somewhat of the odour of the flowers from which it has been culled; its colour, its figure, its size are apparent; it is hard, cold, easily handled, and if you strike it with the finger, it will emit a sound. Finally all the things which are requisite to cause us distinctly to recognise a body are met with in it. But notice that while I speak and approach the fire what remained of the taste is exhaled, the smell evaporates, the colour alters, the figure is destroyed, the size increases, it becomes liquid, it heats, scarcely can one handle it, and when one strikes it, no sound is emitted. Does the same wax remain after this change? We must confess that it remains; none would judge otherwise. What then did I know so distinctly in this piece of wax? It could certainly be nothing of all that the senses brought to my notice, since all these things which fall under taste, smell, sight, touch, and hearing, are found to be changed, and yet the same wax remains.

Perhaps it was what I now think, viz. that this wax was not that sweetness of honey, nor that agreeable scent of flowers, nor that particular whiteness, nor that figure, nor that sound, but simply a body which a little while before appeared to me as perceptible under these forms, and which is now perceptible under others. But what, precisely, is it that I imagine when I form such conceptions? Let us attentively consider this, and, abstracting from all that does not belong to the wax, let us see what remains. Certainly nothing remains excepting a certain extended thing which is flexible and movable. But what is the meaning of flexible and movable? Is it not that I imagine that this piece of wax being round is capable of becoming square and of passing from a square to a triangular figure? No, certainly it is not that, since I imagine it admits of an infinitude of similar changes, and I nevertheless do not know how to compass the infinitude by my imagination, and consequently this conception which I have of the wax is not brought about by the faculty of imagination. What now is this extension? Is it not also unknown? For it becomes greater when the wax is melted, greater when it is boiled, and greater still when the heat increases; and I should not conceive according to truth what wax is, if I did not think that even this piece that we are considering is capable of receiving more variations in extension than I have ever imagined. We must then grant that I could not even understand through the imagination what this piece of wax is, and that it is my mind alone which perceives it. I say this piece of wax in particular, for as to wax in general it is yet clearer. But what is this piece of wax which cannot be understood excepting by the mind? It is certainly the same that I see, touch, imagine, and finally it is the same which I have always believed it to be from the beginning. But what must particularly be observed is that its perception is neither an act of vision, nor of touch, nor of imagination, and has never been such although it may have appeared formerly to be so, but only an intuition of the mind, which may be imperfect and confused as it was formerly, or clear and distinct as it is at present, according as my attention is more or less directed to the elements which are found in it, and of which it is composed.

Yet in the meantime I am greatly astonished when I consider [the mind's] proneness to fall into error; for although without giving expression to my thoughts I consider all this in my own mind, words often impede me and I am almost deceived by the terms of ordinary language. For we say that we see the same wax, if it is present, and not that we simply judge that it is the same from its having the same colour and figure. From this I should conclude that I knew the wax by means of vision and not simply by the intuition of the mind; unless by chance I remember that, when looking from a window and saying I see men who pass in the street, I really do not see them, but infer that what I see is men, just as I say that I see wax. And yet what do I see from the window but hats and coats which may cover automatic machines? Yet I judge these to be men. And similarly solely by the faculty of judgment which rests in my mind, I comprehend that which I believed I saw with my eyes.

A man who makes it his aim to raise his knowledge above the common should be ashamed to derive the occasion for doubting from the forms of speech invented by the vulgar; I prefer to pass on and consider whether I had a more evident and perfect conception of what the wax was when I first perceived it, and when I believed I knew it by means of the external senses or at least by the common sense as it is called, that is to say by the imaginative faculty, or whether my present conception is clearer now that I have most carefully examined what it is, and in what way it can be known. It would certainly be absurd to doubt as to this. For what was there in this first perception which was distinct? What was there which might not as well have been perceived by any of the animals? But when I distinguish the wax from its external forms, and when, just as if I had taken from it its vestments, I consider it quite naked, it is certain that although some error may still be found in my judgment, I can nevertheless not perceive it thus without a human mind.

But finally what shall I say of this mind, that is, of myself, for up to this point I do not admit in myself anything but mind? What then, I who seem to perceive this piece of wax so distinctly, do I not know myself, not only with much more truth and certainty, but also with much more distinctness and clearness? For if I judge that the wax is or exists from the fact that I see it, it certainly follows much more clearly that I am or that I exist myself from the fact that I see it. For it may be that what I see is not really wax; it may also be that I do not possess eyes with which to see anything; but it cannot be that when I see, or (for I no longer take account of the distinction) when I think I see, that I myself who think am nought. So if I judge that the wax exists from the fact that I touch it, the same thing will follow, to wit, that I am; and if I judge that my imagination, or some other cause, whatever it is, persuades me that the wax exists, I shall still conclude the same. And what I have here remarked of wax may be applied to all other things which are external to me. And further, if the perception of wax has seemed to me clearer and more distinct, not only after the sight or the touch, but also after many other causes have rendered it quite manifest to me, with how much more distinctness must it be said that I now know myself, since all the reasons which contribute to the knowledge of wax, or any other body whatever, are yet better proofs of the nature of my mind! And there are so many other things in the mind itself which may contribute to the elucidation of its nature, that those which depend on body such as these just mentioned hardly merit being taken into account.

But finally here I am, having insensibly reverted to the point I desired, for, since it is now manifest to me that even bodies are not properly speaking known by the senses or by the faculty of imagination, but by the understanding only, and since they are not known from the fact that they are seen or touched, but only because they are understood, I see clearly that there is nothing which is easier for me to know than my mind. But because it is difficult to rid oneself so promptly of an opinion to which one was accustomed for so long, it will be well that I should halt a little at this point, so that by the length of my meditation I may more deeply imprint on my memory this new knowledge.

MEDITATION III

Of God: That He Exists.

I shall now close my eyes, I shall stop my ears, I shall call away all my senses, I shall efface even from my thoughts all the images of corporeal things, or at least (for that is hardly possible) I shall esteem them as vain and false; and thus holding converse only with myself and considering my own nature, I shall try little by little to reach a better knowledge of and a more familiar acquaintanceship with myself. I am a thing that thinks, that is to say, that doubts, affirms, denies, that knows a few things, that is ignorant of many, that wills, that desires, that also imagines and perceives; for as I remarked before, although the things which I perceive and imagine are perhaps nothing at all apart from me and in themselves, I am nevertheless assured that these modes of thought that I call perceptions and imaginations, inasmuch only as they are modes of thought, certainly reside in me.

And in the little that I have just said, I think I have summed up all that I really know, or at least all that hitherto I was aware that I knew. In order to try to extend my knowledge further, I shall now look around more care-fully and see whether I cannot still discover in myself some other things which I have not hitherto perceived. I am certain that I am a thing which thinks; but do I not then likewise know what is requisite to render me certain of a truth? Certainly in this first knowledge there is nothing that assures me of its truth, excepting the clear and distinct perception of that which I state, which would not indeed suffice to assure me that what I say is true, if it could ever happen that a thing which I conceived so clearly and distinctly could be false; and accordingly it seems to me that already I can establish as a general rule that all things which I perceive very clearly and very distinctly are true.

At the same time I have before received and admitted many things to be very certain and manifest, which yet I afterwards recognised as being dubious. What then were these things? They were the earth, sky, stars and all other objects which I apprehended by means of the senses. But what did I clearly perceive in them? Nothing more than that the ideas or thoughts of these things were presented to my mind. And not even now do I deny that these ideas are met with in me. But there was yet another thing which I affirmed, and which, owing to the habit which I had formed of believing it, I thought I perceived very clearly, although in truth I did not perceive it at all, to wit, that there were objects outside of me from which these ideas proceeded, and to which they were entirely similar. And it was in this that I erred, or, if perchance my judgment was correct, this was not due to any knowledge arising from my perception.

But when I took anything very simple and easy in the sphere of arithmetic or geometry into consideration, e.g. that two and three together made five, and other things of the sort, were not these present to my mind so clearly as to enable me to affirm that they were true? Certainly if I judged that since such matters could be doubted, this would not have been so for any other reason than that it came into my mind that perhaps a God might have endowed me with such a nature that I may have been deceived even concerning things which seemed to me most manifest. But every time that this preconceived opinion of the sovereign power of a God presents itself to my thought, I am constrained to confess that it is easy to Him, if He wishes it, to cause me to err, even in matters in which I believe myself to have the best evidence. And, on the other hand, always when I direct my attention to things which I believe myself to perceive very clearly, I am so persuaded of their truth that I let myself break out into words such as these: Let who will deceive me, He can never cause me to be nothing while I think that I am, or some day cause it to be true to say that I have never been, it being true now to say that I am, or that two and three make more or less than five, or any such thing in which I see a manifest con-tradiction. And, certainly, since I have no reason to believe that there is a God who is a deceiver, and as I have not yet satisfied myself that there is a God at all, the reason for doubt which depends on this opinion alone is very slight, and so to speak metaphysical. But in order to be able altogether to remove it, I must inquire whether there is a God as soon as the occasion presents itself; and if I find that there is a God, I must also inquire whether He may be a deceiver; for without a knowledge of these two truths I do not see that I can ever be certain of anything.

And in order that I may have an opportunity of inquiring into this in an orderly way it is requisite that I should here divide my thoughts into certain kinds, and that I should consider in which of these kinds there is, properly speaking, truth or error to be found. Of my thoughts some are so to speak images of the things, and to these alone is the title "idea" properly applied; examples are my thought of a man or of a chimera, of heaven, of an angel, or of God. But other thoughts possess other forms as well. For example in willing, fearing, approving, denying, though I always perceive something as the subject of the action of my mind, yet by this action I always add something else to the idea which I have of that thing; and of the thoughts of this kind some are called volitions or affections, and others judgments.

Now as to what concerns ideas, if we consider them only in themselves and do not relate them to anything else beyond themselves, they cannot properly speaking be false; for whether I imagine a goat or a chimera, it is not less true that I imagine the one than the other. We must not fear likewise that falsity can enter into will and into affections, for although I may desire evil things, or even things that never existed, it is not the less true that I desire them. Thus there remains no more than the judgments which we make, in which I must take the greatest care not to deceive myself. But the principal error and the commonest which we may meet with in them, consists in my judging that the ideas which are in me are similar or conformable to the things which are outside me; for without doubt if I considered the ideas only as certain modes of my thoughts, without trying to relate them to anything beyond, they could scarcely give me material for error.

But among these ideas, some appear to me to be innate, some adventitious, and others to be formed by myself; for, as I have the power of understanding what is called a thing, or a truth, or a thought, it appears to me that I hold this power from no other source than my own nature. But if I now hear some sound, if I see the sun, or feel heat, I have hitherto judged that these sensations proceeded from certain things that exist outside of me; and finally it appears to me that sirens, hippogryphs, and the like, are formed out of my own mind. But again I may possibly persuade myself that all these ideas are of the nature of those which I term adventitious, or else that they are all innate, or all fictitious: for I have not yet clearly discovered their true origin.

And my principal task in this place is to consider, in respect to those ideas which appear to me to proceed from certain objects that are outside me, what are the reasons which cause me to think them similar to these objects. It seems indeed in the first place that I am taught this lesson by nature; and, secondly, I experience in myself that these ideas do not depend on my will nor therefore on myself—for they often present themselves to my mind in spite of my will. Just now, for instance, whether I will or whether I do not will, I feel heat, and thus I persuade myself that this feeling, or at least this idea of heat, is produced in me by something which is different from me, i.e. by the heat of the fire near which I sit. And nothing seems to me more obvious than to judge that this object imprints its likeness rather than anything else upon me.

Now I must discover whether these proofs are sufficiently strong and convincing. When I say that I am so instructed by nature, I merely mean a certain spontaneous inclination which impels me to believe in this connection, and not a natural light which makes me recognise that it is true. But these two things are very different; for I cannot doubt that which the natural light causes me to believe to be true, as, for example, it has shown me that I am from the fact that I doubt, or other facts of the same kind. And I possess no other faculty whereby to distinguish truth from falsehood, which can teach me that what this light shows me to be true is not really true, and no other faculty that is equally trustworthy. But as far as natural impulses are concerned, I have frequently remarked, when I had to make active choice between virtue and vice, that they often enough led me to the part that was worse; and this is why I do not see any reason for following them in what regards truth and error.

And as to the other reason, which is that these ideas must proceed from objects outside me, since they do not depend on my will, I do not find it any the more convincing. For just as these impulses of which I have spoken are found in me, notwithstanding that they do not always concur with my will, so perhaps there is in me some faculty fitted to produce these ideas without the assistance of any external things, even though it is not yet known by me; just as, apparently, they have hitherto always been found in me during sleep without the aid of any external objects.

And finally, though they did proceed from objects different from myself, it is not a necessary consequence that they should resemble these. On the contrary, I have noticed that in many cases there was a great difference between the object and its idea. I find, for example, two completely diverse ideas of the sun in my mind; the one derives its origin from the senses, and should be placed in the category of adventitious ideas; according to this idea the sun seems to be extremely small; but the other is derived from astronomical reasonings, i.e. is elicited from certain notions that are innate in me, or else it is formed by me in some other manner; in accordance with it the sun appears to be several times greater than the earth. These two ideas cannot, indeed, both resemble the same sun, and reason makes me believe that the one which seems to have originated directly from the sun itself is the one which is most dissimilar to it.

All this causes me to believe that until the present time it has not been by a judgment that was certain, but only by a sort of blind impulse that I believed that things existed outside of, and different from me, which, by the organs of my senses, or by some other method whatever it might be, conveyed these ideas or images to me.

But there is yet another method of inquiring whether any of the objects of which I have ideas within me exist outside of me. If ideas are only taken as certain modes of thought, I recognise amongst them no difference or inequality, and all appear to proceed from me in the same manner; but when we consider them as images, one representing one thing and the other another, it is clear that they are very different one from the other. There is no doubt that those which represent to me substances are something more, and contain so to speak more objective reality within them than those that simply represent modes or accidents; and that idea again by which I understand a supreme God, eternal, infinite, omniscient, omnipotent, and Creator of all things which are outside of Himself, has certainly more objective reality in itself than those ideas by which finite substances are represented.

Now it is manifest by the natural light that there must at least be as much reality in the efficient and total cause as in its effect. For, pray, whence can the effect derive its reality, if not from its cause? And in what way can this cause communicate this reality to it, unless it possessed it in itself? And from this it follows, not only that something cannot proceed from nothing, but likewise that what is more perfect—that is to say, which has more reality within itself— cannot proceed from the less perfect. And this is not only evidently true of those effects which possess actual or formal reality, but also of the ideas in which we consider merely what is termed objective reality. To take an example, the stone which has not yet existed not only cannot now commence to be unless it has been produced by something which possesses within itself, either formally or eminently, all that enters into the composition of the stone, and heat can only be produced in a subject in which it did not previously exist by a cause that is of an order at least as perfect as heat, and so in all other cases. But further, the idea of heat, or of a stone, cannot exist in me unless it has been placed within me by some cause which possesses within it at least as much reality as that which I conceive to exist in the heat or the stone. For although this cause does not transmit anything of its actual or formal reality to my idea, we must not for that reason imagine that it is necessarily a less real cause; we must remember that its nature is such that it demands of itself no other formal reality than that which it borrows from my thought, of which it is only a mode. But in order that an idea should contain some one certain objective reality rather than another, it must without doubt derive it from some cause in which there is at least as much formal reality as this idea contains of objective reality. For if we imagine that something is found in an idea which is not found in the cause, it must then have been derived from nought; but however imperfect may be this mode of being by which a thing is objectively in the understanding by its idea, we cannot certainly say that this mode of being is nothing, nor, consequently, that the idea derives its origin from nothing.

Nor must I imagine that, since the reality that I consider in these ideas is only objective, it is not essential that this reality should be formally in the causes of my ideas, but that it is sufficient that it should be found objectively. For just as this mode of objective existence pertains to ideas by their proper nature, so does the mode of formal existence pertain to the causes of those ideas (this is at least true of the first and principal) by the nature peculiar to them. And although it may be the case that one idea gives birth to another idea, that cannot continue to be so indefinitely; for in the end we must reach an idea whose cause shall be so to speak an archetype, in which the whole reality which is so to speak objectively in these ideas is contained formally. Thus the light of nature causes me to know clearly that the ideas in me are like images which can, in truth, easily fall short of the perfection of the objects from which they have been derived, but which can never contain anything greater or more perfect.

And the longer and the more carefully that I investigate these matters, the more clearly and distinctly do I recognise their truth. But what am I to conclude from it all in the end? It is this, that if the objective reality of any one of my ideas is of such a nature as clearly to make me recognise that it is not in me either formally or eminently, and that consequently I cannot myself be the cause of it, it follows of necessity that I am not alone in the world, but that there is another being which exists, or which is the cause of this idea. On the other hand, had no such an idea existed in me, I should have had no sufficient argument to convince me of the existence of any being beyond myself; for I have made very careful investigation everywhere and up to the present time have been able to find no other ground.

But of my ideas, beyond that which represents me to myself, as to which there can here be no difficulty, there is another which represents a God, and there are others representing corporeal and inanimate things, others angels, others animals, and others again which represent to me men similar to myself.

As regards the ideas which represent to me other men or animals, or angels, I can however easily conceive that they might be formed by an admixture of the other ideas which I have of myself, of corporeal things, and of God, even although there were apart from me neither men nor animals, nor angels, in all the world.

And in regard to the ideas of corporeal objects, I do not recognise in them anything so great or so excellent that they might not have possibly proceeded from myself; for if I consider them more closely, and examine them individually, as I yesterday examined the idea of wax, I find that there is very little in them which I perceive clearly and distinctly. Magnitude or extension in length, breadth, or depth, I do so perceive; also figure which results from a termination of this extension, the situation which bodies of different figure preserve in relation to one another, and movement or change of situation; to which we may also add substance, duration and number. As to other things such as light, colours, sounds, scents, tastes, heat, cold and the other tactile qualities, they are thought by me with so much obscurity and confusion that I do not even know if they are true or false, i.e. whether the ideas which I form of these qualities are actually the ideas of real objects or not. For although I have before remarked that it is only in judgments that falsity, properly speaking, or formal falsity, can be met with, a certain material falsity may nevertheless be found in ideas, i.e. when these ideas represent what is nothing as though it were something. For example, the ideas which I have of cold and heat are so far from clear and distinct that by their means I cannot tell whether cold is merely a privation of heat, or heat a privation of cold, or whether both are real qualities, or are not such. And inasmuch as there cannot be any ideas which do not appear to represent some things, if it is correct to say that cold is merely a privation of heat, the idea which represents it to me as something real and positive will not be improperly termed false, and the same holds good of other similar ideas.

To these it is certainly not necessary that I should attribute any author other than myself. For if they are false, i.e. if they represent things which do not exist, the light of nature shows me that they issue from nought, that is to say, that they are only in me in so far as something is lacking to the perfection of my nature. But if they are true, nevertheless because they exhibit so little reality to me that I cannot even clearly distinguish the thing represented from non-being, I do not see any reason why they should not be produced by myself.

As to the clear and distinct idea which I have of corporeal things, some of them seem as though I might have derived them from the idea which I possess of myself, as those which I have of substance, duration, number, and such like. For when I think that a stone is a substance, or at least a thing capable of existing of itself, and that I am a substance also, although I conceive that I am a thing that thinks and not one that is extended, and that the stone on the other hand is an extended thing which does not think, and that thus there is a notable difference between the two conceptions—they seem, never-theless, to agree in this, that both represent substances. In the same way, when I perceive that I now exist and further recollect that I have in former times existed, and when I remember that I have various thoughts of which I can recognise the number, I acquire ideas of duration and number which I can afterwards transfer to any object that I please. But as to all the other qualities of which the ideas of corporeal things are composed, to wit, extension, figure, situation and motion, it is true that they are not formally in me, since I am only a thing that thinks; but because they are merely certain modes of substance and because I myself am also a substance, it would seem that they might be contained in me eminently.

Hence there remains only the idea of God, concerning which we must consider whether it is something which cannot have proceeded from me my-self. By the name God I understand a substance that is infinite, independent, all-knowing, all-powerful, and by which I myself and everything else, if any-thing else does exist, have been created. Now all these characteristics are such that the more diligently I attend to them, the less do they appear capable of proceeding from me alone; hence, from what has been already said, we must conclude that God necessarily exists.

For although the idea of substance is within me owing to the fact that I am substance, nevertheless I should not have the idea of an infinite substance—since I am finite—if it had not proceeded from some substance which was veritably infinite.

Nor should I imagine that I do not perceive the infinite by a true idea, but only by the negation of the finite, just as I perceive repose and darkness by the negation of movement and of light; for, on the contrary, I see that there is manifestly more reality in infinite substance than in finite, and therefore that in some way I have in me the notion of the infinite earlier than the finite—to wit, the notion of God before that of myself. For how would it be possible that I should know that I doubt and desire, that is to say, that something is lacking to me, and that I am not quite perfect, unless I had within me some idea of a Being more perfect than myself, in comparison with which I should recognise the deficiencies of my nature?

And we cannot say that this idea of God is perhaps materially false and that consequently I can derive it from nought, as I have just said is the case with ideas of heat, cold and other such things; for, on the contrary, as this idea is very clear and distinct and contains within it more objective reality than any other, there can be none which is of itself more true, nor any in which there can be less suspicion of falsehood. The idea, I say, of this Being who is absolutely perfect and infinite, is entirely true; for although, perhaps, we can imagine that such a Being does not exist, we cannot nevertheless imagine that His idea represents nothing real to me, as I have said of the idea of cold. This idea is also very clear and distinct; since all that I conceive clearly and distinctly of the real and the true, and of what conveys some perfection, is in its entirety contained in this idea. And this does not cease to be true although I do not comprehend the infinite, or though in God there is an infinitude of things which I cannot comprehend, nor possibly even reach in any way by thought; for it is of the nature of the infinite that my nature, which is finite and limited, should not comprehend it; and it is sufficient that I should understand this, and that I should judge that all things which I clearly perceive and in which I know that there is some perfection, and possibly likewise an infinitude of properties of which I am ignorant, are in God formally or eminently, so that the idea which I have of Him may become the most true, most clear, and most distinct of all the ideas that are in my mind. . . .

MEDITATION IV

Of the True and the False.

I have been well accustomed these past days to detach my mind from my senses, and I have accurately observed that there are very few things that one knows with certainty respecting corporeal objects, that there are many more which are known to us respecting the human mind, and yet more still regarding God Himself; so that I shall now without any difficulty abstract my thoughts from the consideration of imaginable objects, and carry them to those which, being withdrawn from all contact with matter, are purely intelligible. And certainly the idea which I possess of the human mind inasmuch as it is a thinking thing, and not extended in length, width and depth, nor participating in anything pertaining to body, is incomparably more distinct than is the idea of any corporeal thing. And when I consider that I doubt, that is to say, that I am an incomplete and dependent being, the idea of a being that is complete and independent, that is of God, presents itself to my mind with so much distinctness and clearness—and from the fact alone that this idea is found in me, or that I who possess this idea exist, I conclude so certainly that God exists, and that my existence depends entirely on Him in every moment of my life—that I do not think that the human mind is capable of knowing anything with more evidence and certitude. And it seems to me that I now have before me a road which will lead us from the contemplation of the true God (in whom all the treasures of science and wisdom are contained) to the knowledge of the other objects of the universe.

For, first of all, I recognise it to be impossible that He should ever deceive me; for in all fraud and deception some imperfection is to be found, and although it may appear that the power of deception is a mark of subtility or power, yet the desire to deceive without doubt testifies to malice or feebleness, and accordingly cannot be found in God.

In the next place I experienced in myself a certain capacity for judging which I have doubtless received from God, like all the other things that I possess; and as He could not desire to deceive me, it is clear that He has not given me a faculty that will lead me to err if I use it aright. . . .

Whereupon, regarding myself more closely, and considering what are my errors (for they alone testify to there being any imperfection in me), I answer that they depend on a combination of two causes, to wit, on the faculty of knowledge that rests in me, and on the power of choice or of free will—that is to say, of the understanding and at the same time of the will. For by the understanding alone I apprehend the ideas of things as to which I can form a judgment. But no error is properly speaking found in it, provided the word error is taken in its proper signification; and though there is possibly an infinitude of things in the world of which I have no idea in my understanding, we cannot for all that say that it is deprived of these ideas, but simply it does not possess these; because in truth there is no reason to prove that God should have given me a greater faculty of knowledge than He has given me; and however skilful a workman I represent Him to be, I should not for all that consider that He was bound to have placed in each of His works all the perfections which He may have been able to place in some. I likewise cannot complain that God has not given me a free choice or a will which is sufficient, ample and perfect, since as a matter of fact I am conscious of a will so extended as to be subject to no limits. And what seems to me very remarkable in this regard is that of all the qualities which I possess there is no one so perfect and so comprehensive that I do not very clearly recognise that it might be yet greater and more perfect. For, to take an example, if I consider the faculty of comprehension which I possess, I find that it is of very small extent and extremely limited, and at the same time I find the idea of another faculty much more ample and even infinite, and seeing that I can form the idea of it, I recognise from this very fact that it pertains to the nature of God. If in the same way I examine the memory, the imagination, or some other faculty, I do not find any which is not small and circumscribed, while in God it is immense. It is free will alone or liberty of choice which I find to be so great in me that I can conceive no other idea to be more great; it is indeed the case that it is for the most part this will that causes me to know that in some manner I bear the image and similitude of God. For although the power of will is incomparably greater in God than in me, both by reason of the knowledge and the power which, conjoined with it, render it stronger and more efficacious, and by reason of its object, inasmuch as in God it extends to a great many things; it nevertheless does not seem to me greater if I consider it formally and precisely in itself: for the faculty of will consists alone in our having the power of choosing to do a thing or choosing not to do it (that is, to affirm or deny, to pursue or to shun it), or rather it consists alone in the fact that in order to affirm or deny, pursue or shun those things placed before us by the understanding, we act so that we are unconscious that any outside force constrains us in doing so. For in order that I should be free it is not necessary that I should be indifferent as to the choice of one or the other of two contraries; but contrariwise the more I lean to the one—whether I recognise clearly that the reasons of the good and true are to be found in it, or whether God so disposes my inward thought—the more freely do I choose and embrace it. And undoubtedly both divine grace and natural knowledge, far from diminishing my liberty, rather increase it and strengthen it. Hence this indifference which I feel, when I am not swayed to one side rather than to the other by lack of reason, is the lowest grade of liberty, and rather evinces a lack or negation in knowledge than a perfection of will: for if I always recognised clearly what was true and good, I should never have trouble in deliberating as to what judgment or choice I should make, and then I should be entirely free without ever being indifferent.

From all this I recognise that the power of will which I have received from God is not of itself the source of my errors—for it is very ample and very perfect of its kind—any more than is the power of understanding; for since I understand nothing but by the power which God has given me for understanding, there is no doubt that all that I understand, I understand as I ought, and it is not possible that I err in this. Whence then come my errors? They come from the sole fact that since the will is much wider in its range and compass than the understanding, I do not restrain it within the same bounds, but extend it also to things which I do not understand: and as the will is of itself indifferent to these, it easily falls into error and sin, and chooses the evil for the good, or the false for the true. . . .

MEDITATION VI

Of the Existence of Material Things, and of the Real Distinction between the Soul and Body of Man.

Nothing further now remains but to inquire whether material things exist. And certainly I at least know that these may exist in so far as they are considered as the objects of pure mathematics, since in this aspect I perceive them clearly and distinctly. For there is no doubt that God possesses the power to produce everything that I am capable of perceiving with distinctness, and I have never deemed that anything was impossible for Him, unless I found a contradiction in attempting to conceive it clearly. . . .

But I am in the habit of imagining many other things besides this corporeal nature which is the object of pure mathematics, to wit, the colours, sounds, scents, pain, and other such things, although less distinctly. And inasmuch as I perceive these things much better through the senses, by the medium of which, and by the memory, they seem to have reached my imagination, I believe that, in order to examine them more conveniently, it is right that I should at the same time investigate the nature of sense perception, and that I should see if from the ideas which I apprehend by this mode of thought, which I call feeling, I cannot derive some certain proof of the existence of corporeal objects.

And first of all I shall recall to my memory those matters which I hitherto held to be true, as having perceived them through the senses, and the foundations on which my belief has rested; in the next place I shall examine the reasons which have since obliged me to place them in doubt; in the last place I shall consider which of them I must now believe.

First of all, then, I perceived that I had a head, hands, feet, and all other members of which this body—which I considered as a part, or possibly even as the whole, of myself—is composed. Further I was sensible that this body was placed amidst many others, from which it was capable of being affected in many different ways, beneficial and hurtful, and I remarked that a certain feeling of pleasure accompanied those that were beneficial, and pain those which were harmful. And in addition to this pleasure and pain, I also experienced hunger, thirst, and other similar appetites, as also certain corporeal inclinations towards joy, sadness, anger, and other similar passions. And outside myself, in addition to extension, figure, and motions of bodies, I remarked in them hardness, heat, and all other tactile qualities, and, further, light and colour, and scents and sounds, the variety of which gave me the means of distinguishing the sky, the earth, the sea, and generally all the other bodies, one from the other. And certainly, considering the ideas of all these qualities which presented themselves to my mind, and which alone I perceived properly or immediately, it was not without reason that I believed myself to perceive objects quite different from my thought, to wit, bodies from which those ideas proceeded; for I found by experience that these ideas presented themselves to me without my consent being requisite, so that I could not perceive any object, however desirous I might be, unless it were present to the organs of sense; and it was not in my power not to perceive it, when it was present. And because the ideas which I received through the senses were much more lively, more clear, and even, in their own way, more distinct than any of those which I could of myself frame in meditation, or than those I found impressed on my memory, it appeared as though they could not have proceeded from my mind, so that they must necessarily have been produced in me by some other things. And having no knowledge of those objects excepting the knowledge which the ideas themselves gave me, nothing was more likely to occur to my mind than that the objects were similar to the ideas which were caused. And because I likewise remembered that I had formerly made use of my senses rather than my reason, and recognised that the ideas which I formed of myself were not so distinct as those which I perceived through the senses, and that they were most frequently even composed of portions of these last, I persuaded myself easily that I had no idea in my mind which had not formerly come to me through the senses. Nor was it without some reason that I believed that this body (which by a certain special right I call my own) belonged to me more properly and more strictly than any other; for in fact I could never be separated from it as from other bodies; I experienced in it and on account of it all my appetites and affections, and finally I was touched by the feeling of pain and the titillation of pleasure in its parts, and not in the parts of other bodies which were separated from it. But when I inquired, why, from some, I know not what, painful sensation, there follows sadness of mind, and from the pleasurable sensation there arises joy, or why this mysterious pinching of the stomach which I call hunger causes me to desire to eat, and dryness of throat causes a desire to drink, and so on, I could give no reason excepting that nature taught me so; for there is certainly no affinity (that I at least can understand) between the craving of the stomach and the desire to eat, any more than between the perception of whatever causes pain and the thought of sadness which arises from this perception. And in the same way it appeared to me that I had learned from nature all the other judgments which I formed regarding the objects of my senses, since I remarked that these judgments were formed in me before I had the leisure to weigh and consider any reasons which might oblige me to make them.

But afterwards many experiences little by little destroyed all the faith which I had rested in my senses; for I from time to time observed that those towers which from afar appeared to me to be round, more closely observed seemed square, and that colossal statues raised on the summit of these towers appeared as quite tiny statues when viewed from the bottom; and so in an infinitude of other cases I found error in judgments founded on the external senses. And not only in those founded on the external senses, but even in those founded on the internal as well; for is there anything more intimate or more internal than pain? And yet I have learned from some persons whose arms or legs have been cut off, that they sometimes seemed to feel pain in the part which had been amputated, which made me think that I could not be quite certain that it was a certain member which pained me, even although I felt pain in it. And to those grounds of doubt I have lately added two others, which are very general; the first is that I never have believed myself to feel anything in waking moments which I cannot also sometimes believe myself to feel when I sleep, and as I do not think that these things which I seem to feel in sleep proceed from objects outside of me, I do not see any reason why I should have this belief regarding objects which I seem to perceive while awake. The other was that being still ignorant, or rather supposing myself to be ignorant, of the author of my being, I saw nothing to prevent me from having been so constituted by nature that I might be deceived even in matters which seemed to me to be most certain. And as to the grounds on which I was formerly persuaded of the truth of sensible objects, I had not much trouble in replying to them. For since nature seemed to cause me to lean towards many things from which reason repelled me, I did not believe that I should trust much to the teachings of nature. And although the ideas which I receive by the senses do not depend on my will, I did not think that one should for that reason conclude that they proceeded from things different from myself, since possibly some faculty might be discovered in me—though hitherto unknown to me—which produced them.

But now that I begin to know myself better, and to discover more clearly the author of my being, I do not in truth think that I should rashly admit all the matters which the senses seem to teach us, but, on the other hand, I do not think that I should doubt them all universally.

And first of all, because I know that all things which I apprehend clearly and distinctly can be created by God as I apprehend them, it suffices that I am able to apprehend one thing apart from another clearly and distinctly in order to be certain that the one is different from the other, since they may be made to exist in separation at least by the omnipotence of God; and it does not signify by what power this separation is made in order to compel me to judge them to be different: and, therefore, just because I know certainly that I exist, and that meanwhile I do not remark that any other thing necessarily pertains to my nature or essence, excepting that I am a thinking thing, I rightly conclude that my essence consists solely in the fact that I am a thinking thing. And although possibly (or rather certainly, as I shall say in a moment) I possess a body with which I am very intimately conjoined, yet because, on the one side, I have a clear and distinct idea of myself inasmuch as I am only a thinking and unextended thing, and as, on the other, I possess a distinct idea of body, inasmuch as it is only an extended and unthinking thing, it is certain that this I is entirely and absolutely distinct from my body, and can exist without it.

I further find in myself faculties employing modes of thinking peculiar to themselves, to wit, the faculties of imagination and feeling, without which I can easily conceive myself clearly and distinctly as a complete being; while, on the other hand, they cannot be so conceived apart from me, that is without an intelligent substance in which they reside; for in their formal concept, some kind of intellection is comprised, from which I infer that they are distinct from me as its modes are from a thing. I observe also in me some other faculties such as that of change of position, the assumption of different figures and such like, which cannot be conceived, any more than can the preceding, apart from some substance to which they are attached, and consequently cannot exist without it; but it is very clear that these faculties, if it be true that they exist, must be attached to some corporeal or extended substance, and not to an intelligent substance, since in the clear and distinct conception of these there is some sort of extension found to be present, but no intellection at all. There is certainly further in me a certain passive faculty of perception, that is, of receiving and recognising the ideas of sensible things, but this would be useless to me, if there were not either in me or in some other thing another active faculty capable of forming and producing these ideas. But this active faculty cannot exist in me seeing that it does not presuppose thought, and also that those ideas are often produced in me without my contributing in any way to the same, and often even against my will; it is thus necessarily the case that the faculty resides in some substance different from me in which all the reality which is objectively in the ideas that are produced by this faculty is formally or eminently contained, as I remarked before. And this substance is either a body, that is, a corporeal nature in which there is contained formally all that which is objectively in those ideas, or it is God Himself, or some other creature more noble than body in which that same is contained eminently. But, since God is no deceiver, it is very manifest that He does not communicate to me these ideas immediately and by Himself, nor yet by the intervention of some creature in which their reality is not formally, but only eminently, contained. For since He has given me no faculty to recognise that this is the case, but, on the other hand, a very great inclination to believe that they are conveyed to me by corporeal objects, I do not see how He could be defended from the accusation of deceit if these ideas were produced by causes other than corporeal objects. Hence we must allow that corporeal things exist. However, they are perhaps not exactly what we perceive by the senses, since this comprehension by the senses is in many instances very obscure and confused; but we must at least admit that all things which I conceive in them clearly and distinctly, that is to say, all things which, speaking generally, are comprehended in the object of pure mathematics are truly to be recognised as external objects.

As to other things, however, which are either particular only, as, for example, that the sun is of such and such a figure, etc., or which are less clearly and distinctly conceived, such as light, sound, pain and the like, it is certain that although they are very dubious and uncertain, yet on the sole ground that God is not a deceiver, and that consequently He has not permitted any falsity to exist in my opinion which He has not likewise given me the faculty of correcting, I may assuredly hope to conclude that I have within me the means of arriving at the truth even here. And first of all there is no doubt that in all things which nature teaches me there is some truth contained; for by nature, considered in general, I now understand no other thing than either God Himself or else the order and disposition which God has established in created things; and by my nature in particular I understand no other thing than the complexus of all the things which God has given me.

But there is nothing which this nature teaches me more expressly than that I have a body which is adversely affected when I feel pain, which has need of food or drink when I experience the feelings of hunger and thirst, and so on; nor can I doubt there being some truth in all this.

Nature also teaches me by these sensations of pain, hunger, thirst, etc., that I am not only lodged in my body as a pilot in a vessel, but that I am very closely united to it, and so to speak so intermingled with it that I seem to compose with it one whole. For if that were not the case, when my body is hurt, I, who am merely a thinking thing, should not feel pain, for I should perceive this wound by the understanding only, just as the sailor perceives by sight when something is damaged in his vessel; and when my body has need of drink or food, I should clearly understand the fact without being warned of it by confused feelings of hunger and thirst. For all these sensations of hunger, thirst, pain, etc., are in truth none other than certain confused modes of thought which are produced by the union and apparent intermingling of mind and body.

Moreover, nature teaches me that many other bodies exist around mine of which some are to be avoided, and others sought after. And certainly from the fact that I am sensible of different sorts of colours, sounds, scents, tastes, heat, hardness, etc., I very easily conclude that there are in the bodies from which all these diverse sense-perceptions proceed certain variations which answer to them, although possibly these are not really at all similar to them. And also from the fact that amongst these different sense-perceptions some are very agreeable to me and others disagreeable, it is quite certain that my body (or rather myself in my entirety, inasmuch as I am formed of body and soul) may receive different impressions agreeable and disagreeable from the other bodies which surround it. . . .

From this it is quite clear that, notwithstanding the supreme goodness of God, the nature of man, inasmuch as it is composed of mind and body, cannot be otherwise than sometimes a source of deception. For if there is any cause which excites, not in the foot but in some part of the nerves which are extended between the foot and the brain, or even in the brain itself, the same movement which usually is produced when the foot is detrimentally affected, pain will be experienced as though it were in the foot, and the sense will thus naturally be deceived; for since the same movement in the brain is capable of causing but one sensation in the mind, and this sensation is much more frequently excited by a cause which hurts the foot than by another existing in some other quarter, it is reasonable that it should convey to the mind pain in the foot rather than in any other part of the body. And although the parchedness of the throat does not always proceed, as it usually does, from the fact that drinking is necessary for the health of the body, but sometimes comes from quite a different cause, as is the case with dropsical patients, it is yet much better that it should mislead on this occasion than if, on the other hand, it were always to deceive us when the body is in good health; and so on in similar cases.

And certainly this consideration is of great service to me, not only in enabling me to recognise all the errors to which my nature is subject, but also in enabling me to avoid them or to correct them more easily. For knowing that all my senses more frequently indicate to me truth than falsehood respecting the things which concern that which is beneficial to the body, and being able almost always to avail myself of many of them in order to examine one particular thing, and, besides that, being able to make use of my memory in order to connect the present with the past, and of my understanding which already has discovered all the causes of my errors, I ought no longer to fear that falsity may be found in matters every day presented to me by my senses. And I ought to set aside all the doubts of these past days as hyperbolical and ridiculous, particularly that very common uncertainty respecting sleep, which I could not distinguish from the waking state; for at present I find a very notable difference between the two, inasmuch as our memory can never connect our dreams one with the other, or with the whole course of our lives, as it unites events which happen to us while we are awake. And, as a matter of fact, if someone, while I was awake, quite suddenly appeared to me and disappeared as fast as do the images which I see in sleep, so that I could not know from whence the form came nor whither it went, it would not be without reason that I should deem it a spectre or a phantom formed by my brain, rather than a real man. But when I perceive things as to which I know distinctly both the place from which they proceed, and that in which they are, and the time at which they appeared to me, and when, without any interruption, I can connect the perceptions which I have of them with the whole course of my life, I am perfectly assured that these perceptions occur while I am waking and not during sleep. And I ought in no wise to doubt the truth of such matters, if, after having called up all my senses, my memory, and my understanding, to examine them, nothing is brought to evidence by any one of them which is repugnant to what is set forth by the others. For because God is in no wise a deceiver, it follows that I am not deceived in this. But because the exigencies of action often oblige us to make up our minds before having leisure to examine matters carefully, we must confess that the life of man is very frequently subject to error in respect to individual objects, and we must in the end acknowledge the infirmity of our nature.

Questions

1. State the grounds on which Descartes attempts to doubt the senses as a basis for genuine knowledge. Give your reasons for thinking that he succeeded, or that he failed, in this attempt.

2. State the grounds on which Descartes attempts to doubt that "two and three together always form five." Give your reasons for thinking that he succeeded, or that he failed, in this attempt.

3. Why does Descartes find that the mind (or self) and God are more easily known than any other thing?

4. Descartes' famous conclusion, "I think; therefore, I am," has been criticized as meaning no more than "There is a thought." How do you think that he might reply to such a criticism?

5. What is Descartes trying to show about our knowledge of the world by his discussion of knowing a piece of wax? (p. 52)

6. State all the premises Descartes must accept in order to prove that God exists. Tested by his own method of doubt, is his proof of God's existence acceptable? Why or why not?

7. According to Descartes, what part does God play in our knowledge of the world? Why are we sometimes mistaken in our knowledge?

8. How does Descartes prove that corporeal objects exist? What is his final justification of perceptual knowledge? Does it square with his rationalist theory of knowledge? *p. 46*

9. How do you know you are not dreaming right now? Does Descartes offer a satisfactory resolution of this dilemma?

2

An Essay Concerning Human Understanding

John Locke

(1632-1704)

John Locke was born at Wrington, Somerset, in England, and was educated at Westminster School and Oxford. He was a friend of the chemist Robert Boyle, and was himself an amateur in chemistry; but he finally expressed his scientific bent in the study and practice of medicine. He was a close associate of Thomas Sydenham, a famous physician, who was endeavoring to introduce into England a science of medicine based on observation and taught by demonstration. Through his writings Locke made important contributions to the cause of civil liberty and religious toleration in England, and his political ideas had a great influence on the Founding Fathers of the United States. (For Locke's political ideas, see the selection beginning on page 613.) As for philosophy, Locke said that Descartes' books were the first to give him a relish for philosophical studies. His principal writings are: *Two Treatises of Government* (1690); *Letters on Toleration* (1689, 1690); and *An Essay Concerning Human Understanding* (1690).

In this reading and in the following two readings we are given the classic modern statements of the theory of knowledge known as *empiricism*. The principle of empiricism may be stated as follows: All knowledge of the world comes from, and is based on, experience. This principle is to be understood in two ways. First, it is a psychological theory about the origin of knowledge. Second, it is a philosophical theory about the criteria of knowledge (i.e., about how we are to decide whether or not we really know something). The philosophical theory of empiricism consists in the claim that our having knowledge about the world is determined solely by the test of experience: If we can give evidence in support of our assertions about the world by an appeal to direct experience, we have knowledge. Otherwise, we do not.

The reading begins with Locke's attempt to show how all the ideas which make up our knowledge originate in sense experience and in the mind's "reflection" on its own operations. Locke imagines the mind at birth to be like a blank sheet of paper on which experience begins to write and leave its mark. First the mind has "simple ideas," among which are its ideas of the qualities of objects. Then it builds up "complex ideas," among which are its ideas of the objects ("substances") which have these qualities. Locke goes on to consider the nature of knowledge. Knowledge, he says, is the perception of the agreement or disagreement of our ideas. This raises the question of how we can know whether our knowledge, which is limited to our ideas, does in fact correspond to the real world outside our ideas. The reading concludes with Locke's attempt to answer this question.

The reading is from Books I, II and IV of *An Essay Concerning Human Understanding*. Locke's original chapter titles are retained in this selection.

INTRODUCTION

An inquiry into the understanding, pleasant and useful. Since it is the *understanding* that sets man above the rest of sensible beings, and gives him all the advantage and dominion which he has over them, it is certainly a subject, even for its nobleness, worth our labor to inquire into. The understanding, like the eye, whilst it makes us see and perceive all other things, takes no notice of itself; and it requires art and pains to set it at a distance, and make it its own object. But whatever be the difficulties that lie in the way of this inquiry, whatever it be that keeps us so much in the dark to ourselves, sure I am that all the light we can let in upon our own minds, all the acquaintance we can make with our own understandings, will not only be very pleasant, but bring us great advantage in directing our thoughts in the search of other things. . . .

Method. It is worth while to search out the bounds between opinion and knowledge, and examine by what measures, in things whereof we have no certain knowledge, we ought to regulate our assent, and moderate our persuasions. In order whereunto, I shall pursue this following method:

First, I shall inquire into the original of those *ideas*, notions, or whatever else you please to call them, which a man observes, and is conscious to himself he has in his mind; and the ways whereby the understanding comes to be furnished with them.

Secondly, I shall endeavor to show what *knowledge* the understanding hath by those ideas, and the certainty, evidence, and extent of it. . . .

Our capacity suited to our state and concerns. Though the comprehension of our understandings comes exceeding short of the vast extent of things, yet we shall have cause enough to magnify the bountiful Author of our being for that proportion and degree of knowledge He has bestowed on us, so far above all the rest of the inhabitants of this our mansion. Men have reason to be well satisfied with what God hath thought fit for them, since He has given them, as St. Peter says, whatsoever is necessary for the conveniences of life, and information of virtue; and has put, within the reach of their discovery, the comfortable provision for this life and the way that leads to a better. How short soever their knowledge may come of an universal or perfect comprehension of whatsoever is, it yet secures their great concernments that they have light enough to lead them to the knowledge of their Maker, and the sight of their own duties. . . .

. . . Our business here is not to know all things, but those which concern our conduct. If we can find out those measures whereby a rational creature, put in that state which man is in in this world, may and ought to govern his opinions and actions depending thereon, we need not be troubled that some other things escape our knowledge.

. . . Were the capacities of our understandings well considered, the extent of our knowledge once discovered, and the horizon found which sets the bounds between the enlightened and dark parts of things—between what is and what is not comprehensible by us—men would, perhaps with less scruple, acquiesce in the avowed ignorance of the one, and employ their thoughts and discourse with more advantage and satisfaction in the other.

What "idea" stands for. . . . Before I proceed on to what I have thought on this subject, I must here, in the entrance, beg pardon of my reader for the frequent use of the word "idea" which he will find in the following treatise. It being that term which, I think, serves best to stand for whatsoever is the *object* of the understanding when a man thinks, I have used it to express whatever is meant by phantasm, notion, species, or whatever it is which the mind can be employed about in thinking; and I could not avoid frequently using it.

I presume it will be easily granted me, that there are such *ideas* in men's minds. Everyone is conscious of them in himself; and men's words and actions will satisfy him that they are in others.

Our first inquiry, then, shall be, how they come into the mind.

OF IDEAS IN GENERAL, AND THEIR ORIGINAL

Idea is the object of thinking. Every man being conscious to himself that he thinks, and that which his mind is applied about whilst thinking being the ideas that are there, it is past doubt that men have in their minds several ideas, such as are those expressed by the words whiteness, hardness, sweetness, thinking, motion, man, elephant, army, drunkenness, and others: it is in the first place then to be inquired, How he comes by them? . . .

All ideas come from sensation or reflection. Let us then suppose the mind to be, as we say, white paper, void of all characters, without any ideas; how comes it to be furnished? Whence comes it by that vast store, which the busy and boundless fancy of man has painted on it with an almost endless variety? Whence has it all the materials of reason and knowledge? To this I answer, in one word, from experience. In that all our knowledge is founded, and from that it ultimately derives itself. Our observation, employed either about external sensible objects, or about the internal operations of our minds, perceived and reflected on by ourselves, is that which supplies our understandings with all the materials of thinking. These two are the fountains of knowledge, from whence all the ideas we have, or can naturally have, do spring.

The objects of sensation, one source of ideas. First, our senses, conversant about particular sensible objects, do convey into the mind several distinct perceptions of things, according to those various ways wherein those objects do affect them; and thus we come by those ideas we have of yellow, white, heat, cold, soft, hard, bitter, sweet, and all those which we call sensible qualities; which when I say the senses convey into the mind, I mean, they from external objects convey into the mind what produces there those perceptions. This great source of most of the ideas we have, depending wholly upon our senses, and derived by them to the understanding, I call *sensation.*

The operations of our minds, the other source of them. Secondly, the other fountain, from which experience furnisheth the understanding with ideas, is the perception of the operations of our own mind within us, as it is employed about the ideas it has got; which operations, when the soul comes to reflect on and consider, do furnish the understanding with another set of ideas which could not be had from things without; and such are perception, thinking, doubting, believing, reasoning, knowing, willing, and all the different actings of our own minds; which we, being conscious of, and observing in ourselves, do from these receive into our understandings as distinct ideas, as we do from bodies affecting our senses. This source of ideas every man has wholly in himself; and though it be not sense as having nothing to do with external objects, yet it is very like it, and might properly enough be called *internal sense.* But as I call the other sensation, so I call this *reflection,* the ideas it affords being such only as the mind gets by reflecting on its own operations within itself. By reflection, then, in the following part of this discourse, I would be understood to mean that notice which the mind takes of its own operations, and the manner of them, by reason whereof there come to be ideas of these operations in the understanding. These two, I say, viz., external material things as the object of sensation, and the operations of our own minds within as the objects of reflection, are, to me, the only originals from whence all our ideas take their beginnings. The term *operations* here, I use in a large sense, as comprehending not barely the actions of the mind about its ideas, but some sort of passions arising sometimes from them, such as is the satisfaction or uneasiness arising from any thought. . . .

OF SIMPLE IDEAS

Uncompounded appearances. The better to understand the nature, manner, and extent of our knowledge, one thing is carefully to be observed concerning the ideas we have; and that is, that some of them are *simple,* and some *complex.*

Though the qualities that affect our senses are, in the things themselves, so united and blended that there is no separation, no distance between them; yet it is plain the ideas they produce in the mind enter by the senses simple and unmixed. For though the sight and touch often take in from the same object, at the same time, different ideas—as a man sees at once motion and color, the hand feels softness and warmth in the same piece of wax—yet the simple ideas thus united in the same subject are as perfectly distinct as those that come in by different senses; the coldness and hardness which a man feels in a piece of ice being as distinct ideas in the mind as the smell and whiteness of a lily, or as the taste of sugar and smell of a rose: and there is nothing can be plainer to a man than the clear and distinct perception he has of those simple ideas; which, being each in itself uncompounded, contains in it nothing but *one uniform appearance or conception in the mind,* and is not distinguishable into different ideas.

The mind can neither make nor destroy them. These simple ideas, the materials of all our knowledge, are suggested and furnished to the mind only by those two ways above mentioned, viz., sensation and reflection. When the understanding is once stored with these simple ideas, it has the power to repeat, compare, and unite them, even to an almost infinite variety, and so can make at pleasure new complex ideas. But it is not in the power of the most exalted wit or enlarged understanding, by any quickness or variety of thought, to *invent* or *frame* one new simple idea in the mind, not taken in by the ways before mentioned; nor can any force of the understanding *destroy* those that are there: the dominion of man, in this little world of his own understanding, being much-what the same as it is in the great world of visible things; wherein his power, however managed by art and skill, reaches no farther than to compound and divide the materials that are made to his hand but can do nothing towards the making the least particle of new matter, or destroying one atom of what is already in being. The same inability will everyone find in himself, who shall go about to fashion in his understanding any simple idea not received in by his senses from external objects, or by reflection from the operations of his own mind about them. I would have anyone try to fancy any taste which had never affected his palate, or frame the idea of a scent he had never smelt; and when he can do this, I will also conclude that a blind man hath *ideas* of colors, and a deaf man true, distinct notions of sounds. . . .

OF SIMPLE IDEAS OF REFLECTION

Simple ideas of reflection are the operations of the mind about its other ideas. The mind, receiving the ideas mentioned in the foregoing chapters from without, when it turns its view inward upon itself, and observes its own actions about those ideas it has, takes from thence other ideas, which are as capable to be the objects of its contemplation as any of those it received from foreign things.

The idea of perception, and idea of willing, we have from reflection. The two great and principal actions of the mind, which are most frequently considered, and which are so frequent that everyone that pleases may take notice of them in himself, are these two: *perception* or *thinking,* and *volition* or *willing.* . . .

OF SIMPLE IDEAS OF BOTH
SENSATION AND REFLECTION

Ideas of pleasure and pain. There be other simple ideas which convey themselves into the mind by all the ways of sensation and reflection: viz., pleasure or delight, and its opposite, pain or uneasiness; power, existence, unity.

SOME FARTHER CONSIDERATIONS CONCERNING
OUR SIMPLE IDEAS OF SENSATION

Ideas in the mind, qualities in bodies. To discover the nature of our ideas the better, and to discourse of them intelligibly, it will be convenient to distinguish them, as they are *ideas or perceptions in our minds,* and as they are *modifications of matter in the bodies that cause such perception in us:* that so we may not think (as perhaps usually is done) that they are exactly the images and resemblances of something inherent in the subject; most of those of sensation being in the mind no more the likeness of something existing without us than the names that stand for them are the likeness of our ideas, which yet upon hearing they are apt to excite in us.

Whatsoever the mind perceives in itself, or is the immediate object of perception, thought, or understanding, that I call *idea;* and the power to produce any idea in our mind, I call *quality* of the subject wherein that power is. Thus a snowball having the power to produce in us the ideas of white, cold, and round, the powers to produce those ideas in us as they are in the snowball, I call qualities; and as they are sensations or perceptions in our understandings, I call them ideas; which ideas, if I speak of them sometimes as in the things themselves, I would be understood to mean those qualities in the objects which produce them in us.

Primary qualities. Qualities thus considered in bodies are: *First* such as are utterly inseparable from the body, in what estate soever it be; and such as, in all the alterations and changes it suffers, all the force can be used upon it, it constantly keeps; and such as sense constantly finds in every particle of matter which has bulk enough to be perceived, and the mind finds inseparable from every particle of matter, though less than to make itself singly be perceived by our senses: v.g., take a grain of wheat, divide it into two parts, each part has still solidity, extension, figure, and mobility; divide it again, and it retains still the same qualities: and so divide it on till the parts become insensible, they must retain still each of them all those qualities. For, division (which is all that a mill or pestle or any other body does upon another, in reducing it to insensible parts) can never take away either solidity, extension, figure, or mobility from any body, but only makes two or more distinct separate masses of matter of that which was but one before; all which distinct masses, reckoned as so many distinct bodies, after division, make a certain number. These I call *original* or *primary qualities* of body, which I think we may observe to produce simple ideas in us, viz., solidity, extension, figure, motion or rest, and number.

Secondary qualities. Secondly, such qualities, which in truth are nothing in the objects themselves, but powers to produce various sensations in us by their primary qualities, i.e., by the bulk, figure, texture, and motion of their insensible parts, as colors, sounds, tastes, etc., these I call *secondary* qualities. To these might be added a third sort, which are allowed to be barely powers, though they are as much real qualities in the subject as those which I, to comply with the common way of speaking, call qualities, but, for distinction, *secondary* qualities. For, the power in fire to produce a new color or consistency in wax or clay, by its primary qualities, is as much a quality in fire as the power it has to produce in me a new idea or sensation of warmth or burning, which I felt not before, by the same primary qualities, viz., the bulk, texture, and motion of its insensible parts.

How primary qualities produce ideas in us. The next thing to be considered is how bodies produce ideas in us; and that is manifestly by impulse, the only way we can conceive bodies to operate in.

If, then, external objects be not united to our minds when they produce ideas therein, and yet we perceive these original qualities in such of them as singly fall under our senses, it is evident that some motion must be thence continued by our nerves, or animal spirits, by some parts of our bodies, to the brain or the seat of sensation, there to produce in our minds the particular ideas we have of them. And since the extension, figure, number, and motion of bodies of an observable bigness, may be perceived at a distance by the sight, it is evident some singly imperceptible bodies must come from them to the eyes, and thereby convey to the brain some motion which produces these ideas which we have of them in us.

How secondary. After the same manner that the ideas of these original qualities are produced in us, we may conceive that the ideas of secondary qualities are also produced, viz., by the operation of insensible particles on our senses. For it being manifest that there are bodies, and good store of bodies, each whereof are so small that we cannot by any of our senses discover either their bulk, figure, or motion (as is evident in the particles of the air and water, and others extremely smaller than those, perhaps as much smaller than the particles of air or water as the particles of air or water are smaller than peas or hailstones): let us suppose at present that the different motions and figures, bulk and number, of such particles, affecting the several organs of our senses, produce in us these different sensations which we have from the colors and smells of bodies, v.g., that a violet, by the impulse of such insensible particles of matter of peculiar figures and bulks, and in different degrees and modifications of their motions, causes the ideas of the blue color and sweet scent of that flower to be produced in our minds; it being no more impossible to conceive that God should annex such ideas to such motions, with which they have no similitude, than that He should annex the idea of pain to the motion of a piece of steel dividing our flesh, with which the idea hath no resemblance.

What I have said concerning colors and smells may be understood also of tastes and sounds, and other the like sensible qualities; which, whatever reality we by mistake attribute to them, are in truth nothing in the objects themselves, but powers to produce various sensations in us, and depend on those primary qualities, viz., bulk, figure, texture, and motion of parts as I have said.

Ideas of primary qualities are resemblances; of secondary, not. From whence I think it is easy to draw this observation, that the ideas of primary qualities of bodies are resemblances of them, and their patterns do really exist in the bodies themselves; but the ideas produced in us by these secondary qualities have no resemblance of them at all. There is nothing like our ideas existing in the bodies themselves. They are, in the bodies we denominate from them, only a power to produce those sensations in us; and what is sweet, blue, or warm in idea, is but the certain bulk, figure, and motion of the insensible parts in the bodies themselves, which we call so.

Flame is denominated hot and light; snow, white and cold; and manna, white and sweet, from the ideas they produce in us, which qualities are commonly thought to be the same in those bodies that those ideas are in us, the one the perfect resemblance of the other, as they are in a mirror; and it would by most men be judged very extravagant, if one should say otherwise. And yet he that will consider that the same fire that at one distance produces in us the sensation of warmth, does at a nearer approach produce in us the far different sensation of pain, ought to bethink himself what reason he has to say that this idea of warmth, which was produced in him by the fire, is actually in the fire, and his idea of pain which the same fire produced in him the same way is not in the fire. Why are whiteness and coldness in snow and pain not, when it produces the one and the other idea in us, and can do neither but by the bulk, figure, number, and motion of its solid parts?

The particular bulk, number, figure, and motion of the parts of fire or snow are really in them, whether anyone's senses perceive them or no; and therefore they may be called *real* qualities, because they really exist in those bodies. But light, heat, whiteness, or coldness, are no more really in them than sickness or pain is in manna. Take away the sensation of them; let not the eyes see light or colors, nor the ears hear sounds; let the palate not taste, nor the nose smell; and all colors, tastes, odors, and sounds, as they are such particular ideas, vanish and cease, and are reduced to their causes, i.e., bulk, figure, and motion of parts. . . .

Pound an almond, and the clear white color will be altered into a dirty one, and the sweet taste into an oily one. What real alteration can the beating of the pestle make in any body, but an alteration of the texture of it?

Ideas being thus distinguished and understood, we may be able to give an account how the same water, at the same time, may produce the idea of cold by one hand, and of heat by the other; whereas it is impossible that the same water, if those ideas were really in it, should at the same time be both hot and cold. For if we imagine warmth as it is in our hands, to be nothing but a certain sort and degree of motion in the minute particles of our nerves or animal spirits, we may understand how it is possible that the same water may at the same time produce the sensation of heat in one hand, and cold in the other; which yet figure never does, that never producing the idea of a square by one hand which has produced the idea of a globe by another. But if the sensation of heat and cold be nothing but the increase or diminution of the motion of the minute parts of our bodies, caused by the corpuscles of any other body, it is easy to be understood that if that motion be greater in one hand than in the other, if a body be applied to the two hands, which has in its minute particles a greater motion than in those of one of the hands, and a less than in those of the other, it will increase the motion of the one hand, and lessen it in the other, and so cause the different sensations of heat and cold that depend thereon. . . .

Three sorts of qualities in bodies. The qualities then that are in bodies, rightly considered, are of three sorts:

First, the bulk, figure, number, situation, and motion or rest of their solid parts; those are in them, whether we perceive them or not; and when they are of that size that we can discover them, we have by these ideas of the thing as it is in itself, as is plain in artificial things. These I call *primary qualities.*

Secondly, the power that is in any body, by reason of its insensible primary qualities, to operate after a peculiar manner on any of our senses, and thereby produce in us the different ideas of several colors, sounds, smells, tastes, etc. These are usually called *sensible qualities.*

Thirdly, the power that is in any body, by reason of the particular constitution of its primary qualities, to make such a change in the bulk, figure, texture, and motion of another body, as to make it operate on our senses differently from what it did before. Thus the sun has a power to make wax white, and fire, to make lead fluid. These are usually called *powers.*

The first of these, as has been said, I think may be properly called real, original, or primary qualities, because they are in the things themselves, whether they are perceived or no; and upon their different modifications it is that the secondary qualities depend.

The other two are only powers to act differently upon other things, which powers result from the different modifications of those primary qualities. . . .

OF OUR COMPLEX IDEAS OF SUBSTANCES

Ideas of particular substances, how made. The mind being, as I have declared, furnished with a great number of the simple ideas conveyed in by the senses, as they are found in exterior things, or by reflections on its own operations, takes notice, also, that a certain number of these simple ideas go constantly together; which being presumed to belong to one thing, and words being suited to common apprehensions, and made use of for quick despatch, are called, so united in one subject, by one name; which, by inadvertency, we are apt afterward to talk of and consider as one simple idea, which indeed is a complication of many ideas together: because, as I have said, not imagining how these simple ideas can subsist by themselves, we accustom ourselves to suppose some *substratum* wherein they do subsist, and from which they do result; which therefore we call *substance*.

Our obscure idea of substance in general. So that if anyone will examine himself concerning his notion of pure substance in general, he will find he has no other idea of it at all, but only a supposition of he knows not what support of such qualities which are capable of producing simple ideas in us; which qualities are commonly called accidents. If anyone should be asked, what is the subject wherein color or weight inheres, he would have nothing to say but, the solid extended parts. And if he were demanded, what is it that solidity and extension inhere in, he would not be in a much better case than the Indian who, saying that the world was supported by a great elephant, was asked what the elephant rested on; to which his answer was, a great tortoise; but being again pressed to know what gave support to the broad-backed tortoise, replied—something, he knew not what. And thus here, as in all other cases where we use words without having clear and distinct ideas, we talk like children: who, being questioned what such a thing is which they know not, readily give this satisfactory answer, that it is *something;* which in truth signifies no more, when so used, either by children or men, but that they know not what; and that the thing they pretend to know and talk of is what they have no distinct idea of at all, and so are perfectly ignorant of it, and in the dark. The idea, then, we have, to which we give the *general* name substance, being nothing but the supposed, but unknown, support of those qualities we find existing, which we imagine cannot subsist *sine re substante,* "without something to support them," we call that support *substantia;* which, according to the true import of the word, is, in plain English, standing under, or upholding.

Of the sorts of substances. An obscure and relative idea of substance in general being thus made, we come to have the ideas of particular sorts of substances, by collecting such combinations of simple ideas as are by experience and observation of men's senses taken notice of to exist together, and are therefore supposed to flow from the particular internal constitution or unknown essence of that substance. Thus we come to have the ideas of a man, horse, gold, water, etc., of which substances, whether anyone has any other clear idea, farther than of certain simple ideas coexistent together, I appeal to everyone's own experience. It is the ordinary qualities observable in iron or a diamond, put together, that make the true complex idea of those substances, which a smith or a jeweler commonly knows better than a philosopher; who, whatever substantial forms he may talk of, has no other idea of those substances than what is framed by a collection of those simple ideas which are to be found in them. Only we must take notice that our complex ideas of substances, besides all these simple ideas they are made up of, have always the confused idea of something to which they belong, and in which they subsist: and therefore when we speak of any sort of substance, we say it is a thing having such or such qualities; as, body is a thing that is extended, figured, and capable of motion; spirit, a thing capable of thinking; and so hardness, friability, and power to draw iron, we say, are qualities to be found in a loadstone. These and the like fashions of speaking intimate that the substance is supposed always something, besides the extension, figure, solidity, motion, thinking, or other observable ideas, though we know not what it is.

No clear or distinct idea of substance in general. Hence, when we talk or think of any particular sort of corporeal substances, as horse, stone, etc., though the idea we have of either of them be but the complication or collection of those several simple ideas of sensible qualities which we used to find united in the thing called horse or stone; yet because we cannot conceive how they should subsist alone, nor one in other, we suppose them existing in, and supported by, some common subject; which support we denote by the name substance, though it be certain we have no clear or distinct idea of that thing we suppose a support.

As clear an idea of spirit as body. The same happens concerning the operations of the mind; viz., thinking, reasoning, fearing, etc., which we, concluding not to subsist of themselves, nor apprehending how they can belong to body, or be produced by it, we are apt to think these the actions of some other substance, which we call *spirit;* whereby yet it is evident, that having no other idea or notion of matter but something wherein those many sensible qualities which affect our senses do subsist; by supposing a substance wherein thinking, knowing, doubting, and a power of moving, etc., do subsist, we have as clear a notion of the substance of spirit as we have of body: the one being supposed to be (without knowing what it is) the *substratum* to those simple ideas we have from without; and the other supposed (with a like ignorance of what it is) to be the *substratum* to those operations which we experiment in ourselves within. It is plain, then, that the idea of *corporeal substance* in matter is as remote from our conceptions and apprehensions as that of *spiritual substance,* or spirit; and therefore, from our not having any notion of the substance of spirit, we can no more conclude its nonexistence than we can, for the same reason, deny the existence of body: it being as rational to affirm there is no body, because we have no clear and distinct idea of the substance of matter, as to say there is no spirit, because we have no clear and distinct idea of the substance of a spirit.

Our ideas of particular sorts of substances. Whatever therefore be the secret and abstract nature of substance in general, all the ideas we have of particular, distinct sorts of substances, are nothing but several combinations of simple ideas coexisting in such, though unknown, cause of their union, as makes the whole subsist of itself. It is by such combinations of simple ideas, and nothing else, that we represent particular sorts of substances to ourselves; such are the ideas we have of their several species in our minds; and such only do we, by their specific names, signify to others, v.g., man, horse, sun, water, iron; upon hearing which words everyone who understands the language, frames in his mind a combination of those several simple ideas which he has usually observed or fancied to exist together under that denomination; all which he supposes to rest in, and be, as it were, adherent to, that unknown common subject, which inheres not in anything else. Though in the meantime it be manifest, and everyone upon inquiry into his own thoughts will find, that he has no other idea of any substance, v.g., let it be gold, horse, iron, man, vitriol, bread, but what he has barely of those sensible qualities which he supposes to inhere with a supposition of such a *substratum* as gives, as it were, a support to those qualities, or simple ideas, which he has observed to exist united together. Thus, the idea of the sun—what is it but an aggregate of those several simple ideas—bright, hot, roundish, having a constant regular motion, at a certain distance from us, and perhaps some other: as he who thinks and discourses of the sun has been more or less accurate in observing those sensible qualities, ideas, or properties which are in that thing which he calls the sun.

Power, a great part of our complex ideas of substances. For he has the perfectest idea of any of the particular sorts of substances who has gathered and put together most of those simple ideas which do exist in it, among which are to be reckoned its active powers and passive capacities; which, though not simple ideas, yet in this respect, for brevity's sake, may conveniently enough be reckoned amongst them. Thus, the power of drawing iron is one of the ideas of the complex one of that substance we call a loadstone, and a power to be so drawn is a part of the complex one we call iron; which powers pass for inherent qualities in those subjects. . . .

Three sorts of ideas make our complex ones of substances. The ideas that make our complex ones of corporeal substances are of these three sorts. First, the ideas of the primary qualities of things which are discovered by our senses, and are in them even when we perceive them not; such as the bulk, figure, number, situation, and motion of the parts of bodies, which are really in them, whether we take notice of them or no. Secondly, the sensible secondary qualities which, depending on these, are nothing but the powers those substances have to produce several ideas in us by our senses; which ideas are not in the things themselves otherwise than as anything is in its cause. Thirdly, the aptness we consider in any substance to give or receive such alterations of primary qualities as that the substance so altered should produce in us different ideas from what it did before; these are called active and passive powers: all which powers, as far as we have any notice or notion of them, terminate only in sensible simple ideas. . . .

Our faculties of discovery suited to our state. The infinitely wise contriver of us, and all things about us, hath fitted our senses, faculties, and organs, to the conveniences of life, and the business we have to do here. We are able, by our senses, to know and distinguish things; and to examine them so far, as to apply them to our uses, and several ways to accommodate the exigencies of this life. We have insight enough into their admirable contrivances and wonderful effects, to admire and magnify the wisdom, power, and goodness of their author. Such a knowledge as this, which is suited to our present condition, we want not faculties to attain. But it appears not that God intended we should have a perfect, clear, and adequate knowledge of them: that perhaps is not in the comprehension of any finite being. We are furnished with faculties (dull and weak as they are) to discover enough in the creatures to lead us to the knowledge of the Creator, and the knowledge of our duty; and we are fitted well enough with abilities to provide for the conveniences of living: these are our business in this world. . . .

Idea of God. If we examine the idea we have of the incomprehensible Supreme Being, we shall find that we come by it the same way; and that the complex ideas we have both of God and separate spirits are made of the simple ideas we receive from reflection: v.g., having, from what we experiment in ourselves, got the ideas of existence and duration, of knowledge and power, of pleasure and happiness, and of several other qualities and powers which it is better to have than to be without; when we would frame an idea the most suitable we can to the Supreme Being, we enlarge every one of these with our idea of infinity; and so, putting them together, make our complex idea of God.

If I find that I know some few things, and some of them, or all, perhaps, imperfectly; I can frame an idea of knowing twice as many, which I can double again as often as I can add to number; and thus enlarge my idea of knowledge, by extending its comprehension to all things existing or possible. The same also I can do of knowing them more perfectly, i.e., all their qualities, powers, causes, consequences, and relations, etc., till all be perfectly known that is in them, or can any way relate to them; and thus frame the idea of infinite or boundless knowledge. The same may also be done of power, till we come to that we call infinite; and also of the duration of existence without beginning or end; and so frame the idea of an eternal being. The degrees or extent, wherein we ascribe existence, power, wisdom, and all other perfections (which we can have any ideas of), to that Sovereign Being which we call God, being all boundless and infinite, we frame the best idea of Him our minds are capable of: all which is done, I say, by enlarging those simple ideas we have taken from the operations of our own minds by reflection, or by our senses from exterior things, to that vastness to which infinity can extend them. . . .

OF CAUSE AND EFFECT

Whence their ideas got. In the notice that our senses take of the constant vicissitude of things, we cannot but observe that several particular both qualities and substances begin to exist; and that they receive this their existence from the due application and operation of some other being. From this observation we get our ideas of cause and effect. *That which produces any simple or complex idea,* we denote by the general name *cause; and that which is produced, effect.* Thus finding that in that substance which we call "wax" fluidity, which is a simple idea that was not in it before, is constantly produced by the application of a certain degree of heat, we call the simple idea of heat, in relation to fluidity in wax, the cause of it, and fluidity the effect. So also finding that the substance, wood, which is a certain collection of simple ideas so called, by the application of fire is turned into another substance called ashes, i.e., another complex idea, consisting of a collection of simple ideas, quite different from that complex idea which we call wood, we consider fire, in relation to ashes, as cause, and the ashes, as effect. So that whatever is considered by us to conduce or operate to the producing any particular simple idea, or collection of simple ideas, whether substance or mode, which did not before exist, hath thereby in our minds the relation of a cause, and so is denominated by us. . . .

OF KNOWLEDGE IN GENERAL

Our knowledge conversant about our ideas only. Since the mind, in all its thoughts and reasonings, hath no other immediate object but its own ideas, which it alone does or can contemplate, it is evident that our knowledge is only conversant about them.

Knowledge is the perception of the agreement or disagreement of two ideas. Knowledge then seems to me to be nothing but the perception of the connection of and agreement, or disagreement and repugnancy, of any of our ideas. In this alone it consists. Where this perception is, there is knowledge; and where it is not, there, though we may fancy, guess, or believe, yet we always come short of knowledge. For, when we know that white is not black, what do we else but perceive that these two ideas do not agree? When we possess ourselves with the utmost security of the demonstration that the three angles of a triangle are equal to two right ones, what do we more but perceive that equality to two right ones does necessarily agree to, and is inseparable from, the three angles of a triangle? . . .

OF THE EXTENT OF HUMAN KNOWLEDGE

Knowledge, as has been said, lying in the perception of the agreement or disagreement of any of our ideas, it follows from hence that,

(i) *No farther than we have ideas.* First, we can have knowledge no farther than we have ideas.

(ii) *No farther than we can perceive their agreement or disagreement.* Secondly, that we can have no knowledge farther than we can have perception of that agreement or disagreement: which perception being (1) either by intuition, or the immediate comparing any two ideas, or (2) by reason, examining the agreement or disagreement of two ideas by the intervention of some others, or (3) by sensation, perceiving the existence of particular things; hence it also follows,

(iii) *Intuitive knowledge extends itself not to all the relations of all our ideas.* Thirdly, that we cannot have an intuitive knowledge that shall extend itself to all our ideas, and all that we would know about them; because we cannot examine and perceive all the relations they have one to another by juxtaposition, or an immediate comparison one with another. Thus having the ideas of an obtuse and an acute-angled triangle, both drawn from equal bases and between parallels, I can by intuitive knowledge perceive the one not to be the other, but cannot that way know whether they be equal or no: because their agreement or disagreement in equality can never be perceived by an immediate comparing them; the difference of figure makes their parts incapable of an exact immediate application; and therefore there is need of some intervening qualities to measure them by, which is demonstration or rational knowledge.

(iv) *Nor demonstrative knowledge.* Fourthly, it follows also, from what is above observed, that our rational knowledge cannot reach to the whole extent of our ideas: because between two different ideas we would examine, we cannot always find such mediums as we can connect one to another with an intuitive knowledge, in all the parts of the deduction; and wherever that fails, we come short of knowledge and demonstration.

(v) *Sensitive knowledge narrower than either.* Fifthly, sensitive knowledge, reaching no farther than the existence of things actually present to our senses, is yet much narrower than either of the former. . . .

OF THE REALITY OF HUMAN KNOWLEDGE

Objection. Knowledge placed in ideas may be all bare vision. I doubt not but my reader by this time may be apt to think that I have been all this while only building a castle in the air; and be ready to say to me, "To what purpose all this stir? 'Knowledge,' say you, 'is only the perception of the agreement or disagreement of our own ideas'; but who knows what those ideas may be?

Is there anything so extravagant as the imaginations of men's brains? Where is the head that has no chimeras in it? Or if there be a sober and a wise man, what difference will there be, by your rules, between his knowledge, and that of the most extravagant fancy in the world? They both have their ideas, and perceive their agreement or disagreement one with another. If there be any difference between them, the advantage will be on the warm-headed man's side, as having the more ideas, and the more lively. And so, by your rules, he will be the more knowing. If it be true that all knowledge lies only in the perception of the agreement or disagreement of our own ideas, the visions of an enthusiast, and the reasonings of a sober man, will be equally certain. It is no matter how things are: so a man observe but the agreement of his own imaginations, and talk conformably, it is all truth, all certainty. Such castles in the air will be as strongholds of truth as the demonstrations of Euclid. That an harpy is not a centaur is by this way as certain knowledge, and as much a truth, as that a square is not a circle.

"But of what use is all this fine knowledge of men's own imaginations to a man that inquires after the reality of things? It matters not what men's fancies are, it is the knowledge of things that is only to be prized; it is this alone gives a value of our reasonings, and preference to one man's knowledge over another's, that it is of things as they really are, and not of dreams and fancies."

Answer. Not so, where ideas agree with things. To which I answer, that if our knowledge of our ideas terminate in them, and reach no farther, where there is something farther intended, our most serious thoughts will be of little more use than the reveries of a crazy brain; and the truths built thereon of no more weight than the discourses of a man who sees things clearly in a dream, and with great assurance utters them. But I hope before I have done to make it evident that this way of certainty, by the knowledge of our own ideas, goes a little farther than bare imagination; and I believe it will appear that all the certainty of general truths a man has lies in nothing else.

It is evident the mind knows not things immediately, but only by the intervention of the ideas it has of them. Our knowledge therefore is real only so far as there is a conformity between our ideas and the reality of things. But what shall be here the criterion? How shall the mind, when it perceives nothing but its own ideas, know that they agree with things themselves? This, though it seems not to want difficulty, yet I think there be two sorts of ideas that we may be assured agree with things.

As (i) *all simple ideas do.* First, the first are simple ideas, which since the mind, as has been showed, can by no means make to itself, must necessarily be the product of things operating on the mind in a natural way, and producing therein those perceptions which by the wisdom and will of our Maker they are ordained and adapted to. From whence it follows that simple ideas are not fictions of our fancies, but the natural and regular productions of things without us really operating upon us, and so carry with them all the conformity which is intended, or which our state requires; for they represent to us things under those appearances which they are fitted to produce in us, whereby we are enabled to distinguish the sorts of particular substances, to discern the states they are in, and so to take them for our necessities, and apply them to our uses. Thus the idea of whiteness or bitterness, as it is in the mind, exactly answering that power which is in any body to produce it there, has all the real conformity it can or ought to have with things without us. And this conformity between our simple ideas and the existence of things is sufficient for real knowledge.

(ii) *All complex ideas except of substances.* Secondly, all our complex ideas except those of substances being archetypes of the mind's own making, not intended to be the copies of anything, not referred to the existence of anything, as to their originals, cannot want any conformity necessary to real knowledge. For that which is not designed to represent anything but itself can never be capable of a wrong representation, nor mislead us from the true apprehension of anything by its dislikeness to it; and such, excepting those of substances, are all our complex ideas: which are combinations of ideas which the mind by its free choice puts together without considering any connection they have in nature. And hence it is, that in all these sorts the ideas themselves are considered as the archetypes, and things [not] otherwise regarded but as they are conformable to them. So that we cannot but be infallibly certain that all the knowledge we attain concerning these ideas is real, and reaches things themselves; because in all our thoughts, reasonings, and discourses of this kind, we intend things no farther than as they are comformable to our ideas. So that in these we cannot miss of a certain and undoubted reality. . . .

(iii) *Ideas of substances have their archetypes without us.* Thirdly, there is another sort of complex ideas, which being referred to archetypes without us may differ from them, and so our knowledge about them may come short of being real. Such are our ideas of substances, which consisting of a collection of simple ideas, supposed taken from the works of nature, may yet vary from them, by having more or different ideas united in them than are to be found united in the things themselves: from whence it comes to pass that they may and often do fail of being exactly conformable to things themselves.

So far as they agree with those, so far our knowledge concerning them is real. . . . But our ideas of substances, being supposed copies, and referred to archetypes without us, must still be taken from something that does or has existed; they must not consist of ideas put together at the pleasure of our thoughts without any real pattern they were taken from, though we can perceive no inconsistence in such a combination. The reason whereof is, because we knowing not what real constitution it is of substances whereon our simple ideas depend, and which really is the cause of the strict union of some of them one with another, and the exclusion of others; there are very few of them that we can be sure are or are not inconsistent in nature, any farther than experience and sensible observation reach. Herein, therefore, is founded the reality of our knowledge concerning substances, that all our complex ideas of them must be such, and such only, as are made up of such simple ones as have been discovered to coexist in nature. And our ideas, being thus true, though not perhaps very exact copies, are yet the subjects of real (as far as we have any) knowledge of them: which, as has been already showed, will not be found to reach very far; but so far as it does, it will still be real knowledge. Whatever ideas we have, the agreement we find they have with others will still be knowledge. If those ideas be abstract, it will be general knowledge. But to make it real concerning substances, the ideas must be taken from the real existence of things. Whatever simple ideas have been found to coexist in any substance, these we may with confidence join together again, and so make abstract ideas of substances. For whatever have once had an union in nature may be united again.

Questions

1. What kinds of ideas does Locke distinguish?

2. What is Locke's model of the mind? How is this model related to his account of the nature of our knowledge of the world? How can one tell whether his way of conceiving the mind is correct or incorrect? For instance, is his account of the mind open to experimental confirmation? Why or why not?

3. How does Locke distinguish between "primary qualities" and "secondary qualities"? What does this distinction tell us about his conception of real existence outside the mind?

4. What does Locke mean by "substance"? Does his conception of substance contradict the principle of empiricism as he formulated it? Why or why not?

5. State Locke's reply to the objection that his view of knowledge is useless to "a man that inquires after the reality of things," and give your reasons for thinking that his reply succeeded, or failed, in answering the objection.

6. Disregarding Locke's psychological account of the origin of knowledge, and considering only his criteria for deciding when we have true knowledge of the world, state the differences between his criteria and those of Descartes (pages 48 ff.). Which set of criteria do you prefer and on what grounds?

3

| *The Principles of*
Human Knowledge | George Berkeley
(1685-1753) |

George Berkeley was born in Ireland and educated at Trinity College, Dublin. He held a number of ecclesiastical positions in the Anglican Church, and finally became Bishop of Cloyne (County Cork, Ireland). His chief works are: *An Essay toward a New Theory of Vision* (1709); *A Treatise Concerning the Principles of Human Knowledge* (1710); and *Three Dialogues between Hylas and Philonous* (1713).

Like Locke, Berkeley believes that all our knowledge comes either from the outward data of our sense experience (colors, sounds, shapes, smells, touch sensations, etc.) or from the inward data of our thoughts and feelings. All of these data are called by Berkeley "ideas," and he makes a sharp distinction between them and the mind which perceives them. Ideas are those things which are perceived; minds are those things which do the perceiving. After stating these principles, Berkeley is ready to propound his famous thesis: That houses, mountains, rivers, and all perceivable objects exist only in our minds. "For," he says, "what are the forementioned objects but the things we perceive by sense? and what do we perceive besides our own ideas and sensations?"

Two views may be taken of this thesis, which is now usually called "subjective idealism." One is that Berkeley is claiming that the only things which exist are minds. Objects that we perceive, such as houses and mountains, tables and chairs, are nothing but groups of ideas in our minds. Therefore nothing exists outside our minds. The other view is that Berkeley is not denying the existence of what are ordinarily called "material objects" at all. He is instead telling us that philosophers use the word "matter" entirely differently from the way it is used by the ordinary man. For the philosopher, "matter" refers to *substance* in which an object's sensible qualities are supposed to inhere, but which cannot itself be perceived by the senses. Substance is that part of an object which provides a "home," as it were, for an object's perceptible qualities. If substance were itself perceptible, then it too would need a "home." Because such a supposition would involve philosophers in an infinite regress of substances underlying substances, those philosophers who talk about substance define it as unperceivable. Since Berkeley believes that only the perceivable exists, he cannot count the philosopher's matter or substance as existing. In contrast with the philosopher's use of "matter," in ordinary life we use the word to refer to objects which are perceivable by the senses. Berkeley says that he does not deny the existence of matter in the latter sense, but only in the former sense. "The only thing whose existence we deny is that which *philosophers* call Matter or corporeal substance." (Berkeley's italics.) Here Berkeley is in direct opposition to Locke, who supposed that *substances* do exist. Thus Berkeley's various arguments against the existence of a material world external to the mind may be interpreted in two ways, as either the claim that nothing exists outside our minds, or as the denial of the existence of *substance*. We leave to the reader the question of whether Berkeley's account of our knowledge of the world may be interpreted in only one or both of these ways.

It is to be noted that Berkeley denies the distinction made by Locke between primary and secondary qualities, according to which only our ideas of primary qualities correspond to the actual properties of real material objects. In order to explain where our ideas of perceivable objects come from and why it is that they do not depend on our will, Berkeley says that there must be a supreme and all powerful mind which puts the ideas in our minds. The reading concludes with Berkeley's defense of his views against four objections.

The reading is from Sections 1-4, 6-11, 14-16, 18-20, 23, 25, 26, 28-35, 50, 51, 58, and 59 of *A Treatise Concerning the Principles of Human Knowledge,* second edition.

It is evident to any one who takes a survey of the *objects* of human knowledge, that they are either ideas actually imprinted on the senses; or else such as are perceived by attending to the passions and operations of the mind; or lastly, ideas formed by help of memory and imagination—either compounding, dividing, or barely representing those originally perceived in the aforesaid ways. By sight I have the ideas of light and colours, with their several degrees and variations. By touch I perceive hard and soft, heat and cold, motion and resistance, and of all these more and less either as to quantity or degree. Smelling furnishes me with odours; the palate with tastes; and hearing conveys sounds to the mind in all their variety of tone and composition. And as several of these are observed to accompany each other, they come to be marked by one name, and so to be reputed as one thing. Thus, for example, a certain colour, taste, smell, figure and consistence having been observed to go together, are accounted one distinct thing, signified by the name *apple;* other collections of ideas constitute a stone, a tree, a book, and the like sensible things—which as they are pleasing or disagreeable excite the passions of love, hatred, joy, grief, and so forth.

But, besides all that endless variety of ideas or objects of knowledge, there is likewise something which knows or perceives them, and exercises divers operations, as willing, imagining, remembering, about them. This perceiving, active being is what I call *mind, spirit, soul,* or *myself.* By which words I do not denote any one of my ideas, but a thing entirely distinct from them, wherein, they exist, or, which is the same thing, whereby they are perceived—for the existence of an idea consists in being perceived.

That neither our thoughts, nor passions, nor ideas formed by the imagination, exist without the mind, is what everybody will allow. And it seems no less evident that the various sensations or ideas imprinted on the sense, however blended or combined together (that is, whatever objects they compose), cannot exist otherwise than in a mind perceiving them—I think an intuitive knowledge may be obtained of this by any one that shall attend to what is meant by the term *exists,* when applied to sensible things. The table I write on I say exists, that is, I see and feel it; and if I were out of my study I should say it existed—meaning thereby that if I was in my study I might perceive it, or that some other spirit actually does perceive it. There was an odour, that is, it was smelt; there was a sound, that is, it was heard; a colour or figure, and it was perceived by sight or touch. This is all that I can understand by these and the like expressions. For as to what is said of the absolute existence of unthinking things without any relation to their being perceived, that seems perfectly unintelligible. Their *esse* is *percipi,* nor is it possible they should have any existence out of the minds or thinking things which perceive them.

It is indeed an opinion, strangely prevailing amongst men, that houses, mountains, rivers, and in a word all sensible objects, have an existence, natural or real, distinct from their being perceived by the understanding. But, with how great an assurance and acquiescence soever this principle may be entertained in the world, yet whoever shall find in his heart to call it in question may, if I mistake not, perceive it to involve a manifest contradiction. For, what are the forementioned objects but the things we perceive by sense? and what do we perceive besides our own ideas or sensations? and is it not plainly repugnant that any one of these, or any combination of them, should exist unperceived? . . .

Some truths there are so near and obvious to the mind that a man need only open his eyes to see them. Such I take this important one to be, viz., that all the choir of heaven and furniture of the earth, in a word all those bodies which compose the mighty frame of the world, have not any subsistence without a mind, that their *being* is to be perceived or known; that consequently so long as they are not actually perceived by me, or do not exist in my mind or that of any other created spirit, they must either have no existence at all, or else subsist in the mind of some Eternal Spirit—it being perfectly unintelligible, and involving all the absurdity of abstraction, to attribute to any single part of them an existence independent of a spirit. To be convinced of which, the reader need only reflect, and try to separate in his own thoughts the *being* of a sensible thing from its *being perceived*.

From what has been said it follows there is not any other Substance than *Spirit,* or that which perceives. But, for the fuller proof of this point, let it be considered the sensible qualities are colour, figure, motion, smell, taste, etc., *i.e.* the ideas perceived by sense. Now, for an idea to exist in an unperceiving thing is a manifest contradiction, for to have an idea is all one as to perceive; that therefore wherein colour, figure, and the like qualities exist must perceive them; hence it is clear there can be no unthinking substance or *substratum* of those ideas.

But, say you, though the ideas themselves do not exist without the mind, yet there may be things like them, whereof they are copies or resemblances, which things exist without the mind in an unthinking substance. I answer, an idea can be like nothing but an idea; a colour or figure can be like nothing but another colour or figure. If we look but never so little into our thoughts, we shall find it impossible for us to conceive a likeness except only between our ideas. Again, I ask whether those supposed originals or external things, of which our ideas are the pictures or representations, be themselves perceivable or no? If they are, then they are ideas and we have gained our point; but if you say they are not, I appeal to any one whether it be sense to assert a colour is like something which is invisible; hard or soft, like something which is intangible; and so of the rest.

Some there are who make a distinction betwixt *primary* and *secondary* qualities. By the former they mean extension, figure, motion, rest, solidity or impenetrability, and number; by the latter they denote all other sensible qualities, as colours, sounds, tastes, and so forth. The ideas we have of these they acknowledge not to be the resemblances of anything existing without the mind, or unperceived, but they will have our ideas of the primary qualities to be patterns or images of things which exist without the mind, in an unthinking substance which they call Matter. By Matter, therefore, we are to understand an inert, senseless substance, in which extension, figure, and motion do actually subsist. But it is evident, from what we have already shown, that extension, figure, and motion are only ideas existing in the mind, and that an idea can be like nothing but another idea, and that consequently neither they nor their archetypes can exist in an unperceiving substance. Hence, it is plain that the very notion of what is called *Matter* or *corporeal substance* involves a contradiction in it.

They who assert that figure, motion, and the rest of the primary or original qualities do exist without the mind in unthinking substances, do at the same time acknowledge that colours, sounds, heat, cold, and suchlike secondary qualities, do not—which they tell us are sensations existing in the mind alone, that depend on and are occasioned by the different size, texture, and motion of the minute particles of matter. This they take for an undoubted truth, which they can demonstrate beyond all exception. Now, if it be certain that those original qualities are inseparably united with the other sensible qualities, and not, even in thought, capable of being abstracted from them, it plainly follows that they exist only in the mind. But I desire any one to reflect and try whether he can, by any abstraction of thought, conceive the extension and motion of a body without all other sensible qualities. For my own part, I see evidently that it is not in my power to frame an idea of a body extended and moving, but I must withal give it some colour or other sensible quality which is acknowledged to exist only in the mind. In short, extension, figure, and motion, abstracted from all other qualities, are inconceivable. Where therefore the other sensible qualities are, there must these be also, to wit, in the mind and nowhere else.

Again, *great* and *small, swift* and *slow,* are allowed to exist nowhere without the mind, being entirely relative, and changing as the frame or position of the organs of sense varies. The extension therefore which exists without the mind is neither great nor small, the motion neither swift nor slow, that is, they are nothing at all. . . . Without extension solidity cannot be conceived; since therefore it has been shewn that extension exists not in an unthinking substance, the same must also be true of solidity. . . .

I shall farther add, that, after the same manner as modern philosophers prove certain sensible qualities to have no existence in Matter, or without the mind, the same thing may be likewise proved of all other sensible qualities whatsoever. Thus, for instance, it is said that heat and cold are affections only of the mind, and not at all patterns of real beings, existing in the corporeal substances which excite them, for that the same body which appears cold to one hand seems warm to another. Now, why may we not as well argue that figure and extension are not patterns or resemblances of qualities existing in Matter, because to the same eye at different stations, or eyes of a different texture at the same station, they appear various, and cannot therefore be the images of anything settled and determinate without the mind? Again, it is proved that sweetness is not really in the sapid thing, because the thing remaining unaltered the sweetness is changed into bitter, as in case of a fever or otherwise vitiated palate. Is it not as reasonable to say that motion is not without the mind, since if the succession of ideas in the mind become swifter, the motion, it is acknowledged, shall appear slower without any alteration in any external object?

In short, let any one consider those arguments which are thought manifestly to prove that colours and taste exist only in the mind, and he shall find they may with equal force be brought to prove the same thing of extension, figure, and motion. Though it must be confessed this method of arguing does not so much prove that there is no extension or colour in an outward object, as that we do not know by sense which is the true extension or colour of the object. But the arguments foregoing plainly show it to be impossible that any colour or extension at all, or other sensible quality whatsoever, should exist in an unthinking subject without the mind, or in truth, that there should be any such thing as an outward object.

But let us examine a little the received opinion. It is said extension is a mode or accident of Matter, and that Matter is the *substratum* that supports it. Now I desire that you would explain to me what is meant by Matter's *supporting* extension. Say you, I have no idea of Matter and therefore cannot explain it. I answer, though you have no positive, yet, if you have any meaning at all, you must at least have a relative idea of Matter; though you know not what it is, yet you must be supposed to know what relation it bears to accidents, and what is meant by its supporting them. It is evident "support" cannot here be taken in its usual or literal sense—as when we say that pillars support a building; in what sense therefore must it be taken? . . .

But, though it were possible that solid, figured, movable substances may exist without the mind, corresponding to the ideas we have of bodies, yet how is it possible for us to know this? Either we must know it by sense or by reason. As for our senses, by them we have the knowledge only of our sensations, ideas, or those things that are immediately perceived by sense, call them what you will: but they do not inform us that things exist without the mind, or unperceived, like to those which are perceived. This the materialists themselves acknowledge. It remains therefore that if we have any knowledge at all of external things, it must be by reason, inferring their existence from what is immediately perceived by sense. But what reason can induce us to believe the existence of bodies without the mind, from what we perceive, since the very patrons of Matter themselves do not pretend there is any necessary connexion betwixt them and our ideas? I say it is granted on all hands (and what happens in dreams, phrensies, and the like, puts it beyond dispute) that it is possible we might be affected with all the ideas we have now, though there were no bodies existing without resembling them. Hence, it is evident the supposition of external bodies is not necessary for the producing our ideas; since it is granted they are produced sometimes, and might possibly be produced always in the same order, we see them in at present, without their concurrence.

But, though we might possibly have all our sensations without them, yet perhaps it may be thought easier to conceive and explain the manner of their production, by supposing external bodies in their likeness rather than otherwise; and so it might be at least probable there are such things as bodies that excite their ideas in our minds. But neither can this be said; for, though we give the materialists their external bodies, they by their own confession are never the nearer knowing how our ideas are produced; since they own themselves unable to comprehend in what manner body can act upon spirit, or how it is possible it should imprint any idea in the mind. Hence it is evident the production of ideas or sensations in our minds can be no reason why we should suppose Matter or corporeal substances, since that is acknowledged to remain equally inexplicable with or without this supposition. If therefore it were possible for bodies to exist without the mind, yet to hold they do so, must needs be a very precarious opinion; since it is to suppose, without any reason at all, that God has created innumerable beings that are entirely useless, and serve to no manner of purpose.

In short, if there were external bodies, it is impossible we should ever come to know it; and if there were not, we might have the very same reasons to think there were that we have now. Suppose—what no one can deny possible—an intelligence without the help of external bodies, to be affected with the same train of sensations or ideas that you are, imprinted in the same order and with like vividness in his mind. I ask whether that intelligence hath not all the reason to believe the existence of corporeal substances, represented by his ideas, and exciting them in his mind, that you can possibly have for believing the same thing? Of this there can be no question—which one consideration were enough to make any reasonable person suspect the strength of whatever arguments he may think himself to have, for the existence of bodies without the mind. . . .

But, say you, surely there is nothing easier than for me to imagine trees, for instance, in a park, or books existing in a closet, and nobody by to perceive them. I answer, you may so, there is no difficulty in it; but what is all this, I beseech you, more than framing in your mind certain ideas which you call books and trees, and the same time omitting to frame the idea of any one that may perceive them? But do not you yourself perceive or think of them all the while? This therefore is nothing to the purpose; it only shews you have the power of imagining or forming ideas in your mind: but it does not shew that you can conceive it possible the objects of your thought may exist without the mind. To make out this, it is necessary that you conceive them existing unconceived or unthought of, which is a manifest repugnancy. When we do our utmost to conceive the existence of external bodies, we are all the while only contemplating our own ideas. But the mind taking no notice of itself, is deluded to think it can and does conceive bodies existing unthought of or without the mind, though at the same time they are apprehended by or exist in itself. A little attention will discover to any one the truth and evidence of what is here said, and make it unnecessary to insist on any other proofs against the existence of *material substance.* . . .

All our ideas, sensations, notions, or the things which we perceive, by whatsoever names they may be distinguished, are visibly inactive—there is nothing of power or agency included in them. So that one idea or object of thought cannot produce or make any alteration in another. To be satisfied of the truth of this, there is nothing else requisite but a bare observation of our ideas. For, since they and every part of them exist only in the mind, it follows that there is nothing in them but what is perceived: but whoever shall attend to his ideas, whether of sense or reflexion, will not perceive in them any power or activity; there is, therefore, no such thing contained in them. A little attention will discover to us that the very being of an idea implies passiveness and inertness in it, insomuch that it is impossible for an idea to do anything, or, strictly speaking, to be the cause of anything: neither can it be the resemblance or pattern of any active being. Whence it plainly follows that extension, figure, and motion cannot be the cause of our sensations. To say, therefore, that these are the effects of powers resulting from the configuration, number, motion, and size of corpuscles, must certainly be false.

We perceive a continual succession of ideas, some are anew excited, others are changed or totally disappear. There is therefore some cause of these ideas, whereon they depend, and which produces and changes them. That this cause cannot be any quality or idea or combination of ideas is clear from the preceding [paragraph]. It must therefore be a substance; but it has been shewn that there is no corporeal or material substance: it remains therefore that the cause of ideas is an incorporeal active substance or Spirit. . . .

I find I can excite ideas in my mind at pleasure, and vary and shift the scene as oft as I think fit. It is no more than willing, and straightway this or that idea arises in my fancy; and by the same power it is obliterated and makes way for another. This making and unmaking of ideas doth very properly denominate the mind active. Thus much is certain and grounded on experience; but when we think of unthinking agents or of exciting ideas exclusive of volition, we only amuse ourselves with words.

But, whatever power I may have over my own thoughts, I find the ideas actually perceived by Sense have not a like dependence on my will. When in broad daylight I open my eyes, it is not in my power to choose whether I shall see or no, or to determine what particular objects shall present themselves to my view; and so likewise as to the hearing and other senses; the ideas imprinted on them are not creatures of my will. There is therefore some *other* Will or Spirit that produces them.

The ideas of Sense are more strong, lively, and distinct than those of the imagination; they have likewise a steadiness, order, and coherence, and are not excited at random, as those which are the effects of human wills often are, but in a regular train or series, the admirable connexion whereof sufficiently testifies the wisdom and benevolence of its Author. Now the set rules or established methods, wherein the Mind we depend on excites in us the ideas of sense, are called the *laws of nature;* and these we learn by experience, which teaches us that such and such ideas are attended with such and such other ideas, in the ordinary course of things.

This gives us a sort of foresight which enables us to regulate our actions for the benefit of life. And without this we should be eternally at a loss; we could not know how to act anything that might procure us the least pleasure, or remove the least pain of sense. That food nourishes, sleep refreshes, and fire warms us; that to sow in the seed-time is the way to reap in the harvest; and in general that to obtain such or such ends, such or such means are conducive— all this we know, not by discovering any necessary connexion between our ideas, but only by the observation of the settled laws of nature, without which we should be all in uncertainty and confusion, and a grown man no more know how to manage himself in the affairs of life than an infant just born.

And yet this consistent uniform working, which so evidently displays the goodness and wisdom of that Governing Spirit whose Will constitutes the laws of nature, is so far from leading our thoughts to Him, that it rather sends them wandering after second causes. For, when we perceive certain ideas of Sense constantly followed by other ideas and we know this is not of our own doing, we forthwith attribute power and agency to the ideas themselves, and make one the cause of another, than which nothing can be more absurd and unintelligible. Thus, for example, having observed that when we perceive by sight a certain round luminous figure we at the same time perceive by touch the idea or sensation called heat, we do from thence conclude the sun to be the cause of heat. And in like manner perceiving the motion and collision of bodies to be attended with sound, we are inclined to think the latter the effect of the former.

The ideas imprinted on the Senses by the Author of nature are called *real things;* and those excited in the imagination being less regular, vivid, and constant, are more properly termed *ideas,* or *images of things,* which they copy and represent. But then our sensations, be they never so vivid and distinct, are nevertheless ideas, that is, they exist in the mind, or are perceived by it, as truly as the ideas of its own framing. The ideas of Sense are allowed to have more reality in them, that is, to be more strong, orderly, and coherent than the creatures of the mind; but this is no argument that they exist without the mind. They are also less dependent on the spirit, or thinking substance which perceives them, in that they are excited by the will of another and more powerful spirit; yet still they are *ideas,* and certainly no idea, whether faint or strong, can exist otherwise than in a mind perceiving it.

Before we proceed any farther it is necessary we spend some time in answering objections which may probably be made against the principles we have hitherto laid down. In doing of which, if I seem too prolix to those of quick apprehensions, I hope it may be pardoned, since all men do not equally apprehend things of this nature, and I am willing to be understood by every one.

First, then, it will be objected that by the foregoing principles all that is real and substantial in nature is banished out of the world, and instead thereof a chimerical scheme of *ideas* takes place. All things that exist, exist only in the mind, that is, they are purely notional. What therefore becomes of the sun, moon and stars? What must we think of houses, rivers, mountains, trees, stones; nay, even of our own bodies? Are all these but so many chimeras and illusions on the fancy? To all which, and whatever else of the same sort may be objected, I answer, that by the principles premised we are not deprived of any one thing in nature. Whatever we see, feel, hear, or anywise conceive or understand remains as secure as ever, and is as real as ever. There is a *rerum natura,* and the distinction between realities and chimeras retains its full force. We have shewn what is meant by *real things* in opposition to *chimeras* or ideas of our own framing; but then they both equally exist in the mind, and in that sense they are alike *ideas.*

I do not argue against the existence of any one thing that we can apprehend either by sense or reflexion. That the things I see with my eyes and touch with my hands do exist, really exist, I make not the least question. The only thing whose existence we deny is that which *philosophers* call Matter or corporeal substance. And in doing of this there is no damage done to the rest of mankind, who, I dare say, will never miss it. The Atheist indeed will want the colour of an empty name to support his impiety; and the Philosophers may possibly find they have lost a great handle for trifling and disputation. . . .

[*Secondly,*] you will say there have been a great many things explained by matter and motion; take away these and you destroy the whole corpuscular philosophy, and undermine those mechanical principles which have been applied with so much success to account for the phenomena. In short, whatever advances have been made, either by ancient or modern philosophers, in the study of nature do all proceed on the supposition that corporeal substance or Matter doth really exist. To this I answer that there is not any one phenomenon explained on that supposition which may not as well be explained without it, as might easily be made appear by an induction of particulars. To explain the phenomena, is all one as to shew why, upon such and such occasions, we are affected with such and such ideas. But how Matter should operate on a Spirit, or produce any idea in it, is what no philosopher will pretend to explain; it is therefore evident there can be no use of Matter in natural philosophy. Besides, they who attempt to account for things do it not by corporeal substance, but by figure, motion, and other qualities, which are in truth no more than mere ideas, and, therefore, cannot be the cause of anything, as hath been already shewn.

[*Thirdly,*] it will upon this be demanded whether it does not seem absurd to take away natural causes, and ascribe everything to the immediate operation of Spirits? We must no longer say upon these principles that fire heats, or water cools, but that a Spirit heats, and so forth. Would not a man be deservedly laughed at, who should talk after this manner? I answer, he would so; in such things we ought to "think with the learned, and speak with the vulgar." They who to demonstration are convinced of the truth of the Copernican system do nevertheless say "the sun rises," "the sun sets," or "comes to the meridian"; and if they affected a contrary style in common talk it would without doubt appear very ridiculous. A little reflexion on what is here said will make it manifest that the common use of language would receive no manner of alteration or disturbance from the admission of our tenets. . . .

[*Fourthly,*] it will be objected that the notions we advance are inconsistent with several sound truths in philosophy and mathematics. For example, the motion of the earth is now universally admitted by astronomers as a truth grounded on the clearest and most convincing reasons. But, on the foregoing principles, there can be no such thing. For, motion being only an idea, it follows that if it be not perceived it exists not; but the motion of the earth is not perceived by sense. I answer, that tenet, if rightly understood, will be found to agree with the principles we have premised; for, the question whether the earth moves or no amounts in reality to no more than this, to wit, whether we have reason to conclude, from what has been observed by astronomers, that if we were placed in such and such circumstances, and such or such a position and distance both from the earth and sun, we should perceive the former to move among the choir of the planets, and appearing in all respects like one of them; and this, by the established rules of nature which we have no reason to mistrust, is reasonably collected from the phenomena.

We may, from the experience we have had of the train and succession of ideas in our minds, often make, I will not say uncertain conjectures, but sure and well-grounded predictions concerning the ideas we shall be affected with pursuant to a great train of actions, and be enabled to pass a right judgment of what would have appeared to us, in case we were placed in circumstances very different from those we are in at present. Herein consists the knowledge of nature, which may preserve its use and certainty very consistently with what hath been said. It will be easy to apply this to whatever objections of the like sort may be drawn from the magnitude of the stars, or any other discoveries in astronomy or nature.

Questions

1. Why does Berkeley believe that there are only two kinds of things that make up the real world: minds and their ideas?

2. How does Berkeley criticize the doctrine of primary and secondary qualities?

3. According to Berkeley, what part does God play in our knowledge of the world? Does the place of God in Berkeley's philosophy resemble the place of God in Descartes' philosophy? Explain your answer.

4. Does Berkeley's belief in the existence of minds, as things which are "entirely distinct from" ideas, contradict the principle of empiricism? Why or why not?

5. State why you think Berkeley's philosophy does, or does not, contradict the findings of physics and chemistry concerning the material world.

6. The following argument has been raised against Berkeley:

"According to Berkeley, we can only know the ideas in our minds. But he claims to have knowledge about what is beyond our minds, since he claims to know that there are no such things as material substances. For to know this, he would have to get beyond the ideas in our minds and somehow see that there are no material objects there, and this contradicts his empiricism. He ought to have said,

'I do not know whether there are any material substances,' instead of saying, 'There are no material substances.' "

State why you think this is, or is not, a valid criticism.

7. In Boswell's *Life of Johnson,* the following passage appears:

> After we came out of the church, we stood talking for some time together of Bishop Berkeley's ingenious sophistry to prove the nonexistence of matter, and that everything in the universe is merely ideal. I observed, that though we are satisfied his doctrine is not true, it is impossible to refute it. I never shall forget the alacrity with which Johnson answered, striking his foot with mighty force against a large stone, till he rebounded from it, "I refute it *thus.*" [1]

State why you think Dr. Johnson did, or did not, successfully refute Berkeley's doctrine.

4

| *An Enquiry Concerning* | David Hume |
| *Human Understanding* | *(1711-1776)* |

David Hume was born in Edinburgh, Scotland, and educated at the University of Edinburgh. At the age of 23, he went to France where he lived for three years; it was during this period that he wrote his great philosophical work, *A Treatise of Human Nature.* Although this was to become one of the most famous and influential books ever written in philosophy, it did not attract much attention during Hume's life, and his fame rested more on his *History of England* and his writings on religion. His principal philosophical writings are: *A Treatise of Human Nature* (1738-1740); *An Enquiry Concerning Human Understanding* (1748; a restatement of the material of Book I of the *Treatise*); *An Enquiry Concerning the Principles of Morals* (1751; a restatement of the material of Book III of the *Treatise*); *The Natural History of Religion* (1757); and *Dialogues Concerning Natural Religion* (published posthumously).

In this reading we are given the essential principles of Hume's theory of knowledge. Following Locke and Berkeley, Hume subscribes to the principle of empiricism which may be stated as follows: All knowledge of the world comes from, and is based on, experience. Hume makes, however, two changes in the empiricism of Locke and Berkeley. The first concerns the nature of the data from which all knowledge of the world is derived. Hume uses the term "impressions"

---

[1] James Boswell, *Life of Johnson,* Oxford University Press (Oxford Standard Edition), N. Y., Vol. 1, 1953, p. 315.

to cover both the sense data which come from our five "outward" senses and the introspective data of our "inward" feelings. He restricts the term "ideas" to those thoughts and images of which we are aware when we "reflect on" our outward and inward impressions. Thus the impressions are the original data, and Hume says that our ideas are copies of our impressions. It should be remembered that what Locke and Berkeley call "ideas" includes both what Hume calls "ideas" and what he calls "impressions." It should also be remembered that what Locke calls "ideas of reflection" (as distinct from "ideas of sensation") include both what Hume calls the "impressions" of our "inward sentiment" and also what Hume calls "ideas."

The second and more important change by Hume is his use of the principle of empiricism as a test for deciding the meaningfulness or meaninglessness of words. Whenever we hear a word being used which we suspect of not having any meaning, Hume says we should ask ourselves from what impressions is derived the idea which the word allegedly stands for. If we cannot discover, or assign, any such impressions, we may conclude that the word is meaningless, since it does not stand for any idea at all. Thus the principle of empiricism is given a dual role in philosophy: It is the basis for the meaningfulness of our language, and it is the basis for the truth (or falsity) of our assertions about the world.

After he explains the nature of ideas and impressions, Hume goes on to state that there are only three ways in which our ideas are associated with one another as they occur in our thinking, remembering, and imagining. These three "principles of association" are resemblance, contiguity, and cause or effect.

Hume then makes a division of all knowledge into two fundamentally different kinds, which he calls "relations of ideas" and "matters of fact." The reader may best understand Hume's distinction between these two kinds of knowledge if he thinks of it as a way of classifying two different kinds of statements: those which express relations of ideas and those which express matters of fact. A statement which expresses a relation of ideas is either a definition or one whose truth or falsity depends on a definition. For example, the statement "A bachelor is a man who has not married" is a definition, or to use Hume's terms expresses a "relation of ideas." Thus the word "bachelor" is interchangeable with the phrase "a man who has not married," and hence is not interchangeable with the phrase "married man." An important consequence follows from any agreement about the definition of words, which may be illustrated by means of what has just been said about "bachelor." If someone says, "Harry is a bachelor," then we know immediately that the statement "Harry has not married" is true, for this is what "bachelor" means. No one can say first, "Harry is a bachelor," and then say, "Harry is married," because he would be contradicting himself, i.e., making two incompatible statements. For if one abides by the definition of "bachelor," one cannot say that someone is both a bachelor and married. The most important area in which relations of ideas figure is mathematical knowledge, and Hume's examples are drawn from mathematics. When he says that "The square of the hypotenuse is equal to the sum of the squares of the other two sides" (The Pythagorean Theorem) is demonstratively certain, he means that it follows undeniably from the original definitions, axioms and postulates, and the preceding theorems of Euclidean geometry, in the same way that "Harry has no mother-in-law" follows from "Harry is a bachelor."

In contrast with statements which express relations of ideas, statements which express matters of fact depend for their truth or falsity not on our definitions of words, but on our experience of the world. For example, if someone tells us that he has a friend named "Harry," we may think of Harry as being tall or short, thin or fat, married or unmarried; for until we know more about Harry we may think of him in any way we like. Without either being told about Harry or meeting and talking with him, we have no way of deciding whether, for instance, "Harry is married" or its contrary "Harry is not married" is true. Hence, these statements are examples of statements which express matters of fact.

The distinction between relations of ideas and matters of fact is of enormous importance to Hume; for he argues that our knowledge of the world, which he analyzes as our knowledge of causes and their effects, is a knowledge of matters of fact. Hence, we learn the truth of such causal generalizations as "Fire burns," by experience; but when we meet each new instance of fire, we cannot know without approaching it whether it might burn us. For each of the ideas, "it will burn" and "it will not burn," is equally compatible with fire, and only experience will enable us to decide between them. Our past experience may incline us to *expect* a fire to burn us, but we can only *know* that it will in a present experience. So, "Fire burns," and similar statements which summarize our knowledge of the world must never be thought of as definitions or the consequences of definitions, which cannot be false. Unlike mathematical knowledge, our knowledge of the world is not demonstratively certain. Or to use another of Hume's phrases to express this notion, our knowledge of the world is not a priori, i.e., known without experience.

Hume's analysis of our knowledge of cause and effect includes a discussion of what has come to be known as *the principle of the uniformity of nature,* which deserves special notice because of Hume's influence on later philosophy. The principle of the uniformity of nature is also known as *the principle of induction,* for it is assumed whenever we make generalizations about the world on the basis of our experience of particulars. When we conclude, "All wood burns," as an (inductive) inference from "This wood burned," "That wood burned," "The other wood burned," etc., we do so only on the assumption that the future will resemble the past. For "All wood burns" is a statement about the wood which we shall experience in the future as well as about the wood which we have experienced in the past.

The question which Hume then asks is: What reasons do we have which could validate the principle of uniformity (that similar causes have similar effects) or of induction (that the future will resemble the past)? He argues that the principle cannot be established as true a priori, and he argues that it cannot be established empirically. (The reader is invited to discover for himself the argument Hume gives in each case.) Since these are the only two ways of knowing, Hume concludes that we must assume this principle without having any reason which justifies our doing so. But even though there are no rational or empirical grounds for making this assumption, we must nevertheless make it whenever we gain knowledge about the world. Hume can only offer us a psychological explanation of how it is that we come to make this assumption, and with this explanation the reading ends.

Hume's skepticism consists in his belief that all of our knowledge of the world rests on a principle which we have no way of verifying or confirming. Ever since Hume raised this point, philosophers have struggled with the fundamental questions it poses concerning the reasonableness of empirical knowledge. The most famous attempt to answer these questions was made by Immanuel Kant (page 116). For a more detailed analysis of the nature of causation as Hume conceived it, the reader is advised to consult the reading by Moritz Schlick (page 193).

This reading is from Sections II, III, IV, and V of *An Enquiry Concerning Human Understanding*. Hume's own section titles are used.

From Hume: *An Inquiry Concerning Human Understanding* (The Library of Liberal Arts No. 49, N. Y., 1955). Reprinted by permission of the publishers, The Liberal Arts Press, Inc.

OF THE ORIGIN OF IDEAS

Everyone will readily allow that there is a considerable difference between the perceptions of the mind when a man feels the pain of excessive heat or the pleasure of moderate warmth, and when he afterwards recalls to his memory this sensation or anticipates it by his imagination. These faculties may mimic or copy the perceptions of the senses, but they never can entirely reach the force and vivacity of the original sentiment. The utmost we say of them, even when they operate with greatest vigor, is that they represent their object in so lively a manner that we could *almost* say we feel or see it. But, except the mind be disordered by disease or madness, they never can arrive at such a pitch of vivacity as to render these perceptions altogether undistinguishable. All the colors of poetry, however splendid, can never paint natural objects in such a manner as to make the description be taken for a real landscape. The most lively thought is still inferior to the dullest sensation.

We may observe a like distinction to run through all the other perceptions of the mind. A man in a fit of anger is actuated in a very different manner from one who only thinks of that emotion. If you tell me that any person is in love, I easily understand your meaning and form a just conception of his situation, but never can mistake that conception for the real disorders and agitations of the passion. When we reflect on our past sentiments and affections, our thought is a faithful mirror and copies its objects truly, but the colors which it employs are faint and dull in comparison of those in which our original perceptions were clothed. It requires no nice discernment or metaphysical head to mark the distinction between them.

Here, therefore, we may divide all the perceptions of the mind into two classes or species, which are distinguished by their different degrees of force and vivacity. The less forcible and lively are commonly denominated "thoughts" or "ideas." The other species want a name in our language, and in most others; I suppose, because it was not requisite for any but philosophical purposes to rank them under a general term or appellation. Let us, therefore, use a little freedom and call them "impressions," employing that word in a sense somewhat different from the usual. By the term "impression," then, I mean all our more lively perceptions, when we hear, or see, or feel, or love, or hate, or desire, or will. And impressions are distinguished from ideas, which are the less lively perceptions of which we are conscious when we reflect on any of those sensations or movements above mentioned.

Nothing, at first view, may seem more unbounded than the thought of man, which not only escapes all human power and authority, but is not even restrained within the limits of nature and reality. To form monsters and join incongruous shapes and appearances cost the imagination no more trouble than to conceive the most natural and familiar objects. And while the body is confined to one planet, along which it creeps with pain and difficulty, the thought can in an instant transport us into the most distant regions of the universe, or even beyond the universe into the unbounded chaos where nature is supposed to lie in total confusion. What never was seen or heard of may yet be conceived, nor is anything beyond the power of thought except what implies an absolute contradiction.

But though our thought seems to possess this unbounded liberty, we shall find upon a nearer examination that it is really confined within very narrow limits, and that all this creative power of the mind amounts to no more than the faculty of compounding, transposing, augmenting, or diminishing the materials afforded us by the senses and experience. When we think of a golden mountain, we only join two consistent ideas, "gold" and "mountain," with which we were formerly acquainted. A virtuous horse we can conceive, because, from our own feeling, we can conceive virtue; and this we may unite to the figure and shape of a horse, which is an animal familiar to us. In short, all the materials of thinking are derived either from our outward or inward sentiment; the mixture and composition of these belongs alone to the mind and will, or, to express myself in philosophical language, all our ideas or more feeble perceptions are copies of our impressions or more lively ones.

To prove this, the two following arguments will, I hope, be sufficient. *First,* when we analyze our thoughts or ideas, however compounded or sublime, we always find that they resolve themselves into such simple ideas as were copied from a precedent feeling or sentiment. Even those ideas which at first view seem the most wide of this origin are found, upon a nearer scrutiny, to be derived from it. The idea of God, as meaning an infinitely intelligent, wise, and good Being, arises from reflecting on the operations of our own mind and augmenting, without limit, those qualities of goodness and wisdom. We may prosecute this inquiry to what length we please; where we shall always find that every idea which we examine is copied from a similar impression. Those who would assert that this position is not universally true, nor without exception, have only one, and that an easy, method of refuting it by producing that idea which, in their opinion, is not derived from this source. It will then be incumbent on us, if we would maintain our doctrine, to produce the impression or lively perception which corresponds to it.

Secondly, if it happen, from a defect of the organ, that a man is not susceptible of any species of sensation, we always find that he is as little susceptible of the correspondent idea. A blind man can form no notion of colors, a deaf man of sounds. . . .

Here, therefore, is a proposition which not only seems in itself simple and intelligible, but, if a proper use were made of it, might render every dispute equally intelligible, and banish all that jargon which has so long taken possession of metaphysical reasonings and drawn disgrace upon them. All ideas, especially abstract ones, are naturally faint and obscure. The mind has but a slender hold of them. They are apt to be confounded with other resembling ideas; and when we have often employed any term, though without a distinct meaning, we are apt to imagine it has a determinate idea annexed to it. On the contrary, all impressions, that is, all sensations either outward or inward, are strong and vivid. The limits between them are more exactly determined, nor is it easy to fall into any error or mistake with regard to them. When we entertain, therefore, any suspicion that a philosophical term is employed without any meaning or idea (as is but too frequent), we need but inquire, *from what impression is that supposed idea derived?* And if it be impossible to assign any, this will serve to confirm our suspicion. By bringing ideas in so clear a light, we may reasonably hope to remove all dispute which may arise concerning their nature and reality.

OF THE ASSOCIATION OF IDEAS

It is evident that there is a principle of connection between the different thoughts or ideas of the mind, and that, in their appearance to the memory or imagination, they introduce each other with a certain degree of method and regularity. In our more serious thinking or discourse this is so observable that any particular thought which breaks in upon the regular tract or chain of ideas is immediately remarked and rejected. And even in our wildest and most wandering reveries, nay, in our very dreams, we shall find, if we reflect, that the imagination ran not altogether at adventures, but that there was still a connection upheld among the different ideas which succeeded each other. Were the loosest and freest conversation to be transcribed, there would immediately be observed something which connected it in all its transitions. Or where this is wanting, the person who broke the thread of discourse might still inform you that there had secretly revolved in his mind a succession of thought which had gradually led him from the subject of conversation. Among different languages, even when we cannot suspect the least connection or communication, it is found that the words expressive of ideas the most compounded do yet nearly correspond to each other—a certain proof that the simple ideas comprehended in the compound ones were bound together by some universal principle which had an equal influence on all mankind.

Though it be too obvious to escape observation that different ideas are connected together, I do not find that any philosopher has attempted to enumerate or class all the principles of association—a subject, however, that seems worthy of curiosity. To me there appear to be only three principles of connection among ideas, namely, *Resemblance, Contiguity* in time or place, and *Cause* or *Effect.*

That these principles serve to connect ideas will not, I believe, be much doubted. A picture naturally leads our thoughts to the original.[1] The mention of one apartment in a building naturally introduces an inquiry or discourse concerning the others;[2] and if we think of a wound, we can scarcely forbear reflecting on the pain which follows it.[3] But that this enumeration is complete, and that there are no other principles of association except these, may be difficult to prove to the satisfaction of the reader or even to a man's own satisfaction. All we can do, in such cases, is to run over several instances and examine carefully the principle which binds the different thoughts to each other, never stopping till we render the principle as general as possible. The

---

[1] Resemblance.
[2] Contiguity.
[3] Cause and Effect.

more instances we examine and the more care we employ, the more assurance shall we acquire that the enumeration which we form from the whole is complete and entire.

SKEPTICAL DOUBTS CONCERNING THE OPERATIONS OF THE UNDERSTANDING

Part I

All the objects of human reason or inquiry may naturally be divided into two kinds, to wit, "Relations of Ideas," and "Matters of Fact." Of the first kind are the sciences of Geometry, Algebra, and Arithmetic, and, in short, every affirmation which is either intuitively or demonstratively certain. *That the square of the hypotenuse is equal to the square of the two sides* is a proposition which expresses a relation between these figures. *That three times five is equal to the half of thirty* expresses a relation between these numbers. Propositions of this kind are discoverable by the mere operation of thought, without dependence on what is anywhere existent in the universe. Though there never were a circle or triangle in nature, the truths demonstrated by Euclid would forever retain their certainty and evidence.

Matters of fact, which are the second objects of human reason, are not ascertained in the same manner, nor is our evidence of their truth, however great, of a like nature with the foregoing. The contrary of every matter of fact is still possible, because it can never imply a contradiction and is conceived by the mind with the same facility and distinctness as if ever so conformable to reality. *That the sun will not rise tomorrow* is no less intelligible a proposition and implies no more contradiction than the affirmation *that it will rise*. We should in vain, therefore, attempt to demonstrate its falsehood. Were it demonstratively false, it would imply a contradiction and could never be distinctly conceived by the mind.

It may, therefore, be a subject worthy of curiosity to inquire what is the nature of that evidence which assures us of any real existence and matter of fact beyond the present testimony of our senses or the records of our memory. This part of philosophy, it is observable, had been little cultivated either by the ancients or moderns; and, therefore, our doubts and errors in the prosecution of so important an inquiry may be the more excusable while we march through such difficult paths without any guide or direction. They may even prove useful by exciting curiosity and destroying that implicit faith and security which is the bane of all reasoning and free inquiry. The discovery of defects in the common philosophy, if any such there be, will not, I presume, be a discouragement, but rather an incitement, as is usual, to attempt something more full and satisfactory than has yet been proposed to the public.

All reasonings concerning matter of fact seem to be founded on the relation of *cause* and *effect*. By means of that relation alone we can go beyond the evidence of our memory and senses. If you were to ask a man why he believes any matter of fact which is absent, for instance, that his friend is in the country or in France, he would give you a reason, and this reason would be some other fact: as a letter received from him or the knowledge of his former resolutions and promises. A man finding a watch or any other machine in a desert island would conclude that there had once been men in that island. All our reasonings concerning fact are of the same nature. And here it is constantly supposed that there is a connection between the present fact and that which is inferred from it. Were there nothing to bind them together, the inference would be entirely precarious. The hearing of an articulate voice and rational discourse in the dark assures us of the presence of some person. Why? Because these are the effects of the human make and fabric, and closely connected with it. If we anatomize all the other reasonings of this nature, we shall find that they are founded on the relation of cause and effect, and that this relation is either near or remote, direct or collateral. Heat and light are collateral effects of fire, and the one effect may justly be inferred from the other.

If we would satisfy ourselves, therefore, concerning the nature of that evidence which assures us of matters of fact, we must inquire how we arrive at the knowledge of cause and effect.

I shall venture to affirm, as a general proposition which admits of no exception, that the knowledge of this relation is not, in any instance, attained by reasonings *a priori,* but arises entirely from experience, when we find that any particular objects are constantly conjoined with each other. Let an object be presented to a man of ever so strong natural reason and abilities—if that object be entirely new to him, he will not be able, by the most accurate examination of its sensible qualities, to discover any of its causes or effects. Adam, though his rational faculties be supposed, at the very first, entirely perfect, could not have inferred from the fluidity and transparency of water that it would suffocate him, or from the light and warmth of fire that it would consume him. No object ever discovers, by the qualities which appear to the senses, either the causes which produced it or the effects which will arise from it; nor can our reason, unassisted by experience, ever draw any inference concerning real existence and matter of fact.

This proposition, *that causes and effects are discoverable, not by reason, but by experience,* will readily be admitted with regard to such objects as we remember to have once been altogether unknown to us, since we must be conscious of the utter inability which we then lay under of foretelling what would arise from them. Present two smooth pieces of marble to a man who has no tincture of natural philosophy; he will never discover that they will adhere together in such a manner as to require great force to separate them in a direct line, while they make so small a resistance to a lateral pressure. Such events as bear little analogy to the common course of nature are also readily confessed to be known only by experience, nor does any man imagine that the explosion of gunpowder or the attraction of a loadstone could ever be discovered by arguments *a priori.* In like manner, when an effect is supposed to depend upon an intricate machinery or secret structure of parts, we make no difficulty in attributing all our knowledge of it to experience. Who will assert that he can give the ultimate reason why milk or bread is proper nourishment for a man, not for a lion or tiger?

But the same truth may not appear at first sight to have the same evidence with regard to events which have become familiar to us from our first appearance in the world, which bear a close analogy to the whole course of nature, and which are supposed to depend on the simple qualities of objects without any secret structure of parts. We are apt to imagine that we could discover these effects by the mere operation of our reason without experience. We fancy that, were we brought on a sudden into this world, we could at first have inferred that one billiard ball would communicate motion to another upon impulse, and that we needed not to have waited for the event in order to pronounce with certainty concerning it. Such is the influence of custom that where it is strongest it not only covers our natural ignorance but even conceals itself, and seems not to take place, merely because it is found in the highest degree.

But to convince us that all the laws of nature and all the operations of bodies without exception are known only by experience, the following reflections may perhaps suffice. Were any object presented to us, and were we required to pronounce concerning the effect which will result from it without consulting past observation, after what manner, I beseech you, must the mind proceed in this operation? It must invent or imagine some event which it ascribes to the object as its effect; and it is plain that this invention must be entirely arbitrary. The mind can never possibly find the effect in the supposed cause by the most accurate scrutiny and examination. For the effect is totally different from the cause, and consequently can never be discovered in it. Motion in the second billiard ball is a quite distinct event from motion in the first, nor is there anything in the one to suggest the smallest hint of the other. A stone or piece of metal raised into the air and left without any support immediately falls. But to consider the matter *a priori,* is there anything we discover in this situation which can beget the idea of a downward rather than an upward or any other motion in the stone or metal?

And as the first imagination or invention of a particular effect in all natural operations is arbitrary where we consult not experience, so must we also esteem the supposed tie or connection between the cause and effect which binds them together and renders it impossible that any other effect could result from the operation of that cause. When I see, for instance, a billiard ball moving in a straight line toward another, even suppose motion in the second ball should by accident be suggested to me as the result of their contact or impulse, may I not conceive that a hundred different events might as well follow from that cause? May not both these balls remain at absolute rest? May not the first ball return in a straight line or leap off from the second in any line or direction? All these suppositions are consistent and conceivable. Why, then, should we give the preference to one which is no more consistent or conceivable than the rest? All our reasonings *a priori* will never be able to show us any foundation for this preference.

In a word, then, every effect is a distinct event from its cause. It could not, therefore, be discovered in the cause, and the first invention or conception of it, *a priori,* must be entirely arbitrary. And even after it is suggested, the conjunction of it with the cause must appear equally arbitrary, since there are always many other effects which, to reason, must seem fully as consistent and natural. In vain, therefore, should we pretend to determine any single event or infer any cause or effect without the assistance of observation and experience.

Hence we may discover the reason why no philosopher who is rational and modest has ever pretended to assign the ultimate cause of any natural operation, or to show distinctly the action of that power which produces any single effect in the universe. It is confessed that the utmost effort of human reason is to reduce the principles productive of natural phenomena to a greater simplicity, and to resolve the many particular effects into a few general causes, by means of reasonings from analogy, experience, and observation. But as to the causes of these general causes, we should in vain attempt their discovery, nor shall we ever be able to satisfy ourselves by any particular explication of them. These ultimate springs and principles are totally shut up from human curiosity and inquiry. Elasticity, gravity, cohesion of parts, communication of motion by impulse—these are probably the ultimate causes and principles which we shall ever discover in nature; and we may esteem ourselves sufficiently happy if, by accurate inquiry and reasoning, we can trace up the particular phenomena to, or near to, these general principles. The most perfect philosophy of the natural kind only staves off our ignorance a little longer, as perhaps the most perfect philosophy of the moral or metaphysical kind serves only to discover larger portions of it. Thus the observation of human blindness and weakness is the result of all philosophy, and meets us, at every turn, in spite of our endeavors to elude or avoid it.

Nor is geometry, when taken into the assistance of natural philosophy, ever able to remedy this defect or lead us into the knowledge of ultimate causes by all that accuracy of reasoning for which it is so justly celebrated. Every part of mixed mathematics proceeds upon the supposition that certain laws are established by nature in her operations, and abstract reasonings are employed either to assist experience in the discovery of these laws or to determine their influence in particular instances where it depends upon any precise degree of distance and quantity. Thus it is a law of motion, discovered by experience, that the moment or force of any body in motion is in the compound ratio or proportion of its solid contents and its velocity, and, consequently, that a small force may remove the greatest obstacle or raise the greatest weight if by any contrivance or machinery we can increase the velocity of that force so as to make it an overmatch for its antagonist. Geometry assists us in the application of this law by giving us the just dimensions of all the parts and figures which can enter into any species of machine, but still the discovery of the law itself is owing merely to experience; and all the abstract reasonings in the world could never lead us one step toward the knowledge of it. When we reason *a priori* and consider merely any object or cause as it appears to the mind, independent of all observation, it never could suggest to us the notion of any distinct object, such as its effect, much less show us the inseparable and inviolable connection between them. A man must be very sagacious who could discover by reasoning that crystal is the effect of heat, and ice of cold, without being previously acquainted with the operation of these qualities.

Part II

But we have not yet attained any tolerable satisfaction with regard to the question first proposed. Each solution still gives rise to a new question as difficult as the foregoing and leads us on to further inquiries. When it is asked, *What is the nature of all our reasonings concerning matter of fact?* the proper answer seems to be, That they are founded on the relation of cause and effect. When again it is asked, *What is the foundation of all our reasonings and conclusions concerning that relation?* it may be replied in one word, *experience.* But if we still carry on our sifting humor and ask, *What is the foundation of all conclusions from experience?* this implies a new question which may be of more difficult solution and explication. Philosophers that give themselves airs of superior wisdom and sufficiency have a hard task when they encounter persons of inquisitive dispositions, who push them from every corner to which they retreat, and who are sure at last to bring them to some dangerous dilemma. The best expedient to prevent this confusion is to be modest in our pretensions and even to discover the difficulty ourselves before it is objected to us. By this means we may make a kind of merit of our very ignorance.

I shall content myself in this section with an easy task and shall pretend only to give a negative answer to the question here proposed. I say, then, that even after we have experience of the operations of cause and effect, our conclusions from that experience are *not* founded on reasoning or any process of the understanding. This answer we must endeavor both to explain and to defend.

It must certainly be allowed that nature has kept us at a great distance from all her secrets and has afforded us only the knowledge of a few superficial qualities of objects, while she conceals from us those powers and principles on which the influence of these objects entirely depends. Our senses inform us of the color, weight, and consistency of bread, but neither sense nor reason can ever inform us of those qualities which fit it for the nourishment and support of the human body. Sight or feeling conveys an idea of the actual motion of bodies, but as to that wonderful force or power which would carry on a moving body forever in a continued change of place, and which bodies never lose but by communicating it to others, of this we cannot form the most distant conception. But notwithstanding this ignorance of natural powers and principles, we always presume when we see like sensible qualities that they have like secret powers, and expect that effects similar to those which we have experienced will follow from them. If a body of like color and consistency with that bread which we have formerly eaten be presented to us, we make no scruple of repeating the experiment and foresee with certainty like nourishment and support. Now this is a process of the mind or thought of which I would willingly know the foundation. It is allowed on all hands that there is no known connection between the sensible qualities and the secret powers, and, consequently, that the mind is not led to form such a conclusion concerning their constant and regular conjunction by anything which it knows of their nature. As to past *experience,* it can be allowed to give *direct* and *certain* information of those precise objects only, and that precise period of time which fell under its cognizance: But why this experience should be extended to future times and to other objects which, for aught we know, may be only in appearance similar, this is the main question on which I would insist. The bread which I formerly ate nourished me; that is, a body of such sensible qualities was, at that time, endued with such secret powers. But does it follow that other bread must also nourish me at another time, and that like sensible qualities must always be attended with like secret powers? The consequence seems nowise necessary. At least, it must be acknowledged that there is here a consequence drawn by the mind that there is a certain step taken, a process of thought, and an inference which wants to be explained. These two propositions are far from being the same: *I have found that such an object has always been attended with such an effect,* and *I foresee that other objects which are in appearance similar will be attended with similar effects.* I shall allow, if you please, that the one proposition may justly be inferred from the other: I know, in fact, that it always is inferred. But if you insist that the inference is made by a chain of reasoning, I desire you to produce that reasoning. The connection between these propositions is not intuitive. There is required a medium which may enable the mind to draw such an inference, if indeed it be drawn by reasoning and argument. What that medium is I must confess passes my comprehension; and it is incumbent on those to produce it who assert that it really exists and is the original of all our conclusions concerning matter of fact.

This negative argument must certainly, in process of time, become altogether convincing if many penetrating and able philosophers shall turn their inquiries this way, and no one be ever able to discover any connecting proposition or intermediate step which supports the understanding in this conclusion. But as the question is yet new, every reader may not trust so far to his own penetration as to conclude, because an argument escapes his inquiry, that therefore it does not really exist. For this reason it may be requisite to venture upon a more difficult task, and, enumerating all the branches of human knowledge, endeavor to show that none of them can afford such an argument.

All reasonings may be divided into two kinds, namely, demonstrative reasoning, or that concerning relations of ideas, and moral reasoning, or that concerning matter of fact and existence. That there are no demonstrative argu ments in the case seems evident, since it implies no contradiction that the course of nature may change and that an object, seemingly like those which we have experienced, may be attended with different or contrary effects. May I not clearly and distinctly conceive that a body, falling from the clouds and which in all other respects resembles snow, has yet the taste of salt or feeling of fire? Is there any more intelligible proposition than to affirm that all the trees will flourish in December and January, and will decay in May and June? Now, whatever is intelligible and can be distinctly conceived implies no contradiction and can never be proved false by any demonstrative argument or abstract reasoning *a priori.*

If we be, therefore, engaged by arguments to put trust in past experience and make it the standard of our future judgment, these arguments must be probable only, or such as regard matter of fact and real existence, according to the division above mentioned. But that there is no argument of this kind must appear if our explication of that species of reasoning be admitted as solid and satisfactory. We have said that all arguments concerning existence are founded on the relation of cause and effect, that our knowledge of that relation is derived entirely from experience, and that all our experimental conclusions proceed upon the supposition that the future will be conformable to the past. To endeavor, therefore, the proof of this last supposition by probable arguments, or arguments regarding existence, must be evidently going in a circle and taking that for granted which is the very point in question.

In reality, all arguments from experience are founded on the similarity which we discover among natural objects, and by which we are induced to expect effects similar to those which we have found to follow from such objects. And though none but a fool or madman will ever pretend to dispute the authority of experience or to reject that great guide of human life, it may surely be allowed a philosopher to have so much curiosity at least as to examine the principle of human nature which gives this mighty authority to experience and makes us draw advantage from that similarity which nature has placed among different objects. From causes which appear similar, we expect similar effects. This is the sum of all our experimental conclusions. Now it seems evident that, if this conclusion were formed by reason, it would be as perfect at first, and upon one instance, as after ever so long a course of experience; but the case is far otherwise. Nothing [is] so like as eggs, yet no one, on account of this appearing similarity, expects the same taste and relish in all of them. It is only after a long course of uniform experiments in any kind that we attain a firm reliance and security with regard to a particular event. Now, where is that process of reasoning which, from one instance, draws a conclusion so different from that which it infers from a hundred instances that are nowise different from that single one? This question I propose as much for the sake of information as with an intention of raising difficulties. I cannot find, I cannot imagine any such reasoning. But I keep my mind still open to instruction if anyone will vouchsafe to bestow it on me.

Should it be said that, from a number of uniform experiments, we *infer* a connection between the sensible qualities and the secret powers, this, I must confess, seems the same difficulty, couched in different terms. The question still occurs, On what process of argument is this *inference* founded? Where is the medium, the interposing ideas which join propositions so very wide of each other? It is confessed that the color, consistency, and other sensible qualities of bread appear not of themselves to have any connection with the secret powers of nourishment and support; for otherwise we could infer these secret powers from the first appearance of these sensible qualities without the aid of experience, contrary to the sentiment of all philosophers, and contrary to plain matter of fact. Here, then, is our natural state of ignorance with regard to the powers and influence of all objects. How is this remedied by experience? It only shows us a number of uniform effects resulting from certain objects, and teaches us that those particular objects, at that particular time, were endowed with such powers and forces. When a new object endowed with similar sensible qualities is produced, we expect similar powers and forces, and look for a like effect. From a body of like color and consistency with bread, we expect like nourishment and support. But this surely is a step or progress of the mind which wants to be explained. When a man says, *I have found, in all past instances, such sensible qualities, conjoined with such secret powers,* and when he says, *similar sensible qualities will always be conjoined with similar secret powers,* he is not guilty of a tautology, nor are these propositions in any respect the same. You say that the one proposition is an inference from the other; but you must confess that the inference is not intuitive, neither is it demonstrative. Of what nature is it then? To say it is experimental is begging the question. For all inferences from experience suppose, as their foundation, that the future will resemble the past and that similar powers will be conjoined with similar sensible qualities. If there be any suspicion that the course of nature may change, and that the past may be no rule for the future, all experience becomes useless and can give rise to no inference or conclusion. It is impossible, therefore, that any arguments from experience can prove this resemblance of the past to the future, since all these arguments are founded on the supposition of that resemblance. Let the course of things be allowed hitherto ever so regular, that alone, without some new argument or inference, proves not that for the future it will continue so. In vain do you pretend to have learned the nature of bodies from your past experience. Their secret nature, and consequently all their effects and influence, may change without any change in their sensible qualities. This happens sometimes, and with regard to some objects. Why may it not happen always, and with regard to all objects? What logic, what process of argument secures you against this supposition? My practice, you say, refutes my doubts. But you mistake the purport of my question. As an agent, I am quite satisfied in the point; but as a philosopher who has some share of curiosity, I will not say skepticism, I want to learn the foundation of this inference. No reading, no inquiry has yet been able to remove my difficulty or give me satisfaction in a matter of such importance. Can I do better than propose the difficulty to the public, even though, perhaps, I have small hopes of obtaining a solution? We shall at least, by this means, be sensible of our ignorance, if we do not augment our knowledge. . . .

SKEPTICAL SOLUTION OF THESE DOUBTS

Suppose a person, though endowed with the strongest faculties of reason and reflection, to be brought on a sudden into this world; he would, indeed, immediately observe a continual succession of objects and one event following another, but he would not be able to discover anything further. He would not at first, by any reasoning, be able to reach the idea of cause and effect, since the particular powers by which all natural operations are performed never appear to the senses; nor is it reasonable to conclude, merely because one event in one instance precedes another, that therefore the one is the cause, the other the effect. The conjunction may be arbitrary and casual. There may be no reason to infer the existence of one from the appearance of the other: and, in a word, such a person without more experience could never employ his conjecture or reasoning concerning any matter of fact or be assured of anything beyond what was immediately present to his memory or senses.

Suppose again that he has acquired more experience and has lived so long in the world as to have observed similar objects or events to be constantly conjoined together—what is the consequence of this experience? He immediately infers the existence of one object from the appearance of the other, yet he has not, by all his experience, acquired any idea or knowledge of the secret power by which the one object produces the other, nor is it by any process of reasoning he is engaged to draw this inference; but still he finds himself determined to draw it, and though he should be convinced that his understanding has no part in the operation, he would nevertheless continue in the same course of thinking. There is some other principle which determines him to form such a conclusion.

This principle is *custom* or *habit*. For wherever the repetition of any particular act or operation produces a propensity to renew the same act or operation without being impelled by any reasoning or process of the understanding, we always say that this propensity is the effect of *custom*. By employing that word we pretend not to have given the ultimate reason of such a propensity. We only point out a principle of human nature which is universally acknowledged, and which is well known by its effects. Perhaps we can push our inquiries no further or pretend to give the cause of this cause, but must rest contented with it as the ultimate principle which we can assign of all our conclusions from experience. It is sufficient satisfaction that we can go so far without repining at the narrowness of our faculties, because they will carry us no further. And it is certain we here advance a very intelligible proposition at least, if not a true one, when we assert that after the constant conjunction of two objects, heat and flame, for instance, weight and solidity, we are determined by custom alone to expect the one from the appearance of the other. This hypothesis seems even the only one which explains the difficulty why we draw from a thousand instances an inference which we are not able to draw from one instance that is in no respect different from them. Reason is incapable of any such variation. The conclusions which it draws from considering one circle are the same which it would form upon surveying all the circles in the universe. But no man, having seen only one body move after being impelled by another, could infer that every other body will move after a like impulse. All inferences from experience, therefore, are effects of custom, not of reasoning.

Custom, then, is the great guide of human life. It is that principle alone which renders our experience useful to us and makes us expect, for the future, a similar train of events with those which have appeared in the past. Without the influence of custom we should be entirely ignorant of every matter of fact beyond what is immediately present to the memory and senses. We should never know how to adjust means to ends or to employ our natural powers in the production of any effect. There would be an end at once of all action as well as of the chief part of speculation.

But here it may be proper to remark that though our conclusions from experience carry us beyond our memory and senses and assure us of matters of fact which happened in the most distant places and most remote ages, yet some fact must always be present to the senses or memory from which we may first proceed in drawing these conclusions. A man who should find in a desert country the remains of pompous buildings would conclude that the country had, in ancient times, been cultivated by civilized inhabitants; but did nothing of this nature occur to him, he could never form such an inference. We learn the events of former ages from history, but then we must peruse the volume in which this instruction is contained, and thence carry up our inferences from one testimony to another, till we arrive at the eyewitnesses and spectators of these distant events. In a word, if we proceed not upon some fact present to the memory or senses, our reasonings would be merely hypothetical; and however the particular links might be connected with each other, the whole chain of inferences would have nothing to support it, nor could we ever, by its means, arrive at the knowledge of any real existence. If I ask why you believe any particular matter of fact which you relate, you must tell me some reason; and this reason will be some other fact connected with it. But as you cannot proceed after this manner *in infinitum,* you must at last terminate in some fact which is present to your memory or senses or must allow that your belief is entirely without foundation.

What, then, is the conclusion of the whole matter? A simple one, though, it must be confessed, pretty remote from the common theories of philosophy. All belief of matter of fact or real existence is derived merely from some object present to the memory or senses and a customary conjunction between that and some other object; or, in other words, having found, in many instances, that any two kinds of objects, flame and heat, snow and cold, have always been conjoined together: if flame or snow be presented anew to the senses, the mind is carried by custom to expect heat or cold, and to *believe* that such a quality does exist and will discover itself upon a nearer approach. This belief is the necessary result of placing the mind in such circumstances. It is an operation of the soul, when we are so situated, as unavoidable as to feel the passion of love, when we receive benefits; or hatred, when we meet with injuries. All these operations are a species of natural instincts, which no reasoning or process of the thought and understanding is able either to produce or to prevent.

Questions

1. It has been claimed that Hume shows our knowledge of causes and effects to depend only on the two principles of the association of ideas which he calls "resemblance" and "contiguity." How would each of these principles operate in such knowledge if this claim were correct? If you think the claim is not correct, why do you think Hume inserted the section, "Of the Association of Ideas," in his essay on knowledge?

2. Explain in your own words the difference between "relations of ideas" and "matters of fact." Why is the latter *empirical* knowledge, and not the former? Why does all knowledge of matters of fact rest on the assumption of the uniformity of nature (that similar causes will lead to similar effects)?

3. Are the following statements about relations of ideas or matters of fact? Give reasons for classifying each statement as you do.
   a. One-half of twelve is twice three.
   b. Two gloves, one made for the right hand and the other for the left, and which are of the same size, color, and pattern, make a pair.
   c. My two gloves are a pair.
   d. Sheep are wool-bearing mammals.
   e. My sheep bear wool.
   f. My sheep bear silk.
   g. The woman was wearing a silk dress made out of wool.
   h. The Eiffel Tower is in Washington, D. C.
   i. There are only two kinds of things: minds and their ideas. (Berkeley)
   j. Whatever I conceive clearly and distinctly exists. (Descartes)
   k. If I have an idea of something, then my idea must be a copy of an impression or set of impressions. (Hume)
   l. Every effect has a cause.
   m. When I push the button, the bell rings.
   n. When I push the button, I push the button.
   o. Fire burns.
   p. Every body perseveres in its state of rest, or of uniform motion in a right line, unless it is compelled to change that state by forces impressed thereon. (Newton)

4. What is Hume's argument to show that the principle of the uniformity of nature is not true a priori? What is his argument to show that the principle is not true a posteriori (i.e., is not empirically true)? If you think there are flaws in these arguments, state what they are. If you do not think there are flaws in these arguments, state why you agree, or disagree, with the claim: "Hume has shown us that all empirical science rests on a blind faith that the future will be like the past."

5. If you accepted Hume's version of the principle of empiricism as a test of meaningfulness as well as truth, how would you criticize Locke's and Berkeley's views of knowledge and existence? (For Locke's and Berkeley's views, see pages 70 and 87.)

5

(Prefaces)

~~Prolegomena~~ to *Any Future Metaphysics* | Immanuel Kant
| (*1724-1804*)

Immanuel Kant was born in Königsberg, Germany, where he lived all his life. He attended the University of Königsberg and in 1755 received the degree of doctor of philosophy there. He became a lecturer at the University, and finally professor of metaphysics and logic. Kant's philosophical works have had a profound influence on all fields of philosophy since his time. He is perhaps most famous for his *Critique of Pure Reason* (1781). Kant wrote his *Prolegomena to Any Future Metaphysics* (1783), from which the present reading is taken, as a more readable and concise version of the *Critique of Pure Reason*. In these works he presents his theory of knowledge. Much of the lively discussion among contemporary philosophers concerning the nature of knowledge stems directly from these works. Similarly, Kant's writings in moral philosophy have had a powerful impact on the study of ethics today. The moral philosophy which Kant expounded in his *Fundamental Principles of the Metaphysic of Morals* (1785) and in his *Critique of Practical Reason* (1788) is still of vital concern to all who are interested in the problem of moral knowledge. The greater part of the *Fundamental Principles of the Metaphysic of Morals* is contained in Chapter 6 in this book.

In his *Critique of Pure Reason* and *Prolegomena to Any Future Metaphysics,* Kant was trying to define the exact nature of metaphysical knowledge. He was concerned with two problems. One arose from the fact that in the history of philosophy many metaphysical theories were constructed which were meant to tell us the ultimate nature of reality, but none of them seemed to make any real advance over other previous theories. Unlike the empirical sciences, metaphysics did not seem to be a gradually increasing body of well established knowledge. Yet there were always philosophers who would claim to have the truth about the fundamental characteristics of all existence, and who would claim that other metaphysical views were false. Examples of metaphysics are given in the present chapter of this book in the selections by Descartes (pages 54 ff.), and by Royce (page 129). Since each writer appears to say something different about the nature of reality, how is it possible to make a choice among their different views? Kant sought a solution to this problem by making a careful examination of the kind of knowledge metaphysicians were claiming to have when they spoke about reality or existence. He thought that once he had made clear what sort of knowledge was possible in metaphysics and what sort was not possible, other philosophers could proceed to "do metaphysics" and gain the kind of knowledge which he had stated to be possible. Hence he calls his briefer study of metaphysical knowledge "prolegomena," that is, preliminary statements or prefaces, to any future metaphysics.

The second problem with which Kant was concerned in writing(2) his *Prolegomena* and his *Critique of Pure Reason* was the problem raised by David Hume concerning our knowledge of the world. Hume had shown that all knowledge of the world rests on the assumption that similar causes will have similar effects (page 111). He then argued that although the mind must make this assumption in order to gain knowledge of the world, no reasons can be found which would validate it. Kant saw that Hume's argument implied a denial of the possibility of metaphysics, since this assumption and others of the same type (for example, that there was a beginning to the universe, that every event has a cause, that substance is infinitely divisible, etc.) were precisely what metaphysics claimed to establish on absolutely certain grounds. In the *Prolegomena* and the *Critique of Pure Reason* Kant tries to give an account of metaphysical knowledge which is not open to Hume's criticisms. We may call such knowledge "legitimate metaphysical knowledge," to distinguish it from that kind of metaphysical knowledge which Kant believed to be impossible.

In order to make clear the nature of legitimate metaphysical knowledge, Kant begins with two classifications of judgments. The first classification of judgments is as either *analytical* or *synthetical,* the second as either *a priori* or *a posteriori.* The first classification is concerned with the *meaning* of judgments, the second with the kinds of grounds on which judgments are *justified.*

A judgment is made up of a subject and a predicate. In order to understand what a judgment means, we must understand both the subject and the predicate. Let us suppose we do understand the subject and predicate of a given judgment. Then we can tell whether the judgment is analytical or synthetical in the following way. If in understanding the predicate we merely make explicit one of the ideas already contained in our idea of the subject, the judgment is analytical (i.e., its meaning is an analysis of a complex idea). If in understanding the predicate we add a new idea to our idea of the subject, then the judgment is synthetical (i.e., its meaning is a synthesis of different ideas). Let us take an example. The judgment, "A person six feet tall is taller than a person five feet tall," is analytical since the predicate "being taller than" does not add any new idea to the idea of the relation of a six-footer to a five-footer. But the judgment, "Christopher Columbus was six feet tall," is a synthetical judgment since we can know who Christopher Columbus was without knowing that he was six feet tall. (Indeed, he might not have been six feet tall, but this would not mean he was not Christopher Columbus.) Kant uses the following example. Every time we think of a physical body, we must think of it as taking up some space. Thus in the judgment, "All bodies are extended," the predicate does not add any new idea to the subject, but is already contained in the subject. Therefore the judgment is analytical. But when we think of a physical body we do not have to think of it as having weight (for instance, when we think of it as "floating" in space outside the gravitational pull of any celestial body). Thus the judgment, "All bodies have weight," is a synthetical judgment because the idea of weight adds something to the idea of a body.

Let us turn to the second classification of judgments, according to which judgments are either *a priori* or *a posteriori*. A judgment is a priori (or, as it is sometimes said, a judgment is true a priori or false a priori) when we can know that it is true or false without relying upon the evidence of experience. We can know it by pure reason alone and our knowledge of it is absolutely certain. In every case of an a priori judgment, the judgment is necessarily true or necessarily false. In Kant's terminology, the judgment is "apodictic." A judgment is a posteriori (true a posteriori or false a posteriori) when we can know that it is true or false only empirically, that is, only by appealing to the evidence of our experience. Thus we may call an a posteriori judgment simply an empirical judgment. A posteriori judgments correspond to Hume's "matters of fact"; a priori judgments to his "relations of ideas" (page 105).

Now there are four possible combinations of the different kinds of judgments: (1) analytical a priori, (2) analytical a posteriori, (3) synthetical a posteriori, and (4) synthetical a priori. Kant says that all analytical judgments are a priori, and therefore there are no such things as judgments of type (2). But he believes that synthetical judgments may be either a posteriori or a priori. Synthetical a posteriori judgments are all the empirical judgments of the sciences. Synthetical a priori judgments belong to two branches of knowledge: mathematics and metaphysics. Kant explains to his own satisfaction why mathematical propositions are synthetical and a priori. He then propounds his principal thesis: *If there is such a thing as metaphysical knowledge it must consist of synthetical a priori judgments.* His argument assumes that the task of legitimate metaphysical knowledge is to give us information about the world by means of purely rational (nonempirical) judgments which possess absolute certainty and necessity. If metaphysics claims to give us knowledge of a reality beyond all possible experience, it is mere speculation and not legitimate knowledge at all. But if it claims to give us knowledge about a reality within the limits of possible experience, then it must be knowledge derived a priori from pure reason; for otherwise it would yield the merely probable a posteriori judgments of the empirical sciences.

In our present reading Kant is setting up the problem which he later tries to solve in the main body of the *Prolegomena* and the *Critique of Pure Reason*. The problem is this: How is legitimate metaphysical knowledge possible? And we have seen that this means: How is it possible to gain a priori knowledge of the world of experience?

We may briefly summarize the solution which Kant offers in the main body of his works. We can derive from reason alone, by means of a "deduction," the necessary conditions of all possible experience. Legitimate metaphysical knowledge is knowledge of the a priori presuppositions of all possible experience (and hence of all empirical knowledge). These presuppositions are the formal concepts imposed by the rational mind upon the manifold material supplied by our sensations. We can experience (and thus know) the world only through the union of rational form (concepts) and empirical matter (percepts).

For further discussion of the role of a priori concepts in our knowledge of the world, the reader is advised to consult the reading by C. I. Lewis (page 177).

This reading is from Kant's own Introduction and Preamble to the *Prolegomena to Any Future Metaphysics*. The translation from the German is by Lewis White Beck. Kant's own section titles are used.

From Kant: *Prolegomena to Any Future Metaphysics,* the Mahaffy-Carus translation revised by Lewis White Beck (The Library of Liberal Arts No. 27, N. Y., 1950). Reprinted by permission of the publishers, The Liberal Arts Press, Inc.

INTRODUCTION

My purpose is to persuade all those who think metaphysics worth studying that it is absolutely necessary to pause a moment and, regarding all that has been done as though undone, to propose first the preliminary question, "Whether such a thing as metaphysics be even possible at all?"

If it be science, how is it that it cannot, like other sciences, obtain universal and lasting recognition? If not, how can it maintain its pretensions and keep the human mind in suspense with hopes never ceasing, yet never fulfilled? Whether then we demonstrate our knowledge or our ignorance in this field, we must come once for all to a definite conclusion respecting the nature of this so-called science, which cannot possibly remain on its present footing. It seems almost ridiculous, while every other science is continually advancing, that in this, which pretends to be wisdom incarnate, for whose oracle everyone inquires, we should constantly move round the same spot, without gaining a single step. And so its votaries having melted away, we do not find men confident of their ability to shine in other sciences venturing their reputation here, where everybody, however ignorant in other matters, presumes to deliver a final verdict, because in this domain there is actually as yet no standard weight and measure to distinguish sound knowledge from shallow talk.

After all it is nothing extraordinary in the elaboration of a science that, when men begin to wonder how far it has advanced, the question should at last occur whether and how such a science is possible at all. Human reason so delights building that it has several times built up a tower and then razed it to see how the foundation was laid. It is never too late to become reasonable and wise; but if the knowledge comes late, there is always more difficulty in starting a reform. . . .

Since the *Essays* of Locke and Leibniz, or rather since the origin of metaphysics so far as we know its history, nothing has ever happened which could have been more decisive to its fate than the attack made upon it by David Hume. He threw no light on this species of knowledge, but he certainly struck a spark by which light might have been kindled had it caught some inflammable substance and had its smouldering fire been carefully nursed and developed.

Hume started chiefly from a single but important concept in metaphysics, namely, that of the connection of cause and effect (including its derivatives force and action, and so on). He challenged reason, which pretends to have given birth to this concept of herself, to answer him by what right she thinks anything could be so constituted that if that thing be posited, something else also must necessarily be posited; for this is the meaning of the concept of cause. He demonstrated irrefutably that it was perfectly impossible for reason to think, *a priori* and by means of concepts, such a combination, for it implies necessity. We cannot at all see why, in consequence of the existence of one thing, another must necessarily exist or how the concept of such a combination can arise *a priori*. Hence he inferred that reason was altogether deluded with reference to this concept, which she erroneously considered as one of her own children, whereas in reality it was nothing but a bastard of imagination, impregnated by experience, which subsumed certain representations under the law of association and mistook a subjective necessity (habit) for an objective necessity arising from insight. Hence he inferred that reason had no power to think such combinations, even in general, because her concepts would then be purely fictitious and all her pretended *a priori* cognitions nothing but common experiences marked with a false stamp. In plain language, this means that there is not and cannot be any such thing as metaphysics at all.

However hasty and mistaken Hume's inference may appear, it was at least founded upon investigation, and this investigation deserved the concentrated attention of the brighter spirits of his day as well as determined efforts on their part to discover, if possible, a happier solution of the problem in the sense proposed by him, all of which would have speedily resulted in a complete reform of the science.

But Hume suffered the usual misfortune of metaphysicians, of not being understood. It is positively painful to see how utterly his opponents, Reid, Oswald, Beattie, and lastly Priestley, missed the point of the problem; for while they were ever taking for granted that which he doubted, and demonstrating with zeal and often with impudence that which he never thought of doubting, they so misconstrued his valuable suggestion that everything remained in its old condition, as if nothing had happened. The question was not whether the concept of cause was right, useful, and even indispensable for our knowledge of nature, for this Hume had never doubted; but whether that concept could be thought by reason *a priori,* and consequently whether it possessed an inner truth, independent of all experience, implying a perhaps more extended use not restricted merely to objects of experience. This was Hume's problem. It was solely a question concerning the *origin,* not concerning the *indispensable* need of using the concept. Were the former decided, the conditions of the use and the sphere of its valid application would have been determined as a matter of course.

But to satisfy the conditions of the problem, the opponents of the great thinker should have penetrated very deeply into the nature of reason, so far as it is concerned with pure thinking—a task which did not suit them. They found a more convenient method of being defiant without any insight, namely, the appeal to *common sense.* It is indeed a great gift of God to possess right or (as they now call it) plain common sense. But this common sense must be shown in action by well-considered and reasonable thoughts and words, not by appealing to it as an oracle when no rational justification for one's position can be advanced. To appeal to common sense when insight and science fail, and no sooner—this is one of the subtle discoveries of modern times, by means of which the most superficial ranter can safely enter the lists with the most thorough thinker and hold his own. But as long as a particle of insight remains, no one would think of having recourse to this subterfuge. Seen clearly, it is but an appeal to the opinion of the multitude, of whose applause the philosopher is ashamed, while the popular charlatan glories and boasts in it. I should think that Hume might fairly have laid as much claim to common sense as Beattie and, in addition, to a critical reason (such as the latter did not possess), which keeps common sense in check and prevents it from speculating, or, if speculations are under discussion, restrains the desire to decide because it cannot satisfy itself concerning its own premises. By this means alone can common sense remain sound. Chisels and hammers may suffice to work a piece of wood, but for etching we require an etcher's needle. Thus common sense and speculative understanding are each serviceable, but each in its own way: the former in judgments which apply immediately to experience; the latter when we judge universally from more concepts, as in metaphysics, where that which calls itself, in spite of the inappropriateness of the name, sound common sense, has no right to judge at all.

I openly confess my recollection of David Hume was the very thing which many years ago first interrupted my dogmatic slumber and gave my investigations in the field of speculative philosophy a quite new direction. I was far from following him in the conclusions at which he arrived by regarding, not the whole of his problem, but a part, which by itself can give us no information. If we start from a well-founded, but undeveloped, thought which another has bequeathed to us, we may well hope by continued reflection to advance farther than the acute man to whom we owe the first spark of light.

I therefore first tried whether Hume's objection could not be put into a general form, and soon found that the concept of the connection of cause and effect was by no means the only concept by which the understanding thinks the connection of things *a priori,* but rather that metaphysics consists altogether of such concepts. I sought to ascertain their number; and when I had satisfactorily succeeded in this by starting from a single principle, I proceeded to the deduction of these concepts, which I was now certain were not derived from experience, as Hume had attempted to derive them, but sprang from the pure understanding. This deduction (which seemed impossible to my acute predecessor, which had never even occurred to anyone else, though no one had hesitated to use the concepts without investigating the basis of their objective validity) was the most difficult task which ever could have been undertaken in the service of metaphysics; and the worst was that metaphysics, such as it is, could not assist me in the least because this deduction alone can render metaphysics possible. But as soon as I had succeeded in solving Hume's problem, not merely in a particular case, but with respect to the whole faculty of pure reason, I could proceed safely, though slowly, to determine the whole sphere of pure reason completely and from universal principles, in its boundaries as well as in its contents. This was required for metaphysics in order to construct its system according to a safe plan. . . .

PREAMBLE ON THE PECULIARITIES OF
ALL METAPHYSICAL KNOWLEDGE
Of the Sources of Metaphysics

First, as concerns the sources of metaphysical knowledge, its very concept implies that they cannot be empirical. Its principles (including not only its maxims but its basic notions) must never be derived from experience. It must not be physical but metaphysical knowledge, namely, knowledge lying beyond experience. It can therefore have for its basis neither external experience, which is the source of physics proper, nor internal, which is the basis of empirical psychology. It is therefore *a priori* knowledge, coming from pure understanding and pure reason. . . .

Concerning the Kind of Knowledge Which Can Alone Be Called Metaphysical

On the Distinction between Analytical and Synthetical Judgments in General.

The peculiarity of its sources demands that metaphysical knowledge must consist of nothing but *a priori* judgments. But whatever be their origin or their logical form, there is a distinction in judgments, as to their content, according to which they are either merely *explicative,* adding nothing to the content of knowledge, or *expansive,* increasing the given knowledge. The former may be called *analytical,* the latter *synthetical,* judgments.

Analytical judgments express nothing in the predicate but what has been already actually thought in the concept of the subject, though not so distinctly or with the same (full) consciousness. When I say: "All bodies are extended," I have not amplified in the least my concept of body, but have only analyzed it, as extension was really thought to belong to that concept before the judgment was made, though it was not expressed. This judgment is therefore analytical. On the contrary, this judgment, "All bodies have weight," contains in its predicate something not actually thought in the universal concept of body; it amplifies my knowledge by adding something to my concept, and must therefore be called synthetical.

The Common Principle of All Analytical Judgments Is the Law of Contradiction.

All analytical judgments depend wholly on the law of contradiction, and are in their nature *a priori* cognitions, whether the concepts that supply them with matter be empirical or not. For the predicate of an affirmative analytical judgment is already contained in the concept of the subject, of which it cannot be denied without contradiction. In the same way its opposite is necessarily denied of the subject in an analytical, but negative, judgment, by the same law of contradiction. Such is the nature of the judgments: "All bodies are extended," and "No bodies are unextended (that is, simple)."

For this very reason all analytical judgments are *a priori* even when the concepts are empirical, as, for example, "Gold is a yellow metal"; for to know this I require no experience beyond my concept of gold as a yellow metal. It is, in fact, the very concept, and I need only analyze it without looking beyond it.

Synthetical Judgments Require a Different Principle from the Law of Contradiction.

There are synthetical *a posteriori* judgments of empirical origin; but there are also others which are certain *a priori,* and which spring from pure understanding and reason. Yet they both agree in this, that they cannot possibly spring from the principle of analysis, namely, the law of contradiction, alone. They require a quite different principle from which they may be deduced, subject, of course, always to the law of contradiction, which must never be violated, even though everything cannot be deduced from it. I shall first classify synthetical judgments.

Judgments of Experience are always synthetical. For it would be absurd to base an analytical judgment on experience, as our concept suffices for the purpose without requiring any testimony from experience. That body is extended is a judgment established *a priori,* and not an empirical judgment. For before appealing to experience, we already have all the conditions of the judgment in the concept, from which we have but to elicit the predicate according to the law of contradiction, and thereby to become conscious of the necessity of the judgment, which experience could not in the least teach us.

Mathematical Judgments are all synthetical. This fact seems hitherto to have altogether escaped the observation of those who have analyzed human reason; it even seems directly opposed to all their conjectures, though it is incontestably certain and most important in its consequences. For as it was found that the conclusions of mathematicians all proceed according to the law of contradiction (as is demanded by all apodictic certainty), men persuaded themselves that the fundamental principles were known from the same law. This was a great mistake, for a synthetical proposition can indeed be established by the law of contradiction, but only by presupposing another synthetical proposition from which it follows, but never by that law alone.

First of all, we must observe that all strictly mathematical judgments are *a priori,* and not empirical, because they carry with them necessity, which cannot be obtained from experience. But if this be not conceded to me, very good; I shall confine my assertion to *pure mathematics,* the very notion of which implies that it contains pure *a priori* and not empirical knowledge.

It must at first be thought that the proposition $7 + 5 = 12$ is a mere analytical judgment, following from the concept of the sum of seven and five, according to the law of contradiction. But on closer examination it appears that the concept of the sum of $7 + 5$ contains merely their union in a single number, without its being at all thought what the particular number is that unites them. The concept of twelve is by no means thought by merely thinking of the combination of seven and five; and, analyze this possible sum as we may, we shall not discover twelve in the concept. We must go beyond these concepts, by calling to our aid some intuition which corresponds to one of the concepts—that is, either our five fingers or five points (as Segner has it in his *Arithmetic*)—and we must add successively the units of the five given in the intuition to the concept of seven. Hence our concept is really amplified by the proposition $7 + 5 = 12$, and we add to the first concept a second concept not thought in it. Arithmetical judgments are therefore synthetical, and the more plainly according as we take larger numbers; for in such cases it is clear that, however closely we analyze our concepts without calling intuition to our aid, we can never find the sum by such mere dissection.

Just as little is any principle of geometry analytical. That a straight line is the shortest path between two points is a synthetical proposition. For my concept of straight contains nothing of quantity, but only a quality. The concept "shortest" is therefore altogether additional and cannot be obtained by any analysis of the concept "straight line." Here, too, intuition must come to aid us. It alone makes the synthesis possible. What usually makes us believe that the predicate of such apodictic judgments is already contained in our concept, and that the judgment is therefore analytical, is the duplicity of the expression. We must think a certain predicate as attached to a given concept, and necessity indeed belongs to the concepts. But the question is not what we must join in thought *to* the given concept, but what we actually think together with and in it, though obscurely; and so it appears that the predicate belongs to this concept necessarily indeed, yet not directly but indirectly by means of an intuition which must be present.

Some other principles, assumed by geometers, are indeed actually analytical, and depend on the law of contradiction; but they only serve, as identical propositions, as a method of concatenation, and not as principles—for example $a = a$, the whole is equal to itself, or $a + b > a$, the whole is greater than its part. And yet even these, though they are recognized as valid from mere concepts, are admitted in mathematics only because they can be represented in some intuition.

The essential and distinguishing feature of pure mathematical knowledge among all other *a priori* knowledge is that it cannot at all proceed from concepts, but only by means of the construction of concepts. As therefore in its propositions it must proceed beyond the concept to that which its corresponding intuition contains, these propositions neither can, nor ought to, arise analytically, by dissection of the concept, but are all synthetical.

I cannot refrain from pointing out the disadvantage resulting to philosophy from the neglect of this easy and apparently insignificant observation. Hume being prompted to cast his eye over the whole field of *a priori* cognitions in which human understanding claims such mighty possessions (a calling he felt worthy of a philosopher) heedlessly severed from it a whole, and indeed its most valuable, province, namely, pure mathematics; for he imagined its nature or, so to speak, the state constitution of this empire depended on totally different principles, namely, on the law of contradiction alone; and although he did not divide judgments in this manner formally and universally as I have done here, what he said was equivalent to this: that mathematics contains only analytical, but metaphysics synthetical, *a priori* propositions. In this, however, he was greatly mistaken, and the mistake had a decidedly injurious effect upon his whole conception. But for this, he would have extended his question concerning the origin of our synthetical judgments far beyond the metaphysical concept of causality and included in it the possibility of mathematics *a priori* also, for this latter he must have assumed to be equally synthetical. And then he could not have based his metaphysical propositions on mere experience without subjecting the axioms of mathematics equally to experience, a thing which he was far too acute to do. The good company into which metaphysics would thus have been brought would have saved it from the danger of a contemptuous ill-treatment, for the thrust intended for it must have reached mathematics, which was not and could not have been Hume's intention. Thus that acute man would have been led into considerations which must needs be similar to those that now occupy us, but which would have gained inestimably by his inimitably elegant style.

Metaphysical Judgments, properly so called, are all synthetical. We must distinguish judgments pertaining to metaphysics from metaphysical judgments properly so called. Many of the former are analytical, but they only afford the means for metaphysical judgments, which are the whole end of the science and which are always synthetical. For if there be concepts pertaining to metaphysics (as, for example, that of substance), the judgments springing from simple analysis of them also pertain to metaphysics, as, for example, substance is that which only exists as subject, etc.; and by means of several such analytical judgments we seek to approach the definition of the concepts. But as the analysis of a pure concept of the understanding (the kind of concept pertaining to metaphysics) does not proceed in any different manner from the dissection of any other, even empirical, concepts, not belonging to metaphysics (such as, air is an elastic fluid, the elasticity of which is not destroyed by any known degree of cold), it follows that the concept indeed, but not the analytical judgment, is properly metaphysical. This science has something peculiar in the production of its *a priori* cognitions, which must therefore be distinguished from the features it has in common with other rational knowledge. Thus the judgment that all the substance in things is permanent is a synthetical and properly metaphysical judgment.

If the *a priori* concepts which constitute the materials and tools of metaphysics have first been collected according to fixed principles, then their analysis will be of great value; it might be taught as a particular part (as a *philosophia definitiva*), containing nothing but analytical judgments pertaining to metaphysics, and could be treated separately from the synthetical which constitute metaphysics proper. For indeed these analyses are not of much value except in metaphysics, that is, as regards the synthetical judgments which are to be generated by these previously analyzed concepts.

The conclusion drawn in this section then is that metaphysics is properly concerned with synthetical propositions *a priori,* and these alone constitute its end, for which it indeed requires various dissections of its concepts, namely, analytical judgments, but wherein the procedure is not different from that in every other kind of knowledge, in which we merely seek to render our concepts distinct by analysis. But the generation of *a priori* knowledge by intuition as well as by concepts, in fine, of synthetical propositions *a priori,* especially in philosophical knowledge, constitutes the essential subject of metaphysics. . . .

The General Problem: How Is Knowledge from
Pure Reason Possible?

We have already learned the significant distinction between analytical and synthetical judgments. The possibility of analytical propositions was easily comprehended, being entirely founded on the law of contradiction. The possibility of synthetical *a posteriori* judgments, of those which are gathered from experience, also requires no particular explanations, for experience is nothing but a continued synthesis of perceptions. There remain therefore only synthetical propositions *a priori,* of which the possibility must be sought or investigated, because they must depend upon other principles than the law of contradiction.

But here we need not first establish the possibility of such propositions so as to ask whether they are possible. For there are enough of them which indeed are of undoubted certainty; and, as our present method is analytical, we shall start from the fact that such synthetical but purely rational knowledge actually exists; but we must now inquire into the ground of this possibility and ask *how* such knowledge is possible, in order that we may, from the principles of its possibility, be enabled to determine the conditions of its use, its sphere and its limits. The real problem upon which all depends, when expressed with scholastic precision, is therefore: "How are synthetic propositions *a priori* possible?"

For the sake of popular understanding I have above expressed this problem somewhat differently, as an inquiry into purely rational knowledge, which I could do for once without detriment to the desired insight, because, as we have only to do here with metaphysics and its sources, the reader will, I hope, after the foregoing reminders, keep in mind that when we speak of knowing by pure reason we do not mean analytical but synthetical knowledge.

Metaphysics stands or falls with the solution of this problem; its very existence depends upon it. Let anyone make metaphysical assertions with ever so much plausibility, let him overwhelm us with conclusions; but if he has not previously proved able to answer this question satisfactorily, I have a right to say: This is all vain, baseless philosophy and false wisdom. You speak through pure reason and claim, as it were, to create cognitions *a priori* not only by dissecting given concepts, but also by asserting connections which do not rest upon the law of contradiction, and which you claim to conceive quite independently of all experience; how do you arrive at this, and how will you justify such pretensions? . . .

All metaphysicians are therefore solemnly and legally suspended from their occupations till they shall have adequately answered the question, "How are synthetic cognitions *a priori* possible?" For the answer contains the only credentials which they must show when they have anything to offer us in the name of pure reason. But if they do not possess these credentials, they can expect nothing else of reasonable people, who have been deceived so often, than to be dismissed without further inquiry.

If they, on the other hand, desire to carry on their business, not as a science, but as an art of wholesome persuasion suitable to the common sense of man, this calling cannot in justice be denied them. They will then speak the modest language of a rational belief; they will grant that they are not allowed even to conjecture, far less to know, anything which lies beyond the bounds of all possible experience, but only to assume (not for speculative use, which they must abandon, but for practical use only) the existence of something possible and even indispensable for the guidance of the understanding and of the will in life. In this manner alone can they be called useful and wise men, and the more so as they renounce the title of metaphysicians. For the latter profess to be speculative philosophers; and since, when judgments *a priori* are under discussion, poor probabilities cannot be admitted (for what is declared to be known *a priori* is thereby announced as necessary), such men cannot be permitted to play with conjectures, but their assertion must be either science or nothing at all. . . .

Questions

1. What is metaphysics, according to Kant? What is his diagnosis of the ills of metaphysics? What is his remedy?

2. For Kant, what kind of judgment is analytical? What kind of judgment is synthetical?

3. How does Kant use the terms "a priori" and "a posteriori"? Give examples of (a) analytical, (b) synthetical a posteriori, and (c) synthetical a priori judgments.

4. The crucial question about Kant's program to show that metaphysics is possible is "Can one make synthetical a priori judgments?" How would you answer this question?

5. Kant says that "7 + 5 = 12" is a synthetical judgment. Yet it has been argued that in his terms such an arithmetical equation expresses "nothing in the predicate but what has been already actually thought in the concept of the subject." State why you think he was, or was not, mistaken about his classification of "7 + 5 = 12."

6. Kant says that "All bodies have weight" is a synthetical judgment. Yet it has been argued that we would not call something a body if it were weightless. State why you think he was, or was not, mistaken about the classification of the above statement.

7. Using Kant's classes of synthetical and analytical judgments, how would you classify the following judgments? Give your reasons for classifying them as you do. Are any of them synthetical a priori judgments?

    a. Things equal to the same thing are equal to each other.

    b. A pair of gloves is two matching gloves, one of which is for the right hand and the other for the left.

    c. If I am wearing a pair of gloves, then I am wearing two gloves.

    d. Every effect has a cause.

    e. Every event has a cause.

    f. Water is wet.

    g. At sea level, water freezes when the temperature is 32° F.

    h. At sea level, water freezes when it gets cold enough.

    i. This is a hot day. (A judgment made by someone when the temperature is 80° F.)

    j. A room is warm at 60° F. (A private judgment.)

k. A room is warm at 60° F. (A legal definition in a city ordinance governing landlords who are responsible for providing heat in their buildings.)

l. All red objects are red.

m. Every body perseveres in its state of rest, or of uniform motion in a
right line, unless it is compelled to change that state by forces impressed
thereon. (Newton)

8. Read the selection by David Hume (page 98). Kant claims that Hume's
philosophy is an attack on metaphysics. State why you agree or disagree with this
claim. Is Hume himself writing metaphysics? What do you think Hume would
say about the possibility of synthetical a priori judgments?

9. Read the selection on scientific method (page 210) and the selection by
Royce (page 129). Taking Royce as an example of metaphysics, what would you
say were the basic differences between science and metaphysics?

6

Reality and Idealism	Josiah Royce
	(1855-1916)

Josiah Royce was educated at the University of California and at Johns
Hopkins University. In 1882 he joined the faculty of Harvard University and taught philosophy there until his death. He was the leading
American exponent of the philosophy known as objective or absolute
idealism. Royce's principal works are: *The Spirit of Modern Philosophy* (1892); *The World and the Individual* (1900-1902); and *The
Philosophy of Loyalty* (1908).

In this reading Royce distinguishes two types of idealism, which
have come to be known as "subjective idealism" and "objective idealism." The first type of idealism is that of George Berkeley (page 87).
Royce tries to show how the second type of idealism is a logical development from Berkeley's point of view. Royce begins by expounding
the subjective idealism of Berkeley, according to which all our ideas
are derived from experience (the principle of empiricism) and our
conception of the world is simply a system of ideas in our own minds.
There is no such thing as a material world beyond our actual or possible experiences. To say that we live in a real world means that we
now have certain experiences and that they are systematically connected
with other possible experiences we *could* have. The only kind of reality
that could possibly exist outside our minds would be another mind, a
universal mind to whose "standard" ideas our ideas would have to
correspond in order to be true. For if external reality were something
entirely different from a mind, it would be theoretically impossible
(not merely practically impossible) to know it. And this would mean

that any statement about it would be meaningless. We literally would not know what we were talking about.

Royce then argues that our knowledge of the world presupposes the existence of a reality which is outside our minds, but is nevertheless like our minds. This is the second type of idealism: objective idealism. It consists in the belief that the whole of existence is one universal mind whose system of ideas is what we mean by the real world. Whereas for Berkeley, the subjective idealist, the whole of existence is made up of our human minds and their ideas, and the mind of God who puts the sense-ideas into our minds, for Royce, the objective idealist, the whole of existence is made up of our human minds and their ideas, and the one universal mind which does not *cause* us to have ideas but which is the ultimate object to which all our ideas *refer*. Within this metaphysical framework Royce also explains what it means to say that our ideas are true or false.

This reading is from Lecture XI of *The Spirit of Modern Philosophy*.

From *The Spirit of Modern Philosophy*, by Josiah Royce, edited by Ralph Barton Perry, George Braziller, Inc., N. Y., 1955. Reprinted by permission of the publisher.

. . . Idealism has two aspects. It is, for the first, a kind of analysis of the world, an analysis which so far has no absolute character about it, but which undertakes, in a fashion that might be acceptable to any skeptic, to examine what you mean by all the things, whatever they are, that you believe in or experience. This idealistic analysis consists merely in a pointing out, by various devices, that the world of your knowledge, whatever it contains, is through and through such stuff as ideas are made of, that you never in your life believed in anything definable *but* ideas, that, as Berkeley put it, "this whole choir of heaven and furniture of earth" is nothing for any of us but a system of ideas which govern our belief and our conduct. . . . In this aspect idealism is already a little puzzling to our natural consciousness, but it becomes quickly familiar, in fact almost commonplace, and seems after all to alter our practical faith or to solve our deeper problems very little.

The other aspect of idealism is the one which gives us our notion of the absolute Self. To it the first is only preparatory. . . .

I begin with the first and the less significant aspect of idealism. Our world, I say, whatever it may contain, is such stuff as ideas are made of. This preparatory sort of idealism is the one that, as I just suggested, Berkeley made prominent, and, after a fashion, familiar. I must state it in my own way, although one in vain seeks to attain novelty in illustrating so frequently described a view.

. . . Is the outer world, as it exists outside of your ideas, or of anybody's ideas, something having shape, filling space, possessing solidity, full of moving things? That would in the first place seem evident. The sound isn't outside of me, but the sound-waves, you say, are. The colors are ideal facts; but the ether-waves don't need a mind to know them. Warmth is ideal, but the physical fact called heat, this playing to and fro of molecules, is real, and is there apart from any mind. But *is* this so evident? What do I *mean* by the shape of anything, or by the size of anything? Don't I mean just the idea of shape or of size that I am obliged to get under certain circumstances? What is the meaning of any property that I give to the real outer world? How can I express that property except in case I think it in terms of my ideas? As for the sound-waves and the ether-waves, what are they but things ideally conceived to explain the facts of nature? The conceptions have doubtless their truth, but it is an ideal truth. What I mean by saying that the things yonder have shape and size and trembling molecules, and that there is air with sound-waves, and ether with light-waves in it—what I *mean* by all this is that experience forces upon me, directly or indirectly, a vast system of ideas, which may indeed be founded in truth beyond me, which in fact *must* be founded in such truth if my experience has any sense, but which, like my ideas of color and of warmth, are simply expressions of how the world's order must appear to me, and to anybody constituted like me. Above all, is this plain about space. The real things, I say, outside of me, fill space, and move about in it. But what do I mean by space? Only a vast system of ideas which experience and my own mind force upon me. Doubtless these ideas have a validity. They have *this* validity, that I, at all events, when I look upon the world, am bound to see it in space, as much bound as the king in *Hamlet* was, when he looked within, to see himself as guilty and unrepentant. But just as his guilt was an idea—a crushing, an irresistible, an overwhelming idea—but still just an idea, so, too, the space in which I place my world is one great formal idea of mine. That is just why I can describe it to other people. "It has three dimensions," I say, "length, breadth, depth." I describe each. I form, I convey, I construct, an idea of it through them. I know space, as an idea, very well. I can compute all sorts of unseen truths about the relations of its parts. I am sure that you, too, share this idea. But, then, for all of us alike it is just an idea; and when we put our world into space, and call it real there, we simply think one idea into another idea, not voluntarily, to be sure, but inevitably, and yet without leaving the realm of ideas.

Thus, all the reality that *we* attribute to our world, in so far as *we* know and can tell what we mean thereby, becomes ideal. There is, in fact, a certain system of ideas, forced upon us by experience, which we have to use as the guide of our conduct. This system of ideas we can't change by our wish; it is for us as overwhelming a fact as guilt, or as the bearing of our fellows towards us, but we know it only *as* such a system of ideas. And we call it the world of matter. John Stuart Mill very well expressed the puzzle of the whole thing, as we have now reached the statement of this puzzle, when he called matter a mass of "permanent possibilities of experience" for each of us. Mill's definition has its faults, but it is a very fair beginning. You know matter as something that either now gives you this idea or experience, or that would give you some other idea or experience under other circumstances. A fire, while it burns, is for you a permanent possibility of either getting the idea of an agreeable warmth, or of getting the idea of a bad burn, and you treat it accordingly. A precipice amongst mountains is a permanent possibility of your experiencing a fall, or of your getting a feeling of the exciting or of the sublime in mountain scenery. You have no experience just now of the tropics or of the poles, but both tropical and polar climates exist in your world as permanent possibilities of experience. When you call the sun 92,000,000 miles away, you mean that between you and the sun (that is, between your present experience and the possible experience of the sun's surface) there would inevitably lie the actually inaccessible, but still numerically conceivable series of experiences of distance expressed by the number of miles in question. In short, your whole attitude towards the real world may be summed up by saying: "I have experiences now which I seem bound to have, experiences of color, sound, and all the rest of my present ideas; and I am also bound by experience to believe that in case I did certain things (for instance, touched the wall, traveled to the tropics, visited Europe, studied physics), I then should get, in a determinate order, dependent wholly upon *what* I had done, certain other experiences (for instance, experiences of the wall's solidity, or of a tropical climate, or of the scenes of an European tour, or of the facts of physics)." And this acceptance of actual experience, this belief in possible experience, constitutes all that you mean by your faith in the outer world.

But, you say, Is not, then, all this faith of ours after all well founded? Isn't there really something yonder that corresponds in fact to this series of experiences in us? Yes, indeed, there no doubt is. But what if this, which so shall correspond without us to the ideas within us, what if this hard and fast reality should itself be a system of ideas, outside of our minds but not outside of every mind? As the maiden's disdain is outside the rejected lover's mind, unchangeable so far for him, but not on that account the less ideal, not the less a fact in a mind, as, to take afresh a former fashion of illustration, the price of a security or the objective existence of this lecture is an ideal fact, but real and external for the individual person—even so why might not this world beyond us, this "permanent possibility of experience," be in essence itself a system of ideal experiences of some standard thought of which ours is only the copy? Nay, must it not be such a system in case it has any reality at all? For, after all, isn't this precisely what our analysis brings us to? Nothing whatever can I say about my world yonder that I do not express in terms of mind. *What* things are, extended, moving, colored, tuneful, majestic, beautiful, holy, *what* they are in any aspect of their nature, mathematical, logical, physical, sensuously pleasing, spiritually valuable, all this must mean for me only something that I have to express in the fashion of ideas. The more I am to know my world, the more of a mind I must have for the purpose. The closer I come to the truth about the things, the more ideas I get. Isn't it plain, then, that *if* my world yonder is anything knowable at all, it must be in and for itself essentially a mental world? Are my ideas to *resemble* in any way the world? Is the truth of my thought to consist in its *agreement* with reality? And am I thus capable, as common sense supposes, of *conforming* my ideas to things? Then reflect. What can, after all, so well agree with an idea as another idea? To what can things that go on in my mind conform unless it be to another mind? If the more my mind grows in mental clearness, the nearer it gets to the nature of reality, then surely the reality that my mind thus resembles must be in itself mental.

After all, then, would it deprive the world here about me of reality, nay, would it not rather save and assure the reality and the knowableness of my world of experience, if I said that this world, as it exists outside of my mind, and of any other human minds, exists in and for a standard, an universal mind, whose system of ideas simply constitutes the world? Even if I fail to prove that there is such a mind, do I not at least thus make plausible that, as I said, our world of common sense has no fact in it which we cannot interpret in terms of ideas, so that this world is throughout such stuff as ideas are made of? To say this, as you see, in no wise deprives our world of its due share of reality. If the standard mind knows now that its ideal fire has the quality of burning those who touch it, and if I in my finitude am bound to conform in my experiences to the thoughts of this standard mind, then in case I touch that fire I shall surely get the idea of a burn. The standard mind will be at least as hard and fast and real in its ideal consistency as is the maiden in her disdain for the rejected lover; and I, in presence of the ideal stars and the oceans, will see the genuine realities of fate as certainly as the lover hears his fate in the voice that expresses her will.

What I have desired thus far is merely to give each of you, as it were, the sensation of being an idealist in this first and purely analytical sense of the word idealism. The sum and substance of it all is, you see, this: you know your world in fact as a system of ideas about things, such that from moment to moment you find this system forced upon you by experience. Even matter you know just as a mass of coherent ideas that you cannot help having. Space and time, as you think them, are surely ideas of yours. Now, what more natural than to say that *if* this be so, the real world beyond you must in itself be a system of somebody's ideas? If it is, then you can comprehend what its existence means. If it isn't, then since all you can know of it is ideal, the real world must be utterly unknowable, a bare x. Minds I can understand, because I myself am a mind. An existence that has no mental attribute is wholly opaque to me. So far, however, from such a world of ideas, existent beyond me in another mind, seeming to coherent thought essentially *un*real, ideas and minds and their ways are, on the contrary, the hardest and stubbornest facts that we can name. *If* the external world is in itself mental, then, be this reality a standard and universal thought, or a mass of little atomic minds constituting the various particles of matter, in any case one can comprehend what it is, and will have at the same time to submit to its stubborn authority as the lover accepts the reality of the maiden's moods. If the world *isn't* such an ideal thing, then indeed all our science, which is through and through concerned with our mental interpretations of things, can neither have objective validity, nor make satisfactory progress towards truth. For as science is concerned with ideas, the world beyond all ideas is a bare x.

. . . There lies now just ahead of us the goal of a synthetic idealistic conception, which will not be content with this mere analysis of the colors and forms of things, and with the mere discovery that all these are for us nothing but ideas. In this second aspect, idealism grows bolder, and fears not the profoundest doubt that may have entered your mind as to whether there is any world at all, or as to whether it is in any fashion knowable. State in full the deepest problem, the hardest question about the world that your thought ever conceived. In this new form idealism offers you a suggestion that indeed will not wholly answer nor do away with every such problem, but that certainly will set the meaning of it in a new light. What this new light is, I must in conclusion seek to illustrate.

Note the point we have reached. *Either,* as you see, your real world yonder is through and through a world of ideas, an outer mind that you are more or less comprehending through your experience, *or else,* in so far as it is real and outer it is unknowable, an inscrutable $x,$ an absolute mystery. The dilemma is perfect. There is no third alternative. Either a mind yonder, or else the unknowable; that is your choice. . . . Problems are, after a fashion, rather familiar things, that is, in the world of ideas. There are problems soluble and problems insoluble in that world of ideas. It is a soluble problem if one asks what whole number is the square root of 64. The answer is 8. It is an insoluble problem if one asks me to find what whole number is the square root of 65. There is, namely, no such whole number. If one asks me to name the length of a straight line that shall be equal to the circumference of a circle of a known radius, that again, in the world of ideas, is an insoluble problem, because, as can be proved, the circumference of a circle is a length that cannot possibly be exactly expressed in terms of any statable number when the radius is of a stated length. So in the world of ideas, problems are definite questions which can be asked in knowable terms. Fair questions of this sort either may be fairly answered in our present state of knowledge, or else they could be answered if we knew a little or a good deal more, or finally they could not possibly be answered. But in the latter case, if they could not possibly be answered, they always must resemble the problem how to square the circle. They then always turn out, namely, to be absurdly stated questions, and it is their absurdity that makes these problems absolutely insoluble. Any fair question could be answered by one who knew enough. No fair question has an unknowable answer. But now, *if* your unknowable world out there is a thing of wholly, of absolutely problematic and inscrutable nature, is it so because you don't *yet* know enough about it, or because in its very nature and essence it is an absurd thing, an x that *would* answer a question, which actually it is nonsense to ask? Surely one must choose the former alternative. The real world may be unknown; it can't be essentially unknowable.

This subtlety is wearisome enough, I know, just here, but I shall not dwell long upon it. Plainly *if* the unknowable world out there is through and through in its nature a really inscrutable problem, this must mean that in nature it resembles such problems as, What is the whole number that is the square root of 65? Or, What two adjacent hills are there that have no valley between them? For in the world of thought such are the *only* insoluble problems. All others either may now be solved, or would be solved if we knew more than we now do. But, once more, *if* this unknowable is only just the real world as now unknown to us, but capable some time of becoming known, then remember that, as we have just seen, only a mind can ever become an object known to a mind. If I know you as external to me, it is only because you are minds. If I can come to know *any* truth, it is only in so far as this truth is essentially mental, is an idea, is a thought, that I can ever come to know it. Hence, if that so-called unknowable, that unknown outer world there, ever could, by any device, come within our ken, then it is already an ideal world. For just that is what our whole idealistic analysis has been proving. Only ideas are knowable. And nothing absolutely unknowable can exist. For the absolutely unknowable, the x pure and simple, . . . simply cannot be admitted. The notion of it is nonsense. The assertion of it is a contradiction. Round-squares, and sugar salt-lumps, and Snarks, and Boojums, and Jabberwocks, and Abracadabras; such, I insist, are the only unknowables there are. The unknown, that which our human and finite selfhood hasn't grasped, exists spread out before us in a boundless world of truth; but the unknowable is essentially, confessedly, *ipso facto* a fiction.

The nerve of our whole argument in the foregoing is now pretty fairly exposed. We have seen that the outer truth must be, if anything, a "possibility of experience." But we may now see that a *bare* "possibility" as such is, like the unknowable, something meaningless. That which, whenever I come to know it, turns out to be through and through an idea, an experience, must be in itself, before I know it, either somebody's idea, somebody's experience, or it must be nothing. What is a "possibility" of experience that is outside of me, and that is still nothing *for* any one else than myself? Isn't it a bare x, a nonsense phrase? Isn't it like an unseen color, an untasted taste, an unfelt feeling? In proving that the world is one of "possible" experience, we have proved that in so far as it is real it is one of actual experience.

Once more, then, to sum up here, *if*, however vast the world of the unknown, only the essentially knowable can exist, and *if* everything knowable is an idea, a mental somewhat, the content of some mind, then once for all we are the world of ideas. Your deepest doubt proves this. Only the nonsense of that inscrutable x, of that Abracadabra, of that Snark, the Unknowable of whose essence you make your real world, prevents you from seeing this.

To return, however, to our dilemma. *Either* idealism, we said, *or* the unknowable. What we have now said is that the absolutely unknowable is essentially an absurdity, a nonexistent. For any fair and statable problem admits of an answer. *If* the world exists yonder, its essence is then already capable of being known by some mind. If capable of being known by a mind, this essence is then already essentially ideal and mental. A mind that knew the real world would, for instance, find it a something possessing qualities. But qualities are ideal existences, just as much as are the particular qualities called odors or tones or colors. A mind knowing the real world would again find in it relations, such as equality and inequality, attraction and repulsion, likeness and unlikeness. But such relations have no meaning except as objects of a mind. In brief, then, the world as known would be found to be a world that had all the while been ideal and mental, even before it became known to the particular mind that we are to conceive as coming into connection with it. Thus, then, we are driven to the second alternative. The real world must be a mind, or else a group of minds.

But with this result we come in presence of a final problem. All this, you say, depends upon my assurance that there is after all a real and therefore an essentially knowable and rational world yonder. Such a world would have to be in essence a mind, or a world of minds. But after all, how does one ever escape from the prison of the inner life? Am I not in all this merely wandering amidst the realm of my own ideas? *My* world, of course, isn't and can't be a mere *x,* an essentially unknowable thing, just because it *is my* world, and I have an idea of it. But then does not this mean that *my* world is, after all, forever just *my* world, so that I never get to any truth beyond myself? Isn't this result very disheartening? My world is thus a world of ideas, but alas! how do I then ever reach those ideas of the minds beyond me?

The answer is a simple, but in one sense a very problematic, one. You, in one sense, namely, never *do* or *can* get beyond your own ideas, nor ought you to wish to do so, because in truth all those other minds that constitute your outer and real world are in essence one with your own self. This whole world of ideas is essentially *one* world, and so it is essentially the world of one self and *That art Thou.*

The truth and meaning of this deepest proposition of all idealism is now not at all remote from us. The considerations, however, upon which it depends are of the driest possible sort, as commonplace as they are deep.

Whatever objects you may think about, whether they are objects directly known to you, or objects infinitely far removed, objects in the distant stars, or objects remote in time, or objects near and present—such objects, then, as a number with fifty places of digits in it, or the mountains on the other side of the moon, or the day of your death, or the character of Cromwell, or the law of gravitation, or a name that you are just now trying to think of and have forgotten, or the meaning of some mood or feeling or idea now in your mind— all such objects, I insist, stand in a certain constant and curious relation to your mind whenever you are thinking about them—a relation that we often miss because it is so familiar. What is this relation? Such an object, while you think about it, needn't be, as popular thought often supposes it to be, the *cause* of your thoughts concerning it. Thus, when you think about Cromwell's character, Cromwell's character isn't just now *causing* any ideas in you—isn't, so to speak, doing anything to you. Cromwell is dead, and after life's fitful fever his character is a very inactive thing. Not as the *cause,* but as the *object* of your thought is Cromwell present to you. Even so, if you choose now to think of the moment of your death, that moment is somewhere off there in the future, and you can make it your object, but it isn't now an active cause of your ideas. The moment of your death has no present physical existence at all, and just now causes nothing. So, too, with the mountains on the other side of the moon. When you make them the object of your thought, they remain indifferent to you. They do not affect you. You never saw them. But all the same you can think about them.

Yet this thinking *about* things is, after all, a very curious relation in which to stand to things. In order to think *about* a thing, it is *not* enough that I should have an idea in me that merely resembles that thing. This last is a very important observation. I repeat, it is *not* enough that I should merely have an idea in me that resembles the thing whereof I think. I have, for instance, in me the idea of a pain. Another man has a pain just like mine. Say we both have toothache; or have both burned our finger-tips in the same way. Now my idea of pain is just like the pain in him, but I am not on that account neces- sarily thinking about *his* pain, merely because what I am thinking about, namely, my own pain, resembles his pain. No; to think about an object you must not merely have an idea that resembles the object, but you must *mean* to have your idea resemble that object. Stated in other form, to think of an object you must consciously aim at that object, you must pick out that object, you must already in some measure possess that object enough, namely, to identify it as what you mean. But how can you *mean,* how can you *aim at,* how can you *possess,* how can you *pick out,* how can you *identify* what is not already present in essence to your own hidden self? Here is surely a deep question. When you aim at yonder object, be it the mountains in the moon or the day of your death, you really say, "I, as my real self, as my larger self, as my complete consciousness, already in deepest truth possess that object, have it, own it, identify it. And that, and that alone, makes it possible for me in my transient, my individual, my momentary personality, to mean yonder object, to inquire about it, to be partly aware of it and partly ignorant of it." You can't mean what is utterly foreign to you. You mean an object, you assert about it, you talk about it, yes, you doubt or wonder about it, you admit your private and individual ignorance about it, only in so far as your larger self, your deeper personality, your total of normal consciousness already *has* that object. Your momentary and private wonder, ignorance, inquiry, or assertion about the object implies, asserts, presupposes that your total self is in full and immediate possession of the object. This, in fact, is the very nature of that curious relation of a thought to an object which we are now considering. The self that is doubt- ing or asserting, or that is even feeling its private ignorance about an object, and that still, even in consequence of all this, is *meaning,* is *aiming at* such object, is in essence identical with the self for which this object exists in its complete and consciously known truth.

So paradoxical seems this final assertion of idealism that I cannot hope in one moment to make it very plain to you. But what I intend by thus saying that the self which thinks about an object, which really, even in the midst of the blindest ignorance and doubt concerning its object still means the object— that this self is identical with the deeper self which possesses and truly knows the object—what I intend hereby I can best illustrate by simple cases taken from your own experience. You are in doubt, say, about a name that you have forgotten, or about a thought that you just had, but that has now escaped you. As you hunt for the name or the lost idea, you are all the while sure that you mean just one particular name or idea and no other. But you don't yet know what name or idea this is. You try, and reject name after name. You query, "Was this what I was thinking of, or this?" But after searching you erelong find the name or the idea, and now at once you *recognize* it. "Oh, that," you say, "was what I meant all along, only—I didn't know what I meant." Did not know? Yes, in one sense you knew all the while—that is, your deeper self, your true consciousness knew. It was your momentary self that did not know. But when you found the long-sought name, recalled the lost idea, you recognized it at once, because it was all the while your own, because you, the true and larger self, who owned the name or the idea and were aware of what it was, now were seen to include the smaller and momentary self that sought the name or tried to recall the thought. Your deeper consciousness of the lost idea was all the while there. In fact, did you not presuppose this when you sought the lost idea? How can I mean a name, or an idea, unless I in truth am the self who knows the name, who possesses the idea? In hunting for the name or the lost idea, I am hunting for my own thought. Well, just so I know nothing about the far-off stars in detail, but in so far as I mean the far-off stars at all, as I speak of them, I am identical with that remote and deep thought of my own that already knows the stars. When I study the stars, I am trying to find out what I really mean by them. To be sure, only experience can tell me, but that is because only experience can bring me into relation with my larger self. The escape from the prison of the inner self is simply the fact that the inner self is through and through an appeal to a larger self. The self that inquires, either inquires without meaning, or if it has a meaning, this meaning exists in and for the larger self that knows.

Here is a suggestion of what I mean by Synthetic Idealism. No truth, I repeat, is more familiar. That I am always meaning to inquire into objects beyond me, what clearer fact could be mentioned? That only in case it is already I who, in deeper truth, in my real and hidden thought, *know* the lost object yonder, the object whose nature I seek to comprehend, that only in this case I can truly *mean* the thing yonder—this, as we must assert, is involved in the very idea of *meaning*. That is the logical analysis of it. You can mean what your deeper self knows; you cannot mean what your deeper self doesn't know. To be sure, the complete illustration of this most critical insight of idealism belongs elsewhere. Few see the familiar. Nothing is more common than for people to think that they mean objects that have nothing to do with themselves. Kant it was, who, despite his things in themselves, first showed us that nobody really means an object, really knows it, or doubts it, or aims at it, unless he does so by aiming at a truth that is present to his own larger self. Except for the unity of my true self, taught Kant, I have no objects. And so it makes no difference whether I know a thing or am in doubt about it. So long as I really *mean* it, that is enough. The self that *means* the object is identical with the larger self that possesses the object, just as when you seek the lost idea you are already in essence with the self that possesses the lost idea.

In this way I suggest to you the proof which a rigid analysis of the logic of our most commonplace thought would give for the doctrine that in the world there is but *one* Self, and that it is *his* world which we all alike are truly meaning, whether we talk of one another or of Cromwell's character or of the fixed stars or of the far-off æons of the future. The relation of my thought to its object has, I insist, this curious character, that *unless* the thought and its object are parts of one larger thought, I can't even be *meaning* that object yonder, can't even be in error about it, can't even doubt its existence. You, for instance, are part of one larger self with me, or else I can't even be meaning to address you as outer beings. You are part of one larger self along with the most mysterious or most remote fact of nature, along with the moon, and all the hosts of heaven, along with all truth and all beauty. Else could you not even intend to speak of such objects beyond you. For whatever you speak of you will find that your world is meant by you as just your world. Talk of the unknowable, and it forthwith becomes your unknowable, your problem, whose solution, unless the problem be a mere nonsense question, your larger self must own and be aware of. The deepest problem of life is, "What is this deeper self?" And the only answer is, *It is the self that knows in unity all truth.* This, I insist, is no hypothesis. It is actually the presupposition of your deepest doubt. And that is why I say: Everything finite is more or less obscure, dark, doubtful. Only the Infinite Self, the problem-solver, the complete thinker, the one who knows what we mean even when we are most confused and ignorant, the one who includes us, who has the world present to himself in unity, before whom all past and future truth, all distant and dark truth is clear in one eternal moment, to whom far and forgot is near, who thinks the whole of nature, and in whom are all things, the Logos, the world-possessor—only his existence, I say, is perfectly sure.

Yet I must not state the outcome thus confidently without a little more analysis and exemplification. Let me put the whole matter in a slightly different way. When a man believes that he knows any truth about a fact beyond his present and momentary thought, what is the position, with reference to that fact, which he gives himself? We must first answer, He believes that one who really knew his, the thinker's, thought, and compared it with the fact yonder, would perceive the agreement between the two. Is this *all*, however, that the believer holds to be true of his own thought? No, not so, for he holds not only that his thought, as it is, agrees with *some* fact outside his present self (as my thought, for instance, of my toothache may agree with the fact yonder called my neighbor's toothache), but also that his thought agrees with the fact with which it *meant* to agree. To *mean* to agree, however, with a specific fact beyond my present self, involves such a relation to that fact that if I could somehow come directly into the presence of the fact itself, could somehow absorb it into my present consciousness, I should become immediately aware of it as the fact that I all along had meant. Our previous examples have been intended to bring clearly before us this curious and in fact unique character of the relation called *meaning* an object of our thought. To return, then, to our supposed believer: he believes that he *knows* some fact beyond his present consciousness. This involves, as we have now seen, the assertion that he believes himself to stand in such an actual relation to the fact yonder that were it in instead of out of his present consciousness, he would recognize it both as the object *meant* by his present thought, and also as in agreement therewith; and it is all this which, as he believes, an immediate observer of his own thought and of the object— that is, an observer who should include our believer's present self, and the fact yonder, and who should reflect on their relations—would find as the real relation. Observe, however, that only by *reflection* would this higher observer find out that real relation. Nothing but Reflective Self-consciousness could discover it. To believe that you know anything beyond your present and momentary self, is, therefore, to believe that you do stand in such a relation to truth as only a larger and reflectively observant self, that included you and your object, could render intelligible. Or once more, so to believe is essentially to appeal confidently to a possible larger self for approval. But now to say, I know a truth, and yet to say, This larger self to whom I appeal is appealed to only as to a possible self that needn't be real—all this involves just the absurdity against which our whole idealistic analysis has been directed in case of all the sorts of fact and truth in the world. To believe is to say, I stand in a *real* relation to truth, a relation which transcends wholly my present momentary self; and this real relation is of such a curious nature that only a larger inclusive self, which consciously reflected upon my meaning and consciously possessed the object that I mean, could know or grasp the reality of the relation. If, however, this *relation* is a real one, it must, like the colors, the sounds, and all the other things of which we spoke before, be real *for* somebody. Bare possibilities are nothing. Really possible things are already in some sense real. If, then, my relation to the truth, this complex relation of meaning an object and conforming to it, when the object, although at this moment meant by me, is not now present to my momentary thought—if this relation is genuine, and yet is such as only a possible larger self could render intelligible, then my possible larger self must be real in order that my momentary self should in fact possess the truth in question. Or, in briefest form, The relation of conforming one's thought to an outer object meant by this thought is a relation which only a Reflective Larger Self could grasp or find real. If the relation is real, the larger self is real, too.

So much, then, for the case when one *believes* that one has grasped a truth beyond the moment. But now for the case when one is actually in *error* about some object of his momentary and finite thought. Error is the actual failure to agree, not with any fact taken at random, but with just the fact that one had meant to agree with. Under what circumstances, then, is error possible? Only in case one's real thought, by virtue of its meaning, does transcend his own momentary and in so far ignorant self. As the true believer, meaning the truth that he believes, must be in real relation thereto, even so the blunderer, really meaning, as he does, the fact yonder, in order that he should be able even to blunder about it, must be, in so far, in the same real relation to truth as the true believer. His error lies in missing that conformity with the meant object at which he aimed. None the less, however, did he really mean and really aim; and, therefore, is he in error, because his real and larger self finds him to be so. True thinking and false thinking alike involve, then, the same fundamental conditions, in so far as both are carried on in moments; and in so far as, in both cases, the false moment and the true are such by virtue of being organic parts of a larger, critical, reflective, and so conscious self. . . .

Flee where we will, then, the net of the larger Self ensnares us. We are lost and imprisoned in the thickets of its tangled labyrinth. The moments are not at all in themselves, for as moments they have no meaning; they exist only in relation to the beyond. The larger Self alone is, and they are by reason of it, organic parts of it. They perish, but it remains; they have truth or error only in its overshadowing presence.

And now, as to the unity of this Self. Can there be many such organic selves, mutually separate unities of moments and of the objects that these moments mean? Nay, were there *many* such, would not their manifoldness be a truth? Their relations, would not these be real? Their distinct places in the world-order, would not these things be objects of possible true or false thoughts? If so, must not there be once more the inclusive real Self for whom these truths were true, these separate selves interrelated, and their variety absorbed in the organism of its rational meaning?

There is, then, at last, but one Self, organically, reflectively, consciously inclusive of all the selves, and so of all truth. I have called this self, Logos, problem-solver, all-knower. Consider, then, last of all, his relation to problems. We questioned the whole seeming world of the outer order; we wondered as to space and time, as to nature and evolution, as to the beginning and the end of things. Now he who wonders is like him who doubts. Has his wonder any rationality about it? Does he *mean* anything by his doubt? Then the truth that he means, and about which he wonders, has its real constitution. As wonderer, he in the moment possesses not this solving truth; he appeals to the self who can solve. That self must possess the solution just as surely as the problem has a meaning. The real nature of space and time, the real beginning of things, where matter was at any point of time in the past, what is to become of the world's energy: these are matters of truth, and truth is necessarily present to the Self as in one all-comprehending self-completed moment, beyond which is naught, within which is the world.

The world, then, is such stuff as ideas are made of. Thought possesses all things. But the world isn't unreal. It extends infinitely beyond our private consciousness, because it is the world of an universal mind. What facts it is to contain only experience can inform us. There is no magic that can anticipate the work of science. Absolutely the *only* thing sure from the first about this world, however, is that it is intelligent, rational, orderly, essentially comprehensible, so that all its problems are somewhere solved, all its darkest mysteries are known to the supreme Self. This Self infinitely and reflectively transcends our consciousness, and therefore, since it includes us, it is at the very least a person, and more definitely conscious than we are; for what it possesses is self-reflecting knowledge, and what is knowledge aware of itself, but consciousness? Beyond the seeming wreck and chaos of our finite problems, its eternal insight dwells, therefore, in absolute and supreme majesty. Yet it is not far from every one of us. There is no least or most transient thought that flits through a child's mind, or that troubles with the faintest line of care a maiden's face, and that still does not contain and embody something of this divine Logos.

Questions

1. What are the two aspects of idealism which Royce recognizes? What does he mean by "idea"? By "the larger Self"?

2. Make clear the differences between Berkeley's views and Royce's views on our knowledge of the world. (For Berkeley's views, see page 87.) What reasons lead you to agree with one and not the other, or to agree with neither?

3. State why you think that the scientific method could, or could not, be used to decide whether Royce's views of the world were true. (For a description of the scientific method, see page 210.)

4. What is objective idealism's theory of truth? Is there any difference in the way in which Royce would account for the truth of "2 + 3 = 5" and the truth of "There is a study lamp on my work table"? Explain your answer.

5. We call Royce a metaphysician because he presents a view of the ultimate nature of the world or of reality. Do you find that there is in this selection by Royce any implicit distinction between metaphysics and religion? If you were to distinguish between metaphysics and religion for yourself, how would you do so? Do you think that there is a distinction between metaphysics and religion implicit in the selections by Descartes (page 43) and Berkeley (page 87)?

7

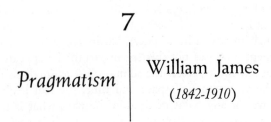

Pragmatism

William James

(1842-1910)

William James received his M.D. from Harvard Medical School and was appointed to the Harvard faculty in 1872 as an instructor in comparative anatomy and physiology. He then became interested in psychology and was appointed as professor of philosophy and psychology at Harvard in 1885. In 1890 he published his famous *Principles of Psychology*. By 1897 he had begun writing on the philosophy of pragmatism, which is the only major philosophical viewpoint to originate in America. James's chief philosophical works are: *The Will to Believe* (1897); *The Varieties of Religious Experience* (1902); *Pragmatism* (1907); *A Pluralistic Universe* (1909); and *Essays in Radical Empiricism* (1912).

There are three things discussed in this exposition of pragmatism by William James. First, there is the pragmatic test for determining the *meaning* of ideas and statements. Second, there is the pragmatic theory of *truth*. And third, there are the pragmatic *arguments against rationalism and objective idealism*. It will be helpful to consider these three parts of pragmatism in turn in order to arrive at a clear and adequate conception of the pragmatic view of our knowledge of the world.

The pragmatic test for meaning was first formulated by the American philosopher, Charles Sanders Peirce. It may be considered both as a test for the meaning of words (or ideas) and as a test for the meaning of declarative sentences (or assertions). The meaning of a word is determined by stating how a person would act (or be prepared to act) both if he believes that something has the property named by the word and if he believes that something does not have the property named by the word. If it makes no difference in a person's actions (or expectations) whether he believes that something has or does not have the property allegedly named by a word, the word actually names no property at all and is therefore meaningless. The meaning of a sentence is determined by stating how a person would act (or be prepared to act) if he believes the sentence to be true and if he believes the sentence to be false. If it makes no difference in a person's actions (or expectations) whether he believes a sentence to be true or to be false, the sentence is meaningless.

The basic principle of the pragmatic theory of truth is: A belief is true if and only if it is useful. However, James often adds qualifications to this principle, and sometimes he defines truth not in terms of usefulness at all but in terms of verification. In the latter case the reader must try to decide whether James wants to claim that "truth" means two distinct things: either usefulness or verification, or whether he wants to claim that in fact all beliefs which can be verified are useful and all useful beliefs can be verified. The reader must also try to make explicit what end or ends James is referring to when he discusses truth in terms of usefulness; for whenever we say that something is useful, we implicitly refer to some end to which the thing is useful as a means.

The arguments which James raises against the "intellectualism" of rationalists and objective idealists are (1) that rationalists believe in pure abstractions which are not related to concrete reality; (2) that belief in an Absolute (the universal mind or "Larger Self") has no, or at best very little, relevance to practical life; (3) that, according to both rationalism and objective idealism, truth is "an inert static relation"; (4) that the rationalist and idealist conception of "agreement with reality," which makes our ideas true, is not a practical or useful "agreement"; and (5) that the rationalist and idealist views of truth do not correspond to the way people actually do verify their beliefs. In order to make a fair appraisal of these criticisms, the reader should consult the views of a rationalist by reading the selection by Descartes (page 43), and the views of an objective idealist by reading the selection by Royce (page 129).

This reading is from Lectures II and VI of *Pragmatism*.

From *Pragmatism,* by William James, Longmans, Green and Co., N. Y., 1907. Copyright © 1907 by William James, 1934 by Henry James. Reprinted by permission of Paul R. Reynolds and Son, 599 Fifth Ave., New York 17, N. Y.

Some years ago, being with a camping party in the mountains, I returned from a solitary ramble to find every one engaged in a ferocious metaphysical dispute. The *corpus* of the dispute was a squirrel—a live squirrel supposed to be clinging to one side of a tree-trunk; while over against the tree's opposite side a human being was imagined to stand. This human witness tries to get sight of the squirrel by moving rapidly round the tree, but no matter how fast he goes, the squirrel moves as fast in the opposite direction, and always keeps the tree between himself and the man, so that never a glimpse of him is caught. The resultant metaphysical problem now is this: *Does the man go round the squirrel or not?* He goes round the tree, sure enough, and the squirrel is on the tree; but does he go round the squirrel? In the unlimited leisure of the wilderness, discussion had been worn threadbare. Every one had taken sides, and was obstinate; and the numbers on both sides were even. Each side, when I appeared therefore appealed to me to make it a majority. Mindful of the scholastic adage that whenever you meet a contradiction you must make a distinction, I immediately sought and found one, as follows: "Which party is right," I said, "depends on what you *practically mean* by 'going round' the squirrel. If you mean passing from the north of him to the east, then to the south, then to the west, and then to the north of him again, obviously the man does go round him, for he occupies these successive positions. But if on the contrary you mean being first in front of him, then on the right of him, then behind him, then on his left, and finally in front again, it is quite as obvious that the man fails to go round him; for by the compensating movements the squirrel makes, he keeps his belly turned towards the man all the time, and his back turned away. Make the distinction, and there is no occasion for any farther dispute. You are both right and both wrong according as you conceive the verb 'to go round' in one practical fashion or the other."

Although one or two of the hotter disputants called my speech a shuffling evasion, saying they wanted no quibbling or scholastic hairsplitting, but meant just plain honest English "round," the majority seemed to think that the distinction had assuaged the dispute.

I tell this trivial anecdote because it is a peculiarly simple example of what I wish now to speak of as *the pragmatic method*. The pragmatic method is primarily a method of settling metaphysical disputes that otherwise might be interminable. Is the world one or many? fated or free? material or spiritual? Here are notions either of which may or may not hold good of the world; and disputes over such notions are unending. The pragmatic method in such cases is to try to interpret each notion by tracing its respective practical consequences. What difference would it practically make to any one if this notion rather than that notion were true? If no practical difference whatever can be traced, then the alternative means practically the same thing, and all dispute is idle. Whenever a dispute is serious, we ought to be able to show some practical difference that must follow from one side or the other's being right.

A glance at the history of the idea will show you still better what pragmatism means. The term is derived from the same Greek word πρᾶγμα, meaning action, from which our words "practice" and "practical" come. It was first introduced into philosophy by Mr. Charles Peirce in 1878. In an article entitled "How to Make Our Ideas Clear," in the *Popular Science Monthly* for January of that year, Mr. Peirce, after pointing out that our beliefs are really rules for action, said that, to develop a thought's meaning, we need only determine what conduct it is fitted to produce: that conduct is for us its sole significance. And the tangible fact at the root of all our thought-distinctions, however subtle, is that there is no one of them so fine as to consist in anything but a possible difference of practice. To attain perfect clearness in our thoughts of an object, then, we need only consider what conceivable effects of a practical kind the object may involve—what sensations we are to expect from it, and what reactions we must prepare. Our conception of these effects, whether immediate or remote, is then for us the whole of our conception of the object, so far as that conception has positive significance at all.

This is the principle of Peirce, the principle of pragmatism. It lay entirely unnoticed by any one for twenty years, until I, in an address before Professor Howison's philosophical union at the University of California, brought it forward again and made a special application of it to religion. By that date (1898) the times seemed ripe for its reception. The word "pragmatism" spread, and at present it fairly spots the pages of the philosophic journals. On all hands we find the "pragmatic movement" spoken of, sometimes with respect, sometimes with contumely, seldom with clear understanding. It is evident that the term applies itself conveniently to a number of tendencies that hitherto have lacked a collective name, and that it has "come to stay."

To take in the importance of Peirce's principle, one must get accustomed to applying it to concrete cases. I found a few years ago that Ostwald, the illustrious Leipzig chemist, had been making perfectly distinct use of the principle of pragmatism in his lectures on the philosophy of science, though he had not called it by that name.

"All realities influence our practice," he wrote me, "and that influence is their meaning for us. I am accustomed to put questions to my classes in this way: In what respects would the world be different if this alternative or that were true? If I can find nothing that would become different, then the alternative has no sense."

That is, the rival views mean practically the same thing, and meaning, other than practical, there is for us none. Ostwald in a published lecture gives this example of what he means. Chemists have long wrangled over the inner constitution of certain bodies called "tautomerous." Their properties seemed equally consistent with the notion that an instable hydrogen atom oscillates inside of them, or that they are instable mixtures of two bodies. Controversy raged, but never was decided. "It would never have begun," says Ostwald, "if the combatants had asked themselves what particular experimental fact could have been made different by one or the other view being correct. For it would then have appeared that no difference of fact could possibly ensue; and the quarrel was as unreal as if, theorizing in primitive times about the raising of dough by yeast, one party should have invoked a 'brownie,' while another insisted on an 'elf' as the true cause of the phenomenon."

It is astonishing to see how many philosophical disputes collapse into insignificance the moment you subject them to this simple test of tracing a concrete consequence. There can *be* no difference anywhere that doesn't *make* a difference elsewhere—no difference in abstract truth that doesn't express itself in a difference in concrete fact and in conduct consequent upon that fact, imposed on somebody, somehow, somewhere, and somewhen. The whole function of philosophy ought to be to find out what definite difference it will make to you and me, at definite instants of our life, if this world-formula or that world-formula be the true one. . . .

Pragmatism represents a perfectly familiar attitude in philosophy, the empiricist attitude, but it represents it, as it seems to me, both in a more radical and in a less objectionable form than it has ever yet assumed. A pragmatist turns his back resolutely and once for all upon a lot of inveterate habits dear to professional philosophers. He turns away from abstraction and insufficiency, from verbal solutions, from bad *a priori* reasons, from fixed principles, closed systems, and pretended absolutes and origins. He turns towards concreteness and adequacy, towards facts, towards action and towards power. That means the empiricist temper regnant and the rationalist temper sincerely given up. It means the open air and possibilities of nature, as against dogma, artificiality, and the pretence of finality in truth.

At the same time it does not stand for any special results. It is a method only. But the general triumph of that method would mean an enormous change in what I called the "temperament" of philosophy. Teachers of the ultrarationalistic type would be frozen out, much as the courtier type is frozen out in republics, as the ultramontane type of priest is frozen out in Protestant lands.

Science and metaphysics would come much nearer together, would in fact work absolutely hand in hand.

Metaphysics has usually followed a very primitive kind of quest. You know how men have always hankered after unlawful magic, and you know what a great part in magic *words* have always played. If you have his name, or the formula of incantation that binds him, you can control the spirit, genie, afrite, or whatever the power may be. Solomon knew the names of all the spirits, and having their names, he held them subject to his will. So the universe has always appeared to the natural mind as a kind of enigma, of which the key must be sought in the shape of some illuminating or power-bringing word or name. That word names the universe's *principle,* and to possess it is after a fashion to possess the universe itself. "God," "Matter," "Reason," "the Absolute," "Energy," are so many solving names. You can rest when you have them. You are at the end of your metaphysical quest.

But if you follow the pragmatic method, you cannot look on any such word as closing your quest. You must bring out of each word its practical cash-value, set it at work within the stream of your experience. It appears less as a solution, then, than as a program for more work, and more particularly as an indication of the ways in which existing realities may be *changed.*

Theories thus become instruments, not answers to enigmas, in which we can rest. We don't lie back upon them, we move forward, and, on occasion, make nature over again by their aid. Pragmatism unstiffens all our theories, limbers them up and sets each one at work. Being nothing essentially new, it harmonizes with many ancient philosophic tendencies. It agrees with nominalism, for instance, in always appealing to particulars; with utilitarianism in emphasizing practical aspects; with positivism in its disdain for verbal solutions, useless questions and metaphysical abstractions.

All these, you see, are *anti-intellectualist* tendencies. Against rationalism as a pretension and a method pragmatism is fully armed and militant. But, at the outset, at least, it stands for no particular results. It has no dogmas, and no doctrines save its method. As the young Italian pragmatist Papini has well said, it lies in the midst of our theories, like a corridor in a hotel. Innumerable chambers open out of it. In one you may find a man writing an atheistic volume; in the next some one on his knees praying for faith and strength; in a third a chemist investigating a body's properties. In a fourth a system of idealistic metaphysics is being excogitated; in a fifth the impossibility of metaphysics is being shown. But they all own the corridor, and all must pass through it if they want a practicable way of getting into or out of their respective rooms.

No particular results then, so far, but only an attitude of orientation, is what the pragmatic method means. *The attitude of looking away from first things, principles, "categories," supposed necessities, and of looking towards last things, fruits, consequences, facts.*

So much for the pragmatic method! Meanwhile the word pragmatism has come to be used in a still wider sense, as meaning also a certain *theory of truth*.

. . . "Truth" in our ideas and beliefs means the same thing that it means in science. It means nothing but this, *that ideas (which themselves are but parts of our experience) become true just in so far as they help us to get into satisfactory relation with other parts of our experience,* to summarize them and get about among them by conceptual short-cuts instead of following the interminable succession of particular phenomena. Any idea upon which we can ride, so to speak; any idea that will carry us prosperously from any one part of our experience to any other part, linking things satisfactorily, working securely, simplifying, saving labor, is true for just so much, true in so far forth, true *instrumentally.* This is the "instrumental" view of truth taught so successfully at Chicago, the view that truth in our ideas means their power to "work" promulgated so brilliantly at Oxford.

Messrs. Dewey, Schiller [1] and their allies in reaching this general conception of all truth have only followed the example of geologists, biologists and philologists. In the establishment of these other sciences, the successful stroke was always to take some simple process actually observable in operation—as denudation by weather, say, or variation from parental type, or change of dialect by incorporation of new words and pronunciations—and then to generalize it, making it apply to all times, and produce great results by summating its effects through the ages.

The observable process which Schiller and Dewey particularly singled out for generalization is the familiar one by which any individual settles into *new opinions.* The process here is always the same. The individual has a stock of old opinions already, but he meets a new experience that puts them to a strain. Somebody contradicts them; or in a reflective moment he discovers that they contradict each other; or he hears of facts with which they are incompatible; or desires arise in him which they cease to satisfy. The result is an inward trouble to which his mind till then had been a stranger, and from which he seeks to escape by modifying his previous mass of opinions. He saves as much of it as he can, for in this matter of belief we are all extreme conservatives. So he tries to change first this opinion, and then that (for they resist change very variously), until at last some new idea comes up which he can graft upon the ancient stock with a minimum of disturbance of the latter, some idea that mediates between the stock and the new experience and runs them into one another most felicitously and expediently.

This new idea is then adopted as the true one. It preserves the older stock of truths with a minimum of modification, stretching them just enough to make them admit the novelty, but conceiving that in ways as familiar as the case leaves possible. An *outrée* explanation, violating all our preconceptions, would never pass for a true account of a novelty. We should scratch round industriously till we found something less excentric. The most violent revolutions in an individual's beliefs leave most of his old order standing. Time and space, cause and effect, nature and history, and one's own biography remain un-

[1] [John Dewey was teaching philosophy at the University of Chicago and F. C. S. Schiller, at Oxford when James wrote these lectures.—Eds.]

touched. New truth is always a go-between, a smoother-over of transitions. It marries old opinion to new fact so as ever to show a minimum of jolt, a maximum of continuity. We hold a theory true just in proportion to its success in solving this "problem of maxima and minima." But success in solving this problem is eminently a matter of approximation. We say this theory solves it on the whole more satisfactorily than that theory; but that means more satisfactorily to ourselves, and individuals will emphasize their points of satisfaction differently. To a certain degree, therefore, everything here is plastic.

The point I now urge you to observe particularly is the part played by the older truths. Failure to take account of it is the source of much of the unjust criticism levelled against pragmatism. Their influence is absolutely controlling. Loyalty to them is the first principle—in most cases it is the only principle; for by far the most usual way of handling phenomena so novel that they would make for a serious rearrangement of our preconception is to ignore them altogether, or to abuse those who bear witness for them. . . .

Such then would be the scope of pragmatism—first, a method; and second, a genetic theory of what is meant by truth. . . .

You will probably be surprised to learn that Messrs. Schiller's and Dewey's theories have suffered a hailstorm of contempt and ridicule. All rationalism has risen against them. In influential quarters Mr. Schiller, in particular, has been treated like an impudent schoolboy who deserves a spanking. I should not mention this, but for the fact that it throws so much sidelight upon that rationalistic temper to which I have opposed the temper of pragmatism. Pragmatism is uncomfortable away from facts. Rationalism is comfortable only in the presence of abstractions. This pragmatist talk about truths in the plural, about their utility and satisfactoriness, about the success with which they "work," etc., suggests to the typical intellectualist mind a sort of coarse, lame, second-rate, makeshift article of truth. Such truths are not real truth. Such tests are merely subjective. As against this, objective truth must be something nonutilitarian, haughty, refined, remote, august, exalted. It must be an absolute correspondence of our thoughts with an equally absolute reality. It must be what we *ought* to think unconditionally. The conditioned ways in which we *do* think are so much irrelevance and matter for psychology. Down with psychology, up with logic, in all this question!

See the exquisite contrast of the types of mind! The pragmatist clings to facts and concreteness, observes truth at its work in particular cases, and generalizes. Truth, for him, becomes a class-name for all sorts of definite working-values in experience. For the rationalist it remains a pure abstraction, to the bare name of which we must defer. When the pragmatist undertakes to show in detail just *why* we must defer, the rationalist is unable to recognize the concretes from which his own abstraction is taken. He accuses us of *denying* truth; whereas we have only sought to trace exactly why people follow it and always ought to follow it. Your typical ultra-abstractionist fairly shudders at concreteness: other things equal, he positively prefers the pale and spectral. If the two universes were offered, he would always choose the skinny outline rather than the rich thicket of reality. It is so much purer, clearer, nobler.

Men who are strongly of the fact-loving temperament are liable to be kept at a distance by the small sympathy with facts which that philosophy from the present-day fashion of idealism offers them. It is far too intellectualistic. Old fashioned theism was bad enough, with its notion of God as an exalted monarch, made up of a lot of unintelligible or preposterous "attributes"; but, so long as it held strongly by the argument from design, it kept some touch with concrete realities. Since, however, Darwinism has once for all displaced design from the minds of the "scientific," theism has lost that foothold; and some kind of an immanent or pantheistic deity working *in* things rather than above them is, if any, the kind recommended to our contemporary imagination. Aspirants to a philosophic religion turn, as a rule, more hopefully nowadays towards idealistic pantheism than towards the older dualistic theism, in spite of the fact that the latter still counts able defenders.

But the brand of pantheism offered is hard for them to assimilate if they are lovers of facts, or empirically minded. It is the absolutistic brand, spurning the dust and reared upon pure logic. It keeps no connexion whatever with concreteness. Affirming the Absolute Mind, which is its substitute for God, to be the rational presupposition of all particulars of fact, whatever they may be, it remains supremely indifferent to what the particular facts in our world actually are. Be they what they may, the Absolute will father them. Like the sick lion in Aesop's fable, all footprints lead into his den, but *nulla vestigia retrorsum.* You cannot redescend into the world of particulars by the Absolute's aid, or deduce any necessary consequences of detail important for your life from your idea of his nature. He gives you indeed the assurance that all is well with *Him,* and for his eternal way of thinking; but thereupon he leaves you to be finitely saved by your own temporal devices. . . .

Now pragmatism, devoted though she be to facts, has no such materialistic bias as ordinary empiricism labors under. Moreover, she has no objection whatever to the realizing of abstractions, so long as you get about among particulars with their aid and they actually carry you somewhere. Interested in no conclusions but those which our minds and our experiences work out together, she has no *a priori* prejudices against theology. *If theological ideas prove to have a value for concrete life, they will be true, for pragmatism, in the sense of being good for so much. For how much more they are true will depend entirely on their relations to the other truths that also have to be acknowledged.*

What I said just now about the Absolute, of transcendental idealism, is a case in point. First, I called it majestic and said it yielded religious comfort to a class of minds, and then I accused it of remoteness and sterility. But so far as it affords such comfort, it surely is not sterile; it has that amount of value; it performs a concrete function. As a good pragmatist, I myself ought to call the Absolute true "in so far forth," then; and I unhesitatingly now do so. . . .

I am well aware how odd it must seem to some of you to hear me say that an idea is "true" so long as to believe it is profitable to our lives. That it is *good,* for as much as it profits, you will gladly admit. If what we do by its aid is good, you will allow the idea itself to be good in so far forth, for we are the better for possessing it. But is it not a strange misuse of the word "truth," you will say, to call ideas also "true" for this reason?

To answer this difficulty fully is impossible at this stage of my account. You touch here upon the very central point of Messrs. Schiller's, Dewey's and my own doctrine of truth. Let me now say only this, that truth is *one species of good,* and not, as is usually supposed, a category distinct from good, and co-ordinate with it. *The true is the name of whatever proves itself to be good in the way of belief, and good, too, for definite, assignable reasons.* Surely you must admit this, that if there were *no* good for life in true ideas, or if the knowledge of them were positively disadvantageous and false ideas the only useful ones, then the current notion that truth is divine and precious, and its pursuit a duty, could never have grown up or become a dogma. In a world like that, our duty would be to *shun* truth, rather. But in this world, just as certain foods are not only agreeable to our taste, but good for our teeth, our stomach, and our tissues; so certain ideas are not only agreeable to think about, or agreeable as supporting other ideas that we are fond of, but they are also helpful in life's practical struggles. If there be any life that it is really better we should lead, and if there be any idea which, if believed in, would help us to lead that life, then it would be really *better for us to believe in that idea, unless, indeed, belief in it incidentally clashed with other greater vital benefits.*

"What would be better for us to believe!" This sounds very like a definition of truth. It comes very near to saying "what we *ought* to believe": and in *that* definition none of you would find any oddity. Ought we ever not to believe what it is *better for us* to believe? And can we then keep the notion of what is better for us, and what is true for us, permanently apart?

Pragmatism says no, and I fully agree with her. Probably you also agree, so far as the abstract statement goes, but with a suspicion that if we practically did believe everything that made for good in our own personal lives, we should be found indulging all kinds of fancies about this world's affairs, and all kinds of sentimental superstitions about a world hereafter. Your suspicion here is undoubtedly well founded, and it is evident that something happens when you pass from the abstract to the concrete that complicates the situation.

I said just now that what is better for us to believe is true *unless the belief incidentally clashes with some other vital benefit.* Now in real life what vital benefits is any particular belief of ours most liable to clash with? What indeed except the vital benefits yielded by *other beliefs* when these prove incompatible with the first ones? In other words, the greatest enemy of any one of our truths may be the rest of our truths. . . .

I fully expect to see the pragmatist view of truth run through the classic stages of a theory's career. First, you know, a new theory is attacked as absurd; then it is admitted to be true, but obvious and insignificant; finally it is seen to be so important that its adversaries claim that they themselves discovered it. Our doctrine of truth is at present in the first of these three stages, with symptoms of the second stage having begun in certain quarters. I wish that this lecture might help it beyond the first stage in the eyes of many of you.

Truth, as any dictionary will tell you, is a property of certain of our ideas. It means their "agreement," as falsity means their disagreement, with "reality." Pragmatists and intellectualists both accept this definition as a matter of course. They begin to quarrel only after the question is raised as to what may precisely be meant by the term "agreement," and what by the term "reality," when reality is taken as something for our ideas to agree with.

In answering these questions the pragmatists are more analytic and painstaking, the intellectualists more offhand and irreflective. The popular notion is that a true idea must copy its reality. Like other popular views, this one follows the analogy of the most usual experience. Our true ideas of sensible things do indeed copy them. Shut your eyes and think of yonder clock on the wall, and you get just such a true picture or copy of its dial. But your idea of its "works" (unless you are a clock maker) is much less of a copy, yet it passes muster, for it in no way clashes with the reality. Even though it should shrink to the mere word "works," that word still serves you truly; and when you speak of the "time-keeping function" of the clock, or of its spring's "elasticity," it is hard to see exactly what your ideas can copy.

You perceive that there is a problem here. Where your ideas cannot copy definitely their object, what does agreement with that object mean? Some idealists seem to say that they are true whenever they are what God means that we ought to think about that object. Others hold the copy-view all through, and speak as if our ideas possessed truth just in proportion as they approach to being copies of the Absolute's eternal way of thinking.

These views, you see, invite pragmatistic discussion. But the great assumption of the intellectualists is that truth means essentially an inert static relation. When you've got your true idea of anything, there's an end of the matter. You're in possession, you *know:* you have fulfilled your thinking destiny. You are where you ought to be mentally; you have obeyed your categorical imperative; and nothing more need follow on that climax of your rational destiny. Epistemologically you are in stable equilibrium.

Pragmatism, on the other hand, asks its usual question. "Grant an idea or belief to be true," it says, "what concrete difference will its being true make in any one's actual life? How will the truth be realized? What experiences will be different from those which would obtain if the belief were false? What, in short, is the truth's cash-value in experimental terms?"

The moment pragmatism asks this question, it sees the answer: *True ideas are those that we can assimilate, validate, corroborate and verify. False ideas are those that we can not.* That is the practical difference it makes to us to have true ideas; that, therefore, is the meaning of truth, for it is all that truth is known as.

This thesis is what I have defended. The truth of an idea is not a stagnant property inherent in it. Truth *happens* to an idea. It *becomes* true, is *made* true by events. Its verity *is* in fact an event, a process; the process, namely, of its verifying itself, its veri*fication*. Its validity is the process of its valid*ation*.

But what do the words verification and validation themselves pragmatically mean? They again signify certain practical consequences of the verified and validated idea. It is hard to find any one phrase that characterizes these consequences better than the ordinary agreement-formula—just such consequences being what we have in mind whenever we say that our ideas "agree" with reality. They lead us, namely, through the acts and other ideas which they instigate, into or up to, or towards, other parts of experience with which we feel all the while—such feeling being among our potentialities—that the original ideas remain in agreement. The connexions and transitions come to us from point to point as being progressive, harmonious, satisfactory. This function of agreeable leading is what we mean by an idea's verification. Such an account is vague and it sounds at first quite trivial, but it has results which it will take the rest of my hour to explain.

Let me begin by reminding you of the fact that the possession of true thoughts means everywhere the possession of invaluable instruments of action; and that our duty to gain truth, so far from being a blank command from out of the blue, or a "stunt" self-imposed by our intellect, can account for itself by excellent practical reasons.

The importance to human life of having true beliefs about matters of fact is a thing too notorious. We live in a world of realities that can be infinitely useful or infinitely harmful. Ideas that tell us which of them to expect count as the true ideas in all this primary sphere of verification, and the pursuit of such ideas is a primary human duty. The possession of truth so far from being here an end in itself is only a preliminary means towards other vital satisfactions. If I am lost in the woods and starved, and find what looks like a cow-path, it is of the utmost importance that I should think of a human habitation at the end of it; for if I do so and follow it, I save myself. The true thought is useful here because the house which is its object is useful. The practical value of true ideas is thus primarily derived from the practical importance of their objects to us. Their objects are, indeed, not important at all times. I may on another occasion have no use for the house; and then my idea of it, however verifiable, will be practically irrelevant, and had better remain latent. Yet since almost any object may some day become temporarily important, the advantage of having a general stock of *extra* truths, of ideas that shall be true of merely possible situations, is obvious. We store such extra truths away in our memories, and with the overflow we fill our books of reference. Whenever such an extra truth becomes practically relevant to one of our emergencies, it passes from cold-storage to do work in the world and our belief in it grows active. You can say of it then either that "it is useful because it is true" or that "it is true because it is useful." Both of these phrases mean exactly the same thing, namely, that here is an idea that gets fulfilled and can be verified. True is the name for whatever idea starts the verification-process; useful is the name for its completed function in experience. True ideas would never have been singled out as such, would never have acquired a class-name, least of all a name suggesting value, unless they had been useful from the outset in this way.

From this simple cue pragmatism gets her general notion of truth as something essentially bound up with the way in which one moment in our experience may lead us towards other moments which it will be worth while to have been led to. Primarily, and on the common-sense level, the truth of a state of mind means this function of *a leading that is worth while.* When a moment in our experience, of any kind whatever, inspires us with a thought that is true, that means that sooner or later we dip by that thought's guidance into the particulars of experience again and make advantageous connexion with them. This is a vague enough statement, but I beg you to retain it, for it is essential.

Our experience meanwhile is all shot through with regularities. One bit of it can warn us to get ready for another bit, can "intend" or be "significant of" that remoter object. The object's advent is the significance's verification. Truth, in these cases, meaning nothing but eventual verification, is manifestly incompatible with waywardness on our part. Woe to him whose beliefs play fast and loose with the order which realities follow in his experience; they will lead him nowhere or else make false connexions.

By "realities" or "objects" here, we mean either things of common sense, sensibly present, or else common-sense relations, such as dates, places, distances, kinds, activities. Following our mental image of a house along the cow-path, we actually come to see the house; we get the image's full verification. *Such simply and fully verified leadings are certainly the originals and prototypes of the truth-process.* Experience offers indeed other forms of truth-process, but they are all conceivable as being primary verifications arrested, multiplied or substituted one for another.

Take, for instance, yonder object on the wall. You and I consider it to be a "clock," although no one of us has seen the hidden works that make it one. We let our notion pass for true without attempting to verify. If truths mean verification-process essentially, ought we then to call such unverified truths as this abortive? No, for they form the overwhelmingly large number of the truths we live by. Indirect as well as direct verifications pass muster. Where circumstantial evidence is sufficient, we can go without eye-witnessing. Just as we here assume Japan to exist without ever having been there, because it *works* to do so, everything we know conspiring with the belief, and nothing interfering, so we assume that thing to be a clock. We *use* it as a clock, regulating the length of our lecture by it. The verification of the assumption here means its leading to no frustration or contradiction. Verifi*ability* of wheels and weights and pendulum is as good as verification. For one truth-process completed there are a million in our lives that function in this state of nascency. They turn us *towards* direct verification; lead us into the *surroundings* of the objects they envisage; and then, if everything runs on harmoniously, we are so sure that verification is possible that we omit it, and are usually justified by all that happens.

Truth lives, in fact, for the most part on a credit system. Our thoughts and beliefs "pass" so long as nothing challenges them just as bank-notes pass so long as nobody refuses them. But this all points to direct face-to-face verifications somewhere, without which the fabric of truth collapses like a financial system with no cash-basis whatever. You accept my verification of one thing, I yours of another. We trade on each other's truth. But beliefs verified concretely by *somebody* are posts of the whole superstructure.

Another great reason—beside economy of time—for waiving complete verification in the usual business of life is that all things exist in kinds and not singly. Our world is found once for all to have that peculiarity. So that when we have once directly verified our ideas about one specimen of a kind, we consider ourselves free to apply them to other specimens without verification. A mind that habitually discerns the kind of thing before it, and acts by the law of the kind immediately, without pausing to verify, will be a "true" mind in ninety-nine out of a hundred emergencies, proved so by its conduct fitting everything it meets, and getting no refutation.

Indirectly or only potentially verifying processes may thus be true as well as full verification-processes. They work as true processes would work, give us the same advantages, and claim our recognition for the same reasons. All this on the common-sense level of matters of fact, which we are alone considering.

But matters of fact are not our only stock in trade. *Relations among purely mental ideas* form another sphere where true and false beliefs obtain, and here the beliefs are absolute, or unconditional. When they are true they bear the name either of definitions or of principles. It is either a principle or a definition that 1 and 1 make 2, that 2 and 1 make 3, and so on; that white differs less from gray than it does from black; that when the cause begins to act the effect also commences. Such propositions hold of all possible "ones," of all conceivable "whites" and "grays" and "causes." The objects here are mental objects. Their relations are perceptually obvious at a glance, and no sense-verification is necessary. Moreover, once true, always true, of those same mental objects. Truth here has an "eternal" character. If you can find a concrete thing anywhere that is "one" or "white" or "gray" or an "effect," then your principles will everlastingly apply to it. It is but a case of ascertaining the kind, and then applying the law of its kind to the particular object. You are sure to get truth if you can but name the kind rightly, for your mental relations hold good of everything of that kind without exception. If you then, nevertheless, failed to get truth concretely, you would say that you had classed your real objects wrongly.

In this realm of mental relations, truth again is an affair of leading. We relate one abstract idea with another, framing in the end great systems of logical and mathematical truth, under the respective terms of which the sensible facts of experience eventually arrange themselves, so that our eternal truths hold good of realities also. This marriage of fact and theory is endlessly fertile. What we say is here already true in advance of special verification, *if we have subsumed our objects rightly.* Our ready-made ideal framework for all sorts of possible objects follows from the very structure of our thinking. We can no more play fast and loose with these abstract relations than we can do so with our sense-experiences. They coerce us; we must treat them consistently, whether or not we like the results. The rules of addition apply to our debts as rigorously as to our assets. The hundredth decimal of π, the ratio of the circumference to its diameter, is predetermined ideally now, though no one may have computed it. If we should ever need the figure in our dealings with an actual circle we should need to have it given rightly, calculated by the usual rules; for it is the same kind of truth that those rules elsewhere calculate.

Between the coercions of the sensible order and those of the ideal order, our mind is thus wedged tightly. Our ideas must agree with realities, be such realites concrete or abstract, be they facts or be they principles, under penalty of endless inconsistency and frustration.

So far, intellectualists can raise no protest. They can only say that we have barely touched the skin of the matter.

Realities mean, then, either concrete facts, or abstract kinds of things and relations perceived intuitively between them. They furthermore and thirdly mean, as things that new ideas of ours must no less take account of, the whole body of other truths already in our possession. But what now does "agreement" with such threefold realities mean?—to use again the definition that is current.

Here it is that pragmatism and intellectualism begin to part company. Primarily, no doubt, to agree means to copy, but we saw that the mere word "clock" would do instead of a mental picture of its works, and that of many realities our ideas can only be symbols and not copies. "Past time," "power," "spontaneity"—how can our mind copy such realities?

To "agree" in the widest sense with a reality *can only mean to be guided either straight up to it or into its surroundings, or to be put into such working touch with it as to handle either it or something connected with it better than if we disagreed.* But either intellectually or practically! And often agreement will only mean the negative fact that nothing contradictory from the quarter of that reality comes to interfere with the way in which our ideas guide us elsewhere. To copy a reality is, indeed, one very important way of agreeing with it, but it is far from being essential. The essential thing is the process of being guided. Any idea that helps us to *deal,* whether practically or intellectually, with either the reality or its belongings, that doesn't entangle our progress in frustrations, that *fits,* in fact, and adapts our life to the reality's whole setting, will agree sufficiently to meet the requirement. It will hold true of that reality. . . .

"*The true,*" to put it very briefly, is only the expedient in the way of our thinking, just as "*the right*" is only the expedient in the way of our behaving. Expedient in almost any fashion; and expedient in the long run and on the whole of course; for what meets expediently all the experience in sight won't necessarily meet all farther experiences equally satisfactorily. Experience, as we know, has ways of *boiling over,* and making us correct our present formulas.

The "absolutely" true, meaning what no farther experience will ever alter, is that ideal vanishing-point towards which we imagine that all our temporary truths will some day converge. It runs on all fours with the perfectly wise man, and with the absolutely complete experience; and, if these ideals are ever realized, they will all be realized together. Meanwhile we have to live to-day by what truth we can get to-day, and be ready to-morrow to call it falsehood. Ptolemaic astronomy, Euclidean space, Aristotelian logic, scholastic metaphysics were expedient for centuries, but human experience has boiled over those limits, and we now call these things only relatively true, or true within those borders of experience. "Absolutely" they are false; for we know that those limits were casual, and might have been transcended by past theorists just as they are by present thinkers. . . .

The most fateful point of difference between being a rationalist and being a pragmatist is now fully in sight. Experience is in mutation and our psychological ascertainments of truth are in mutation—so much rationalism will allow; but never that either reality itself or truth itself is mutable. Reality stands complete and ready-made from all eternity, rationalism insists, and the agreement of our ideas with it is that unique unanalyzable virtue in them of which she has already told us. As that intrinsic excellence, their truth has nothing to do with our experiences. It adds nothing to the content of experience. It makes no difference to reality itself; it is supervenient, inert, static, a reflexion merely. It doesn't *exist,* it *holds* or *obtains,* it belongs to another dimension from that of either facts or fact-relations, belongs, in short, to the epistemological dimension—and with that big word rationalism closes the discussion.

Thus, just as pragmatism faces forward to the future, so does rationalism here again face backward to a past eternity. True to her inveterate habit, rationalism reverts to "principles," and thinks that when an abstraction once is named, we own an oracular solution.

Questions

1. What is the principle of pragmatism? How does James's story about the squirrel illustrate the pragmatic method?

2. When you apply the principle of pragmatism (or the pragmatic method) to the following sentences, how many of them are found to be meaningful?
   a. The chemical formula for water is H_2O.
   b. Water freezes at 32° F.
   c. The water in my home town tastes salty.
   d. The water in my home town tastes awful.
   e. Everyone tends to do what is least painful to him.
   f. Everyone seeks his own good.
   g. A warm bath will often make a tired person feel refreshed. (From a personal health manual.)
   h. A bath in our soap will give you that fresh feeling. (From a soap advertisement.)

    i. Wear a real man's shirt. Wear our shirts. (From a shirt advertisement.)
    j. Our soup contains ingredients. (Sign in a restaurant.)
    k. The furniture of the world is nothing but ideas. (Berkeley)
    l. The world is the world of a universal mind. (Royce)
    m. The only things that exist are the things I can perceive. (An empiricist.)
    n. God will take care of you.
    o. Parallel lines never meet.
    p. Every body perseveres in its state of rest, or of uniform motion in a right line, unless it is compelled to change that state by forces impressed thereon. (Newton)

    3. What is the pragmatic theory of truth? How does it compare with the objective idealist's theory of truth (pages 139 ff.)? Would there ever be any agreement (or conflict) in the ways in which these theories account for the truth of a law in physics, or a theorem in geometry? How would you explain such agreement (or conflict)?

    4. "I am well aware how odd it must seem to some of you to hear me say that an idea is 'true' so long as to believe it is profitable to our lives." (James, page 150.) Which of the following statements express ideas that you think are true? (What do you mean by "true"?) Which express ideas that you think might be profitable to someone? (What do you mean by "profitable"?) Which express ideas that you think may be both true and profitable?

    a. A dollar is worth one hundred cents.
    b. Fire burns.
    c. It hurts to have a dentist's drill in your teeth.
    d. Words will never hurt me.
    e. Chocolate ice cream is delicious.
    f. A stitch in time saves nine.
    g. I have nothing to fear. (Said by a soldier as he goes into battle.)
    h. You only live once. (Said by someone prepared to fight to the last ditch.)
    i. You only live once. (Said by someone who surrenders as soon as the enemy takes the field.)
    j. God will take care of you.

8

Critique of the Pragmatic Theory of Truth

G. E. Moore, o.m.
(1873-1958)

George Edward Moore taught philosophy at Cambridge University from 1911 until his retirement in 1939. He has had a great influence on contemporary British and American philosophy. His published work includes: *Principia Ethica* (1903); *Ethics* (1912); and *Philosophical Studies* (1922).

    In this reading Professor Moore begins by presenting four assertions which he believes William James intended to make when he propounded the pragmatic theory of truth. (For James's views, see the preceding selection in this chapter.) The four assertions are (1) that all true ideas are verifiable; (2) that all verifiable ideas are true; (3) that all true ideas are useful; and (4) that all useful ideas are true. Professor Moore proceeds to examine these four assertions one by one and to state why he accepts one of them (the second) but rejects the other three. He then goes on to consider other assertions about truth made by James and to give his reasons for also rejecting them. All of his arguments rest on the assumption that a theory of truth ought to clarify what is meant when we say in ordinary speech that a statement is true. The final standard for deciding whether to accept a theory of truth thus depends on the meaning or meanings which people ordinarily have in mind when they use the word "true." Professor Moore always appeals to common sense examples of true statements to see whether the pragmatic view of truth would apply to these examples. Whether the arguments which Professor Moore gives for accepting or rejecting the pragmatist's assertions are logically sound, and whether William James could satisfactorily reply to them, is left to the reader's considered judgment.

This reading is from the essay, "William James' 'Pragmatism,'" first published in *Proceedings of the Aristotelian Society* (1907-1908), and reprinted in *Philosophical Studies*.

From "Professor James' 'Pragmatism,'" by G. E. Moore, *Proceedings of the Aristotelian Society,* 1907-1908. Reprinted by permission of the author and The Aristotelian Society.

Apparently, Professor James wishes to assert that *all* our true ideas are or can be verified—that *all* are useful. And certainly this is not a truism like the proposition that *many* of them are so. Even if this were all that he meant, it would be worth discussing. But even this, I think, is not all. The very first proposition in which he expresses his theory is the following. "True ideas," he says, "are those that we can assimilate, validate, corroborate and verify. False ideas are those that we cannot." And what does this mean? Let us, for brevity's sake, substitute the word "verify" alone for the four words which Professor James uses, as he himself subsequently seems to do. He asserts, then, that true ideas are *those which* we can verify. And plainly he does not mean by this merely that *some* of the ideas which we can verify are true, while plenty of others, which we can verify, are not true. The plain meaning of his words is that *all* the ideas which we can verify are true. No one would use them who did not mean this. Apparently, therefore, Professor James means to assert not merely that we can verify all our true ideas; but also that all the ideas, which we can verify, are true. And so, too, with utility or usefulness. He seems to mean not merely that all our true ideas are useful; but that all those which are useful are true. This would follow, for one thing, from the fact that he seems to use the words "verification" or "verifiability" and "usefulness" as if they came to the same thing. But, in this case too, he asserts it in words that have but one plain meaning. "The true," he says, "is only the expedient in the way of our thinking." "The true" is *the* expedient: that is, *all* expedient thinking is true. Or again: "An idea is 'true' so long as to believe it is profitable to our lives." That is to say, *every* idea, which is profitable to our lives, is, while it is so, true. These words certainly have a plain enough meaning. Apparently, therefore, Professor James means to assert not merely that all true ideas are useful, but also that all useful ideas are true.

Professor James's words, then, do at least suggest that he wishes to assert all four of the following propositions. He wishes to assert, it would seem:

1. That we can verify all those of our ideas, which are true.
2. That all those among our ideas, which we can verify, are true.
3. That all our true ideas are useful.
4. That all those of our ideas, which are useful, are true.

These four propositions are what I propose first to consider. He does mean to assert them, at least. Very likely he wishes to assert something more even than these. He does, in fact, suggest that he means to assert, in addition, that these properties of "verifiability" and "utility" are the *only* properties (beside that of being properly *called* "true") which belong to all our true ideas and to none but true ideas. But this obviously cannot be true, unless all these four propositions are true. And therefore we may as well consider them first.

First, then, can we verify all our true ideas?

I wish only to point out the plainest and most obvious reasons why I think it is doubtful whether we can.

We are very often in doubt as to whether we did or did not do a certain thing in the past. We may have the idea that we did, and also the idea that we did not; and we may wish to find out which idea is the true one. Very often, indeed, I may believe very strongly, that I did do a certain thing; and somebody else, who has equally good reason to know, may believe equally strongly that I did not. For instance, I may have written a letter, and may believe that I used certain words in it. But my correspondent may believe that I did not. Can we always verify either of these ideas? Certainly sometimes we can. The letter may be produced, and prove that I did use the words in question. And I shall then have verified my idea. Or it may prove that I did not use them. And then we shall have verified my correspondent's idea. But, suppose the letter has been destroyed; suppose there is no copy of it, nor any trustworthy record of what was said in it; suppose there is no other witness as to what I said in it, beside myself and my correspondent? Can we then always verify which of our ideas is the true one? I think it is very doubtful whether we can *nearly* always. Certainly we may often try to discover any possible means of verification, and be quite unable, for a time at least, to discover any. Such cases, in which we are unable, for a time at least, to verify either of two contradictory ideas, occur very commonly indeed. Let us take an even more trivial instance than the last. Bad whist-players often do not notice at all carefully which cards they have among the lower cards in a suit. At the end of a hand they cannot be certain whether they had or had not the seven of diamonds, or the five of spades. And, after the cards have been shuffled, a dispute will sometimes arise as to whether a particular player had the seven of diamonds or not. His partner may think that he had, and he himself may think that he had not. Both may be uncertain, and the memory of both, on such a point, may be well known to be untrustworthy. And, moreover, neither of the other players may be able to remember any better. Is it always possible to verify which of these ideas is the true one? Either the player did or did not have the seven of diamonds. This much is certain. One person thinks that he did, and another thinks he did not; and both, so soon as the question is raised, have before their minds both of these ideas—the idea that he did, and the idea that he did not. This also is certain. And it is certain that one or other of these two ideas is true. But can they always verify either of them? Sometimes, no doubt, they can, even after the cards have been shuffled. There may have been a fifth person present, overlooking the play, whose memory is perfectly trustworthy, and whose word may be taken as settling the point. Or the players may themselves be able, by recalling other incidents of play, to arrive at such a certainty as may be said to verify the one hypothesis or the other. But very often neither of these two things will occur. And, in such a case, is it always possible to verify the true idea? Perhaps, theoretically, it may be still possible. Theoretically, I suppose, the fact that one player, and not any of the other three, had the card in his hand, may have made some difference to the card, which *might* be discovered by some possible method of scientific investigation. Perhaps some such difference may remain even after the same card has been repeatedly used in many subsequent games. But suppose the same question arises again, a week after the original game was played. Did you, or did you not, last week have the seven of diamonds in that particular hand? The question has not been settled in the meantime; and now, perhaps, the original pack of cards has been destroyed. Is it still possible to verify either idea? Theoretically, I suppose, it may be still possible. But even this, I think, is very doubtful. And surely it is plain that, humanly and practically speaking, it will often have become quite impossible to verify either idea. In all probability it never will be possible for any man to verify whether I had the card or not on this particular occasion. No doubt we are here speaking of an idea, which some man *could have* verified at one time. But the hypothesis I am considering is the hypothesis that we never have a true idea, which we *cannot* verify; that is to say, which we cannot verify *after* the idea has occurred. And with regard to this hypothesis, it seems to me quite plain that *very often indeed* we have two ideas, one or other of which is certainly true; and yet that, in all probability, it is no longer possible and never will be possible for any man to verify either.

It seems to me, then, that we very often have true ideas which we cannot verify; true ideas, which, in all probability, no man ever will be able to verify. . . .

When, therefore, Professor James tells us that "True ideas are those that we can assimilate, validate, corroborate and verify. False ideas are those that we cannot," there seems to be a serious objection to part of what these words imply. . . .

But to another part of what he implies by the words quoted above, there is, I think, no serious objection. There is reason to object to the statement that we can verify all our true ideas; but to the statement that all ideas, which we can "assimilate, validate, corroborate and verify," are true, I see no serious objection. Here, I think, we might say simply that all ideas which we can verify are true. To this, which is the second of the four propositions, which I distinguished above as what Professor James seems to wish to assert, there is, I think, no serious objection, if we understand the word "verify" in its proper and natural sense. We may, no doubt, sometimes say that we have verified an idea or an hypothesis, when we have only obtained evidence which proves it to be probable, and does not prove it to be certain. And, if we use the word in this loose sense for incomplete verification, it is obviously the case that we may verify an idea which is not true. But it seems scarcely necessary to point this out. And where we really can *completely* verify an idea or an hypothesis, there, undoubtedly, the idea which we can verify is always true. The very meaning of the word "verify" is to find evidence which does really prove an idea to be true; and where an idea can be really proved to be true, it is, of course, always true.

This is all I wish to say about Professor James's first two propositions, namely:

1. That no ideas of ours are true, except those which we can verify.
2. That all those ideas, which we can verify, are true.

The first seems to me extremely doubtful—in fact, almost certainly untrue; the second on the other hand, certainly true, in its most obvious meaning. And I shall say no more about them. The fact is, I doubt whether either of them expresses anything which Professor James is really anxious to assert. I have mentioned them, only because his words do, in fact, imply them and because he gives those words a very prominent place. But I have already had occasion to notice that he seems to speak as if to say that we can verify an idea came to the same thing as saying it is useful to us. And it is the connection of truth with usefulness, not its connection with "verification," that he is, I think, really anxious to assert. He talks about "verification" only, I believe, because he thinks that what he says about it will support his main view that truth is what "works," is "useful," is "expedient," "pays." It is this main view we have now to consider. We have to consider the two propositions:

3. That all our true ideas are useful.
4. That all ideas, which are useful, are true.

First, then: Is it the case that all our true ideas are useful? Is it the case that none of our ideas are true, except those which are useful?

. . . There seems to be an immense number of true ideas, which occur but once and to one person, and never again either to him or to anyone else. I may, for instance, idly count the number of dots on the back of a card, and arrive at a true idea of their number; and yet, perhaps, I may never think of their number again, nor anybody else ever know it. We are all, it seems to me, constantly noticing trivial details, and getting true ideas about them, of which we never think again, and which nobody else ever gets. And is it quite certain that all these true ideas are useful? It seems to me perfectly clear, on the contrary, that many of them are not. Just as it is clear that many men sometimes waste their time in acquiring information which is useful to others but not to them, surely it is clear that they sometimes waste their time in acquiring information, which is useful to nobody at all, because nobody else ever acquires it. I do not say that it is never useful idly to count the number of dots on the back of a card. Plainly it is sometimes useful to be idle, and one idle employment may often be as good as another. But surely it is true that men *sometimes* do these things, when their time would have been better employed otherwise? Surely they sometimes get into the habit of attending to trivial truths, which it is as great a disadvantage that they should attend to as that they should constantly be thinking of their own thoughts and blemishes? I cannot see my way to deny that this is so; and therefore I cannot see my way to assert positively that all our true ideas are useful, even so much as on *one occasion*. It seems to me that there are many true ideas which occur but once, and which are not useful when they do occur. And if this be so, then it is plainly not true that *all* our true ideas are useful in any sense at all. . . .

But now, what are we to say of the converse proposition—the proposition that all those among our ideas, which are useful, are true? That we never have a useful idea, which is not true?

I confess the matter seems to me equally clear here. The assertion should mean that every idea, which is at any time useful, is true; that no idea, which is not true, is ever useful. And it seems hardly possible to doubt that this assertion is false. It is, in the first place, commonly held that it is sometimes right positively to deceive another person. In war, for instance, it is held that one army is justified in trying to give the enemy a false idea as to where it will be at a given time. Such a false idea is sometimes given, and it seems to me quite clear that it is sometimes useful. In such a case, no doubt, it may be said that the false idea is useful to the party who have given it, but not useful to those who actually believe in it. And the question whether it is useful on the whole will depend upon the question which side it is desirable should win. But it seems to me unquestionable that the false idea is sometimes useful on the whole. Take, for instance, the case of a party of savages, who wish to make a night attack and massacre a party of Europeans but are deceived as to the position in which the Europeans are encamped. It is surely plain that such a false idea is sometimes useful on the whole. But quite apart from the question whether deception is ever justifiable, it is not very difficult to think of cases where a false idea, not produced by deception, is plainly useful—and useful, not merely on the whole, but to the person who has it as well. A man often thinks that his watch is right, when, in fact, it is slow, and his false idea may cause him to miss his train. And in such cases, no doubt, his false idea is *generally* disadvantageous. But, in a particular case, the train which he would have caught but for his false idea may be destroyed in a railway accident, or something may suddenly occur at home, which renders it much more useful that he should be there, than it would have been for him to catch his train. Do such cases never occur? And is not the false idea sometimes useful in some of them? It seems to me perfectly clear that it is *sometimes* useful for a man to think his watch is right when it is wrong. And such instances would be sufficient to show that it is not the case that every idea of ours, which is ever useful, is a true idea. But let us take cases, not, like these, of an idea, which occurs but a few times or to one man, but of ideas which have occurred to many men at many times. It seems to me very difficult to be sure that the belief in an eternal hell has not been often useful to many men, and yet it may be doubted whether this idea is true. And so, too, with the belief in a happy life after death, or the belief in the existence of a God; it is, I think, very difficult to be sure that these beliefs have not been, and are not still, often useful, and yet it may be doubted whether they are true. These beliefs, of course, are matters of controversy. Some men believe that they are both useful and true; and others, again, that they are neither. And I do not think we are justified in giving them as certain instances of beliefs, which are not true, but, nevertheless, have often been useful. But there is a view that these beliefs, though not true, have, nevertheless, been often useful; and this view seems to me to deserve respect, especially since, as we have seen, some beliefs, which are not true, certainly are sometimes useful. Are we justified in asserting positively that it is false? Is it perfectly certain that beliefs, which have often been useful to many men, may not, nevertheless, be untrue? Is it perfectly certain that beliefs, which are not true, have not often been useful to many men? The certainty may at least be doubted, and in any case it seems certain that some beliefs, which are not true, are, nevertheless, sometimes useful.

For these reasons, it seems to me almost certain that *both* the assertions which I have been considering are false. It is almost certainly false that all our true ideas are useful, and almost certainly false that all our useful ideas are true. . . .

. . . But now, supposing Professor James does not mean to assert either of these two things, what else can he mean to assert? What else can he mean, that would account for the interest and importance he seems to attach to his assertion of connection between truth and utility? Let us consider the alternatives.

And, first of all, he might mean that *most* of our true ideas are useful, and *most* of our useful ideas true. He might mean that most of our true ideas are useful at some time or other; and even that most of them are useful, whenever they actually occur. And he might mean, moreover, that if we consider the whole range of ideas, which are useful to us, we shall find that by far the greater number of them are true ones; that true ideas are far more often useful to us, than those which are not true. And all this, I think, may be readily admitted to be true. If this were all that he meant, I do not think that anyone would be very anxious to dispute it. But is it conceivable that this is *all* that he means? Is it conceivable that he should have been so anxious to insist upon this admitted commonplace? Is it conceivable that he should have been offering us this, and nothing more, as a theory of what truth means, and a theory worth making a fuss about, and being proud of? It seems to me quite inconceivable that this should have been *all* that he meant. He must have had something more than this in his mind. But, if so, what more? I think very likely that here Professor James was only thinking of ideas.

In the passage which I quoted at the beginning, as showing that he does mean to assert that *all* useful ideas are true, he immediately goes on to assert a qualification, which must now be noticed. "The true," he says, "is only the expedient in the way of our thinking." But he immediately adds: "Expedient in the long run, and on the whole, of course; for what meets expediently all the experience in sight won't necessarily meet all further experiences equally satisfactorily." Here, therefore, we have something else that he might mean. What is expedient *in the long run,* he means to say, is true. And what exactly does this mean? It seems to mean that an idea, which is not true, may be expedient *for some time.* That is to say, it may occur *once,* and be expedient then; and again, and be expedient then; and so on, over a considerable period. But (Professor James seems to prophesy) if it is not true, there will come a time, when it will cease to be expedient. If it occurs again and again over a long *enough* period, there will at last, if it is not true, come a time when it will (for once at least) fail to be useful, and will (perhaps he means) *never* be useful again. This is, I think, what Professor James means in this passage. He means, I think, that though an idea, which is not true, may for some time be repeatedly expedient, there will at last come a time when its occurrence will, perhaps, *never* be expedient again, certainly will, for a time, not be *generally* expedient. And this is a view which, it seems to me, may possibly be true. It is certainly possible that a time may come, in the far future, when ideas, which are not true, will hardly ever, if ever, be expedient. And this is all that Professor James seems here positively to mean. He seems to mean that, if you take time *enough,* false ideas will some day cease to be expedient. And it is very difficult to be sure that this is not true; since it is very difficult to prophesy as to what may happen in the far future. I am sure I hope that this prophecy will come true. But in the meantime (Professor James seems to admit) ideas, which are not true, may, for an indefinitely long time, again and again be expedient. And is it conceivable that a theory, which admits this, is *all* that he has meant to assert? Is it conceivable that what interests him, in his theory of truth, is merely the belief that, some day or other, false ideas will cease to be expedient? "In the long run, *of course,*" he says, as if this were what he had meant all along. But I think it is quite plain that this is *not* all that he has meant. This may be one thing which he is anxious to assert, but it certainly does not explain the whole of his interest in his theory of truth.

And, in fact, there is quite a different theory which he seems plainly to have in his mind in other places. When Professor James says, "in the long run, *of course,*" he implies that ideas which are expedient only for a *short* run are very often not true. But in what he says elsewhere he asserts the very opposite of this. He says elsewhere that a belief is true "*so long as* to believe it is profitable to our lives." That is to say, a belief will be true, *so long as* it is useful, even if it is *not* useful in the long run! This is certainly quite a different theory; and, strictly speaking, it implies that an idea, which is useful even *on one occasion,* will be true. But perhaps this is only a verbal implication. I think very likely that here Professor James was only thinking of ideas, which can be said *to have a run,* though only a comparatively short one—of ideas, that is, which are expedient, not merely on one occasion, but *for some time.* That is to say, the theory which he now suggests is that ideas, which occur again and again, perhaps to one man only, perhaps to several different people, over some space of time are, if they are expedient on most occasions within that space of time, true. This is a view which he is, I think, really anxious to assert; and if it were true, it would, I think, be important. And it is difficult to find instances which show, with certainty, that it is false. I believe that it is false; but it is difficult to prove it, because, in the case of some ideas it is so difficult to be certain that they ever were useful, and in the case of others so difficult to be certain that they are not true. A belief such as I spoke of before—the belief in eternal hell—is an instance. I think this belief has been, for a long time, useful, and that yet it is false. But it is, perhaps, arguable that it never has been useful; and many people on the other hand, would still assert that it is true. It cannot, therefore, perhaps, fairly be used as an instance of a belief, which is certainly not true, and yet has for some time been useful. But whether this view that all beliefs, which are expedient for some time, are true, be true or false; can it be all that Professor James means to assert? Can it constitute the whole of what interests him in his theory of truth?

I do not think it can.

. . . We have seen that he seems sometimes to hold that beliefs are true, *so long as* they are "profitable to our lives." And this implies, as we have seen, the doubtful proposition that any belief which is useful for some length of time, is true. But this is not all that it implies. It also implies that beliefs are true *only* so long as they are profitable. Nor does Professor James appear to mean by this that they *occur,* only so long as they are profitable. He seems to hold, on the contrary, that beliefs, which are profitable for some time, do sometimes finally occur at a time when they are not profitable. He implies, therefore, that a belief, which occurs at several different times, may be true at some of the times at which it occurs, and yet untrue at others. I think there is no doubt that this view is what he is sometimes thinking of. And this, we see, constitutes a quite new view as to the connection between truth and utility—

a view quite different from any that we have hitherto considered. This view asserts not that every true idea is useful at some time, or in the long run, or for a considerable period; but that the truth of an idea may come and go, as its utility comes and goes. It admits that one and the same idea sometimes occurs at times when it is useful, and sometimes at times when it is not; but it maintains that this same idea is true, at those times when it is useful, and not true, at those when it is not. And the fact that Professor James seems to suggest this view constitutes, I think, a second most serious objection to what he says about the connection of truth and utility. It seems so obvious that utility is a property which comes and goes—which belongs to a given idea at one time, and does not belong to it at another, that anyone who says that the true is the useful naturally seems not to be overlooking this obvious fact, but to be suggesting that truth is a property which comes and goes in the same way. It is, in this way I think, that the "instrumental" view of truth is connected with the view that truth is "mutable." Professor James does, I think, imply that truth is mutable in just this sense—namely, that one and the same idea may be true at some of the times at which it occurs, and not true at others, and this is the view which I have next to consider.

. . . Is it the case that an idea which exists at one time, and is true then, ever exists at any other time, without being true? Is it the case that any idea ever changes from true to false? That it has the property of being true on one of the occasions when it exists, and that it has *not* this property, but that of being false instead, on some other occasion when it exists?

In order to answer this question clearly, it is, I think, necessary to make still another distinction. It does certainly seem to be true, *in a sense,* that a given idea may be true on one occasion and false on another. We constantly speak as if there were cases in which a given thing was true on one occasion and false on another; and I think it cannot be denied that, when we so speak, we are often expressing in a perfectly proper and legitimate manner something which is undeniably true. It is true now, I might say, that I am in this room; but tomorrow this will not be true. It is true now that men are often very miserable; but perhaps in some future state of society this will not be true. These are perfectly natural forms of expression, and what they express is something which certainly may be true. And yet what they do apparently assert is that something or other, which is true at one time, will not, or *perhaps* will not, be true at another. We constantly use such expressions, which imply that what is true at one time is not true at another; and it is certainly legitimate to use them. And hence, I think, we must admit that, *in a sense,* it is true that a thing may be true at one time which is not true at another; in that sense, namely, in which we use these expressions. And it is, I think, also plain that these things, which may be true at one time and false at another, may, *in a sense,* be ideas. We might even say: The idea that I am in this room is true now; but tomorrow it will not be true. We might say this without any strain on language. In any ordinary book—indeed, in any philosophical book, where the subject we are at present discussing was not being expressly discussed—

such expressions do, I think, constantly occur. And we should pass them, without any objection. We should at once understand what they meant, and treat them as perfectly natural expressions of things undeniably true. We must, then, I think, admit that, *in a sense,* an idea may be true at one time, and false at another. The question is: In what sense? What is the truth for which these perfectly legitimate expressions stand?

It seems to me that in all these cases, so far as we are not merely talking of *facts,* but of true *ideas,* that the "idea," which we truly say to be true at one time and false at another, is merely the idea of a *sentence*—that is, of certain *words.* And we do undoubtedly call *words* "true." The words "I am at a meeting of the Aristotelian Society" are true, if I use them now; but if I use the same words tomorrow, they would not be true. The words "George III is king of England" were true in 1800, but they are not true now. That is to say, a given set of words may undoubtedly be true at one time, and false at another; and since we may have ideas of words as well as of other things, we may, in this sense, say the same of certain of our "ideas." We may say that some of our "ideas" (namely those of words) are true at one time and not true at another.

But is it conceivable that Professor James *merely* meant to assert that the same *words* are sometimes true at one time and false at another? Can this be *all* he means by saying that truth is mutable? I do not think it can possibly be so. No one, I think, in definitely discussing the mutability of truth, could say that true ideas were mutable, and yet mean (although he did not say so) that this proposition applied *solely* to ideas of words. Professor James must, I think, have been sometimes thinking that *other* ideas, and not merely ideas of words, do sometimes change from true to false. And this is the proposition which I am concerned to dispute. It seems to me that if we mean by an idea, not merely the idea of certain words, but the kind of idea which words express, it is very doubtful whether such an idea ever changes from true to false— whether any such idea is ever true at one time and false at another.

And plainly, in the first place, the mere fact that the same set of words, as in the instances I have given, really are true at one time and false at another, does not afford any presumption that anything which they stand for is true at one time and false at another. For the same words may obviously be used in different senses at different times; and hence though the same words, which formerly expressed a truth, may cease to express one, that may be because they now express a *different* idea, and not because the idea which they formerly expressed has ceased to be true. And that, in instances such as I have given, the words *do* change their meaning according to the time at which they are uttered or thought of is, I think, evident. If I use now the words "I am in this room," these words certainly express (among other things) the idea that my being in this room is contemporary with my present use of the words; and if I were to use the same words tomorrow, they would express the idea that my being in this room tomorrow, was contemporary with the use of them *then.* And since my use of them then would not be the same fact as my use of them now, they would certainly then express a different idea from that which they express now. And in general, whenever we use the present tense in its primary sense, it seems to me plain that we do mean something different by it each time we use it. We always mean (among other things) to express the idea that a given event is contemporary with our actual use of it; and since our actual use of it on one occasion is always a different fact from our actual use of it on another, we express by it a different idea each time we use it. And similarly with the past and future tenses. If anybody had said in 1807 "Napoleon is dead," he would certainly have meant by these words something different from what I mean by them when I use them now. He would have meant that Napoleon's death occurred at a time previous to *his* use of those words; and this would not have been true. But in this fact there is nothing to show that if he *had* meant by them what I mean now, his idea would not have been as true then as mine is now. And so, if I say "It will rain tomorrow," these words have a different meaning today from what they would have if I used them tomorrow. What we mean by "tomorrow" is obviously a different day, when we use the word on one day, from what we mean by it when we use it on another. But in this there is nothing to show that if the idea, which I *now* mean by "It will rain tomorrow," *were* to occur again tomorrow, it would not be true then, if it is true now. All this is surely very obvious. But, if we take account of it, and if we concentrate our attention not on the words but on what is meant by them, is it so certain that what we mean by them on any one occasion ever changes from true to false? If there were to occur to me tomorrow the very same idea which I now express by the words "I am in this room," is it certain that this idea would not be as true then as it is now? It is perhaps true that the *whole* of what I mean by such a phrase as this never does recur. But part of it does, and that a part which is true. Part of what I mean is certainly identical with part of what I should mean tomorrow by saying, "I *was* in that room last night." And this part would be as true then, as it is now. And is there *any* part, which, if it were to recur at any time, would *not* then be true, though it is true now? In the case of all ideas or parts of ideas, which ever do actually recur, can we find a single instance of one, which is plainly true at one of the times when it occurs, and yet not true at another? I cannot think of any such instance. . . .

It seems to me, then, that if we mean by an idea, not mere words, but the kind of idea which words express, any idea, which is true at one time when it occurs, *would* be true at any time when it were to occur; and that this is so, even though it is an idea, which refers to facts which are mutable. My being in this room is a fact which is now, but which certainly has not been at every time and will not be at every time. And the words "I *am* in this room," though they express a truth now, would not have expressed one if I had used them yesterday, and will not if I use them tomorrow. But if we consider the idea which these words *now* express—namely, the idea of the connection of my being in this room with this particular time—it seems to me evident that anybody who had thought of that connection at any time in the past would have been thinking truly, and that anybody who were to think of it at any time in the future would be thinking truly. This seems to me to be the sense in which truths are immutable—in which no idea can change from true to false. And I think Professor James means to deny of truths generally, if not of all truths, that they are immutable even in this sense. If he does not mean this there seems nothing left for him to mean, when he says that truths are mutable, except (1) that some *facts* are mutable, and (2) that the same *words* may be true at one time and false at another. And it seems to me impossible that he could speak as he does, if he meant *nothing more* than these two things. I believe, therefore, that he is really thinking that ideas which have been once true (*ideas,* and not merely words) do sometimes afterwards become false: that the very same idea is at one time true and at another false. But he certainly gives no instance which shows that this does ever occur. And how far does he mean his principle to carry him? Does he hold that this idea that Julius Cæsar was murdered in the Senate-House, though true now, may, at some future time cease to be true, if it should be more profitable to the lives of future generations to believe that he died in his bed? Things like this are what his words seem to imply; and, even if he does hold that truths like this are *not* mutable, he never tries to tell us to what kinds of truths he would limit mutability, nor how they differ from such as this.

Questions

1. What are Professor Moore's arguments against the assertions that *all* true ideas are useful and that *all* useful ideas are true? How might William James have replied to Professor Moore in defense of these two assertions?

2. Do you think Professor Moore distorted James's intended meaning when the latter said: "The true is only the expedient in the way of our thinking. . . . And expedient in the long run and on the whole of course"? What are Professor Moore's objections to this passage? State why you agree, or disagree, with Professor Moore.

3. After reading both William James and Professor Moore, give your reasons for accepting, or rejecting, the statement, "Truth is mutable." Make clear what you take the statement to mean.

4. Analyze what you think the word "true" would mean if it were applied to each of the following statements. (If you think the word would have different meanings for different kinds of statements, make clear what these differences are.)

    a. Ice does not heat water.
    b. There is no whole number between 8 and 9.
    c. William James was an American.
    d. A four-sided triangle will never be discovered by man.
    e. As time goes by we all get older.
    f. A pound of iron does not weigh more than a pound of butter.
    g. Boys will be boys.

Suggested Further Reading	*Introductory Studies*

Berlin, Isaiah, *The Age of Enlightenment, The Eighteenth Century Philosophers,* New American Library, N. Y., 1956.

Hampshire, Stuart, *The Age of Reason, The Seventeenth Century Philosophers,* New American Library, N. Y., 1956.

Hospers, John, *An Introduction to Philosophical Analysis,* Prentice-Hall, Englewood Cliffs, N. J., 1953; especially Chaps. 2, "Necessary Knowledge"; 3, "Empirical Knowledge"; 4, "Law, Cause and Freedom"; and 6, "Perceiving the World."

Jones, W. T., *A History of Western Philosophy,* Harcourt, Brace, N. Y., 1952; especially Chaps. 23, "Descartes"; 26, "Locke"; 27, "Berkeley"; 28, "Hume"; and 30, "Kant."

MacNabb, D. G. C., *David Hume, His Theory of Knowledge and Morality,* Hutchinson's University Library, London, 1951.

O'Connor, D. J., *John Locke,* Penguin Books, Harmondsworth, Middlesex, Eng., 1952.

Richardson, Moses, *Fundamentals of Mathematics,* Macmillan, N. Y., 1954; especially Chaps. II, "Logic, Mathematics, and Science"; IX, "Analytic Geometry"; XVI, "Euclidean and Non-Euclidean Geometry"; and XVIII, "The Nature of Mathematics."

Russell, Bertrand, *The Problems of Philosophy,* Oxford University Press, N. Y., 1912.

Warnock, G. J., *Berkeley,* Penguin Books, Harmondsworth, Middlesex, Eng., 1953.

Weldon, Thomas D., *Introduction to Kant's Critique of Pure Reason,* Clarendon Press, Oxford, 1945.

Woozley, A. D., *Theory of Knowledge,* Hutchinson's University Library, London, 1949.

| *Advanced Studies*

Ayer, A. J., *The Problem of Knowledge,* Penguin Books, Harmondsworth, Middlesex, Eng., 1956; especially Chaps. 1, "Philosophy and Knowledge"; 2, "Scepticism and Certainty"; and 3, "Perception."

Buchler, Justus, ed., *The Philosophy of Peirce, Selected Writings,* Harcourt, Brace, N. Y., 1940.

Gallie, W. B., *Peirce and Pragmatism,* Penguin Books, Harmondsworth, Middlesex, Eng., 1952.

Haldane, Elizabeth S., and Ross, G. R. T., eds., *The Philosophical Works of Descartes,* Cambridge University Press, Cambridge, Eng., 1934, 2 vols., Vol. 2. This volume contains the "Objections and Replies," seven sets of exchanges between Descartes and some of his contemporaries, among them Thomas Hobbes and Pierre Gassendi, concerning the *Meditations.*

Lean, Martin E., *Sense-Perception and Matter,* Routledge and Kegan Paul, London, 1953.

Perry, Ralph Barton, *The Thought and Character of William James,* Little, Brown, Boston, 1936.

Reichenbach, Hans, *The Rise of Scientific Philosophy,* University of California Press, Berkeley, 1951.

Ryle, Gilbert, *The Concept of Mind,* Hutchinson's University Library, London, 1949.

Santayana, George, *Character and Opinion in the United States, with Reminiscences of William James and Josiah Royce and Academic Life in America,* Scribner's, N. Y., 1920.

Chapter Two

THE
PROBLEM
OF
Scientific Knowledge

The Two Kinds of Sciences

All scientific knowledge may be divided into the empirical sciences and the formal sciences. Physics, chemistry, and biology are examples of empirical sciences. Arithmetic, geometry, and algebra are examples of formal sciences. The distinction between these kinds of sciences is based on the differences in the proof of their statements. In an empirical science, the proof of its statements is based on an appeal to experiences which show that the statements correctly describe the world. In a formal science, the proof of its statements is based on an appeal to their consistency with the science's initial assumptions and definitions. This distinction between empirical and formal sciences is similar to Hume's distinction between matters of fact and relations of ideas (page 105) and Kant's distinction between synthetical and analytical judgments (page 123), with which the reader may already be familiar. When we speak of science or scientific knowledge here we shall mean the empirical sciences rather than the formal sciences. Having distinguished empirical and formal sciences, we must notice immediately an important connection between them. Mathematics, the principal family of formal sciences, is one of the tools regularly employed by the empirical scientist in his task of describing the world. The reader will notice that the connection between mathematics and empirical science is a recurring theme in the first three selections in this chapter.

The Problem of Scientific Knowledge

The problem of scientific knowledge is part of the larger problem of our knowledge of the world. The scientific notion of proof involves an appeal to sense experience; and the claim that the sciences give us genuine knowledge rests on the assumption that our sense perceptions inform us of the nature of the world. Thus perceptual knowledge is the foundation of all scientific knowledge, and unless our senses can be shown to be reliable, the claim that the sciences provide knowledge of the world cannot be justified. The reliability of perceptual knowledge is explored at some length in Chapter 1 of this book. The efforts of Locke, Berkeley, Hume, and James to justify our perceptual knowledge are all relevant to the problem of scientific knowledge. However, there are other important aspects of the problem of scientific knowledge, and the present chapter is devoted to these aspects.

The principal questions which we shall be concerned with in this chapter are these: What distinguishes a scientist's way of thinking about the world from other ways of thinking about it? What distinguishes scientific statements about the world from other kinds of statements? Besides perceptual knowledge, what other grounds does a scientist have for his knowledge, and are they good grounds? and, How does scientific knowledge of the world fit in with our everyday, or common sense, knowledge of the world? It is not the aim of this chapter to teach the reader a particular empirical science. Rather, its aim is to throw some light on the second-order question, "What is science?"

It may be profitable to work our way into the problem of scientific knowledge by reminding ourselves of some of the differences between common sense or a person's everyday knowledge of the world, and scientific knowledge. These differences may be only differences of degree, but nonetheless it will be instructive to notice them. The principal distinction between common sense knowledge and scientific knowledge appears to be that common sense is acquired in the ordinary business of living, but scientific knowledge must be pursued deliberately and systematically. This distinction gives rise to differences in point of view, in degree of refinement, and in method.

Despite its name, the viewpoint of common sense is individual; it varies according to person, place, and time. But the scientist aims at a universal point of view. He wants to describe the world in ways that are, in principle, comprehensible to anyone, anywhere, at any time. This difference in point of view is closely related to the difference in degree of refinement. Common sense is concerned with the obvious, with that which "leaps to the eye"; and, as a consequence, common sense knowledge can be expressed in words at the level of "earth," "air," "fire," "water," "animal," "vegetable," and "mineral." But the scientist in his search for a universal viewpoint must analyze the obvious and general by means of concepts that are sharply defined. As a consequence he requires a vocabulary of abstract words like "atom," "wave," "field," "element," "stratum," "cell," and "species." This difference in refinement leads us to say that common sense is vague while scientific knowledge is precise; and one aspect of the problem of scientific knowledge is a consideration of how its preciseness is obtained, and of the advantages and disadvantages of this preciseness.

The difference between common sense and scientific knowledge in degree of refinement is closely related to the presence of method in science and its absence in common sense. Scientists have established procedures for improving and increasing their knowledge of the world, so that yet another difference between science and common sense is one of controlled experiment against uncontrolled experience. The development of scientific knowledge is directed and systematic, while common sense just grows. Indeed, this methodological difference between common sense and science brings us back to the original distinction we noticed: Common sense knowledge seems just to come to us, but scientific knowledge must be pursued deliberately and systematically.

This comparison of scientific with common sense knowledge illuminates the questions which we said earlier characterize the problem of scientific knowledge. To get at the question of what distinguishes a scientist's way of thinking about the world, we must study scientific concepts and discover the ways in which they both differ from and resemble common sense concepts. To get at the question of what distinguishes scientific statements, we must examine the way in which the scientist uses his concepts to formulate his hypotheses. To get at the closely related question of the grounds for scientific statements, we must examine the scientist's method for confirming his hypotheses.

Survey of the Readings

The first two readings in this chapter deal with questions about the concepts with which scientific hypotheses are framed. In "The Nature of the A Priori," Professor C. I. Lewis discusses the way we bring order to our experiences by means of our concepts. His theme is the interplay between our minds and the world, the product of which is our knowledge of the world. Moritz Schlick's essay, "Causality in Everyday Life and in Recent Science," is an elucidation of the concept of causality. But the essay may also be read as a model of the way in which any scientific concept may be elucidated. In the third selection, "Hypotheses and Scientific Method," by Professors Morris R. Cohen and Ernest Nagel, the reader is introduced to the problems of hypothesis-making and hypothesis-confirming, and to the vexing question of what makes a good hypothesis. In the fourth and last selection, "The World of Science and the Everyday World," Professor Gilbert Ryle examines the apparent contradictions between scientific and common sense knowledge of the world. This selection

is a clarification of the ways in which we use both scientific and common sense concepts.

We have already noticed the way in which this chapter is connected with the preceding chapter, "The Problem of Knowledge of the World." The topics considered in this chapter are also closely related to those considered in Chapter 3, "The Problem of Meaning and Verification." Much of the philosophical discussion in recent years concerning the meaning of words and statements has arisen from a study of scientific knowledge and a comparison of the sciences with philosophy. The use of verification as a criterion of meaning, which will be explained in Chapter 3, is a direct result of philosophers' analyzing the distinctive nature of scientific statements.

1

The Nature of the A Priori

C. I. Lewis
(b. 1883)

Clarence Irving Lewis is a professor of philosophy at Harvard University. He has written two books of particular relevance to the problem of scientific knowledge: *Mind and the World Order* (1929) and *An Analysis of Knowledge and Valuation* (1946).

In this reading, Professor Lewis discusses the question of how an observer finds order in what he observes. He puts this question in language which would be appreciated by both Hume (page 98) and Kant (page 116), for he asks, "How does the mind bring order to the chaos of the given?"; and his answer to this question is his effort to solve a problem which was especially acute for these two philosophers.

The given is the chaos of colors, shapes, sounds, tastes, and feelings of which we become aware through our senses. Our minds impose order on these sensations of immediate experience, and enable us to perceive and understand them as a pattern of connected things and events. How do our minds construct an orderly world out of the chaos of our sensations? Professor Lewis answers: By means of our concepts and the rules for thinking with our concepts. These concepts and rules constitute "the a priori," that is, what must be known prior to sense experience in order for sense experience to take "shape." Put in other terms, the a priori consists of our category words and the rules for using them in describing and explaining what we experience. Some of our most basic category words are, for example, "thing" and "property" (or "characteristic"), "cause" and "effect," and "mind" and "body." But these category words lead a double life. For as well as there being a relation between words and the world, there is a relation between words and words, or to use Professor Lewis' terms, between concepts and concepts. This second aspect of the a priori is brought out in Professor Lewis' discussion of mathematics and logic. These are the so-called formal sciences, since the truth of any statement made within one of them depends on its form alone (i.e., the relation of concepts which it expresses). Professor Lewis' discussion of these a priori truths is of interest for two reasons. It serves to point up the difference between a priori truths and truths in the empirical sciences, and it is a preface to his analysis of what he calls "the a priori element" in the empirical sciences. The a priori element in the empirical sciences is an important aspect of what we have already referred to as the relation of words to the world. Professor Lewis finds the a priori in the theories of the empirical sciences, as we use these theories to guide us in "our attack upon the welter of experience." In reading this selection, the reader's main task is to make clear to himself exactly what Professor Lewis claims about the nature of the a priori and its role in the empirical sciences.

This selection is the major part of Chapter VIII, "The Nature of the A Priori, and the Pragmatic Element in Knowledge," from *Mind and the World Order,* first published in 1929.

From *Mind and the World Order* by C. I. Lewis, reprinted through permission by Dover Publications, Inc., New York 10, N. Y. ($1.95, paperbound).

In experience, mind is confronted with the chaos of the given. In the interest of adaptation and control, it seeks to discover within or impose upon this chaos some kind of stable order, through which distinguishable items may become the signs of future possibilities. Those patterns of distinction and relationship which we thus seek to establish are our concepts. These must be determined in advance of the particular experience to which they apply in order that what is given may have meaning. Until the criteria of our interpretation have been fixed, no experience could be the sign of anything or even answer any question. Concepts thus represent what mind brings to experience. That truth which is a priori rises from the concept itself. This happens in two ways. In the first place, there is that kind of truth, exemplified most clearly by pure mathematics, which represents the elaboration of concepts in the abstract, without reference to any particular application to experience. Second, the concept in its application to the given exhibits the predetermined principles of interpretation, the criteria of our distinguishing and relating, of classification, and hence the criteria of reality of any sort. This is most clearly evident in the case of those basic concepts, determining major classes of the real, which may be called the categories, though in less important ways it holds true of concepts in general.

For both these ways in which the truth is fixed, independently of experience or in advance of it, it represents the explication or elaboration of the concept itself. *The a priori is not a material truth, delimiting or delineating the content of experience as such, but is definitive or analytic in its nature.*

Since it is a truth about our own interpretative attitude, it imposes no limitation upon the future possibilities of experience; that is a priori which we can maintain in the face of all experience, come what will. And although it represents the contribution of the mind itself to knowledge, it does not require that this mind be universal, absolute, or a reality of a higher order than the object of its knowledge. The a priori does not need to be conceived as the inscrutable legislation of a transcendent mind, the objects of which, being limited by its forms of intuition, are phenomenal only. Hence the distinction of the legislative mind as ultimate reality from its object which is not thus ultimate falls away, and with it the difficulty of knowing the mind and of recognizing what is a priori as that which is determined by our own active attitude. The a priori is knowable simply through the reflective and critical formulation of our own principles of classification and interpretation. Such legislation can be recognized as our own act because the a priori principle which is definitive, and not a material truth of the content of experience, *has alternatives.* It can be recognized as due to the mind itself by the ordinary criteria of responsibility in general—that a different mode of acting is possible and makes a discoverable difference. Where there is no possibility of refraining from our act or acting otherwise, there can be no discoverable activity—indeed, there is no act. . . . What can be known to be a priori must meet the apparently contradictory requirements that it may be known in advance to hold good for all experience and that it have alternatives. The principle of classification or interpretation meets these requirements, because the alternative to a definition or a rule is not its falsity but merely its abandonment in favor of some other. Thus the determination of the a priori is in some sense like free choice and deliberate action.

If the a priori is something made by mind, mind may also alter it. There will be no assurance that what is a priori will remain fixed and absolute throughout the history of the race or for the developing individual. From the point of view here presented, this is no difficulty at all but the explanation of an interesting historical fact. The rationalist prejudice of an absolute human reason, universal to all men and to all time, has created an artificially exalted and impossible conception of the categories as fixed and unalterable modes of mind. One result has been to limit the usefulness of the conception, so that what we could call, in ordinary parlance, "the categories of physics" or "the categories of biology" would not serve as examples of "the categories" because it is obvious that the fundamental principles and concepts of any natural science change progressively with its development. This, in turn, has served to obscure the large and important part played in science by that element of categorial order which cannot be determined by merely empirical fact but must be provided by the scientist himself in his setting of the problem and fixing the criteria by which the meaning of experimental findings is to be interpreted. Thus the most impressive examples of human knowledge have been too little drawn upon in discussions of epistemology.

The assumption that our categories are fixed for all time by an original human endowment is a superstition comparable to the belief of primitive peoples that the general features of their life and culture are immemorial and of supernatural origin. The grand divisions of our thought-world differ from those of our early ancestors as our modern machines differ from their primitive artifacts and our geographical and astronomical outlook from their world bounded by a distant mountain range or the pillars of Hercules and shut up under the bowl of the sky. Certain fundamental categories are doubtless very ancient and permanent: thing and property, cause and effect, mind and body, and the relations of valid inference, doubtless have their counterparts wherever and whenever the human mind has existed. But even here, the supposition of complete identity and continuity is at variance with facts which should be obvious.

For all primitive peoples, for example, and for some who distinctly are not primitive, the properties of a thing are not localized in time and space, as for us. Almost anything may be a talisman or fetish, whose action takes place (without intermediaries) at a distance and in a time posterior to its destruction by fire or by being eaten. Things also have doubles, inscrutably operating in that other-world whose influence mysteriously interpenetrates the realm which we call "nature." Furthermore, the long-persistent problem in physics of action at a distance increasingly comes back to haunt us and to unite with new problems of physical interpretation which threaten to drive us once more to dissipate the "material thing" throughout all time and space; to find its manifestation and even its very being in a spatio-temporal spread of events indefinitely extended.

That the present distinction of mind and body corresponds only roughly with that division in ancient thought, that body of inert matter and mind which does not occupy space are no older than the advent of that esoteric doctrine which dawned in Europe with the Greek mysteries and Christianity—this can hardly escape us. This mode of distinction contrasts with the tripartite division into body, mind, and spirit, and with the five-fold and *n*-fold divisions of more easterly cultures. It is also obvious that the pressure of modern science in the field of biology, and our present uneasiness about this twofold nature of the individual augur some departure from the clarity of Cartesian dualism.

The *names* of our categories may be very old and stable, but the *concepts,* the modes of classifying and interpreting which they represent, undergo progressive alteration with the advance of thought. . . .

It will be well to make clear that the conception here presented does not imply that because the a priori is something made by mind and capable of alteration, it is therefore arbitrary in the sense of being capriciously determined. That it is not, and cannot be, determined by the given, does not imply that it answers to no criteria whatever. That type of a priori truth which pure mathematics illustrates—that is, the elaboration of concepts in abstraction from all questions of particular applications—answers only to the criteria of self-consistency. Just to the extent that the development of such a purely analytic system is withdrawn from every consideration of useful application, its truth is simply truth to the original meanings embodied in its basic concepts. But when concepts are intended to be applied in experience, and a priori principles are to determine modes of classification and interpretation, the case is different. Here mind is still uncompelled by any possible content of experience. But knowledge has a practical business to perform, the interests of action which it seeks to serve. The mode of the mind's activity answers to our need to understand, in the face of an experience always more or less baffling, and of our need to control. There is also another factor which helps to determine what modes of attempted comprehension will be most easily and most widely useful. While that absolute human reason which the rationalist supposes to be completely and universally possessed by every human is a myth, nevertheless man, being a species of animal, has characteristics which mark him as such, and some of these at least are reflected in the bent of human thought. Some modes of thought are simpler and come more naturally to us than others which still are possible and which might, indeed, be called upon if an enlarged experience should sufficiently alter our problems—just as some modes of bodily translation are more easy and natural, though these may be somewhat altered when the environment includes a sufficient number of automobiles and airplanes. Moreover, the fundamental likeness in our modes of thought, which represents whatever community of nature marks our original mental endowment, is continually enhanced by the fact that the needs of individual humans are mostly served by coöperation with others. "The human mind" is distinctly a social product, and our categories will reflect that fact.

In brief, while the a priori is dictated neither by what is presented in experience nor by any transcendent and eternal factor of human nature, it still answers to criteria of the general type which may be termed pragmatic. The human animal with his needs and interests confronts an experience in which these must be satisfied, if at all. Both the general character of the experience and the nature of the animal will be reflected in the mode of behavior which marks this attempt to realize his ends. This will be true of the categories of his thinking as in other things. And here, as elsewhere, the result will be reached by a process in which attitudes tentatively assumed, disappointment in the ends to be realized, and consequent alteration of behavior will play their part.

Confirmation of this conception of the a priori could only come from comprehensive and detailed examination of at least the major categories of thought and the underlying principles of common-sense and scientific explanation. Such a task cannot be undertaken here; at most only a few illustrations can be offered with the hope that they are typical.

The paradigm of the a priori in general is the definition. It has always been clear that the simplest and most obvious case of truth which can be known in advance of experience is the explicative proposition and those consequences of definition which can be derived by purely logical analysis. These are necessarily true, true under all possible circumstances, because definition is legislative. Not only is the meaning assigned to words more or less a matter of choice—that consideration is relatively trivial—but the manner in which the precise classifications which definition embodies shall be affected, is something not dictated by experience. If experience were other than it is, the definition and its corresponding classification might be inconvenient, useless, or fantastic, but it could not be false. Mind makes classifications and determines meanings; in so doing, it creates that truth without which there could be no other truth.

Traditionally propositions which have been recognized as analytic have often not been classed with the a priori; they have been regarded as too unimportant; sometimes they have even been repudiated as not truth at all but merely verbal statements. The main reasons for this cavalier attitude have been two; in the first place, it has been overlooked that the real itself is a matter of definition and that the dichotomy of real and unreal is that first and basic classification which the mind confronted with experience must make. And second, the powerful sweep and consequence of purely logical analysis has not been understood.

The clearest example of this power of analysis is to be found, of course, in mathematics. The historical importance of mathematics as a paradigm of a priori truth needs no emphasis. Almost one may say that traditional conceptions of the a priori are the historical shadow of Euclidean geometry. But in mathematics much water has gone under the bridge since the time of Kant, and in the light of the changes which have come about, these traditional conceptions are proved totally impossible. The course of this development will be familiar to the reader; only the outstanding features of it need be mentioned.

Though there are anticipations of current mathematical conceptions as far back as Plato, the movement which led to their present acceptance dates principally from the discovery of the non-Euclidean geometries. In developing these systems, it was obviously impossible to depend on intuitions of space, either pure or empirical. If Euclid is true of our space, then no one of these geometries can be; and if Euclid is not true and certain, then the main ground of the supposition that we can rely on intuitions of the spatial is discredited.[1] Hence in developing the non-Euclidean systems, all constructions such as helping-lines, and any step in proof which should depend not upon pure logic but upon the character of space must be dispensed with. If a step in proof cannot be taken by rigorous logic alone, it cannot be taken at all. When it was found thus possible to develop the non-Euclidean systems without appeal to any extralogical aids, a similar revision of Euclid was carried out, eliminating all explicit or implicit reliance upon constructions, superpositions or other appeal to spatial intuition. This new method, together with certain indicated generalizations, constituted the so-called "modern geometry."

Next it was demonstrated that not only geometry but other branches as well can be developed by the deductive method, from a relatively few assumptions, and likewise without reliance upon empirical data. As a result all pure mathematics is found to be abstract, in the sense of being independent of any particular application. Because if all the theorems follow logically from the definitions and postulates, then we can alter at will what we let the terms, such as "point" and "line," denote without in the least disturbing any step in the proofs. *Whatever* "point" and "line" may mean, given these assumptions about them, these consequences—the rest of the system—must also hold of them,

---

[1] Euclid and a non-Euclidean system cannot both be true of space while corresponding denotations of terms are maintained. The discovery that they may both become true of space with systematic difference in the denotation of terms played its part in the logic of modern geometry.

since the theorems follow from the assumptions by rigorous and purely logical deduction.

The question of the truth of the mathematical system *in application* was thus completely separated from its mathematical or logical integrity. Still further changes went along with this. The "truth" of initial assumptions lost all meaning in any other sense than their exhibition of certain patterns of logical relationship to be adhered to throughout. The distinguishing assumptions of a non-Euclidean geometry, for example, so far from being self-evident, were supposedly mere arbitrary falsehoods with respect to their most obvious empirical denotation. The term "axiom" was replaced by "postulate" or "primitive proposition." In the interest of logical simplicity alternative sets of assumptions which would give the same system of propositions were investigated. What should be initially assumed and what proved became a question merely of such logical simplicity. It became customary to speak of the truth of mathematics as hypothetical or to say that what mathematics asserts is only the relation of implication between postulates and theorems. It is truth about certain patterns of logical relationship established by initial definition or postulate.

Further, it became clear that the distinction between those assumptions of the form called "definitions" and those termed "postulates" was relatively arbitrary and unimportant. Logically it makes little difference except for simplicity of procedure, how far the order of a system is set up by propositions in which "is" means logical equivalence and how far by those in which it means only the one-way implication of concepts or subsumption of classes. Since the content of the concepts of pure mathematics is simply that order to which they give rise, that manner of development in which essential relationships are exhibited as the definitive meaning of the concepts is truest to the nature of the subject.

The completion of this last refinement of mathematical method was made by Whitehead and Russell in "Principia Mathematica." It was here proved that the initial assumptions of mathematics can all be dispensed with, except the definitions. The truths of mathematics follow merely from definitions which exhibit the meaning of its concepts, by purely logical deduction. Judgment of such mathematical truth is, thus, completely and exclusively analytic; no synthetic judgment, a priori or otherwise, is requisite to knowledge of pure mathematics. The content of the subject consists entirely of the rigorous logical analysis of abstract concepts, in entire independence of all data of sense or modes of intuition. The definitions which embody these concepts are not required to be true in any other sense than that they should be precise and clear; the formulation of them represents an act of mind which is legislative or creative and in some sense arbitrary; it answers to no criteria save self-consistency and adequacy to whatever purposes the elaboration of the system itself may be supposed to satisfy. It may still be true that "concepts without precepts are empty," but it must be granted that there is a kind of knowledge of "empty" concepts. Or at least such admission can be avoided only by a restriction of the term "knowledge" to exclude pure mathematics and logic. The importance of such a priori analytic knowledge is witnessed by the basic character of these subjects for all other sciences.

Pure mathematics stands between logic on the one side and the empirical application of mathematics on the other. Logic is in some respects the illustration *par excellence* of the a priori, since its laws are the most completely general of any. The laws of logic cannot be proved unless they should first be taken for granted as the principles of their own demonstration. They make explicit the basic principles of all interpretation and of our general modes of classification. And they impose no limitation upon the content of experience. Sometimes we are asked to tremble before the specter of the "alogical" in order that we may thereafter rejoice that we are saved from this by the dependence of reality upon mind. But the "alogical" is pure bogey, a word without a meaning. What kind of experience could defy the principle that everything must either be or not be, that nothing can both be and not be, or that if X is Y and Y is Z, then X is Z? If anything imaginable or unimaginable could violate such laws, then the ever-present fact of change would do it every day. The laws of logic are purely formal; they forbid nothing but what concerns the use of terms and the corresponding modes of classification and analysis. The law of contradiction tells us that nothing can be both white and not white, but it does not and can not tell us whether black is not white or soft or square is not white. To discover what contradicts what we must turn to more particular considerations. Similarly the law of the excluded middle formulates our decision that whatever is not designated by a certain term shall be designated by its negative. It declares our purpose to make, for every name, a complete dichotomy of experience, instead—as we might choose—of classifying on the basis of a tripartite division into opposites and a middle ground between the two. Our rejection of such tripartite division represents only our penchant for simplicity and similar considerations.

Further laws of logic are of like significance. They are principles of procedure, the parliamentary rules of intelligent thought and action. Such laws are independent of the given because they impose no limitations whatever upon it. They are legislative because they are addressed to ourselves—because definition, classification, and inference represent no operation in the world of things, but only our categorial attitudes of mind.

Furthermore, the ultimate criteria of the laws of logic are pragmatic. Indeed, how could they be anything else? The truth of logic is not material truth but a truth about the modes of self-consistency. Since this is so, logic must be the test of its *own* consistency, and hence of its own truth, as well as the test of the consistency of everything else. But if logic tests its own truth, then what can be the test of truth in a genuine issue of logic, which is not a question of mere inadvertence on one side or the other? Those who suppose that there is *a* logic which everyone would agree to if he understood it and understood himself, are more optimistic than those versed in the history of logical discussion have a right to be. The fact is that there are several logics, markedly different, each self-consistent *in its own terms* and such that whoever, using it, avoids false premises, will never reach a false conclusion. Mr. Russell, for example, bases *his* logic on an implication relation such that if twenty sentences be cut from a newspaper and put in a hat, and then two of these be drawn at random, one of them will certainly imply the other, and it is an even chance that the implication will be mutual. Yet upon a foundation so remote from ordinary modes of inference the whole structure of "Principia Mathematica" is built. This logic is utterly self-consistent and valid in its own terms. There are others even more strange of which the same may be said. Genuine issues of logic are those which stand above such questions of the merely self-critical integrity of the logical system. There are such issues, and these cannot be determined—nay, cannot even be argued—except on pragmatic grounds of human bent and intellectual convenience. That we have been blind to this fact, and that much good paper and ink has been wasted by logicians who have tried to argue on some other grounds what are only questions of convenience or of value, itself reflects traditional errors in the conception of the a priori.

Pure mathematics and logic exemplify that type of the a priori which have the highest degree of abstraction from experience—whose concepts are so general that we may call them "empty." Concerning these, there may be a question whether there will not be issues of an entirely different sort when we attempt to apply them in experience. One may say, for example, that when geometry becomes abstract and freed from all necessary reference to our intuitions of the spatial, the question of the *truth about space* becomes an entirely separate one, and one with respect to which there must be reference to forms of intuition or something of the sort, or there will be nothing which is determinable a priori at all. Similarly one may say that if arithmetic as a purely abstract deductive system has no necessary reference to the character of countable objects, then its a priori truth is of no value for the anticipation of the behavior of concrete things. This will be true, of course, and of importance. If there should be a priori truth *only* with respect to concepts in utter abstraction from experience, and if this a priori character were to vanish when these concepts are given a concrete denotation, then the significance of the a priori for the natural sciences and for common practice would be largely, if not completely, lost.

But there *is* an a priori truth of concepts which have concrete denotation. Let us consider the example of arithmetic. Arithmetic depends *in toto* upon the operation of counting or correlating, a procedure which can be carried out in any world containing identifiable things, regardless of the further characters of experience. Mill challenged this a priori character of arithmetic. He asked us to suppose a demon sufficiently powerful and maleficent so that every time two things were brought together with two other things, this demon should always introduce a fifth. The conclusion which he supposed to follow is that under such circumstances $2 + 2 = 5$ would be a universal law of arithmetic. But Mill was quite mistaken. In such a world we should be obliged to become a little clearer than is usual about the distinction between arithmetic and physics, that is all. If two black marbles were put in the same box with two white ones, the demon could take his choice of colors, but it would be evident that there were more black marbles or more white ones than were put in. The same would be true of all objects in any wise identifiable. We should simply find ourselves in the presence of an extraordinary physical law, which we should recognize as universal in our world, that whenever two things were brought into proximity with two others, an additional and similar thing was always created by the process. Mill's world would be physically most extraordinary. The world's work would be enormously facilitated if hats or locomotives or tons of coal could be thus multiplied by anyone possessed originally of two pairs. But the laws of mathematics would not be affected. It is because this is true that arithmetic is a priori. Its laws prevent *nothing;* they are compatible with anything which happens or could conceivably happen in nature. They are true in any possible world. Mathematical addition is not a physical transformation. The only bringing together it implies is in the mind; if translation in general affected numerical alteration, we should always count things *in situ,* but we should count and add as usual. Physical changes which result in an increase or decrease of the countable things involved are matters of everyday occurrence. Such physical processes present us with phenomena in which the purely mathematical has to be separated out by analysis. It is because we shall always separate out that part of the phenomenon not in conformity with arithmetic and designate it by some other category—physical change, chemical reaction, optical illusion—that arithmetic is a priori. *Its laws constitute criteria of our categorial classification and interpretation.* As this example serves to illustrate, such categorial interpretation of the concrete and empirical throws out of court whatever would otherwise violate the a priori principles which embody the category, but it does not thereby legislate anything phenomenal out of existence.

Perhaps, however, we have gone too far. Mill's illustration is of an alteration of experience in general which is too simple and too poorly carried out to make it plausible that our categorial interpretation would be different in such a world. But if translation in general affected numerical alteration then an entirely different mode of categorial interpretation might better serve the purposes. Our present categories would not—*could* not—be prohibited but other modes might more simply reduce the phenomenal to order and facilitate control. Or in such a world, arithmetic might be confined to mental phenomena— since these would be exempt from the effects of change of place—and numerical principles would be laws of psychology. If we were jelly-fish in a liquid world, we should probably not add at all, because the useful purposes served by such conceptions would be so slight. Still if some super-jelly-fish should invent arithmetic by a *jeu d'esprit* (as Hamilton invented quaternions) he would find nothing in any possible experience to controvert it, and he might with some profit apply it to his own distinct ideas. . . .

The a priori element in natural sciences goes much deeper than might be supposed. All order of sufficient importance to be worthy of the name of law depends eventually upon some ordering by mind. Without initial principles by which we guide our attack upon the welter of experience, it would remain forever chaotic and refractory. In every science there are fundamental laws which are a priori because they formulate just such definitive concepts or categorial tests by which alone investigation becomes possible.

A good example of this is to be found in Einstein's little book "Relativity." [2] The question under discussion is the criteria of simultaneity for events at a distance. Suppose the lightning strikes a railroad track at two places, *A* and *B*. How shall we tell whether these events happen at the same time? "We . . . require a definition of simultaneity such that this definition supplies us with a method by which . . . we can decide whether or not the lightning strokes occurred simultaneously. As long as this requirement is not satisfied, I allow myself to be deceived as a physicist (and of course the same applies if I am not a physicist) when I imagine that I am able to attach a meaning to the statement of simultaneity. . . .

"After thinking the matter over for some time you then offer the following suggestion with which to test simultaneity. By measuring along the rails, the connecting line *A B* should be measured up and an observer placed at the mid-point *M* of the distance *A B*. This observer should be supplied with an arrangement (*e. g.,* two mirrors inclined at 90°) which allows him visually to observe both places *A* and *B* at the same time. If the observer perceives the two flashes at the same time, they are simultaneous.

"I am very pleased with this suggestion, but for all that I cannot regard the matter as quite settled, because I feel constrained to raise the following objection: 'Your definition would certainly be right, if I only knew that the light by means of which the observer at *M* perceives the lightning flashes travels along the length *A–M* with the same velocity as along the length *B–M*. But an examination of this supposition would only be possible if we already had at our disposal the means of measuring time. It would thus appear as though we were moving here in a logical circle.'

"After further consideration you cast a somewhat disdainful glance at me—and rightly so—and you declare: 'I maintain my previous definition nevertheless because in reality it assumes nothing whatever about light. There is only *one* demand to be made of the definition of simultaneity, namely, that in every real case it must supply us with an empirical decision as to whether or not the conception which has to be defined is fulfilled. That light requires the same time to traverse the path *A–M* as for the path *B–M* is in reality *neither a supposition nor a hypothesis* about the physical nature of light, but a *stipulation* which I can make of my own free-will in order to arrive at a definition of simultaneity.' . . . We are thus led to a definition of 'time' in physics."

As this example well illustrates, we cannot even ask the questions which discovered law would answer until we have first by a priori stipulation formulated definitive criteria. Such concepts are not verbal definitions nor classifica-

[2] Pp. 26-28: italics are the author's.

tions merely; they are themselves laws which prescribe a certain behavior to whatever is thus named. Such definitive laws are a priori; only so can we enter upon the investigation by which further laws are sought. Yet it should also be pointed out that such a priori laws are subject to abandonment if the structure which is built upon them does not succeed in simplifying our interpretation of phenomena. If, in the illustration given, the relation "simultaneous with," as defined, should not prove transitive—if event *A* should prove simultaneous with *B* and *B* with *C,* but not *A* with *C*—this definition would certainly be rejected.

Indeed *all* definitions and *all* concepts exercise this function of prescribing fundamental law to whatever they denote, because everything which has a name is to be identified with certainty only over some stretch of time. The definition provides criteria of the thing defined which, in application, become necessary or essential laws of its behavior. This is especially evident in the case of scientific definitions because the "things" of science are of a deep-lying sort, representing uniformities of behavior of a high order. If definition is unsuccessful, as early scientific definitions mostly have been, it is because the classification thus set up corresponds with no natural cleavage and does not correlate with sufficiently important uniformities of behavior. Early attempts to reduce phenomena to law are based upon the "things" of common-sense which represent classification according to properties which are relatively easy of direct observation and impressive to the senses. When such attempts fail, it is largely because of this superficiality of initial classification. The alchemist's definitions of the elements, for example, are the clue to his indifferent success; the definitive properties pick out amorphous groups which have little significance of further uniformity. Not until such crucial properties as combining weights become the basis of classification is it possible to arrive at satisfactory laws of chemistry. The earlier definitions can not be said to have been false; they were merely useless, or insufficient to the purposes in hand. A large part of the scientific search is, thus, for *things worth naming.*

We have reached a point today where we understand that the typical procedure of science is neither deduction from what is self-evident or relatively certain nor direct generalization from experience. If any one method is more characteristic of science than another it is that of hypothesis and verification. But we seem still to overlook the fact that the *terms* in which hypothesis and law are framed themselves represent a scientific achievement. We still suffer from the delusion that fixed and eternal categories of human thought on the one side are confronted with equally fixed and given "things" on the other. Is it not obvious, to dispassionate observation, that scientific categories and classifications are subject to progressive modification or even abrupt alteration, and that these have a directive and controlling influence upon the other phases of scientific research? And here, too, as in hypothesis and verification, the development takes place, not by logical derivation from antecedent principles nor by direct formulation of empirical content, but by the hazarding of something by the mind and its retention or repudiation according to the success or nonsuccess of what is based upon it. The test of success here is not, however, simple conformity with experience, as in the testing of hypothesis, but is the achievement of intelligible order amongst the phenomena in question, and responds also to such criteria as intellectual simplicity, economy, and comprehensiveness of principle.

The reader will perhaps feel that, in so far as this is true, what is here represented as a priori is nothing of the sort but is merely something that we learn from experience. But if so, I hope that he will reread the illustration from Einstein, with due regard for the logic of it. However much the give and take between the purposes of science and discovered fact may contribute to alter the procedure by which those aims are sought, and may induce new basic principles and categories, still the naming, classifying, defining activity is at each step prior to the investigation. We cannot even interrogate experience without a network of categories and definitive concepts. Until our meanings are definite and our classifications are fixed, experience cannot conceivably determine anything. We must first be in possession of criteria which tell us what experience would answer what questions, and how, before observation or experiment could tell us anything.

The uniformities which science seeks are of a high order and represent a further reach of those same purposes exhibited on a humbler scale by the uniformities of common-sense comprehension. The categorizing and classifying activity of thought is, thus, more deliberate and self-conscious in the case of science and, by comparison, easier to observe than in the case of common sense. Because scientific categories are in some part built upon more basic distinction, the functioning of them as criteria of the real is less frequent and perhaps less important. It is, nevertheless, sometimes to be observed in the interplay between new principles of scientific interpretation and residual phenomena which are unexplained or reports of observation which are regarded as possibly involving error. If Röntgen had been unable to repeat the experience in which he first saw the bones of his hand, that perception would have been discredited. Because no one but their discoverer could see the "N-rays" with any assurance, and it was found that he saw them when the refracting prism was removed as well as with it, they were discarded as illusory. The phenomena of hypnotism remained for a long time in the limbo of the dubious, and even today offer a difficult problem of separation of veridical phenomenon from illusion, self-deception and the like. The phenomena of "dual personality" would challenge a very fundamental category if only there were not so much doubt about what it is that is "dual" and whether it is genuinely dual. To choose a different sort of example, when the eclipse-photographs which figured in the discussion of relativity were examined, the question was raised whether the star-displacements as measured on them represented simply the bending of light-rays or were due in part to halation of the sensitive film. Thus, for a moment at least, so fundamental a problem as that of abandoning the categories of independent space and time was intertwined with the question whether the position of dots on a photographic plate represented authentic star-photographs or was due to something which took place inside the camera.

What needs to be observed here is at once the continuity of scientific problems of a high order with the apparently simple and fundamental criteria of the real, and the fact that such decisions of reality or unreality are themselves interpretations involving principles of the same order as scientific law. They are such as forbid, for example, the nonbiological transformations and nonphysical successions which occur in dreams. A mouse which disappears where there is no hole is no real mouse; a landscape which recedes as we approach is but illusion. The reality of an object of a particular sort is determined by a certain uniformity of its behavior in experience. The formulation of this uniformity is of the type of natural law. So far, such laws are a priori—for this particular sort of thing; the experience which fails to conform to the law is repudiated as nonveridical.

This situation is most paradoxical; principles of the order of natural law are reached by some generalization from experience—that is, from *veridical* experience; there are no generalizations whatever to be had from the unsorted experience of real and unreal both. But what experience is *veridical,* is determined by the criterion of law. Which is first, then; does the content of experience validate the law or does the law validate the experience in attesting its veridical character? The answer is that the law is first precisely so long as and so far as we are prepared to maintain it as criterion of the real. But the "reality" which is in question is likely to be of a highly specific sort. The authentic photograph of stars and the picture affected by halation, for example, are both real, both physically real, both photographs even, in a certain sense. What is an "authentic photograph" has to be very precisely defined in the case in point and is so defined as to exclude the effect of light reflection from the back of the glass of the photographic plate. The manner of this definition or classification obviously will require a correlation of photograph and thing photographed of the type set forth in certain physical laws. In the particular case, failure to exhibit such lawful relationship condemns the phenomenon as not authentic or not real—that is, not really this very specific sort of thing.

Thus all concepts, and not simply those we should call "categories," function as criteria of reality. Every criterion of classification is criterion of reality of some particular sort. There is no such thing as reality in general; to be real, a thing must be a particular sort of real. Furthermore, what is a priori criterion of reality in one connection may be merely empirical law in some other—for example, the law correlating photograph and thing photographed, or the law of the behavior of solid bodies in translation which condemns the mouse that disappears without a hole, or the laws of perspective which exclude a landscape which recedes as we approach it. *The determination of reality, the classification of phenomena, and the discovery of law, all grow up together.* I will not repeat what has already been said so often about the logical priority of criteria; but it should be observed that this is entirely compatible with the shift of categories and classifications with the widening of human experience. If the criteria of the real are a priori, that is not to say that no conceivable character of experience would lead to alteration of them.

For example, spirits cannot be photographed. But if photographs of spiritistic phenomena, taken under properly guarded conditions, should become sufficiently frequent, this a priori dictum would be called in question. What we should do would be to redefine our terms. Whether "spook" was spirit or matter, whether the definition of "spirit" or of "matter" should be changed; all this would constitute one interrelated problem.

What would prove to you that the relative motion of a body effected a foreshortening of it and altered its mass? If the answer is "no conceivable experience" and you are able to formulate a definition of "mass," a conception of motion, and of ideally exact measurement in terms that do not conflict with one another and with your other physical conceptions, there is no possible ground on which you could be proven wrong. To a mind sufficiently resolute for an independent space and time, no possible experience could prove the principles of relativity. The question, "How long shall we persist in holding to our previous categories, when confronted with star-photographs and the displacement of spectrum-lines (or with spiritistic phenomena or evidence of telepathy)?" is one which has no general answer. A stubborn conservatism can be proved unreasonable only on the pragmatic ground that another method of categorial analysis more successfully reduces all experience of the type in question to order and law. Confronting such a problem, we should reopen together the question of definition or classification, of criteria for this sort of real, and of natural law. And the solution of one of these would probably mean the solution of all. Nothing could *force* a redefinition of "spirit" or of "matter." A sufficiently fundamental relation to human bent or to human interests would guarantee continuance unaltered even in the face of unintelligible and baffling experience. And no equipment of categories and concepts which the mind is likely to achieve will enable us to understand experience completely and in every respect. In such problems, the mind finds itself uncompelled save by its own purposes and needs. What is fixed datum and must be conformed to, is only that welter of the given in which not even the distinction of real and unreal is yet made. The rest is completely and exclusively our problem of interpretation. I *may* categorize experience as I will; but what categorial distinctions will best serve my interests and objectify my own intelligence? What the mixed and troubled experience will be—that is beyond me. But what I shall do with it—that is my own question, when the character of experience is before me. I am coerced only by my own need to understand.

It would indeed be inappropriate to characterize as a priori a law which we are prepared to alter in the light of further experience even though in an isolated case we should discard as nonveridical any experience which failed to conform. But the crux of the matter lies in this; beyond such principles as those of logic and pure mathematics whose permanent stability seems attested, there must be further and more particular criteria of the real prior to any investigation of nature. Such definitions, fundamental principles and criteria the mind itself must supply before experience can even begin to be intelligible. These represent more or less deep-lying attitudes, which the human mind has taken in the light of its total experience up to date. But a newer and wider experience may bring about some alteration of these attitudes even though by themselves they dictate nothing as to the content of experience, and no experience can conceivably prove them invalid.

It is the a priori element in knowledge which is thus pragmatic, not the empirical. The pragmatists generally have neglected to make the separation of concept and immediacy, with the result that they seem to put all truth at once at the mercy of experience and within the power of human decision or in a relation of dependence upon the human mind. But this would be an attempt to have it both ways. The sense in which facts are brute and given cannot be the sense in which the truth about them is made by mind or alterable to human needs. To be sure, this a priori element in knowledge runs very deep; it is present whenever there is classification, interpretation, or the distinction of real from unreal—which means that it is present in all knowledge. So I suppose it must be admitted, in the last analysis, that there can be no more fundamental ground than the pragmatic for a truth of any sort. Nothing—not even direct perception—can force the abandonment of an interpretive attitude, nor indeed *should* move us to such abandonment (since illusion or mistake is always possible) except some demand or purpose of the mind itself. But certain important ends, such as intellectual consistency and economy, completeness of comprehension, and simplicity of interpretation, occupy a place so much higher, for the long-run satisfaction of our needs in general, that they rightfully take precedence over any purpose which is merely personal or transitory. In the popular mind especially, pragmatism too often seems to connote the validity of rather superficial and capricious attitudes—for instance, the justification of belief from no deeper ground than personal desire. It is this insufficient regard for intellectual integrity, this tendency to trench upon high-plane purposes from low-plane motives which marks the kind of "pragmatism" which is to be eschewed. We must all be pragmatists, but pragmatists in the end, not in the beginning.

Questions

1. According to Professor Lewis, a priori truth "imposes no limitation upon the future possibilities of experience." What does he mean by this, and what reasons does he give for saying it?

2. How does Professor Lewis criticize the doctrine that a priori categories remain fixed and absolute?

3. Explain in your own words why geometry is not an empirical science.

4. What is wrong with the following argument?

"We add two apples and two apples and get four apples. Then we add two oranges and two oranges and get four oranges. We do this with other things besides apples and oranges, and we find that every time we add two things to two other things, we get four things. Therefore '2 + 2 = 4' is a generalization from experience, that is, an empirical truth."

5. How does the "success" of a concept or definition in science differ from the truth of a scientific hypothesis? (You may refer to the reading by Professors Cohen and Nagel, beginning on page 210, in answering this question.)

6. According to Professor Lewis, what is the role of the a priori element in knowledge in determining whether something is "real"?

7. Show how Einstein's discussion of the criteria of simultaneity for events at a distance is an illustration of the a priori element in physics.

8. Metaphysics has sometimes been distinguished from science on the ground that metaphysics tells us about the nature of *reality in general,* while science tells us only about this or that real particular object or event. If this were the nature of metaphysics, what would Professor Lewis be likely to say about metaphysics?

9. After reading the selection by William James in Chapter 1 (page 142), show how the pragmatism of Professor Lewis differs from that of James.

10. "It is the a priori element in knowledge which is thus pragmatic, not the empirical." Summarize the main points of the argument which leads Professor Lewis to this conclusion.

11. How is Professor Lewis' account of the nature of the a priori an answer to the problem of synthetical a priori judgments posed by Kant in his *Prolegomena to Any Future Metaphysics* (page 116)?

2

Causality in Everyday Life and in Recent Science | Moritz Schlick (1882-1936)

Moritz Schlick was appointed to the chair in the philosophy of the inductive sciences at the University of Vienna in 1922, a post which he held until his death. In Vienna, he was the leader of a group of philosophers which is often called the Vienna Circle. Their most characteristic doctrine is the verification principle which Schlick states in the reading before us when he says: ". . . [philosophy] discovers the meaning of propositions by finding out just how they are verified, i.e., how their truth or falsity is tested." Schlick employs the principle here when he elucidates the concept of causality by examining the verification of statements in which the concept is used.

This selection may be read on two levels. On the first level it may be read as an elucidation of the concept of causality both in our everyday talk about one event's regularly following another, and in the scientists' talk about Laws of Nature, in which "the vague notions of cause and effect are replaced by the more precise concept of mathematical function." At this level the reader can come to an understanding of the concept of causality in physics and in any science which like physics seeks natural laws expressible as mathematical functions. But by reading this selection at a deeper level, the reader can learn how any scientific concept can be elucidated. For just as Schlick shows how we may come to an understanding of the concept of causality by learning how it is used in verifiable statements about causes and effects, so we may come to an understanding of any scientific concept by learning how it is used in statements that are verifiable. We urge our readers to consider this selection not only as an elucidation of the concept of causality, but also as an example of the way in which any scientific concept can be elucidated.

The reader may compare Schlick's views on causality with those of Hume (pages 109 ff.). The reader should ask whether Hume can be said to be proposing a "theory of causality," in the sense in which Schlick denies that he is proposing such a theory.

This reading consists of the greater part of an essay, "Causality in Everyday Life and in Recent Science," first printed in the University of California *Publications in Philosophy,* 15, 1932.

From "Causality in Everyday Life and in Recent Science," by Moritz Schlick, *Publications in Philosophy,* 15, University of California Press, Berkeley, 1932. Reprinted by permission of the publisher.

I

There is an old rule, formulated long ago in scholastic philosophy, that warns us against confusing the "post hoc" and the "propter hoc." This means that from the fact that an event E happened after another event C, we must not infer that E happened "because of" C. In other words, the rule maintains that the meaning of the proposition "E follows C" is entirely different from the meaning of the proposition "E is the effect of the cause C." But what *is* the difference between the two meanings? This question, it seems to me, is the philosophical problem of Causality.

I call it philosophical, because it is a question of meaning only, not of truth. It deals with the signification of the word "propter" or "because of"; we have to know what these words signify in order to understand the mere meaning of the principle of causality; the question whether this principle (if we can discover any meaning in it) is true or false would be a scientific problem, i.e., it could be decided only by observation and experience.

Our rule seems to presuppose that we are already acquainted with the signification of the words *post* and *propter;* for if we were not, there would be no possibility of ever applying the rule to any particular case. At best it would yield us an information of an entirely negative nature: it would tell us that the causal relation is *not* merely the relation of temporal succession, but something more; yet it would not give the slightest hint as to the positive essence of the causal relation.

Now there is no doubt that we do apply the rule continually and that it is a perfectly good and sound rule which people ought to follow even much more frequently than they do. If we take a certain medicine and get well after it, it would be very rash to assert that the medicine was the *cause* of our getting well. Or if we try to discover the causes of the depression, we know we are looking for much more than merely for events which *preceded* the depression. It is evident, therefore, that we actually are in possession of some kind of criterion which enables us to distinguish between events that merely follow each other and events that cause each other; for we do make this distinction every day, and we make it with a sufficient accuracy to have nearly all our behavior guided by it.

We simply have to observe how this distinction is actually made in order to find out the meaning of the concept of causality as it is used in our daily experience. This simple proceeding will surely not be difficult, and yet it is the general method—and I am convinced the only method—of philosophy: it discovers the meaning of propositions by finding out just how they are verified, i.e., how their truth or falsity is tested.

This is what I propose to do with propositions in which the concept of causality is used. I shall certainly not propose any "theory of causality"; I believe there can be no such thing. There are no theories and hypotheses in philosophy; hypotheses are the material out of which the sciences are constructed, and I believe that philosophy is something different from the sciences.

How, then, do we verify the statement that the taking of some medicine was not only the antecedent but also the *cause* of the recovery of the patient?

At a first glance there seem to be two different ways of such a verification (remember, we do not ask how it *should* be done, but how it is really done in practice):

1. We try the medicine many times and perhaps on many different patients. If we find that in every single case a person suffering from a particular complaint is cured, we shall say: the recovery after the use of the medicine was not a mere *chance,* but was *caused* by it. In other words: if the event E *always* occurs after the event C has occurred before, if C never occurs without being followed by E, then we do not hesitate to call C the cause and E the effect. It is important to notice that we do this whether we are able to "explain" the cure or not; there are cases in which we just know that a medicine is good without knowing how it works.

This is a fact; and I should like to express it, as it has often been expressed by thinkers of the positivist school, by saying that the difference between a mere temporal sequence and a causal sequence is the regularity, the uniformity of the latter. If C is *regularly* followed by E, then C is the cause of E; if E only "happens" to follow C now and then, the sequence is called a mere chance. And since (as we just saw) the observation of the regularity was, in this case, the *only* thing that was done, it was necessarily the *only* reason for speaking of cause and effect, it was the *sufficient* reason. The word cause, as used in everyday life, implies *nothing but* regularity of sequence, because *nothing else* is used to verify the propositions in which it occurs.

I am sure the reader must feel very much disappointed to have me repeat these old "positivistic" statements which have been discussed and, some believe, refuted so many times. I appeal to his patience and hope he will presently see the import of these remarks for the higher aspects of the problem of causality as they are presented by recent science.

Metaphysicians will, of course, find fault with our representation of the facts. Although they will admit, I think, that in the above example the verification consisted entirely in the observation of uniformity and nothing else, they will probably maintain that even the most unprejudiced observer never thinks that the regularity of sequence constitutes the whole of causality, but regards it only as a sign or as the consequence of something else, of some "real connection" or some peculiar "intimacy" between cause and effect, or by whatever name he may call the unobservable "tie" which he believes to be present in causation.

I do not deny that this may be so, but I answer: we are not concerned with what any observer thinks or says; our investigation of meaning is concerned only with what he *does* and can show us. Speaking, thinking, believing implies interpretation; we must not discuss interpretations or the results of philosophical analysis; we have to do with verification only, which is always an act or an activity. With regard to meaning we have to be pragmatists, whatever we may be with regard to the conception of truth. If the existence of that mysterious "tie" is verified *only* by the observation of regular sequence, then this regularity will be all the meaning the word "tie" actually has, and no thinking, believing, or speaking can add anything to it.

Perhaps the best known objection against the identification of causality and regularity is the remark that nothing is more regular than the succession of day and night, and yet we do not call the one the cause of the other. But this is simply accounted for by the fact that "day" and "night" are really not names for "events" at all in the sense in which this word is used in science. And as soon as we analyze day and night into the series of natural events for which these names stand, we find that the sequence of those events must be regarded as a very good example of "causal connection."

The real difficulties involved in the notion of uniformity are of a different nature and much more serious. We said that E was called the effect of a cause C, if in many cases it was observed to follow C each time without exception. Should we not ask: *how many* times? A physician who has tried a medicine in six cases and has seen the patient get better six times may feel pretty confident that his remedy was the cause of the recovery of his patients (provided, of course, that in his former experience they did not get well without the medicine), but undoubtedly it is possible that in all future cases the remedy will fail to have the desired result; and then we shall say: those first six times were nothing but a chance, the word "chance" meaning simply the negation of causality. If instead of six times the experiment were repeated successfully a hundred times, surely everybody would believe in the beneficial effect of the medicine; nevertheless it must be admitted that the future may bring exceptions and destroy the regularity. A hundred will be considered better than six, but evidently *no* number will be considered absolutely satisfactory; for if in one single case only C were not followed by E, one would feel no longer justified to call C the cause of E, and for all we know such a crucial case might always occur in the future.

So this is the state of affairs: the proposition "C is the cause of E" seemed to mean nothing but "C is always followed by E"; but this latter proposition can unfortunately never be verified on account of the unfortunate "always" it contains. Verification would be possible only if a finite number is substituted for "always," but no finite number is satisfactory, because it does not exclude the possibility of exceptions.

This difficulty has been pointed out about as many times as the problem of induction has been discussed, and the conclusion has usually been that causality cannot be explained as meaning simply uniformity, but that it must mean something else. Perhaps so. But we must insist: it *can* mean something else only if there is a way of verifying causal judgments different from the one we have described. What shall we do if no such way is discovered?

We can do nothing but stick to the facts with absolute frankness. Since the meaning of a proposition lies entirely in its verification, it will have meaning only *in so far* as it is verified.[1] And if the verification is never considered complete and final, if we never declare a certain C to be the cause of a certain E without reserving the right of revocation (and this, it is important to notice, not on account of any incorrect observation or similar "mistake"), then we shall have to admit that we simply have no clear concept of causality. Where there is no definite verification, there can be no definite meaning. The function of the word "cause" will be vague. A sentence containing this word may serve a very good purpose in the practice of everyday life as well as of science, but it will have no theoretical meaning.

There is a very curious way in which the difficulty hidden in the word "always" is sometimes apparently overcome. It consists in saying: if it cannot be verified that E *always* follows C, it can also never be falsified; for the cases in which it does not seem to be the case can be explained as mere appearances, and so our belief in the causal relation between C and E can never be proved to be false. A physician, for instance, who has had complete success with a cure in ninety-nine cases but finds it to fail in the hundredth case, will by no means give up his belief that his treatment has been the "cause" of the ninety-nine recoveries, but will explain that in the negative case there must have been a circumstance which intervened and prevented the effect. And we shall very likely accept this explanation as very natural, just as we would not blame a medicine for not making a patient well, if five minutes after taking it he were killed by an automobile accident. Theoretically, and in a very crude symbolism, we might say that in the negative case the cause is not any more C at all, but $C + C'$, where C' is the intervening circumstance, and $C + C'$ does *not* have the effect E, which C alone would have had. This statement must, of course, be capable of being verified by really observing C'; if we were to admit un-

---

[1] [This seems to be a slip. Schlick must have intended to say "verifiable." Emendation suggested by Profs. H. Feigl and W. Sellars.—Eds.]

observable C's we could consider *any* event to be the cause of any other event by merely assuming the existence of convenient C's, and then surely our judgments about causal relations would lose all meaning. There are certain philosophers, those who advocate the doctrine of "conventionalism," who believe that this is really the nature of all our causal judgments; in their opinion all these judgments—which would include all laws of nature—have no real meaning; they do not say anything about the world, but only indicate the way in which we select, or even arbitrarily invent, events in order to make them fit into a preconceived scheme, which we have decided to use as our most convenient means of describing nature. Among famous scientists the astronomer A. S. Eddington may be mentioned as holding similar views.

We must note here that the interpretation of negative cases by means of disturbing influences—intervening C's—does *not* offer any criterion of causality other than uniformity of sequence; on the contrary, it saves causality only by substituting a hidden regularity for an apparent irregularity.

The regularity may at first be hidden, but it must be discoverable, if we are not to fall into the snares of conventionalism; that is, we must be able to find a C' such that C and C' together will always be followed by an E' which is different from E. And if there should be cases in which C + C' is not followed by E', we have to find a new event C", and so on. Evidently it would be a great advantage and would help to elucidate special cases of causality, if there were a way of making sure that no further C's could possibly intervene. There would be no hope of doing this, if *any* event in the world could eventually play the rôle of the C' for which we are looking. But if these events were restricted in a certain way so that it would be possible to examine *all* of them, then we would know that no other disturbing element could come into question, and verification would become more satisfactory.

Now it has usually been assumed by science that the possible causes were indeed very definitely restricted. In looking for the cause of a given event E it was thought that we could exclude all events happening *long before* E, and all events happening *at a great distance* from E (events occurring *after* E had, of course, been already ruled out by prescientific thinking). Assuming these conditions in their most rigorous and consistent form one arrived at the idea that no event could be regarded as the proper cause of E unless it occurred in the immediate spatial and temporal vicinity of E. So the causal relation between two events C and E was thought to imply their contiguity in space and time. Action-at-a-distance (temporal as well as spatial distance) was considered impossible. If this were so, one would have to look for the causes of any event only in its immediate neighborhood, there would indeed be no time and no room for any other event to interfere. It is irrelevant that this view was supported by *a priori* arguments such as "an event can act only at the place where it occurs, and nowhere else"; nevertheless such arguments show that one believed one could *understand* the causal relation better if there was contiguity; if cause and effect were separated from each other, their relation appeared to be more mysterious. This brings us to the consideration of the second way in which the existence of a causal relation seems to be established (the first one being observation of uniformity of sequence).

2. Supposing there were a case in which we believed we really and completely "understood" the working of a certain treatment or medicine in the human body: in such a case we should not have to wait for any repetition of the sequence treatment-recovery in order to assert a causal relation between these two events; we could assert it even before it occurred a single time, because our "understanding" of this particular causation would imply our conviction that the first event would entail the second one, or, as it is often put, C would *necessarily* be followed by E. If a surgeon amputates a man's leg, he will know beforehand that the man will be one-legged afterwards. Nobody thinks that we must wait for a long series of experiences in order to know that amputation results in the loss of a limb. We feel we "understand" the whole process and therefore know its result without having experienced it.

So there seems to be a second way of verifying a causal judgment independent of observation of regularity: it consists in simply pointing to the "understanding" of the particular causal relation. And those who believe in this second way will immediately add that it is the only real way, the only legitimate method, and that our first criterion—uniformity of occurrence—was nothing but an untrustworthy symptom, which might be good enough for an empiristic scientist, but could never satisfy the philosopher.

But let us examine what exactly is meant by "understanding" as the word is used here.

It is usually supposed to be a matter of "pure reason." Now, the only sense I can find for this term is the purely logical, which would mean the same as the purely deductive, the merely analytical. And there is indeed a purely logical element in the case we have just been examining. That amputation of a leg causes a man to be one-legged is an identical inference; it is, like all logical inferences, a mere tautology. But it is easy to see, unfortunately, that this has nothing to do with causation. The causal connection is hidden in the word "amputation." We usually believe we understand this connection, because we think we comprehend the process, say, of a saw cutting through a bone: the hard particles of the steel are in immediate contact with the soft particles of the bone, and the latter somehow must give way to the former. Here again we have contiguity in space and time, which appears to flatter our imagination, but apart from that we have again nothing but a sequence of events which we have often observed to happen in a similar way and which we therefore expect to happen again. For aught we know we might some day come across a bone that would resist any saw and that no human power would be able to cut in two.

So we see that, at least in our example, we were led to think we understood or comprehended the causal nexus: partly by a misinterpretation of the way in which logical inference entered into our thought, and partly by analyzing the causal process into a spatial and temporal continuity of events. This means that our second criterion is really only a hidden application of the first one; it is not different, and consequently not any better.

The examination of any other example leads to the same result. What, for instance, is the difference between a case in which we *understand* that a certain medicine must have a certain effect, and another case in which we just know by experience that it does have that effect? It is evidently this: in the second case we observe only two events, the application of the drug and, after a reasonable lapse of time, the recovery of the patient; in the first case we know how the gap between cause and effect is filled by an unbroken chain of events which are contiguous in space and time. The drug, e.g., is injected into the veins; we know it comes into immediate contact with the blood particles; we know that these will then undergo a certain chemical change; they will travel through the body; they will come into contact with a certain organ; this organ will be changed in a particular way; and so on. In this way we infer that in the end the patient *must* be healed, *if* all the other events follow each other in the way we have assumed. And how do we know that they do follow each other so? All we know is that in former experiences in the laboratory this has always been the regular course of things.

From all this we must draw the negative conclusion that it is impossible—at least in so far as the judgments of everyday life and of qualitative science are concerned—to find any meaning for the word "causation," except that it implies regularity of sequence. And this is rather vague, because there is no rule as to how many instances have to be observed in order to justify our speaking of regularity.

But the two chief things we can learn from the foregoing considerations seem to me to be these:

1. The "understanding" of a causal relation is not a process of logical reasoning; what is called causal necessity is absolutely different from logical necessity (which is nothing but identity). But at the same time we see why former philosophers so frequently made the mistake of confusing the two and believing that the effect could be logically inferred from the cause. The only serious philosopher of our present time, who still believes that there must be some kind of identity of cause and effect and therefore believes the relation between them to be in some way rational or logical, is (so far as I know) E. Meyerson. He tries to prove this historically by analyzing the statements of famous philosophers and scientists; but the psychological explanation of his view lies in the fact that he started as a chemist, who is used to thinking in terms of identical substances, whereas the physicist, who goes more deeply into the explanation of nature, has to think in terms of events.

2. We learn that the causal relation between two separate events is actually explained or understood when we can conceive the two as being connected by a chain of intermediate events. If some of these are still separated, we have to look for new events between them, and so on, until all the gaps are filled out and the chain has become perfectly continuous in space and time. But evidently *we can go no further,* and it would be nonsense to expect more of us. If we look for the causal link that links two events together, we cannot find anything but another event (or perhaps several). Whatever can be observed and shown

in the causal chain will be the links, but it would be nonsense to look for the linkage.

This shows that we are perfectly right when we think of cause and effect as *connected* by a causal chain, but that we are perfectly wrong when we think that this chain could consist of anything but events, that it could be a kind of mysterious tie called "causality." The conception of such a "tie," which is really not a concept but a mere word, is due to a faulty process of thinking that is very common in the history of philosophy: the continuation of a thought beyond its logical limit; we transcend the region in which a word makes sense and necessarily find ourselves in the region of nonsense. After the scientist has successfully filled up all the gaps in his causal chains by continually interpolating new events, the philosopher wants to go on with this pleasant game after all the gaps are filled. So he invents a kind of glue and assures us that in reality it is only his glue that holds the events together at all. But we can never find the glue; there is no room for it, as the world is already completely filled by events which leave no chinks between them. Even in our times there are some philosophers who say that we directly experience causation, e.g., in the act of volition, or even in the feeling of muscular effort. But whatever such feelings of willing or of effort may be, they are certainly events in the world; they can be glued to other events, but they cannot be the glue.

All this has of course been seen very clearly by Hume when he said that it was impossible to discover any "impression" for the idea of causal nexus. Only we can express this even more strongly by saying that we are already committing a kind of nonsense when we try to *look* for such an impression. At this point we find complete agreement between Hume and Kant. Kant applauded Hume for seeing that when we speak of causation we cannot possibly mean a sort of tie which connects the events or establishes a kind of intimacy between them, and he conceived causality as something entirely different, namely as a Principle of Order. He believed that the human mind imposed a certain order on the events of its experience, and that causality was one of the principles according to which this was done. And according to him, the human mind did this because it could not help doing it; the Principle was simply part of its metaphysical nature.

Although we must of course reject the latter part of Kant's view, we can most heartily consent to his opinion that if causality is anything at all it can be nothing but a Principle of Order.

II

It is the object of science to discover Order in the world. This is done by finding and formulating Laws of Nature. So there must be a relationship between causality and the laws of nature, and it is easy to see what it is. The principle of causality seems to assert that every definite cause will have a definite effect, and a law of nature tells us, what will be the particular event that belongs to a given cause as its effect. So the principle of causality itself is not a law but can be regarded as the statement that all events in nature are subject to laws. And this must not be interpreted as if a law of nature were something imposed upon reality, compelling nature to behave in a certain way, just as a civic law would force a certain behavior upon the citizens. Laws of nature do not *prescribe* a certain order *to* the world, but simply *de*scribe the order *of* the world; they do not command what must happen, but simply formulate what does happen. The "necessity" which we attribute to them must not be misunderstood as a kind of compulsion (this term would imply the possibility of "obedience" and "disobedience"), but it means only that there is *no exception* to the laws, that they hold in *all* cases.

From what I said a moment ago we might expect all laws of nature to have the form: "the cause so-and-so has the effect so-and-so"; but if we look at the actual formulations in science we do not find a single law of this form, wherever the expression is perfectly precise, as is the case in theoretical physics. What we do find there is always a mathematical equation. The vague notions of cause and effect have been replaced by the more precise concept of mathematical function. Cause and effect are both names for events, and one of the reasons why it seems impossible to use them with the necessary scientific precision lies in the fact that it is impossible to *isolate* events. If I drop my pencil on the table, this would be considered as one event in everyday language; but think of the innumerable facts it involves: the motions of all the molecules of my fingers, of the table, of the surrounding air! It would be hopeless to give a complete description of such an "event," and still more impossible to find its complete *cause;* we know that, for instance, the position of the moon would somehow enter into the cause, as the presence of the moon contributes to the gravitational field in which the pencil is falling.

So science does not speak of causes and effects, but of functional relations between measurable quantities; it starts with measurement of quantities rather than with description of occurrences. And it seems to be the essence of every law of nature that it states the way in which the values of some quantities measured at certain places and times depend on the values of some other quantities measured at certain other places and times.

This introduction of mathematical functions is an enormous advantage, but we must not believe that all our difficulties in interpreting causality can be overcome by simply abandoning the use of the terms cause and effect.

In the first place it must be remembered that the scientific conception of nature as a system of functional relations is a sort of idealized scheme which acquires physical meaning only by being applied or attached to reality; it is referred to reality only by observation, of course; and every observation is an observation of an event (such as the change of color of a liquid in a chemical experiment or the motion of the mercury in a thermometer), which will be regarded as isolated and as causally connected with other events (e.g., certain manipulations of the observer). In this way the old concepts which have been eliminated from the system of science seem to reappear when we examine the actual experiences on which science is based. It is true that a careful analysis would show that this is not a very serious predicament in itself, and it is also true that the difficulties connected with the isolation of events can be minimized by careful experimental arrangements; but the recent development of physics has shown that there is a definite limit to this isolation, and the consequences of this fact *are* serious.

In the second place, we must not rejoice too much in the replacement of the concept of causality by the concept of law, before we are quite sure that we know exactly what we mean by the word *law*. Is it really a satisfactory explanation to say (as we did a little while ago) that a law of nature is a function between measured quantities? I think it is not sufficient. In order to show this let us consider a special form of law which corresponds to the ideas of classical physics (but our arguments would remain true in a more general case).

Let us suppose that there is no "action-at-a-distance," so that the occurrence of any event at a given point of space and at a given time would depend only on what happened immediately before and in the immediate vicinity of that point. The laws describing such a kind of dependence would be expressed by differential equations. Now consider a physical system within a closed surface, the happenings in which were completely governed by these laws: then it seemed possible for classical physics to give a perfectly precise expression of the Principle of Causality for such a system. It used to be given by the following statement: "The state of the system (i.e., the totality of the events within our surface) at any time t is completely determined by its state at some other time t_0 and by all the events which happen *on* the closed boundary during the whole time-interval $t-t_0$." (If *nothing* were happening at the boundary—i.e., if we had a completely isolated system—or if there were no boundary—which would be the case if our system were the whole universe, as Laplace considered it in his famous formula—then the same statement could be made more simple by saying that the state of the system at *any* particular time determines its states at *all* other times.) This is, of course, a formulation of determinism.

We must analyze very carefully what can be meant by this statement. The clue must evidently be found in the word "determine," which is used here. The word indicates a certain relation between two states of the system: one which determines and one which is determined. This is, of course, nothing but our *causal* relation, and we see that the word determination has taken the place of the word causation. This does not seem to be a great advantage; but let us see how the scientist uses the word determination—then we shall find out what he *means* by it. When he says that the state E at the time t is determined by the state C at the time t_0, he means that his differential equations (his Laws) enable him to *calculate* E, if C and the boundary conditions are known to him. Determination therefore means Possibility of Calculation, *and nothing else*.

It does *not* mean that C in some magic way *produces* E. And yet we can now understand how the idea of production comes in and what justification can be given for it. "To produce" literally means to bring forth; and in a very definite sense the calculation does "bring out" if not E, at least the complete description of E, i.e., the values of all the physical quantities which are characteristic of E. From the logical point of view a mathematical computation is a process of analysis which can bring out only what is already contained in the presuppositions; and in fact, the description of the initial state C (and of the boundary conditions) together with the Laws do logically contain the description of all the succeeding states E, in the same sense in which all the terms of a series may be said to be contained in the law of the series together with its first term.

Here again it might seem as if the causal relation were in some way reduced to a sort of logical inherence of the effect in the cause, and as if a logical interpretation of "production" were found; but a moment's thought shows the futility of such an interpretation. For calculation can only show what will occur *if* certain laws are valid, but it can never show that they *are* valid. In other words: the logical equivalence does not hold between cause and effect, or in fact between anything in reality, but it holds only between the two propositions: (1) State C has been observed and certain states E will follow; and (2) State C has been observed and certain laws L are valid. The meaning of these two propositions is identical (if the proper substitutions are made for E and L), and the calculation is nothing but the analytic method of transforming one into the other. Mathematical analysis teaches us how to express a sequence of events by means of a Law, *if* there is a certain order in nature; the principle of causality asserts that there *is* order in nature. These are two entirely different and independent things. Logical necessity and "production" belong to calculus, causality belongs to real nature.

We see again that laws of nature must not be thought of as supernatural powers forcing nature into a certain behavior and thereby "producing" the effects of given causes, but simply as abbreviated expressions of the order in which events do follow each other. . . .

We now return to our analysis of the concept of determination. We found it to mean "possibility of calculation"; and from what we have seen thus far it seems that possibility of calculation implied nothing but the existence of some mathematical functions which connect the values of the quantities that describe different states of a physical system at different times. But here we strike a serious difficulty. It is this: whatever the succeeding states of a physical system may be—after we have observed them it is *always* possible to find functions connecting them in such a way that if one of those states is given, all the rest of them can be computed by means of those functions. The mathematician assures us that he has no difficulty in constructing analytical functions which with any desired degree of approximation will represent any succeeding states of the system, however chaotic it may be. This proves that we cannot identify Law with functional relations; for if *any* sequence of events can be described by functions, then the possibility of such a description cannot be used to distinguish an orderly or causal sequence from a chaotic or noncausal one. The principle of causality would always be true: whatever happened, it would be a mere tautology which says nothing about nature.

We conclude that "possibility of calculation" cannot simply mean possibility of description by functions; something more is needed. It is usually thought that what is needed is some kind of specification of the functions, so that laws of nature must be defined by functions possessing some special property.

The first property which presents itself here is *simplicity*. Many writers hold that the difference between a causal chain of events and a noncausal one is this, that the former can be described by simple function, the latter only by complicated ones. I do not doubt for a moment that all the laws we know, and probably even all the laws we shall ever know, do comply with this criterion, which I usually call the aesthetic criterion, because simplicity seems to be an aesthetic rather than a scientific concept. Nevertheless, it is entirely unsatisfactory from the logical point of view, and this for two reasons. The first one is that we cannot give a strict definition that will enable us to distinguish between simple and complicated functions; I suppose the latter ones are those that can be handled successfully only by a very skilful mathematician—but evidently no such definition could have the necessary objectivity and clarity. The second reason is that we can easily imagine circumstances in which nobody would refuse to regard even the most complicated function as a perfectly good law of nature. This would be the case if all the predictions made by the complicated formula were found to be true, and no simpler function of equal efficiency could be discovered. For these reasons the logician must dismiss the criterion of simplicity as inadequate.

Another criterion of causality that might be chosen consists in postulating that the functional relations describing the flow of events must not contain the space and time coördinates in an explicit form. This sounds rather technical, but it is nothing but the mathematical formulation of the principle: Same cause, same effect. It means that if under certain circumstances at a particular place and time a certain sequence of events is observed, then a similar sequence of events will be observed if similar circumstances occur at some other place and some other time. This postulate has been adopted by such a great authority as Maxwell, and it may perhaps be regarded as a special form of the simplicity principle, as the absence of explicit space and time values could be considered as a particular kind of simplicity of the functions. The postulate is fulfilled if space and time enter only as the independent variables of differential equations, and this is true in our present-day physics.

Now again I certainly expect that all laws of nature will actually conform to Maxwell's criterion just as well as to the general criterion of simplicity (if they did not it would mean that we should have to change our views concerning the nature of space and time considerably)—none the less it remains theoretically possible that a future physics might have to introduce formulae which contain space and time in an explicit form, so that the same cause would never have the same effect, but the effect would also depend, in a definite way, e.g., on the date, and would be different tomorrow, or next month, or next year.

However improbable this may seem to be—the philosopher has to take into account all possibilities, no matter how remote they are; he must never tie himself down to the particular state of science at this time, which is always only one of many possible states; his realm is the field of possibilities, because it is the realm of all meaningful propositions. In our case he must ask himself: would we regard the universe as noncausal or chaotic, if it did not conform to Maxwell's criterion? And the answer is: by no means! If we knew formulae which we could use just as successfully for the description of that strange universe as we use our present scientific formulae to describe the actual world, we should have to say that both worlds were completely orderly. This brings us to the essential point, at last: we have to see how the formulae are actually *used*.

Instead of inventing definitions of *law,* which always prove more or less artificial, we must direct our attention to the way in which the scientist really tests a formula in each particular case and tries to verify whether or not it represents the law for which he is looking. He first constructs a function by connecting all the observed data, and he will certainly try to construct it so that it obeys Maxwell's criterion as well as that of simplicity—but he is not content with this. His success in finding a function of this nature is not a sufficient, and not even a necessary, reason for him to be convinced that the Law is found. He will proceed to apply it to *new* data, which have not been used for the construction of his formula. If observation shows that the function fits the new data he will triumph and believe that it expresses the real law. He will *believe* it; he will never be absolutely sure, because new data may come up in the future which will not fit into the formula. But, of course, his faith will grow with the number of verifications. The mathematician can always construct an analytic formula that will cover all the observed data, but he can never guarantee that it will also fit future data which he does not know yet and which nature will furnish after having been asked to do so by the skilful experiments and observations of the scientist.

Now at last we know what is meant by the "possibility of calculation" which we found to be the essence of causality or "determination." It does not mean possibility of finding a function with particular mathematical properties, but it means possibility of *applying* a function with *any* properties to such data (or "events" or "states of a physical system") as have not been used for its construction. The technical term for this procedure is "extrapolation," and so we can now say that in science causality stands for possibility of extrapolation. From the way in which we introduce the term "possibility" it is clear that it implies correspondence with observation or (which is saying the same thing) with reality: when we say that it is possible to extrapolate from a physical formula we mean that the extrapolated values will correspond to the values which are really observed. This process of computing values which are confirmed by future experience is usually called *prediction,* and so we may say quite simply: a Law is a formula which allows us to make true predictions.

The criterion of causality is successful prediction. That is all we can say. It is not much more than what we said in the beginning, after analyzing causality in everyday life, where we ended by speaking of regularity of sequences. Regularity of occurrence in the ordinary sense is just a particular case in which the method of prediction is especially easy to grasp. Our former difficulty in understanding causality was that we were unable to say when a causal judgment should be considered definitely verified, and therefore could give no definite meaning to it. This difficulty has not been overcome by our analysis of scientific law. Even in science there is no way of ever establishing a law as absolutely valid and thereby proving the existence of causation in any particular case. We can never be sure that *all* predictions from a law will come true. Although in practice a small number of successful predictions will suffice to cause a very strong belief in a law, and sometimes even one single verification will be regarded as sufficient: from the strictly logical point of view all our formulae will always remain hypotheses, theoretically it will always remain possible to say that the verifications were just "chance."

There is no room to discuss the logical consequences of this situation and we must turn to the most recent development of science in order to see whether it agrees with the results of our analysis. Does it support the view that the *only* criterion, and therefore the only meaning, of causality is successful prediction?

It is gratifying to state that the recent discussions of causality in connection with the quantum theory afford a very striking confirmation of our view. As is well known, the quantum theory in its present form asserts that a strictly deterministic description of nature is impossible; in other words, that physics has to abandon the Principle of Causality.

What does physics mean when it thus denies causality? In order to find this out we need only examine the specific reasons which are given for this denial.

If causality were defined by simplicity of mathematical functions, as was done by the aesthetic criterion, then its denial would mean that it is impossible to describe nature by simple functions. Does science assert this? Does it despair of causality because the formulae it has to use are too complicated? Certainly not! Therefore its rejection of determinism is not guided by the aesthetic criterion.

If causality were essentially defined by Maxwell's criterion, i.e., by the principle that the describing functions must not contain space and time coordinates in an explicit form (which, as we saw it, is equivalent to the rule "same cause, same effect"), then denial of determinism would mean: it is impossible to describe nature by equations in which space and time do not occur explicitly. And is this the great revelation made by the quantum theory? By no means! Therefore violation of Maxwell's criterion is not the reason why determinism is rejected.

What *is* the real reason? None other but that it is found impossible to *predict* phenomena with perfect accuracy. Within certain well-defined limits it is impossible to construct functions that can be used for extrapolation. This is the essential consequence of Heisenberg's famous Uncertainty Principle, and it proves that the physicist in his actual proceeding has adopted just that view of causality which we have been advocating.

It is true that the formulation given by most physicists seems to be a little different. They usually insist on the impossibility, not of prediction of future states, but of complete description of the present state of a physical system. But an easy analysis shows that this must be interpreted as involving incapacity of extrapolation. For the sake of simplicity we may assume that a description of a system would be complete if it included the positions of all the electric particles composing the system at the present moment, and the velocities of all these particles at the same moment. But what is "velocity"? What does it mean in actual experience when we assert that a certain particle moves with a certain velocity? It means nothing but that the particle which at one moment has been observed at a definite particular place will, after a definite short interval of time, be observed at another definite place. Thus assigning a certain velocity to a particle at a given moment means predicting its position at a given future moment. Theoretically, the Principle of Indeterminacy does not make it impossible to observe two succeeding positions of a particle in a short interval of time and assign to it a velocity equal to the ratio of the distance and the time interval, but in this way we have described only the *past* behavior of the particle—or, I should rather say, its *observed* behavior. As soon as we try to use this value of velocity for an extrapolation in order to get a future position of the particle, the Uncertainty Principle steps in to tell us that our attempt is in vain; our value of velocity is no good for such a prediction; our own observation will have changed the velocity in an unknown way, therefore the particle will probably not be found in the predicted place, and there is no possibility of knowing where it could be found.

In this way the concept of velocity is connected with prediction, and only because there is no predictability here, does the ordinary procedure of science (which is implied by the words Law and Causation) become inapplicable.

Perhaps it is not unnecessary to remind the reader that these consequences of the Uncertainty Principle become practically serious only when we are concerned with very small particles whose position we try to describe with unlimited accuracy. If we are content to determine the position with a certain approximation we shall be able to predict future positions with a probability the exact amount of which is stated by Heisenberg's formula. And if we have to do with larger particles, such as molecules for instance, not to speak of rifle bullets or billiard balls, the approximation and the probability reach such enormous amounts that the certainty of our predictions becomes incomparably greater than the accuracy of our most perfect observations.

This is very fortunate from the practical point of view; for it means that for all ordinary purposes of science and everyday life the deterministic attitude not only remains justified, but is the only one compatible with our knowledge of nature. If it were otherwise, if Planck's constant h, which in a way measures the uncertainty of our predictions, were more than 10^{30} times greater than it actually is, then the Principle of Indeterminacy would make our lives very difficult, because hardly anything could ever be planned ahead. If human beings could exist at all in a world of so much disorder, they would have to give up many pursuits, such as medicine, engineering, and they would have to give up morality. For there can be no morals without responsibility, and there could be no responsibility if human actions were simply random events in the world. (Lack of determination means pure chance, randomness; the alternative "either determination or chance" is a logical one, there is no escape from it, no third possibility.) A serious amount of indeterminism would be nothing to rejoice about; it would mean fatal disorder. Such considerations make us wonder why metaphysicians so often thought it necessary to defend indeterminism for ethical or religious reasons; they have been misled by a strange confusion concerning the terms necessity and law, freedom and determinism. But we are not concerned with this here.

The situation is a little different in the case of those philosophical writers and philosophizing scientists who have derived great satisfaction from the recent development of science because the indeterminism to which it leads is a *physical* indeterminism. They rejoice in the incomplete determination of nature by physical laws because it seems to leave room for Mind in the universe. If there are little gaps in physical causation, why should they not be filled by the activity of mental factors, such as thoughts or feelings, which would in this way have some influence on the course of events?

If this view were logically sound it would mean that the happenings in the physical world which modern physics leaves partly undetermined could be made deterministic again by the introduction of mental events (either partly, if only some of the gaps were supposed to be filled, or wholly, if mental factors were believed to be at work everywhere). Reduced to sober scientific language this would mean that the psychologist could make exact predictions in cases where the physicist must fail; if, e.g., the laws of physics could not tell him where a certain electron was going, he would still be able to predict the future position of this electron by consulting certain psychological laws.

I admit that there might be some intellectual satisfaction in this restoration, or partial restoration, of determinism; but I fail to see why the metaphysician should welcome it as satisfying his deepest desires. It is only through some secret additions and misinterpretations that this view could seem so valuable to him. But in reality I am convinced that the whole view is logically unsound. To regard physical and mental events as two different entities which between themselves determine the course of the universe in the described manner seems to me to be a particularly shallow and crude attempt to deal with the so-called Psycho-physical Problem, and to rest on a very naïve and uncritical use of the terms "physical" and "mental." A view that succeeds in finding a place for Mind in the universe only with the utmost difficulty and only after physics has discovered the principle of indeterminacy—such a view, I am sure, must be based on an analysis of the term "mind" which is fundamentally wrong. The true analysis of the terms "physical" and "mental" (with which we are not concerned here) will show that they cannot be used in this dualistic way without severe violation of the rules of philosophical grammar, and that the understanding of the real meaning of these terms has nothing to do with any particular theory of physics and is quite independent of any present doctrines and of the progress of science.

No metaphysical conclusion can be drawn from the discoveries of recent science—as indeed such conclusions cannot be drawn from *anything*. Science, as the pursuit of truth, can and must stimulate philosophy, as the pursuit of meaning, but one of these can never be the explanation of the other.

We found that recent science confirmed the view that causality must be understood as meaning "possibility of extrapolation," because we found that this was exactly the sense in which the word is used in quantum physics. But, of course, our view and our analysis in no way presuppose the truth of the present state of quantum physics. If future science should abandon the principle of indeterminacy and should return to a deterministic interpretation of nature, our result would not be affected. For determinism could be restored only by showing that the laws of nature did not set any finite limit to the accuracy of our predictions. This would mean that we should have no more reason definitely to lose confidence in the applicability of our extrapolations, and it would presuppose just that view of causality which I have been trying to explain here.

Questions

1. In Schlick's account, how does our thinking about causality in everyday life differ from our thinking about it in science?

2. Why is the concept of causality important to a scientific view of the world? Is a scientific view of the world possible without it?

3. Follow Schlick's example and show the relation between our everyday and scientific concepts of weight, length, heat, and color. Are the everyday and scientific versions of these concepts related (or not related) in the same way that the everyday and scientific versions of causality are related? If there is a difference, why is there?

4. Could Schlick's method of elucidating the scientific concept of causality be used in elucidating any other scientific concepts? The reader might try applying Schlick's method to the following scientific concepts: gravity, force, osmosis, species, stratum, and element.

5. Could Schlick's method of elucidating scientific concepts be used in elucidating any other kinds of concepts? The reader might try applying Schlick's method to the following concepts: intelligence, idea, love, hate, angel.

6. Judging by this essay, what would you say that Schlick's conception of a philosophical problem is? Why should a philosopher not propose a "theory of causality"? Does Hume (pages 109 ff.) propose such a theory? Explain your answer.

3

Hypotheses and Scientific Method

Morris R. Cohen
(1880-1947)
and Ernest Nagel
(b. 1901)

Morris Cohen taught philosophy at the City College in New York City from 1912 until he retired in 1938. Ernest Nagel, one of Professor Cohen's former students, is a professor of philosophy at Columbia University. As well as being a joint author of *An Introduction to Logic and Scientific Method* from which this reading is taken, each of these men published separately books relevant to the problem of scientific knowledge. Professor Cohen is the author of *Reason and Nature, An Essay on the Meaning of Scientific Method* (1931); and Professor Nagel is the author of *Sovereign Reason, and Other Studies in the Philosophy of Science* (1954).

In this reading Cohen and Nagel discuss the invention and verification of hypotheses in the natural sciences. According to one view, our scientific knowledge consists of hypotheses about the natural world. The question for the reader then is: How are scientific hypotheses different from other kinds of statements? With regard to scientific hypotheses themselves the appropriate question is: What is a good hypothesis? Because they have taken the making and testing of hypotheses in the whole of natural science as their subject, the authors' remarks are necessarily very general. The reader who is acquainted with a particular natural science should both supplement what Cohen and Nagel have to say from his own knowledge, and test what they say against his own knowledge of the making and testing of hypotheses.

This reading is taken from *An Introduction to Logic and Scientific Method,* Chapter XI, "Hypotheses and Scientific Method," with slight omissions. The revised edition of 1936 has been used, and the authors' section headings have been retained.

"Those who refuse to go beyond fact rarely get as far as fact. . . . Almost every great step [in the history of science] has been made by the 'anticipation of nature,' that is, by the invention of hypotheses which, though verifiable, often had very little foundation to start with."–T. H. HUXLEY.

"How odd it is that anyone should not see that all observation must be for or against some view, if it is to be of any service."–CHARLES DARWIN.

THE OCCASION AND THE FUNCTION OF INQUIRY

In the second book of his fascinating *History,* Herodotus recounts the sights that met him on his travels to Egypt. The river Nile aroused his attention:

"Now the Nile, when it overflows, floods not only the Delta, but also the tracts of country on both sides the stream which are thought to belong to Libya and Arabia, in some places reaching to the extent of two days' journey from its banks, in some even exceeding that distance, but in others falling short of it.

"Concerning the nature of the river, I was not able to gain any information either from the priests or from others. I was particularly anxious to learn from them why the Nile, at the commencement of the summer solstice, begins to rise, and continues to increase for a hundred days—and why, as soon as that number is past, it forthwith retires and contracts its stream, continuing low during the whole of the winter until the summer solstice comes around again. On none of these points could I obtain any explanation from the inhabitants, though I made every inquiry, wishing to know what was commonly reported—they could neither tell me what special virtue the Nile has which makes it so opposite in its nature to all other streams, nor why, unlike every other river, it gives forth no breezes from its surface.

"Some of the Greeks, however, wishing to get a reputation for cleverness, have offered explanations of the phenomena of the river, for which they have accounted in three different ways. Two of these I do not think it worth while to speak of, further than simply to mention what they are. One pretends that the Etesian winds [the northwest winds blowing from the Mediterranean] cause the rise of the river by preventing the Nile-water from running off into the sea. But in the first place it has often happened, when the Etesian winds did not blow, that the Nile has risen according to its usual wont; and further, if the Etesian winds produced the effect, the other rivers which flow in a direction opposite to those winds ought to present the same phenomena as the Nile, and the more so as they are all smaller streams, and have a weaker current. But these rivers, of which there are many both in Syria and in Libya, are entirely unlike the Nile in this respect.

"The second opinion is even more unscientific than the one just mentioned, and also, if I may so say, more marvellous. It is that the Nile acts so strangely because it flows from the ocean, and that the ocean flows all round the earth.

"The third explanation, which is very much more plausible than either of the others, is positively the furthest from the truth; for there is really nothing in what it says, any more than in the other theories. It is that the inundation of the Nile is caused by the melting of snows. Now, as the Nile flows out of Libya [Central Africa], through Ethiopia into Egypt, how is it possible that it can be formed of melted snow, running, as it does, from the hottest regions of the world into cooler countries? Many are the proofs whereby anyone capable of reasoning on the subject may be convinced that it is most unlikely this should be the case. The first and strongest argument is furnished by the winds, which always blow hot from these regions. The second is that rain and frost are unknown there. Now, whenever snow falls, it must of necessity rain within five days; so that, if there were snow, there must be rain also in those parts. Thirdly, it is certain that the natives of the country are black with the heat, that the kites and the swallows remain there the whole year, and that the cranes, when they fly from the rigors of a Scythian winter, flock thither to pass the cold season. If then, in the country whence the Nile has its source, or in that through which it flows, there fell ever so little snow, it is absolutely impossible that any of these circumstances could take place.

"As for the writer who attributes the phenomenon to the ocean, his account is involved in such obscurity, that it is impossible to disprove it by argument. For my part I know of no river called Ocean, and I think that Homer, or one of the earlier poets, invented the name and introduced it into his poetry." [1]

Herodotus then goes on to state his own explanation of the behavior of the Nile.

Has the reader ever been guilty of believing or saying that the way to find out what the truth is, is to "study the facts" or to "let the facts speak for themselves"? Then let him examine this quotation for the light it may throw on the nature of the circumstances under which contributions to knowledge are made. Unless habitual beliefs are shaken into doubt by alterations in our familiar environment or by our curiosity, we either do no thinking at all, or our thinking, such as it is, has a routine character. We wish now to reinforce this suggestion and indicate its importance in understanding the nature of reflective or scientific method.

This excerpt from Herodotus illustrates clearly the Greek zest for scientific knowledge and speculation. But it also illustrates the great difference between the habit of simple acceptance of apparently stray, disconnected information, and the attitude that searches for some order in facts which are only superficially isolated. The observable inundation of the Nile was to many a brute fact, unconnected with other familiar but isolated facts. For Herodotus, however, the behavior of the Nile was not simply a brute fact. It presented a *problem* that could be resolved only by finding some general *connection* between the periodic inundation of the Nile and *other* facts.

It is an utterly superficial view, therefore, that the truth is to be found by "studying the facts." It is superficial because no inquiry can even get under way until and unless *some difficulty is felt* in a practical or theoretical situation. It is the difficulty, or problem, which guides our search for some *order among the facts,* in terms of which the difficulty is to be removed. We could not possibly discover the *reasons* for the inundation of the Nile unless we first recognized in the inundation a *problem* demanding solution.

If some problem is the occasion for inquiry, the *solution* of the problem is the goal and function of the inquiry. What constitutes a satisfactory solution of a problem, and in particular of the problem: Why does the Nile overflow its banks? The sort of answer for which Herodotus was looking was the discovery of a connection between the fact of the Nile's behavior and *other* facts; in virtue of that connection, apparently isolated facts would be seen to be *ordered* facts. And in general, scientific investigations must begin with some problem, and aim at an order connecting what at first sight may seem unrelated facts. But the ability to perceive in some brute experience the occasion for a problem, and especially a problem *whose solution has a bearing on the solution of other problems,* is not a common talent among men. For no rule can be given by means of which men can learn to ask significant questions. It is a mark of scientific genius to be sensitive to difficulties where less gifted people pass by untroubled with doubt.

[1] *History,* tr. by George Rawlinson, 1859, 4 vols., Vol. II, pp. 24-29.

THE FORMULATION OF RELEVANT HYPOTHESES

How does such a search for an order among facts proceed? The reader must note in the first place that a problem cannot even be *stated* unless we are somewhat familiar with the subject matter in which we discover the problem. The Greeks found a problem in the behavior of the Nile because, among other reasons, they were acquainted with the behavior of other rivers, and because the behavior of these other rivers was known to them to be connected with such things as wind, snowfall, and evaporation.

In order to state some obscurely felt difficulty in the form of a determinate problem, we must be able to *pick out,* on the basis of *previous knowledge,* certain elements in the subject matter as *significant.* Thus Herodotus noted the *distance covered* by the overflowing waters, the *time* at which the inundation *begins,* the *time* at which the overflow reaches its *maximum,* and the absence of *breezes* at the river's surface. It was in terms of such distinguishable and repeatable elements in the total situation known as "the inundation of the Nile" that Herodotus stated his difficulty. But his attention was drawn to these elements, rather than to others, because he was familiar with certain *theories* dealing with the behavior of rivers. It was his familiarity with such theories which made him look to facts like the winds, snowfall, or evaporation, rather than to other facts in order to find a connection between them and the Nile's behavior.

We cannot take a single step forward in any inquiry unless we begin with a *suggested* explanation or solution of the difficulty which originated it. Such tentative explanations are suggested to us by something in the subject matter and by our previous knowledge. When they are formulated as propositions, they are called *hypotheses.*

The function of a hypothesis is to *direct* our search for the order among facts. The suggestions formulated in the hypothesis *may* be solutions to the problem. *Whether* they are, is the task of the inquiry. No one of the suggestions need necessarily lead to our goal. And frequently some of the suggestions are incompatible with one another, so that they cannot all be solutions to the same problem.

We shall discuss below the formal conditions a satisfactory hypothesis must fulfill. The reader should note at this point that Herodotus examined three hypotheses (besides his own) for solving the problem of the Nile's periodic inundation. He accepted his own, after rejecting the other three. As a matter of fact, all four explanations are false. Nevertheless, the procedure he followed in rejecting some hypotheses and accepting others is still a model of scientific method.

How important hypotheses are in directing inquiry will be seen clearly if we reflect once more on the frequent advice: "Let the facts speak for themselves." For what *are* the facts, and *which* facts should we study? Herodotus could have observed the rise and retreat of the Nile until the end of time without finding in that particular repeated fact the sort of connections he was looking for—the relations of the inundation to the rainfall in Central Africa, for example. His problem could receive a solution only with the discovery of an invariable connection between the overflow of the Nile and some other fact. But *what* other fact? The number of other facts is endless, and an undirected observation of the Nile may never reveal either the other facts or their mode of connection. Facts must be *selected* for study on the basis of a hypothesis.

In directing an inquiry, a hypothesis must of necessity regard some facts as *significant* and others as not. It would have been humanly impossible for Herodotus to examine the relations of the Nile to *every other* class of events. Such a task, however, would have been regarded by him as preposterous. For most of these other facts, such as the number of prayers offered by the Egyptians every day, or the number of travelers visiting Naucratis each season, were judged by him to be *irrelevant*.

What is meant by saying that some hypotheses express "relevant" connection of facts, and others do not? The melting of snows is a relevant fact for understanding the Nile's behavior, Herodotus might have explained, because *on the basis of previous knowledge* melting snow can be regarded as related more or less constantly and in some determinate manner with the volume of rivers. But the number of visitors in Naucratis each season is not relevant to the Nile's behavior, because no such relation is known to exist between changes in the visiting population of a city and variations in the volume of rivers. A hypothesis is believed to be relevant to a problem if it expresses determinate modes of connections between a set of facts, including the fact investigated; it is irrelevant otherwise.

No rules can be stated for "hitting upon" relevant hypotheses. A hypothesis may often be believed to be relevant which subsequent inquiry shows to be not so. Or we may believe that certain facts are irrelevant to a problem although subsequent inquiry may reveal the contrary. *In the absence of knowledge concerning a subject matter, we can make no well-founded judgments of relevance.*

It follows that the valuable suggestions for solving a problem can be made only by those who are familiar with the kinds of connections which the subject matter under investigation is capable of exhibiting. Thus the explanation of the Nile's periodic overflow as due to heavy rainfall would not be very likely to occur to anyone not already familiar with the relation between rain and swollen rivers. The hypotheses which occur to an investigator are therefore a function, in part at least, of his previous knowledge.

THE DEDUCTIVE DEVELOPMENT OF HYPOTHESES

Let us now reëxamine the procedure of Herodotus in terms of the distinctions already familiar.

The search for an explanation of the Nile's behavior was a search for a *general rule* which asserts a *universal* connection between facts of that kind and other facts of different kind. The task of Herodotus was to show that the general rule which was suggested to him in the form of a hypothesis *did truly and in fact* apply to the specific problem at hand. How did he perform it?

The argument which Herodotus employed to reject the first theory may be stated as follows: The defender of the theory offers the following argument:

If the Etesian winds blow, the Nile rises (*general rule*).

The Nile rises for one hundred days beginning with the summer solstice (*observed fact*).

∴ The Etesian winds blow, beginning with the summer solstice (*inferred event*).

The inference is, of course, invalid as a conclusive proof. But its proponent may claim that the reasoning is a *presumptive probable inference,* so that the conclusion is probable on the evidence. Herodotus shows that this is not the case. He points out that we can find an occasion when the Nile rises (*observed case*) and the Etesian winds do not blow. Such a case is obviously not explained by our general rule. He therefore concludes that the hypothesis of the winds will not *always* account for the inundation of the river. But he is not content with this, for the defender of the theory may perhaps be satisfied with an explanation of the overflow which is not invariable. Herodotus showed further that the logical consequences of the Etesian wind theory were *contrary* to the known facts. In order to do this, he had therefore to point out some of the other consequences of that theory by discovering what it *implied*.

His argument continues:

If the blowing of the Etesian winds produced inundations, other rivers should behave as the Nile does (*elaborated rule*).

These other rivers do not overflow their banks (*observed fact*).

∴ The blowing of the Etesian winds does not invariably produce inundations.

This inference is a valid mixed hypothetical syllogism. Herodotus has therefore shown that the Etesian-wind theory cannot be regarded as a satisfactory explanation of the problem.

In this rejection of the first theory, Herodotus was compelled to elaborate it deductively. The importance of this step can be seen even more clearly by considering his rejection of the third theory. This may be stated as follows: If there are periodic melting snows in the interior of Africa, then the Nile will inundate periodically. Herodotus rejects this explanation not because he can *actually observe* the absence of snow in Central Africa, but because he can observe what he believes to be the consequences of Central Africa's being a warm country. And since he rejects the possibility of snowfall in warm places, he also rejects the theory of melting snows as the cause of the Nile's behavior. Let us restate part of his argument:

If hot winds blow from a region, then that region itself is hot (*general rule*).

Hot winds blow from the interior of Africa (*observed fact*).

∴ The interior of Africa is hot (*inferred fact*).

If snow falls in a region, then that region cannot have a hot climate (*rule*).

The interior of Africa *is* hot (*inferred fact from the previous inference*).

∴ Snow does not fall in the interior of Africa (*inferred fact*).

From this analysis we may conclude that the deductive elaboration of a hypothesis must follow its formulation. For we can discover the full meaning of a hypothesis, whether it is relevant and whether it offers a satisfactory solution of the problem, only by discovering what it *implies*. It is worth noting that Herodotus rejected the second theory simply on the ground that it was obscurely stated, so that it was impossible to find out what it did imply.

We are therefore already in the position to appreciate how important the technique of deduction is for scientific method. By attending to a few more relatively simple examples the reader can appreciate the indispensability for scientific procedure of developing a hypothesis deductively.

Galileo's study on falling bodies is one of the most far-reaching in modern times. He had shown that if we neglect the resistance of air, the velocity with which bodies fall to the ground does not depend on their weight. It was known that bodies pick up speed as they approach the ground. But it was not known what the relation is between the velocity, the space traveled, and the time required for the fall. Of what general law could the fall of a body be regarded as an instance?

Galileo considered two hypotheses. According to the first, the increase in the velocity of a freely falling body is proportional to the *space* traversed. But Galileo argued (mistakenly, as we now know) that one consequence of this assumption is that a body should travel *instantaneously* through a portion of its path. He believed this was impossible, and therefore rejected the proposed law of the increase in velocity.

Galileo next considered the hypothesis that the change in velocity of a freely falling body during an interval of time is proportional to that interval. This assumption may be expressed in modern notation as: $v = at$, where v represents the velocity, a the velocity acquired in one second, and t the number of seconds the body has fallen. It may also be expressed by saying that the acceleration of a falling body (defined as the change in velocity during any unit interval of time) is constant.

But the assumption that the acceleration is constant could not be put to the test *directly*. Galileo was compelled to strengthen his argument by *deducing other consequences* from the acceleration hypothesis, and showing that these consequences were capable of direct verification. The argument was strengthened because these consequences had not previously been known to be true. For example, he deduced from the hypothesis $v = at$, the proposition: The distances freely falling bodies traverse are proportional to the square of the time of their fall.

Instances of this rule can be established experimentally. Thus a body which falls for two seconds travels four times as far as a body which falls only one second; and a body falling three seconds travels nine times as far as a body falling one second. This, therefore, strengthens the evidence for the hypothesis that bodies fall so that their acceleration is constant.

In a similar fashion, Galileo deduced other propositions from the acceleration hypothesis, all of which he could verify with much precision. In this way the evidence for that hypothesis was increased. *But it was possible to increase it only after exploring its directly verifiable implications.*

Nevertheless, the evidence for the acceleration hypothesis always remains only *probable*. The hypothesis is only probable on the evidence because it is always logically possible to find some other hypothesis from which all the verified propositions are consequences. Nevertheless, it shows itself the best available so long as it enables us to infer and discover an ever greater variety of true propositions. A comprehensive theory is established as true with a high probability by showing that various *samplings* from its logical consequences are empirically true.

Let us now summarize the general features of Galileo's procedure. We find that he *selected* some *portion* of his experiences for study. His experiments from the Tower of Pisa resolved some of his doubts. But the resolution of these doubts only raised others. If the behavior of freely falling bodies did not depend upon their weight, upon what did it depend? The ancients, as well as his own contemporaries, had already isolated some properties of bodies as *irrelevant* to their behavior in falling. The temperature, the smell, the color, the shapes of the bodies, were tacitly assumed to be irrelevant qualities. The ancients also regarded the distance and the duration of fall as unimportant. But this assumption Galileo refused to make. And he ventured to formulate hypotheses in which these properties of bodies were the determining factors of their behavior.

This selection of the relevant factors was in part based on his previous knowledge. Galileo, like the ancients, neglected the color and smell of bodies because general experience seemed to indicate that their color or smell could vary without corresponding changes in their behavior when falling. In part, however, the selection was based on a tentative guess that properties heretofore regarded as unimportant were in fact relevant. Galileo had already made successful researches in physics, in which the quantitative relations exclusively studied by the mathematics of his day played a fundamental rôle. He was also well read in ancient philosophy, and had an unbounded confidence that the "Book of Nature" was written in geometric characters. It was not, therefore, with an *unbiased* mind, it was not with a mind empty of strong convictions and interesting suggestions, that Galileo tried to solve for himself the problems of motion. It was a conviction with him that the only relevant factors in the study of motion were velocity, time, distance, and certain constant proportions.

We may thus distinguish two sets of ideas which Galileo employed in studying the motions of bodies. One set, by far the larger, consisted of his mathematical, physical, and philosophical convictions, which determined his choice of subjects and their relevant properties. The other set consisted of the *special* hypotheses he devised for discovering the relations between the relevant factors. The first set was a relatively stable collection of beliefs and prejudices. It is very likely Galileo would have held on to these, even if neither of his two hypotheses on falling bodies had been confirmed by experiment. The second set, especially at the stage of scientific development in Galileo's time, was a more unsettled collection of suggestions and beliefs. Thus Galileo might easily have sacrificed his very simple equations between velocity, time, distance, and acceleration for somewhat more complex ones if his experiments had demanded the latter.

It is these special assumptions which become formulated consciously as hypotheses or theories. And it is to a more careful study of the conditions which such hypotheses must meet that we now turn.

THE FORMAL CONDITIONS FOR HYPOTHESES

1. In the first place, a hypothesis must be formulated in such a manner that deductions can be made from it and that consequently a decision can be reached as to whether it does or does not explain the facts considered. This condition may be discussed from two points of view.

a. It is often the case—indeed the most valuable hypotheses of science are of this nature—that a hypothesis cannot be directly verified. We cannot establish directly by any simple observation that two bodies attract each other inversely as the square of their distances. The hypothesis must therefore be stated so that by means of the well-established techniques of logic and mathematics its implications can be clearly traced, and then subjected to experimental confirmation. Thus the hypothesis that the sun and the planet Mars attract each other proportionally to their masses, but inversely as the square of their distances, cannot be directly confirmed by observation. But one set of consequences from this hypothesis, that the orbit of Mars is an ellipse with the sun at the focus, and that therefore, given certain initial conditions, Mars should be observable at different points of the ellipse on stated occasions, is capable of being verified.

b. Unless each of the constituent terms of a hypothesis denotes a determinate experimental procedure, it is impossible to put the hypothesis to an experimental test. The hypothesis that the universe is shrinking in such a fashion that all lengths contract in the same ratio is empirically meaningless if it can have no consequences which are verifiable. In the same way the hypothesis that belief in a Providence is a stronger force making for righteous living than concern for one's fellow man can have no verifiable consequences unless we can assign an experimental process for measuring the relative strength of the "forces" involved.

2. A second, very obvious, condition which a hypothesis must satisfy is that it should provide the answer to the problem which generated the inquiry.

Thus the theory that freely falling bodies fall with constant accelerations accounts for the known behavior of bodies near the surface of the earth.

Nevertheless, it would be a gross error to suppose that false hypotheses—that is, those whose logical consequences are not all in agreement with observation—are always useless. A false hypothesis may direct our attention to unsuspected facts or relations between facts, and so increase the evidence for other theories. The history of human inquiry is replete with hypotheses that have been rejected as false but which have had a useful purpose. The phlogiston theory in chemistry, the theory of caloric, or specific heat substance, the corpuscular theory of light, the one-fluid theory of electricity, the contract theory of the state, the associationist theory of psychology—these are a few examples of such useful hypotheses. A more obvious illustration is the following: The ancient Babylonians entertained many false notions about the magical properties of the number seven. Nevertheless, because of their belief that the heavenly bodies visible to the naked eye which move among the fixed stars had to be seven in number, they were led to look for and find the rarely seen planet Mercury. . . .

3. A very important further condition must be imposed upon hypotheses. As we have seen, Galileo's theory of acceleration enabled him not only to account for what he already knew when he formulated it, but also to *predict* that observation would reveal certain propositions to be true whose truth was not known or even suspected at the time the prediction was made. He was able to show, for example, that if the acceleration of a freely falling body was constant, then the path of projectiles fired from a gun inclined to the horizon would have to be a parabola. A hypothesis becomes *verified,* but of course *not proved* beyond every doubt, through the successful predictions it makes.

Let us change the illustration to make the point clearer. Let us imagine a very large bag which contains an enormous number of slips of paper. Each piece of paper, moreover, has a numeral written upon it. Suppose now we draw from the bag without replacing it one slip of paper at a time, and record the numeral we find written on each. The first numeral we draw, we continue to imagine, is 3, the second is 9. We are now offered a fortune if we can state what the five successive numerals beginning with the hundredth drawing will be.

What reply shall we give to the implied question? We may say, perhaps, that one answer is as good as another, because we suspect that the order in which the numerals appear is completely random. We may, however, entertain the hypothesis that the numeral we obtain on one drawing is *not* unrelated to the numeral we obtain on another drawing. We may then look for an *order* in which the numerals appear. On the *general* hypothesis that there is such an order we may then offer a *special* hypothesis to account for the sequence of the numerals. For it is clear that we can *try* to formulate such a law of sequence, even if in fact the numerals do not appear in any determinate sequence. The supposition we may make at this time, that the numerals appear in an ordered array, need not prevent us at some subsequent time from affirming, on the basis of better evidence, that they do not.

Let us accept the general hypothesis of order. The problem then is to find the *particular* order. Now the particular law or formula that we may entertain will be largely determined by our previous knowledge and our familiarity with mathematical series. On the basis of such familiarity it may appear plausible that the numeral drawn is connected with the *number of the drawing*. Other modes of connection may, of course, be entertained; the numerals drawn may be supposed connected with the *time* at which they are drawn, for example. Let us, however, accept the suggestion that the numeral is a function of the number of the drawing. Several formulae expressing this mode of connection will occur to everyone familiar with algebra. Thus we may offer as the law of the series the formula $y_1 = 3^n$, where n is the number of the drawing and y_1 the numeral drawn. When $n = 1$, y_1 is 3; and when $n = 2$, y_1 is 9. This hypothesis, therefore, completely accounts for the known facts.

But we know several other hypotheses which will also completely account for the known facts. $y_2 = 6n - 3$; $y_3 = \frac{3}{2}(n^2 + n)$; $y_4 = 2n^2 + 1$; $y_5 = (n^3/3) + (11n/3) - 1$, are four other formulae which will do so. And it is easy to show that an endless number of different expressions can be found which will perform the same function. If we reject this multitude of hypotheses without even a cursory examination, it is because we think we have some *relevant knowledge* for considering only these five.

But are all these five formulae equally "good"? If the discovery of an order determining the numerals *already drawn* were the only condition imposed upon a hypothesis, there would indeed be no reason for preferring one formula to another. However, we desire that our laws or formulae should be truly *universal*: they must express the *invariable* relations in which the numerals stand to one another. Hence the hypothesis to be preferred is the one which can *predict* what will happen, and from which we can infer what has *already* happened, even if we did not know what has happened when the hypothesis was formulated. Accordingly, we can calculate that if any one of these five formulae is universally applicable to the series of drawings, then on the third drawing from the bag we should obtain the following numerals: 27 if the first is true; 15 if the second is true; 18 if the third is true; 19 if the fourth is true; and 19 if the fifth is true.

It is extremely important to state the hypothesis and its consequences *before* any attempt at verification. For in the first place, until the hypothesis is stated we do not know what it is we are trying to verify. And in the second place, if we deliberately choose the hypothesis so that it will in fact be confirmed by a set of instances, we have no guarantee that it will be confirmed by other instances. In such a case we have not guarded against the fallacy of selection, and the "verification" is not a test or check upon the hypothesis so chosen. The logical function of prediction is to permit a genuine verification of our hypotheses by indicating, prior to the actual process of verification, instances which may verify them.

If, therefore, in our illustration the third numeral to be drawn should happen to be 19, the first three formulae would be eliminated. The remaining two would have faced the challenge of a larger body of experience. Nevertheless, we cannot be sure that these two formulae are the *only* two which could have expressed the order of the sequence of the numerals.

It becomes evident that a function of verification is to supply satisfactory evidence for eliminating some or all of the hypotheses we are considering. We are supposing we have been left with the two formulae: y_4 and y_5. Both have been imagined to be successful in predicting the third numeral. However, what we have said of what is necessary for a hypothesis to predict successfully applies not only to the third drawing, but to all subsequent drawings. If a hypothesis expresses a universal connection it must maintain itself and not be eliminated in the face of *every possible* attempt at verification. But since, as in our illustration, it is often the case that more than one hypothesis is left in the field after a finite number of verifications, we cannot affirm one such hypothesis to the *exclusion* of the others. We can *try,* however, by repeating the process, to eliminate all the relevant alternatives to some *one* hypothesis. This is an ideal which guides our inquiry, but it can rarely, if ever, be realized. And we are fortunate indeed if the hypotheses we had initially regarded as relevant are not all eliminated in the development of the inquiry.

To say that a hypothesis must be so formulated that its material consequences can be discovered means, then, that a hypothesis must be *capable of verification*. At the time a hypothesis is developed, it may be impossible to verify it actually because of practical or technical difficulties. The logical consequences of a hypothesis may be such that much time may have to elapse between the time of drawing the inference and the time of the predicted consequence. Thus a total eclipse of the sun was required for testing one of the consequences of the theory of relativity. But while a hypothesis is frequently incapable of immediate verification, and while it can never be *demonstrated* if it asserts a truly universal connection, it must be *verifiable*. Its consequences, as we have already observed, must be stated in terms of *determinate* empirical operations.

It follows that unless a hypothesis is explicitly or implicitly *differentiating* in the order it specifies, it cannot be regarded as adequate. A hypothesis must be *capable of being refuted* if it specifies one order of connection rather than another.

Consider the proposition *All men are mortal,* which is a hypothesis to account for the behavior of men. Is this a satisfactory formulation? If we should find a man who is two hundred years old, need this instance cast any doubt on the universality of the mortality theory of men? Certainly a defender of the theory would not have to think so. But what if we found a gentleman as old as one of the Struldbrugs? The defender of the theory could still maintain that his hypothesis is perfectly compatible with such an instance. We may reflect, however, that the hypothesis is so stated that *no matter how aged a man we could produce,* the hypothesis would not be refuted. The hypothesis, to be satisfactory, must be modified so that an experimental determination is possible between it and any contrary alternative.

A hypothesis, if it has verifiable consequences, cannot pretend to explain *no matter what* may happen: the consequences which are capable of being observed if the hypothesis is true cannot all be the same as the verifiable consequences of a contrary hypothesis. In our example, the hypothesis receives the proper modification if it is stated in the form *All men die before they reach the two-hundredth anniversary of their birth*. In this form, a five-hundred-year-old gentleman would definitely refute the hypothesis.

Many theories which have a wide popular appeal fail to meet the condition we have specified. Thus the theory that whatever happens is the work of Providence, or the will of the unconscious self, is unsatisfactory from the point of view we are now considering. For that theory is *not* verified, if *after* the "happening" we can interpret the event as the work of Providence or of the unconscious self. In fact, the theory is so poorly formulated that we cannot state what its logical consequences are, and therefore what should be the nature of some future event. The theory does not enable us to predict. It is not verifiable. It does not differentiate between itself and any apparently contrary theory, such as that whatever happens is fortuitous.

4. One further condition for satisfactory hypotheses remains to be considered. In our artificial illustration we found that after the third drawing, two hypotheses still remained in the field. How are we to decide between them? The answer seems not to be difficult in this case. Since the formula y_4 will yield a different numeral for $n = 4$ than will the formula y_5, the fourth drawing will enable us to verify one of them and eliminate the other, or perhaps eliminate both. But what if we should be dealing with two hypotheses of which all the consequences we can actually verify are the same?

We must distinguish two cases in which this may happen. Suppose, as the first case, that two investigators wish to determine the nature of a closed curved line they find traced on a piece of ground. One says it is a curve such that the distances from points on it to a certain fixed point are all equal. The other says the curve is such that the area inclosed by it is the largest one that can be inclosed by a curve of that length. It can be shown, however, that all the logical consequences of the first hypothesis are the same as those of the second. Indeed, the two hypotheses are not different logically. If the two investigators should quarrel about their respective theories, they would be quarreling either about words or about their esthetic preferences for the different formulations of what is essentially the same theory.

It may happen, however, that two theories are not logically equivalent although the consequences in which they differ are incapable of being tested experimentally. Such a situation may arise when our methods of observation are not sensitive enough to distinguish between the logically distinct consequences. For example, the Newtonian theory of gravitation asserts that two bodies attract each other inversely as the "second power" of their distances; an alternative theory may assert that the attraction is inversely proportional to the 2.00000008 power of their distances. We cannot detect experimentally the difference between the two theories. What further condition must be imposed so that we may be able to decide in such cases between rival hypotheses?

The answer we shall examine is that the *simpler* one of two hypotheses is the more satisfactory. We may cite as a familiar example the heliocentric theory formulated by Copernicus to account for the apparent motions of the sun, moon, and planets. The geocentric theory of Ptolemy had been formulated for the same purpose. Both theories enable us to account for these motions, and in the sixteenth century, apart from the question of the phases of Venus, neither theory permitted a prediction which could not be made by the other theory. Indeed, it has been shown that for many applications the two theories are mathematically equivalent. Moreover, the theory of Ptolemy had the advantage that it did not go counter to the testimony of the senses: men could "see" the sun rise in the east and sink in the west; the heliocentric view, from the point of view of "common sense," is a very sophisticated explanation. Nevertheless, Copernicus and many of his contemporaries found the heliocentric theory "simpler" than the ancient theory of Ptolemy, and therefore to be preferred. What are we to understand by this? We must try to analyze what is meant by "simplicity."

a. "Simplicity" is often confused with "familiarity." Those not trained in physics and mathematics doubtless find a geocentric theory of the heavens simpler than a heliocentric theory, since in the latter case we must revise habitual interpretations of what it is we are supposed to see with our eyes. The theory that the earth is flat is simpler than the theory that it is round, because the untutored man finds it difficult to conceive of people at the antipodes walking on the surface of the earth without falling off. But "simplicity" so understood can be no guide for choosing between rival hypotheses. A new and therefore unfamiliar hypothesis would never be chosen for its simplicity. What is simple to one person is not so to another. To say that Einstein's theory of relativity is simpler (in this sense) than Newton's physics is clearly absurd.

b. One hypothesis is said to be simpler than another if the number of independent types of elements in the first is smaller than in the second. Plane geometry may be said to be simpler than solid geometry, not merely because most people find the first easier to master than the second, but also because configurations in three independent dimensions are studied in the latter and only two are studied in the former. Plane projective geometry is simpler in this sense than plane metric geometry, because only those transformations are studied in the first which leave invariant the colinearity of points and the concurrence of lines, while in the second type of geometry there is added the study of transformations which leave invariant the congruence of segments, angles, and areas. So also theories of physics are simpler than theories of biology, and these latter simpler than the theories of the social sciences.

A theory of human behavior which postulates a single unlearned impulse, for example, sex desire, or self-preservation, is often believed to be simpler in this sense than a theory which assumes several independent unlearned impulses.

But this belief is mistaken, because in theories of the first type it is necessary to introduce special assumptions or qualifications of the single impulse in order to account for the observed variety of types of human behavior. Unless, therefore, *all* the assumptions of a hypothesis are explicitly stated, together with the relations between them, it is impossible to say whether it is in fact simpler than another hypothesis.

c. We are thus led to recognize another sense of simplicity. Two hypotheses may be both capable of introducing order into a certain domain. But one theory may be able to show that various facts in the domain are related on the basis of the *systematic implications of its assumptions.* The second theory, however, may be able to formulate an order only on the basis of special assumptions formulated *ad hoc* which are unconnected in any systematic fashion. The first theory is then said to be simpler than the second. Simplicity in this sense is the *simplicity of system.* A hypothesis simple in this sense is characterized by *generality.* One theory will therefore be said to be more simple or general than another if the first can, while the second cannot, exhibit the connections it is investigating as *special instances* of the relations it takes as fundamental.

The heliocentric theory, especially as it was developed by Newton, is systematically simpler than the theory of Ptolemy. We can account for the succession of day and night and of the seasons, for solar and lunar eclipses, for the phases of the moon and of the interior planets, for the behavior of gyroscopes, for the flattening of the earth at the poles, for the precession of the equinoxes, and for many other events, in terms of the fundamental ideas of the heliocentric theory. While a Ptolemaic astronomy can also account for these things, *special* assumptions have to be made in order to explain some of them, and such assumptions are not systematically related to the type of relation taken as fundamental.

Systematic simplicity is the kind sought in the advanced stages of scientific inquiry. Unless we remember this, the changes that are taking place in science must seem to us arbitrary. For changes in theory are frequently made for the sole purpose of finding some more general theory which will explain what was heretofore explained by two different and unconnected theories. And when it is said we should prefer the simpler one of two theories, it is systematic simplicity which must be understood. As we shall see presently, it is not easy at an advanced stage in a science to find a satisfactory hypothesis in order to explain some difficulty. For not every hypothesis will do. The explanation demanded is one in terms of a theory *analogous* in certain ways to theories already recognized in other domains. Such a demand is clearly reasonable, because if it is satisfied we are one step nearer to the ideal of a coherent *system* of explanations for an extensive domain of facts. In this sense, Einstein's general theory of relativity, although its mathematics is more difficult than that of the Newtonian theory of gravitation, is simpler than the latter. Unlike the latter, it does not introduce forces *ad hoc.*

It must be said, however, that it is difficult to differentiate between the relative systematic simplicity of two theories at an advanced stage of science. Is the Schrödinger wave theory more or less simple than the Heisenberg matrix theory of the atom? Here we must allow for an incalculable esthetic element in the choice between rival theories. But while there is an element of arbitrariness in thus choosing between very general theories, the arbitrariness is limited, for the theory chosen is still subject to the other formal conditions we have examined.

FACTS, HYPOTHESES, AND CRUCIAL EXPERIMENTS
Observation

A hypothesis, we have said, must be verifiable, and verification takes place through experiment or sense observation. Observation, however, is not so simple a matter as is sometimes believed. A study of what is involved in making observations will enable us to offer the *coup de grâce* to the utterly misleading view that knowledge can be advanced by merely collecting facts.

1. Even apparently random observation requires the use of hypothesis to interpret what it is we are sensing. We can claim, indeed, that we "see" the fixed stars, the earth eclipsing the moon, bees gathering nectar for honey, or a storm approaching. But we shall be less ready to maintain that we simply and literally *see* these things, unaided by any theory, if we remember how comparatively recent in human history are these explanations of *what* it is we see. Unless we identify observation with an immediate, ineffable experience, we must employ hypotheses even in observation. For the objects of our seeing, hearing, and so on, acquire meaning for us only when we link up what is directly given in experience with what is not. This brilliant white spot of light against the deep-blue background—it has an incommunicable quality; but it also *means* a star many light-years away. In significant observation we *interpret* what is immediately given in sense. We *classify* objects of perception (calling this a "tree," that a "star") in virtue of noted similarities between things, similarities which are believed to be significant because of the theories we hold. Thus, a whale is classified as a mammal, and not as a fish, in spite of certain superficial resemblances between whales and fish.

2. Observation may be erroneous. The contradictory testimony of witnesses claiming to have "seen" the same occurrence is a familiar theme of applied psychology. Every day in our courts of law men swear in good faith to having seen things which on cross-examination they admit they were not in a position to observe. This is satirized in Anatole France's *Penguin Island* in the replies given by the villagers of Alca when they were asked for the color of the dragon who had brought destruction in the darkness of the night before. They answered:

"Red."

"Green."

"Blue."

"Yellow."

"His head is bright green, his wings are brilliant orange tinged with pink, his limbs are silver grey, his hind-quarters and his tail are striped with brown and pink bands, his belly bright yellow spotted with black."

"His color? He has no color."

"His is the color of a dragon." [2]

No wonder, after hearing this testimony, the Elders remained uncertain as to what should be done! But if uninterpreted sense experience were observation, how could error ever arise?

3. The hypothesis which *directs* observation also determines in large measure what factors in the subject matter are noted. For this reason, unless the conditions under which an observation is made are known, the observation is very unreliable, if not worthless. Changes are most satisfactorily studied when only a single factor is varied at a time. Of what value, then, is an observation that a certain liquid boils at 80° C., if we do not also observe its density and the atmospheric pressure? But, clearly, only some theory will lead us to observe all the relevant factors; only a theory will indicate whether atmospheric pressure is a single factor, or whether it may be distinguished into several others, as force is into magnitude and direction.

4. All but primitive observations are carried on with the aid of specially devised instruments. The nature and limitations of such instruments must be known. Their readings must be "corrected" and interpreted in the light of a comprehensive theoretical system.

These points are made in a striking manner by the French physicist Pierre Duhem. "Enter a laboratory; approach the table crowded with an assortment of apparatus, an electric cell, copper wire covered with silk, small cups of mercury, spools of wire, an iron bar carrying a mirror; an experimenter is plugging into small openings the metal end of a pin whose head is ebony; the iron oscillates, and by means of a mirror which is attached to it, throws upon a celluloid scale a luminous band; the forward and backward motion of this luminous spot enables the physicist to observe minutely the oscillations of the iron bar. But ask him what he is doing. Will he answer, 'I am studying the oscillations of an iron bar which carries a mirror?' No, he will answer that he is measuring the electric resistance of the spools. If you are astonished, if you ask him what his words mean, what relation they have with the phenomena he has been observing and which you have noted at the same time as he, he will answer that your question requires a long explanation, and that you should take a course in electricity." [3]

Is it not imperative, therefore, that the sharp distinction frequently made between fact and hypothesis be overhauled? Facts, we have seen, are not obtained by simply using our organs of sense. What, then, are facts? Are they, as is sometimes asserted, hypotheses for which evidence is considerable? But

[2] Translation by A. W. Evans, Bk. II, Chap. VI.
[3] *La théorie physique,* p. 218.

in that case does this evidence consist only of *other* hypotheses for which the evidence is considerable, and so on *ad infinitum?*

Facts

We must, obviously, distinguish between the different senses of "fact." It denotes at least four distinct things.

1. We sometimes mean by "facts" certain discriminated elements in sense perception. That which is denoted by the expressions "This band of color lies between those two bands," "The end of this pointer coincides with that mark on the scale," are facts in this sense. But we must note that no inquiry *begins* with facts so defined. Such sensory elements are *analytically sought out by us,* for the purpose of finding reliable signs which will enable us to test the inferences we make. All observation appeals ultimately to certain *isolable* elements in sense experience. We search for such elements because concerning them universal agreement among all people is obtainable.

2. "Fact" sometimes denotes the propositions which *interpret* what is given to us in sense experience. *This is a mirror, That sound is the dinner bell, This piece of gold is malleable,* are facts in this sense. All inquiry must take for granted a host of propositions of this sort, although we may be led to reject some of them as false as the inquiry progresses.

3. "Fact" also denotes propositions which truly assert an invariable sequence or conjunction of characters. *All gold is malleable, Water solidifies at zero degree Centigrade, Opium is a soporific,* are facts in this sense, while, *Woman is fickle,* is not a fact, or at least is a disputed fact. What is *believed* to be a fact in this (or even in the second) sense depends clearly upon the evidence we have been able to accumulate; ultimately, upon facts in the first sense noted, together with certain assumed universal connections between them. Hence, whether a proposition shall be called a fact or a hypothesis depends upon the state of our evidence. The proposition *The earth is round* at one time had no known evidence in its favor; later, it was employed as a hypothesis to *order* a host of directly observable events; it is now regarded as a fact because to doubt it would be to throw into confusion other portions of our knowledge.

4. Finally, "fact" denotes those things existing in space or time, together with the relations between them, in virtue of which a proposition is true. Facts in this sense are neither true nor false; they simply *are:* they can be apprehended by us in part through the senses; they may have a career in time, may push each other, destroy each other, grow, disappear; or they may be untouched by change. Facts in this fourth sense are distinct from the hypotheses we make about them. A hypothesis is true, and is a fact in the second or third sense, when it does state *what* the fact in this fourth sense is.

Consequently, the distinction between fact and hypothesis is never sharp when by "fact" is understood a proposition which may indeed be true, but for which the evidence can never be complete. It is the function of a hypothesis to reach the facts in our fourth sense. However, at any stage of our knowledge this function is only partially fulfilled. Nevertheless, as Joseph Priestley remarked: "Very lame and imperfect theories are sufficient to suggest useful experiments which serve to correct those theories, and give birth to others more perfect. These, then, occasion farther experiments, which bring us still nearer to the truth; and in this method of *approximation,* we must be content to proceed, and we ought to think ourselves happy, if, in this slow method, we make any real progress." [4]

Crucial Experiments

In the light of these remarks on the distinction between fact and hypothesis, we must reconsider, and qualify, our previous discussion of the verification of hypotheses. It is a common belief that a *single crucial experiment* may often decide between two rival theories. For if one theory implies an experimentally certifiable proposition which contradicts a proposition implied by a second theory, by carrying out the experiment, the argument runs, we can definitely eliminate one of the theories.

Consider two hypotheses: H_1, the hypothesis that light consists of very small particles traveling with enormous speeds, and H_2, the hypothesis that light is a form of wave motion. Both hypotheses explain a class of events E, for example, the rectilinear propagation of light, the reflection of light, the refraction of light. But H_1 implies the proposition p_1 that the velocity of light in water is *greater* than in air; while H_2 implies the proposition p_2 that the velocity of light in water is *less* than in air. Now p_1 and p_2 cannot both be true. Here, apparently, is an ideal case for performing a crucial experiment. If p_2 should be confirmed by experiment, p_1 would be refuted, and we could then argue, *and argue validly,* that the hypothesis H_1 cannot be true. By 1850 experimental technique in physical optics had become very refined, and Foucault was able to show that light travels faster in air than in water. According to the doctrine of crucial experiments, the corpuscular hypothesis of light should have been banished to limbo once for all.

Unfortunately, matters are not so simple: contemporary physics has revived Newton's corpuscular hypothesis in order to explain certain optical effects. How can this be? What is wrong with the apparently impeccable logic of the doctrine of crucial experiments?

The answer is simple, but calls our attention once more to the intimate way in which observation and theory are interrelated. In order to deduce the proposition p_1 from H_1, and in order that we may be able to perform the experiment of Foucault, many *other* assumptions, K, must be made about the nature of light and the instruments we employ in measuring its velocity. Consequently, it is not the hypothesis H_1 alone which is being put to the test by the experiment—it is H_1 and K. The logic of the crucial experiment therefore is as follows: If H_1 and K, then p_1; but p_1 is false; therefore either H_1 is false or K (in part or completely) is false. Now if we have good grounds for believing

[4] *The History . . . of Discoveries Relating to Vision, Light, and Colours,* 1772, p. 181.

that K is not false, H_1 is refuted by the experiment. Nevertheless the experiment really tests both H_1 *and* K. If in the interest of the coherence of our knowledge it is found necessary to revise the assumptions contained in K, the crucial experiment must be reinterpreted, and it need not then decide against H_1.

Every experiment, therefore, tests not an isolated hypothesis, but the *whole body* of relevant knowledge logically involved. If the experiment is claimed to refute an isolated hypothesis, this is because the rest of the assumptions we have made are believed to be well founded. But this belief may be mistaken.

This point is important enough to deserve another illustration. Let us suppose we wish to discover whether our "space" is Euclidean, that is, whether the angle sum of a physical triangle is equal to two right angles. We select as vertices of such a triangle three fixed stars, and as its sides the paths of rays traveling from vertex to vertex. By making a series of measurements we can *calculate* the magnitude of the angles of this triangle and so obtain the angle sum. Suppose the sum is less than two right angles. *Must* we conclude that Euclidean geometry is not true? Not at all! There are at least three alternatives open to us:

1. We may explain the discrepancy between the theoretical and "observed" values of the angle sum on the hypothesis of errors in measurement.

2. We may conclude that Euclidean geometry is not physically true.

3. We may conclude that the "lines" joining the vertices of the triangle with each other and with our measuring instruments are not "really" straight lines; that is, Euclidean geometry is physically true, but light does not travel in Euclidean straight lines in stellar space.

If we accept the second alternative, we do so on the assumption that light is propagated rectilinearly, an assumption which, although supported by much evidence, is nevertheless not indubitable. If we accept the third alternative, it may be because we have some independent evidence for denying the rectilinear propagation of light; or it may be because a greater coherence or system is introduced into the body of our physical knowledge as a consequence of this denial.

"Crucial experiments," we must conclude, are crucial against a hypothesis only if there is a relatively stable set of assumptions which we do not wish to abandon. But no guarantees can be given, for reasons we have stated, that some portion of such assumptions will never be surrendered.

THE ROLE OF ANALOGY IN THE
FORMATION OF HYPOTHESES

The reader of this [essay], noticing that it is nearing its end, may perhaps finally lose his patience. "You have told me what a hypothesis means, how central a position it occupies in all inquiry, and what the requirements for a hypothesis are. For all this I thank you. But why don't you tell me how I am to discover a satisfactory hypothesis—what rules I should follow?"

. . . We must perhaps try the reader's patience still further, first, by quoting what a great wit replied to a similar question, and second, by considering critically a piece of advice that is sometimes given as an aid in discovering hypotheses. The wit is De Morgan. "A hypothesis must have been started," he wrote, "not by rule, but by that sagacity of which no description can be given, precisely because the very owners of it do not act under laws perceptible to themselves. The inventor of hypothesis, if pressed to explain his method, must answer as did Zerah Colburn [a Vermont calculating boy of the early nineteen-hundreds] when asked for his mode of instantaneous calculation. When the poor boy had been bothered for some time in this manner, he cried out in a huff, 'God put it into my head, and I can't put it into yours.'" [5]

The advice is that analogies or resemblances should be noted between the facts we are trying to explain and other facts whose explanation we already know. But which analogies, we are tempted to ask? We can always find *some* resemblances, although not all of them are significant. What we have already said about relevance is applicable here. Nevertheless, it is true enough that if previously established knowledge can be used in new settings, analogies must be noted and exploited.

It is a mistake, however, to suppose that we always explicitly notice precise analogies and then rationally develop their consequences. We generally begin with an unanalyzed feeling of vague resemblance, which is discovered to involve an explicit analogy in structure or function *only by a careful inquiry*. We do not *start* by noting the structural identity in the bend of a human arm and the bend of a pipe, and then go on to characterize the latter as an "elbow." Nor do we notice first the slant of the eyes and thinness of the lips of Orientals, and then conclude that they look alike. Usually it is rather the other way.

Moreover, considerations of analogy are not always on hand when we wish to formulate a satisfactory hypothesis. For though a hypothesis is generally satisfactory only when it does have certain *structural analogies* to other well-established theories, it is not easy to formulate hypotheses which meet this condition. When we study the behavior of gases, we wish to find a theory analogous to those *already* established to account for the behavior of matter in motion. This is not an easy task, as the history of the kinetic theory of gases shows. The analogy of a hypothesis to others is therefore a *condition we impose* upon it, in the interest of the systematic simplicity of all our knowledge, before such analogy can aid in any discovery. And when we succeed in formulating a hypothesis analogous to others, this is an *achievement,* and the starting-point of further inquiry.

Questions

1. Why is the view that scientific truth is to be found by "studying the facts" a superficial one?

2. How does a scientific hypothesis differ from any other kind of statement? What makes a given hypothesis *relevant* to a problem? Why is it indispensable for scientific procedure to develop a hypothesis deductively? Name and illustrate

---

[5] *A Budget of Paradoxes,* Vol. I, p. 86.

the authors' four formal conditions for a scientific hypothesis. Explain the importance of each of these conditions.

3. What is a fact in science? Consider whether Bertrand Russell accurately represents the relation of facts to scientific hypotheses when he writes:

> . . . Science, though it starts from observation of the particular, is not concerned essentially with the particular, but with the general. A fact, in science, is not a mere fact, but an instance.[1]

4. Which of the following statements are facts, or hypotheses, or both? Explain how you are using the words "fact" and "hypothesis." Can you distinguish different kinds of facts, or different degrees of sophistication in hypotheses, or both? Perhaps you can use some of the following statements to illustrate the distinctions you may wish to make in answering this last question.

   a. The sun shines.
   b. The sun is a luminous body.
   c. The sun is a mass of burning gases.
   d. The sun is a mass of radiant energy.
   e. The sun is a process in which hydrogen is converted to helium.
   f. On earth, night follows day.
   g. The earth rotates on its axis.
   h. The earth revolves around the sun.
   i. The sun goes around the earth.
   j. The earth is flat.
   k. The earth is a sphere.

5. Hiero, the ruler of Syracuse, ordered Archimedes to discover, without destroying the crown, whether a gold crown contained silver alloy. Archimedes noticed one day while taking a bath that his body seemed lighter, and it occurred to him that any body immersed in a liquid loses a weight equal to the weight of the displaced liquid.

   Show that this suggestion is sufficient to solve the problem put to Archimedes.

   (From Cohen and Nagel)

6. Before the eighteenth century, heat was regarded as an "imponderable fluid" or caloric, which lodged in the pores of substances. According to this, when an object gets colder the caloric fluid flows out, and conversely it flows in when the objects gets warmer. This theory accounted for all known facts about heat. But an alternative theory of heat was suggested, according to which heat is a form of motion. This theory also explained the known facts. At the beginning of the nineteenth century, however, Sir Humphry Davy performed an experiment which was allegedly crucial between the two theories. The experiment consisted in rubbing together two pieces of ice which were isolated from all sources of heat. The ice melted, and according to the caloric theory it must have combined with the caloric fluid to produce water. The caloric theory, however, could not explain the source of this caloric. On the other hand, the melting of the ice was easily explained on the kinetic theory of heat. Hence Davy's experiment is regarded as a crucial one.

   In what sense does this claim hold?

   (From Cohen and Nagel)

7. Show that an important condition for hypotheses is not fulfilled by the part of Freud's theory discussed in the following:

> [Freud declares that] "the *libido is regularly and lawfully of a masculine nature, be it in the man or in the woman; and if we consider its object, this may be either the man or the woman.*" . . . Those individuals whose sex life seeks an object he calls the anaclitic type, and this is essentially a mas-

[1] Bertrand Russell, *The Scientific Outlook*, Norton, N. Y., 1931, pp. 57-58.

culine type, since it is originally the woman who tends the infant. . . .
*Later on he states that where woman is anaclitic or object-loving in her
makeup, in that degree is she masculine.* This is a perfect example of the
unassailable position, and has its analogs in much of male estimation of
woman. Woman is primarily unintelligent, many men from Plato's time
have said. But if they are shown a woman who is intelligent, their answer
is, well, in that respect she is masculine! [2]

(From Cohen and Nagel)

4

| The World of Science and the Everyday World | Gilbert Ryle (b. 1900) |

Gilbert Ryle is Waynflete Professor of Metaphysical Philosophy in
Oxford University. He is the editor of *Mind,* and the author of *The
Concept of Mind* (1949) and *Dilemmas* (1954), from which this read-
ing is taken.

Professor Ryle's topic is the relation between scientific knowledge
of the world and our "everyday" knowledge of the world. Their relation is puzzling because they often seem incompatible and even contradictory, so that we appear to be faced with a dilemma in which we
have to choose between the world of science and the world of real life
or common sense. We can understand each of these "worlds" when we
think of them separately; but when we think of them together, the
conflict in our concepts (i.e., the words we use to talk about these
worlds) leads us to the perplexing conclusion that one of these worlds
is a counterfeit of the other. But must we come to such a conclusion?

In the first part of this reading, "The Two Worlds," Professor
Ryle explores at some length the conflicts which arise in our concepts,
when we try to think of these worlds together. In the second part of
this reading, "Technical and Untechnical Concepts," Professor Ryle
shows that the dilemma of the relations of "the world of science" and
"the everyday world" is to be resolved in part by our noticing the ways
in which different concepts, though applying to the same subjects,
apply to them differently. When I suppose that my statement, "My desk
has a solid top," is contradicted by my statement, "My desk is made of
atoms in motion," I am confused about the ways in which the concepts
"solid" and "made of atoms" apply to my desk. Conceptual short cir-

[2] Abraham Myerson, "Freud's Theory of Sex," in *Sex in Civilization,* ed. by V. F.
Calverton and S. D. Schmalhausen, 1929, pp. 519, 520.

cuits can be avoided by noticing that "solid" and "made of atoms" belong to two different circuits. Neither circuit crosses the other, nor can either circuit replace the other. What the reader must do is study Professor Ryle's account of how conceptual conflicts may arise and may be sorted out, and then decide whether he has resolved the dilemma of the apparent contradiction between "the world of science" and "the everyday world." In addition the reader may consider whether Professor Ryle's resolution of this dilemma might be generalized as a method for resolving other dilemmas with conceptual origins.

This reading is taken from *Dilemmas,* Chapter V, "The World of Science and the Everyday World," and Chapter VI, "Technical and Untechnical Concepts," first published in 1954.

From *Dilemmas,* by Gilbert Ryle, Cambridge University Press, Cambridge, Eng., 1954. Reprinted by permission of the publisher.

THE TWO WORLDS

We often worry ourselves about the relations between what we call "the world of science" and "the world of real life" or "the world of common sense." Sometimes we are even encouraged to worry about the relations between "the desk of physics" and the desk on which we write.

When we are in a certain intellectual mood, we seem to find clashes between the things that scientists tell us about our furniture, clothes and limbs and the things that we tell about them. We are apt to express these felt rivalries by saying that the world whose parts and members are described by scientists is different from the world whose parts and members we describe ourselves, and yet, since there can be only one world, one of these seeming worlds must be a dummy-world. Moreover, as no one nowadays is hardy enough to say "Boo" to science, it must be the world that we ourselves describe which is the dummy-world. . . . I want to persuade you that this notion is the product of an influential variety of cross-purposes between theories, and to show you some of the sources of these cross-purposes.

As a preface to the serious part of the argument I want to deflate two over-inflated ideas, from which derives not the cogency but some of the persuasiveness of the argument for the irreconcilability of the world of science with the everyday world. One is the idea of *science,* the other that of *world*.

a. There is no such animal as "Science." There are scores of sciences. Most of these sciences are such that acquaintanceship with them or, what is even more captivating, hearsay knowledge about them has not the slightest tendency to make us contrast their world with the everyday world. Philology is a science, but not even popularizations of its discoveries would make anyone feel that the world of philology cannot be accommodated by the world of familiar people, things and happenings. Let philologists discover everything discoverable about the structures and origins of the expressions that we use; yet their discoveries have no tendency to make us write off as mere dummies the expressions that we use and that philologists also use. The sole dividedness of mind that is induced in us by learning any of the lessons of philology is akin to that which we sometimes experience when told, say, that our old, familiar paperweight was once an axe-head used by a prehistoric warrior. Something utterly ordinary becomes also, just for the moment, charged with history. A mere paperweight becomes also, just for the moment, a death-dealing weapon. But that is all.

Nor do most of the other sciences give us the feeling that we live our daily lives in a bubble-world. Botanists, entomologists, meteorologists, and geologists do not seem to threaten the walls, floors and ceilings of our common dwelling-place. On the contrary, they seem to increase the quantity and improve the arrangement of its furniture. Nor even, as might be supposed, do all branches of physical science engender in us the idea that our everyday world is a dummy-world. The discoveries and theories of astronomers and astrophysicists may make us feel that the earth is very small, but only by making us feel that the heavens are very big. The gnawing suspicion that both the terrestrial and the superterrestrial alike are merely painted stage-canvas is not begotten by even hearsay knowledge of the physics of the immense. It is not begotten, either, by hearsay knowledge of the physics of the middle-sized. The theory of the pendulum, the cannon ball, the water pump, the fulcrum, the balloon and the steam engine does not by itself drive us to vote between the everyday world and the so-called world of science. Even the comparatively minute can be accommodated by us without theoretical heart-searchings in our everyday world. Pollen grains, frost crystals and bacteria, though revealed only through the microscope, do not by themselves make us doubt whether middle-sized and immense things may not belong where rainbows and mirages or even dreams belong. We always knew that there were things too small to be seen with the naked eye; the magnifying glass and the microscope have surprised us not by establishing their existence, but by disclosing their variety and, in some cases, their importance.

Now, there are, I think, two branches of science which, especially when in collusion with one another, produce what I may describe as the "poison-pen effect," the effect of half persuading us that our best friends are really our worst enemies. One is the physical theory of the ultimate elements of matter; the other is that one wing of human physiology which investigates the mechanism and functioning of our organs of perception. I do not think it makes much difference to the issue whether these ultimate elements of matter are described as the Greek atomists described them or as the twentieth-century nuclear physicist describes them. Nor do I think that it makes much difference whether we consider old-fashioned guesses or recent conclusive discoveries about the mechanism of perception. The upsetting moral drawn by Epicurus, Galileo, Sydenham and Locke is precisely that drawn by Eddington, Sherrington and

Russell. The fact that this upsetting moral was once drawn from a piece of speculation and is now drawn from well-established scientific theory makes no difference. The moral drawn is not a piece of good science now, and it was not a piece of bad science then.

So the so-called world of science which, we gather, has the title to replace our everyday world is, I suggest, the world not of science in general but of atomic and subatomic physics in particular, enhanced by some slightly incongruous appendages borrowed from one branch of neurophysiology.

b. The other idea which needs prefatory deflation is that of *world*. When we hear that there is a grave disparity between our everyday world and the world of science or, a little more specifically, the world of one wing of physical science, it is difficult for us to shake off the impression that there are some physicists who by dint of their experiments, calculations and theorizing have qualified themselves to tell us everything that is really important about the cosmos, whatever that may be. Where theologians used to be the people to tell us about the creation and management of the cosmos, now these physicists are the experts—for all that in the articles and books that they write for their colleagues and pupils the word "world' seldom occurs, and the grand word "cosmos," I hope, never occurs. There is some risk of a purely verbal muddle here. We know that a lot of people are interested in poultry and would not be surprised to find in existence a periodical called "The Poultry World." Here the word "world" is not used as theologians use it. It is a collective noun used to label together all matters pertaining to poultry-keeping. It could be paraphrased by "field" or "sphere of interest" or "province." In this use there could be no question of a vendetta between the poultry world and the Christian world, since, while "world" could be paraphrased by "cosmos" in the phrase "Christian world," it could not be so paraphrased in the other.

It is obviously quite innocuous to speak of the physicist's world, if we do so in the way in which we speak of the poultry-keeper's world or the entertainment world. We could correspondingly speak of the bacteriologist's world and the marine zoologist's world. In this use there is no connotation of cosmic authority, for the word "world" in this use does not mean *"the* world" or "the cosmos." On the contrary, it means the *department* of interests which physicists' interests constitute.

But this is not the whole story. For while there are hosts of interests, scientific, political, artistic, etc., from which the interests peculiar to physicists are distinguished, while, that is, there are hosts of provinces of interest, which are different from without being rivals of the physicist's province, there remains an important respect in which the subject matters of fundamental physical theory do comprehend or cover the subject matters of all the other natural sciences. The specimens collected by the marine biologist, though of no special interest to the physical theorist, are still, in an indirect way, specimens of what he is specially interested in. So too are the objects studied by the geologist, the mycologist and the philatelist. There is nothing that any natural scientist studies of which the truths of physics are not true; and from this it is tempting to infer that the physicist is therefore talking about everything, and so that he is, after all, talking about the cosmos. So, after all, the cosmos must be described only in his terms, and can only be misdescribed in the terms of any of these other more special sciences or, more glaringly, in theological terms, or most glaringly of all, in the terms of everyday conversation.

Let me remind you that . . . I am not now finding fault with the theories of physicists when I argue that they tell neither lies nor the truth about the world, in any awe-inspiring sense of "the world." . . .

Least of all am I trying to expound or contribute to any scientific theory. I have not got the competence and, if I had, I hope that I would not have the inclination. My sole concern is to show how certain nonscientific morals seem to be but are not consequential upon a certain sort of scientific theory. I am questioning nothing that any scientist says on weekdays in his working tone of voice. But I certainly am questioning most of what a very few of them say in an edifying tone of voice on Sundays.

I am now going to try to bring out the underlying logical pattern of the view that the truths of physical theory leave no room for the truths of daily life, and this I do by means of a long drawn out analogy with which I hope you will bear for some little time. An undergraduate member of a college is one day permitted to inspect the college accounts and to discuss them with the auditor. He hears that these accounts show how the college has fared during the year. "You will find," he is told, "that all the activities of the college are represented in these columns. Undergraduates are taught, and here are the tuition fees that they pay. Their instructors teach, and here are the stipends that they receive. Games are played, and here are the figures; so much for rent of the ground, so much for the wages of the groundsman, and so on. Even your entertainments are recorded; here is what was paid out to the butchers, grocers and fruiterers, here are the kitchen charges, and here is what you paid in your college battels." At first the undergraduate is merely mildly interested. He allows that these columns give him a different sort of view of the life of the college from the patchwork-quilt of views that he had previously acquired from his own experiences of working in the library, playing football, dining with his friends, and the rest. But then under the influence of the auditor's grave and sober voice he suddenly begins to wonder. Here everything in the life of the college is systematically marshalled and couched in terms which, though colourless, are precise, impersonal and susceptible of conclusive checking. To every plus there corresponds an equal and opposite minus; the entries are classified; the origins and destinations of all payments are indicated. Moreover, a general conclusion is reached; the financial position of the college is exhibited and compared with its position in previous years. So is not this expert's way, perhaps, the right way in which to think of the life of the college, and the other muddled and emotionally charged ways to which he had been used the wrong ways?

At first in discomfort he wriggles and suggests "May not these accounts give us just one part of the life of the college? The chimney sweep and the inspector of electricity meters see their little corners of the activities of the col-

lege; but no one supposes that what they have to tell is more than a petty frag-
ment of the whole story. Perhaps you, the auditor, are like them and see only a
small part of what is going on." But the auditor rejects this suggestion. "No,"
he says, "here are the payments to the chimney sweep at so much per chimney
swept, and here are the payments to the Electricity Board at so much a unit.
Everybody's part in the college life, including my own, is down here in figures.
There is nothing departmental in the college accounts. Everything is covered.
What is more, the whole system of accountancy is uniform for all colleges and
is, at least in general pattern, uniform for all businesses, government departments and town councils. No speculations or hypotheses are admitted; our
results are lifted above the horizons of opinion and prejudice by the sublime
Principle of Double Entry. These accounts tell the objective truth about the
entire life of the whole college; the stories that you tell about it to your brothers
and sisters are only picturesque travesties of the audited facts. They are only
dreams. Here are the realities." What is the undergraduate to reply? He cannot
question the accuracy, comprehensiveness or exhaustiveness of the accounts. He
cannot complain that they cover five or six sides of college life, but do not cover
the other sixteen sides. All the sides that he can think of are indeed duly covered.

Perhaps he is acute enough to suspect that there has been some subtle
trick played by this word "covered." The tuition he had received last term from
the lecturer in Anglo-Saxon was indeed covered, yet the accounts were silent
about what had been taught and the auditor betrayed no inquisitiveness about
what progress the student had made. He, too, the undergraduate himself, had
been covered in scores of sections of the accounts, as a recipient of an Exhibition, as a pupil of the lecturer in Anglo-Saxon and so on. He had been covered,
but not characterized or mischaracterized. Nothing was said about him that
would not have fitted a much taller Exhibitioner or a much less enthusiastic
student of Anglo-Saxon. Nothing had been said about him personally at all.
He has not been described, though he has been financially accounted for.

Take a special case. In one way the auditor is very much interested in the
books that the librarian buys for the college library. They must be scrupulously
accounted for, the price paid for each must be entered, the fact of the actual
receipt of the book must be recorded. But in another way the auditor need not
be at all interested in these books, since he need not have any idea what the
books contain or whether anybody reads them. For him the book is merely
what is indicated by the price mark on its jacket. For him the differences between one book and another are differences in shillings. The figures in the
section devoted to library accounts do indeed cover every one of the actual books
bought; yet nothing in these figures would have been different had these books
been different in subject matter, language, style and binding, so long as their
prices were the same. The accounts tell neither lies nor the truth about the
contents of any of the books. In the reviewer's sense of "describe," they do
not describe any of the books, though they scrupulously cover all of the books.

Which, now, is the real and which the bubble-book, the book read by the
undergraduate or the book whose price is entered in the library accounts?

Clearly there is no answer. There are not two books, nor yet one real book, side by side with another bubble-book—the latter, queerly, being the one that is useful for examinations. There is just a book available for students, and an entry in the accounts specifying what the college paid for it. There could have been no such entry had there not been the book. There could not be a library stocked with mere book-prices; though also there could not be a well-conducted college which had a library full of books but required no library accounts to be kept.

The library used by the student is the same library as that accounted for by the accountant. What the student finds in the library is what the accountant tells the pounds, shillings and pence of. I am suggesting, you see, that it is in partially the same way that the world of the philologist, the marine biologist, the astronomer and the housewife is the same world as that of the physicist; and what the pedestrian and the bacteriologist find in the world is what the physicist tells [them] about in his double-entry notation.

I do not want to press the analogy beyond a certain point. I am not arguing that a scientific theory is in all or many respects like a balance sheet, but only that it is like a balance sheet in one important respect, namely that the formulae of the one and the financial entries of the other are constitutionally speechless about certain sorts of matters, just because they are *ex officio* explicit about other, but connected matters. Everything that the student says about the books in the library may be true, and everything that the accountant says about them may be true. The student's information about the books is greatly unlike the accountant's, and neither is it deducible from the accountant's information, nor vice versa. Yet the student's information is covered, in an important way, by the accounts, although these are constitutionally speechless about the literary and scholarly qualities of books which are just what interest the student. . . . For though the accountant is, in some very general sense, telling the college about the books in the library, he is not, in the reviewer's sense of the word, describing or, of course, misdescribing these books at all. He is exhibiting the arithmetical relations holding during the financial year between the total bills paid to the booksellers for books and, somewhat indirectly, the total bills paid to the college for the use of those books. That there are such bills to record and, consequently, such arithmetical relations between their totals, itself logically presupposes that there are books in the library, actually bought from booksellers and actually available for reading by students. It logically presupposes that there are things of which the student's descriptions are either true or false, though these descriptions cannot be read out of the library accounts. Not only can the full history of the life of the college during the year accommodate both of these kinds of information about the books, but it could not include a page for either kind without having a page for the other. It is not a question of two rival libraries, or of two rival descriptions of one library, but of two different but complementary ways of giving information of very different sorts about the one library.

Popularizers of physical theories sometimes try to make us feel at home in their theories by saying that these theories tell us about chairs and tables. This does make us feel comfortable, just for the moment. But only for the moment, since in the next breath we hear that what these theories have to say about chairs and tables is totally unlike what we say about them to the parlourmaid and what the joiner says about them to us. Worse still, we are given the impression that what we and the joiner say about them is unscientific and will not do, while what they say about them is scientific and has got to do. In fact, of course, physical theorists do not describe chairs and tables at all, any more than the accountant describes the books bought for the library. The accountant talks about book-bills and so refers indirectly to the books paid for. But this indirect reference is not a description; nor therefore a description which vies for acceptance with the student's description; and not therefore a description the correctness of which involves the incorrectness of the student's description. What is true or false of book-bills is not true or false of books, or vice versa, and yet the fact that one statement is true of the book-bills itself requires that there are the other quite different statements which are true of the books. The corresponding thing holds in the other field. A bit of the theory of ultimate particles has no place in it for a description or misdescription of chairs and tables, and a description of chairs and tables has no place in it for a description or misdescription of ultimate particles. A statement that is true *or* false of the one is *neither* true *nor* false of the other. It cannot therefore be a rival of the other. The very fact that some statement in physical theory is true requires that some statement or other (it cannot be deduced which) about such things as chairs and tables [is] true.

A popularizing accountant might try to make us feel at home in his parallel columns by saying that a certain entry contained the audited truth about books. If successful, he might get us to feel that books have suddenly been deprived of their readable contents and become pale shadows of book-bills. One cannot say "Boo" to accountancy, but one can and should say "Boo" to the accountant who leaves his ledgers to edify us with the moral he pretends to draw from his accounts, namely that books are nothing but entries in columns of pounds, shillings and pence.

I hope that this protracted analogy has satisfied you at least that there is a genuine logical door open for us; that at least there is no general logical objection to saying that physical theory, while it covers the things that the more special sciences explore and the ordinary observer describes, still does not put up a rival description of them; and even that for it to be true in its way, there must be descriptions of these other kinds which are true in their quite different way or ways. It need not be a matter of rival worlds of which one has to be a bubble-world, nor yet a matter of different sectors or provinces of one world, such that what is true of one sector is false of the other.

In the way in which a landscape painter paints a good or bad picture of a range of hills, the geologist does not paint a rival picture, good or bad, of those hills, though what he tells us the geology of are the same hills that the painter depicts or misdepicts. The painter is not doing bad geology and the geologist is not doing good or bad landscape painting. In the way in which the joiner tells us what a piece of furniture is like and gets his description right or wrong (no matter whether he is talking about its colour, the wood it is made of, its style, carpentry or period), the nuclear physicist does not proffer a competing description, right or wrong, though what he tells us the nuclear physics of covers what the joiner describes. They are not giving conflicting answers to the same questions or to the same sort of question, though the physicist's questions are, in a rather artificial sense of "about," about what the joiner gives his information about. The physicist does not mention the furniture; what he does mention are, so to speak, bills for such goods as, *inter alia,* bits of furniture.

Part of this point is sometimes expressed in this way. As the painter in oils on one side of the mountain and the painter in water colours on the other side of the mountain produce very different pictures, which may still be excellent pictures of the same mountain, so the nuclear physicist, the theologian, the historian, the lyric poet and the man in the street produce very different, yet compatible and even complementary pictures of one and the same "world." But this analogy is perilous. It is risky enough to say that the accountant and the reviewer both give descriptions of the same book, since in the natural sense of "describe" in which the reviewer does describe or misdescribe the book, the accountant does neither. But it is far riskier to characterize the physicist, the theologian, the historian, the poet and the man in the street as all alike producing "pictures," whether of the same object or of different objects. The highly concrete word "picture" smothers the enormous differences between the businesses of the scientist, historian, poet and theologian even worse than the relatively abstract word "description" smothers the big differences between the businesses of the accountant and the reviewer. It is just these smothered differences which need to be brought out into the open. If the seeming feuds between science and theology or between fundamental physics and common knowledge are to be dissolved at all, their dissolution can come not from making the polite compromise that both parties are really artists of a sort working from different points of view and with different sketching materials, but only from drawing uncompromising contrasts between their businesses. To satisfy the tobacconist and the tennis coach that there need be no professional antagonisms between them, it is not necessary or expedient to pretend that they are really fellow workers in some joint but unobvious missionary enterprise. It is better policy to remind them how different and independent their trades actually are. Indeed, this smothering effect of using notions like *depicting, describing, explaining,* and others to cover highly disparate things reinforces other tendencies to assimilate the dissimilar and unsuspiciously to impute just those parities of reasoning, the unreality of which engenders dilemmas.

But you will not and should not be satisfied with this mere promise of a lifebelt. Can it be actually produced and thrown to us in the precise stretch of surf where we are in difficulties? To one particular place where the surf is boiling round us I shall now turn.

TECHNICAL AND UNTECHNICAL CONCEPTS

Galileo, whose lead was quickly followed by Descartes and Newton, showed that a scientific theory has no place in it for terms which cannot appear among the data or the results of calculations. But colours, tastes, smells, noises and felt warmth and cold cannot, it seems, appear there. So there is no place for them in scientific theories. What the thermometer records has its place there, but not what the fingers or the lips register; the frequencies and amplitudes of the vibrations propagated through air, but not the notes that constitute heard melodies. To us it makes a big difference whether we are blind, colour-blind, or dazzled, and whether we look at things in sunlight or moonlight, through white glass or tinted glass; but the facts about light recorded and organized in the theory of optics are indifferent to these personal differences to us. The chemist, the geneticist and the wielder of the Geiger counter, in apparent defiance of this ostracism of sensible qualities, may indeed base their special theories on the smells and tastes of chemical compounds, on the colours of sweet peas and on the clicks heard from the Geiger counter, but this does not suffice to reinstate these sensible qualities in the aristocracy of genuine physical facts. It shows only that they can, in certain conditions and when plenty of precautions are taken, be a reliable index to these facts, somewhat, perhaps, as a stomach-ache can be a reliable index to the presence of strychnine in the food consumed, though the food did not and could not incorporate any stomach-aches. Since scientific truths are about what can carry and be carried by calculations, colours, tastes and smells which cannot be so carried must belong not to the facts of physics, but elsewhere, namely either to the facts of human and animal physiology or to the facts of human and animal psychology. Colours are either in the eye of the beholder or else in the mind of the beholder. They are his rejected gift to the world. Here and here only can the iridescences of the bubble enjoy their slippery existence.

This doctrine has had a great influence and there is something in it which is true and important. It brings out into the open a fundamental logical property of the formulae that can be ingredients in an exact scientific theory. But we need to notice one or two possible traps. First, even if it is true that physical theory cannot accommodate mentions of the colours or tastes of things, this does not by itself prove that mentions of the colours and tastes of things are to be construed as mentions of things existing or happening in people's physiological or psychological insides. Certainly our insides are always a convenient limbo in which to bundle our miscellanea. The human mind in particular is traditionally the "Pending" tray for theorists' unanswered letters. But so far as the argument has yet gone, it need not be the right tray. That it is the right tray follows, or seems to follow, only from some further, much more specific arguments, some of which we shall consider later.

Next, the fact that mentions of colours and tastes cannot occur in the formulae of physical theory does not by itself prove that these formulae may not *cover* or *apply to,* without *describing,* just those things the describing of which requires the mention of colours and tastes. You cannot get mentions of the brands or the origins of wines into the arithmetic of the pipes, gallons and pints of wine for which ship space is wanted by the shipper. For him the differences between two gallons of red, vintage wine and five gallons of cheap, white wine is three gallons, *sans phrase.* Yet the gallons to be shipped cannot conceivably be mere gallons *sans phrase;* they are, for example, gallons of wine, and of wine with discoverable chemical as well as dinner-table properties. It is not true that what is not and cannot be mentioned in a formula is denied by that formula. If a supercargo's quota of cubic feet in the hold is given, for example, a vintner's implementation, then it is capable of that implementation among others. What it is not capable of is unimplementability. A public car-park need not have in it this or that particular car, or any cars of this or that make, or even any cars at all. But one thing it must have, and that is *room* for cars, no matter whose and no matter of which makes. The one thing it cannot have is a barrier against the entry of cars. It is not because it is totally inhospitable but because it is totally hospitable, that its notice boards are silent about my and your car, and about Rolls Royces and Morris Minors. Again, it is not because algebraical equations will have nothing to do with numbers, that they mention none of them. Rather it is because they are impartially receptive of any numbers you please. x is not a rival to 7; it is a hotel for 7 or for any other number. So the logically necessary silence of physical formulae about mahogany and oak or about colours and tastes need not be construed as proclaiming a shut door. It can be construed instead as proclaiming a wide open door. Precisely this is the way that we had, I think, to construe the silence of the college accounts about the contents of the books bought for its library. Only book-prices were mentioned, but this restriction was not merely compatible with the books that were bought for these prices having other properties than these prices; it was actually incompatible with books being nothing more than the vehicles of purchase prices. An object could not be merely something costing half-a-crown. The accounts were indeed entirely silent about the literary and scholarly merits and demerits of the books, but the silence was not a denial of the existence of any such qualities but, so to speak, a declaration of total indifference to which of these and other qualities belonged to which of the books. Pounds, shillings and pence are common denominators, and common denominators cannot be exclusive.

It is worth while indicating one intellectual motive for what I argue to be this error of construing a logically necessary impartiality as a logically necessary hostility. The hold of Aristotelian logic was, for both good and ill, very strong on seventeenth- and eighteenth-century theorists. So it seemed to be beyond question that the measurable dimensions of an object, say its thermometer temperature or its speed in yards per second, characterized it in the same general sort of way as its colour or taste were naïvely supposed to do. It seemed natural to list them both as Qualities. It then seemed necessary to draw a line between the qualities which have to be mentioned and operated with in physical theory and the qualities which cannot. They were in fact so distinguished—first, I believe, by Boyle—as the "Primary" and "Secondary Qualities" respectively. But then the scientifically blue-blooded Primary Qualities could not tolerate sharing a bench with the rude Secondary Qualities, and these had, in consequence, to be deprived of their title to be qualities of things at all. Clearly the mistake was to put them on the same bench at the start, but Aristotle's economy in benches was not yet recognized to be a piece of personal stinginess. Perhaps even we have inherited something of this stinginess. For we are still able to be influenced by the argument that as the description of a table given by a physicist mentions and can mention nothing of what enters into the joiner's description, therefore the joiner's description must be abandoned. In letting this argument influence us, we are supposing that there is just one rather short bench for everything that we can call "descriptions." . . . The undiscriminating employment of smother expressions, like "Quality," "Property," "Predicate," "Attribute," "Characteristic," "Description" and "Picture" reinforces our other temptations to treat as like one another concepts which in their daily jobs do not work at all like one another. It is their refusals to play the parts assigned to them which constitute dilemmas.

What I want to do now is to bring out more clearly some ways in which different concepts, though applying to the same subjects, apply to them in very different manners. The parts they play are not rival parts.

Are the cards with which we play Poker the same as those with which we play Bridge or are they different? Certainly they are the same. But are the properties or attributes of the cards which the Poker-player notices or misses the same as those which the Bridge-player notices or misses? Do these players give the same descriptions of them, or different and even conflicting descriptions of them? This is not so easy to answer. For while both may notice that a certain card is the Queen of Hearts, one of them realizes, or perhaps fails to realize, that it is the last surviving trump card, while the other has no such expression even, in his Poker vocabulary. He realizes, on the contrary, or perhaps fails to realize, that it is the card which will complete his straight flush—an attribute of which the Bridge-player knows nothing. Well, is one of them right and the other wrong? Is the player who lists the card as a trump card the victim of an illusion from which the Poker-player is exempt? Or is he, on the other hand, a specially acute observer or diagnostician, in contrast with the Poker-player who is put off with mere superficial appearances? Is the Poker-player, unhappily, trump-blind? Is the Queen of Hearts really, though not manifestly, endowed with the important property or attribute of being a trump card; or is it just the Bridge-player's systematic delusion that this is so, since it is really, say, the completion of a straight flush? Or is it really neither of these things, but just a Queen of Hearts? Obviously this is not a genuine perplexity. The question whether this Queen of Hearts is, at a particular moment, a trump card or not depends on the prior question whether four people are playing Bridge with the pack containing this card; and what makes Hearts, or some other suit, trumps is nothing occult or latent behind the glossy faces of the cards, but simply the general nature of the game of Bridge and the particular turn the bidding has taken during a particular stretch of the game.

The only perplexing thing in the situation is whether we ought to say that being a trump card is a "property" or "attribute" of the Queen of Hearts. We know how to find out whether it is a trump or not, and we know what we can do with it if it is a trump that we cannot do with it if it is not. What is not so clear—and is also quite immaterial to the play—is whether or not we should classify this knowledge as knowledge of a "property" or "attribute" of the card. This is not a Bridge-player's worry but a logician's worry. The fact that this is an invented and frivolous worry even for logicians does not matter, since we shall see, I hope, that it is of a piece with some kindred worries which are not invented or frivolous.

The question what the Queen of Hearts can and cannot do cannot be answered at all unless we know the game in which it is being employed, and specific information about what she can and cannot do in a certain state of the game requires some specific knowledge about what has been going on since the last deal.

The corresponding thing is true at a more elementary level still. A child, who could recognize the card for a picture of a queen, oddly decorated with red, heart-shaped patterns, might have as yet no idea how packs or suits of cards are composed, much less any idea that there are games the rules of which allot different values or powers to the different members of a suit. The notion that most often a Queen is "higher" than a Jack but "lower" than a King would not yet have dawned on him.

The rules of Bridge were man-invented and can be amended when we like. Nor need we play Bridge or any other game at all. But if Bridge is being played, then the question whether a given card is a trump card or not is not itself conventional. We cannot then have it which way we like. It is not a matter of mere arbitrary dubbing. We can forget and be reminded what are trumps; we can make mistakes about what are trumps and be corrected or penalized; a spectator can infer correctly or incorrectly to what are trumps from the way the hands are played. It is an objective, public fact that a given card is a trump card, though its being so is a matter of some highly arbitrary conventions being voluntarily conformed to and applied.

The same sorts of considerations apply to the familiar marketing concepts which we employ when thinking about shopping. It is not difficult to see that while having such and such a market price can be called a property or attribute of a commercial article, such logicians' appellations need to be hedged with the same sorts of precautions. There might not have been such a thing as money; there can be money where there are no pounds, shillings or pence; the purchasing power of pounds, shillings and pence can be modified by policy as well as from other causes; and retailers have some margin of freedom within which to fix the prices of their goods. None the less, in the context of the monetary system we have, the way it is working, and the retailer's decision, it is a public, objective fact that the commodity costs so many pounds, shillings and pence. We have to discover its price, and we cannot get a different price attached to it by private fiats. Moreover, where we can abstain from playing Bridge, we are bound to take part in the marketing game—only, of course, for that very reason among others, it is not a game. Here too, there can be no question of the price of a commodity being construed as an invisible quality of the thing, whose detection requires some mysterious superperceptive faculties or some abnormal diagnostic powers. We all know how to find out what things cost and we all know what is involved in their costing what they do. To know this we have merely to get the hang of an apparatus of financial and commercial terms, and to apply these to particular cases. It would be absurd to imagine, say, an Esquimau researcher, who had no monetary terminology and no grasp of simple arithmetic, finding or even looking for the prices of articles. It would be absurd, too, to doubt whether an article could both be worth 2s. 6d. and be palatable; or to ask which of these properties was a real and which a merely apparent property of the article. There could be no logical rivalry between them. They are not jealous applicants for seats on the same bench.

The thinking in which we operate with the terms or concepts of Bridge is considering how to win the game. The thinking in which we operate with the terms or concepts of commerce is considering how to make the best bargains. But the thinking in which we operate with the terms or concepts of a scientific theory is directed not towards victories or profits but towards knowledge. This gives us an extra and important motive for taking the terms of a scientific theory to stand for genuine qualities or properties of things. It also gives us a powerful inducement to overlook the numerous ways in which our operations with these terms is like our operations with the terms of Bridge and the terms of retail or wholesale trade. Where we are not seriously perplexed by the question whether behind the features of the Queen of Hearts which the child can see, there do not covertly reside some grander properties which he fails to detect, such as the card's being a trump card, we can be seriously perplexed by the question whether behind the warmth of the bath water which the child feels with his hand, there does not covertly reside some grander property which he fails to detect, namely the thermometer temperature of the water.

Where no one, unless while taking part in logicians' debates, feels any inclination to ascribe greater or deeper reality to the price than to the taste of a loaf of bread, we all of us feel strongly inclined, in certain intellectual moods, to ascribe greater or deeper truth to a formula giving the chemical composition of the bread than to the baker's or the consumer's information about it. Here we feel a kind of logical rivalry; there we did not feel it, though we could, with our logical tongues in our cheeks, build up the semblance of a case for there being such a rivalry. The case there was transparently hollow; the case here, even if hollow, is less transparently hollow.

Part of the general point that I am trying to make can be put in this way. Though phonetically and grammatically the phrase "trump card" is even shorter and simpler than the phrase "Queen of Hearts," the concept of *trump card* incorporates over and above the moderate complexities of that of *Queen of Hearts* or *three of Diamonds* all the extra complexities which constitute what we have to learn in order to be able to operate in games of Bridge with the term "trump." This huge difference in level of complexity is smothered if we very earnestly employ for concepts of the two very different levels the same umbrella words "property," "quality" and "attribute." The even more hospitable umbrella word "concept" also helps to hide the differences between the heads that it covers. But even if we employ no such logicians' smother words, we are still under some intellectual pressure to overassimilate the complex and elaborate to the simple and manageable, or the not yet scheduled to the already scheduled. That is to say, when we are not at the moment playing Bridge, but standing back and considering Bridge terms and playing-card terms together, we can, in a way, momentarily forget what we know quite well while playing, and begin to wonder how truths of the one level tie in with truths of the other; to wonder, even, if assertions of the one level are not disqualified from being true by the truth of assertions of the other level. How, for instance, can a card which was a trump card ten minutes ago, not be one now without having undergone a real change of intrinsic nature? Naturally in this particular field such moments are short and our wonderings only quarter serious. For we can deliberately join a game and as deliberately leave it. It is our sport; we are not its sport. Its control over our thinking and acting is brief and easily rescinded. Moreover, it is only one of dozens of different sorts of card games. We can without intellectual embarrassment switch in a moment from operating with the entire conceptual apparatus of Bridge to operating with the entire conceptual apparatus of Poker or Old Maid. There are no such rescindings or transfers of the controls exercised over our thinking and acting by the conceptual apparatus of established scientific theories. Here we have no similar opportunities for, so to speak, standing on the platform to wave "good-bye for the present" to the departing team of special concepts. We have no holiday from one another. Where we can often and easily get a detached view of the sort of work done, in its card-table setting, by a concept like *trump,* we cannot often or easily get a detached view of the sort of work done by a concept like *thermometer temperature* or *Vitamin B.*

Influential, too, is the fact that we can look up the codes of Bridge which fix the roles of the concepts of Bridge; and we can compare these codes word by word and phrase by phrase with the codes of other games. We have no such manuals in which to look up the codes which fix the roles of the concepts of a science, or the concepts of untechnical life. We have to read the unwritten codes of their conduct out of their conduct and we have no works of reference to tell us whether we have misread.

It is clear, I hope, how the meanings of the terms used by Bridge-players and Poker-players are heavy with the systems or schemes of those games. It would be absurd to suppose someone learning what is meant by "straight flush" without learning even the rudiments of Poker, or learning all about Poker without learning what a straight flush is. For brevity, let me describe the term "straight flush" as a "Poker-laden" term. In the same general sort of way the special terms of a science are more or less heavy with the burthen of the theory of that science. The technical terms of genetics are theory-laden, laden, that is, not just with theoretical luggage of some sort or other but with the luggage of genetic theory. Their meanings change with changes in the theory. Knowing their meanings requires some grasp of the theory.

So we can say, now, that it is relatively easy for an ordinary Poker-player to explain in words the differences between the quantity and type of luggage carried by an expression like "straight flush" and the quantity and type of luggage carried by an expression like "Queen of Hearts." But the corresponding task in some other fields is far from easy. Precisely how much more theoretical luggage is carried by such a term as "light wave" than is carried by such a term as "pink" or "blue"? But at least one can discern very often that there is this important difference between one term and another, namely that one of them carries some of the luggage of a specific theory, while the other carries none from that theory, since, for example, the latter is properly handled by people who know nothing even of the rudiments of that theory. "Queen of Hearts," for example, carries no Bridge luggage. So at least in some important respects the terms peculiar to Bridge will be mismanaged if construed as being on an equal footing with terms which are not Bridge-laden. They cannot be treated as fellow occupants of one bench, or as rivals for occupancy of one bench.

Our alarming and initially paralysing question was this: "How is the World of Physics related to the Everyday World?" I have tried to reduce its terrors and dispel its paralysing effect, by asking you to reconstrue the question thus, "How are the concepts of physical theory logically related to the concepts of everyday discourse?" I have asked you to see this question as having much in common with the questions "How are the special terms of Bridge or Poker logically related to the terms in which the observant child describes the cards that are shown to him?" and "How are the special terms of traders logically related to the terms in which we describe their commodities after we have brought them home?"

I shall not be surprised if you feel some impatience with the lengthy and somewhat factitious illustrations by which I have tried to disclose some of the kinds of difference in level and complexity between, for example, the concept of *trump* and that of *Queen of Hearts,* or between the concept of *thermometer temperature* and that of *warmth*. I expect some of you to feel that I have or *ex officio* ought to have in my reportoire some neat, strict and systematized docketing labels, by means of which I could just tell you, without relying on unreliable analogies, what the differences are between concepts and concepts, between, say, the technical concepts of a scientific theory and the semitechnical or untechnical concepts of the pavement. But I have no such packet of labels. They would do no good if I constructed a packet of them. The welter of technical concepts with which a scientist operates and the welter of untechnical and semitechnical concepts with which we all operate are welters not of homogeneous, but heterogeneous concepts. Even the relatively few technical terms of cricket or Bridge are highly variegated in kind.

Questions

1. Professor Ryle illustrates "the underlying logical pattern of the view that the truths of physical theory leave no room for the truths of daily life" by means of a conversation between an undergraduate and the college auditor. What does this conversation show about "conflicts" between physical theory and the truths of daily life?

2. How does Professor Ryle's discussion of the concepts of "trump" and "Queen of Hearts" illustrate the way concepts of physical theory are logically related to concepts of everyday discourse?

3. How does transforming the question "How is the world of physics related to the everyday world?" into the question "How are the concepts of physical theory logically related to the concepts of everyday discourse?" reduce the terrors and dispel the paralyzing effect of the first question?

4. How does a "dilemma" in Professor Ryle's sense differ from (a) a scientific problem (e.g., What chemical reactions are taking place in the center of the sun?); and (b) a philosophical problem (e.g., How do we know God exists?)?

5. How would you argue in an effort to dispel the following "dilemmas":
   a. The painter's apprentice quit his job when the firm got a contract for painting yellow lines down the center of highways, because his geometry teacher had told him that straight lines are never found in the world.
   b. A physiology student refused to use such expressions as "I have changed my mind," "I'll keep it in mind," and "What's on your mind?" after he learned that no physiologist had ever discovered in the course of his dissections an organ that could be called the mind.
   c. A student of biology could say a great deal about biological organisms and biological processes, but despaired of ever being able to answer the question "What is life?"
   d. A man who learned something about the tenets of psychoanalysis decided that he must give up his old methods of greeting his friends, and now say to each of them, "Good day. How are you, and how is your psyche?" (Suggested by Professor G. Ryle.)
   e. An economics student despaired of ever making sense of his science when he read that at the present economists believe the dollar to be worth fifty-eight cents.

6. Have you met in your reading thus far any philosophical problems which may be resolved by avoiding conceptual "dilemmas"? For example, explain why you agree or disagree with the following statements:
   a. Descartes is caught in a conceptual "dilemma" when he tries to extend the concept of truth in mathematics to sense experience. (See pages 52 ff.)

    b. Berkeley is caught in a conceptual "dilemma" in the new use he proposes for the word "idea." (See pages 89 ff.)

    c. James is caught in a conceptual "dilemma" when he argues that statements which it is profitable to believe are true. (See pages 150 ff.)

| Suggested Further Reading | Introductory Studies |

Bergmann, Gustav, *Philosophy of Science,* University of Wisconsin Press, Madison, 1957.

Bridgman, Percy W., *The Logic of Modern Physics,* Macmillan, N. Y., 1927.

Conant, James Bryant, ed., *Harvard Case Studies in Experimental Science,* Harvard University Press, Cambridge, Mass., 1957, 2 vols.

Einstein, Albert, and Leopold Infeld, *The Evolution of Physics,* Cambridge University Press, Cambridge, Eng., 1947.

Holton, Gerald, *Introduction to Concepts and Theories in Physical Science,* Addison-Wesley, Reading, Mass., 1953; especially Chaps. 8, "The Nature of Scientific Theory"; 12, "Concepts"; 13, "The Growth of Science"; 14, "Laws."

Toulmin, Stephen, *The Philosophy of Science,* Hutchinson's University Library, London, 1953.

| | Advanced Studies |

Burtt, Edwin A., *The Metaphysical Foundations of Modern Physical Science,* rev. ed., Doubleday, N. Y., 1955.

Feigl, Herbert, and Wilfrid Sellars, eds., *Readings in Philosophical Analysis,* Appleton-Century-Crofts, N. Y., 1949.

Feigl, Herbert, and May Brodbeck, eds., *Readings in the Philosophy of Science,* Appleton-Century-Crofts, N. Y., 1953.

Kneale, William, *Probability and Induction,* Oxford University Press, N. Y., 1949.

Mach, Ernst, *The Science of Mechanics, A Critical and Historical Account of Its Development,* 5th ed., Open Court, La Salle, Ill., 1942.

Munitz, Milton K., *Space, Time and Creation, Philosophical Aspects of Scientific Cosmology,* Free Press, Glencoe, Ill., 1957.

———, ed., *Theories of the Universe,* Free Press, Glencoe, Ill., 1957.

Nagel, Ernest, ed., *John Stuart Mill's Philosophy of Scientific Method,* Hafner, N. Y., 1950.

Schlick, Moritz, *Philosophy of Nature,* Philosophical Library, N. Y., 1949.

Chapter Three

THE
PROBLEM
OF

Meaning and Verification

Philosophical Questions about Meaning

The problem of meaning and verification consists of two closely connected questions: How do we find out what is the meaning of a statement? and, How do we find out whether a statement is true or false? Both of these are second-order questions. In order to answer them we must make statements about the meaning and truth of other statements. We cannot answer them by making (first-order) statements about what exists or what ought to exist. First-order statements have meaning and are either true or false, but the *study* of their meaning and of their truth or falsity is a second-order study. To answer questions about the meaning and truth of statements is not to gain knowledge of the world but to gain knowledge of the language and thoughts in which we express our knowledge of the world.

The question of meaning has several different aspects: What does it mean to say that a word or sentence has meaning? Can a word or sentence ever be meaningless, and if so, under what circumstances? How is meaning given to a word or sentence? What different kinds of meaning are there?

Although these philosophical questions about meaning are all second-order questions, they are directly relevant to first-order questions about existence and values. For once a person understands what meaning is, how our statements acquire meaning, and how we can know what our statements mean, he is in possession of criteria of meaning which can be applied to any first-order statement to test whether it has meaning, and, if it

has, what precisely its meaning is. The philosophical study of meaning thus prepares the way for the clarification of all our statements. It helps us avoid meaninglessness, vagueness, ambiguity, and inconsistency in the way we use words, and thereby helps us be clear and precise in our own thinking. It also enables us to recognize when others are not using language clearly and consistently.

Misunderstanding and lack of understanding between persons have a number of causes, some stemming from psychological or emotional conflict, some from cultural differences, and some from semantic failures. We shall here point out four main types of semantic failures. First, we may be doubtful or confused *1.* about what someone means by what he says because he is actually uttering meaningless words or sentences. (How this is possible we shall see below.) Second, we *2.* may not be familiar with the words the person is using. Although there are well established and unambiguous rules which govern the proper use of the words, we do not know what they are. This is the case when we hear a specialist using technical terms. His statements have meaning, but not to us. Third, we may *3.* be doubtful about the meaning of a statement because the person who makes the statement is not being clear. The statement is vague or means something other than what the speaker intended by it because the speaker is violating or misapplying the rules which state how the words of the language are to be used. A fourth reason for doubt and confusion about the meaning of a statement is the fact that the rules of correct linguistic *4.* usage are not always precise (At what point, precisely, can we say that a person is drunk?); they are continually changing (Shakespeare used English words which in his time were given meanings different from their present meanings.); and there is disagreement about what the rules are in certain areas of discourse (What a literary critic says in his criticism may not only be unintelligible to the ordinary man, but may also be unintelligible to other literary critics.).

The philosophical investigation of meaning, then, attempts to understand the nature of meaning and to arrive at specific criteria for determining the presence or absence of meaning (meaningfulness or meaninglessness), for determining what particular meaning is present when *some* meaning is present, and for determining whether the meaning is precise or vague, univocal or equivocal, and contextually appropriate or inappropriate.

Meaning and Verification

The reader has undoubtedly noticed that the philosophical problem of this chapter is called the problem of meaning *and verification*. How does "verification" fit into the problem? Verification is the process of finding out whether a statement is true or false. For any scientific statement, verification consists in some procedure or procedures of the scientific method, the general character of which is analyzed in Chapter 2 of this book. For nonscientific statements there are no universally accepted verification procedures. But whatever verification procedure is used, its purpose is always to decide whether the grounds on which the statement rests are good grounds. And this is true for all statements, scientific or nonscientific.

The grounds on which a statement

rests are the reasons which would be given in support of the statement if it were challenged. If the verification procedure shows that the grounds on which a statement rests are good, then we are justified in accepting the statement as true. If the verification procedure shows that the grounds are not good, then we do not know whether the statement is true or false. The verification procedure may, however, show that there are good grounds for *rejecting* the statement, and in that case we are justified in counting it as false.

To verify a statement as true, that is, to give good reasons for accepting the statement, is to describe the conditions under which the statement would be true and then to show that those conditions do exist. For example, the conditions under which the statement "The Appalachian Mountains are older than the Rocky Mountains" is true are that two events occurred, one of which was the origin of the Appalachians and the other the origin of the Rockies, and that the former event took place before the latter. Now we have good reasons for making the statement if and only if we have good reasons for believing that those events did occur as described. Such good reasons would be found in the *evidence* which geologists appeal to in support of the statement. But how did we know what conditions would make the statement true? We only knew those conditions because we understood what the statement meant. In fact the meaning of the statement consists in giving these conditions.

If we now generalize this last point to apply to any statement whatever, we have what is called "the verification principle." This principle may be formulated thus: The meaning of a statement is the set of conditions which, if they exist, show that the statement is true, and if they do not exist, show that the statement is false. Since it is by means of a verification procedure that we find out whether the conditions exist or not, we get the alternative formula: The meaning of a statement is to be found in the way in which it is verified. It follows from this view of meaning that if a person who makes a statement cannot give the conditions under which the statement would be true (or false), then he is uttering a meaningless string of words and is not really saying anything at all. The reader will gain a fuller understanding of the verification principle when he reads the selections by Professor A. J. Ayer and Dr. Friedrich Waismann in this chapter.

The importance of the verification principle can be seen at once if we consider certain kinds of statements whose meaning has been the subject of great dispute among philosophers. Such statements include "metaphysical" statements or statements about the ultimate nature of reality ("Matter does not exist." "There is a First Cause of the universe." "Nothing can break the rigid causal order of the world."), value statements ("Our duty is to bring about the greatest happiness of the greatest number." "Democracy is better than totalitarianism."), and statements which combine both metaphysical and valuational elements ("All men are created equal." "The class struggle is a manifestation of the dialectical process of history."). When the verification principle is applied to these statements, the results are of great importance to philosophy. For it is difficult to state what conditions would make these statements true (or false) and many people who utter them do not say how they would verify them. But unless they do give us this information we do not know what their statements mean and our failure to understand them is not our fault. It is not we who are thickheaded, it is they who are muddleheaded! What is more, for all we know their statements might be meaningless. If neither they nor anyone else can possibly tell us how to verify their statements, there is simply no meaning to be understood.

The Verification Principle in Recent Philosophy

The verification principle was originally formulated by a group of philosophers, known as "the Vienna Circle," who were active at the University of Vienna between the years 1922 and 1938. They were primarily interested in introducing into philosophy the clarity and logical rigor of the sciences. To this end they advocated the use of the verification principle as a correct criterion both for determining the presence or absence of meaning in sentences and for determining precisely what the meaning of a sentence is, if it is meaningful. In this chapter Professor Ayer states the Vienna Circle's principle in his own words:

. . . A sentence is factually significant to any given person, if, and only if, he knows how to verify the proposition which it purports to express—that is, if he knows what observations would lead him, under certain conditions, to accept the proposition as being true, or reject it as being false.

In recent philosophy there have been two developments which, although they originated independently of the Vienna Circle, bear certain resemblances to its general outlook. These are the developments of philosophical pragmatism in America and philosophical analysis in England. The conception of meaning advanced by the American pragmatists is set forth in the selection titled "Pragmatism," by William James, in Chapter 1 (page 142). James attributes the pragmatic conception of meaning to the American philosopher, Charles Peirce, and states it in this way:

To attain perfect clearness in our thoughts of an object . . . we need only consider what conceivable effects of a practical kind the object may involve— what sensations we are to expect from it, and what reactions we must prepare. Our conception of these effects, whether immediate or remote, is then for us the whole of our conception of the object, so far as that conception has positive significance at all.

The reader will find certain similarities between this conception of meaning and that which is contained in the verification principle if he compares William James's discussion of meaning with those of Professor Ayer and Dr. Waismann in this chapter.

The second development in recent philosophy which has certain affinities with the aims (if not with the actual views) of the Vienna Circle is that of British philosophical analysis, led by Professor G. E. Moore of Cambridge University. Professor Moore's method of philosophizing is illustrated in Chapter 1 (page 158) by his painstaking examination of the words and sentences in which William James expounds the pragmatic theory of truth. Other selections in this book which belong within the development of British philosophical analysis and which exemplify its concern with the precise meaning of words and sentences are: "The World of Science and the Everyday World," by

Gilbert Ryle (Chapter 2, page 233); "Free Will and Moral Responsibility," by P. H. Nowell-Smith (Chapter 5, page 463); "Moral Reasoning," by R. M. Hare (Chapter 6, page 583); "Natural Rights," by Margaret Macdonald (Chapter 7, page 641); and "Criticism of Kant's Philosophy of History," by W. H. Walsh (Chapter 8, page 679). The primary aim that inspires all of these meticulous analytical studies is clarity of thought, and it is this same aim which motivated the members of the Vienna Circle to adopt the verification principle as a test for the meaning of sentences.

Contents of this Chapter

In this chapter are three contributions to the problem of meaning and verification. In the first selection Professor John Hospers discusses the meaning of words as distinct from the meaning of sentences. What Professor Hospers says about the use of words and the nature of language in general can be applied to the utterances of all the philosophers represented in this book. The reader will find it enlightening to refer to Professor Hospers' "Words and the World" from time to time as he is reading other selections in the book.

In the second selection Professor A. J. Ayer expounds the verification principle as the criterion of the meaning of "factually significant" sentences. Professor Ayer's views on the meaning of sentences which express moral judgments are given in another selection of this book (page 575). In the present reading Professor Ayer uses the verification principle as a weapon against metaphysics, that is, against the making of statements about the nature of the whole of existence and about the reality of things beyond the perceivable world.

In the third selection Dr. Friedrich Waismann makes certain qualifications in the concept of verification as it is used in the verification principle. He is particularly interested in how the way we use words to describe the world affects the verification of our statements about the world. He endeavors to show that there is no sharp dichotomy between the world we look at and the words we use to talk about it.

The discussions of meaning offered by Professors Hospers and Ayer and by Dr. Waismann are various ways of dealing with the questions we have mentioned in this introduction. The significance of their views can be understood by seeing what happens when they are applied to specific statements of everyday common sense talk, of scientific language, of theological and metaphysical discourse, of the language of morals and political theory, and of historical interpretation. Thus the three readings in this chapter have a bearing on all the other chapters in this book.

Words and the World | John Hospers
(*b. 1918*)

John Hospers teaches philosophy at Brooklyn College. He is the author of *Meaning and Truth in the Arts* (1946) and *An Introduction to Philosophical Analysis* (1953).

In this reading Professor Hospers analyzes certain fundamental aspects of the relation between the world and the language we use to talk about it. He begins with a discussion of what a word is and how it is given meaning. He then examines the nature of a definition of a word, and finally the various ways words may be related to the world.

Professor Hospers' treatment of these topics owes much to the work of the Vienna Circle and the British school of philosophical analysis, two groups discussed in the introduction to this chapter. Professor Hospers makes explicit much of what is implicit in the methods which these groups use in dealing with philosophical problems.

This reading is taken from *An Introduction to Philosophical Analysis,* Chapter I, "Words and the World."

THE RELATION OF WORDS TO THINGS

Signs and symbols.   Every day of our lives we encounter situations in which one thing stands for, or means, another. A red light at a traffic intersection means that we are required to stop; a red flag means that danger is nearby; a wailing siren means that an ambulance is approaching; one kind of bell means that someone is at the door; another, that class is over. The second member of each of these pairs is the thing in which we are really interested; but the first is more convenient or accessible, so we use it to stand for the second.

In all of these cases, human beings have decided that the first member of each pair shall be made to stand for the second. But not all cases of one thing standing for another are like this. Some things stand for others regardless of what human beings decide. Clouds of a certain kind stand for rain—that is, they indicate that rain can be expected; a twister in the sky means that a tornado is approaching; a sudden drop in the barometric pressure means that a storm is on the way; and so on. We have not invented or devised these relationships; they are already there—we merely find them and record them. They are the same for all people and in all languages.

Sometimes these are known as *natural symbols,* as opposed to the first kind, which are known as *arbitrary symbols.* But more often things of the second kind are called *signs*—thus nimbus clouds are signs, not symbols, of rain—while things of the first kind are called simply *symbols.* This is the usage which we shall employ here. We shall use the word ("symbol") to refer only to those cases of standing-for in which one thing has been *made* to stand for another, by a decision of some human being or group of human beings.

Such symbols are called arbitrary because it is simply a matter of choice which item in experience is chosen to stand for the thing in question. We could have used something other than a red light as a stop signal at an intersection; there is no *natural* relationship, or relationship in nature, between the light and what it stands for as there is between clouds and what they stand for. Nor is there any reason why people had to make three dots and a dash stand for the letter *V* in the Morse code. All such things are the result of human decisions.

These symbols are also called *conventional* because after one person or group decided to use this to stand for that, other people decided to do the same thing, and the practice spread: that is, these symbols were adopted by common *convention,* and thus were made into conventional symbols. (A symbol that you alone decided upon, such as a white chalk-mark on a fencepost that you want to replace next spring, would be arbitrary—arbitrarily selected by you—but not conventional.) If people did not agree to use the same symbol for the same thing, communication would be vastly more difficult than it is. Thus, to avoid confusion, people in many nations use the red light to mean "stop," the red flag to stand for danger, the white flag to indicate peace overtures, and so on.

Sometimes symbols are used in complicated groups, or systems. Musical notation is an example. There are symbols standing for quarter tones and whole tones, sharps and flats, repeats, and so on. So precise is this system of symbols at its most complete, when it includes metronomic readings, changes of tempo, and variations in dynamics, that from reading what is on a page of music we can pretty well gather what the composer intended the music to sound like, leaving aside certain elements of musical interpretation that are dependent on technique and which are virtually impossible to indicate on paper.

The most complicated of all systems of symbols is *language.* It is because of language that we are discussing symbols here. Words are symbols, and every language (English, French, Sanskrit, and so forth) is a system of symbols. Every symbol in these systems stands for something because human beings have made them do so. Human beings have devised noises and made them into symbols. Unless people had taken and made them stand for things in the world, they would be *merely* noises, not words. Different noises are made to stand for different things, and a large body of people comes to use these noises in the same way. In this way, the words, begun as arbitrary symbols, become conventional symbols. When they are thus given meanings, the noises *become words*; the noise is, as it were, baptized into a word.

Words stand for things.   When we say that words stand for things, we do not mean that all words stand for physical things such as tables, trees, and automobiles; we are using the word "thing" in a very broad sense, such as when we say, "A funny thing happened yesterday" or "I'll tell him a thing or two." Some words stand for psychological states: "fear," "drowsiness," and so on. Other words stand for abstractions—things which (in the opinion of most people) would not exist unless there were concrete things for them to belong to: "whiteness," "intelligence." Thus far, all our examples have been nouns; but there are also the noun-substitutes, or pronouns—"you," "he," "that," and so forth—whose meaning in a particular case depends on the time, place, and other circumstances in which they are uttered. Some words stand for actions— "run," "eat," "think"; these are the verbs. Adjectives usually stand for qualities: "white," "heavy," "virtuous," "superior." Adverbs usually stand for manners of doing things: "slowly," "fastidiously." Prepositions stand for relations: "in," "above," "between," and the like.

Even so, not all words stand for things, at least not in the same way that the above kinds of words do. (1) There are *connective* words—the conjunctions—such as "and," "or," "because," "therefore." If this were a book on logic we would have to give a detailed account of the functions of such words. Here it is enough to point out that, while they do not stand for things themselves, they serve to connect words and combinations of words that do. They make a great deal of difference to the total meaning of sentences: thus, "She is going *and* I am going" is quite different in meaning from "She is going *or* I am going." (2) There are *emotive* words: words which do not stand for things but serve to release certain feelings in the speaker and/or evoke certain feelings in the listener. The purest emotive words are the interjections: "hurrah," "phooey," "whoopee," and so on. Most emotive words are also used to stand for things, and therefore are impure examples of emotive words: "nasty," "beautiful," "contemptible." . . . We should [also] be careful to distinguish *emotive* words from *emotion* words: thus, "sadness" is an emotion word because it names an emotion, while "alas" is an emotive word because the use of it tends to express and evoke an emotion.

The meanings of words are given, not discovered.   A woman once remarked, "I don't see how the astronomers found the names of all those stars." The error is obvious: astronomers have discovered many things about the stars, but not their names; for these names were not discovered but *given*. The words naming the stars are noises which, by arbitrary choice and then by convention, came to be used to stand for the various stars. The names are not related to the objects named in the way that twisters in the sky are related to tornadoes. People *discovered* that twisters are connected with tornadoes, but they *assigned* the meanings to noises which made them words. Here is a man-made relationship: human beings, by stipulating meanings for noises, caused this relationship to exist; they did not discover it already existing.

But don't you and I discover the meanings of words? Didn't we discover, for example, what the names of different stars are? *We* didn't name this one "Arcturus"; we learned, or discovered, its name. Again the answer should be obvious: we, you and I, did not name this star "Arcturus"; we discovered it; but what we discovered was simply the fact that other human beings already used this noise to stand for this star—and we simply fell in with this same usage. People used this noise to stand for this star long before we were born; these people, in turn, learned it from others before them—and so on back until we arrive at the individual or group of individuals who did not discover or learn the name, but *gave* it. In the case of most words, these individuals are now unknown or forgotten.

No right and wrong words for things.   Whoever started using one of the noises that now constitute the English language to stand for some thing, was not using the right or the wrong noise with which to do it: he was merely selecting one of an infinite multitude of possible noises and arbitrarily making it stand for that thing. His choice might be inconvenient, for example, if he selected a noise fifteen syllables long to stand for something he wanted to talk about a hundred times a day. Even so, it would not be the *wrong* noise. There are no right or wrong words for things.

But aren't certain words wrong? Suppose the name "Finns" has been used to stand for a certain people; then isn't the land they live in rightly called "Finland" and wrongly called anything else?

It would not be wrong to call it something else: some other noise might have been given instead, and it would not have been the wrong noise. But *once some names have already been given,* it is often most *convenient* to be guided in the rest of the name-giving process by those names which are already there. If the name "Finns" has already been given to a certain people, and the word "land" means what it does now, what is more convenient than to call the land "Finland," "land of the Finns"? Although it is easiest to remember that way, there are many cases where this has not been done, but other entirely unrelated names have been given, and these names are not wrong. The word "Finland" is still not a *natural* symbol for that country: the "natural" relation here is not one of resemblance between the word and the country, but between the word "Finland" and the other words "Finn" and "land."

But surely it is wrong to call some things by certain names? If I called the thing on which I am sitting a lamp instead of a chair, surely that would be wrong, wouldn't it?

Yes, it would be wrong *if* we meant by the noise "lamp" what people who speak English *already mean* by it, something that (among other things) serves to give light. You are surely not sitting on a thing that gives light, and to say that you did would be wrong: more precisely, it would be false. But of course you *could* use the noise "lamp" to stand for it if you wanted to; to do so would only be extremely confusing to other people because they already use the word "lamp" to stand for something different. We would then have *two* meanings for the noise "lamp," the one you just gave it and the conventional one which those who speak English have used for generations. In order not to mislead them, you would (if you wanted to stick to your new usage) have to tell them in advance that you were not using the noise "lamp" to mean the same thing that they were. Even so, the situation would be greatly complicated by your new usage: every time you used the noise "lamp" they would have to remember that you were using it to mean something different from the thing *they* had used the word to mean for many years. Moreover, such complication would be needless: it would serve no purpose; there would be nothing to be said for it and everything to be said against it. Nevertheless it would not be wrong: if you used the noise in this queer way it would only be unnecessarily confusing. It would only be wrong (false) if you said "I'm sitting on a lamp" and used the word "lamp" in this sentence in the conventional sense you had just rejected. The error in it would be that of using a noise to stand for a thing which by convention had been referred to by a *different* noise, and then turning right around and using this noise (perhaps unconsciously) in its conventional sense. You would be stipulating one meaning for a noise and actually using it with a different meaning.

The moral of this is that if you want to avoid unnecessary confusion in the use of language, you had better refer to a thing by the same noise that other people already use in referring to it.

Freedom of stipulation.   Still, you don't have to; no law forces you to. If you want to be different and use a different noise for the same thing that others use the noise "lamp" to refer to, you are welcome to do so. "Anybody can use any noise he wants to refer to anything he wants, as long as he makes clear what he is using the noise to refer to." This is the rule of freedom of stipulation. Its results, as we have seen, would be confusing if you made use of this freedom anywhere but on an island of which you were the sole inhabitant; for wherever there are people, there are already certain noises made to stand for certain things. If you lived alone all your life, or if there were no other people in the world, there would be no objection whatever; but in such a situation you would not need any language at all. However, your freedom to stipulate is always there; the only question is whether it is practical or useful in any way to avail yourself of it.

The rule of common usage.   Because of the unnecessary confusion and inconvenience that would be brought about if you tried to inflict a set of symbols of your own invention upon society and everyone else did the same, the rule that is usually suggested for your employment of words is that you *follow common usage*. This is what we ordinarily do without being told to do it, simply because it would be pointless to invent a new noise to stand for a thing when another noise is already being used by everyone around us. We find it easier simply to fall in line with a usage which is already established. When we *do* employ a word in a way contrary to common usage, we should inform our hearers of what we *are* using it to mean. Conversely, when we do not inform our hearers of what we are using our words to mean, they have a right to take for granted that we are using them in their conventional sense—in other words, that we are following common usage. . . .

Exceptions to the rule of common usage.   Should one *always* stick to common usage of a word? There are several qualifications we might wish to add to the rule of common usage:

1. There may not be a word for what you want to talk about. In this case, you cannot stick to common usage of a word because there is no word to stick to. Perhaps then you undertake to make one up: that is, to take a noise and use it to refer to something that has not been given a name in your language before. This, then, will be a new arbitrary symbol. If your usage catches on and other people adopt it, your noise will have become a conventional symbol; it will then have attained common usage. When the mathematician Kasner found that he wanted to refer frequently to the tenth power of ten, he asked his little grandson, "What would *you* call it?" "Googol," was the immediate response. And so the noise (now a word) "googol" has attained common usage in writings on popular mathematics.

2. Sometimes there is a common usage for a word, but you want to depart from it because the thing that the word stands for already has another word standing for it. For example, some persons now tend to use the word "God" to refer simply to nature as a whole. The word "God" already has a common usage, to refer to a supernatural Being. The word "nature" also has a common usage, to refer to the totality of things, events, and processes in the universe. Even though the word "God" were very commonly used in this new sense, you might want to resist this tendency; you would want to depart from this increasingly common usage because its results would be confusing. Word 1 stands for Thing 1; Word 2 stands for Thing 2; why complicate the matter by trying to make Word 1 also stand for Thing 2? Sometimes common usage may tend to do this, and when it does, it may well be in the interest of clarity to resist such usage.

More often, however, when a word or phrase is used in violation of common usage this is not done in the interest of clarity, but in the interest of beguiling you into accepting an unwarranted conclusion. Thus, if someone said, "There are no democracies left in the world," you might be misled by his assertion, until you discovered that he was using the word "democracy" to apply only to governments in which every citizen is a voting member of a national legislature (instead of voting for representatives to do this). You and he may argue at cross-purposes until you realize that he is using the word in this rather unusual sense. Similarly, if someone said to you, "There aren't really any material objects in the world—there are only spirits," you might be surprised at this "information," then skeptical, then inclined to deny it vehemently. But your surprise would vanish if you found that he was using the word "spirits" in such a broad way as to include trees, houses, planets, and so on—the very thing to which common usage already assigns the phrase "material objects." Often people, perhaps without knowing what they are doing, will flaunt one of their assertions as a new discovery about the universe, whereas in reality they are merely manipulating words and employing them in violation of common usage without informing their hearers of the fact.

(3.) Sometimes, and this is perhaps the most important case of all, a word does stand for something in common usage, but is employed with such haziness and indefiniteness that you are not satisfied in following common usage by continuing to use the word. The word "good," for example, is considered (by some people) so indefinite in its reference as to make its continued use confusing and unprofitable. They feel that the word as now used is simply a blanket term covering a nest of confusions, and they want to avoid this situation in the interest of clarity, even at the expense of ignoring common usage.

When it seems to you that you would only be perpetuating confusion by continuing to follow common usage of a word, you can do either of two things: (1) you can drop the word altogether, and try to say what you want to say more precisely by using different words; or (2) you can keep on using the same word but try to purify it by using it in some special and more precise sense—generally by restricting it rather arbitrarily to some specific portion of the hazy area of reference which it now has. (If you were going to use it to mean something entirely different, there would be no point in continuing to use the same word at all: thus, there would be no point in using the word "good" to mean "two or more feet high.") . . .

DEFINING CHARACTERISTICS AND DEFINITIONS

Denotation and designation.   By convention, words stand for things, and unless they are proper names they stand for classes of things. But we have also talked as if words stood rather for *characteristics*. Which of these is correct?

Both of them: words stand for both, but not in the same way. Words de-note, and they also designate. The word "cow" denotes Bossy, Dewdrop, and all the particular things to which the word "cow" is applicable; and the entire class of these particular things is called its *denotation*. But it *designates* a set of characteristics, namely, those characteristics which a thing must have in order for the word "cow" to be applicable to it.

Of the two, designation is by far the more important; for the characteristics which a word designates will determine what the particular things are which the word denotes. If we know what a word designates, we know the *conditions of applicability* of the word; we know under what conditions we can apply the word to a given particular thing in the world and under what conditions we cannot. "When a thing has characteristics A, B, and C, then the word 'X' (in our language) is applicable to it; otherwise, it is not."

Knowing only the denotation of a word is not enough. If we had never heard the word "city," but were told that New York is a city, Chicago is a city, Paris is a city, and so on, we might suspect that being a center of population and containing a large number of people had something to do with a thing's being called a city, since Coyote Canyon and Buzzard Gulch were never listed as cities. Even if we had before us the *total denotation* of the word—a complete list of all the cities in the world—we would still want some *criterion* which would enable us to tack the label "city" on some things and not others. In other words, even if we had a complete list of cities, we would still want to know why, *by virtue of what characteristics,* these were included on the list and others excluded. It would become especially urgent to know this if we wanted to talk about some center of population in the distant future, or one of your imagination, with *possible* and not merely *actual* ones. What would entitle them to be called cities? Here the list of actual cities will not help; we must know the criterion for the use of the word "city": "What are the characteristics whose presence *would* entitle something to the word 'city,' whether that something actually exists or not?" In short, we must know not merely what things the word denotes, but what characteristics it designates. When we state all the characteristics it designates, we are giving its *definition.*

Defining and accompanying characteristics.   Usually a definition comprises several *defining characteristics.* Everything in the world has an indefinitely large (some would say an infinitely large) number of characteristics; but those characteristics *without* which the thing would not be labeled by a certain word are the characteristics which *define* that word—its defining characteristics. A sentence which lists the complete set of defining characteristics is the *definition* of the word. Those characteristics of a thing without which the word would still apply to it are its *accompanying* characteristics.[1]

For example, triangles have many characteristics. Some are large, some small. Some are scalene, some isosceles, some equilateral. But there is something by virtue of which they are all triangles, and without which they would not be triangles; these characteristics are the defining ones, which together constitute the definition of "triangle." Having three sides is a defining characteristic; for anything that did not have this would not be called a triangle. Being a plane figure is another, being a closed figure another, being bounded by straight lines still another. But being at least two inches high is not; for something could still be a triangle without being at least two inches high.

The test of whether a certain characteristic is defining is always this: would the same word still apply if the thing lacked the characteristic? If the answer is no, the characteristic is defining; if the answer is yes, it is merely accompanying. Can a triangle have unequal sides and still be a triangle? Yes. Then having equal sides is not a defining characteristic of triangles. Can a triangle have unequal sides and still be an equilateral triangle? No. Then having equal

[1] Sometimes the defining characteristics are called *essential,* and the accompanying ones *accidental,* characteristics.

Sometimes a thing's characteristics are called its *properties.* This is a usage often employed in philosophy, but unfortunately the word "properties" is ambiguous: it is also used to mean (1) *only* those characteristics which are defining, and (2) *only* those characteristics which a thing would have in isolation from other things (its intrinsic as opposed to its relational characteristics).

sides is defining of equilateral triangles. A defining characteristic is a *sine qua non* (literally "without which not"). Would this thing still be an X if it didn't have characteristic A? If it would not, then having A is a *sine qua non* of its being an X—it is defining.

This is not the same question as "Would it still have A if it weren't an X?" The answer to this last question might well be yes even if the answer to the first one was no. Would it still be a triangle if it weren't a plane figure? No. Would it still be a plane figure if it weren't a triangle? It very well might: it could be a square, a parallelogram, a pentagon, etc. Having A is essential to its being an X, but being an X is not essential to its having A. Y and Z may also have A. In other words, there are many classes of things in the world that have *some* defining characteristics in common. The characteristic of being solid is defining of many things—chairs, trees, ice, etc.

Clearly this does not mean (imply) that all these words have the same definition. A definition states *all* the defining characteristics, and two words would not have the same definition unless *all* the defining characteristics were the same. The words "asteroid" and "planetoid" have the same definition and therefore designate the same total set of characteristics. But there are not many words like this; it would obviously be a pointless duplication of language. One word may be defined by characteristics A, B, and C, and another word by characteristics A, B, and D; but two words will not often have the same total set of defining characteristics, and hence the same definition. . . .

When we are distinguishing defining from accompanying characteristics, we should be particularly careful about the *universally accompanying* characteristics: when D *always* accompanies A, B, and C, we may think that it belongs in the definition. But let us then ask ourselves, "Even though D always accompanies A, B, and C, *if* sometime D did *not* accompany A, B, and C, would the thing in question still be called an X?" If the answer is yes, the characteristic is still accompanying and not defining. (Even if all right acts produced happiness and all acts producing happiness were right, it would not follow that "being right" and "producing happiness" mean the same: for the producing of happiness may be only a universal accompaniment of being right.)

Shifts in defining characteristics.   The tendency, however, is for a universally accompanying characteristic to become defining. This does not mean that one characteristic is both defining and accompanying at the same time; it means only that the designation of the word sometimes shifts gradually in the history of a language, so that the word does not designate the same characteristics at all times. The most usual direction of this shift is for universally accompanying characteristics to become incorporated (perhaps unconsciously) into the definition. Let us suppose that the word "whale" was once used to apply to anything that had characteristics A, B, and C. But then it was discovered that the creatures that had A, B, and C, also had another characteristic, D—they were mammals. This came to be added to the list of defining characteristics, for today nothing that was nonmammalian would be called a whale. (Let no one say that in discovering that whales were mammals we *found* the correct definition of the word "whale." We *could* have kept on using the word "whale" in the old way, so that if a creature having A, B, and C turned up without D, we would have called it a whale in spite of its non-mammalian character. But much zoological classification had already taken place on the basis of whether the creatures were mammalian or not, and it was most convenient simply to shift this definition a bit to accommodate the existing classification.)

Verbal disputes. Often, when we use a word, we do not have clearly in mind what characteristics the word is being used to designate, and as a result we get into unnecessary confusions and disputes.

Example. Here is a table. Would it still be a table if I painted it a different color? Yes—nobody would use color (in the case of tables) as a defining characteristic. Would it still be a table if I used it for a different purpose? Yes. Would it still be a table if I somehow petrified the wood into stone? Yes—what it is made of is not a defining characteristic. Would it still be a table if I took off one of its legs? Yes, probably we would still call it a table. Suppose I took off all four legs? Then it would not be called a table but a table-top. (Thus, having legs—at least one—is a defining characteristic of "table"; without legs it is not a table; that is, we would not use the *word* "table" to apply to it.) Suppose I chopped it to pieces; would it still be a table? No, it would be pieces of wood that had been a table but were so no longer. We so use the word "table" that the general form or shape of the thing is essential to its being called a table, but not its material composition; we use the one characteristic as defining, the other not. Of course we *could* have chosen the defining characteristics differently: we simply found this one the most convenient; for we needed a class name to talk about objects of a certain general shape, regardless of what they were made of. Had our interests been different, we would have made the word designate a different set of characteristics.

The issue, "When is it a table and when isn't it?" is a *verbal* issue—one which involves only the meanings of words, in this case the word "table." There is no dispute about the *facts*—whether the object can be painted, chopped to pieces, etc. Different people might witness the whole series of operations and yet disagree on "when it stopped being a table." Nor is the dispute clarified by assertions that "we are here searching for the *essence* of a table (or tablehood)" or that "we are trying to find *the real nature of* a table." One can use this language if he likes, provided he realizes that all we are doing is trying to bring to light what the characteristics are which we take as defining of the word, and get them all together into a definition, so that we shall know exactly when to apply the word and when not to do so. Once it is made clear what characteristics are being used as defining, the whole controversy dissolves. . . .

Just as many disputes can be resolved by clearing up words, so can *questions*. It is not always clear from the wording of a question whether it is information about *things* or about *words* that would answer it. Questions be-

ginning with "What *is the nature of* . . ." are usually (whether the ques-
tioners are aware of it or not) requests for defining characteristics. Sometimes, when we ask, "What is the nature of cats?" or "What is the nature of
water?" we are asking for accompanying characteristics as well as defining
ones: we want to know what some of the most usual or important characteristics of cats or water are, whether defining or not. But more often when we
want to know about the nature of X, we want to know the defining characteristics of X, those characteristics in the absence of which we would not call the
thing an X. The same holds for "essence-questions." "What *is the essence of*
X?" is usually a disguised request for the definition, or at least some of the
defining characteristics, of X. Those characteristics without which something
would not be an X are the characteristics which constitute "the essence" of
X. . . .

Why the relation of words to the world is not precise. Thus far, we
have talked as if all we had to do was to separate out clearly the defining from
the accompanying characteristics, so that we could mark out exactly the area
of the world to which each word applied. This is, indeed, extremely important,
for the reasons we have discussed. But often in practice it is unfortunately
impossible to do this with precision. Why is this so? What are the difficulties
in the way?

The fact that words are ambiguous can hardly be listed as one of them.
If this were our only difficulty, we would have only to state that word X in
one sense designates characteristics A, B, and C, word X in another sense
designates characteristics A, D, and E, and so on. Each word would still mark
out a precise area of the world, so long as we distinguished one sense of the
word from another.

1. There is, however, one very pervasive difficulty, namely *vagueness*. In
a general sense, all the difficulties we shall consider can be said to belong
under the heading of vagueness; but the term "vagueness" in philosophy and
semantics is more often restricted, so that words are said to be vague only when
there are *continua* (plural of "continuum") in the world. There is a continuum
of colors: red shades into orange, orange into yellow. By gradations the difficult becomes the easy, the hot becomes the cold, the fast becomes the slow. No
sharp boundary line can conveniently be drawn for the use of the word. You
cannot say that the word is applicable to everything in this area and inapplicable to everything outside it; there is a penumbra or "twilight-zone" in which
it is not clear whether the word applies or not.

A · ———————————— C · ———————————— B ·

.D
.E
.F

Going from A to B in a straight line, you would cross C; C without doubt
would be said to be *between* A and B. But would D be between A and B? We

might feel more hesitation here. "Well, not *directly* between. But close enough. Let's say it is between." Ordinarily, for example, we would say that Cleveland is between New York and Chicago, even though it is not on a straight line connecting them. (In that strict sense, *no* city would be between New York and Chicago, for a straight line between them would pass through the interior of the earth. Even if you choose some other strict sense of "between," such as "on the arc of a great circle connecting them," probably there is no city right on the line traced by this arc.)

Suppose our answer then is yes; now what of E? Is it between A and B? Well, if D is, you can hardly say that E is not—after all it is so close to D, it would be a bit arbitrary to say that D is but E is not. Then what of F? The same principle would apply again: E is between A and B, and F is right next to E, so F must be too . . . and so on until we have a point ten thousand miles away still between A and B!

Well, *that* point—call it X—isn't between A and B, surely. Yet E is, by our own admission. What can we make of this? Drawing the line between E and F seems unjustified: E would be between and F wouldn't, and they are so close together. But so is the line between F and G, between G and H, and so forth. There is *no* place where it is satisfactory to draw a boundary line. This is the "difficulty of the slippery slope": you want to go down from the top (you want to admit more than just C as being between A and B); but once you start down the slope, you can't seem to stop short of the bottom; yet you don't want to land *there* either. Set the boundary line anywhere you like, but you will fly in the face of common usage of the word.

You might say that this particular source of difficulty is nature's fault and not ours. We cannot draw a boundary line, except very arbitrarily, for the area of application of a word, simply because nature has presented us with a continuum which makes it impossible to do it satisfactorily.

Sometimes, for one special purpose or another, we have to do it, even though we feel uncomfortable about it. We have to draw the line between passing grades and failing grades, say, at 60, even though there is not much difference between a grade of 59 and a grade of 61—certainly far less than there is between the two passing grades of 61 and 100! But we are forced to draw it somewhere. . . .

2. Consider an ordinary word like "gold," the name of a chemical element, a metal. What are its characteristics? It is yellow, it has a certain definite melting-point, it has certain characteristic spectral lines, it combines chemically with such-and-such other elements in such-and-such combinations, it has a certain atomic weight, it is used chiefly in coins and jewelry. Now which of these characteristics are defining?

Some are fairly easy to exclude, for instance the use in coins and jewelry; clearly if gold were used for something else it would still be gold. (That is, it would still be *called* "gold," because we, in common usage, have not *made* its use a defining characteristic. Let us never forget that while the characteristics are there, it is we who make them defining. We could have used the noise in another way, to designate a different set of characteristics.) But of some characteristics we are not so certain. Does gold *have* to be yellow? Is this a defining characteristic? Before we reply yes, let us ask not whether all gold *is* yellow but whether it *has* to be—whether we would refuse to call any nonyellow thing gold, even if it had *all the other* characteristics associated with the word "gold." Suppose we came across something that had the required weight, melting point, ductility, and chemical properties, but was not yellow. Would it be gold? are we so sure that being yellow is defining?

Suppose we decide then that it is not really necessary, that being yellow is perhaps a universally accompanying characteristic, but not really a defining one. Now we might lean over to the other extreme: practically every characteristic that gold has is accompanying. We might say: "All that is required is that it have a certain atomic wieght. This is the only characteristic that really belongs in the definition; all the rest are merely accompanying. The chemist identifies and defines gold by whether it has this particular weight. That is all that really matters—that is what keeps gold where it is in the table of the elements. If it has this atomic weight it's gold, and if it doesn't it isn't. Things like color don't matter at all."

But is this any more satisfactory? Suppose that the chemist came across an element that had the required weight, but was purple in color, liquid at ordinary temperatures, had a whole new group of spectral lines, and so forth. Surely he would be reluctant, and so would you, to call it by the name "gold." Or suppose he came across something that was yellow, had the required melting-point, the usual spectral lines, and so forth, but did *not* have the required weight. Wouldn't it still be gold? Wouldn't he feel more inclined to call it gold than the thing that had only the required weight and *none* of the other characteristics?

Suppose, then, he sat down to make a list of all the characteristics that were really necessary, really defining, and *only* these. (He is aware by now that chemistry books often do not distinguish between the two—they list the characteristics of gold but do not say which are accompanying and which are defining.) If he listed only the atomic weight (call this characteristic A), he would feel unsatisfied—the specter of something that had all the other characteristics and not A would haunt him. If he listed a number of properties but not A, however, he would feel even more unsatisfied; he would feel that A was *more* essential than they were. Suppose, then, he listed all of them: not only the weight but the color (B), the spectral lines (C), the melting-point (D), and so on perhaps half a dozen others, he would feel that he had included too much: "Surely not all *this* is necessary?" If he did include all these, then if a thing lacked even *one* of them, it would not be gold! And surely that wouldn't be so! If something had A, B, C, D, E, and F, wouldn't he call it gold even though it lacked G? Then G was not defining. But this wouldn't prove that the first six were defining and G not; for if it had A, B, C, D, E, and G, he would still want to call it "gold" even though it lacked F. So apparently F wasn't defining either. And in the same way he could run through the whole list of characteristics, with none of them being defining. But surely that is absurd! You can't have a thing, or class of things, with *no* defining characteristics whatever! That would mean that there was *no* rule for the word's use—no characteristics that the word designated!

There are many words like this, in which if we are asked what characteristics are really defining, what characteristics the thing *has* to have to be this kind of thing, there is *no* characteristic which we can point to—there is no characteristic which we absolutely cannot do without. But this does not imply that there is no rule of usage, *no* conditions to be fulfilled in order for the word to be applicable—what it implies is that *no single characteristic is essential, as long as the other ones are there.* . . .

Under an analysis like this words display enormous ambiguity. You and I might think we had the same characteristics in mind in using the word "gold," since we never disagreed on the denotation of the word, but when it came down to it you might continue to call it gold even though it was not yellow (in the presence, say, of three of the other characteristics) and I might not. . . .

[3.] But now a new complication descends upon us, the most sweeping of them all. Suppose we define "dragon" as "fire-breathing serpent." This sounds clear enough: two defining characteristics, and that's the end of the matter. But not so: for the questions we asked of the term can now be asked of each term in the *definition*. What is it to be a serpent? could it be a serpent and have one leg? or thicker than it was long? and what must something be like exactly to merit the word "fire"? and suppose the process weren't breathing exactly, but something like it in certain ways, maybe "breathing" would do. . . . And then of each of these words in turn: what is it exactly to have a leg? what kind of protuberance exactly must it be? would this (drawing a picture) be a leg? . . . And so on.

You triumphantly define "murder" as "unjustified killing." But under what conditions exactly is something unjustified? And what is killing? if you leave your child to die of exposure, is that killing? if you drive your wife to suicide, is that killing? or running down a pedestrian in an automobile because you hadn't bothered (or hadn't had the money) to get your car serviced? To kill must you commit a physical act? must you have a certain state of mind or intention? or is it enough that the person be dead because of you, regardless of what you intended or overtly did? And if you decide on the last-mentioned, what is the criterion for "person being dead because of you"? And so on. If "X" is defined in terms of characteristics A and B (an ideally clear situation, as we have seen!), then we must ask what A and B are defined in terms of. A is defined in terms of F, G, H, and B in terms of I, J, K. Then what are F, G, H, I, J, and K defined in terms of? Well, F is defined in terms of M, N, O. . . . But we shall soon run out of letters of the alphabet, and the point is becoming painfully clear.

Thus, even if we have solved the difficulties about one term, "X," and think we have achieved a clear definition, with definite defining characteristics, the presence of which will entitle the thing to be called "X" and the absence of which will prohibit it, we still find the same indefiniteness we were trying so hard to get rid of infesting the words we used in the definition to state these defining characteristics; and the same for those words in turn; and so on. Thus, suppose you call it a house if it has a roof, four walls, and so on; but even if we can agree on a set of defining characteristics for "house," we find that the same questions that confronted us with the word occur all over again with the words used in defining it. What exactly is it to be a roof? Is there one set of characteristics defining *that*? Whatever definition we arrive at for it, the same difficulty will recur for the words in the definition. A definition is no stronger than the words in it, just as a chain is no stronger than its weakest link. Every time you think you have an airtight rule for "X," it can turn out that the very constituents of the rule are not airtight themselves; the plugs that have been put in to fill up the gaps have to be filled up themselves. This phenomenon is sometimes called *"open texture of language."*

This is just the way language is built. As long as words are built up on the basis of previous imprecise words, and those in turn on others, this phenomenon will continue. The mathematical words are, in general, the least subject to it. Second, perhaps, are the words devised for special purposes in the various sciences. (Even here, words in the definition present more difficulty than at first might appear.) The only way to avoid this difficulty would be to invent an artificial language and not use a "natural language" such as English at all. In an artificial language we would start with a few words, left undefined ("primitive terms"), and then would define others in terms of these, and still others in terms of these, being sure at each stage not to use any words which had not been defined in terms of the primitive terms or other words defined at a prior stage in the process. . . .

Stipulative and reportive definitions. When we define a word, we are indicating (presumably to someone else) what the word means. But this phrase should now sound suspicious. A word, as we have repeatedly observed, doesn't just "mean" something. A word is an arbitrary symbol which is given meaning by human beings. What, then, are we doing when we "indicate what a word means"? We are doing one of two things: either (1) we are stating what *we* are going to mean by it, or (2) we are reporting what people in general, more specifically those who use the language we are speaking, or sometimes some segment of those who use that language, already mean by it. In the first case we are stipulating a meaning, and we have a *stipulative* definition. In the second case we are reporting the usage of others, and we have a *reportive,* or *lexical,* definition.

Usually when we state definitions we state lexical or reportive definitions— the kind we generally get from a dictionary, which reports what meanings are actually attached to different words by the users of a language. (Only rarely does a dictionary try to stipulate or legislate meanings.) . . .

Do we give definitions or do we find them? In the case of stipulative definitions, clearly we give them. In the case of reportive definitions, we find them in the sense that we find what meanings *other human beings have given* to the words. No one ever found a definition that somebody before him had not given.

People do sometimes speak of trying to discover a definition when no definition has yet been found. One is tempted to ask, "If nobody ever *gave* a definition to a word (or to a noise, to make it a word), how did it ever *acquire* one? Words don't have definitions 'just naturally.' What definition could a word have other than what people give it? Once again, to state a definition is to state what characteristics a word designates—in other words, to state its meaning in one sense of 'meaning.' Surely no one can deny that a word has only as much meaning as its users give it? If no meaning has been given it, it is just a noise."

All this will be admitted; nevertheless, there is a school of thought which holds that it is not merely words, but *things,* that people define. "All you have said applies to defining words; but more important than defining words is defining things."

What kind of activity is defining things supposed to be? We know what it is like to define a word; but what is it like to define a thing? Surely, we might think, the word "definition" applies only to symbols. This, however, is a verbal matter: *we* may prefer to restrict the word "definition" to symbols, while someone else may prefer to extend the use of the word "definition" to cover things as well as symbols. And surely he can extend the use of the word if he so desires (freedom of stipulation). The question is not "Can he extend the use of the word 'definition'?" but rather, "What kind of activity is one engaging in when he claims to be giving definitions of things?" The person who claims to do this is said to be a believer in *real definitions*. In that case, what are real definitions?

1. "Real definitions give us the meanings of things." The word "meaning" can be used to apply to things as well as to words; we may discover the meaning of a thing in the sense of its cause, its explanation, its inner structure, and so forth. But is it not misleading to speak of this as definition? It is misleading enough to speak of it as meaning!

2. Real definitions tell us the essence of things, the true nature of things. Usually when we ask for the essence of something we are asking for its *most essential* characteristics—those in terms of which the word naming it is defined. "What is the essence of X?" we are asked; and we reply by stating some or all of the defining characteristics of X. In these cases, what is defined is always a word or a phrase—a symbol. The language of "essence," however, may mislead us into thinking that we are defining things.

3. Sometimes it happens that the most important, the most fundamental (in some sense) of the characteristics of a thing or group of things has not yet been discovered, and that once this characteristic is discovered, it is made defining. When this happens, it may be said that "the real definition" of the thing has been found. For example, a psychologist may say, "For years we have hunted for the definition of schizophrenia, and now we have found it."

What has been found? For years trained observers have found certain patterns of behavior recurring, not every one of them in every case, but most of them: A, B, C, D. . . . Now another characteristic, M, is found, and M is more important than the rest, since knowing that M is present enables psychologists to explain *why* some or all of the other characteristics are present—just as knowing the atomic structure of an element explains some of its chemical properties. M is so important to this whole set of characteristics that the word "X" (in this case "schizophrenia") is now defined partially in terms of M: in other words, M is made a defining characteristic. Now, one might describe this situation by saying that he had *found* the definition of X. It would be less misleading, however, if he said merely that he had found a new characteristic of X, the presence of which explained the presence of previously observed characteristics, and therefore it became convenient to shift the definition a bit in order to make M a defining characteristic.

Word-word definitions and word-thing definitions.   There are two kinds of definition of words which we may give: (1) word-word definitions, in which we say that a certain word means the same as a certain other word or words; (2) word-thing definitions, in which we say what characteristics a thing must have in order to be labeled by the word.

It is word-thing definitions which we have been discussing so far, for we have been discussing the relation of words to the world. In word-thing definitions, we either stipulate that the word shall, or report that the word does, designate the characteristics a thing must have for the word to apply to it.

In word-word definitions we merely relate the word to other words. For example, "dog" means the same as "chien." We could know that this English word means the same as that French word without knowing what *things* either of them applied to, or what characteristics the word designates. Again—this example is taken from within one language—to be told that "asteroid" means the same as "planetoid" is not to be told what either one of them means. Usually, of course, when we are told that this expression means the same as that, we already know what the first one designates. But it is possible that someone might know about every word in one language its equivalent in another language, without knowing what is designated by a single word in either. Such a person would have a system of word-word definitions but would be quite unable to relate these words to the world: he would have no word-thing definitions.

Ways of relating words to the world.   [1.] The clearest and most precise *word-thing* way of relating a word to the world is to state its (word-thing) definition—to state what characteristics it designates. This gives, as we have seen, a criterion for the use of the word. In common usage there is often no single clear criterion, and to make the application of the word precise we must often stipulate a definition rather than report one already in use.

[2.] Sometimes it is difficult or even impossible to state exactly what the word means, but we are able to take the whole sentence in which it is em- *contextual* bedded and state what *it* means. Thus, we say what the word "brother" means if we say, "X is the brother of Y means that X is a male having the same parents as Y." This is known as a *contextual* definition of "brother," or sometimes as a *definition-in-use*.

denotation

[3.] We can show what a word means by listing some of the things denoted by it. Thus one might say, " 'Bird?' That means robins, chickadees, sparrows, wrens, and so on." This method, of course, does not give us a criterion for the application of the word to the world; it simply tells us what a few of its applications are. Moreover, it may be misleading: we might conclude from a list of things denoted by the word that flying is a defining characteristic of birds, and this conclusion would be false. Incomplete and misleading though it is, however, denotation is often employed as a method of showing how a word applies to the world.

Ostensive definition

[4.] Thus far all the methods have involved the use of words. *Ostensive definition*, however, does not employ words at all. (One might say that it is not definition at all. That is a terminological matter concerning how broadly we wish to use the word "definition." But whether we call it definition or not, it is a way of connecting words with the world.) Ostensive definition, as the name implies, *shows* you, *confronts* you with, an instance or instances of the word's denotation. Showing someone a beech tree would be giving him an ostensive definition of the term "beech tree." No words except "beech tree" (with an act of pointing) need be used. All the other ways of applying words to the world involve words: they are verbal.

It would seem that the meanings of at least *some* of the words in a language have to be indicated ostensively. Suppose for a moment that we have only verbal definitions. Each word is defined, and in doing so, other words are used, This will help us only if we already know what these other words mean. How will we find out what they mean? By having their meaning explained by the use of still other words. And so on. But how can this process go on forever? Must we not eventually come to the point where we directly connect words with things, and not with other words, lest we be caught up forever in the circle of our own words? If we do not sooner or later come to a point where we directly connect a word with a thing—sometimes by pointing, sometimes by more complicated nonverbal means—then the realm of words would be forever separated from the realm of things. To connect words with the world, we need ostensive definition. How, otherwise, would we have *begun* to learn the meanings of words? . . .

The business of giving ostensive definitions, and of learning them, is much more detailed than just pointing to something and pronouncing a word. At the least, it consists of a series of successive pointings and pronouncings, so that you can reflect on what the things given the same name had in common which weren't shared by those not given the same name. Indeed, with just one act of pointing to a table you wouldn't know what was meant—the table itself, its color, its shape, its upright position, what it was made of, or some other characteristic. . . .

Nor is it always pointing that will do the trick. You certainly can't point to thoughts, emotions, or acts of willing. You can't point to fear or anxiety—you can only point to manifestations of them. You can't indicate the meaning of these terms directly at all—you can't enter your son's mind when he is afraid and say "That's fear"; but you can watch him when he gives every indication of being afraid and say "When you act that way, you're afraid." In doing this we rely on the assumption that when one person feels fear he behaves pretty much like another does when he feels fear, at least enough so that it is safe to use the same word for both persons' states. Because you cannot always tell, you sometimes label something "fear" which closer inspection or observation makes you label "anxiety."

Even the meanings of abstract words, like "change" and "again," can be indicated ostensively—we certainly never learned *them* verbally. (Try to define them verbally!) When you saw the neighbor's car parked every day in front of your house, and finally it parked next door, Mother said, "Now it's in a different place"; but she may also have said, "Well! that's a change." And lest you think that "change" just meant "cars parking in a different place," she used the same word the next day to label something quite different—the turning of the weather, or the sudden increase in the price of eggs. By a gradual process of abstraction you learned how to use the word "change." Or, when the car had a blowout in front of your house, and the next day it happened to another car there, Mother said, "Why, it's happened *again*." But you learned that it had nothing to do with cars having blowouts when she used the word after you spilled soup on the table for the second time. And so on—by this gradual process of repetition and abstraction you came to know (though not in these words of course) that the word "again" has to do not with any event or type of event, but with the general *repetitiveness* of the events. And in every case, you learned the meanings of the words ostensively—it was a long time before you could grasp the meaning of a word verbally, without being confronted with an instance of its application.

Questions

[From *Introduction to Philosophical Analysis,* by John Hospers, Chap. I.]

1. "Isn't the word 'cat' the *right* word for this pet of mine that meows and purrs? Surely it would be applying the wrong name to it if I called it a buffalo!" "Well, there aren't any right and wrong names for things, so it would be equally right if you called it a buffalo." Resolve the argument.

2. Answer this objection:
   "Nothing can be determined by appealing to common usage of language. You can't decide on an issue by showing how people use words! *Common usage may be wrong.* Suppose we tried to settle the question whether the earth is round by this method. In the Middle Ages one might have used the rule to prove that the earth is flat. Yet, as we know, that wouldn't prove for a moment that the earth really is flat."

3. Defining and accompanying characteristics. Which of the following state defining characteristics (and thus are statements about what the word means) and

which state accompanying characteristics (and thus make statements about the thing named by the word)?

    a. Triangles have three sides.
    b. Tigers are native to India.
    c. Dogs are carnivorous.
    d. Steel is used for purposes of construction.
    e. Books contain paper.
    f. Swooning isn't the sort of thing you can plan in advance.
    g. Human beings are less than twenty feet tall.
    h. A good player seldom loses a game.
    i. An axe is an instrument used for cutting.
    j. When you run you always go fast.
    k. Ladies don't use vulgar words.

    4. Consider the following verbal issues, using your knowledge of defining and accompanying characteristics to clarify the controversy in each case:

    a. Is this still a table if I cut off its legs? If I cut it up for firewood?
    b. Is it still water even if it's not liquid now?
    c. Is it still wood after I've burned it?
    d. Is he an adult before he is 21 years old?
    e. Is this still the same train, even though it's a different set of cars?
    f. Is this still the same train, even though it leaves the station at a different time each day?
    g. Is this iron even though it's not magnetic?
    h. Is this a zebra even though it has no stripes?
    i. Am I the same person as ten years ago, though all the cells that were then in my body have been replaced by others?
    j. Is this a watch even though it has no dial?
    k. Is this a hill or a mountain?
    l. Is it still grass after the cow has eaten it?

    5. Are the following disputes verbal? How would you proceed to settle them?

    a. You have an old Ford car. One part is defective and you get a new part to replace it. The next day you do the same with another part, and so on for each part until you have replaced every part in the entire car. Is what you have left at the end of this process the same car as when you began the replacements?
    b. Jack said to his brother Dick, "When I die I'll leave you my money." Next day he changed his mind and decided to leave it to his wife instead, so he wrote in his will, "All my money I leave to my next of kin" (his wife). But unknown to Jack, his wife had died. Next day Jack himself died, and his money went to his next of kin, his brother Dick. The question is: Did Jack keep his promise to Dick or didn't he?

    6. Which of the following words, in your opinion, share with the word "gold" the fact that no characteristics by themselves are defining, but the greater number of a cluster of characteristics must be present? Chair; run; eat; house; book; dog; radio; circle; smoke.

    7. Evaluate each of the following assertions. Clear up whatever confusions they may contain.

    a. Controversies about the nature of beauty or the nature of justice are silly and futile. People can define the words "beauty" and "justice" any way they want to, can't they? They have freedom of stipulation, so what are they arguing about?
    b. "This author defines one's religion as whatever values one holds highest in life. This of course is a *false* definition; this isn't what religion really is at all." "But a person can use the word 'religion' to mean that if he

wants to. Nor is his statement false; for he is stating a definition, and definitions can't be true or false."

c. For generations scientists tried to discover what pneumonia really is. At last they discovered it. It is a special kind of virus disease. So now at least we have the true definition of "pneumonia."

d. No one has yet found an answer to the question: How can a human being change and yet remain the same human being that he was before?

e. You can't step into the same river twice; for the water that was there the previous time has already flowed downstream.

f. This egg before me would not be the egg that it is if it had not been laid by this hen, at this time, at this place, if it were not being seen by me now, and about to be eaten by me. (Everything is what it is because of *everything* that ever happened to it and *all* the conditions under which it exists.)

2

The Verification Principle | A. J. Ayer
| *(b. 1910)*

Alfred Jules Ayer is Grote Professor of the Philosophy of Mind and Logic in the University of London. He is the editor of the Pelican Philosophy Series and the author of *Language, Truth and Logic* (1936); *The Foundations of Empirical Knowledge* (1940); *Philosophical Essays* (1954); and *The Problem of Knowledge* (1956).

This reading is from *Language, Truth and Logic,* a book in which Professor Ayer expresses his own version of the doctrines of the group known as "the Vienna Circle," which was mentioned in the introduction to this chapter.

In this reading, Professor Ayer describes the Vienna Circle's chief philosophical tool, the verification principle, and shows its use in one of the Circle's early objectives, the elimination of metaphysics. In the Preface to the first edition of *Language, Truth and Logic,* Professor Ayer makes certain observations about the origin of the verification principle, which will help the reader place it in the history of philosophy. Berkeley and Hume, to whom Professor Ayer refers, are represented in this book (pages 87 and 98). Professor Ayer writes:

The views which are put forward in this treatise derive from the doctrines of Bertrand Russell and Wittgenstein, which are themselves the logical outcome of the empiricism of Berkeley and David Hume. Like Hume, I divide all genuine propositions into two classes: those which, in his terminology, concern "relations of ideas," and those which concern "matters of fact." The former class comprises the *a priori* propositions of logic and pure mathematics, and these I allow to be necessary and certain only because they are analytic. That is, I maintain that the reason why these propositions cannot be confuted in experience is that they do not make any assertion about the empirical world, but simply record our determination to use symbols in a certain fashion. Propositions concerning empirical matters of fact, on the other hand, I hold to be hypotheses, which can be probable but never certain. And in giving an account of the method of their validation I claim also to have explained the nature of truth.

To test whether a sentence expresses a genuine empirical hypothesis, I adopt what may be called a modified verification principle. For I require of an empirical hypothesis, not indeed that it should be conclusively verifiable, but that some possible sense-experience should be relevant to the determination of its truth or falsehood. If a putative proposition fails to satisfy this principle, and is not a tautology, then I hold that it is metaphysical, and that, being metaphysical, it is neither true nor false but literally senseless. It will be found that much of what ordinarily passes for philosophy is metaphysical according to this criterion, and, in particular, that it can not be significantly asserted that there is a nonempirical world of values, or that men have immortal souls, or that there is a transcendent God.

Professor Ayer makes use of the term "tautology" in the above quotation to mean any statement which is necessarily and always true, such as a mathematical equation or a geometrical theorem. The denial of a tautology would be self-contradictory. In the terminology of David Hume, a tautology is a statement expressing a "relation of ideas." (See the selection by Hume in Chapter 1, page 98.) In the terminology of Immanuel Kant, a tautology is an "analytical judgment." (See the selection by Kant in Chapter 1, page 116.)

This selection has been divided into three parts. Part I is a discussion of metaphysics as "knowledge of a reality transcending the world of science and common sense." Examples of metaphysics in this sense are the selection by Josiah Royce in Chapter 1 (page 129) and most of the writings of theologians (see Chapter 4). Part II of this selection is a statement of the verification principle and a discussion of the way in which it is to be used in distinguishing between meaningful statements and nonsense sentences. This passage reveals what admirers of the Vienna Circle have always regarded as their strong point, and their critics have always regarded as their most serious error, namely, their parsimony about what they will permit philosophers to say. Part III is an account of what leads philosophers to make metaphysical assertions. Professor Ayer argues that through misunderstanding the structure and function of sentences, metaphysicians believe they can say more than the semantical rules of a language permit them to say. When they violate those rules, their sentences become nonsense.

The reader's task is first to learn what the verification principle is and how it is to be used. He may then consider for himself whether its use eliminates metaphysics, and whether it places proper limits on the meaningfulness of sentences.

This reading is from Chapter I of *Language, Truth and Logic.*

From *Language, Truth and Logic,* by Alfred Jules Ayer, reprinted through permission by the author and by Dover Publications, Inc., New York 10, N. Y. ($1.25, paperbound).

I

The traditional disputes of philosophers are, for the most part, as unwarranted as they are unfruitful. The surest way to end them is to establish beyond question what should be the purpose and method of a philosophical enquiry. And this is by no means so difficult a task as the history of philosophy would lead one to suppose. For if there are any questions which science leaves it to philosophy to answer, a straightforward process of elimination must lead to their discovery.

We may begin by criticising the metaphysical thesis that philosophy affords us knowledge of a reality transcending the world of science and common sense. Later on, when we come to define metaphysics and account for its existence, we shall find that it is possible to be a metaphysician without believing in a transcendent reality; for we shall see that many metaphysical utterances are due to the commission of logical errors, rather than to a conscious desire on the part of their authors to go beyond the limits of experience. But it is convenient for us to take the case of those who believe that it is possible to have knowledge of a transcendent reality as a starting-point for our discussion. The arguments which we use to refute them will subsequently be found to apply to the whole of metaphysics.

One way of attacking a metaphysician who claimed to have knowledge of a reality which transcended the phenomenal world would be to enquire from what premises his propositions were deduced. Must he not begin, as other men do, with the evidence of his senses? And if so, what valid process of reasoning can possibly lead him to the conception of a transcendent reality? Surely from empirical premises nothing whatsoever concerning the properties, or even the existence, of anything super-empirical can legitimately be inferred. But this objection would be met by a denial on the part of the metaphysician that his assertions were ultimately based on the evidence of his senses. He would say that he was endowed with a faculty of intellectual intuition which enabled him to know facts that could not be known through sense-experience. And even if it could be shown that he was relying on empirical premises, and that his venture into a nonempirical world was therefore logically unjustified, it would not follow that the assertions which he made concerning this nonempirical world could not be true. For the fact that a conclusion does not follow from its putative premise is not sufficient to show that it is false. Consequently one cannot overthrow a system of transcendent metaphysics merely by criticising the way in which it comes into being. What is required is rather a criticism of the nature of the actual statements which comprise it. And this is the line of argument which we shall, in fact, pursue. For we shall maintain that no statement which refers to a "reality" transcending the limits of all possible sense-experience can possibly have any literal significance; from which it must follow that the labours of those who have striven to describe such a reality have all been devoted to the production of nonsense.

It may be suggested that this is a proposition which has already been proved by Kant. But although Kant also condemned transcendent metaphysics, he did so on different grounds. For he said that the human understanding was so constituted that it lost itself in contradictions when it ventured out beyond the limits of possible experience and attempted to deal with things in themselves. And thus he made the impossibility of a transcendent metaphysic not, as we do, a matter of logic, but a matter of fact. He asserted, not that our minds could not conceivably have had the power of penetrating beyond the phenomenal world, but merely that they were in fact devoid of it. And this leads the critic to ask how, if it is possible to know only what lies within the bounds of sense-experience, the author can be justified in asserting that real things do exist beyond, and how he can tell what are the boundaries beyond which the human understanding may not venture, unless he succeeds in passing them himself. As Wittgenstein says, "In order to draw a limit to thinking, we should have to think both sides of this limit,"[1] a truth to which Bradley gives a special twist in maintaining that the man who is ready to prove that metaphysics is impossible is a brother metaphysician with a rival theory of his own.[2]

Whatever force these objections may have against the Kantian doctrine, they have none whatsoever against the thesis that I am about to set forth. It cannot here be said that the author is himself overstepping the barrier he maintains to be impassable. For the fruitlessness of attempting to transcend the limits of possible sense-experience will be deduced, not from a psychological hypothesis concerning the actual constitution of the human mind, but from the rule which determines the literal significance of language. Our charge against the metaphysician is not that he attempts to employ the understanding in a field where it cannot profitably venture, but that he produces sentences which fail to conform to the conditions under which alone a sentence can be literally significant. Nor are we ourselves obliged to talk nonsense in order to show that all sentences of a certain type are necessarily devoid of literal significance. We need only formulate the criterion which enables us to test whether a sentence expresses a genuine proposition about a matter of fact, and then point out that the sentences under consideration fail to satisfy it. And this we shall

---

[1] *Tractatus Logico-Philosophicus*, Preface.
[2] Bradley, *Appearance and Reality*, 2nd ed., p. 1.

now proceed to do. We shall first of all formulate the criterion in somewhat vague terms, and then give the explanations which are necessary to render it precise.

II

The criterion which we use to test the genuineness of apparent statements of fact is the criterion of verifiability. We say that a sentence is factually significant to any given person, if, and only if, he knows how to verify the proposition which it purports to express—that is, if he knows what observations would lead him, under certain conditions, to accept the proposition as being true, or reject it as being false. If, on the other hand, the putative proposition is of such a character that the assumption of its truth, or falsehood, is consistent with any assumption whatsoever concerning the nature of his future experience, then, as far as he is concerned, it is, if not a tautology, a mere pseudo-proposition. The sentence expressing it may be emotionally significant to him; but it is not literally significant. And with regard to questions the procedure is the same. We enquire in every case what observations would lead us to answer the question, one way or the other; and, if none can be discovered, we must conclude that the sentence under consideration does not, as far as we are concerned, express a genuine question, however strongly its grammatical appearance may suggest that it does.

. . . This procedure needs to be examined in detail.

In the first place, it is necessary to draw a distinction between practical verifiability, and verifiability in principle. Plainly we all understand, in many cases believe, propositions which we have not in fact taken steps to verify. Many of these are propositions which we could verify if we took enough trouble. But there remain a number of significant propositions, concerning matters of fact, which we could not verify even if we chose; simply because we lack the practical means of placing ourselves in the situation where the relevant observations could be made. A simple and familiar example of such a proposition is the proposition that there are mountains on the farther side of the moon.[3] No rocket has yet been invented which would enable me to go and look at the farther side of the moon, so that I am unable to decide the matter by actual observation. But I do know what observations would decide it for me, if, as is theoretically conceivable, I were once in a position to make them. And therefore I say that the proposition is verifiable in principle, if not in practice, and is accordingly significant. On the other hand, such a metaphysical pseudo-proposition as "The Absolute enters into, but is itself incapable of, evolution and progress"[4] is not even in principle verifiable. For one cannot conceive of an observation which would enable one to determine whether the Absolute did, or did not, enter into evolution and progress. Of course it is possible that the author of such a remark is using English words in a way in which they are

[3] This example has been used by Professor Schlick to illustrate the same point.
[4] A remark taken at random from *Appearance and Reality,* by F. H. Bradley.

not commonly used by English-speaking people, and that he does, in fact, intend to assert something which could be empirically verified. But until he makes us understand how the proposition that he wishes to express would be verified, he fails to communicate anything to us. And if he admits, as I think the author of the remark in question would have admitted, that his words were not intended to express either a tautology or a proposition which was capable, at least in principle, of being verified, then it follows that he has made an utterance which has no literal significance even for himself.

A further distinction which we must make is the distinction between the "strong" and the "weak" sense of the term "verifiable." A proposition is said to be verifiable, in the strong sense of the term, if, and only if, its truth could be conclusively established in experience. But it is verifiable, in the weak sense, if it is possible for experience to render it probable. In which sense are we using the term when we say that a putative proposition is genuine only if it is verifiable?

It seems to me that if we adopt conclusive verifiability as our criterion of significance, as some positivists have proposed,[5] our argument will prove too much. Consider, for example, the case of general propositions of law—such propositions, namely, as "Arsenic is poisonous"; "All men are mortal"; "A body tends to expand when it is heated." It is of the very nature of these propositions that their truth cannot be established with certainty by any finite series of observations. But if it is recognised that such general propositions of law are designed to cover an infinite number of cases, then it must be admitted that they cannot, even in principle, be verified conclusively. And then, if we adopt conclusive verifiability as our criterion of significance, we are logically obliged to treat these general propositions of law in the same fashion as we treat the statements of the metaphysician.

In face of this difficulty, some positivists[6] have adopted the heroic course of saying that these general propositions are indeed pieces of nonsense, albeit an essentially important type of nonsense. But here the introduction of the term "important" is simply an attempt to hedge. It serves only to mark the authors' recognition that their view is somewhat too paradoxical, without in any way removing the paradox. Besides, the difficulty is not confined to the case of general propositions of law, though it is there revealed most plainly. It is hardly less obvious in the case of propositions about the remote past. For it must surely be admitted that, however strong the evidence in favour of historical statements may be, their truth can never become more than highly probable. And to maintain that they also constituted an important, or unimportant, type of nonsense would be unplausible, to say the very least. Indeed, it will be our contention that no proposition, other than a tautology, can possibly be anything more than a probable hypothesis. And if this is correct, the principle that

[5] E.g., M. Schlick, "Positivismus und Realismus," *Erkenntnis*, Vol. I, 1930. F. Waismann, "Logische Analyse des Warscheinlichkeitsbegriffs," *Erkenntnis*, Vol. I, 1930.

[6] E.g., M. Schlick, "Die Kausalität in der gegenwärtigen Physik," *Naturwissenschaft*, Vol. 19, 1931.

a sentence can be factually significant only if it expresses what is conclusively verifiable is self-stultifying as a criterion of significance. For it leads to the conclusion that it is impossible to make a significant statement of fact at all.

Nor can we accept the suggestion that a sentence should be allowed to be factually significant if, and only if, it expresses something which is definitely confutable by experience.[7] Those who adopt this course assume that, although no finite series of observations is ever sufficient to establish the truth of a hypothesis beyond all possibility of doubt, there are crucial cases in which a single observation, or series of observations, can definitely confute it. But, as we shall show later on, this assumption is false. A hypothesis cannot be conclusively confuted any more than it can be conclusively verified. For when we take the occurrence of certain observations as proof that a given hypothesis is false, we presuppose the existence of certain conditions. And though, in any given case, it may be extremely improbable that this assumption is false, it is not logically impossible. We shall see that there need be no self-contradiction in holding that some of the relevant circumstances are other than we have taken them to be, and consequently that the hypothesis has not really broken down. And if it is not the case that any hypothesis can be definitely confuted, we cannot hold that the genuineness of a proposition depends on the possibility of its definite confutation.

Accordingly, we fall back on the weaker sense of verification. We say that the question that must be asked about any putative statement of fact is not, Would any observations make its truth or falsehood logically certain? but simply, Would any observations be relevant to the determination of its truth or falsehood? And it is only if a negative answer is given to this second question that we conclude that the statement under consideration is nonsensical.

To make our position clearer, we may formulate it in another way. Let us call a proposition which records an actual or possible observation an experiential proposition. Then we may say that it is the mark of a genuine factual proposition, not that it should be equivalent to an experiential proposition, or any finite number of experiential propositions, but simply that some experiential propositions can be deduced from it in conjunction with certain other premises without being deducible from those other premises alone.

This criterion seems liberal enough. In contrast to the principle of conclusive verifiability, it clearly does not deny significance to general propositions or to propositions about the past. Let us see what kinds of assertion it rules out.

A good example of the kind of utterance that is condemned by our criterion as being not even false but nonsensical would be the assertion that the world of sense-experience was altogether unreal. It must, of course, be admitted that our senses do sometimes deceive us. We may, as the result of having certain sensations, expect certain other sensations to be obtainable which are, in fact, not obtainable. But, in all such cases, it is further sense-experience that informs us of the mistakes that arise out of sense-experience. We say that the senses sometimes deceive us, just because the expectations to which our sense-experi-

[7] This has been proposed by Karl Popper in his *Logik der Forschung*.

ences give rise do not always accord with what we subsequently experience. That is, we rely on our senses to substantiate or confute the judgements which are based on our sensations. And therefore the fact that our perceptual judgements are sometimes found to be erroneous has not the slightest tendency to show that the world of sense-experience is unreal. And, indeed, it is plain that no conceivable observation, or series of observations, could have any tendency to show that the world revealed to us by sense-experience was unreal. Consequently, anyone who condemns the sensible world as a world of mere appearance, as opposed to reality, is saying something which, according to our criterion of significance, is literally nonsensical.

An example of a controversy which the application of our criterion obliges us to condemn as fictitious is provided by those who dispute concerning the number of substances that there are in the world. For it is admitted both by monists, who maintain that reality is one substance, and by pluralists, who maintain that reality is many, that it is impossible to imagine any empirical situation which would be relevant to the solution of their dispute. But if we are told that no possible observation could give any probability either to the assertion that reality was one substance or to the assertion that it was many, then we must conclude that neither assertion is significant. There are genuine logical and empirical questions involved in the dispute between monists and pluralists. But the metaphysical question concerning "substance" is ruled out by our criterion as spurious.

A similar treatment must be accorded to the controversy between realists and idealists, in its metaphysical aspect. A simple illustration, which I have made use of in a similar argument elsewhere,[8] will help to demonstrate this. Let us suppose that a picture is discovered and the suggestion made that it was painted by Goya. There is a definite procedure for dealing with such a question. The experts examine the picture to see in what way it resembles the accredited works of Goya, and to see if it bears any marks which are characteristic of a forgery; they look up contemporary records for evidence of the existence of such a picture, and so on. In the end, they may still disagree, but each one knows what empirical evidence would go to confirm or discredit his opinion. Suppose, now, that these men have studied philosophy, and some of them proceed to maintain that this picture is a set of ideas in the perceiver's mind, or in God's mind, others that it is objectively real. What possible experience could any of them have which would be relevant to the solution of this dispute one way or the other? In the ordinary sense of the term "real," in which it is opposed to "illusory," the reality of the picture is not in doubt. The disputants have satisfied themselves that the picture is real, in this sense, by obtaining a correlated series of sensations of sight and sensations of touch. Is there any similar process by which they could discover whether the picture was real, in the sense in which the term "real" is opposed to "ideal"? Clearly there is none. But, if that is so, the problem is fictitious according to our criterion. This does not mean that the realist-idealist controversy may be dismissed without further

[8] Vide "Demonstration of the Impossibility of Metaphysics," *Mind,* 1934, p. 339.

ado. For it can legitimately be regarded as a dispute concerning the analysis of existential propositions, and so as involving a logical problem which, as we shall see, can be definitively solved. What we have just shown is that the question at issue between idealists and realists becomes fictitious when, as is often the case, it is given a metaphysical interpretation.

There is no need for us to give further examples of the operation of our criterion of significance. For our object is merely to show that philosophy, as a genuine branch of knowledge, must be distinguished from metaphysics. We are not now concerned with the historical question how much of what has traditionally passed for philosophy is actually metaphysical. We shall, however, point out later on that the majority of the "great philosophers" of the past were not essentially metaphysicians, and thus reassure those who would otherwise be prevented from adopting our criterion by considerations of piety.

. . . All propositions which have factual content are empirical hypotheses; and the function of an empirical hypothesis is to provide a rule for the anticipation of experience. And this means that every empirical hypothesis must be relevant to some actual, or possible, experience, so that a statement which is not relevant to any experience is not an empirical hypothesis, and accordingly has no factual content. But this is precisely what the principle of verifiability asserts.

It should be mentioned here that the fact that the utterances of the metaphysician are nonsensical does not follow simply from the fact that they are devoid of factual content. It follows from that fact, together with the fact that they are not *a priori* propositions. . . . *A priori* propositions, which have always been attractive to philosophers on account of their certainty, owe this certainty to the fact that they are tautologies. We may accordingly define a metaphysical sentence as a sentence which purports to express a genuine proposition, but does, in fact, express neither a tautology nor an empirical hypothesis. And as tautologies and empirical hypotheses form the entire class of significant propositions, we are justified in concluding that all metaphysical assertions are nonsensical. Our next task is to show how they come to be made.

III

The use of the term "substance," to which we have already referred, provides us with a good example of the way in which metaphysics mostly comes to be written. It happens to be the case that we cannot, in our language, refer to the sensible properties of a thing without introducing a word or phrase which appears to stand for the thing itself as opposed to anything which may be said about it. And, as a result of this, those who are infected by the primitive superstition that to every name a single real entity must correspond assume that it is necessary to distinguish logically between the thing itself and any, or all, of its sensible properties. And so they employ the term "substance" to refer to the thing itself. But from the fact that we happen to employ a single word to refer to a thing, and make that word the grammatical subject of the sentences in which we refer to the sensible appearances of the thing, it does not by any means follow that the thing itself is a "simple entity," or that it cannot be defined in terms of the totality of its appearances. It is true that in talking of "its" appearances we appear to distinguish the thing from the appearances, but that is simply an accident of linguistic usage. Logical analysis shows that what makes these "appearances" the "appearances of" the same thing is not their relationship to an entity other than themselves, but their relationship to one another. The metaphysician fails to see this because he is misled by a superficial grammatical feature of his language.

A simpler and clearer instance of the way in which a consideration of grammar leads to metaphysics is the case of the metaphysical concept of Being. The origin of our temptation to raise questions about Being, which no conceivable experience would enable us to answer, lies in the fact that, in our language, sentences which express existential propositions and sentences which express attributive propositions may be of the same grammatical form. For instance, the sentences "Martyrs exist" and "Martyrs suffer" both consist of a noun followed by an intransitive verb, and the fact that they have grammatically the same appearance leads one to assume that they are of the same logical type. It is seen that in the proposition "Martyrs suffer," the members of a certain species are credited with a certain attribute, and it is sometimes assumed that the same thing is true of such a proposition as "Martyrs exist." If this were actually the case, it would, indeed, be as legitimate to speculate about the Being of martyrs as it is to speculate about their suffering. But, as Kant pointed out,[9] existence is not an attribute. For, when we ascribe an attribute to a thing, we covertly assert that it exists: so that if existence were itself an attribute, it would follow that all positive existential propositions were tautologies, and all negative existential propositions self-contradictory; and this is not the case.[10] So that those who raise questions about Being which are based on the assumption that existence is an attribute are guilty of following grammar beyond the boundaries of sense.

A similar mistake has been made in connection with such propositions as "Unicorns are fictitious." Here again the fact that there is a superficial grammatical resemblance between the English sentences "Dogs are faithful" and "Unicorns are fictitious," and between the corresponding sentences in other languages, creates the assumption that they are of the same logical type. Dogs must exist in order to have the property of being faithful, and so it is held that unless unicorns in some way existed they could not have the property of being fictitious. But, as it is plainly self-contradictory to say that fictitious objects exist, the device is adopted of saying that they are real in some nonempirical sense—that they have a mode of real being which is different from the mode of being of existent things. But since there is no way of testing whether an

---

[9] Vide *The Critique of Pure Reason*, "Transcendental Dialectic," Book II, Chapter iii, section 4.

[10] This argument is well stated by John Wisdom, *Interpretation and Analysis*, pp. 62, 63.

object is real in this sense, as there is for testing whether it is real in the ordinary sense, the assertion that fictitious objects have a special nonempirical mode of real being is devoid of all literal significance. It comes to be made as a result of the assumption that being fictitious is an attribute. And this is a fallacy of the same order as the fallacy of supposing that existence is an attribute, and it can be exposed in the same way.

In general, the postulation of real nonexistent entities results from the superstition, just now referred to, that, to every word or phrase that can be the grammatical subject of a sentence, there must somewhere be a real entity corresponding. For as there is no place in the empirical world for many of these "entities," a special nonempirical world is invoked to house them. To this error must be attributed, not only the utterances of a Heidegger, who bases his metaphysics on the assumption that "Nothing" is a name which is used to denote something peculiarly mysterious,[11] but also the prevalence of such problems as those concerning the reality of propositions and universals whose senselessness, though less obvious, is no less complete.

These few examples afford a sufficient indication of the way in which most metaphysical assertions come to be formulated. They show how easy it is to write sentences which are literally nonsensical without seeing that they are nonsensical. And thus we see that the view that a number of the traditional "problems of philosophy" are metaphysical, and consequently fictitious, does not involve any incredible assumptions about the psychology of philosophers.

Among those who recognise that if philosophy is to be accounted a genuine branch of knowledge it must be defined in such a way as to distinguish it from metaphysics, it is fashionable to speak of the metaphysician as a kind of misplaced poet. As his statements have no literal meaning, they are not subject to any criteria of truth or falsehood: but they may still serve to express, or arouse, emotion, and thus be subject to ethical or æsthetic standards. And it is suggested that they may have considerable value, as means of moral inspiration, or even as works of art. In this way, an attempt is made to compensate the metaphysician for his extrusion from philosophy.

I am afraid that this compensation is hardly in accordance with his deserts. The view that the metaphysician is to be reckoned among the poets appears to rest on the assumption that both talk nonsense. But this assumption is false. In the vast majority of cases the sentences which are produced by poets do have literal meaning. The difference between the man who uses language scientifically and the man who uses it emotively is not that the one produces sentences which are incapable of arousing emotion, and the other sentences which have no sense, but that the one is primarily concerned with the expression of true propositions, the other with the creation of a work of art. Thus, if a work of science contains true and important propositions, its value as a work of science will hardly be diminished by the fact that they are inelegantly expressed. And similarly, a work of art is not necessarily the worse for the fact that all the propositions comprising it are literally false. But to say that many literary works

[11] Vide *Was ist Metaphysik?* by Heidegger.

are largely composed of falsehoods, is not to say that they are composed of pseudo-propositions. It is, in fact, very rare for a literary artist to produce sentences which have no literal meaning. And where this does occur, the sentences are carefully chosen for their rhythm and balance. If the author writes nonsense, it is because he considers it most suitable for bringing about the effects for which his writing is designed.

The metaphysician, on the other hand, does not intend to write nonsense. He lapses into it through being deceived by grammar, or through committing errors of reasoning, such as that which leads to the view that the sensible world is unreal. But it is not the mark of a poet simply to make mistakes of this sort. There are some, indeed, who would see in the fact that the metaphysician's utterances are senseless a reason against the view that they have æsthetic value. And, without going so far as this, we may safely say that it does not constitute a reason for it.

It is true, however, that although the greater part of metaphysics is merely the embodiment of humdrum errors, there remain a number of metaphysical passages which are the work of genuine mystical feeling; and they may more plausibly be held to have moral or æsthetic value. But, as far as we are concerned, the distinction between the kind of metaphysics that is produced by a philosopher who has been duped by grammar, and the kind that is produced by a mystic who is trying to express the inexpressible, is of no great importance: what is important to us is to realise that even the utterances of the metaphysician who is attempting to expound a vision are literally senseless; so that henceforth we may pursue our philosophical researches with as little regard for them as for the more inglorious kind of metaphysics which comes from a failure to understand the workings of our language.

Questions

1. What is the verification principle, and how is it to be used in distinguishing between meaningful statements and meaningless utterances?

2. Use the verification principle in deciding whether the following are meaningful: *p. 283 (top 4)*

+a. The universe contains other solar systems resembling our own.
+b. Darkest Africa contains wild animals unknown to modern science.
+c. New York City is the capital of the United States.
—d. The woman wore a blue dress that was yellow all over.
—e. The round tower is square.
— *f. How high is up?
+g. Electricity is running through the cord of my lighted desk lamp.
+h. Please shake hands with my invisible, intangible, inaudible friend, who
possibly has aroma → has been waiting for you to greet him for the last fifteen minutes.
+i. The meaning of a statement is its method of verification.
+j. The world extends infinitely beyond our private consciousness, because it is the world of a universal mind. (Royce)

3. What does Professor Ayer mean by "metaphysics"? How does he believe that it can be eliminated?

4. Compare this selection by Professor Ayer with the reading titled "The Emotive Theory" (page 575), also by him. How is his verification principle related

to his "emotive theory" of ethics? Attack or defend the statement: "Professor Ayer destroys all philosophy by eliminating both metaphysics and ethics as rational attempts to solve genuine problems."

5. Professor Ayer claims that his views are "the logical outcome of the empiricism of Berkeley and David Hume." After reading either the selection by Berkeley in Chapter 1 (page 87), or the selection by Hume in Chapter 1 (page 98), or both, state why you agree or disagree with Professor Ayer's claim.

6. How might Professor Ayer reply to the following objection? Defend (or attack) the reply you construct as an adequate (or inadequate) answer to the objection.

"You say that those who have tried to describe a reality which transcends all sense experience have merely produced nonsense. But all you can justifiably assert from the failure of these attempts is that no one has yet gained knowledge of such a reality. You should say only that *we do not know* the nature of such a reality. You should not say that the attempt to describe it is nonsense."

7. Explain by means of examples the difference between "practical verifiability" *p. 281* and "verifiability in principle." What is the consequence of using this distinction in deciding whether sentences are meaningful or meaningless?

8. Explain by means of examples the difference between the "strong" and the "weak" sense of the term "verifiable." Which of the two senses does Professor Ayer adopt as a criterion of meaning, and why?

9. ". . . It is plain that no conceivable observation, or series of observations, could have any tendency to show that the world revealed to us by sense experience was unreal." Do you agree? Why or why not?

10. Show why the dispute whether reality is one substance or many substances is meaningless, when tested by the verification principle.

11. How are metaphysicians deceived by grammar, according to Professor Ayer? Explain what is meant by "grammar" in this discussion.

3

Verifiability | Friedrich Waismann
(b. 1896)

Friedrich Waismann is Senior Lecturer in the Philosophy of Mathematics in Oxford University. He was a prominent member of the Vienna Circle, a group of philosophers whose basic viewpoint was described in the introduction to the preceding selection, "The Verification Principle," by Professor A. J. Ayer (page 277). In this selection Dr. Waismann comments on the interpretation and use of the verification principle: "The meaning of a statement is the method of its verification."

This reading is divided into two parts. Part I is a discussion of the way in which a material object statement is verified by someone's finding out the truth of sense-datum statements which it implies. "The tickets are on the desk" is an example of a material object statement. "Two small, orange, oblong patches are in the middle of that brown surface over there" is an example of a sense-datum statement which it implies. Dr. Waismann shows that the relation between the truth of a material object statement and a sense-datum statement which it implies is complicated by two features of our language. The first of these is what he calls the "open texture" of the words we use to talk about the world, and the second is the essential incompleteness of any description of something we can experience. Part II of this reading is a discussion of the supposed dichotomy between a world of facts and the words which describe these facts. Through a series of examples Dr. Waismann illustrates his view that language ". . . contributes to the formation and participates in the constitution of a fact."

In its original form this essay was a contribution to a symposium on verifiability, and was first published in the *Aristotelian Society Supplementary Volume 19,* "Analysis and Metaphysics," 1945. It was subsequently reprinted, with the editorial alterations necessary to make it independent of the original symposium, in *Essays on Logic and Language, First Series,* edited by Professor Antony Flew (1951). Part I of our selection is drawn from Part I of the original; and Part II is drawn from Part III of the original.

From "Verifiability," by Friedrich Waismann, *Aristotelian Society Supplementary Volume 19,* 1945. Reprinted by permission of the author and The Aristotelian Society.

I

When we reflect on such a sentence as "The meaning of a statement is the method of its verification," we should, first of all, be quite clear as to what we mean by the term "method of verification." From a logical point of view we are not interested in the various activities that are involved in verifying a statement. What, then, is it we have in mind when we talk of such things? Take an example. Suppose there is a metal ball in front of me, and I have the task of finding out whether the ball is charged with electricity. To do that I connect the ball with an electroscope and watch whether the gold leaves diverge. The statement "The gold leaves of the instrument diverge" (*s*) describes the verification of the statement "The ball is charged" (*p*). Now what exactly am I doing when I describe the verification of the statement *p*? I establish a connection between two statements by declaring that the one (*s*) is to follow from the other (*p*). In other words, I lay down a *rule of inference* which allows me to pass from the statement "The ball is charged with electricity" to another that describes an observable situation. By doing this I connect the statement with another one, I make it part of a system of operations, I incorporate it into language, in short, *I determine the way it is to be used*. In this sense giving the verification of a statement is an important part of giving its use, or, to put it differently, explaining its verification is a contribution to its grammar.

In everyday life we understand sentences without bothering much as to the way they are verified. We understand them because we understand the single words which occur in them and grasp the grammatical structure of the sentence as a whole. The question of the verification arises only when we come across a new sort of combination of words. If, for instance, someone were to tell us that he owned a dog that was able to think, we should at first not quite understand what he was talking about and would ask him some further questions. Suppose he described to us in detail the dog's behaviour in certain circumstances, then we should say "Ah, now we understand you, that's what you call thinking." There is no need to inquire into the verification of such sentences as "The dog barks," "He runs," "He is playful," and so on, as the words are then used as we may say in their *normal* way. But when we say "The dog thinks," we create a new context, we step outside the boundaries of common speech, and then the question arises as to what is meant by such a word series. In such cases explaining the verification is explaining the meaning, and changing the verification is changing the meaning. Obviously meaning and verification *are* connected—so why say they are not?

But when I say that the statement p is connected with the statements s_1, $s_2 \ldots s_n$ which describe evidences for it, I do *not* say that p is *identical* with $s_1, s_2 \ldots s_n$ or their conjunction. To say this would only be true if $s_1, s_2 \ldots s_t$ or their conjunction entailed p. Now is that so? There *may* be statements which are nothing more than abbreviations for all that which is unfolded in their verification. There are, however, other sorts of statements of which this is certainly not true. Recent discussions on phenomenalism, for example, tend to show that no conjunction or disjunction of sense-datum statements, however complex, entails the existence or the nonexistence of a certain material object. If that is so, a material object statement, though it *is* connected with sense-datum statements, is not just an abbreviation for them; rather has it a logical status of its own, and is not equivalent to any truth-function of the latter ones. I think that the result of these discussions is essentially right, and I ask for permission, to make my point quite clear, to add one word more.

The failure of the phenomenalist to translate a material object statement into terms of sense-data is not, as has been suggested, due to the poverty of our language which lacks the vocabulary for describing all the minute details of sense experience, nor is it due to the difficulties inherent in producing an *infinite* combination of sense-datum statements though all these things may contribute to it. In the main it is due to a factor which, though it is very important and really quite obvious, has to my knowledge never been noticed—to the "open texture" [1] of most of our empirical concepts. What I mean is this: Suppose I

[1] I owe this term to Mr. Kneale who suggested it to me as a translation of *Porosität der Begriffe*, a term coined by me in German.

have to verify a statement such as "There is a cat next door"; suppose I go over to the next room, open the door, look into it and actually see a cat. Is this enough to prove my statement? Or must I, in addition to it, touch the cat, pat him and induce him to purr? And supposing that I had done all these things, can I then be absolutely certain that my statement was true? Instantly we come up against the well-known battery of sceptical arguments mustered since ancient times. What, for instance, should I say when that creature later on grew to a gigantic size? Or if it showed some queer behaviour usually not to be found with cats, say, if, under certain conditions, it could be revived from death whereas normal cats could not? Shall I, in such a case, say that a new species has come into being? Or that it was a cat with extraordinary properties? Again, suppose I say "There is my friend over there." What if on drawing closer in order to shake hands with him he suddenly disappeared? "Therefore it was not my friend but some delusion or other." But suppose a few seconds later I saw him again, could grasp his hand, etc. What then? "Therefore my friend was nevertheless there and his disappearance was some delusion or other." But imagine after a while he disappeared again, or seemed to disappear—what shall I say now? Have we rules ready for all imaginable possibilities?

An example of the first sort tends to show that we can think of situations in which we couldn't be certain whether something was a cat or some other animal (or a *jinni*). An example of the second sort tends to show that we can consider circumstances in which we couldn't be certain whether something was real or a delusion. The fact that in many cases there is no such thing as a conclusive verification is connected with the fact that most of our empirical concepts are not delimited in all possible directions. Suppose I come across a being that looks like a man, speaks like a man, behaves like a man, and is only one span tall—shall I say it *is* a man? Or what about the case of a person who is so old as to remember King Darius? Would you say he is an immortal? Is there anything like an exhaustive definition that finally and once for all sets our mind at rest? "But are there not exact definitions at least in science?" Let's see. The notion of gold seems to be defined with absolute precision, say by the spectrum of gold with its characteristic lines. Now what would you say if a substance was discovered that looked like gold, satisfied all the chemical tests for gold, whilst it emitted a new sort of radiation? "But such things do not happen." Quite so; but they *might* happen, and that is enough to show that we can never exclude altogether the possibility of some unforeseen situation arising in which we shall have to modify our definition. Try as we may, no concept is limited in such a way that there is no room for any doubt. We introduce a concept and limit it in *some* directions; for instance, we define gold in contrast to some other metals such as alloys. This suffices for our present needs, and we do not probe any farther. We tend to *overlook* the fact that there are always other directions in which the concept has not been defined. And if we did, we could easily imagine conditions which would necessitate new limitations. In short, it is not possible to define a concept like gold with absolute precision, i.e. in such a way that every nook and cranny is blocked against entry of doubt. That is what is meant by the open texture of a concept.

Vagueness should be distinguished from *open texture*. A word which is actually used in a fluctuating way (such as "heap" or "pink") is said to be vague; a term like "gold," though its actual use may not be vague, is non-exhaustive or of an open texture in that we can never fill up all the possible gaps through which a doubt may seep in. Open texture, then, is something like *possibility of vagueness*. Vagueness can be remedied by giving more accurate rules, open texture cannot. An alternative way of stating this would be to say that definitions of open terms are *always* corrigible or emendable.

Open texture is a very fundamental characteristic of most, though not of all, empirical concepts, and it is this texture which prevents us from verifying conclusively most of our empirical statements. Take any material object statement. The terms which occur in it are nonexhaustive; that means that we cannot foresee completely all possible conditions in which they are to be used; there will always remain a possibility, however faint, that we have not taken into account something or other that may be relevant to their usage; and that means that we cannot foresee completely all the possible circumstances in which the statement is true or in which it is false. There will always remain a margin of uncertainty. Thus the absence of a conclusive verification is directly due to the open texture of the terms concerned.

This has an important consequence. Phenomenalists have tried to translate what we mean by a material object statement into terms of sense experience. Now such a translation would be possible only if the terms of a material object statement were completely definable. For only then could we describe completely all the possible evidences which would make the statement true or false. As this condition is not fulfilled, the programme of phenomenalism falls flat, and in consequence the attempts at analysing chairs and tables into patterns of sense-data—which has become something of a national sport in this country —are doomed to fail. Similar remarks apply to certain psychological statements such as "He is an intelligent person"; here again it is due to the open texture of a term like "intelligent" that the statement cannot be reduced to a conjunction or disjunction of statements which specify the way a man would behave in such-and-such circumstances.

It may have been a dim awareness of this fact that induced Locke to insist on corporeal, and Berkeley on mental substance. Doing away with their metaphysical fog, we may restate what seems to be the grain of truth in their views by saying that a material object statement, or a psychological statement has a logic of its own, and for this reason cannot be reduced to the level of other statements.

But there is a deeper reason for all that, and this consists in what I venture to call the *essential incompleteness* of an empirical description. To explain more fully: If I had to describe the right hand of mine which I am now holding up, I may say different things of it: I may state its size, its shape, its colour, its tissue, the chemical compound of its bones, its cells, and perhaps add some more particulars; but however far I go, I shall never reach a point where my description will be completed: logically speaking, it is always possible to extend the description by adding some detail or other. Every description stretches, as it were, into a horizon of open possibilities: however far I go, I shall always carry this horizon with me. Contrast this case with others in which completeness is attainable. If, in geometry, I describe a triangle, e.g. by giving its three sides, the description is *complete:* nothing can be added to it that is not included in, or at variance with, the data. Again, there is a sense in which it may be said that a melody is described completely in the musical notation (disregarding, for the moment, the question of its interpretation); a figure on a carpet, viewed as an ornament, may be described in some geometrical notation; and in this case, too, there is a sense in which the description may be called complete. (I do not mean the *physical* carpet, but its pattern.) The same applies to a game of chess: it can be described, move by move, from the beginning to the end. Such cases serve merely to set off the nature of an empirical description by the contrast: there is no such thing as completeness in the case in which I describe my right hand, or the character of a person; I can never exhaust all the details nor foresee all possible circumstances which would make me modify or retract my statement. (This was already seen by Leibniz when he said that anything actual is always inexhaustible in its properties and a true image of the Infinite Mind.)

The situation described has a direct bearing on the open texture of concepts. A term is defined when the sort of situation is described in which it is to be used. Suppose for a moment that we were able to describe situations completely without omitting anything (as in chess), then we could produce an exhaustive list of all the circumstances in which the term is to be used so that nothing is left to doubt; in other words, we could construct a *complete definition,* i.e. a thought model which anticipates and settles once for all every possible question of usage. As, in fact, we can never eliminate the possibility of some unforeseen factor emerging, we can never be quite sure that we have included in our definition everything that should be included, and thus the process of defining and refining an idea will go on without ever reaching a final stage. In other words, every definition stretches into an open horizon. Try as we may, the situation will always remain the same: no definition of an empirical term will cover all possibilities. Thus the result is that the incompleteness of our verification is rooted in the incompleteness of the definition of the terms involved, and the incompleteness of the definition is rooted in the incompleteness of empirical description; that is one of the grounds why a material object statement p can *not* be verified conclusively, nor be resolved into statements $s_1, s_2 \ldots s_n$ which describe evidences for it. (In mathematics such a reduction is often possible: thus a statement about rational numbers *can,* without loss of meaning, be translated into statements about integers; but here you have complete description, complete definition and conclusive proof and refutation.)

One word more. Why is it that, as a rule, an experiential statement is not verifiable in a conclusive way? Is it because I can never exhaust the description of a material object or of a situation, since I may always add something to it—something that, in principle, can be foreseen? Or is it because something quite new and unforeseen may occur? In the first case, though I know all the tests, I may still be unable to perform them, say, for lack of time. In the second case I cannot even be sure that I know all the tests that may be required; in other words, the difficulty is to state completely what a verification would be in this case. (Can you foresee all circumstances which would turn a putative fact into a delusion?) Now the answer to the question is that *both factors combine* to prevent a verification from being conclusive. *But they play a very different part*. It is due to the first factor that, in verifying a statement, we can never finish the job. But it is the second that is responsible for the open texture of our terms which is so characteristic of all factual knowledge. To see this more clearly, compare the situation in mathematics: here a theorem, say Goldbach's hypothesis, which says that every even number can be represented as the sum of two primes, may be undecidable as we cannot go through all the integers in order to try it out. But this in no way detracts from the *closed* texture of the mathematical concepts. If there was no such thing as the (always present) possibility of the emergence of something new, there could be nothing like the open texture of concepts; and if there was no such thing as the open texture of concepts, verification would be incomplete only in the sense that it could never be finished (just as in the case of Goldbach).

To sum up: An experiential statement is, as a rule, not conclusively verifiable for two different reasons:

(1) because of the existence of an unlimited number of tests;
(2) because of the open texture of the terms involved.

These two reasons correspond to two different senses of "incompleteness." The first is related to the fact that I can never conclude the description of a material object, or of a situation. I may, for instance, look at my table from ever new points in space without ever exhausting all the possibilities. The second (and more exciting one) is due to the fact that our factual knowledge is incomplete in another dimension: there is always a chance that something unforeseen may occur. That again may mean two different things:

(1) that I should get acquainted with some totally new experience such as at present I cannot even imagine;
(2) that some new discovery was made which would affect our whole interpretation of certain facts.

An illustration of the first sort would be supplied by a man born blind who later obtained the experience of seeing. An illustration of the second sort would be the change brought about by the discovery of a new agent of nature, such as electricity. In this case we perceive that the data of observation are connected in a new and unforeseen way, that, as it were, new lines can now be traced through the field of experience. So we can say more exactly that the open texture of concepts is rooted in that particular incompleteness of our factual knowledge which I have just adumbrated.

What I have said modifies to a more or less extent the account I have given of verification. I said that in giving the method of verification we lay down a rule (or rules) of inference. We should, however, feel grave doubts whether that is so. If a material object statement were to entail a sense-datum statement, to entail it in a strictly *logical* sense, then the premiss would be cancelled together with the conclusion: or, to put it differently, a single negative instance would suffice to refute the premiss. Suppose someone told me, "Look, there is your friend, he is just crossing the street." Now if I looked in the direction indicated, but failed to perceive the person who is my friend, would I say that the statement was refuted beyond the shadow of a doubt? There may be cases in which I may say that. But there are others in which I would certainly not think that the statement was refuted on the strength of such a single glance (for instance, when I was led to expect my friend at this hour, or received a letter from him saying that he will arrive at that time, and the like). A discrepancy between a material object statement and a single sense experience may always be explained away by some accessory assumption: I haven't looked thoroughly, my friend happened in this very second to be behind someone else, he just stepped into a doorway, and so on, not to mention more fanciful theories. I can never exclude the possibility that, though the evidence was against it, the statement may be true.

Whoever considers these facts with unbiassed eyes will, I trust, assent to the conclusion that a single sense experience, strictly speaking, never excludes a material object statement in the sense in which the negation of p excludes p. That means that no sense-datum statement s can ever come into *sharp logical conflict* with a material object statement p; in other words: $p . \sim s$ [p and not s] never represents a *contradiction* in the sense that $p . \sim p$ [p and not p] does. In the light of this we can no longer adhere to the view that p entails s. How, then, should we formulate the "method of verification"—that is, the connection between a proposition p and the statements $s_1, s_2 \ldots s_n$ which are evidences for it? I propose to say that the evidences $s_1, s_2 \ldots s_n$ *speak for* or *against* the proposition p, that they *strengthen* or *weaken* it, which does not mean that they prove or disprove it strictly. . . .

II

People are inclined to think that there is a world of facts as opposed to a world of words which describe these facts. I am not too happy about that. Consider an example. We are accustomed to see colour as a "quality" of objects. That is, colour cannot subsist by itself, but must inhere in a thing. This conception springs from the way we express ourselves. When colour is rendered by an adjective, colour is conceived as an attribute of things, i.e. as something that can have no independent existence. That, however, is not the only way of conceiving colour. There are languages such as Russian, German, Italian, which render colour by means of verbs. If we were to imitate this usage in English by allowing some such form as "The sky blues," we should come face to face with the question, Do I mean the same fact when I say "The sky blues" as when I say "The sky is blue"? I don't think so. We say "The sun shines," "Jewels glitter," "The river shimmers," "Windows gleam," "Stars twinkle," etc.; that is, in the case of phenomena of lustre we make use of a verbal mode of expression. Now in rendering colour phenomena by verbs we assimilate them more closely to the phenomena of lustre; and in doing so we alter not only our manner of speaking but our entire way of apprehending colour. We *see* the blue differently now—a hint that language affects our whole mode of apprehension. In the word "blueing" we are clearly aware of an active, verbal element. On that account "being blue" is not quite equivalent to "blueing," since it lacks what is peculiar to the verbal mode of expression. The sky which "blues" is seen as something that continually brings forth blueness—it radiates blueness, so to speak; blue does not inhere in it as a mere quality, rather is it felt as the vital pulse of the sky; there is a faint suggestion of the operating of some force behind the phenomenon. It's hard to get the feel of it in English; perhaps it may help you to liken this mode of expression to the impressionist way of painting which is at bottom a new way of seeing: the impressionist sees in colour an immediate manifestation of reality, a free agent no longer bound up with things.

There are, then, different linguistic means of rendering colour. When this is done by means of adjectives, colour is conceived as an attribute of things. The learning of such a language involves for everyone who speaks it his being habituated to see colour as a "quality" of objects. This conception becomes thus incorporated into his picture of the world. The verbal mode of expression detaches colour from things: it enables us to see colour as a phenomenon with a life of its own. Adjective and verb thus represent two different worlds of thought.

There is also an adverbial way of talking about colour. Imagine a language with a wealth of expressions for all shades of lustre, but without adjectives for colours; colours, as a rule, are ignored; *when* they are expressed, this is done by adding an adverb to the word that specifies the sort of lustre. Thus the people who use this sort of language would say, "The sea is glittering golden in the sunshine," "The evening clouds glow redly," "There in the depth a shadow greenly gleams." In such phrases colour would lose the last trace of independence and be reduced to a mere modification of lustre. Just as we in our language cannot say "That's very," but only some such thing as "That's very brilliant," so in the language considered we could not say "That's bluish," but only, e.g., "That's shining bluishly." There can be little doubt that, owing to this circumstance, the users of such language would find it very hard to see colour as a quality of things. For them it would not be the *things* that are coloured, rather colour would reside in the lustre as it glows and darkens and changes—evidence that they would see the world with different eyes.

"But isn't it still true to say that I have the same experience whenever I look up at the sky?" You would be less happy if you were asked, "Do you have the same experience when you look at a picture puzzle and see a figure in it as before, when you didn't see it?" You may, perhaps, say you see the same lines, though each time in a different arrangement. Now what exactly corresponds to this different arrangement in the case when I look up at the sky? One might say: we are aware of the blue, but this awareness is itself tinged and coloured by the whole linguistic background which brings into prominence, or weakens and hides certain analogies. In this sense language does affect the whole manner in which we become aware of a fact: the fact articulates itself differently, so to speak. In urging that you *must* have the same experience whenever you look at the sky you forget that the term "experience" is itself ambiguous: whether it is taken, e.g., to include or to exclude all the various analogies which a certain mode of expression calls up. . . .

I have observed that when the clock strikes in the night and I, already half asleep, am too tired to count the strokes, I am seized by an impression that the sequence will never end—as though it would go on, stroke after stroke, in an unending measureless procession. The whole thing vanishes as soon as I *count*. Counting frees me, as it were, from the dark formlessness impending over me. (Is this not a parable of the rational?) It seems to me that one could say here that counting *alters* the quality of the experience. Now is it the same fact which I perceive when counting and when not counting?

Again, suppose there is a tribe whose members count "one, two, three, a few, many." Suppose a man of this tribe looking at a flock of birds said "A few birds" whereas I should say "Five birds"—is it the same fact for him as it is for me? If in such a case I pass to a language of a different structure, I can no longer describe "the same" fact, but only another one more or less resembling the first. What, then, is the objective reality supposed to be described by language?

What rebels in us against such a suggestion is the feeling that the fact is there objectively no matter in which way we render it. I perceive something that exists and put it into words. From this it seems to follow that fact is something that exists independent of, and prior to language; language merely serves the end of communication. What we are liable to overlook here is that the way we see a fact—i.e. what we emphasize and what we disregard—is *our* work. "The sun-beams trembling on the floating tides" (Pope). Here a fact is something that emerges out from, and takes shape against a background. The background may be, e.g., my visual field; something that rouses my attention detaches itself from this field, is brought into focus and apprehended linguistically; that is what we call a fact. A fact is noticed; and by being noticed it becomes a fact. "Was it then no fact before you noticed it?" It was, if I *could* have noticed it. In a language in which there is only the number series "one, two, three, a few, many," a fact such as "There are five birds" is imperceptible.

To make my meaning still clearer consider a language in which description does not take the form of sentences. Examples of such a description would be supplied by a map, a picture language, a film, the musical notation. A map, for instance, should not be taken as a conjunction of single statements each of which describes a separate fact. For what, would you say, is the boundary of a fact? Where does the one end and the other begin? If we think of such types of description, we are no longer tempted to say, that a country, or a story told in a film, or a melody must consist of "facts." Here we begin to see how confusing the idea is according to which the world is a cluster of facts—just as if it were a sort of mosaic made up of little coloured stones. Reality is undivided. What we may have in mind is perhaps that *language* contains units, viz. *sentences*. In describing reality, by using sentences, we draw, as it were, lines through it, limit a part and call what corresponds with such a sentence a fact. In other words, language is the knife with which we cut out facts. (This account is oversimplified as it doesn't take notice of *false* statements.)

Reality, then, is not made up of facts in the sense in which a plant is made up of cells, a house of bricks, a stone of molecules; rather, if you want a simile, a fact is present, in much the same sense in which a character manifests itself in a face. Not that I invent the character and read it into the face; no, the character is somehow written on the face but no one would on that account say that a face is "made up" of features symbolic of such-and-such traits. Just as we have to interpret a face, so we have to interpret reality. The elements of such an interpretation, without our being aware of it, are already present in language—for instance, in such moulds as the notion of thinghood, of causality, of number, or again in the way we render colour, etc.

Noticing a fact may be likened to seeing a face in a cloud, or a figure in an arrangement of dots, or suddenly becoming aware of the solution of a picture puzzle: one views a complex of elements as one, reads a sort of unity into it, etc. Language supplies us with a means of comprehending and categorizing; and different languages categorize differently.

"But surely noticing a face in a cloud is not inventing it?" Certainly not; only you might not have noticed it unless you had already had the experience of human faces somewhere else. Does this not throw a light on what constitutes the noticing of facts? I would not dream for a moment of saying that I *invent* them; I might, however, be unable to perceive them if I had not certain moulds of comprehension ready at hand. These forms I borrow from language. Language, then, *contributes to the formation and participates in the constitution* of a fact; which, of course, does not mean that it *produces* the fact.

Questions

1. What does Dr. Waismann mean by the open texture of an empirical concept? Why does he say that "cat" is open-textured, but that "pink" and "heap" are vague? Explain by means of examples whether an empirical concept can be both open-textured and vague.

2. What does Dr. Waismann mean by the essential incompleteness of an empirical description? Try to give a complete description of your left shoe. Where does your attempt at completeness break down? Is your description incomplete because

of a lack of knowledge about your left shoe, or is it incomplete in principle? Explain this difference, and defend your answer.

3. How does Dr. Waismann show that language contributes to the formation and participates in the constitution of a fact? In what way is Dr. Waismann's point similar to, and in what way is it different from, the point which Professor C. I. Lewis makes about the a priori element in natural science (pages 186 ff.)?

4. Show how Dr. Waismann's conception of the verification principle differs from Professor Ayer's (pages 281 ff.). Under Dr. Waismann's interpretation of the verification principle, would adoption of the principle lead to the elimination of metaphysics? Why or why not?

5. Dr. Waismann says that when we describe the verification of a statement we "determine the way it is to be used." State in your own words the connection he finds between the verification of a statement and its use.

6. Explain what Dr. Waismann means by saying that empirical evidence "speaks for or against" a proposition but does not "prove or disprove" it. Give examples.

Suggested Further Reading | *Introductory Studies*

Carnap, Rudolph, *Philosophy and Logical Syntax,* Routledge and Kegan Paul, London, 1935.

Feigl, Herbert, and Wilfrid Sellars, eds., *Readings in Philosophical Analysis,* Appleton-Century-Crofts, N. Y., 1949. This book contains the following three studies in the problem of meaning and verification: "Logical Empiricism," by Herbert Feigl; "Experience and Meaning," by C. I. Lewis; and "Meaning and Verification," by Moritz Schlick.

Harris, Robert T., and James L. Jarrett, *Language and Informal Logic,* Longmans, Green, N. Y., 1956.

Lewis, C. I., *An Analysis of Knowledge and Valuation,* Book I, Open Court, La Salle, Ill., 1946.

Reichenbach, Hans, *Experience and Prediction,* University of Chicago Press, Chicago, 1938, Chap. I.

| *Advanced Studies*

Ayer, A. J., ed., *Logical Positivism,* Free Press, Glencoe, Ill., 1957.

Holloway, John, *Language and Intelligence,* Macmillan, London, 1951.

Lazerowitz, Morris, *The Structure of Metaphysics,* Humanities Press, N. Y., 1955, Chaps. I-VI.

Russell, Bertrand, *An Inquiry Into Meaning and Truth,* Norton, N. Y., 1940.

Wisdom, John, *Other Minds,* Blackwell, Oxford, 1952.

Wittgenstein, Ludwig, *Philosophical Investigations,* tr. by G. E. M. Anscombe, Blackwell, Oxford, 1953.

Chapter Four

THE
PROBLEM
OF

Knowledge of God

Religion and Philosophy

We may introduce the problem of knowledge of God by asking the reader to consider the following religious statements. In the Twenty-third Psalm King David says, "The Lord is my shepherd; I shall not want." In many Christian churches the members of the congregation say together, "I believe in God the Father, Creator of Heaven and Earth. . . ." These are statements about God, and are examples of the most important variety of religious statement. Now the philosopher's questions about religious statements are the questions which he asks about any statement: What are the grounds for believing it? and, Do we have good grounds for believing it? But because of the nature of religion, the philosopher's questions must be qualified in certain ways.

First, we must notice that we are confronted not with religion, but with religions. What is more, unlike the sciences, these religions cannot be harmonized in the way in which chemistry and physics support one another. Nor do they treat of different subject matters as geology and biology do. Rather, the relation of religions appears to be such that if someone accepts one, he must reject the others. Because of the magnitude of the subject, we can do nothing here to examine the claims of any one religion over all others. Hence we have thought it best to confine ourselves to the problem of knowledge of God as it has arisen in connection with Christianity and Judaism, the religions which we suppose are most likely to interest our readers.

Judaism and Christianity are theistic, indeed monotheistic religions. A theistic religion is based on a belief in a god or gods. A monotheistic religion is based on a belief in a single god. There are also nontheistic religions, of which Buddhism is an example. By limiting ourselves to the problem of the knowledge of God as it has arisen in connection with Judaism and Christianity, we refrain from the philosophical consideration of the doctrines of other monotheistic religions (such as Islam) and of all polytheistic and nontheistic religions. In addition, we shall limit ourselves to the examination of the problem of knowledge of God as it occurs in those forms of Judaism and Christianity which are based on a belief in a *transcendent* god, that is, a god who is thought of as prior to and apart from the world, who in some sense created the world and can bring about changes in it. Finally, we shall confine our philosophical study to theists' claims to have knowledge of a transcendent god's existence and of the relation of this god to the world. By limiting our study to these claims we are focusing our attention upon the central philosophical problems of theistic religion.

Our first question, then, concerns the way in which statements of a transcendent theistic religion are to be believed. Are they to be believed on grounds similar to those for our belief that $2 + 2 = 4$? Or on grounds similar to those for our belief that fire burns? Or on grounds similar to those for our belief that the earth revolves around the sun? Or are religious statements to be believed on grounds that are neither definitional, nor empirical, nor scientific, but of some fourth kind? The traditional answer to questions about the grounds for religious statements is that for some statements the ground is a divine revelation, and for others the grounds may be reason as well as revelation. Let us examine these grounds more closely.

Reason and Revelation

When reason is considered as a ground of religious knowledge, the word "reason" is used to mean any attempt by the human mind alone, without divine assistance, to know the truth of a religious statement. It means knowing that a religious statement is true by an inference from either our experience of the world, our conception of God, or our conception of the world. Giving reason a place in religion raises these questions: Can my religious beliefs be confirmed (or disproved) by my experience of the world? and, Can my religious beliefs be proved (or disproved) on the basis of my conceptions of God or of the world?

When we turn to revelation as a basis for religious knowledge, the following questions confront us: What is revelation? How does one know that an experience of one's own or of someone else is a revelation? and, What is the relation of reason to revelation? In this chapter the selections which are primarily concerned with these questions about reason and revelation are "Faith and Reason: Their Distinct Provinces," by John Locke, "Prophecy and Prophets," by Benedict de Spinoza, and "The Ways of Knowing Divine Truths," by St. Thomas Aquinas.

Locke holds that when any religious statement is offered to us as a revelation, we may at the very least use reason to ascertain whether the statement is in origin a revelation. What is more, he believes that if the content of the statement is contrary to reason, we have a sufficient case for not counting it as a revelation because God is too good to be the author of unreason. Locke believes that there may be some religious truths above reason, but we leave it to the reader to decide whether truths above reason would be intelligible by Locke's standards of meaningfulness.

In the selection on "Prophecy and Prophets" Spinoza analyzes the revelations of the Old Testament prophets by the criteria of reason. Although Spinoza wrote before Locke, this selection may nonetheless be read as an illustration of the Lockean principle that reason may evaluate the credentials of a revelation and pass on whether its content is reasonable.

In "The Ways of Knowing Divine Truths" Aquinas takes a position which differs from that of Locke and Spinoza, but is not in direct opposition to it. Many Christians, who want to find a place for reason in religion, regard Aquinas as the most persuasive defender of the view that reason may support at least some religious truths. Indeed, Aquinas' advocacy of reason is often regarded as the crucial demonstration of the possibility of natural theology, the discovery of truths about God by human faculties alone. Aquinas argues for the possibility of natural theology by pointing out that reason as well as revelation is a gift of God. Its origin, then, is a guarantee of reason's reliability, and we are justified in using it to establish the truth of the statement, "God exists," and of certain statements about God's nature. The success of Aquinas' introduction of reason into religion turns largely on his claim that reason and revelation will never be incompatible because reason cannot be used to determine the authenticity of an alleged revelation. This is the point at which Locke and Spinoza may be found to be in opposition to Aquinas. While Locke recognizes the possibility of revealed truths, he nonetheless allows that reason may be used to examine the claim that a given statement is revealed, and this seems to be assigning reason a greater task than Aquinas advocates. Spinoza's treatment of the Old Testament prophets is an example of the reasonable analysis of the content of revelations, a practice Locke also recommends; this too seems to be a larger use of reason than Aquinas advocates. Whether there are irremediable incompatibilities in the positions of Locke and Spinoza, on the one hand, and Aquinas, on the other, is a question we shall leave to the reader's consideration.

The frequent occurrence of the terms "revelation," "faith," and "reason" in the readings in this chapter makes these terms deserving of some further general comment. We shall begin with "revelation." Locke distinguishes between direct revelation and traditional revelation. In a direct revelation God reveals himself to someone immediately. When someone believes that he is having a direct revelation, it is legitimate to ask, "Is God revealing himself to me?" The reader may turn to Spinoza on "Prophecy and Prophets" for a discussion of the ways in which the Old Testament prophets reassured themselves on this point. The reader may ask himself whether any better tests of direct revelation than theirs might be devised.

Traditional revelation is a first person's revelation described to a second person, so that the second person knows what was revealed to the first person. But how can someone say that he knows what has been revealed to another person? Consider the dilemma which Locke finds in this question. The direct ex-perience of God is extraordinary. But if someone has had an extraordinary experience, he can hardly describe it in everyday language; for everyday language is designed to describe ordinary experiences. On the other hand, if he devises a language to describe his extraordinary experience, how can someone who has not had the experiences which give his words meaning understand what is being talked about? Locke's dilemma seems ineludible, and thus makes us question the reasonableness of regarding revelation as a source of knowledge.

In practice, of course, no religious teacher or believer feels the force of Locke's reasonable criticism of discourse based on divine revelation; and our question remains, "How can someone say that he knows what has been revealed to another?" The answer which is often given by religious people is that they believe by faith.

The view of faith which we shall take here is that to believe a religious statement on faith is to believe it because of trust in the authority who makes the statement. This relationship of trust between a religious believer and a religious authority is a defining characteristic of theistic religion, and one which must be understood in order to know what it is to be religious in a theistic sense. The supreme religious authority for theism is God. But not all believers claim to know God directly. Hence a human religious authority must be relied on. Such an authority may be a living person or a group of living persons, or it may be a book. If the authority is a living person, he is trusted because it is believed that he is God's agent, capable of receiving divine revelations. Trust in a group of persons is to be understood in the same way. If the authority is a book, it is trusted because it is believed to be a record of the lives and revelations of people who were God's agents when they lived on earth, that is, who were religious authorities themselves. So we come to this conclusion: The supreme religious authority is God. But because of the difficulty of knowing God directly, many believers rely on a religious authority who is believed to be God's agent, capable of receiving revelations. Even when this person is no longer living, he continues to be a religious authority when his revelations are remembered or are recorded in a book and believers continue to heed them. In what follows we shall discuss religious authority as a person rather than as God.

It is important to notice that the authoritativeness of a religious authority is of a particular kind. The religious authority is an authority only to those who trust him, and he remains an authority to them only so long as he is trusted. Trust is the ratification of authority. Thus, the religious person's reliance on a religious authority is unlike what we ordinarily understand as someone's reliance on an expert. Consider, for example, a car owner's reliance on a mechanic's opinion about his car. It is true that the car owner trusts the mechanic's opinion because he believes that the mechanic knows more than he does about both his car in particular and the science of automobile mechanics in general. But the car owner believes that in principle both his car and the science of automobile mechanics are knowable to anyone who takes the trouble to study them. What the mechanic knows is not something that is necessarily hidden from others. Thus, the mechanic's opinion is testable against the opinion of other me-

chanics, and, in the end, the opinions of all mechanics are testable against the science of automobile mechanics. So it is not the car owner's trust, but the mechanic's knowledge that makes the mechanic an expert. A similar account of expertness can be given for others such as lawyers, physicians, detectives, and antique dealers who are regarded as masters of their fields.

But the relation between a religious person and his authority is a very different one. In principle what the authority knows is unknown to the believer, for this is why he seeks an authority. What is more there can be no appeal to other authorities. For when a religious person accepts what an authority says, he makes what the authority says his religion. To seek the confirmation of one's religion by additional authorities is to run the risk of having it denied. In one sense, of course, a denial of someone's religion is meaningless to him; for he has no context in which to understand the denial. But the apparent denial of one's religion can be unsettling to a religious person, and one of the characteristics of a highly organized religion is that in it there is one and only one source of doctrinal authority.

The reader must not suppose, however, that a religious believer's reliance on a religious authority is a unique sort of relation between a seeker of knowledge and an authority. There is a similar relation, for example, between a person who comes to a court of law for justice and his judge, and between a person and judges of other matters such as beauty, artistic excellence, and etiquette. In all of these matters the judge's position as a judge depends on his being regarded as such by those who seek his judgments. What is more those persons who seek a judge's opinion cannot know what it will be until he delivers it. What they seek to know is hidden until the judge makes it plain. In these ways the relation between a person and a judge whose opinion he has asked is similar to the relation between a person and a religious authority whom he has asked about God. It might be argued that these judges differ from religious authorities in that the most respected judges are those who can give good reasons for their decisions, while a religious authority gives no reasons for what he says other than to claim that what he says is said for God. It must be noticed, however, that the ultimate good reasons which a judge can offer for his judgments are the canons of his field; so that the ultimate reason for accepting the opinion of a judge of beauty, for example, is that one *accepts* the canons of beauty in accordance with which the judge speaks; and similarly, one accepts what a religious authority says because one *accepts* the proposition that he speaks for God. There is one important difference here, however. While one might eventually learn to apply canons for one's self, as someone must when he becomes a judge, the theory behind religious authority is that there is no learning to speak for God. Rather God chooses to speak through the person who thus becomes an authority.

So much for the positive side of faith. We must now notice three misconceptions of faith, which we may deal with in the light of our positive account of it. (1) It is sometimes said that faith is nothing but someone's saying that he believes things which are unbelievable. But we ask, "What is the criterion of belief (or disbelief)?" The criterion can hardly be either empirical or experimental; for religious authorities presumably do not speak, as authorities, about the realm of either everyday experience or science. The realm about which they do speak is in some sense outside everyday experience and scientific experiment. It is just this characteristic of the divine which makes the religious person turn to an authority. It is true that the religious person may believe what someone else finds unbelievable. But this only shows that the religious person's criterion of belief is his authority, and that the other person refuses to accept this criterion.

(2) It is sometimes said that a religious person who believes on faith believes without evidence. But here we may ask, "What is meant by 'evidence'?" Religion is not the sort of subject for which there is independent evidence. For the religious person does not accept something as evidence of the divine until his authority tells him that it is, and then he accepts it as evidence because his authority has told him that it is. Anyone who approaches religion in the scientific spirit of independent evidence is bound to be appalled. For the religious person believes what he is told by his authority and whatever he is told by that authority he believes. But this characteristic of religion is simply one of the ways in which it differs from science.

(3) It is sometimes said that a religious person's faith is his believing despite evidence to the contrary. But here we must ask, "What is to count as evidence to the contrary?" We must say that for a religious person, evidence to the contrary must be defined by his authority. To understand why something is not evidence to the contrary one must accept the religion in connection with which the question about evidence to the

contrary has arisen. Only when one sees the evidence as the religious authority sees it will one understand how to count it. Consider the case of someone who believes that God is a kindly father, and who continues to believe this no matter what dreadful calamities befall him. His friends urge him to accept the calamities as evidence against the fatherliness of God. Thus they say that his religious belief is contrary to the evidence. But to the believer the calamities are not evidence that God hates him, or that God is indifferent. Notice that the believer and his friends do not dispute about what they see. The believer's calamities are real enough. The issue between them is how to interpret religiously what they see, and the believer interprets his calamities in accordance with his religion. It is only because his friends judge his belief outside the context of his religion that they can say that he speaks contrary to the evidence. But then we may ask, "Do they understand the evidence?"

Proving That God Exists

Having looked closely at the place of revelation, authority, and faith in religious belief, let us examine some of the ways religious believers have used reason as a ground for their belief. In theistic religion, the basic belief which some theologians have tried to prove by reasonable arguments is the belief that God exists.

In this chapter the proof of God's existence through the use of reason is considered by St. Anselm, St. Thomas Aquinas, and David Hume. Each considers the problem from a different point of view.

Anselm believes as a matter of faith that God exists. But he tries to prove that God exists as a matter of intellectual curiosity. We say as a matter of intellectual curiosity, because his success is in no way crucial to his belief. Whether he succeeds or fails, he will continue to believe on faith.

Aquinas, too, believes as a matter of faith that God exists. But he tries to prove by reason that God exists, so that he may convince nonbelievers by undeniable arguments that they ought to believe in God's existence.

Hume does not believe that God's existence can be proved by reason, and he uses reason to demolish those arguments which are supposed to prove that God exists.

It can be seen that Anselm, who is proving to himself by reason a belief which he already holds on faith, will not have much of interest to say to Aquinas who is trying to prove God's existence to people who do not believe at all. Aquinas and Hume are, of course, working in direct contradiction, the one expecting to support the statement, "God exists," by reason, the other expecting to show its untenability on reasonable grounds.

We must notice the sort of question which the question "Is there a God?" is not like. It is not like the question "Are there okapis?" For this question can be finally answered by showing the questioner an okapi. But if, as many theists suppose (and here we shall follow their supposition), God is outside the world, is a transcendent being, then we cannot look for God in the world. So we cannot answer the question "Is there a God?" by pointing to something in the world, as we can answer the question "Are there okapis?" by pointing to an okapi.

How then do theists who believe in a transcendent God prove his existence?

In this chapter we offer examples of their efforts which may be classified under three heads: Proofs from the Nature of God, Proofs from the Nature of the World, and the Proof by Analogy. Proofs from the nature of God are designed to show that God's nature is such that once we understand it, we can see it implies his existence. Proofs from the nature of the world show that the world has some quality (motion, beauty, order, etc.) which it could not have given itself and which implies the existence of a source, namely, God. The proof by analogy is designed to show that there is a resemblance between the world and machines and that just as machines have inventors so the world must have a maker, who is God. In this chapter we offer Anselm's proof from the nature of God, Aquinas' proofs from the nature of the world, and Hume's discussion of the proof by analogy. Just after each of these ways of proving by reason that God exists, the reader will find an equally reasonable criticism which may be leveled against the proof.

Whether these attempts to argue for or against God's existence on the ground of reason alone are misdirected or inappropriate is a question which must be raised by every reader. The justifiability of using reason in theistic religion is considered in a different way in the final selection in the chapter, and we shall return to this issue in the last part of this introduction. But first we must consider briefly the use of reason to support (or attack) the belief that God intervenes in the world.

God in the World

The theist contends that while God is outside the world, he is nonetheless capable of intervening in the course of world events. Two of the problems which arise from this theistic contention are the problem of miracles and the problem of evil. The problem of miracles centers on the question of whether God does intervene in the world. The problem of evil centers on the question of why, if the world is God's creation and God can intervene in the world, there is evil. In this chapter these problems are discussed under the assumption that God exists. To deny God's existence is, of course, to deny these problems.

We have included in this chapter readings on the problem of miracles by Hume, who argues that miracles are impossible, and by Professor C. S. Lewis, who argues that miracles are possible. These authors mean by the word "miracle" any interruption of the order of nature which must be accounted for as a divine suspension of the laws of nature. The reader should be careful to distinguish this meaning of "miracle" from another common use of the word. "Miracle" is sometimes used to mean any natural event which causes wonder, any event which is, as we say, "improbable but not impossible"; and people do sometimes say that God is the cause of events of this kind too. But this last sense of "miracle" is not the sense in which our authors are interested in the possibility of miracles.

Hume's argument against miracles is based on his conception of the character of our knowledge of the world. What we call the order of nature is the sum of our experiences of the world. Now when someone asks us to believe that a miracle, an interruption of the order of nature, has occurred, he is asking us to believe something which contradicts our experience of the world. Notice that we are not being asked to believe something that is simply unknown to us by experience but is nonetheless not incompatible with our experience, as if we were asked to believe that a certain man always walks on his hands, sleeps during the day and stays awake at night, and dines by eating nuts first and soup last. When we are asked to believe a miracle we are being asked to believe something on the order of a man's dying and then coming to life again, an alleged state of affairs that is contradictory to our experience. This very contradiction is its own disproof. So, Hume argues, every claim that a miracle has occurred requires our disbelief. In direct opposition to Hume we offer Professor C. S. Lewis' argument for miracles. Professor Lewis' case rests on a criticism of Hume's account of the improbability of miracles and his own defense of their probability. We leave to the reader the task of deciding between Hume and Professor Lewis.

Let us now turn to the second problem arising from the claim that God can enter into the world. This is the problem of evil, which has long perplexed the theist. Epicurus (342?-270 B.C.) is credited with inventing the following dilemma about God and evil: Either God would remove evil out of this world, and cannot; or he can, and will not; or he has not the power nor will; or, lastly, he has both the power and will. If he has the will, and not the power, this shows weakness, which is contrary to the nature of God. If he has the power, and not the will, it is malignity; and this is no less contrary to his nature. If he is neither able nor willing, he is both impotent and malignant, and consequently cannot be God. If he be both willing and able (which alone is consonant to the nature

of God), whence comes evil, or why does he not prevent it?

If there is evil in the world it is difficult for the theist to maintain the claim that God is benevolent. But if God is not benevolent, can he be God? In this chapter we offer two readings on the problem of evil, one by Leibniz and the other by Hume. Leibniz meets the theistic dilemma of evil in the world by questioning whether there *is* evil in the world, and thus saves the theist's belief in a benevolent God. Hume, on the other hand, is inclined to the view that "the original source of all things" is indifferent to the propagation of either good or evil in the world. But such a view renders any ordinary sort of theism absurd.

The questions which lie behind the problem of evil are these: Can any observation of the world render theism false? Does the existence of evil render theism false? Would the absence of evil from the world render theism true? These are questions which we must leave to the reader's consideration. But we must also remind him of the second-order question: Is theism (or even religion in general) the sort of subject which can be true or false? It is to this last question that we must now address ourselves.

A Reconsideration of the Grounds for Religious Statements

We have now surveyed in a rapid and introductory fashion the question of the relation of revelation and reason, and the question of whether reason can be used to establish religious statements. The religious statements which we are interested in are "God exists," "God does (does not) work miracles," and "God is (is not) responsible for the evil in the world." Thus, the philosophers of religion whom we have been considering have treated religious statements as though they were about some sort of matters of fact to be confirmed (or disproved) by an appeal to reason, understood in a very broad sense.

In the epilogue of this chapter, Mr. Alasdair MacIntyre explores the nature of religious statements, and hence, religion, from a radically different point of view. He believes that religion is neither a kind of science, nor a would-be science. Thus, religious statements cannot be examined and criticized by criteria suitable to the sciences. Religion is an independent, self-contained area of thought to be discussed and understood on its own terms, namely, faith. In its independence religion is like morals, politics, and, of course, the sciences, which are also to be discussed and understood on their own terms. Mr. MacIntyre argues for the unique character of religion, by showing the ways in which our use of religious statements is unlike our use of any other statements, and hence shows how they are intelligible only in their own context, which is religion itself. In effect, Mr. MacIntyre is arguing for the view that if the philosopher is to understand the grounds of religious statements, he must work out their basis in faith rather than in scientifically conceived reason. This is not to say that faith does not have a logic of its own; but its logic, its grounds for belief and disbelief, must be recognized as its own.

1

Faith and Reason: Their Distinct Provinces

John Locke
(1632-1704)

[A general introductory note on Locke may be found on page 70.]

It is generally known that Locke's contributions to the theory of knowledge have given him a secure place in the history of philosophy; but it is not always remembered that the implications of his epistemology for the problem of religious knowledge have also earned him a small but significant place in the history of religion, particularly in the history of the Christianity of the English-speaking world. Locke believed that reason has a place in religion. He assigned it the task of certifying the divine origin of revelations, and of guaranteeing their content against unreasonableness. Whether any revelation can survive such a scrutiny by reason is a question which we leave to the reader. Locke claims that faith and reason are not opposed to each other, and this claim depends largely on his view that there are some propositions whose content is "above reason" but not "contrary to reason." Without such propositions the religious person would of course have nothing to believe on faith. Whether Locke succeeds in leaving room for such propositions is an additional question which we leave to the reader's consideration.

This selection is drawn from Locke's *Essay Concerning Human Understanding* (1690), Chapters XVI, XVII, and XVIII. The original chapter titles have been retained as subtitles in this selection.

The bare testimony of revelation is the highest certainty.   There is one sort of propositions that challenge the highest degree of our assent upon bare testimony, whether the thing proposed agree or disagree with common experience and the ordinary course of things, or no. The reason whereof is, because the testimony is of such an one, as cannot deceive, nor be deceived, and that is God himself. This carries with it an assurance beyond doubt, evidence beyond exception. This is called by a peculiar name, revelation; and our assent to it, faith; which as absolutely determines our minds, and as perfectly excludes all wavering, as our knowledge itself; and we may as well doubt of our own being, as we can, whether any revelation from God be true. So that faith is a settled and sure principle of assent and assurance, and leaves no manner of room for doubt or hesitation. Only we must be sure that it be a divine revelation, and that we understand it right: else we shall expose ourselves to all the extravagancy of enthusiasm, and all the error of wrong principles, if we have faith and assurance in what is not divine revelation. And therefore in those cases, our assent can be rationally no higher than the evidence of its being a revelation, and that this is the meaning of the expressions it is delivered in. If the evidence of its being a revelation, or that this is its true sense, be only on probable proofs: our assent can reach no higher than an assurance or diffidence, arising from the more or less apparent probability of the proofs. But of faith, and the precedency it ought to have before other arguments of persuasion, I shall speak more hereafter, where I treat of it, as it is ordinarily placed, in contradistinction to reason; though in truth it be nothing else but an assent founded on the highest reason.

OF REASON

Various significations of the word reason. The word "reason" in the English language has different significations: sometimes it is taken for true and clear principles; sometimes for clear and fair deductions from those principles; and sometimes for the cause, and particularly the final cause. But the consideration I shall have of it here is in a signification different from all these; and that is, as it stands for a faculty in man, that faculty whereby man is supposed to be distinguished from beasts, and wherein it is evident he much surpasses them.

Wherein reasoning consists. If general knowledge, as has been shown, consists in a perception of the agreement or disagreement of our own ideas, and the knowledge of the existence of all things without us (except only of a God, whose existence every man may certainly know and demonstrate to himself from his own existence) be had only by our senses: what room is there for the exercise of any other faculty, but outward sense and inward perception? What need is there of reason? Very much; both for the enlargement of our knowledge, and regulating our assent; for it hath to do both in knowledge and opinion, and is necessary and assisting to all our other intellectual faculties, and indeed contains two of them, viz., sagacity and illation. By the one, it finds out; and by the other, it so orders the intermediate ideas, as to discover what connection there is in each link of the chain, whereby the extremes are held together; and thereby, as it were, to draw into view the truth sought for, which is that which we call illation or inference, and consists in nothing but the perception of the connection there is between the ideas, in each step of the deduction, whereby the mind comes to see either the certain agreement or disagreement of any two ideas, as in demonstration, in which it arrives at knowledge; or their probable connection, on which it gives or withholds its assent, as in opinion. Sense and intuition reach but a very little way. The greatest part of our knowledge depends upon deductions and intermediate ideas: and in those cases, where we are fain to substitute assent instead of knowledge, and take propositions for true, without being certain they are so, we have need to find out, examine, and compare the grounds of their probability. In both these cases, the faculty which finds out the means, and rightly applies them to discover certainty in the one, and probability in the other, is that which we call reason. For as reason perceives the necessary and indubitable connection of all the ideas or proofs one to another, in each step of any demonstration that produces knowledge: so it likewise perceives the probable connection of all the ideas or proofs one to another, in every step of a discourse, to which it will think assent due. This is the lowest degree of that which can be truly called reason. For where the mind does not perceive this probable connection, where it does not discern whether there be any such connection or no; there men's opinions are not the product of judgment, or the consequence of reason, but the effects of chance and hazard, of a mind floating at all adventures, without choice and without direction.

Its four parts.   So that we may in reason consider these four degrees; the first and highest is the discovering and finding out of truths; the second, the regular and methodical disposition of them, and laying them in a clear and fit order, to make their connection and force be plainly and easily perceived; the third is the perceiving their connection; and the fourth, a making a right conclusion. . . .

Above, contrary, and according to reason.   By what has been before said of reason, we may be able to make some guess at the distinction of things, into those that are according to, above, and contrary to reason. (1) According to reason are such propositions, whose truth we can discover by examining and tracing those ideas we have from sensation and reflection: and by natural deduction find to be true or probable. (2) Above reason are such propositions, whose truth or probability we cannot by reason derive from those principles. (3) Contrary to reason are such propositions, as are inconsistent with, or irreconcilable to, our clear and distinct ideas. Thus the existence of one God is according to reason; the existence of more than one God, contrary to reason; the resurrection of the dead above reason. Farther, as above reason may be taken in a double sense, viz., either as signifying above probability, or above certainty; so in that large sense also, contrary to reason is, I suppose, sometimes taken.

Reason and faith not opposite.   There is another use of the word reason, wherein it is opposed to faith; which though it be in itself a very improper way of speaking, yet common use has so authorized it, that it would be folly either to oppose or hope to remedy it: only I think it may not be amiss to take notice that however faith be opposed to reason, faith is nothing but a firm assent of the mind: which if it be regulated, as is our duty, cannot be afforded to anything but upon good reason; and so cannot be opposite to it. He that believes, without having any reason for believing, may be in love with his own fancies; but neither seeks truth as he ought, nor pays the obedience due to his Maker, who would have him use those discerning faculties he has given him, to keep him out of mistake and error. He that does not this to the best of his power, however he sometimes lights on truth, is in the right but by chance; and I know not whether the luckiness of the accident will excuse the irregularity of his proceeding. This at least is certain, that he must be accountable for whatever mistakes he runs into: whereas he that makes use of the light and faculties

God has given him, and seeks sincerely to discover truths by those helps and abilities he has, may have this satisfaction in doing his duty as a rational creature, that, though he should miss truth, he will not miss the reward of it. For he governs his assent right, and places it as he should, who, in any case or matter whatsoever, believes or disbelieves, according as reason directs him. He that doth otherwise transgresses against his own light, and misuses those faculties which were given him to no other end, but to search and follow the clearer evidence and greater probability. But, since reason and faith are by some men opposed, we will so consider them in the following chapter.

OF FAITH AND REASON, AND THEIR DISTINCT PROVINCES

Necessary to know their boundaries.   It has been above shown: (1) That we are of necessity ignorant, and want knowledge of all sorts, where we want ideas. (2) That we are ignorant, and want rational knowledge, where we want proofs. (3) That we want certain knowledge and certainty, as far as we want clear and determined specific ideas. (4) That we want probability to direct our assent in matters where we have neither knowledge of our own, nor testimony of other men, to bottom our reason upon.

From these things thus premised, I think we may come to lay down the measures and boundaries between faith and reason; the want whereof may possibly have been the cause, if not of great disorders, yet at least of great disputes, and perhaps mistakes in the world. For till it be resolved, how far we are to be guided by reason, and how far by faith, we shall in vain dispute, and endeavor to convince one another in matters of religion.

Faith and reason what, as contradistinguished.   I find every sect, as far as reason will help them, make use of it gladly; and where it fails them, they cry out, it is matter of faith, and above reason. And I do not see how they can argue with anyone, or ever convince a gainsayer who makes use of the same plea, without setting down strict boundaries between faith and reason; which ought to be the first point established in all questions, where faith has anything to do.

Reason, therefore, here, as contradistinguished to faith, I take to be the discovery of the certainty or probability of such propositions or truths, which the mind arrives at by deduction made from such ideas, which it has got by the use of its natural faculties, viz., by sensation or reflection.

Faith, on the other side, is the assent to any proposition, not thus made out by the deductions of reason; but upon the credit of the proposer, as coming from God, in some extraordinary way of communication. This way of discovering truths to men we call revelation.

No new simple idea can be conveyed by traditional revelation.   First, then, I say that no man inspired by God can by any revelation communicate to others any new simple ideas, which they had not before from sensation or reflection. For whatsoever impressions he himself may have from the immediate hand of God, this revelation, if it be of new simple ideas, cannot be conveyed to another, either by words, or any other signs. Because words, by their immediate operation on us, cause no other ideas, but of their natural sounds: and it is by the custom of using them for signs, that they excite and revive in our minds latent ideas; but yet only such ideas as were there before. For words, seen or heard, recall to our thoughts those ideas only, which to us they have been wont to be signs of; but cannot introduce any perfectly new and formerly unknown simple ideas. The same holds in all other signs, which cannot signify to us things, of which we have before never had any idea at all. Thus whatever things were discovered to St. Paul, when he was rapt up into the third heaven, whatever new ideas his mind there received, all the description he can make to others of that place is only this, that there are such things, "as eye hath not seen, nor ear heard, nor hath it entered into the heart of man to conceive." And supposing God should discover to anyone, supernaturally, a species of creatures inhabiting, for example, Jupiter or Saturn (for that it is possible there may be such, nobody can deny), which had six senses; and imprint on his mind the ideas conveyed to theirs by that sixth sense; he could no more, by words, produce in the minds of other men those ideas, imprinted by that sixth sense, than one of us could convey the idea of any color by the sounds of words into a man who, having the other four senses perfect, had always totally wanted the fifth of seeing. For our simple ideas then, which are the foundation and sole matter of all our notions and knowledge, we must depend wholly on our reason, I mean our natural faculties; and can by no means receive them, or any of them, from traditional revelation; I say, traditional revelation, in distinction to original revelation. By the one, I mean that first impression, which is made immediately by God, on the mind of any man, to which we cannot set any bounds; and by the other, those impressions delivered over to others in words, and the ordinary ways of conveying our conceptions one to another.

Traditional revelation may make us know propositions knowable also by reason, but not with the same certainty that reason doth.   Secondly, I say that the same truths may be discovered, and conveyed down from revelation, which are discoverable to us by reason, and by those ideas we naturally may have. So God might, by revelation, discover the truth of any proposition of Euclid; as well as men, by the natural use of their faculties, come to make the discovery themselves. In all things of this kind, there is little need or use of revelation, God having furnished us with natural and surer means to arrive at the knowledge of them. For whatsoever truth we come to the clear discovery of, from the knowledge and contemplation of our own ideas, will always be certainer to us than those which are conveyed to us by traditional revelation. For the knowledge we have, that this revelation came at first from God, can never be so sure as the knowledge we have from the clear and distinct perception of the agreement or disagreement of our own ideas; v. g., if it were revealed some ages since, that the three angles of a triangle were equal to two right ones, I might assent to the truth of that proposition, upon the credit of the tradition that it was revealed; but that would never amount to so great a certainty as the knowledge of it, upon the comparing and measuring my own ideas of two right angles, and the three angles of a triangle. The like holds in matter of fact knowable by our senses; v. g., the history of the deluge is conveyed to us by writings, which had their original from revelation: and yet nobody, I think, will say he has as certain and clear a knowledge of the flood, as Noah that saw it; or that he himself would have had, had he then been alive and seen it. For he has no greater assurance than that of his senses, that it is writ in the book supposed writ by Moses inspired: but he has not so great an assurance that Moses writ that book, as if he had seen Moses write it. So that the assurance of its being a revelation is less still than the assurance of his senses.

Revelation cannot be admitted against the clear evidence of reason.   In propositions then, whose certainty is built upon the clear perception of the agreement or disagreement of our ideas, attained either by immediate intuition as in self-evident propositions, or by evident deductions of reason in demonstrations, we need not the assistance of revelation as necessary to gain our assent, and introduce them into our minds. Because the natural ways of knowledge could settle them there, or had done it already; which is the greatest assurance we can possibly have of anything, unless where God immediately reveals it to us: and there too our assurance can be no greater than our knowledge is that it is a revelation from God. But yet nothing, I think, can, under that title, shake or overrule plain knowledge; or rationally prevail with any man to admit it for true, in a direct contradiction to the clear evidence of his own understanding. For since no evidence of our faculties, by which we receive such revelations, can exceed, if equal, the certainty of our intuitive knowledge, we can never receive for a truth anything that is directly contrary to our clear and distinct knowledge; v. g., the ideas of one body, and one place, do so clearly agree, and the mind has so evident a perception of their agreement, that we can never assent to a proposition that affirms the same body to be in two distant places at once, however it should pretend to the authority of a divine revelation: since the evidence, first, that we deceive not ourselves in ascribing it to God; secondly, that we understand it right; can never be so great as the evidence of our own intuitive knowledge, whereby we discern it impossible for the same body to be in two places at once. And therefore no proposition can be received for divine revelation, or obtain the assent due to all such, if it be contradictory to our clear intuitive knowledge. Because this would be to subvert the principles and foundations of all knowledge, evidence, and assent whatsoever: and there would be left no difference between truth and falsehood, no measures of credible and incredible in the world, if doubtful propositions shall take place before self-evident; and what we certainly know give way to what we may possibly be mistaken in. In propositions therefore contrary to the clear perception of the agreement or disagreement of any of our ideas, it will be in vain to urge them as matters of faith. They cannot move our assent, under that or any other title whatsoever. For faith can never convince us of anything that contradicts our knowledge. Because though faith be founded on the testimony of God (who cannot lie) revealing any proposition to us, yet we cannot have an assurance of the truth of its being a divine revelation, greater than our own knowledge: since the whole strength of the certainty depends upon our knowledge that God revealed it, which in this case, where the proposition supposed revealed contradicts our knowledge or reason, will always have this objection hanging to it, viz., that we cannot tell how to conceive that to come from God, the bountiful Author of our being, which, if received for true, must overturn all the principles and foundations of knowledge he has given us; render all our faculties useless; wholly destroy the most excellent part of his workmanship, our understandings; and put a man in a condition, wherein he will have less light, less conduct than the beast that perisheth. For if the mind of man can never have a clearer (and perhaps not so clear) evidence of anything to be a divine revelation, as it has of the principles of its own reason, it can never have a ground to quit the clear evidence of its reason, to give a place to a proposition, whose revelation has not a greater evidence than those principles have.

Traditional revelation much less.   Thus far a man has use of reason, and ought to hearken to it, even in immediate and original revelation, where it is supposed to be made to himself: but to all those who pretend not to immediate revelation, but are required to pay obedience, and to receive the truths revealed to others, which by the tradition of writings, or word of mouth, are conveyed down to them, reason has a great deal more to do, and is that only which can induce us to receive them. For matter of faith being only divine revelation, and nothing else, faith, as we use the word (called commonly divine faith) has to do with no propositions, but those which are supposed to be divinely revealed. So that I do not see how those, who make revelation alone the sole object of faith, can say that it is a matter of faith, and not of reason, to believe that such or such a proposition, to be found in such or such a book, is of divine inspiration; unless it be revealed that that proposition, or all in that book, was communicated by divine inspiration. Without such a revelation, the believing, or not believing, that proposition or book to be of divine authority can never be matter of faith, but matter of reason; and such as I must come to an assent to, only by the use of my reason, which can never require or enable me to believe that which is contrary to itself: it being impossible for reason ever to produce any assent to that which to itself appears unreasonable.

In all things, therefore, where we have clear evidence from our ideas, and those principles of knowledge I have above mentioned, reason is the proper judge; and revelation, though it may in consenting with it confirm its dictates, yet cannot in such cases invalidate its decrees: nor can we be obliged, where we have the clear and evident sentence of reason, to quit it for the contrary opinion, under a pretence that it is matter of faith; which can have authority against the plain and clear dictates of reason.

Things above reason.   But, thirdly, there being many things, wherein we have very imperfect notions, or none at all; and other things, of whose past, present, or future existence, by the natural use of our faculties, we can have no knowledge at all: these, as being beyond the discovery of our natural faculties, and above reason, are, when revealed, the proper matter of faith. Thus, that part of the angels rebelled against God, and thereby lost their first happy state; and that the dead shall rise, and live again: these, and the like, being beyond the discovery of reason, are purely matters of faith; with which reason has directly nothing to do.

Or not contrary to reason, if revealed, are matter of faith.   But since God in giving us the light of reason has not thereby tied up his own hands from affording us, when he thinks fit, the light of revelation in any of those matters, wherein our natural faculties are able to give a probable determination; revelation, where God has been pleased to give it, must carry it against the probable conjectures of reason. Because the mind, not being certain of the truth of that it does not evidently know but only yielding to the probability that appears in it, is bound to give up its assent to such a testimony; which, it is satisfied, comes from one who cannot err, and will not deceive. But yet it still belongs to reason to judge of the truth of its being a revelation, and of the signification of the words wherein it is delivered. Indeed, if anything shall be thought revelation, which is contrary to the plain principles of reason, and the evident knowledge the mind has of its own clear and distinct ideas; there reason must be hearkened to, as to a matter within its province: since a man can never have so certain a knowledge that a proposition, which contradicts the clear principles and evidence of his own knowledge, was divinely revealed, or that he understands the words rightly wherein it is delivered; as he has that the contrary is true: and so is bound to consider and judge of it as a matter of reason, and not swallow it, without examination, as a matter of faith.

Revelation in matters where reason cannot judge, or but probably, ought to be hearkened to.   First, whatever proposition is revealed, of whose truth our mind, by its natural faculties and notions, cannot judge; that is purely matter of faith, and above reason.

Secondly, all propositions, whereof the mind, by the use of its natural faculties, can come to determine and judge from naturally acquired ideas, are matter of reason; with this difference still, that in those concerning which it has but an uncertain evidence, and so is persuaded of their truth only upon probable grounds, which still admit a possibility of the contrary to be true, without doing violence to the certain evidence of its own knowledge, and overturning the principles of its own reason; in such probable propositions, I say, an evident revelation ought to determine our assent even against probability. For where the principles of reason have not evidenced a proposition to be certainly true or false, there clear revelation as another principle of truth, and ground of assent, may determine; and so it may be matter of faith, and be also above reason. Because reason, in that particular matter, being able to reach no higher than probability, faith gave the determination where reason came short; and revelation discovered on which side the truth lay.

In matters where reason can afford certain knowledge that is to be hearkened to.   Thus far the dominion of faith reaches, and that without any violence or hindrance to reason, which is not injured or disturbed, but assisted and improved, by new discoveries of truth coming from the eternal fountain of all knowledge. Whatever God hath revealed is certainly true; no doubt can be made of it. This is the proper object of faith: but whether it be a divine revelation or no, reason must judge; which can never permit the mind to reject a greater evidence to embrace what is less evident, nor allow it to entertain probability in opposition to knowledge and certainty. There can be no evidence that any traditional revelation is of divine original, in the words we receive it, and in the sense we understand it, so clear and so certain, as that of the principles of reason: and therefore nothing that is contrary to, and inconsistent with, the clear and self-evident dictates of reason has a right to be urged or assented to as a matter of faith, wherein reason hath nothing to do. Whatsoever is divine revelation ought to overrule all our opinions, prejudices, and interest, and hath a right to be received with full assent. Such a submission as this, of our reason to faith, takes not away the landmarks of knowledge: this shakes not the foundations of reason, but leaves us that use of our faculties, for which they were given us.

If the boundaries be not set between faith and reason, no enthusiasm or extravagancy in religion can be contradicted. If the provinces of faith and reason are not kept distinct by these boundaries, there will, in matters of religion, be no room for reason at all; and those extravagant opinions and ceremonies that are to be found in the several religions of the world will not deserve to be blamed. For, to this crying up of faith, in opposition to reason, we may, I think, in good measure ascribe those absurdities that fill almost all the religions which possess and divide mankind. For men, having been principled with an opinion that they must not consult reason in the things of religion, however apparently contradictory to common sense and the very principles of all their knowledge, have let loose their fancies and natural superstition; and have been by them let into so strange opinions, and extravagant practices in religion, that a considerate man cannot but stand amazed at their follies, and judge them so far from being acceptable to the great and wise God, that he cannot avoid thinking them ridiculous, and offensive to a sober good man. So that in effect religion, which should most distinguish us from beasts, and ought most peculiarly to elevate us, as rational creatures, above brutes, is that wherein men often appear most irrational and more senseless than beasts themselves. *"Credo, quia impossibile est,"* I believe, because it is impossible, might in a good man pass for a sally of zeal; but would prove a very ill rule for men to choose their opinions or religion by.

Questions

1. What does Locke mean by "reason" and by "faith"? How does he show that in religion reason and faith are not opposed?

2. What is Locke's distinction between propositions which are "above reason" and those which are "contrary to reason"? Illustrate the distinction with examples. Using these categories, how would you classify the following propositions (explain your answers):

a. The dead man came to life again.
b. Triangles do not have three sides.

3. When Locke says that "the existence of more than one God [is] contrary to reason," does he speak as a reasonable man, or as a believing Christian, or both? Explain your answer.

4. What does Locke mean by "revelation"? In what areas does he allow reason to be the critic of revelation? On what matters can revelation be independent of reason? How does Locke answer the question of whether someone's revelation about a matter independent of reason can be intelligible to another person?

5. In what respects is it a just (or unjust) criticism of Locke to say that while he permits us to have original revelations if we can, he assures us that we can never understand anyone else's revelation whose subject is God's nature or will; so he makes it impossible for religion to be discussed?

2

Prophecy and	Benedict de Spinoza
Prophets	*(1634-1677)*

Spinoza was born a Jew, in Holland. He was given an education in the Torah, the Talmud, and the works of such commentators as Abraham ibn Ezra and Maimonides, studies which would have fitted him to be a rabbi. But these studies led him to express views on the nature of God, on immortality, and on the scientific authority of the Sacred Scriptures, which differed sharply from the views of the Jewish community in Amsterdam. Spinoza argued that there is nothing in the Scriptures to contradict the views that God is material and that the soul is not immortal. What is more he held that on matters determinable by reason, the Scriptures should be subject to examination by reason, and should be criticized when found contrary to it. The expression of these views led to Spinoza's excommunication. The reason for his excommunication may, however, have been more political than doctrinal. Spinoza's ideas might not have alarmed his fellow Jews if they had not thought his opinions might disturb the religious sensibilities of the rulers of Holland, and thus might bring an end to the toleration which the Jews were enjoying there.

Having suffered from a religious intolerance associated with political fears, Spinoza set out to show that the safety of the state is best secured "by allowing every man to think what he likes, and say what he thinks." He argues for freedom of religious thought in his *Tractatus Theologico-Politicus,* by showing that there is ". . . nothing taught expressly by Scripture, which does not agree with our understanding, or which is repugnant thereto. . . ." Hence, for a Christian or Jew, the freedom to exercise his reason is not incompatible with his religion, and may even be essential to it.

The reading that follows is drawn from Spinoza's examination of prophecy and prophets. These topics are vital to a religion based on what Locke calls "traditional revelation." For a religious believer's views on prophets and the methods of prophets determine what he can believe on faith. Spinoza discusses here those aspects of prophecy which are subject to examination by reason and those which must be accepted on faith.

This reading is drawn from Chapters I and II of the *Tractatus Theologico-Politicus* (1670). The translation from the Latin is by R. H. M. Elwes.

Prophecy, or revelation, is sure knowledge revealed by God to man. A prophet is one who interprets the revelations of God to those who are unable to attain to sure knowledge of the matters revealed, and therefore can only apprehend them by simple faith. . . .

. . . The prophets were endowed with unusually vivid imaginations, and not with unusually perfect minds. This conclusion is amply sustained by Scripture, for we are told that Solomon was the wisest of men, but had no special faculty of prophecy. Heman, Calcol, and Dara, though men of great talent, were not prophets, whereas uneducated countrymen, nay, even women, such as Hagar, Abraham's handmaid, were thus gifted. Nor is this contrary to ordinary experience and reason. Men of great imaginative power are less fitted for abstract reasoning, whereas those who excel in intellect and its use keep their imagination more restrained and controlled, holding it in subjection, so to speak, lest it should usurp the place of reason.

Thus to suppose that knowledge of natural and spiritual phenomena can be gained from the prophetic books is an utter mistake, which I shall endeavour to expose, as I think philosophy, the age, and the question itself demand. I care not for the girdings of superstition, for superstition is the bitter enemy of all true knowledge and true morality. Yes; it has come to this! Men who openly confess that they can form no idea of God, and only know Him through created things, of which they know not the causes, can unblushingly accuse philosophers of Atheism.

Treating the question methodically, I will show that prophecies varied, not only according to the imagination and physical temperament of the prophet, but also according to his particular opinions; and further that prophecy never rendered the prophet wiser than he was before. But I will first discuss the assurance of truth which the prophets received.

Imagination does not, in its own nature, involve any certainty of truth, such as is implied in every clear and distinct idea, but requires some extrinsic reason to assure us of its objective reality: hence prophecy cannot afford certainty, and the prophets were assured of God's revelation by some sign, and not by the fact of revelation, as we may see from Abraham, who, when he had heard the promise of God, demanded a sign, not because he did not believe in God, but because he wished to be sure that it was God Who made the promise. The fact is still more evident in the case of Gideon: "Show me," he says to God, "show me a sign, that I may know that it is Thou that talkest with me." God also says to Moses: "And let this be a sign that I have sent thee." Hezekiah, though he had long known Isaiah to be a prophet, none the less demanded a sign of the cure which he predicted. It is thus quite evident that the prophets always received some sign to certify them of their prophetic imaginings; and for this reason Moses bids the Jews (Deut. xviii.) ask of the prophets a sign, namely, the prediction of some coming event. In this respect, prophetic knowledge is inferior to natural knowledge, which needs no sign, and in itself implies certitude. Moreover, Scripture warrants the statement that the certitude of the prophets was not mathematical, but moral. Moses lays down the punishment of death for the prophet who preaches new gods, even though he confirm his doctrine by signs and wonders (Deut. xiii.); "For," he says, "the Lord also worketh signs and wonders to try His people." And Jesus Christ warns His disciples of the same thing (Matt. xxiv. 24). Furthermore, Ezekiel (xiv. 9) plainly states that God sometimes deceives men with false revelations; and Micaiah bears like witness in the case of the prophets of Ahab.

Although these instances go to prove that revelation is open to doubt, it nevertheless contains, as we have said, a considerable element of certainty; for God never deceives the good, nor His chosen, but (according to the ancient proverb, and as appears in the history of Abigail and her speech) God uses the good as instruments of goodness, and the wicked as means to execute His wrath. This may be seen from the case of Micaiah above quoted; for although God had determined to deceive Ahab, through prophets, He made use of lying prophets; to the good prophet He revealed the truth, and did not forbid his proclaiming it.

Still the certitude of prophecy remains, as I have said, merely moral; for no one can justify himself before God, nor boast that he is an instrument for God's goodness. . . .

The whole question of the certitude of prophecy was based on these three considerations:

1. That the things revealed were imagined very vividly, affecting the prophets in the same way as things seen when awake.
2. The presence of a sign.
3. Lastly and chiefly, that the mind of the prophet was given wholly to what was right and good.

Although Scripture does not always make mention of a sign, we must nevertheless suppose that a sign was always vouchsafed; for Scripture does not always relate every condition and circumstance (as many have remarked), but rather takes them for granted. We may, however, admit that no sign was needed when the prophecy declared nothing that was not already contained in the law of Moses, because it was confirmed by that law. For instance, Jeremiah's prophecy of the destruction of Jerusalem was confirmed by the prophecies of other prophets, and by the threats in the law, and, therefore, it needed no sign; whereas Hananiah, who, contrary to all the prophets, foretold the speedy restoration of the state, stood in need of a sign, or he would have been in doubt as to the truth of his prophecy, until it was confirmed by facts. "The prophet which prophesieth of peace, when the word of the prophet shall come to pass, then shall the prophet be known that the Lord hath truly sent him."

As, then, the certitude afforded to the prophet by signs was not mathematical (*i.e.* did not necessarily follow from the perception of the thing perceived or seen), but only moral, and as the signs were only given to convince the prophet, it follows that such signs were given according to the opinions and capacity of each prophet, so that a sign which would convince one prophet would fall far short of convincing another who was imbued with different opinions. Therefore the signs varied according to the individual prophet.

So also did the revelation vary, as we have stated, according to individual disposition and temperament, and according to the opinions previously held.

It varied according to disposition, in this way: if a prophet was cheerful, victories, peace, and events which make men glad, were revealed to him; in that he was naturally more likely to imagine such things. If, on the contrary, he was melancholy, wars, massacres, and calamities were revealed; and so, according as a prophet was merciful, gentle, quick to anger, or severe, he was more fitted for one kind of revelation than another. It varied according to the temper of imagination in this way: if a prophet was cultivated he perceived the mind of God in a cultivated way, if he was confused he perceived it confusedly. And so with revelations perceived through visions. If a prophet was a countryman he saw visions of oxen, cows, and the like; if he was a soldier he saw generals and armies; if a courtier, a royal throne; and so on.

Lastly, prophecy varied according to the opinions held by the prophets; for instance, to the Magi, who believed in the follies of astrology, the birth of Christ was revealed through the vision of a star in the East. To the augurs of Nebuchadnezzar the destruction of Jerusalem was revealed through entrails, whereas the king himself inferred it from oracles and the direction of arrows which he shot into the air. To prophets who believed that man acts from free choice and by his own power, God was revealed as standing apart from and ignorant of future human actions. . . .

The style of the prophecy also varied according to the eloquence of the individual prophet. The prophecies of Ezekiel and Amos are not written in a cultivated style like those of Isaiah and Nahum, but more rudely. Any Hebrew scholar who wishes to inquire into this point more closely, and compares chapters of the different prophets treating of the same subject, will find great dissimilarity of style. Compare, for instance, chap. i. of the courtly Isaiah, verse

11 to verse 20, with chap. v. of the countryman Amos, verses 21-24. Compare also the order and reasoning of the prophecies of Jeremiah, written in Idumæa (chap. xlix.), with the order and reasoning of Obadiah. Compare, lastly, Isa. xl. 19, 20, and xliv. 8, with Hosea viii. 6, and xiii. 2. And so on.

A due consideration of these passages will clearly show us that God has no particular style in speaking, but, according to the learning and capacity of the prophet, is cultivated, compressed, severe, untutored, prolix, or obscure.

There was, moreover, a certain variation in the visions vouchsafed to the prophets, and in the symbols by which they expressed them; for Isaiah saw the glory of the Lord departing from the Temple in a different form from that presented to Ezekiel. The Rabbis, indeed, maintain that both visions were really the same, but that Ezekiel, being a countryman, was above measure impressed by it, and therefore set it forth in full detail; but unless there is a trustworthy tradition on the subject, which I do not for a moment believe, this theory is plainly an invention. Isaiah saw seraphim with six wings, Ezekiel beasts with four wings; Isaiah saw God clothed and sitting on a royal throne, Ezekiel saw Him in the likeness of a fire; each doubtless saw God under the form in which he usually imagined Him.

Further, the visions varied in clearness as well as in details; for the revelations of Zechariah were too obscure to be understood by the prophet without explanation, as appears from his narration of them; the visions of Daniel could not be understood by him even after they had been explained, and this obscurity did not arise from the difficulty of the matter revealed (for being merely human affairs, these only transcended human capacity in being future), but solely in the fact that Daniel's imagination was not so capable for prophecy while he was awake as while he was asleep; and this is further evident from the fact that at the very beginning of the vision he was so terrified that he almost despaired of his strength. Thus, on account of the inadequacy of his imagination and his strength, the things revealed were so obscure to him that he could not understand them even after they had been explained. . . .

Everyone has been strangely hasty in affirming that the prophets knew everything within the scope of human intellect; and, although certain passages of Scripture plainly affirm that the prophets were in certain respects ignorant, such persons would rather say that they do not understand the passages than admit that there was anything which the prophets did not know; or else they try to wrest the Scriptural words away from their evident meaning.

If either of these proceedings is allowable we may as well shut our Bibles; for vainly shall we attempt to prove anything from them if their plainest passages may be classed among obscure and impenetrable mysteries, or if we may put any interpretation on them which we fancy. For instance, nothing is more clear in the Bible than that Joshua, and perhaps also the author who wrote his history, thought that the sun revolves round the earth, and that the earth is fixed, and further that the sun for a certain period remained still. Many, who will not admit any movement in the heavenly bodies, explain away the passage till it seems to mean something quite different; others, who have learned to philosophize more correctly, and understand that the earth moves while the sun is still, or at any rate does not revolve round the earth, try with all their might to wrest this meaning from Scripture, though plainly nothing of the sort is intended. Such quibblers excite my wonder! Are we, forsooth, bound to believe that Joshua the soldier was a learned astronomer? or that a miracle could not be revealed to him, or that the light of the sun could not remain longer than usual above the horizon, without his knowing the cause? To me both alternatives appear ridiculous, and therefore I would rather say that Joshua was ignorant of the true cause of the lengthened day, and that he and the whole host with him thought that the sun moved round the earth every day, and that on that particular occasion it stood still for a time, thus causing the light to remain longer; and I would say that they did not conjecture that, from the amount of snow in the air (see Josh. x. 11), the refraction may have been greater than usual, or that there may have been some other cause which we will not now inquire into. . . .

Not only in matters of this kind, but in others more important, the prophets could be, and in fact were, ignorant; for they taught nothing special about the Divine attributes, but held quite ordinary notions about God, and to these notions their revelations were adapted, as I will demonstrate by ample Scriptural testimony; from all which one may easily see that they were praised and commended, not so much for the sublimity and eminence of their intellect as for their piety and faithfulness.

Adam, the first man to whom God was revealed, did not know that He is omnipotent and omniscient; for he hid himself from Him, and attempted to make excuses for his fault before God, as though he had had to do with a man; therefore to him also was God revealed according to his understanding— that is, as being unaware of his situation or his sin; for Adam heard, or seemed to hear, the Lord walking in the garden, calling him and asking him where he was; and then, on seeing his shamefacedness, asking him whether he had eaten of the forbidden fruit. Adam evidently only knew the Deity as the Creator of all things. To Cain also God was revealed, according to his understanding, as ignorant of human affairs, nor was a higher conception of the Diety required for repentance of his sin.

To Laban the Lord revealed Himself as the God of Abraham, because Laban believed that each nation had its own special divinity (see Gen. xxxi. 29). Abraham also knew not that God is omnipresent, and has foreknowledge of all things; for when he heard the sentence against the inhabitants of Sodom, he prayed that the Lord should not execute it till He had ascertained whether they all merited such punishment; for he said (see Gen. xviii. 24), "Peradventure there be fifty righteous within the city," and in accordance with this belief God was revealed to him; as Abraham imagined, He spake thus: "I will go down now, and see whether they have done altogether according to the cry of it which is come unto Me; and, if not, I will know." Further, the Divine testimony concerning Abraham asserts nothing but that he was obedient, and that he "commanded his household after him that they should keep the way of the Lord" (Gen. xviii. 19); it does not state that he held sublime conceptions of the Deity.

Moses, also, was not sufficiently aware that God is omniscient, and directs human actions by His sole decree, for although God Himself says that the Israelites should hearken to Him, Moses still considered the matter doubtful and repeated, "But if they will not believe me, nor hearken unto my voice." To him in like manner God was revealed as taking no part in, and as being ignorant of, future human actions: the Lord gave him two signs and said, "And it shall come to pass that if they will not believe thee, neither hearken to the voice of the first sign, that they will believe the voice of the latter sign; but if not, thou shalt take of the water of the river," etc. Indeed, if any one considers without prejudice the recorded opinions of Moses, he will plainly see that Moses conceived the Deity as a Being Who has always existed, does exist, and always will exist, and for this cause he calls Him by the name Jehovah, which in Hebrew signifies these three phases of existence: as to His nature, Moses only taught that He is merciful, gracious, and exceeding jealous, as appears from many passages in the Pentateuch. Lastly, he believed and taught that this Being was so different from all other beings, that He could not be expressed by the image of any visible thing; also, that He could not be looked upon, and that not so much from inherent impossibility as from human infirmity; further, that by reason of His power He was without equal and unique. . . . Further it is related (Ex. xxxiii. 18) that Moses asked of God that he might behold Him, but as Moses (as we have said) had formed no mental image of God, and God (as I have shown) only revealed Himself to the prophets in accordance with the disposition of their imagination, He did not reveal Himself in any form. This, I repeat, was because the imagination of Moses was unsuitable; for other prophets bear witness that they saw the Lord; for instance, Isaiah, Ezekiel, Daniel, etc. For this reason God answered Moses, "Thou canst not see My face"; and inasmuch as Moses believed that God can be looked upon—that is, that no contradiction of the Divine nature is therein involved (for otherwise he would never have preferred his request)— it is added, "For no one shall look on Me and live," thus giving a reason in accordance with Moses' idea; for it is not stated that a contradiction of the Divine nature would be involved, as was really the case, but that the thing would not come to pass because of human infirmity. . . .

Lastly, as Moses believed that God dwelt in the heavens, God was revealed to him as coming down from heaven on to a mountain, and in order to talk with the Lord Moses went up the mountain, which he certainly need not have done if he could have conceived of God as omnipresent. . . .

We have now more than sufficiently proved our point, that God adapted revelations to the understanding and opinions of the prophets, and that in matters of theory without bearing on charity or morality the prophets could be, and in fact were, ignorant, and held conflicting opinions. It therefore follows that we must by no means go to the prophets for knowledge, either of natural or of spiritual phenomena.

We have determined, then, that we are only bound to believe in the prophetic writings, the object and substance of the revelation; with regard to the details, every one may believe or not, as he likes. . . .

Questions

1. What does Spinoza mean by "prophecy" or "revelation"?
2. How does Spinoza characterize prophets? How does he explain the prophets' differing conceptions of God?
3. What are Spinoza's tests for the certitude of prophecy? How does one determine whether the mind of the prophet was given wholly to what was right and good?
4. In what matters does Spinoza permit reason to criticize prophecy or revelation? In what ways does he resemble (or differ from) Locke here? What matters, if any, does Spinoza allow to be "above reason"? How is he like (or unlike) Locke here? (For Locke's views, see the reading beginning on page 312.)

3

The Ways of Knowing Divine Truths

St. Thomas Aquinas
(1225?-1274)

Thomas Aquinas was a Dominican friar. The Dominican order was founded to preach Christianity throughout the world. The order was confirmed by Pope Honorius III in 1216, and Thomas joined it in 1244, when the order was in its twenty-eighth year. These dates are mentioned to place Aquinas' writings in the context of his order and its missionary purposes. His great works are the *Summa Contra Gentiles,* written during the years 1259 to 1264, and the *Summa Theologica,* begun in 1265 and left unfinished at his death. The "summa" in the titles means "summary" or "compendium." The "gentiles" against whom the first summa is written are those who do not believe in Christianity. Both of the summas are comprehensive surveys of Christian doctrine, but each is written from a different point of view. The *Summa Contra Gentiles* is written to convince non-Christian readers of the truth of Christianity on reasonable grounds. It contains the sort of material which a Christian missionary would find useful in preaching to nonbelievers. The *Summa Theologica* is written for the benefit of those who are already believers. A preacher would find it useful in his task of offering orderly expositions of Christian beliefs to his congregation. In both of the summas, however, Aquinas adheres to his opinion that reason, as well as faith, has a place in religion.

Aquinas is one of the most notable members of a philosophical movement called "Scholasticism," which flourished among the Christian clergy of Western Europe from the ninth through the fourteenth centuries. The Scholastics' program was to use reason to organize, harmonize, and justify Christian doctrines. One of the principal causes of interest in such a program was the clergy's new knowledge of Greek philosophy. Greek philosophy presented an intellectual challenge to Christian belief, which the Scholastics proposed to meet by rationalizing Christianity. Aquinas was particularly interested in this aspect of the Scholastic program, and he endeavored to carry it out in a remarkable way. He adapted the philosophy of the pagan, but supremely reasonable, Aristotle to the support of a Christianity which Aquinas believed was consistent with reason.

In this reading, Aquinas justifies his attempt to write a reasonable exposition of Christianity. Aquinas' case depends on his being able to show that there are two kinds of truths about God (truths which exceed human reason, and truths which can be known by reason), and that these truths are not inconsistent. This selection may also be read as a preface to Aquinas' proofs of God's existence (page 347); for these proofs are one of the fruits of his conviction that reason can confirm religion.

This reading is drawn from the *Summa Contra Gentiles,* Book I, Chapters 3 through 8. The original chapter titles are used as subtitles in this reading. The translation from the Latin is by Professor Anton C. Pegis.

From *On the Truth of the Catholic Faith, Book One: God,* by Saint Thomas Aquinas, translated by Anton C. Pegis. Copyright ©, 1955, by Doubleday & Co., Inc., N. Y. Reprinted by permission of the publishers.

ON THE WAY IN WHICH DIVINE TRUTH IS TO BE MADE KNOWN

The way of making truth known is not always the same, and, as the Philosopher has very well said, "it belongs to an educated man to seek such certitude in each thing as the nature of that thing allows." But, since such is the case, we must first show what way is open to us in order that we may make known the truth which is our object.

There is a twofold mode of truth in what we profess about God. Some truths about God exceed all the ability of the human reason. Such is the truth that God is triune. But there are some truths which the natural reason also is able to reach. Such are that God exists, that He is one, and the like. In fact, such truths about God have been proved demonstratively by the philosophers, guided by the light of the natural reason.[1]

That there are certain truths about God that totally surpass man's ability appears with the greatest evidence. Since, indeed, the principle of all knowledge that the reason perceives about some thing is the understanding of the very substance of that being (for according to Aristotle "what a thing is" is the principle of demonstration), it is necessary that the way in which we understand the substance of a thing determines the way in which we know what belongs to it. Hence, if the human intellect comprehends the substance of some thing, for example, that of a stone or of a triangle, no intelligible characteristic belonging to that thing surpasses the grasp of the human reason. But this does not happen to us in the case of God. For the human intellect is not able to reach a comprehension of the divine substance through its natural power. For, according to its manner of knowing in the present life, the intellect depends on the sense for the origin of knowledge; and so those things that do not fall under the senses cannot be grasped by the human intellect except in so far as the knowledge of them is gathered from sensible things. Now, sensible things cannot lead the human intellect to the point of seeing in them the nature of the divine substance; for sensible things are effects that fall short of the power of their cause. Yet, beginning with sensible things, our intellect is led to the point of knowing about God that He exists, and other such characteristics that must be attributed to the First Principle. There are, consequently, some intelligible truths about God that are open to the human reason; but there are others that absolutely surpass its power.

We may easily see the same point from the gradation of intellects. Consider the case of two persons of whom one has a more penetrating grasp of a thing by his intellect than does the other. He who has the superior intellect understands many things that the other cannot grasp at all. Such is the case with a very simple person who cannot at all grasp the subtle speculations of philosophy. But the intellect of an angel surpasses the human intellect much more than the intellect of the greatest philosopher surpasses the intellect of the most uncultivated simple person; for the distance between the best philosopher and a simple

---

[1] [In the *Summa Contra Gentiles*, Book I, Chapter 2, Aquinas qualifies the use of natural reason in divine matters in the following way:

"To proceed against individual errors is a difficult business, and this for two reasons. In the first place, it is difficult because the sacrilegious remarks of individual men who have erred are not so well known to us so that we may use what they say as the basis of proceeding to a refutation of their errors. This is, indeed, the method that the ancient Doctors of the Church used in the refutation of the errors of the Gentiles. For they could know the positions taken by the Gentiles since they themselves had been Gentiles, or at least had lived among the Gentiles and had been instructed in their teaching. In the second place, it is difficult because some of them, such as the Mohammedans and the pagans, do not agree with us in accepting the authority of any Scripture, by which they may be convinced of their error. Thus, against the Jews we are able to argue by means of the Old Testament, while against heretics we are able to argue by means of the New Testament. But the Mohammedans and the pagans accept neither the one nor the other. We must, therefore, have recourse to the natural reason, to which all men are forced to give their assent. However, it is true, in divine matters the natural reason has its failings."—Eds.]

person is contained within the limits of the human species, which the angelic intellect surpasses. For the angel knows God on the basis of a more noble effect than does man; and this by as much as the substance of an angel, through which the angel in his natural knowledge is led to the knowledge of God, is nobler than sensible things and even than the soul itself, through which the human intellect mounts to the knowledge of God. The divine intellect surpasses the angelic intellect much more than the angelic surpasses the human. For the divine intellect is in its capacity equal to its substance, and therefore it understands fully what it is, including all its intelligible attributes. But by his natural knowledge the angel does not know what God is, since the substance itself of the angel, through which he is led to the knowledge of God, is an effect that is not equal to the power of its cause. Hence, the angel is not able, by means of his natural knowledge, to grasp all the things that God understands in Himself; nor is the human reason sufficient to grasp all the things that the angel understands through his own natural power. Just as, therefore, it would be the height of folly for a simple person to assert that what a philosopher proposes is false on the ground that he himself cannot understand it, so (and even more so) it is the acme of stupidity for a man to suspect as false what is divinely revealed through the ministry of the angels simply because it cannot be investigated by reason.

The same thing, moreover, appears quite clearly from the defect that we experience every day in our knowledge of things. We do not know a great many of the properties of sensible things, and in most cases we are not able to discover fully the natures of those properties that we apprehend by the sense. Much more is it the case, therefore, that the human reason is not equal to the task of investigating all the intelligible characteristics of that most excellent substance.

The remark of Aristotle likewise agrees with this conclusion. He says that "our intellect is related to the prime beings, which are most evident in their nature, as the eye of an owl is related to the sun."

Sacred Scripture also gives testimony to this truth. We read in Job: "Peradventure thou wilt comprehend the steps of God, and wilt find out the Almighty perfectly?" (11:7). And again: "Behold, God is great, exceeding our knowledge" (Job 36:26). And St. Paul: "We know in part" (I Cor. 13:9).

We should not, therefore, immediately reject as false, following the opinion of the Manicheans and many unbelievers, everything that is said about God even though it cannot be investigated by reason.

THAT THE TRUTH ABOUT GOD TO WHICH THE NATURAL REASON REACHES IS FITTINGLY PROPOSED TO MEN FOR BELIEF

Since, therefore, there exists a twofold truth concerning the divine being, one to which the inquiry of the reason can reach, the other which surpasses the whole ability of the human reason, it is fitting that both of these truths be proposed to man divinely for belief. This point must first be shown concerning the truth that is open to the inquiry of the reason; otherwise, it might perhaps seem to someone that, since such a truth can be known by the reason, it was uselessly given to men through a supernatural inspiration as an object of belief.

Yet, if this truth were left solely as a matter of inquiry for the human reason, three awkward consequences would follow.

The first is that few men would possess the knowledge of God. For there are three reasons why most men are cut off from the fruit of diligent inquiry which is the discovery of truth. Some do not have the physical disposition for such work. As a result, there are many who are naturally not fitted to pursue knowledge; and so, however much they tried, they would be unable to reach the highest level of human knowledge which consists in knowing God. Others are cut off from pursuing this truth by the necessities imposed upon them by their daily lives. For some men must devote themselves to taking care of temporal matters. Such men would not be able to give so much time to the leisure of contemplative inquiry as to reach the highest peak at which human investigation can arrive, namely, the knowledge of God. Finally, there are some who are cut off by indolence. In order to know the things that the reason can investigate concerning God, a knowledge of many things must already be possessed. For almost all of philosophy is directed towards the knowledge of God, and that is why metaphysics, which deals with divine things, is the last part of philosophy to be learned. This means that we are able to arrive at the inquiry concerning the aforementioned truth only on the basis of a great deal of labor spent in study. Now, those who wish to undergo such a labor for the mere love of knowledge are few, even though God has inserted into the minds of men a natural appetite for knowledge.

The second awkward effect is that those who would come to discover the abovementioned truth would barely reach it after a great deal of time. The reasons are several. There is the profundity of this truth, which the human intellect is made capable of grasping by natural inquiry only after a long training. Then, there are many things that must be presupposed, as we have said. There is also the fact that, in youth, when the soul is swayed by the various movements of the passions, it is not in a suitable state for the knowledge of such lofty truth. On the contrary, "one becomes wise and knowing in repose," as it is said in the *Physics*.[2] The result is this. If the only way open to us for the knowledge of God were solely that of the reason, the human race would remain in the blackest shadows of ignorance. For then the knowledge of God, which especially renders men perfect and good, would come to be possessed only by a few, and these few would require a great deal of time in order to reach it.

The third awkward effect is this. The investigation of the human reason for the most part has falsity present within it, and this is due partly to the weakness of our intellect in judgment, and partly to the admixture of images.

---

[2] Aristotle, *Physics*, VII, 3 (247b 9).

The result is that many, remaining ignorant of the power of demonstration, would hold in doubt those things that have been most truly demonstrated. This would be particularly the case since they see that, among those who are reputed to be wise men, each one teaches his own brand of doctrine. Furthermore, with the many truths that are demonstrated, there sometimes is mingled something that is false, which is not demonstrated but rather asserted on the basis of some probable or sophistical argument, which yet has the credit of being a demonstration. That is why it was necessary that the unshakeable certitude and pure truth concerning divine things should be presented to men by way of faith.[3]

Beneficially, therefore, did the divine Mercy provide that it should instruct us to hold by faith even those truths that the human reason is able to investigate. In this way, all men would easily be able to have a share in the knowledge of God, and this without uncertainty and error.

Hence it is written: "Henceforward you walk not as also the Gentiles walk in the vanity of their mind, having their understanding darkened" (Eph. 4:17-18). And again: "All thy children shall be taught of the Lord" (Isa. 54:13).

THAT THE TRUTHS THE HUMAN REASON IS NOT ABLE TO INVESTIGATE ARE FITTINGLY PROPOSED TO MEN FOR BELIEF

Now, perhaps some will think that men should not be asked to believe what the reason is not adequate to investigate, since the divine Wisdom provides in the case of each thing according to the mode of its nature. We must therefore prove that it is necessary for man to receive from God as objects of belief even those truths that are above the human reason.

No one tends with desire and zeal towards something that is not already known to him. But men are ordained by the divine Providence towards a higher good than human fragility can experience in the present life. That is why it was necessary for the human mind to be called to something higher than the human reason here and now can reach, so that it would thus learn to desire something and with zeal tend towards something that surpasses the whole state of the present life. This belongs especially to the Christian religion, which in a unique way promises spiritual and eternal goods. And so there are many things proposed to men in it that transcend human sense. The Old Law,

---

[3] [Although St. Thomas does not name Maimonides or his *Guide for the Perplexed* (*Dux neutrorum*), there are evident points of contact between the Catholic and the Jewish theologian. On the reasons for revelation given here, on our knowledge of God, on creation and the eternity of the world, and on Aristotelianism in general, St. Thomas has Maimonides in mind both to agree and to disagree with him. By way of background for *SCG*, I, the reader can usefully consult the references to Maimonides in E. Gilson, *History of Christian Philosophy in the Middle Ages* [Random House], New York, 1955, pp. 649-51.—A. C. Pegis]

on the other hand, whose promises were of a temporal character, contained very few proposals that transcended the inquiry of the human reason. Following this same direction, the philosophers themselves, in order that they might lead men from the pleasure of sensible things to virtue, were concerned to show that there were in existence other goods of a higher nature than these things of sense, and that those who gave themselves to the active or contemplative virtues would find much sweeter enjoyment in the taste of these higher goods.

It is also necessary that such truth be proposed to men for belief so that they may have a truer knowledge of God. For then only do we know God truly when we believe Him to be above everything that it is possible for man to think about Him; for the divine substance surpasses the natural knowledge of which man is capable. Hence, by the fact that some things about God are proposed to man that surpass his reason, there is strengthened in man the view that God is something above what he can think.

Another benefit that comes from the revelation to men of truths that exceed the reason is the curbing of presumption, which is the mother of error. For there are some who have such a presumptuous opinion of their own ability that they deem themselves able to measure the nature of everything; I mean to say that, in their estimation, everything is true that seems to them so, and everything is false that does not. So that the human mind, therefore, might be freed from this presumption and come to a humble inquiry after truth, it was necessary that some things should be proposed to man by God that would completely surpass his intellect.

A still further benefit may also be seen in what Aristotle says in the *Ethics*. There was a certain Simonides who exhorted people to put aside the knowledge of divine things and to apply their talents to human occupations. He said that "he who is a man should know human things, and he who is mortal, things that are mortal." Against Simonides Aristotle says that "man should draw himself towards what is immortal and divine as much as he can." And so he says in the *De animalibus* that, although what we know of the higher substances is very little, yet that little is loved and desired more than all the knowledge that we have about less noble substances. He also says in the *De caelo et mundo* that when questions about the heavenly bodies can be given even a modest and merely plausible solution, he who hears this experiences intense joy. From all these considerations it is clear that even the most imperfect knowledge about the most noble realities brings the greatest perfection to the soul. Therefore, although the human reason cannot grasp fully the truths that are above it, yet, if it somehow holds these truths at least by faith, it acquires great perfection for itself.

Therefore it is written: "For many things are shown to thee above the understanding of men" (Ecclus. 3:25). Again: "So the things that are of God no man knoweth but the Spirit of God. But to us God hath revealed them by His Spirit" (I Cor. 2:11, 10).

THAT TO GIVE ASSENT TO THE TRUTHS OF
FAITH IS NOT FOOLISHNESS EVEN THOUGH
THEY ARE ABOVE REASON

Those who place their faith in this truth, however, "for which the human reason offers no experimental evidence," do not believe foolishly, as though "following artificial fables" (II Peter 1:16). For these "secrets of divine Wisdom" (Job 11:6) the divine Wisdom itself, which knows all things to the full, has deigned to reveal to men. It reveals its own presence, as well as the truth of its teaching and inspiration, by fitting arguments; and in order to confirm those truths that exceed natural knowledge, it gives visible manifestation to works that surpass the ability of all nature. Thus, there are the wonderful cures of illnesses, there is the raising of the dead, and the wonderful immutation in the heavenly bodies; and what is more wonderful, there is the inspiration given to human minds, so that simple and untutored persons, filled with the gift of the Holy Spirit, come to possess instantaneously the highest wisdom and the readiest eloquence. When these arguments were examined, through the efficacy of the abovementioned proof, and not the violent assault of arms or the promise of pleasures, and (what is most wonderful of all) in the midst of the tyranny of the persecutors, an innumerable throng of people, both simple and most learned, flocked to the Christian faith. In this faith there are truths preached that surpass every human intellect; the pleasures of the flesh are curbed; it is taught that the things of the world should be spurned. Now, for the minds of mortal men to assent to these things is the greatest of miracles, just as it is a manifest work of divine inspiration that, spurning visible things, men should seek only what is invisible. Now, that this has happened neither without preparation nor by chance, but as a result of the disposition of God, is clear from the fact that through many pronouncements of the ancient prophets God had foretold that He would do this. The books of these prophets are held in veneration among us Christians, since they give witness to our faith.

The manner of this confirmation is touched on by St. Paul: "Which," that is, human salvation, "having begun to be declared by the Lord, was confirmed unto us by them that hear Him: God also bearing them witness of signs, and wonders, and divers miracles, and distributions of the Holy Ghost" (Heb. 2:3-4).

This wonderful conversion of the world to the Christian faith is the clearest witness of the signs given in the past; so that it is not necessary that they should be further repeated, since they appear most clearly in their effect. For it would be truly more wonderful than all signs if the world had been led by simple and humble men to believe such lofty truths, to accomplish such difficult actions, and to have such high hopes. Yet it is also a fact that, even in our own time, God does not cease to work miracles through His saints for the confirmation of the faith.

On the other hand, those who founded sects committed to erroneous doctrines proceeded in a way that is opposite to this. The point is clear in the case of Mohammed. He seduced the people by promises of carnal pleasure to which the concupiscence of the flesh goads us. His teaching also contained precepts that were in conformity with his promises, and he gave free rein to carnal pleasure. In all this, as is not unexpected, he was obeyed by carnal men. As for proofs of the truth of his doctrine, he brought forward only such as could be grasped by the natural ability of anyone with a very modest wisdom. Indeed, the truths that he taught he mingled with many fables and with doctrines of the greatest falsity. He did not bring forth any signs produced in a supernatural way, which alone fittingly gives witness to divine inspiration; for a visible action that can be only divine reveals an invisibly inspired teacher of truth. On the contrary, Mohammed said that he was sent in the power of his arms—which are signs not lacking even to robbers and tyrants. What is more, no wise men, men trained in things divine and human, believed in him from the beginning. Those who believed in him were brutal men and desert wanderers, utterly ignorant of all divine teaching, through whose numbers Mohammed forced others to become his followers by the violence of his arms. Nor do divine pronouncements on the part of preceding prophets offer him any witness. On the contrary, he perverts almost all the testimonies of the Old and New Testaments by making them into fabrications of his own, as can be seen by anyone who examines his law. It was, therefore, a shrewd decision on his part to forbid his followers to read the Old and New Testaments, lest these books convict him of falsity. It is thus clear that those who place any faith in his words believe foolishly.

THAT THE TRUTH OF REASON IS NOT OPPOSED TO THE TRUTH OF THE CHRISTIAN FAITH

Now, although the truth of the Christian faith which we have discussed surpasses the capacity of the reason, nevertheless that truth that the human reason is naturally endowed to know cannot be opposed to the truth of the Christian faith. For that with which the human reason is naturally endowed is clearly most true; so much so, that it is impossible for us to think of such truths as false. Nor is it permissible to believe as false that which we hold by faith, since this is confirmed in a way that is so clearly divine. Since, therefore, only the false is opposed to the true, as is clearly evident from an examination of their definitions, it is impossible that the truth of faith should be opposed to those principles that the human reason knows naturally.

Furthermore, that which is introduced into the soul of the student by the teacher is contained in the knowledge of the teacher—unless his teaching is fictitious, which it is improper to say of God. Now, the knowledge of the principles that are known to us naturally has been implanted in us by God; for God is the Author of our nature. These principles, therefore, are also contained by the divine Wisdom. Hence, whatever is opposed to them is opposed to the divine Wisdom, and, therefore, cannot come from God. That which we hold by faith as divinely revealed, therefore, cannot be contrary to our natural knowledge.

Again. In the presence of contrary arguments our intellect is chained, so that it cannot proceed to the knowledge of the truth. If, therefore, contrary knowledges were implanted in us by God, our intellect would be hindered from knowing truth by this very fact. Now, such an effect cannot come from God.

And again. What is natural cannot change as long as nature does not. Now, it is impossible that contrary opinions should exist in the same knowing subject at the same time. No opinion or belief, therefore, is implanted in man by God which is contrary to man's natural knowledge.

Therefore, the Apostle says: "The word is nigh thee, even in thy mouth and in thy heart. This is the word of faith, which we preach" (Rom. 10:8). But because it overcomes reason, there are some who think that it is opposed to it: which is impossible.

The authority of St. Augustine also agrees with this. He writes as follows: "That which truth will reveal cannot in any way be opposed to the sacred books of the Old and the New Testament."

From this we evidently gather the following conclusion: whatever arguments are brought forward against the doctrines of faith are conclusions incorrectly derived from the first and self-evident principles imbedded in nature. Such conclusions do not have the force of demonstration; they are arguments that are either probable or sophistical. And so, there exists the possibility to answer them.

HOW THE HUMAN REASON IS RELATED TO THE TRUTH OF FAITH

There is also a further consideration. Sensible things, from which the human reason takes the origin of its knowledge, retain within themselves some sort of trace of a likeness to God. This is so imperfect, however, that it is absolutely inadequate to manifest the substance of God. For effects bear within themselves, in their own way, the likeness of their causes, since an agent produces its like; yet an effect does not always reach to the full likeness of its cause. Now, the human reason is related to the knowledge of the truth of faith (a truth which can be most evident only to those who see the divine substance) in such a way that it can gather certain likenesses of it, which are yet not sufficient so that the truth of faith may be comprehended as being understood demonstratively or through itself. Yet it is useful for the human reason to exercise itself in such arguments, however weak they may be, provided only that there be present no presumption to comprehend or to demonstrate. For to be able to see something of the loftiest realities, however thin and weak the sight may be, is, as our previous remarks indicate, a cause of the greatest joy.

The testimony of Hilary agrees with this. Speaking of this same truth, he writes as follows in his De Trinitate: "Enter these truths by believing, press forward, persevere. And though I may know that you will not arrive at an end, yet I will congratulate you in your progress. For, though he who pursues the infinite with reverence will never finally reach the end, yet he will always progress by pressing onward. But do not intrude yourself into the divine secret, do not, presuming to comprehend the sum total of intelligence, plunge yourself into the mystery of the unending nativity; rather, understand that these things are incomprehensible."

Questions

1. What are the two kinds of truth about God which Aquinas distinguishes? Try to extend his list of examples of these two kinds of truth.

2. What does Aquinas mean by "the natural reason"? Why does he believe that it is possible to know that God exists by the natural reason?

3. What awkward consequences would follow if truths about God knowable by reason could not be "proposed to man divinely for belief"?

4. What does Aquinas mean by a truth about God which exceeds "all the ability of the human reason"?

5. How does Aquinas seek to show that it is not foolish to believe a truth about God which is above human reason? On what grounds can one accept (or reject) his criterion of foolishness?

6. Why does Aquinas believe that what is known about God by reason cannot be opposed by what is accepted on faith? In what respects does his account of the relation between faith and reason resemble (or differ from) the accounts of Locke (page 312) and of Spinoza (page 321)?

7. Consider the following argument:

"If the boundary between what can be known by reason and what must be believed on faith is drawn by reason, then reason is the arbiter of faith. But for the limits of faith to be defined by reason is a contradiction which destroys faith. On the other hand, if the boundary between faith and reason is drawn by faith, then faith is the arbiter of reason. But it is a manifest contradiction for the nonreasonable to define the reasonable. Thus a man can be either reasonable or faithful, but he can never be both."

State your own reasons for accepting, or rejecting, the above argument. How do you think that Locke, or Spinoza, or Aquinas would reply to this argument?

4

Faith Seeking Understanding | St. Anselm (*1033?-1109*)

Anselm was first Prior and then Abbot of the Monastery of Bec, in Normandy, which was in his time the greatest center of learning in all Europe. He spent the last six years of his life as Archbishop of Canterbury in England. We remember him today as a Scholastic theologian. His most famous contribution to religious thought is probably his proof of God's existence based on God's nature (or being), and his statement of this proof is the subject of the reading before us. This proof is commonly called the ontological argument (from "ontology," the science of being) and it owes much to the theology of the early Christian writer, St. Augustine (354-430 A.D.). Augustine's theology in turn owes much to the philosophy of Plato. Anselm is, however, to be credited with making the definitive statement of the ontological argument, and everyone turns to him to read the argument in its original form.

A typical example of a proof of God's existence by arguing from his nature follows. The clue to God's nature is the way we talk about him, and we say that God is a perfect being. Now, it is an imperfection not to exist. But God is perfect; so he has no imperfections. Therefore, since he is perfect, he must exist.

The reader must see that this argument turns on unpacking the word "perfect." It is being used in an equivocal way, that is, with several meanings, one of which is "existent." Thus, when we say that God is perfect, we are also saying that God exists. The critical questions, then, which may be asked about this argument are these: Must we say that "perfect" means "existent"? and, Must we say that God is perfect? As Aquinas points out in his criticism of this kind of argument (in the reading which immediately follows this one; see page 343), we need say neither of these things. So, the appeal of any proof of God's existence by an inference from his nature is strictly limited to those who are willing to talk of God as the argument prescribes. But there is yet a more serious question to be asked about any proof of God's existence drawn from his nature: Isn't it an effort to define God into existence? The fact that we know how to talk about unicorns, and could identify one if we saw it in the garden, does not mean that we should ever expect to see one. As Aquinas remarks, it is one thing to define a word; it is a separate and independent move to claim that what the word can be used to talk about exists. So, we may define "God" as meaning "a perfect being," but it is another thing to claim that God exists. Of course, the theists, who take the proof of God's existence from his nature seriously, point out that God is unique in being the one entity, the inconceivability of whose nonexistence is shown as soon as his nature is properly conceived. But this is a contention whose value we must leave the reader to consider for himself.

This selection is drawn from the *Proslogion* (1077-1078), Preface and Chapters I through IV. The original chapter titles are retained as subtitles in this reading. The translation from the Latin is by Professor Eugene R. Fairweather.

From *A Scholastic Miscellany,* by Eugene R. Fairweather, editor and translator, The Westminster Press, Phila., 1956. Used by permission.

PREFACE

Some time ago, at the urgent request of some of my brethren, I published a brief work,[1] as an example of meditation on the grounds of faith. I wrote it in the role of one who seeks, by silent reasoning with himself, to learn what he does not know. But when I reflected on this little book, and saw that it was put together as a long chain of arguments, I began to ask myself whether *one* argument might possibly be found, resting on no other argument for its proof, but sufficient in itself to prove that God truly exists, and that he is the supreme good, needing nothing outside himself, but needful for the being and well-being of all things. I often turned my earnest attention to this problem, and at times I believed that I could put my finger on what I was looking for, but at other times it completely escaped my mind's eye, until finally, in despair, I decided to give up searching for something that seemed impossible to find. But when I tried to put the whole question out of my mind, so as to avoid crowding out other matters, with which I might make some progress, by this useless preoccupation, then, despite my unwillingness and resistance, it began to force itself on me more persistently than ever. Then, one day, when I was worn out by my vigorous resistance to the obsession, the solution I had ceased to hope for presented itself to me, in the very turmoil of my thoughts, so that I enthusiastically embraced the idea which, in my disquiet, I had spurned.

I thought that the proof I was so glad to find would please some readers if it were written down. Consequently, I have written the little work that follows, dealing with this and one or two other matters, in the role of one who strives to raise his mind to the contemplation of God and seeks to understand what he believes. Neither this essay nor the other one I have already mentioned really seemed to me to deserve to be called a book or to bear an author's name; at the same time, I felt that they could not be published without some title that might encourage anyone into whose hands they fell to read them, and so I gave each of them a title. The first I called *An Example of Meditation on the Grounds of Faith,* and the second *Faith Seeking Understanding.*

But when both of them had been copied under these titles by a number of people, I was urged by many people—and especially by Hugh, the reverend archbishop of Lyons, apostolic legate in Gaul, who ordered this with apostolic authority—to attach my name to them. In order to do this more fittingly, I have named the first *Monologion* (or *Soliloquy*), and the second *Proslogion* (or *Address*).

[1] [The *Monologion,* probably Anselm's first work, was written at Bec in the second half of 1076 (cf. Landgraf, *Einführung,* 53). Text in Schmitt, I, 7-87.—E. R. Fairweather]

THE AWAKENING OF THE MIND TO THE
CONTEMPLATION OF GOD

Now then, little man, for a short while fly from your business; hide your-self for a moment from your turbulent thoughts. Break off now your trouble-some cares, and think less of your laborious occupations. Make a little time for God, and rest for a while in him. Enter into the chamber of your mind, shut out everything but God and whatever helps you to seek him, and, when you have shut the door, seek him. Speak now, O my whole heart, speak now to God: "I seek thy face; thy face, Lord, do I desire." [2]

And do thou, O Lord my God, teach my heart where and how to seek thee, where and how to find thee. Lord, if thou art not here, where shall I seek thee who art absent? But if thou art everywhere, why do I not see thee who art present? . . . Let me receive thy light, even from afar, even from the depths. Teach me to seek thee, and when I seek thee show thyself to me, for I cannot seek thee unless thou teach me, or find thee unless thou show me thy-self. Let me seek thee in my desire, let me desire thee in my seeking. Let me find thee by loving thee, let me love thee when I find thee.

I acknowledge, O Lord, with thanksgiving, that thou hast created this thy image in me, so that, remembering thee, I may think of thee, may love thee. But this image is so effaced and worn away by my faults, it is so obscured by the smoke of my sins, that it cannot do what it was made to do, unless thou renew and reform it. I am not trying, O Lord, to penetrate thy loftiness, for I cannot begin to match my understanding with it, but I desire in some measure to understand thy truth, which my heart believes and loves. For I do not seek to understand in order to believe, but I believe in order to understand. For this too I believe, that "unless I believe, I shall not understand."

GOD TRULY IS

And so, O Lord, since thou givest understanding to faith, give me to understand—as far as thou knowest it to be good for me—that thou dost exist, as we believe, and that thou art what we believe thee to be. Now we believe that thou art a being than which none greater can be thought. Or can it be that there is no such being, since "the fool hath said in his heart, 'There is no God'"? But when this same fool hears what I am saying—"A being than which none greater can be thought"—he understands what he hears, and what he understands is in his understanding, even if he does not understand that it exists. For it is one thing for an object to be in the understanding, and another thing to understand that it exists. When a painter considers beforehand what he is going to paint, he has it in his understanding, but he does not suppose that what he has not yet painted already exists. But when he has painted it,

---

[2] [Ps. 26:8 (P.B.V., 27:9); not an exact quotation.—E. R. Fairweather]

he both has it in his understanding and understands that what he has now produced exists. Even the fool, then, must be convinced that a being than which none greater can be thought exists at least in his understanding, since when he hears this he understands it, and whatever is understood is in the understanding. But clearly that than which a greater cannot be thought cannot exist in the understanding alone. For if it is actually in the understanding alone, it can be thought of as existing also in reality, and this is greater. Therefore, if that than which a greater cannot be thought is in the understanding alone, this same thing than which a greater cannot be thought is that than which a greater can be thought. But obviously this is impossible. Without doubt, therefore, there exists, both in the understanding and in reality, something than which a greater cannot be thought.

GOD CANNOT BE THOUGHT OF AS NONEXISTENT

And certainly it exists so truly that it cannot be thought of as nonexistent. For something can be thought of as existing, which cannot be thought of as not existing, and this is greater than that which *can* be thought of as not existing. Thus, if that than which a greater cannot be thought can be thought of as not existing, this very thing than which a greater cannot be thought is *not* that than which a greater cannot be thought. But this is contradictory. So, then, there truly is a being than which a greater cannot be thought—so truly that it cannot even be thought of as not existing.

And *thou* art this being, O Lord our God. Thou so truly art, then, O Lord my God, that thou canst not even be thought of as not existing. And this is right. For if some mind could think of something better than thou, the creature would rise above the Creator and judge its Creator; but this is altogether absurd. And indeed, whatever is, except thyself alone, can be thought of as not existing. Thou alone, therefore, of all beings, hast being in the truest and highest sense, since no other being so truly exists, and thus every other being has less being. Why, then, has "the fool said in his heart, 'There is no God,'" when it is so obvious to the rational mind that, of all beings, thou dost exist supremely? Why indeed, unless it is that he is a stupid fool?

HOW THE FOOL HAS SAID IN HIS HEART WHAT CANNOT BE THOUGHT

But how did he manage to say in his heart what he could not think? Or how is it that he was unable to think what he said in his heart? After all, to say in one's heart and to think are the same thing. Now if it is true—or, rather, since it is true—that he thought it, because he said it in his heart, but did not say it in his heart, since he could not think it, it is clear that something can be said in one's heart or thought in more than one way. For we think of a thing, in one sense, when we think of the word that signifies it, and in another sense, when we understand the very thing itself. Thus, in the first sense God can be thought of as nonexistent, but in the second sense this is quite impossible. For no one who understands what God is can think that God does not exist, even though he says these words in his heart—perhaps without any meaning, perhaps with some quite extraneous meaning. For God is that than which a greater cannot be thought, and whoever understands this rightly must understand that he exists in such a way that he cannot be nonexistent even in thought. He, therefore, who understands that God thus exists cannot think of him as nonexistent.

Thanks be to thee, good Lord, thanks be to thee, because I now understand by thy light what I formerly believed by thy gift, so that even if I were to refuse to believe in thy existence, I could not fail to understand its truth.

Questions

1. How does Anselm endeavor to prove that God exists? Do the steps in his proof appear to be statements of fact, or definitions, or some third kind of statement? If you accept (or reject) the steps in Anselm's proof, what are your grounds for doing so? (The reader may find it easier to answer these questions if he writes out the steps of the proof in 1, 2, 3 order.)

2. What bearing does Anselm's prefacing his proof of God's existence with a prayer have on its validity?

3. How does Anselm account for a "fool's" trying to reject his argument?

4. How would Anselm reply to a person who said:

"I can think of the most perfect society, a Utopia, but that does not mean that a perfect society exists anywhere in the world; therefore, just because I think of a perfect being, namely, God, that does not mean that God exists."?

(Additional questions on Anselm's proof may be found on page 347, after the selection in which Aquinas criticizes proofs of God's existence that are based on his nature.)

5

On the Opinion That God's Existence Is Self-Evident

St. Thomas Aquinas
(1225?-1274)

[A general introductory note on Aquinas may be found on page 328.]

In this selection Aquinas examines and rejects the arguments of those who claim that God's existence is self-evident, and consequently not subject to proof. Aquinas believes that this view is erroneous and that he must clear it away before he can get on with the task of demonstrating that God exists. Aquinas first reports five arguments which are supposed to show that the statement, "God is," is self-evident. Then he offers his refutation of each of these arguments in turn. The first three arguments which Aquinas lists are proofs of God's existence based on his nature. Thus by reading the refutation of these arguments, the reader will find Aquinas' reply to the onto-logical proof of God's existence originally stated by Anselm in the preceding selection. His most telling point against that proof may be this one: ". . . from the fact that that which is indicated by the name God is conceived by the mind, it does not follow that God exists save only in the intellect." Whether this point refutes the ontological argu-ment, particularly Anselm's version of it, is a question which we leave to the reader's consideration.

This selection is drawn from the *Summa Contra Gentiles,* Book I, Chapters 10 and 11. The original chapter titles are retained as sub-titles in this reading. The translation from the Latin is by Professor Anton C. Pegis.

From *On the Truth of the Catholic Faith, Book One: God,* by Saint Thomas Aquinas, translated by Anton C. Pegis. Copyright ©, 1955, by Doubleday & Co., Inc., N. Y. Reprinted by permission of the publishers.

THE OPINION OF THOSE WHO SAY THAT THE EXISTENCE OF GOD, BEING SELF-EVIDENT, CANNOT BE DEMONSTRATED

There are some persons to whom the inquiry seeking to demonstrate that God exists may perhaps appear superfluous. These are the persons who assert that the existence of God is self-evident, in such wise that its contrary cannot be entertained in the mind. It thus appears that the existence of God cannot be demonstrated, as may be seen from the following arguments.

Those propositions are said to be self-evident that are known immediately upon the knowledge of their terms. Thus, as soon as you know the nature of a *whole* and the nature of a *part,* you know immediately that every whole is greater than its part. The proposition *God exists* is of this sort. For by the name *God* we understand something than which a greater cannot be thought. This notion is formed in the intellect by one who hears and understands the name *God.* As a result, God must exist already at least in the intellect. But He cannot exist solely in the intellect, since that which exists both in the intellect and in reality is greater than that which exists in the intellect alone. Now, as the very definition of the name points out, nothing can be greater than God. Consequently, the proposition that God exists is self-evident, as being evident from the very meaning of the name God.

Again, it is possible to think that something exists whose nonexistence cannot be thought. Clearly, such a being is greater than the being whose non-existence can be thought. Consequently, if God Himself could be thought not to be, then something greater than God could be thought. This, however, is contrary to the definition of the name God. Hence, the proposition that God exists is self-evident.

Furthermore, those propositions ought to be the most evident in which the same thing is predicated of itself, for example, *man is man,* or whose predicates are included in the definition of their subjects, for example, *man is an animal.* Now, in God, it is pre-eminently the case that His being is His essence, so that to the question *what is He?* and to the question *is He?* the answer is one and the same. Thus, in the proposition *God exists,* the predicate is consequently either identical with the subject or at least included in the definition of the subject. Hence, that God exists is self-evident.

What is naturally known is known through itself, for we do not come to such propositions through an effort of inquiry. But the proposition that God exists is naturally known since the desire of man naturally tends towards God as towards the ultimate end. The proposition that God exists is, therefore, self-evident.

There is also the consideration that that through which all the rest are known ought itself to be self-evident. Now, God is of this sort. For just as the light of the sun is the principle of all visible perception, so the divine light is the principle of all intelligible knowledge; since the divine light is that in which intelligible illumination is found first and in its highest degree. That God exists, therefore, must be self-evident.

These, then, and others like them are the arguments by which some think that the proposition *God exists* is so self-evident that its contrary cannot be entertained by the mind.

A REFUTATION OF THE ABOVEMENTIONED
OPINION AND A SOLUTION OF THE ARGUMENTS

In part, the above opinion arises from the custom by which from their earliest days people are brought up to hear and to call upon the name of God. Custom, and especially custom in a child, comes to have the force of nature. As a result, what the mind is steeped in from childhood it clings to very firmly, as something known naturally and self-evidently.

In part, however, the above opinion comes about because of a failure to distinguish between that which is self-evident in an absolute sense and that which is self-evident in relation to us. For assuredly that God exists is, absolutely speaking, self-evident, since what God is is His own being. Yet, because we are not able to conceive in our minds that which God is, that God exists remains unknown in relation to us. So, too, that every whole is greater than its part is, absolutely speaking, self-evident; but it would perforce be unknown to one who could not conceive the nature of a whole. Hence it comes about, as it is said in *Metaphysics II,* that "our intellect is related to the most knowable things in reality as the eye of an owl is related to the sun."

And, contrary to the point made by the *first* argument, it does not follow immediately that, as soon as we know the meaning of the name *God,* the existence of God is known. It does not follow first because it is not known to all, even including those who admit that God exists, that God is that than which a greater cannot be thought. After all, many ancients said that this world itself was God. Furthermore, no such inference can be drawn from the interpretations of the name *God* to be found in Damascene. What is more, granted that everyone should understand by the name *God* something than which a greater cannot be thought, it will still not be necessary that there exist in reality something than which a greater cannot be thought. For a thing and the definition of a name are posited in the same way. Now, from the fact that that which is indicated by the name *God* is conceived by the mind, it does not follow that God exists save only in the intellect. Hence, that than which a greater cannot be thought will likewise not have to exist save only in the intellect. From this it does not follow that there exists in reality something than which a greater cannot be thought. No difficulty, consequently, befalls anyone who posits that God does not exist. For that something greater can be thought than anything given in reality or in the intellect is a difficulty only to him who admits that there is something than which a greater cannot be thought in reality.

Nor, again, is it necessary, as the *second* argument advanced, that something greater than God can be thought if God can be thought not to be. For that He can be thought not to be does not arise either from the imperfection or the uncertainty of His own being, since this is in itself most manifest. It arises, rather, from the weakness of our intellect, which cannot behold God Himself except through His effects and which is thus led to know His existence through reasoning.

This enables us to solve the *third* argument as well. For just as it is evident to us that a whole is greater than a part of itself, so to those seeing the divine essence in itself it is supremely self-evident that God exists because His essence is His being. But, because we are not able to see His essence, we arrive at the knowledge of His being, not through God Himself, but through His effects.

The answer to the *fourth* argument is likewise clear. For man naturally knows God in the same way as he naturally desires God. Now, man naturally desires God in so far as he naturally desires beatitude, which is a certain likeness of the divine goodness. On this basis, it is not necessary that God considered in Himself be naturally known to man, but only a likeness of God. It remains, therefore, that man is to reach the knowledge of God through reasoning by way of the likenesses of God found in His effects.

So, too, with the *fifth* argument, an easy solution is available. For God is indeed that by which all things are known, not in the sense that they are not known unless He is known (as obtains among self-evident principles), but because all our knowledge is caused in us through His influence.

Questions

1. What is meant by saying that a proposition is self-evident? Try to give examples of self-evident propositions. What is meant by saying that the proposition, "God is," is self-evident?

2. In what ways does Aquinas criticize arguments to show that "God is" is self-evident? Can you think of any counter arguments which the authors of these arguments might offer?

3. In what ways do you think that the critical points which Aquinas makes against proofs of God's existence from his nature might tell against Anselm's onto-logical argument (pages 341 ff.)?

4. How might Aquinas use his observation, "A thing and the definition of a name are posited in the same way," in refuting the ontological argument? Does Anselm succeed in withstanding this kind of criticism by his account of the fool's reasoning (pages 342 ff.)? Explain your answer.

5. Descartes version of the ontological argument may be found on pages 60 ff. Is it as good a version as Anselm's? How does it fare against Aquinas' objections?

6

| *The Demonstration of God's Existence* | St. Thomas Aquinas (*1225?-1274*) |

[A general introductory note on Aquinas may be found on page 328.]

This selection contains both Aquinas' defense of the claim that it is possible to demonstrate by reason that God exists, and his state-ment of the five arguments which prove that God exists as given in the *Summa Theologica*. In the *Summa Contra Gentiles,* Aquinas acknowledges his debt to Aristotle for the first four of these arguments, and to both St. John Damascene (d. before 754), a theologian of the Greek Church, and Averroës (1126-1198), an Arab philosopher, for the fifth. What is more all of the arguments owe much to Aristotle's doctrine of the four kinds of causes. Thus, to aid the reader, we have appended to this selection a short statement of Aristotle's doctrine of causes taken from his *Metaphysics.*

To appreciate proofs of God's existence from the nature of the world, of which Aquinas' five are the most notable examples, the reader ought to like detective stories, for these proofs are essays in detection. As a reminder of the hazards of detective investigations, it will be helpful to examine the kind of reasoning which occurs in the following situation. When a firm's office manager arrived at his office one morning, he discovered that the door of the office safe had been blown from its hinges, and the safe had been emptied of its contents. Believing that only robbers blow open safes, he immediately telephoned his employer to report the robbery. The employer, however, greeted the manager's news with laughter. For, wanting to get into the safe the previous night and not being able to wait for the time lock to operate, the employer himself had blown open the safe. Disappointed at the evaporation of the robber, the manager reviewed his reasoning to discover his mistake. The exploded safe door undeniably exists, and he was surely right in believing that safes do not blow themselves open. But, the manager noticed, the exploded safe implies the existence of a robber only if one looks at it with robbers in mind, that is, only if one employs the rule of reasoning: "Only robbers blow open safes." Mindful of his new rule, "Employers can blow open safes too," the manager resolved to be more careful in the future about reasoning from what exists to what might exist.

Now theists who try to prove God's existence from the nature of the world argue very much like our manager who argued from the exploded safe door to robbers. The theist who argues from the nature of the world to God's existence points out that the world possesses some characteristic which it could not have given itself. But since the world has the characteristic, it must have been given it by some entity which does have it. Therefore this entity, which the theist calls God, must exist. We may illustrate the strength and weakness of this kind of proof by an argument from what the theist regards as the most basic of the world's characteristics: its existence. Consider the fact that the world exists, a fact which we all accept as indubitably true. The world, however, could not have brought itself into existence. Therefore there must be some source of the existence of the world which is beyond or outside the world. This source of existence we call God.

The reader should notice that for someone to accept this argument he must agree to make two assumptions, without which the conclusion cannot be guaranteed. These assumptions are that the world could not bring itself into existence, and that there is a source of existence which is outside the world and always in existence itself, and which could bring the world into existence. These assumptions work to prove God's existence in the same way that the manager's rules, "Safes do not explode themselves," and "Only robbers blow open safes," worked to prove the existence of a robber. There are, however, certain difficulties in the theist's assumptions. The chief difficulty is that if the success of this argument turns on these assumptions, why must we accept them? For instance, why should we accept the assumption, "The world could not bring itself into existence," rather than the assumption, which is in effect the contradictory of the theist's assumption, "The world has always existed"? To make this last assumption is, of course, to deny that there is any problem about explaining the world's existence, which requires a transcendent God for its answer. Or, consider the difficulties inherent in the theist's second assumption, "There is a source of existence which is outside the world and always in existence, and which could bring the world into existence." First, notice that in the light of the theist's postulating an ultimate source of existence, his opponent's postulating that the world has always existed may not seem too radical a move. Second, when the theist postulates an ultimate source of existence as part of his argument, he seems to assume what he intends to prove, namely, that God exists.

Whether the difficulties listed above render proving God's existence from the nature of the world a hopeless enterprise is a question which we leave to the reader's consideration. David Hume thought that difficulties like these do irreparable damage to theistic proofs from the nature of the world. Indeed he called such proofs "a priori," meaning to point out that their conclusion is assumed in the very statement of the argument. Aquinas, however, regarded the theistic proofs from the nature of the world as a posteriori, that is, as genuine inferences from experience. If they are genuine inferences from experience, then the reader should, of course, be able to conceive the kind of experience that would falsify them. We must add that Aquinas counted the proof of God's existence from his nature as a priori. The reader would do well to scrutinize Aquinas' own arguments for the existence of God based on the nature of the world, to see whether he commits any of the errors in reasoning which he discovers in proofs based on the nature of God.

This selection is the Second and Third Articles of Question II in the First Part of the *Summa Theologica*. The translation from the Latin is by the English Dominican Fathers. The title of each article is a question. In each article Aquinas first reports as objections the answers given to the title question by those authorities with whom he differs. Then he states his own answer to the question and finishes the article by offering his refutations of the objections.

Quoted from the *Summa Theologica,* translation published and copyrighted by Benziger Brothers, Inc., N. Y.

WHETHER IT CAN BE DEMONSTRATED THAT GOD EXISTS?

We proceed thus:

Objection 1.   It seems that the existence of God cannot be demonstrated. For it is an article of faith that God exists. But what is of faith cannot be demonstrated, because a demonstration produces scientific knowledge;

whereas faith is of the unseen (Heb. xi. 1). Therefore it cannot be demonstrated that God exists.

Obj. 2. Further, the essence is the middle term of demonstration. But we cannot know in what God's essence consists, but solely in what it does not consist; as Damascene says (De Fid. Orth. i. 4). Therefore we cannot demonstrate that God exists.

Obj. 3. Further, if the existence of God were demonstrated, this could only be from His effects. But His effects are not proportionate to Him, since He is infinite and His effects are finite; and between the finite and infinite there is no proportion. Therefore, since a cause cannot be demonstrated by an effect not proportionate to it, it seems that the existence of God cannot be demonstrated.

On the contrary, The Apostle says: The invisible things of Him are clearly seen, being understood by the things that are made (Rom. i. 20). But this would not be unless the existence of God could be demonstrated through the things that are made; for the first thing we must know of anything is, whether it exists.

I answer that demonstration can be made in two ways: One is through the cause, and is called a priori, and this is to argue from what is prior absolutely. The other is through the effect, and is called a demonstration a posteriori; this is to argue from what is prior relatively only to us. When an effect is better known to us than its cause, from the effect we proceed to the knowledge of the cause. And from every effect the existence of its proper cause can be demonstrated, so long as its effects are better known to us; because since every effect depends upon its cause, if the effect exists, the cause must pre-exist. Hence the existence of God, in so far as it is not self-evident to us, can be demonstrated from those of His effects which are known to us.

Reply Obj. 1. The existence of God and other like truths about God, which can be known by natural reason, are not articles of faith, but are preambles to the articles; for faith presupposes natural knowledge, even as grace presupposes nature, and perfection supposes something that can be perfected. Nevertheless, there is nothing to prevent a man, who cannot grasp a proof, accepting, as a matter of faith, something which in itself is capable of being scientifically known and demonstrated.

Reply Obj. 2. When the existence of a cause is demonstrated from an effect, this effect takes the place of the definition of the cause in proof of the cause's existence. This is especially the case in regard to God, because, in order to prove the existence of anything, it is necessary to accept as a middle term the meaning of the word, and not its essence, for the question of its essence follows on the question of its existence. Now the names given to God are derived from His effects; consequently, in demonstrating the existence of God from His effects, we may take for the middle term the meaning of the word "God."

Reply Obj. 3. From effects not proportionate to the cause no perfect knowledge of that cause can be obtained. Yet from every effect the existence of the cause can be clearly demonstrated, and so we can demonstrate the existence of God from His effects; though from them we cannot perfectly know God as He is in His essence.

WHETHER GOD EXISTS?

We proceed thus:

Objection 1.   It seems that God does not exist; because if one of two contraries be infinite, the other would be altogether destroyed. But the word "God" means that He is infinite goodness. If, therefore, God existed, there would be no evil discoverable; but there is evil in the world. Therefore God does not exist.

Obj. 2.   Further, it is superfluous to suppose that what can be accounted for by a few principles has been produced by many. But it seems that everything we see in the world can be accounted for by other principles, supposing God did not exist. For all natural things can be reduced to one principle, which is nature; and all voluntary things can be reduced to one principle, which is human reason, or will. Therefore there is no need to suppose God's existence.

On the contrary, it is said in the person of God: I am Who am (Exod. iii. 14).

I answer that the existence of God can be proved in five ways.

The first and more manifest way is the argument from motion. It is certain, and evident to our senses, that in the world some things are in motion. Now whatever is in motion is put in motion by another, for nothing can be in motion except it is in potentiality to that towards which it is in motion; whereas a thing moves inasmuch as it is in act. For motion is nothing else than the reduction of something from potentiality to actuality, except by something in a state of actuality. Thus that which is actually hot, as fire, makes wood, which is potentially hot, to be actually hot, and thereby moves and changes it. Now it is not possible that the same thing should be at once in actuality and potentiality in the same respect, but only in different respects. For what is actually hot cannot simultaneously be potentially hot; but it is simultaneously potentially cold. It is therefore impossible that in the same respect and in the same way a thing should be both mover and moved, i.e., that it should move itself. Therefore, whatever is in motion must be put in motion by another. If that by which it is put in motion be itself put in motion, then this also must needs be put in motion by another, and that by another again. But this cannot go on to infinity, because then there would be no first mover, and, consequently, no other mover; seeing that subsequent movers move only inasmuch as they are put in motion by the first mover; as the staff moves only because it is put in motion by the hand. Therefore it is necessary to arrive at a first mover, put in motion by no other; and this everyone understands to be God.[1]

[1] [In the *Summa Contra Gentiles,* Aquinas states the argument from motion in this way:

"Everything that is moved is moved by another. That some things are in motion— for example, the sun—is evident from sense. Therefore, it is moved by something else that

2.   The second way is from the nature of the efficient cause. In the world of sense we find there is an order of efficient causes. There is no case known (neither is it, indeed, possible) in which a thing is found to be the efficient cause of itself; for so it would be prior to itself, which is impossible. Now in efficient causes it is not possible to go on to infinity, because in all efficient causes following in order, the first is the cause of the intermediate cause, and the intermediate is the cause of the ultimate cause, whether the intermediate cause be several, or one only. Now to take away the cause is to take away the effect. Therefore, if there be no first cause among efficient causes, there will be no ultimate, nor any intermediate cause. But if in efficient causes it is possible to go on to infinity, there will be no first efficient cause, neither will there be an ultimate effect, nor any intermediate efficient causes; all of which is plainly false. Therefore it is necessary to admit a first efficient cause, to which everyone gives the name of God.

3.   The third way is taken from possibility and necessity, and runs thus. We find in nature things that are possible to be and not to be, since they are found to be generated, and to corrupt, and consequently, they are possible to be and not to be. But it is impossible for these always to exist, for that which is possible not to be at some time is not. Therefore, if everything is possible not to be, then at one time there could have been nothing in existence. Now if this were true, even now there would be nothing in existence, because that which does not exist only begins to exist by something already existing. Therefore, if at one time nothing was in existence, it would have been impossible for anything to have begun to exist; and thus even now nothing would be in existence—which is absurd. Therefore, not all beings are merely possible, but there must exist something the existence of which is necessary. But every necessary thing either has its necessity caused by another, as has been already proved in regard to efficient causes. Therefore we cannot but postulate the existence of some being having of itself its own necessity, and not receiving it from another, but rather causing in others their necessity. This all men speak of as God.

4.   The fourth way is taken from the gradation to be found in things. Among beings there are some more and some less good, true, noble, and the like. But "more" and "less" are predicated of different things, according as they resemble in their different ways something which is the maximum, as a thing is said to be hotter according as it more nearly resembles that which is hottest; so that there is something which is truest, something best, something noblest, and, consequently, something which is uttermost being; for those things that are greatest in truth are greatest in being, as it is written in Metaph. ii. Now the maximum in any genus is the cause of all in that genus; as fire, which is the maximum of heat, is the cause of all hot things. Therefore there must

moves it. This mover is itself either moved or not moved. If it is not, we have reached our conclusion—namely, that we must posit some unmoved mover. This we call God. If it is moved, it is moved by another mover. We must, consequently, either proceed to infinity, or we must arrive at some unmoved mover. Now, it is not possible to proceed to infinity. Hence, we must posit some prime unmoved mover."—Eds.]

also be something which is to all beings the cause of their being, goodness, and every other perfection; and this we call God.

The fifth way is taken from the governance of the world. We see that ꜱ things which lack intelligence, such as natural bodies, act for an end, and this is evident from their acting always, or nearly always, in the same way, so as to obtain the best result. Hence it is plain that not fortuitously, but designedly, do they achieve their end. Now whatever lacks intelligence cannot move towards an end, unless it be directed by some being endowed with knowledge and intelligence; as the arrow is shot to its mark by the archer. Therefore some intelligent being exists by whom all natural things are directed to their end; and this being we call God.

Reply Obj. 1.   As Augustine says (Enchir. xi.): Since God is the highest good, He would not allow any evil to exist in His works, unless His omnipotence and goodness were such as to bring good even out of evil. This is part of the infinite goodness of God, that He should allow evil to exist, and out of it produce good.

Reply Obj. 2.   Since nature works for a determinate end under the direction of a higher agent, whatever is done by nature must needs be traced back to God, as to its first cause. So also whatever is done voluntarily must also be traced back to some higher cause other than human reason or will, since these can change and fail; for all things that are changeable and capable of defect must be traced back to an immovable and self-necessary first principle, as was shown in the body of the Article.

APPENDIX TO AQUINAS: The
Demonstration of God's Existence

Aristotle: *Cause*

[A general introductory note on Aristotle may be found on page 491.]
     Aristotle recognizes four types of determining factors or causes. In the *Metaphysics* his account of the four kinds of causes is stated as a four-part definition of the word "cause." The four kinds of causes are usually called by philosophers "the material cause," "the formal cause," "the efficient cause," and "the final cause." These four names correspond to the four denotations of the word "cause" below. The translation from the Greek is by John Warrington.

From Aristotle's *Metaphysics,* edited and translated by John Warrington, Everyman's Library edition published by E. P. Dutton & Co., Inc., N. Y.

CAUSE

"Cause" denotes:

1. That from which (as immanent material) a thing comes into being; e.g. the bronze of a statue, the silver of a drinking-bowl, and the classes [1] to which bronze and silver belong.

2. The form or pattern of a thing (i.e. the formula of its essence), the classes to which it belongs,[2] and its own parts.

3. The starting-point of change or rest. Thus an adviser is the cause of an action, and a father of his child. In general, the maker is the cause of the thing made, and that which changes of that which suffers change.

4. The end, i.e. that for the sake of which a thing is. For example, health is the cause of walking: in answer to the question, Why does one walk? we reply "In order to be healthy"; and in saying so we believe we have assigned the cause. The same is true of all the means which lead from an independent source of motion to its end. Thus, slimming, purging, medicines, surgical appliances, all lead to health; all of them exist for the sake of the end, though they differ one from another in that some of them are instruments and others acts.

There you have practically all the meanings of "cause"; and because the word has a variety of meanings, it follows that a single thing has several causes, and in no accidental sense. Sculptor and bronze are both causes of a statue considered not under two different aspects, but *qua* statue. The two, however, are not causes *in the same way*: bronze is the material, sculptor the efficient cause.

What *causes* a thing in one sense may be its *effect* in another. Thus exercise is the cause of physical fitness, and the latter again of exercise; but *not in the same way,* for in the first case the cause is efficient and in the second final.

Again, a single cause may have opposite effects. That which when present causes one thing is sometimes, when absent, denounced as the cause of the opposite. For instance, we assign the pilot's absence as the cause of a shipwreck, whereas his presence is admitted as the cause of the vessel's safety; so that in either case, whether present or absent, he is the (efficient) cause.

Questions

1. State as carefully as you can the steps in Aquinas' first argument to prove God's existence. Then, state as carefully as you can the assumptions or presuppositions on which the first argument depends. Refer to Aristotle on Cause (page 353)

---

[1] Metal, mineral, etc.

[2] Thus the ratio 2:1 and number in general is the cause of the octave.

where he may be helpful. All arguments depend on assumptions, so it is no criticism of Aquinas to point out that his do too. The proper question then is this: Is there any way in which one of Aquinas' assumptions invalidates his argument by assuming what is to be proved? For instance, when Aquinas follows Aristotle and supposes that one may ask of anything including the world, "What is its efficient cause?", is this a way of assuming God's existence in the premises of his argument? (The reader may examine Aquinas' other arguments in the way outlined above.)

2. When Aquinas promises that "the existence of God . . . can be demonstrated from those of His effects which are known to us" (page 350), what assumption lies behind the phrase "His effects"? How could Aquinas answer the judgment that such an assumption is unwarranted?

3. When Aquinas says that God's existence can be demonstrated, what does he mean by "demonstration"? (Hint: He does not mean by "demonstration" what the vacuum cleaner salesman means when he asks permission to demonstrate his machine.)

4. In what respects do Aquinas' first three arguments follow the same pattern? Can you show that this pattern is also discoverable in the last two arguments?

5. What other characteristics of the world can you think of which might be used as the basis for arguments similar to Aquinas' to prove that God exists? For example, beauty and the moral consciousness of man are two additional characteristics of the world on which arguments to prove God's existence have been based. What are the criteria for choosing a characteristic of the world as a basis for a proof of God's existence? If there are any characteristics which cannot be used in such a proof, what are they, and why can they not be used?

(Additional questions about Aquinas' arguments to prove God's existence may be found on page 359, after the selection in which David Hume criticizes theistic proofs from the nature of the world.)

7

God's Existence Cannot Be Demonstrated | David Hume (1711-1776)

[A general introductory note on Hume may be found on page 98.]

In this reading Hume attacks efforts like those of Aquinas in the preceding selection to demonstrate that God exists. Hume means by the term "demonstration" an argument whose conclusion cannot be doubted. A typical example of a demonstration would be the proof of a theorem in Euclidean geometry. In such a proof one is shown that one must accept the theorem because it follows from the definitions, axioms, postulates, and preceding theorems which one has already accepted. To deny the theorem which follows from all that has gone before would land one in a self-contradiction. But Hume's claim about demonstrative arguments is that a demonstration can never be used to prove existence. For when the conclusion of an argument is "God exists," Hume claims that there is no self-contradiction in someone's saying "God does not exist." Hence, the argument cannot be a demonstration, and its conclusion, "God exists," can never be regarded as proved beyond doubt.

To make Hume's meaning perfectly clear we should add that when he says that demonstrative arguments are a priori, he means that the indubitability of their conclusions derives from the assumptions which one makes prior to framing the argument. Thus, any proof in Euclidean geometry is a priori because the proof of a theorem turns on the definitions, axioms, postulates, and sometimes the previous theorems which are accepted prior to framing the proof in question.

In determining whether Hume's criticism makes arguments like Aquinas' untenable, the reader must decide whether Hume's rule, "Whatever we conceive as existent, we can also conceive as non-existent," applies to a subject like God. What prospect is there for a theist's exempting God from the rule? And what would be the consequences for the status of God, if he did?

This selection is drawn from Part IX of the *Dialogues Concerning Natural Religion* (1779). The speakers in the dialogues are Cleanthes, a theist who believes that God's existence can be proved by an appeal to experience, Demea, a theist who believes God's existence can be proved only by a priori reasoning, and Philo, who is a skeptic.

From *Dialogues Concerning Natural Religion,* by David Hume, edited with introduction by Henry D. Aiken, Hafner Library of Classics, Hafner Publishing Co., Inc., N. Y., 1957.

The argument, [said] Demea, which I would insist on is the common one. Whatever exists must have a cause or reason of its existence, it being absolutely impossible for anything to produce itself or be the cause of its own existence. In mounting up, therefore, from effects to causes, we must either go on in tracing an infinite succession, without any ultimate cause at all, or must at last have recourse to some ultimate cause that is *necessarily* existent. Now that the first supposition is absurd may be thus proved. In the infinite chain or succession of causes and effects, each single effect is determined to exist by the power and efficacy of that cause which immediately preceded; but the whole eternal chain or succession, taken together, is not determined or caused by anything, and yet it is evident that it requires a cause or reason, as much as any particular object which begins to exist in time. The question is still reasonable why this particular succession of causes existed from eternity, and not any other succession or no succession at all. If there be no necessarily existent being, any supposition which can be formed is equally possible; nor is there any more absurdity in *nothing's* having existed from eternity than there is in that succession of causes which constitutes the universe. What was it, then, which determined *something* to exist rather than *nothing,* and bestowed being on a particular possibility, exclusive of the rest? *External causes,* there are supposed to be none. *Chance* is a word without a meaning. Was it *nothing?* But that can never produce anything. We must, therefore, have recourse to a necessarily existent Being who carries the *reason* of his existence in himself, and who cannot be supposed not to exist, without an express contradiction. There is, consequently, such a Being—that is, there is a Deity.

I shall not leave it to Philo, said Cleanthes, though I know that the starting objections is his chief delight, to point out the weakness of this metaphysical reasoning. It seems to me so obviously ill-grounded, and at the same time of so little consequence to the cause of true piety and religion, that I shall myself venture to show the fallacy of it.

I shall begin with observing that there is an evident absurdity in pretending to demonstrate a matter of fact, or to prove it by any arguments *a priori.* Nothing is demonstrable unless the contrary implies a contradiction. Nothing that is distinctly conceivable implies a contradiction. Whatever we conceive as existent, we can also conceive as nonexistent. There is no being, therefore, whose nonexistence implies a contradiction. Consequently there is no being whose existence is demonstrable. I propose this argument as entirely decisive, and am willing to rest the whole controversy upon it.

It is pretended that the Deity is a necessarily existent being; and this necessity of his existence is attempted to be explained by asserting that, if we knew his whole essence or nature, we should perceive it to be as impossible for him not to exist, as for twice two not to be four. But it is evident that this can never happen, while our faculties remain the same as at present. It will still be possible for us, at any time, to conceive the nonexistence of what we formerly conceived to exist; nor can the mind ever lie under a necessity of supposing any object to remain always in being; in the same manner as we lie under a necessity of always conceiving twice two to be four. The words, therefore, *necessary existence* have no meaning or, which is the same thing, none that is consistent.

But further, why may not the material universe be the necessarily existent Being, according to this pretended explication of necessity? We dare not affirm that we know all the qualities of matter; and, for aught we can determine, it may contain some qualities which, were they known, would make its nonexistence appear as great a contradiction as that twice two is five. I find only one argument employed to prove that the material world is not the necessarily existent Being; and this argument is derived from the contingency both of the matter and the form of the world. "Any particle of matter," it is said, "may be *conceived* to be annihilated, and any form may be *conceived* to be altered. Such an annihilation or alteration, therefore, is not impossible." But it seems a great partiality not to perceive that the same argument extends equally to the Deity, so far as we have any conception of him, and that the mind can at least imagine him to be nonexistent or his attributes to be altered. It must be some unknown, inconceivable qualities which can make his nonexistence appear impossible or his attributes unalterable; and no reason can be assigned why these qualities may not belong to matter. As they are altogether unknown and inconceivable, they can never be proved incompatible with it.

Add to this that in tracing an eternal succession of objects it seems absurd to inquire for a general cause or first author. How can anything that exists from eternity have a cause, since that relation implies a priority in time and a beginning of existence?

In such a chain, too, or succession of objects, each part is caused by that which preceded it, and causes that which succeeds it. Where then is the difficulty? But the *whole,* you say, wants a cause. I answer that the uniting of these parts into a whole, like the uniting of several distinct countries into one kingdom, or several distinct members into one body, is performed merely by an arbitrary act of the mind, and has no influence on the nature of things. Did I show you the particular causes of each individual in a collection of twenty particles of matter, I should think it very unreasonable should you afterwards ask me what was the cause of the whole twenty. This is sufficiently explained in explaining the cause of the parts.

3. Though the reasonings which you have urged, Cleanthes, may well excuse me, said Philo, from starting any further difficulties, yet I cannot forbear insisting still upon another topic. It is observed by arithmeticians that the products of 9 compose always either 9 or some lesser product of 9 if you add together all the characters of which any of the former products is composed. Thus, of 18, 27, 36, which are products of 9, you make 9 by adding 1 to 8, 2 to 7, 3 to 6. Thus 369 is a product also of 9; and if you add 3, 6, and 9, you make 18, a lesser product of 9. To a superficial observer so wonderful a regularity may be admired as the effect either of chance or design; but a skilful algebraist immediately concludes it to be the work of necessity, and demonstrates that it must for ever result from the nature of these numbers. Is it not probable, I ask, that the whole economy of the universe is conducted by a like necessity, though no human algebra can furnish a key which solves the difficulty? And instead of admiring the order of natural beings, may it not happen that, could we penetrate into the intimate nature of bodies, we should clearly see why it was absolutely impossible they could ever admit of any other disposition? So dangerous is it to introduce this idea of necessity into the present question! and so naturally does it afford an inference directly opposite to the religious hypothesis!

But dropping all these abstractions, continued Philo, and confining ourselves to more familiar topics, I shall venture to add an observation that the argument *a priori* has seldom been found very convincing, except to people of a metaphysical head who have accustomed themselves to abstract reasoning, and who, finding from mathematics that the understanding frequently leads to truth through obscurity, and contrary to first appearances, have transferred the same habit of thinking to subjects where it ought not to have place. Other people, even of good sense and the best inclined to religion, feel always some deficiency in such arguments, though they are not perhaps able to explain distinctly where it lies—a certain proof that men ever did and ever will derive their religion from other sources than from this species of reasoning.

Questions

1. Why does Hume believe that a matter of fact, such as that God exists, cannot be demonstrated? What are the consequences of regarding (and not regarding) God's existence as a matter of fact? (If the reader is not already acquainted with Hume's account of our knowledge of matters of fact, he may wish to consult pages 105 ff.)

2. In what way does the acceptance of Hume's rule, "Whatever we conceive as existent, we can also conceive as nonexistent," make Aquinas' arguments to prove God's existence untenable? Is there any way in which a theist might exempt the concept of God from Hume's rule? Could the theist escape the charge of making an a priori assumption if he did exempt the concept of God from Hume's rule? Can Hume's rule be objected to on the grounds that it is a priori?

3. What is Hume's argument that the material universe may be necessarily existent? What does this argument show about the character of arguments that God must necessarily exist?

4. What are the consequences for religion of Hume's criticism of arguments like Aquinas' to prove that God exists? If Hume succeeds in showing that religion cannot be founded on reasonable grounds, as Aquinas supposed, what has religion gained (or lost)?

8

An Analysis of the	David Hume
Argument from Design	*(1711-1776)*

[A general introductory note on Hume may be found on page 98.]

In this reading Hume both states, and offers his refutation of, the argument from design. This argument depends on our regarding the universe as a great machine. The possibility of regarding the universe in this way is an outgrowth of the scientific interest in giving mechanistic accounts of physical phenomena, as, for example, Newton's mechanistic account of planetary motion. When the parts of the universe are thought of as machine-like, and all the parts are thought of as fitting together in one vast machine, an interesting analogy follows. If the universe is like a machine, then it must have a characteristic which all machines possess. It must have been made. So, just as a watch implies the existence of a watchmaker, the existence of a universe-machine implies the existence of a universe-machine maker.

Against this argument Hume raises two points which we must leave to the reader's consideration. His first point is that if there is no analogy there is no argument, and Hume finds the resemblance between the universe and a machine too weak to guarantee that God exists. So the first question for the reader is this: Does the universe resemble a machine? Hume's second point is that even if the argument from design rested on a good analogy, the consequent supposition of a resemblance between human machine-makers and God would make our conception of God too absurd to be entertained by any religious person. So the second question for the reader is this: Are the ridiculous consequences which Hume draws from the theistic proof by analogy so devastating that nothing can be salvaged? The reader should notice that Hume's attack on that proof calls into question the very possibility of our having any conception of God at all.

This selection is taken from the *Dialogues Concerning Natural Religion* (1779). Part I of this selection is drawn from Part II of the original *Dialogues;* and Part II of this selection is drawn from Part V of the original. The speakers in the dialogues are Cleanthes, a theist who believes that God's existence can be proved by an appeal to experience, Demea, a theist who believes God's existence can be proved only by a priori reasoning, and Philo, who is a skeptic.

From *Dialogues Concerning Natural Religion,* by David Hume, edited with introduction by Henry D. Aiken, Hafner Library of Classics, Hafner Publishing Co., Inc., N. Y., 1957.

PART I

Not to lose any time in circumlocutions, said Cleanthes, addressing himself to Demea, much less in replying to the pious declamations of Philo, I shall briefly explain how I conceive this matter. Look round the world, contemplate the whole and every part of it: you will find it to be nothing but one great machine, subdivided into an infinite number of lesser machines, which again admit of subdivisions to a degree beyond what human senses and faculties can trace and explain. All these various machines, and even their most minute parts, are adjusted to each other with an accuracy which ravishes into admiration all men who have ever contemplated them. The curious adapting of means to ends, throughout all nature, resembles exactly, though it much exceeds, the productions of human contrivance—of human design, thought, wisdom, and intelligence. Since therefore the effects resemble each other, we are led to infer, by all the rules of analogy, that the causes also resemble, and that the Author of nature is somewhat similar to the mind of man, though possessed of much larger faculties, proportioned to the grandeur of the work which he has executed. By this argument *a posteriori,* and by this argument alone, do we prove at once the existence of a Deity and his similarity to human mind and intelligence.

I shall be so free, Cleanthes, said Demea, as to tell you that from the beginning I could not approve of your conclusion concerning the similarity of the Deity to men; still less can I approve of the mediums by which you endeavour to establish it. What! No demonstration of the Being of God! No abstract arguments! No proofs *a priori!* Are these which have hitherto been so much insisted on by philosophers all fallacy, all sophism? Can we reach no farther in this subject than experience and probability? I will not say that this is betraying the cause of a Deity; but surely, by this affected candour, you give advantages to atheists which they never could obtain by the mere dint of argument and reasoning.

What I chiefly scruple in this subject, said Philo, is not so much that all religious arguments are by Cleanthes reduced to experience, as that they appear not to be even the most certain and irrefragable of that inferior kind. That a stone will fall, that fire will burn, that the earth has solidity, we have observed a thousand and a thousand times; and when any new instance of this nature is presented, we draw without hesitation the accustomed inference. The exact similarity of the cases gives us a perfect assurance of a similar event, and a stronger evidence is never desired nor sought after. But wherever you depart, in the least, from the similarity of the cases, you diminish proportionably the evidence, and may at last bring it to a very weak *analogy,* which is confessedly liable to error and uncertainty. After having experienced the circulation of the blood in human creatures, we make no doubt that it takes place in Titius and Maevius; but from its circulation in frogs and fishes it is only a presumption, though a strong one, from analogy that it takes place in men and other animals. The analogical reasoning is much weaker when we infer the circulation of the sap in vegetables from our experience that the blood circulates in animals; and those who hastily followed that imperfect analogy are found, by more accurate experiments, to have been mistaken.

If we see a house, Cleanthes, we conclude, with the greatest certainty, that it had an architect or builder because this is precisely that species of effect which we have experienced to proceed from that species of cause. But surely you will not affirm that the universe bears such a resemblance to a house that we can with the same certainty infer a similar cause, or that the analogy is here entire and perfect. The dissimilitude is so striking that the utmost you can here pretend to is a guess, a conjecture, a presumption concerning a similar cause; and how that pretension will be received in the world, I leave you to consider.

It would surely be very ill received, replied Cleanthes; and I should be deservedly blamed and detested did I allow that the proofs of a Deity amounted to no more than a guess or conjecture. But is the whole adjustment of means to ends in a house and in the universe so slight a resemblance? the economy of final causes? the order, proportion, and arrangement of every part? Steps of a stair are plainly contrived that human legs may use them in mounting;

and this inference is certain and infallible. Human legs are also contrived for walking and mounting; and this inference, I allow, is not altogether so certain because of the dissimilarity which you remark; but does it, therefore, deserve the name only of presumption or conjecture?

Good God! cried Demea, interrupting him, where are we? Zealous defenders of religion allow that the proofs of a Deity fall short of perfect evidence! And you, Philo, on whose assistance I depended in proving the adorable mysteriousness of the Divine Nature, do you assent to all these extravagant opinions of Cleanthes? For what other name can I give them?

You seem not to apprehend, replied Philo, that I argue with Cleanthes in his own way, and, by showing him the dangerous consequences of his tenets, hope at last to reduce him to our opinion. But what sticks most with you, I observe, is the representation which Cleanthes has made of the argument *a posteriori;* and, finding that that argument is likely to escape your hold and vanish into air, you think it so disguised that you can scarcely believe it to be set in its true light. Now, however much I may dissent, in other respects, from the dangerous principle of Cleanthes, I must allow that he has fairly represented that argument, and I shall endeavour so to state the matter to you that you will entertain no further scruples with regard to it.

Were a man to abstract from everything which he knows or has seen, he would be altogether incapable, merely from his own ideas, to determine what kind of scene the universe must be, or to give the preference to one state or situation of things above another. For as nothing which he clearly conceives could be esteemed impossible or implying a contradiction, every chimera of his fancy would be upon an equal footing; nor could he assign any just reason why he adheres to one idea or system, and rejects the others which are equally possible.

Again, after he opens his eyes and contemplates the world as it really is, it would be impossible for him at first to assign the cause of any one event, much less of the whole of things, or of the universe. He might set his fancy a rambling, and she might bring him in an infinite variety of reports and representations. These would all be possible, but, being all equally possible, he would never of himself give a satisfactory account for his preferring one of them to the rest. Experience alone can point out to him the true cause of any phenomenon.

Now, according to this method of reasoning, Demea, it follows (and is, indeed, tacitly allowed by Cleanthes himself) that order, arrangement, or the adjustment of final causes, is not of itself any proof of design, but only so far as it has been experienced to proceed from that principle. For aught we can know *a priori,* matter may contain the source or spring of order originally within itself, as well as mind does; and there is no more difficulty in conceiving that the several elements, from an internal unknown cause, may fall into the most exquisite arrangement, than to conceive that their ideas, in the great universal mind, from a like internal unknown cause, fall into that arrangement. The equal possibility of both these suppositions is allowed. But, by experience, we find (according to Cleanthes) that there is a difference between them. Throw several pieces of steel together, without shape or form, they will never arrange themselves so as to compose a watch. Stone and mortar and wood, without an architect, never erect a house. But the ideas in a human mind, we see, by an unknown, inexplicable economy, arrange themselves so as to form the plan of a watch or house. Experience, therefore, proves that there is an original principle of order in mind, not in matter. From similar effects we infer similar causes. The adjustment of means to ends is alike in the universe, as in a machine of human contrivance. The causes, therefore, must be resembling.

I was from the beginning scandalized, I must own, with this resemblance which is asserted between the Deity and human creatures, and must conceive it to imply such a degradation of the Supreme Being as no sound theist could endure. With your assistance, therefore, Demea, I shall endeavour to defend what you justly call the adorable mysteriousness of the Divine Nature, and shall refute this reasoning of Cleanthes, provided he allows that I have made a fair representation of it.

When Cleanthes had assented, Philo, after a short pause, proceeded in the following manner.

That all inferences, Cleanthes, concerning fact are founded on experience, and that all experimental reasonings are founded on the supposition that similar causes prove similar effects, and similar effects similar causes, I shall not at present much dispute with you. But observe, I entreat you, with what extreme caution all just reasoners proceed in the transferring of experiments to similar cases. Unless the cases be exactly similar, they repose no perfect confidence in applying their past observation to any particular phenomenon. Every alteration of circumstances occasions a doubt concerning the event; and it requires new experiments to prove certainly that the new circumstances are of no moment or importance. A change in bulk, situation, arrangement, age, disposition of the air, or surrounding bodies—any of these particulars may be attended with the most unexpected consequences. And unless the objects be quite familiar to us, it is the highest temerity to expect with assurance, after any of these changes, an event similar to that which before fell under our observation. The slow and deliberate steps of philosophers here, if anywhere, are distinguished from the precipitate march of the vulgar, who, hurried on by the smallest similitude, are incapable of all discernment or consideration.

But can you think, Cleanthes, that your usual phlegm and philosophy have been preserved in so wide a step as you have taken when you compared to the universe houses, ships, furniture, machines, and, from their similarity in some circumstances, inferred a similarity in their causes? Thought, design, intelligence, such as we discover in men and other animals, is no more than one of the springs and principles of the universe, as well as heat or cold, attraction or repulsion, and a hundred others which fall under daily observation. It is an active cause by which some particular parts of nature, we find, produce alterations on other parts. But can a conclusion, with any propriety, be transferred from parts to the whole? Does not the great disproportion bar all comparison and inference? From observing the growth of a hair, can we learn anything concerning the generation of a man? Would the manner of a leaf's blowing, even though perfectly known, afford us any instruction concerning the vegetation of a tree?

But allowing that we were to take the *operations* of one part of nature upon another for the foundation of our judgment concerning the *origin* of the whole (which never can be admitted), yet why select so minute, so weak, so bounded a principle as the reason and design of animals is found to be upon this planet? What peculiar privilege has this little agitation of the brain which we call *thought,* that we must thus make it the model of the whole universe? Our partiality in our own favour does indeed present it on all occasions, but sound philosophy ought carefully to guard against so natural an illusion.

So far from admitting, continued Philo, that the operations of a part can afford us any just conclusion concerning the origin of the whole, I will not allow any one part to form a rule for another part if the latter be very remote from the former. Is there any reasonable ground to conclude that the inhabitants of other planets possess thought, intelligence, reason, or anything similar to these faculties in men? When nature has so extremely diversified her manner of operation in this small globe, can we imagine that she incessantly copies herself throughout so immense a universe? And if thought, as we may well suppose, be confined merely to this narrow corner and has even there so limited a sphere of action, with what propriety can we assign it for the original cause of all things? The narrow views of a peasant who makes his domestic economy the rule for the government of kingdoms is in comparison a pardonable sophism.

But were we ever so much assured that a thought and reason resembling the human were to be found throughout the whole universe, and were its activity elsewhere vastly greater and more commanding than it appears in this globe, yet I cannot see why the operations of a world constituted, arranged, adjusted, can with any propriety be extended to a world which is in its embryo state, and is advancing towards that constitution and arrangement. By observation we know somewhat of the economy, action, and nourishment of a finished animal, but we must transfer with great caution that observation to the growth of a foetus in the womb, and still more to the formation of an animalcule in the loins of its male parent. Nature, we find, even from our limited experience, possesses an infinite number of springs and principles which incessantly discover themselves on every change of her position and situation. And what new and unknown principles would actuate her in so new and unknown a situation as that of the formation of a universe, we cannot, without the utmost temerity, pretend to determine.

Conclusion →

A very small part of this great system, during a very short time, is very imperfectly discovered to us; and do we thence pronounce decisively concerning the origin of the whole?

Admirable conclusion! Stone, wood, brick, iron, brass, have not, at this time, in this minute globe of earth, an order or arrangement without human art and contrivance; therefore, the universe could not originally attain its order and arrangement without something similar to human art. But is a part of nature a rule for another part very wide of the former? Is it a rule for the whole? Is a very small part a rule for the universe? Is nature in one situation a certain rule for nature in another situation vastly different from the former?

And can you blame me, Cleanthes, if I here imitate the prudent reserve of Simonides, who, according to the noted story, being asked by Hiero, *What God was?* desired a day to think of it, and then two days more; and after that manner continually prolonged the term, without ever bringing in his definition or description? Could you even blame me if I had answered, at first, *that I did not know,* and was sensible that this subject lay vastly beyond the reach of my faculties? You might cry out sceptic and rallier, as much as you pleased; but, having found in so many other subjects much more familiar the imperfections and even contradictions of human reason, I never should expect any success from its feeble conjectures in a subject so sublime and so remote from the sphere of our observation. When two *species* of objects have always been observed to be conjoined together, I can *infer,* by custom, the existence of one wherever I *see* the existence of the other; and this I call an argument from experience. But how this argument can have place where the objects, as in the present case, are single, individual, without parallel or specific resemblance, may be difficult to explain. And will any man tell me with a serious countenance that an orderly universe must arise from some thought and art like the human because we have experience of it? To ascertain this reasoning it were requisite that we had experience of the origin of worlds; and it is not sufficient, surely, that we have seen ships and cities arise from human art and contrivance.

Philo was proceeding in this vehement manner, somewhat between jest and earnest, when he observed some signs of impatience in Cleanthes, and then immediately stopped short. What I had to suggest, said Cleanthes, is only that you would not abuse terms, or make use of popular expressions to subvert philosophical reasonings. You know that the vulgar often distinguish reason from experience, even where the question relates only to matter of fact and existence, though it is found, where that *reason* is properly analyzed, that it is nothing but a species of experience. To prove by experience the origin of the universe from mind is not more contrary to common speech than to prove the motion of the earth from the same principle. And a caviller might raise all the same objections to the Copernican system which you have urged against my reasonings. Have you other earths, might he say, which you have seen to move? Have . . .

Yes! cried Philo, interrupting him, we have other earths. Is not the moon another earth, which we see to turn round its centre? Is not Venus another earth, where we observe the same phenomenon? Are not the revolutions of the sun also a confirmation, from analogy, of the same theory? All the planets, are they not earths which revolve about the sun? Are not the satellites moons which move round Jupiter and Saturn, and along with these primary planets round the sun? These analogies and resemblances, with others which I have not mentioned, are the sole proofs of the Copernican system; and to you it belongs to consider whether you have any analogies of the same kind to support your theory.

In reality, Cleanthes, continued he, the modern system of astronomy is now so much received by all inquirers, and has become so essential a part even of our earliest education, that we are not commonly very scrupulous in examining the reasons upon which it is founded. It is now become a matter of mere curiosity to study the first writers on that subject who had the full force of prejudice to encounter, and were obliged to turn their arguments on every side in order to render them popular and convincing. But if we peruse Galileo's famous *Dialogues*[1] concerning the system of the world, we shall find that that great genius, one of the sublimest that ever existed, first bent all his endeavours to prove that there was no foundation for the distinction commonly made between elementary and celestial substances. The schools, proceeding from the illusions of sense, had carried this distinction very far; and had established the latter substances to be ingenerable, incorruptible, unalterable, impassible; and had assigned all the opposite qualities to the former. But Galileo, beginning with the moon, proved its similarity in every particular to the earth: its convex figure, its natural darkness when not illuminated, its density, its distinction into solid and liquid, the variations of its phases, the mutual illuminations of the earth and moon, their mutual eclipses, the inequalities of the lunar surface, etc. After many instances of this kind, with regard to all the planets, men plainly saw that these bodies became proper objects of experience, and that the similarity of their nature enabled us to extend the same arguments and phenomena from one to the other.

In this cautious proceeding of the astronomers you may read your own condemnation, Cleanthes, or rather may see that the subject in which you are engaged exceeds all human reason and inquiry. Can you pretend to show any such similarity between the fabric of a house and the generation of a universe? Have you ever seen nature in any such situation as resembles the first arrangement of the elements? Have worlds ever been formed under your eye, and have you had leisure to observe the whole progress of the phenomenon, from the first appearance of order to its final consummation? If you have, then cite your experience and deliver your theory.

PART II

But to show you still more inconveniences, continued Philo, in your anthropomorphism, please to take a new survey of your principles. *Like effects prove like causes.* This is the experimental argument; and this, you say too, is the sole theological argument. Now it is certain that the liker the effects are which are seen and the liker the causes which are inferred, the stronger is the

---

[1] [*Dialogo dei due Massimi Sistemi del Mondo* (1632)—H. D. Aiken]

argument. Every departure on either side diminishes the probability and renders the experiment less conclusive. You cannot doubt of the principle; neither ought you to reject its consequences.

All the new discoveries in astronomy which prove the immense grandeur and magnificence of the works of nature are so many additional arguments for a Deity, according to the true system of theism; but, according to your hypothesis of experimental theism, they become so many objections, by removing the effect still farther from all resemblance to the effects of human art and contrivance. . . .

The discoveries by microscopes, as they open a new universe in miniature, are still objections, according to you, arguments, according to me. The further we push our researches of this kind, we are still led to infer the universal cause of all to be vastly different from mankind, or from any object of human experience and observation.

And what say you to the discoveries in anatomy, chemistry, botany? . . . These surely are no objections, replied Cleanthes; they only discover new instances of art and contrivance. It is still the image of mind reflected on us from innumerable objects. Add a mind *like the human,* said Philo. I know of no other, replied Cleanthes. And the liker, the better, insisted Philo. To be sure, said Cleanthes.

Now, Cleanthes, said Philo, with an air of alacrity and triumph, mark the consequences. *First,* by this method of reasoning you renounce all claim to infinity in any of the attributes of the Deity. For, as the cause ought only to be proportioned to the effect, and the effect, so far as it falls under our cognizance, is not infinite, what pretensions have we, upon your suppositions, to ascribe that attribute to the Divine Being? You will still insist that, by removing him so much from all similarity to human creatures, we give in to the most arbitrary hypothesis, and at the same time weaken all proofs of his existence.

Secondly, you have no reason, on your theory, for ascribing perfection to the Deity, even in his finite capacity, or for supposing him free from every error, mistake, or incoherence, in his undertakings. There are many inexplicable difficulties in the works of nature which, if we allow a perfect author to be proved *a priori,* are easily solved, and become only seeming difficulties from the narrow capacity of man, who cannot trace infinite relations. But according to your method of reasoning, these difficulties become all real, and, perhaps, will be insisted on as new instances of likeness to human art and contrivance. At least, you must acknowledge that it is impossible for us to tell, from our limited views, whether this system contains any great faults or deserves any considerable praise if compared to other possible and even real systems. Could a peasant, if the *Aeneid* were read to him, pronounce that poem to be absolutely faultless, or even assign to it its proper rank among the productions of human wit, he who had never seen any other production?

But were this world ever so perfect a production, it must still remain uncertain whether all the excellences of the work can justly be ascribed to the workman. If we survey a ship, what an exalted idea must we form of the ingenuity of the carpenter who framed so complicated, useful, and beautiful a machine? And what surprise must we feel when we find him a stupid mechanic who imitated others, and copied an art which, through a long succession of ages, after multiplied trials, mistakes, corrections, deliberations, and controversies, had been gradually improving? Many worlds might have been botched and bungled, throughout an eternity, ere this system was struck out; much labour lost, many fruitless trials made, and a slow but continued improvement carried on during infinite ages in the art of world-making. In such subjects, who can determine where the truth, nay, who can conjecture where the probability lies, amidst a great number of hypotheses which may be proposed, and a still greater which may be imagined?

And what shadow of an argument, continued Philo, can you produce from your hypothesis to prove the unity of the Deity? A great number of men join in building a house or ship, in rearing a city, in framing a commonwealth; why may not several deities combine in contriving and framing a world? This is only so much greater similarity to human affairs. By sharing the work among several, we may so much further limit the attributes of each, and get rid of that extensive power and knowledge which must be supposed in one deity, and which, according to you, can only serve to weaken the proof of his existence. And if such foolish, such vicious creatures as man can yet often unite in framing and executing one plan, how much more those deities or demons, whom we may suppose several degrees more perfect!

To multiply causes without necessity is indeed contrary to true philosophy, but this principle applies not to the present case. Were one deity antecedently proved by your theory who were possessed of every attribute requisite to the production of the universe, it would be needless, I own (though not absurd), to suppose any other deity existent. But while it is still a question whether all these attributes are united in one subject or dispersed among several independent beings, by what phenomena in nature can we pretend to decide the controversy? Where we see a body raised in a scale, we are sure that there is in the opposite scale, however concealed from sight, some counterpoising weight equal to it; but it is still allowed to doubt whether that weight be an aggregate of several distinct bodies or one uniform united mass. And if the weight requisite very much exceeds anything which we have ever seen conjoined in any single body, the former supposition becomes still more probable and natural. An intelligent being of such vast power and capacity as is necessary to produce the universe, or, to speak in the language of ancient philosophy, so prodigious an animal exceeds all analogy and even comprehension.

But further, Cleanthes: Men are mortal, and renew their species by generation; and this is common to all living creatures. The two great sexes of male and female, says Milton, animate the world. Why must this circumstance, so universal, so essential, be excluded from those numerous and limited deities? Behold, then, the theogeny of ancient times brought back upon us.

And why not become a perfect anthropomorphite? Why not assert the deity or deities to be corporeal, and to have eyes, a nose, mouth, ears, etc.? Epicurus maintained that no man had ever seen reason but in a human figure; therefore, the gods must have a human figure. And this argument, which is deservedly so much ridiculed by Cicero, becomes, according to you, solid and philosophical.

In a word, Cleanthes, a man who follows your hypothesis is able, perhaps, to assert or conjecture that the universe sometime arose from something like design; but beyond that position he cannot ascertain one single circumstance, and is left afterwards to fix every point of his theology by the utmost license of fancy and hypothesis. This world, for aught he knows, is very faulty and imperfect, compared to a superior standard, and was only the first rude essay of some infant deity who afterwards abandoned it, ashamed of his lame performance; it is the work only of some dependent, inferior deity, and is the object of derision to his superiors; it is the production of old age and dotage in some superannuated deity, and ever since his death has run on at adventures, from the first impulse and active force which it received from him. You justly give signs of horror, Demea, at these strange suppositions; but these, and a thousand more of the same kind, are Cleanthes' suppositions, not mine. From the moment the attributes of the Deity are supposed finite, all these have place. And I cannot, for my part, think that so wild and unsettled a system of theology is, in any respect, preferable to none at all.

These suppositions I absolutely disown, cried Cleanthes: they strike me, however, with no horror, especially when proposed in that rambling way in which they drop from you. On the contrary, they give me pleasure when I see that, by the utmost indulgence of your imagination, you never get rid of the hypothesis of design in the universe, but are obliged at every turn to have recourse to it. To this concession I adhere steadily; and this I regard as a sufficient foundation for religion.

Questions

1. What is the argument from design for God's existence? What part does analogy play in this argument? How does one measure the strength of an analogical argument?

2. What specific weaknesses does Hume (Philo) find in the analogy on which the argument from design is based? Do you think these are real weaknesses which undercut the whole argument, or do you think the analogy is still strong enough to give some plausibility to the argument? Defend your answer.

3. Suppose the world *was* very similar to a machine, so that there would be none of the weaknesses in the analogy which Hume (Philo) points out. On what additional grounds would he still challenge the argument from design as a legitimate proof of God's existence?

4. How can Hume (Philo) defend arguments by analogy as a way of learning about the nature of the world, but not about God?

5. Is Cleanthes right when he implies that Hume (Philo) can "never get rid of the hypothesis of design in the universe"? Is this hypothesis indispensable?

9

Can Miracles Be Known to Happen? | David Hume *(1711-1776)*

[A general introductory note on Hume may be found on page 98.]

Hume believed that our knowledge of the world is founded on experience. Thus, if we are to have any knowledge of miracles, it must be by experience. But, Hume asks, can we ever expect to experience a miracle? A miracle is defined as a violation of the laws of nature. Our knowledge of the laws of nature, however, is derived from experience. So to ask us to believe in a miracle is to ask us to believe in something that contradicts our experience. Whether Hume is correct in these statements and whether his argument is sufficient to disprove the possibility of a miracle are questions we leave to the reader's consideration. In addition, we must remind the reader of the much more difficult question which underlies this selection: Is there any other theory of knowledge which both makes knowledge of the world possible and allows for the possibility of miracles?

This reading is drawn from Hume's *Enquiry Concerning Human Understanding* (1748), Section X.

The quotation is from pages 117 through 141 of Hume: *An Inquiry Concerning Human Understanding* (The Library of Liberal Arts No. 49, N. Y., 1955). Reprinted by permission of the publishers, The Liberal Arts Press, Inc.

. . . I flatter myself that I have discovered an argument which, if just, will, with the wise and learned, be an everlasting check to all kinds of superstitious delusion, and consequently will be useful as long as the world endures; for so long, I presume, will the accounts of miracles and prodigies be found in all history, sacred and profane.

Though experience be our only guide in reasoning concerning matters of fact, it must be acknowledged that this guide is not altogether infallible, but in some cases is apt to lead us into errors. One who in our climate should expect better weather in any week of June than in one of December would reason justly and conformably to experience, but it is certain that he may happen, in the event, to find himself mistaken. However, we may observe that in such a case he would have no cause to complain of experience, because it commonly informs us beforehand of the uncertainty by that contrariety of events which we may learn from a diligent observation. All effects follow not with like certainty from their supposed causes. Some events are found, in all countries and all ages, to have been constantly conjoined together; others are found to have been more variable, and sometimes to disappoint our expectations, so that in our reasonings concerning matter of fact there are all imaginable degrees of assurance, from the highest certainty to the lowest species of moral evidence.

A wise man, therefore, proportions his belief to the evidence. In such conclusions as are founded on an infallible experience, he expects the event with the last degree of assurance and regards his past experience as a full *proof* of the future existence of that event. In other cases he proceeds with more caution: he weighs the opposite experiments; he considers which side is supported by the greater number of experiments—to that side he inclines with doubt and hesitation; and when at last he fixes his judgment, the evidence exceeds not what we properly call "probability." All probability, then, supposes an opposition of experiments and observations where the one side is found to overbalance the other and to produce a degree of evidence proportioned to the superiority. A hundred instances or experiments on one side, and fifty on another, afford a doubtful expectation of any event, though a hundred uniform experiments, with only one that is contradictory, reasonably beget a pretty strong degree of assurance. In all cases we must balance the opposite experiments where they are opposite, and deduct the smaller number from the greater in order to know the exact force of the superior evidence.

To apply these principles to a particular instance, we may observe that there is no species of reasoning more common, more useful, and even necessary to human life than that which is derived from the testimony of men and the reports of eyewitnesses and spectators. This species of reasoning, perhaps, one may deny to be founded on the relation of cause and effect. I shall not dispute about a word. It will be sufficient to observe that our assurance in any argument of this kind is derived from no other principle than our observation of the veracity of human testimony and of the usual conformity of facts to the report of witnesses. It being a general maxim that no objects have any discoverable connection together, and that all the inferences which we can draw from one to another are founded merely on our experience of their constant and regular conjunction, it is evident that we ought not to make an exception to this maxim in favor of human testimony whose connection with any event seems in itself as little necessary as any other. Were not the memory tenacious to a certain degree, had not men commonly an inclination to truth and a principle of probity, were they not sensible to shame when detected in a falsehood—were not these, I say, discovered by *experience* to be qualities inherent in human nature, we should never repose the least confidence in human testimony. A man delirious or noted for falsehood and villainy has no manner of authority with us.

And as the evidence derived from witnesses and human testimony is founded on past experience, so it varies with the experience and is regarded either as a *proof* or a *probability,* according as the conjunction between any particular kind of report and any kind of object has been found to be constant or variable. There are a number of circumstances to be taken into consideration in all judgments of this kind; and the ultimate standard by which we determine all disputes that may arise concerning them is always derived from experience and observation. Where this experience is not entirely uniform on any side, it is attended with an unavoidable contrariety in our judgments and with the same opposition and mutual destruction of argument as in every other kind of evidence. We frequently hesitate concerning the reports of others. We balance the opposite circumstances which cause any doubt or uncertainty; and when we discover a superiority on any side, we incline to it, but still with a diminution of assurance, in proportion to the force of its antagonist.

This contrariety of evidence, in the present case, may be derived from several different causes: from the opposition of contrary testimony, from the character or number of the witnesses, from the manner of their delivering their testimony, or from the union of all these circumstances. We entertain a suspicion concerning any matter of fact when the witnesses contradict each other, when they are but few or of a doubtful character, when they have an interest in what they affirm, when they deliver their testimony with hesitation or, on the contrary, with too violent asseverations. There are many other particulars of the same kind which may diminish or destroy the force of any argument derived from human testimony.

Suppose, for instance, that the fact which the testimony endeavors to establish partakes of the extraordinary and the marvelous—in that case the evidence resulting from the testimony admits of a diminution, greater or less in proportion as the fact is more or less unusual. The reason why we place any credit in witnesses and historians is not derived from any *connection* which we perceive *a priori* between testimony and reality, but because we are accustomed to find a conformity between them. But when the fact attested is such a one as has seldom fallen under our observation, here is a contest of two opposite experiences, of which the one destroys the other as far as its force goes, and the superior can only operate on the mind by the force which remains. The very same principle of experience which gives us a certain degree of assurance in the testimony of witnesses gives us also, in this case, another degree of assurance against the fact which they endeavor to establish; from which contradiction there necessarily arises a counterpoise and mutual destruction of belief and authority.

"I should not believe such a story were it told me by Cato" was a proverbial saying in Rome, even during the lifetime of that philosophical patriot. The incredibility of a fact, it was allowed, might invalidate so great an authority.

The Indian prince who refused to believe the first relations concerning the effects of frost reasoned justly, and it naturally required very strong testimony to engage his assent to facts that arose from a state of nature with which he was unacquainted, and which bore so little analogy to those events of which he had had constant and uniform experience. Though they were not contrary to his experience, they were not conformable to it.

But in order to increase the probability against the testimony of witnesses, let us suppose that the fact which they affirm, instead of being only marvelous, is really miraculous; and suppose also that the testimony, considered apart and in itself, amounts to an entire proof—in that case there is proof against proof, of which the strongest must prevail, but still with a diminution of its force, in proportion to that of its antagonist.

A miracle is a violation of the laws of nature; and as a firm and unalterable experience has established these laws, the proof against a miracle, from the very nature of the fact, is as entire as any argument from experience can possibly be imagined. Why is it more than probable that all men must die, that lead cannot of itself remain suspended in the air, that fire consumes wood and is extinguished by water, unless it be that these events are found agreeable to the laws of nature, and there is required a violation of these laws, or, in other words, a miracle to prevent them? Nothing is esteemed a miracle if it ever happens in the common course of nature. It is no miracle that a man, seemingly in good health, should die on a sudden, because such a kind of death, though more unusual than any other, has yet been frequently observed to happen. But it is a miracle that a dead man should come to life, because that has never been observed in any age or country. There must, therefore, be a uniform experience against every miraculous event, otherwise the event would not merit that appellation. And as a uniform experience amounts to a proof, there is here a direct and full *proof,* from the nature of the fact, against the existence of any miracle, nor can such a proof be destroyed or the miracle rendered credible but by an opposite proof which is superior.

The plain consequence is (and it is a general maxim worthy of our attention) that no testimony is sufficient to establish a miracle unless the testimony be of such a kind that its falsehood would be more miraculous than the fact which it endeavors to establish. And even in that case there is a mutual destruction of arguments, and the superior only gives us an assurance suitable to that degree of force which remains after deducting the inferior. When anyone tells me that he saw a dead man restored to life, I immediately consider with myself whether it be more probable that this person should either deceive or be deceived, or that the fact which he relates should really have happened. I weigh the one miracle against the other, and according to the superiority which I discover I pronounce my decision, and always reject the greater miracle. If the falsehood of his testimony would be more miraculous than the event which he relates, then, and not till then, can he pretend to command my belief or opinion.

In the foregoing reasoning we have supposed that the testimony upon which a miracle is founded may possibly amount to entire proof, and that the falsehood of that testimony would be a real prodigy. But it is easy to show that we have been a great deal too liberal in our concession, and that there never was a miraculous event established on so full an evidence.

For, *first*, there is not to be found, in all history, any miracle attested by a sufficient number of men of such unquestioned good sense, education, and learning as to secure us against all delusion in themselves; of such undoubted integrity as to place them beyond all suspicion of any design to deceive others; of such credit and reputation in the eyes of mankind as to have a great deal to lose in case of their being detected in any falsehood, and at the same time attesting facts performed in such a public manner and in so celebrated a part of the world as to render the detection unavoidable—all which circumstances are requisite to give us a full assurance in the testimony of men.

Secondly, we may observe in human nature a principle which, if strictly examined, will be found to diminish extremely the assurance which we might, from human testimony, have in any kind of prodigy. The maxim by which we commonly conduct ourselves in our reasonings is that the objects of which we have no experience resemble those of which we have; that what we have found to be most usual is always most probable; and that where there is an opposition of arguments, we ought to give the preference to such as are founded on the greatest number of past observations. But though, in proceeding by this rule, we readily reject any fact which is unusual and incredible in an ordinary degree, yet in advancing further, the mind observes not always the same rule; but when anything is affirmed utterly absurd and miraculous, it rather the more readily admits of such a fact upon account of that very circumstance which ought to destroy all its authority. The passion of *surprise* and *wonder,* arising from miracles, being an agreeable emotion, gives a sensible tendency toward the belief of those events from which it is derived. And this goes so far that even those who cannot enjoy this pleasure immediately, nor can believe those miraculous events of which they are informed, yet love to partake the satisfaction at second hand, or by rebound, and place a pride and delight in exciting the admiration of others. . . .

Thirdly, it forms a strong presumption against all supernatural and miraculous relations that they are observed chiefly to abound among ignorant and barbarous nations; or if a civilized people has ever given admission to any of them, that people will be found to have received them from ignorant and barbarous ancestors, who transmitted them with that inviolable sanction and authority which always attend received opinions. . . .

I may add, as a *fourth* reason which diminishes the authority of prodigies, that there is no testimony for any, even those which have not been expressly detected, that is not opposed by an infinite number of witnesses, so that not only the miracle destroys the credit of testimony, but the testimony destroys itself. To make this the better understood, let us consider that in matters of religion whatever is different is contrary, and that it is impossible the religions of ancient Rome, of Turkey, of Siam, and of China should all of them be established on any solid foundation. Every miracle, therefore, pretended to have been wrought in any of these religions (and all of them abound in miracles), as its direct scope is to establish the particular system to which it is attributed, so has it the same force, though more indirectly, to overthrow every other system. In destroying a rival system, it likewise destroys the credit of those miracles on which that system was established, so that all the prodigies of different religions are to be regarded as contrary facts, and the evidences of these prodigies, whether weak or strong, as opposite to each other. According to this method of reasoning, when we believe any miracle of Mahomet or his successors, we have for our warrant the testimony of a few barbarous Arabians. And, on the other hand, we are to regard the authority of Titus Livius, Plutarch, Tacitus, and, in short, of all the authors and witnesses, Grecian, Chinese, and Roman Catholic, who have related any miracle in their particular religion—I say we are to regard their testimony in the same light as if they had mentioned the Mahometan miracle and had in express terms contradicted it with the same certainty as they have for the miracle they relate. This argument may appear oversubtile and refined, but is not in reality different from the reasoning of a judge who supposes that the credit of two witnesses maintaining a crime against anyone is destroyed by the testimony of two others who affirm him to have been two hundred leagues distant at the same instant when the crime is said to have been committed. . . .

Upon the whole, then, it appears that no testimony for any kind of miracle has ever amounted to a probability, much less to a proof; and that, even supposing it amounted to a proof, it would be opposed by another proof derived from the very nature of the fact which it would endeavor to establish. It is experience only which gives authority to human testimony, and it is the same experience which assures us of the laws of nature. When, therefore, these two kinds of experience are contrary, we have nothing to do but to subtract the one from the other and embrace an opinion either on one side or the other with that assurance which arises from the remainder. But according to the principle here explained, this subtraction with regard to all popular religions amounts to an entire annihilation; and therefore we may establish it as a maxim that no human testimony can have such force as to prove a miracle and make it a just foundation for any such system of religion.

I beg the limitations here made may be remarked, when I say that a miracle can never be proved so as to be the foundation of a system of religion. For I own that otherwise there may possibly be miracles or violations of the usual course of nature, of such a kind as to admit of proof from human testimony, though perhaps it will be impossible to find any such in all the records of history. Thus suppose all authors, in all languages, agree that from the first of January, 1600, there was a total darkness over the whole earth for eight days; suppose that the tradition of this extraordinary event is still strong and lively among the people; that all travelers who return from foreign countries bring us accounts of the same tradition without the least variation or contradiction—it is evident that our present philosophers, instead of doubting the fact, ought to receive it as certain and ought to search for the causes whence it might be derived. The decay, corruption, and dissolution of nature is an event rendered probable by so many analogies that any phenomenon which seems to have a tendency toward that catastrophe comes within the reach of human testimony if that testimony be very extensive and uniform.

But suppose that all the historians who treat of England should agree that on the first of January, 1600, Queen Elizabeth died; that both before and after her death she was seen by her physicians and the whole court, as is usual with persons of her rank; that her successor was acknowledged and proclaimed by the Parliament; and that, after being interred for a month, she again appeared, resumed the throne, and governed England for three years—I must confess that I should be surprised at the concurrence of so many odd circumstances, but should not have the least inclination to believe so miraculous an event. I should not doubt of her pretended death and of those other public circumstances that followed it; I should only assert it to have been pretended, and that it neither was, nor possibly could be, real. You would in vain object to me the difficulty and almost impossibility of deceiving the world in an affair of such consequence; the wisdom and solid judgment of that renowned Queen, with the little or no advantage which she could reap from so poor an artifice— all this might astonish me, but I would still reply that the knavery and folly of men are such common phenomena that I should rather believe the most extraordinary events to arise from their concurrence than admit of so signal a violation of the laws of nature.

But should this miracle be ascribed to any new system of religion, men in all ages have been so much imposed on by ridiculous stories of that kind that this very circumstance would be a full proof of a cheat and sufficient, with all men of sense, not only to make them reject the fact but even reject it without further examination. Though the Being to whom the miracle is ascribed be in this case Almighty, it does not, upon that account, become a whit more probable, since it is impossible for us to know the attributes or actions of such a Being otherwise than from the experience which we have of his productions in the usual course of nature. This still reduces us to past observation and obliges us to compare the instances of the violation of truth in the testimony of men with those of the violation of the laws of nature by miracles, in order to judge which of them is most likely and probable. As the violations of truth are more common in the testimony concerning religious miracles than in that concerning any other matter of fact, this must diminish very much the authority of the former testimony and make us form a general resolution never to lend any attention to it, with whatever specious pretense it may be covered. . . .

I am the better pleased with the method of reasoning here delivered, as I think it may serve to confound those dangerous friends or disguised enemies to the *Christian religion* who have undertaken to defend it by the principles of human reason. Our most holy religion is founded on *faith*, not on reason; and it is a sure method of exposing it to put it to such a trial as it is by no means fitted to endure. . . .

What we have said of miracles may be applied without any variation to prophecies; and, indeed, all prophecies are real miracles and as such only can be admitted as proofs of any revelation. If it did not exceed the capacity of human nature to foretell future events, it would be absurd to employ any prophecy as an argument for a divine mission or authority from heaven. So that, upon the whole, we may conclude that the Christian religion not only was at first attended with miracles, but even at this day cannot be believed by any reasonable person without one. Mere reason is insufficient to convince us of its veracity. And whoever is moved by *faith* to assent to it is conscious of a continued miracle in his own person which subverts all the principles of his understanding and gives him a determination to believe what is most contrary to custom and experience.

Questions

1. What does Hume mean by "miracle"?
2. How do we obtain our knowledge of the order of nature? What is the difference between something we have never experienced and something which contradicts our experience? Answer this last question by citing examples. For instance, how would you classify the following examples:
   a. A person flies in a rocket to Mars.
   b. A person flies through the air without the help of a machine.
   c. A person turns lead into gold.
   d. A person has X-ray eyes, and can see through walls which everyone else finds opaque.
   e. A man stands on one finger of one hand.
   f. A man jumps ten feet into the air and remains there without any support for ten minutes.
   g. A magician makes a card disappear.
   h. It begins to snow, but the snow is colored red.
   i. A child is born with six toes on each foot.
   j. A child is born with the ability at birth to discuss Einstein's theory of relativity with physicists.
   k. A person dives backward, out of the water up onto the diving board (as appears to happen when a motion picture of diving is reversed).
   l. A man swallows a cupful of nails and broken glass and does not die.
   m. A cube of pure ice in a glass of pure water sinks to the bottom of the glass.
3. Why does Hume believe that a miracle is disproved if its description contradicts our experience of the order of nature?
4. What place does a consideration of evidence by testimony have in a discussion of the possibility of miracles?
5. How does Hume use the rule that "no testimony is sufficient to establish a miracle unless the testimony be of such a kind that its falsehood would be more miraculous than the fact which it endeavors to establish" to disprove the possibility of miracles?
6. Even if we ought not to believe another person's report of a miracle, can we on Hume's principles ever expect to experience a miracle ourselves? Why or why not?

10

The Reasonableness of Believing in Miracles	C. S. Lewis (*b. 1898*)

Clive Staples Lewis is Professor of Medieval and Renaissance English at Cambridge University. He is also the author of more than a half-dozen books of Christian apologetics which are addressed to the common reader and which are noted for their clarity and intellectual vigor. Perhaps the best known of these books is *The Screwtape Letters* (1942).

In this reading Professor Lewis makes a case for the probability of miracles, which is in part deliberately constructed in opposition to David Hume's case against miracles in the preceding selection. The reader should pay close attention to the premises on which Professor Lewis bases his case for miracles, both noticing his differences with Hume, and determining the grounds on which someone might choose between their views.

This reading is drawn from Chapters VIII and XIII of *Miracles: A Preliminary Study,* 1947. The original chapter titles are retained in this reading.

ON PROBABILITY

Probability is founded on the presumption of a resemblance between those objects of which we have had experience and those of which we have had none; and therefore it is impossible that this presumption can arise from probability. HUME, *Treatise of Human Nature,* I, III, vi.

. . . Miracles are possible and . . . there is nothing antecedently ridiculous in the stories which say that God has sometimes performed them. This does not mean, of course, that we are committed to believing all stories of miracles. Most stories about miraculous events are probably false: if it comes to that, most stories about natural events are false. Lies, exaggerations, misunderstandings and hearsay make up perhaps more than half of all that is said and written in the world. We must therefore find a criterion whereby to judge any particular story of the miraculous.

In one sense, of course, our criterion is plain. Those stories are to be accepted for which the historical evidence is sufficiently good. But then . . . the answer to the question, "How much evidence should we require for this story?" depends on our answer to the question, "How far is this story intrinsically probable?" We must therefore find a criterion of probability.

The ordinary procedure of the modern historian, even if he admits the possibility of miracle, is to admit no particular instance of it until every possibility of "natural" explanation has been tried and failed. That is, he will accept the most improbable "natural" explanations rather than say that a miracle occurred. Collective hallucination, hypnotism of unconsenting spectators, widespread instantaneous conspiracy in lying by persons not otherwise known to be liars and not likely to gain by the lie—all these are known to be very improbable events: so improbable that, except for the special purpose of excluding a miracle, they are never suggested. But they are preferred to the admission of a miracle.

Such a procedure is, from the purely historical point of view, sheer midsummer madness *unless* we start by knowing that any miracle whatever is more improbable than the most improbable natural event. Do we know this?

We must distinguish the different kinds of improbability. Since miracles are, by definition, rarer than other events, it is obviously improbable beforehand that one will occur at any given place and time. In that sense every miracle is improbable. But that sort of improbability does not make the story that a miracle *has* happened incredible; for in the same sense all events whatever were once improbable. It is immensely improbable beforehand that a pebble dropped from the stratosphere over London will hit any given spot, or that any one particular person will win a large lottery. But the report that the pebble has landed outside such and such a shop or that Mr. So-and-So has won the lottery is not at all incredible. When you consider the immense number of meetings and fertile unions between ancestors which were necessary in order that you should be born, you perceive that it was once immensely improbable that such a person as you should come to exist: but once you are here, the report of your existence is not in the least incredible. With probability of this kind—antecedent probability of chances—we are not here concerned. Our business is with historical probability.

Ever since Hume's famous *Essay* it has been believed that historical statements about miracles are the most intrinsically improbable of all historical statements. According to Hume, probability rests on what may be called the majority vote of our past experiences. The more often a thing has been known to happen, the more probable it is that it should happen again; and the less often the less probable. Now the regularity of Nature's course, says Hume, is supported by something better than the majority vote of past experiences: it is supported by their unanimous vote, or, as Hume says, by "firm and unalterable experience." There is, in fact, "uniform experience" against Miracle; otherwise, says Hume, it would not be Miracle. A Miracle is therefore the most improbable of all events. It is always more probable that the witnesses were lying or mistaken than that a Miracle occurred.

Now of course we must agree with Hume that if there is absolutely "uniform experience" against miracles, if in other words they have never happened, why then they never have. Unfortunately we know the experience against them to be uniform only if we know that all the reports of them are false. And we can know all the reports to be false only if we know already that miracles have never occurred. In fact, we are arguing in a circle.

There is also an objection to Hume which leads us deeper into our problem. The whole idea of Probability (as Hume understands it) depends on the principle of the Uniformity of Nature. Unless Nature always goes on in the same way, the fact that a thing had happened ten million times would not make it a whit more probable that it would happen again. And how do we know the Uniformity of Nature? A moment's thought shows that we do not know it by experience. We observe many regularities in Nature. But of course all the observations that men have made or will make while the race lasts cover only a minute fraction of the events that actually go on. Our observations would therefore be of no use unless we felt sure that Nature when we are not watching her behaves in the same way as when we are: in other words, unless we believed in the Uniformity of Nature. Experience therefore cannot prove uniformity, because uniformity has to be assumed before experience proves anything. And mere length of experience does not help matters. It is no good saying, "Each fresh experience confirms our belief in uniformity and therefore we reasonably expect that it will always be confirmed"; for that argument works only on the assumption that the future will resemble the past—which is simply the assumption of Uniformity under a new name. Can we say that Uniformity is at any rate very probable? Unfortunately not. We have just seen that all probabilities depend on *it*. Unless Nature is uniform, nothing is either probable or improbable. And clearly the assumption which you have to make before there is any such thing as probability cannot itself be probable.

The odd thing is that no man knew this better than Hume. His *Essay on Miracles* is quite inconsistent with the more radical, and honourable, scepticism of his main work.

The question, "Do miracles occur?" and the question, "Is the course of Nature absolutely uniform?" are the same question asked in two different ways. Hume by sleight of hand, treats them as two different questions. He first answers, "Yes," to the question whether Nature is absolutely uniform: and then uses this "Yes" as a ground for answering, "No," to the question, "Do miracles occur?" The single real question which he set out to answer is never discussed at all. He gets the answer to one form of the question by assuming the answer to another form of the same question.

Probabilities of the kind that Hume is concerned with hold inside the framework of an assumed Uniformity of Nature. When the question of miracles is raised we are asking about the validity or perfection of the frame itself. No study of probabilities inside a given frame can ever tell us how probable it is that the frame itself can be violated. Granted a school time-table with French on Tuesday morning at ten o'clock, it is really probable that Jones, who always skimps his French preparation, will be in trouble next Tuesday, and that he was in trouble on any previous Tuesday. But what does this tell us about the probability of the time-table's being altered? To find that out you must eaves-drop in the masters' common-room. It is no use studying the time-table.

If we stick to Hume's method, far from getting what he hoped (namely, the conclusion that all miracles are infinitely improbable) we get a complete deadlock. The only kind of probability he allows holds exclusively within the frame of uniformity. When uniformity is itself in question (and it is in question the moment we ask whether miracles occur) this kind of probability is suspended. And Hume knows no other. By his method, therefore, we cannot say that uniformity is either probable or improbable; and equally we cannot say that miracles are either probable or improbable. We have impounded *both* uniformity *and* miracles in a sort of limbo where probability and improbability can never come. This result is equally disastrous for the scientist and the theo-logian; but along Hume's lines there is nothing whatever to be done about it.

Our only hope, then, will be to cast about for some quite different kind of Probability. Let us for the moment cease to ask what right we have to believe in the Uniformity of Nature, and ask why in fact men do believe in it. I think the belief has three causes, two of which are irrational. In the first place we are creatures of habit. We expect new situations to resemble old ones. It is a tendency which we share with animals; one can see it working, often to very comic results, in our dogs and cats. In the second place, when we plan our actions, we have to leave out of account the theoretical possibility that Nature might not behave as usual to-morrow, because we can do nothing about it. It is not worth bothering about because no action can be taken to meet it. And what we habitually put out of our minds we soon forget. The picture of uni-formity thus comes to dominate our minds without rival and we believe it. Both these causes are irrational and would be just as effective in building up a false belief as in building up a true one.

But I am convinced that there is a third cause. "In science," said the late Sir Arthur Eddington, "we sometimes have convictions which we cherish but cannot justify; we are influenced by some innate sense of the fitness of things." This may sound a perilously subjective and aesthetic criterion; but can one doubt that it is a principal source of our belief in Uniformity? A universe in which unprecedented and unpredictable events were at every moment flung into Nature would not merely be inconvenient to us: it would be profoundly repugnant. We will not accept such a universe on any terms whatever. It is utterly detestable to us. It shocks our "sense of the fitness of things." In advance of experience, in the teeth of many experiences, we are already enlisted on the side of uniformity. For of course science actually proceeds by concentrating not on the regularities of Nature but on her apparent irregularities. It is the ap-parent irregularity that prompts each new hypothesis. It does so because we refuse to acquiesce in irregularities: we never rest till we have formed and verified a hypothesis which enables us to say that they were not really irregularities at all. Nature as it comes to us looks at first like a mass of irregularities. The stove which lit all right yesterday won't light to-day; the water which was wholesome last year is poisonous this year. The whole mass of seemingly irregular experience could never have been turned into scientific knowledge at all unless from the very start we had brought to it a faith in uniformity which almost no number of disappointments can shake.

This faith—the preference—is it a thing we can trust? Or is it only the way our minds happen to work? It is useless to say that it has hitherto always been confirmed by the event. That is no good unless you (at least silently) add, "And therefore always will be": and you cannot add that unless you know already that our faith in uniformity is well grounded. And that is just what we are now asking. Does this sense of fitness of ours correspond to anything in external reality?

The answer depends on the Metaphysic one holds. If all that exists is Nature, the great mindless interlocking event, if our own deepest convictions are merely the bye-products of an irrational process, then clearly there is not the slightest ground for supposing that our sense of fitness and our consequent faith in uniformity tell us anything about a reality external to ourselves. Our convictions are simply a fact *about us*—like the colour of our hair. If Naturalism is true we have no reason to trust our conviction that Nature is uniform. It can be trusted only if quite a different Metaphysic is true. If the deepest thing in reality, the Fact which is the source of all other facthood, is a thing in some degree like ourselves—if it is a Rational Spirit and we derive our rational spirituality from it—then indeed our conviction can be trusted. Our repugnance to disorder is derived from Nature's Creator and ours. The disorderly world which we cannot endure to believe in is the disorderly world He would not have endured to create. Our conviction that the time-table will not be perpetually or meaninglessly altered is sound because we have (in a sense) eavesdropped in the Master's common-room.

The sciences logically require a metaphysic of this sort. Our greatest natural philosopher thinks it is also the metaphysic out of which they originally grew. Professor Whitehead points out [1] that centuries of belief in a God who combined "the personal energy of Jehovah" with "the rationality of a Greek philosopher" first produced that firm expectation of systematic order which rendered possible the birth of modern science. Men became scientific because they expected Law in Nature, and they expected Law in Nature because they believed in a Legislator. In most modern scientists this belief has died: it will be interesting to see how long their confidence in uniformity survives it. Two significant developments have already appeared—the hypothesis of a lawless subnature, and the surrender of the claim that science is true. We may be living nearer than we suppose to the end of the Scientific Age.

But if we admit God, must we admit Miracle? Indeed, indeed, you have no

[1] *Science and the Modern World*. Chapter II.

security against it. That is the bargain. Theology says to you in effect, "Admit God and with Him the risk of a few miracles, and I in return will ratify your faith in uniformity as regards the overwhelming majority of events." The philosophy which forbids you to make uniformity absolute is also the philosophy which offers you solid grounds for believing it to be general, to be *almost* absolute. The Being who threatens Nature's claim to omnipotence confirms her in her lawful occasions. Give us this ha'porth of tar and we will save the ship. The alternative is really much worse. Try to make Nature absolute and you find that her uniformity is not even probable. By claiming too much, you get nothing. You get the deadlock, as in Hume. Theology offers you a working arrangement, which leaves the scientist free to continue his experiments and the Christian to continue his prayers.

We have also, I suggest, found what we were looking for—a criterion whereby to judge the intrinsic probability of an alleged miracle. We must judge it by our "innate sense of the fitness of things," that same sense of fitness which led us to anticipate that the universe would be orderly. I do not mean, of course, that we are to use this sense in deciding whether miracles in general are possible: we know that they are on philosophical grounds. Nor do I mean that a sense of fitness will do instead of close inquiry into the historical evidence. As I have repeatedly pointed out, the historical evidence cannot be estimated unless we have first estimated the intrinsic probability of the recorded event. It is in making that estimate as regards each story of the miraculous that our sense of fitness comes into play.

If in giving such weight to the sense of fitness I were doing anything new, I should feel rather nervous. In reality I am merely giving formal acknowledgment to a principle which is always used. Whatever men may *say*, no one really thinks that the Christian doctrine of the Resurrection is exactly on the same level with some pious tittle-tattle about how Mother Egarée Louise miraculously found her second best thimble by the aid of St. Antony. The religious and the irreligious are really quite agreed on the point. The whoop of delight with which the sceptic would unearth the story of the thimble, and the "rosy pudency" with which the Christian would keep it in the background, both tell the same tale. Even those who think all stories of miracles absurd think some very much more absurd than others: even those who believe them all (if anyone does) think that some require a specially robust faith. The criterion which both parties are actually using is that of fitness. More than half the disbelief in miracles that exists is based on a sense of their *unfitness:* a conviction (due, as I have argued, to false philosophy) that they are unsuitable to the dignity of God or Nature or else to the indignity and insignificance of man.

MIRACLE AND THE LAWS OF NATURE

The question is whether Nature can be known to be of such a kind that supernatural interferences with her are impossible. She is already known to be, in general, regular: she behaves according to fixed laws, many of which have been discovered, and which interlock with one another. There is, in this discussion, no question of mere failure or inaccuracy to keep these laws on the part of Nature, no question of chancey or spontaneous variation.[2] The only question is whether, granting the existence of a Power outside Nature, there is any intrinsic absurdity in the idea of its intervening to produce within Nature events which the regular "going on" of the whole natural system would never have produced.

Three conceptions of the "Laws" of Nature have been held. (1) That they are mere brute facts, known only by observation, with no discoverable rhyme or reason about them. We know *that* Nature behaves thus and thus; we do not know why she does and can see no reason why she should not do the opposite. (2) That they are applications of the law of averages. The foundations of Nature are in the random and lawless. But the numbers of units we are dealing with are so enormous that the behaviour of these crowds (like the behaviour of very large masses of men) can be calculated with practical accuracy. What we call "impossible events" are events so overwhelmingly improbable—by actuarial standards—that we do not need to take them into account. (3) That the fundamental laws of Physics are really what we call "necessary truths" like the truths of mathematics—in other words, that if we clearly understand what we are saying we shall see that the opposite would be meaningless nonsense. Thus it is a "law" that when one billiard ball shoves another the amount of momentum lost by the first ball must exactly equal the amount gained by the second. People who hold that the laws of Nature are necessary truths would say that all we have done is to split up the single event into two halves (adventures of ball A, and adventures of ball B) and then discover that "the two sides of the account balance." When we understand this we see that of course they *must* balance. The fundamental laws are in the long run merely statements that every event is itself and not some different event.

It will at once be clear that the first of these three theories gives no assurance against Miracles—indeed no assurance that, even apart from Miracles, the "laws" which we have hitherto observed will be obeyed to-morrow. If we have no notion why a thing happens, then of course we know no reason why it should not be otherwise, and therefore have no certainty that it might not some day be otherwise. The second theory, which depends on the law of averages, is in the same position. The assurance it gives us is of the same general kind as our assurance that a coin tossed a thousand times will not give the same result, say, nine hundred times: and that the longer you toss it the more nearly the numbers of Heads and Tails will come to being equal. But this is so only provided the coin is an honest coin. If it is a loaded coin our expectations may be disappointed. But the people who believe in miracles are maintaining precisely that the coin *is* loaded. The expectations based on the law of aver-

[2] If any region of reality is in fact chancey or lawless then it is a region which, so far from admitting Miracle with special ease, renders the word "Miracle" meaningless throughout that region.

ages will work only for *undoctored* Nature. And the question whether miracles occur is just the question whether Nature is ever doctored.

The third view (that Laws of Nature are necessary truths) seems at first sight to present an insurmountable obstacle to miracle. The breaking of them would, in that case, be a self-contradiction and not even Omnipotence can do what is self-contradictory. Therefore the Laws cannot be broken. And therefore, shall we conclude, no miracle can ever occur?

We have gone too quickly. It is certain that the billiard balls will behave in a particular way, just as it is certain that if you divide a shilling unequally between two recipients then A's share must exceed the half and B's share fall short of it by exactly the same amount. Provided, of course, that A does not by sleight of hand steal some of B's pennies at the very moment of the transaction. In the same way, you know what will happen to the two billiard balls —provided nothing interferes. If one ball encounters a roughness in the cloth which the other does not, their motion will not illustrate the law in the way you had expected. Of course what happens as a result of the roughness in the cloth will illustrate the law in some other way, but your original prediction will have been false. Or again, if I snatch up a cue and give one of the balls a little help, you will get a third result: and that third result will equally illustrate the laws of physics, and equally falsify your prediction. I shall have "spoiled the experiment." All interferences leave the law perfectly true. But every prediction of what will happen in a given instance is made under the proviso "other things being equal" or "if there are no interferences." Whether other things *are* equal in a given case and whether interferences may occur is another matter. The arithmetician, as an arithmetician, does not know how likely A is to steal some of B's pennies when the shilling is being divided; you had better ask a criminologist. The physicist, as a physicist, does not know how likely I am to catch up a cue and "spoil" his experiment with the billiard balls; you had better ask someone who knows *me*. In the same way the physicist, as such, does not know how likely it is that some supernatural power is going to interfere with them: you had better ask a metaphysician. But the physicist does know, just because he is a physicist, that if the billiard balls are tampered with by any agency, natural or supernatural, which he had not taken into account, then their behaviour must differ from what he expected. Not because the law is false, but because it is true. The more certain we are of the law, the more clearly we know that if new factors have been introduced the result will vary accordingly. What we do not know, as physicists, is whether Supernatural power might be one of the new factors.

If the laws of Nature are necessary truths, no miracle can break them: but then no miracle needs to break them. It is with them as with the laws of arithmetic. If I put six pennies into a drawer on Monday and six more on Tuesday, the laws decree that—*other things being equal*—I shall find twelve pennies there on Wednesday. But if the drawer has been robbed I may in fact find only two. Something will have been broken (the lock of the drawer or the laws of England) but the laws of arithmetic will not have been broken.

The new situation created by the thief will illustrate the laws of arithmetic just as well as the original situation. But if God comes to work miracles, He comes "like a thief in the night." Miracle is, from the point of view of the scientist, a form of doctoring, tampering, if you like, cheating. It introduces a new factor into the situation, namely supernatural force, which the scientist had not reckoned on. He calculates what will happen, or what must have happened on a past occasion, in the belief that the situation, at that point of space and time, is or was A. But if supernatural force has been added, then the situation really is or was AB. And no one knows better than the scientist that AB *cannot* yield the same result as A. The necessary truth of the laws, far from making it impossible that miracles should occur makes it certain that if the Supernatural is operating they must occur. For if the natural situation by itself, and the natural situation *plus* something else, yielded only the same result, it would be then that we should be faced with a lawless and unsystematic universe. The better you know that two and two make four, the better you know that two and three don't.

This perhaps helps to make a little clearer what the laws of Nature really are. We are in the habit of talking as if they caused events to happen; but they have never caused any event at all. The laws of motion do not set billiard balls moving: they analyse the motion after something else (say, a man with a cue, or a lurch of the liner, or, perhaps, supernatural power) has provided it. They produce no events: they state the pattern to which every event—if only it can be induced to happen—must conform, just as the rules of arithmetic state the pattern to which all transactions with money must conform—if only you can get hold of any money. Thus in one sense the laws of Nature cover the whole field of space and time; in another, what they leave out is precisely the whole real universe—the incessant torrent of actual events which makes up true history. That must come from somewhere else. To think the laws can produce it is like thinking that you can create real money by simply doing sums. For every law, in the last resort, says "If you have A, then you will get B." But first catch your A: the laws won't do it for you.

It is therefore inaccurate to define a miracle as something that breaks the laws of Nature. It doesn't. If I knock out my pipe I alter the position of a great many atoms: in the long run, and to an infinitesimal degree, of all the atoms there are. Nature digests or assimilates this event with perfect ease and harmonises it in a twinkling with all other events. It is one more bit of raw material for the laws to apply to, and they apply. I have simply thrown one event into the general cataract of events and it finds itself at home there and conforms to all other events. If God annihilates or creates or deflects a unit of matter He has created a new situation at that point. Immediately all Nature domiciles this new situation, makes it at home in her realm, adapts all other events to it. It finds itself conforming to all the laws. If God creates a miraculous spermatozoon in the body of a virgin, it does not proceed to break any laws. The laws at once take it over. Nature is ready. Pregnancy follows, according to all the normal laws, and nine months later a child is born. We see every day that physical nature is not in the least incommoded by the daily inrush of events from biological nature or from psychological nature. If events ever come from beyond Nature altogether, she will be no more incommoded by them. Be sure she will rush to the point where she is invaded, as the defensive forces rush to a cut in our finger, and there hasten to accommodate the new-comer. The moment it enters her realm it obeys all her laws. Miraculous wine will intoxicate, miraculous conception will lead to pregnancy, inspired books will suffer all the ordinary processes of textual corruption, miraculous bread will be digested. The divine art of miracle is not an art of suspending the pattern to which events conform but of feeding new events into that pattern. It does not violate the law's proviso, "If A, then B": it says, "But this time instead of A, A2," and Nature, speaking through all her laws, replies, "Then B2," and naturalises the immigrant, as she well knows how. She is an accomplished hostess.

A miracle is emphatically not an event without cause or without results. Its cause is the activity of God: its results follow according to Natural law. In the forward direction (i.e. during the time which follows its occurrence) it is interlocked with all Nature just like any other event. Its peculiarity is that it is not in that way interlocked backwards, interlocked with the previous history of Nature. And this is just what some people find intolerable. The reason they find it intolerable is that they start by taking Nature to be the whole of reality. And they are sure that all reality must be interrelated and consistent. I agree with them. But I think they have mistaken a partial system within reality, namely Nature, for the whole. That being so, the miracle and the previous history of Nature may be interlocked after all but not in the way the Naturalist expected: rather in a much more roundabout fashion. The great complex event called Nature, and the new particular event introduced into it by the miracle, are related by their common origin in God, and doubtless, if we knew enough, most intricately related in His purpose and design, so that a Nature which had had a different history, and therefore been a different Nature, would have been invaded by different miracles or by none at all. In that way the miracle and the previous course of Nature are as well interlocked as any other two realities, but you must go back as far as their common Creator to find the interlocking. You will not find it *within* Nature. The same sort of thing happens with any partial system. The behaviour of fishes which are being studied in a tank makes a relatively closed system. Now suppose that the tank is shaken by a bomb in the neighbourhood of the laboratory. The behaviour of the fishes will now be no longer fully explicable by what was going on in the tank before the bomb fell: there will be a failure of backward interlocking. This does not mean that the bomb and the previous history of events within the tank are totally and finally unrelated. It does mean that to find their relation you must go back to the much larger reality which includes both the tank and the bomb—the reality of war-time England in which bombs are falling but some laboratories are still at work. You would never find it within the history of the tank. In the same way, the miracle is not *naturally* interlocked in the backward direction. To find how it is interlocked with the previous history of Nature you must replace both Nature and the miracle in a larger context. Everything *is* connected with everything else: but not all things are connected by the short and straight roads we expected.

The rightful demand that all reality should be consistent and systematic does not therefore exclude miracles: but it has a very valuable contribution to make to our conception of them. It reminds us that miracles, if they occur, must, like all events, be revelations of the total harmony of all that exists. Nothing arbitrary, nothing simply "stuck on" and left unreconciled with the texture of total reality, can be admitted. By definition, miracles must of course interrupt the usual course of Nature; but if they are real they must, in the very act of so doing, assert all the more the unity and self-consistency of total reality at some deeper level. They will not be like unmetrical lumps of prose breaking the unity of a poem; they will be like that crowning metrical audacity which, though it may be paralleled nowhere else in the poem, yet, coming just where it does, and effecting just what it effects, is (to those who understand) the supreme revelation of the unity in the poet's conception. If what we call Nature is modified by supernatural power, then we may be sure that the capability of being so modified is of the essence of nature—that the total event, if we could grasp it, would turn out to involve, by its very character, the possibility of such modifications. If Nature brings forth miracles then doubtless it is as "natural" for her to do so when impregnated by the masculine force beyond her as it is for a woman to bear children to a man. In calling them miracles we do not mean that they are contradictions or outrages; we mean that, left to her own resources, she could never produce them.

Questions

1. What are the different senses of "natural law" which Professor Lewis notices? What does he mean by "miracle"? How does he show that a miracle is possible in each sense of "natural law" that he distinguishes?

2. How does Professor Lewis attempt to solve the theistic problem of accounting for the intervention in nature of a God who is above nature?

3. What is the difference between an event which "breaks the laws of nature" and an event which "interrupt[s] the usual course of nature"? Illustrate your answer with examples.

4. What is Hume's argument against miracles? (See the selection beginning on page 370.) What argument does Professor Lewis advance against Hume? Decide who has the better case, and justify your decision.

5. How does Professor Lewis use the concept of "fitness" to account for the probability of miracles? What assumptions are required for someone to be able to use Professor Lewis' concept of "fitness" as he does?

11

God and Evil: A Positive View

G. W. Leibniz
(1646-1716)

Leibniz is justly famous as a philosopher, a mathematician, and a theologian. But he is popularly remembered for providing Voltaire with the theme of *Candide* (1759): This is the best of all possible worlds. Whether Leibniz's doctrine is as untenable as Voltaire attempts to show is a question which the reader will be better able to decide after considering this selection. The topic which Leibniz considers here is that of God and evil. Does the existence of evil in the world count against the existence of God? Or, at the very least, does the existence of evil disprove God's benevolence? Leibniz answers both of these questions with a "No," and the reader must be careful to notice the principles which Leibniz believes guarantee his negative answers. The reader must decide whether Leibniz's principles are the only ones which may be invoked, and, further, he must consider the extremely difficult question of how one decides what principles to invoke here.

The first paragraph of this selection is taken from *Principles of Nature and of Grace, Founded on Reason* (1714). The remainder is the last half of *On the Ultimate Origination of Things* (1697). The translation is by Mary Morris.

From the book *Philosophical Writings,* by Leibniz. Everyman's Library Series. Published by E. P. Dutton & Co., Inc. Reprinted by permission of the publishers. Permission also granted by J. M. Dent & Sons, Ltd., London.

It follows from the supreme perfection of God that in producing the universe He chose the best possible plan, containing the greatest variety together with the greatest order; the best arranged situation, place, and time; the greatest effect produced by the simplest means; the most power, the most knowledge, the most happiness and goodness in created things of which the universe admitted. For as all possible things have a claim to existence in the understanding of God in proportion to their perfections, the result of all these claims must be the most perfect actual world which is possible. Otherwise it would not be possible to explain why things have happened as they have rather than other-wise. . . .

. . . The ultimate reason of the reality both of essences and of existences in a Unity must certainly be greater, higher, and prior to the world itself, since through it alone not only the existent things, which the world contains, but also the things that are possible have their reality. It cannot be found except in one single source, because of the interconnection of all these things with one another. It is evident that from this source existent things are continually issuing and being produced, and have been produced, since it is not clear why one state of the world rather than another, yesterday's state rather than today's, should flow from the world itself. It is also evident how God acts not only physically but also freely; and how there lies in Him not only the efficient but also the final cause; and how from Him proceeds the reason not only of the greatness or potency that there is in the mechanism for the universe as now established, but also of the goodness or wisdom involved in the establishing of it.

In case someone may think that moral perfection or goodness is here being confused with metaphysical perfection or greatness, and may admit the latter while denying the former, it should be pointed out that it follows from what has been said not only that the world is the most perfect physically, or, if you prefer it, metaphysically, or in other words that that series of things will be forthcoming which in actual fact affords the greatest quantity of reality, but also that the world should be the most perfect morally, because true moral perfection is physical perfection in minds themselves. Hence the world is not only the most wonderful machine, but also in regard to minds it is the best commonwealth, by whose means there is bestowed on minds the greatest pos-sible amount of felicity or joyfulness; and it is in this that their physical per-fection consists.

But, you will say, we find in the world the very opposite of this. Often the worst of sufferings fall upon the best men; the innocent (I speak not only of the brutes, but of men also) are afflicted, and are slain even with tortures; indeed the world, especially if we look at the government of the human race, seems rather a confused chaos than an affair ordained by some supreme wisdom. So it appears at first sight, I allow: but on deeper examination it must be agreed that the opposite is the case. It is evident *a priori* from those very principles which I have adduced that without doubt there is secured in the world the highest perfection that there could possibly be of all things, and therefore of minds.

And indeed it is unreasonable, as the lawyers say, to give a judgment with-out inspecting the whole law. We have knowledge of a tiny part of that eter-nity which stretches out immeasurably. For how small a thing is the memory of the few thousand years which history hands down to us! And yet out of so little experience we rashly make judgments about the immeasurable and the eternal; just as men who had been born and bred in prison or in the subter-ranean salt-mines of Sarmatia might think that there was no other light in the world than the treacherous flicker of torches, which was hardly sufficient to guide their footsteps. Look at the most lovely picture, and then cover it up, leaving uncovered only a tiny scrap of it. What else will you see there, even if you look as closely as possible, and the more so as you look from nearer and nearer at hand, but a kind of confused medley of colours, without selection, without art! And yet when you remove the covering, and look upon the whole picture from the proper place, you will see that what previously seemed to you to have been aimlessly smeared on the canvas was in fact accomplished with the highest art by the author of the work. What happens to the eyes in painting is equally experienced by the ears in music. The great composers frequently mingle discords with harmonious chords so that the listener may be stimulated and pricked as it were, and may become eager to know what is going to happen; presently when all is restored to order he feels so much the more content. In the same way we may take pleasure in small dangers, or in the experience of ills, from the very sense or proof they give us of our own power or felicity. Or again at the spectacle of rope-walking or sword-dancing we are delighted by the very element of fear that is involved, and we ourselves in play with children hold them as if we were going to throw them out of the window, and half let them go—in very much the same way as the ape carried Christian, King of Denmark, when he was still an infant wrapped in long clothes, to the edge of the roof, and then, when everybody was in terror, turned it into jest and put him back into his cradle safe and sound. On the same principle it has an insipid effect if we always eat sweet things; sharp, acid, and even bitter things should be mixed in to stimulate the taste. He who has not tasted what is bitter has not earned what is sweet, nor will he appreciate it. This is the very law of enjoyment, that positive pleasure does not come from an even course; such things produce weariness, and make men dull, not joyful.

What I have said, however, about the possibility of a part being disturbed without upsetting the harmony of the whole must not be interpreted to mean that no account is taken of the parts; or that it is sufficient for the whole world to be completed at all points, even though it should turn out that the human race was wretched, and that there was in the universe no care for justice and no account was taken of us—as is maintained by some people whose judgment about the sum of things is ill-grounded. For the truth is that, just as in a well-regulated commonwealth care is taken that as far as possible things shall be to the interest of the individual, in the same way the universe would not be sufficiently perfect unless, as far as can be done without upsetting the universal harmony, the good of individual people is considered. Of this there could be established no better measure than the very law of justice itself, which dictates that each should have a part in the perfection of the universe and in his own happiness in proportion to his own virtue and to the extent to which his will is directed towards the common good; by which is fulfilled what we call the charity and love of God, in which alone, according to the judgment of wise theologians also, stands the whole force and power of the Christian religion. Nor ought it to seem remarkable that all this deference should be paid to minds in the universe, since they bear the closest resemblance to the image of the supreme Author, and their relation to Him is not that of machines to their artificer (like the rest of the world) but rather that of citizens to their prince; moreover they will endure as long as the universe itself, and they, in some manner, express and concentrate the whole in themselves; so that it might be said that minds are whole parts.

As for the afflictions of men, and especially of good men, we must hold ourselves assured that they contribute to the greater good of those who suffer them; and this is true not only theologically, but physically also, just as a grain of wheat cast into the earth must suffer before it bears fruit. And in general it is true to say that afflictions are for the time being evil, but in effect good, since they are short cuts to a greater perfection. Similarly in physics the liquids which ferment slowly are also more slowly purified, whereas those in which there is a more violent disturbance throw off the foreign parts with greater force and so more quickly become pure. You might fairly say that this is a case of taking a step back in order to make a stronger leap forward (*reculer pour mieux sauter*). These things must be allowed to be not only pleasant and consoling, but also most true. Indeed in general I hold that there is nothing truer than happiness, and nothing happier and sweeter than truth.

Further, we realize that there is a perpetual and a most free progress of the whole universe in fulfilment of the universal beauty and perfection of the works of God, so that it is always advancing towards a greater development. Thus, even now a great part of our earth has received cultivation, and will receive it more and more. And though it is true that there are times when some parts of it go back again to virgin forest, or are destroyed again and oppressed, this must be understood in the same sense as I just now interpreted the meaning of affliction, namely, that this very destruction and oppression contributes to achieve something greater, so that in some way we receive profit from our very loss.

To the objection that may perhaps be offered that if this were so the world would long ago have become a paradise, the answer is at hand: although many substances have already come to great perfection, yet owing to the infinite divisibility of what is continuous, there always remain in the abyss of things parts that are asleep, and these need to be awakened and to be driven forward into something greater and better—in a word, to a better development. Hence this progress does not ever come to an end.

Questions

1. What sort of thing does Leibniz count as evil? In general, how does one tell when something is evil? Does a judgment of what is evil depend on one's point of view? Explain your answer.

2. How does Leibniz argue that the presence of evil in the world disproves neither God's existence nor his benevolence?

3. In framing his arguments, does Leibniz ask us to accept principles which assume what he is trying to prove? Defend your answer.

12

God and Evil: | David Hume
A Skeptical View | *(1711-1776)*

[A general introductory note on Hume may be found on page 98.]

Hume's contribution to the problem of whether the presence of evil in the world counts for (or against) either the existence or the benevolence of God takes the form of an examination of the following question: Starting solely from our knowledge of the world, is there anything about the world which would lead us to believe that it has been made by a benevolent God? Hume's answer to this question is "No." The reader must decide whether Hume has good grounds for answering this question as he does. In addition the reader ought to contrast Hume's discussion of God and evil with Leibniz's (page 389). For these selections represent opposing points of view about the same topic, and the reader should work out the assumptions on which each point of view depends, the better to see why anyone should choose one point of view rather than the other.

This selection is drawn from the *Dialogues Concerning Natural Religion* (1779), Part XI. It is part of a speech which Hume assigns to his skeptical character, Philo.

From *Dialogues Concerning Natural Religion,* by David Hume, edited with introduction by Henry D. Aiken, Hafner Library of Classics, Hafner Publishing Co., Inc., N. Y., 1957.

My sentiments, [said] Philo, are not worth being made a mystery of; and, therefore, without any ceremony, I shall deliver what occurs to me with regard to the present subject. It must, I think, be allowed that, if a very limited intelligence whom we shall suppose utterly unacquainted with the universe were assured that it were the production of a very good, wise, and powerful Being, however finite, he would, from his conjectures, form *beforehand* a different notion of it from what we find it to be by experience; nor would he ever imagine, merely from these attributes of the cause of which he is informed, that the effect could be so full of vice and misery and disorder, as it appears in this life. Supposing now that this person were brought into the world, still assured that it was the workmanship of such a sublime and benevolent Being, he might, perhaps, be surprised at the disappointment, but would never retract his former belief if founded on any very solid argument, since such a limited intelligence must be sensible of his own blindness and ignorance, and must allow that there may be many solutions of those phenomena which will forever escape his comprehension. But supposing, which is the real case with regard to man, that this creature is not antecedently convinced of a supreme intelligence, benevolent, and powerful, but is left to gather such a belief from the appearances of things—this entirely alters the case, nor will he ever find any reason for such a conclusion. He may be fully convinced of the narrow limits of his understanding, but this will not help him in forming an inference concerning the goodness of superior powers, since he must form that inference from what he knows, not from what he is ignorant of. The more you exaggerate his weakness and ignorance, the more diffident you render him, and give him the greater suspicion that such subjects are beyond the reach of his faculties. You are obliged, therefore, to reason with him merely from the known phenomena, and to drop every arbitrary supposition or conjecture.

Did I show you a house or palace where there was not one apartment convenient or agreeable, where the windows, doors, fires, passages, stairs, and the whole economy of the building were the source of noise, confusion, fatigue, darkness, and the extremes of heat and cold, you would certainly blame the contrivance, without any further examination. The architect would in vain display his subtilty, and prove to you that, if this door or that window were altered, greater ills would ensue. What he says may be strictly true: the alteration of one particular, while the other parts of the building remain, may only augment the inconveniences. But still you would assert in general that, if the architect had had skill and good intentions, he might have formed such a plan of the whole, and might have adjusted the parts in such a manner as would have remedied all or most of these inconveniences. His ignorance, or even your own ignorance of such a plan, will never convince you of the impossibility of it. If you find any inconveniences and deformities in the building, you will always, without entering into any detail, condemn the architect.

In short, I repeat the question: Is the world, considered in general and as it appears to us in this life, different from what a man or such a limited being would, *beforehand,* expect from a very powerful, wise, and benevolent Deity? It must be strange prejudice to assert the contrary. And from thence I conclude that, however consistent the world may be, allowing certain suppositions and conjectures with the idea of such a Deity, it can never afford us an inference concerning his existence. The consistency is not absolutely denied, only the inference. Conjectures, especially where infinity is excluded from the Divine attributes, may perhaps be sufficient to prove a consistency, but can never be foundations for any inference.

There seem to be *four* circumstances on which depend all or the greatest part of the ills that molest sensible creatures; and it is not impossible but all these circumstances may be necessary and unavoidable. We know so little beyond common life, or even of common life, that, with regard to the economy of a universe, there is no conjecture, however wild, which may not be just, nor any one, however plausible, which may not be erroneous. All that belongs to human understanding, in this deep ignorance and obscurity, is to be sceptical or at least cautious, and not to admit of any hypothesis whatever, much less of any which is supported by no appearance of probability. Now this I assert to be the case with regard to all the causes of evil and the circumstances on which it depends. None of them appear to human reason in the least degree necessary or unavoidable, nor can we suppose them such, without the utmost license of imagination.

The *first* circumstance which introduces evil is that contrivance or economy of the animal creation by which pains, as well as pleasures, are employed to excite all creatures to action, and make them vigilant in the great work of self-preservation. Now pleasure alone, in its various degrees, seems to human understanding sufficient for this purpose. All animals might be constantly in a state of enjoyment; but when urged by any of the necessities of nature, such as thirst, hunger, weariness, instead of pain, they might feel a diminution of pleasure by which they might be prompted to seek that object which is necessary to their subsistence. Men pursue pleasure as eagerly as they avoid pain; at least, they might have been so constituted. It seems, therefore, plainly possible to carry on the business of life without any pain. Why then is any animal ever rendered susceptible of such a sensation? If animals can be free from it an hour, they might enjoy a perpetual exemption from it, and it required as particular a contrivance of their organs to produce that feeling as to endow them with sight, hearing, or any of the senses. Shall we conjecture that such a contrivance was necessary, without any appearance of reason, and shall we build on that conjecture as on the most certain truth?

But a capacity of pain would not alone produce pain were it not for the *second* circumstance, viz., the conducting of the world by general laws; and this seems nowise necessary to a very perfect Being. It is true, if everything were conducted by particular volitions, the course of nature would be perpetually broken, and no man could employ his reason in the conduct of life. But might not other particular volitions remedy this inconvenience? In short, might not the Deity exterminate all ill, wherever it were to be found, and produce all good, without any preparation or long progress of causes and effects?

Besides, we must consider that, according to the present economy of the world, the course of nature, though supposed exactly regular, yet to us appears not so, and many events are uncertain, and many disappoint our expectations. Health and sickness, calm and tempest, with an infinite number of other accidents whose causes are unknown and variable, have a great influence both on the fortunes of particular persons and on the prosperity of public societies; and indeed all human life, in a manner, depends on such accidents. A being, therefore, who knows the secret springs of the universe might easily, by particular volitions, turn all these accidents to the good of mankind and render the whole world happy, without discovering himself in any operation. A fleet whose purposes were salutary to society might always meet with a fair wind. Good princes enjoy sound health and long life. Persons born to power and authority be framed with good tempers and virtuous dispositions. A few such events as these, regularly and wisely conducted, would change the face of the world, and yet would no more seem to disturb the course of nature or confound human conduct than the present economy of things where the causes are secret and variable and compounded. Some small touches given to Caligula's brain in his infancy might have converted him into a Trajan. One wave, a little higher than the rest, by burying Caesar and his fortune in the bottom of the ocean, might have restored liberty to a considerable part of mankind. There may, for aught we know, be good reasons why Providence interposes not in this manner, but they are unknown to us; and, though the mere supposition that such reasons exist may be sufficient to *save* the conclusion concerning the Divine attributes, yet surely it can never be sufficient to *establish* that conclusion.

3.   If everything in the universe be conducted by general laws, and if animals be rendered susceptible of pain, it scarcely seems possible but some ill must arise in the various shocks of matter and the various concurrence and opposition of general laws; but this ill would be very rare were it not for the *third* circumstance which I proposed to mention, viz., the great frugality with which all powers and faculties are distributed to every particular being. So well adjusted are the organs and capacities of all animals, and so well fitted to their preservation, that, as far as history or tradition reaches, there appears not to be any single species which has yet been extinguished in the universe. Every animal has the requisite endowments, but these endowments are bestowed with so scrupulous an economy that any considerable diminution must entirely destroy the creature. Wherever one power is increased, there is a proportional abatement in the others. Animals which excel in swiftness are commonly defective in force. Those which possess both are either imperfect in some of their senses or are oppressed with the most craving wants. The human species, whose chief excellence is reason and sagacity, is of all others the most necessitous, and the most deficient in bodily advantages, without clothes, without arms, without food, without lodging, without any convenience of life, except what they owe to their own skill and industry. In short, nature seems to have formed an exact calculation of the necessities of her creatures, and, like a *rigid master,* has afforded them little more powers or endowments than what are strictly sufficient to supply those necessities. An *indulgent parent* would have bestowed a large stock in order to guard against accidents, and secure the happiness and welfare of the creature in the most unfortunate concurrence of circumstances. Every course of life would not have been so surrounded with precipices that the least departure from the true path, by mistake or necessity, must involve us in misery and ruin. Some reserve, some fund, would have been provided to ensure happiness, nor would the powers and the necessities have been adjusted with so rigid an economy. The Author of nature is incon-

ceivably powerful; his force is supposed great, if not altogether inexhaustible, nor is there any reason, as far as we can judge, to make him observe this strict frugality in his dealings with his creatures. It would have been better, were his power extremely limited, to have created fewer animals, and to have endowed these with more faculties for their happiness and preservation. A builder is never esteemed prudent who undertakes a plan beyond what his stock will enable him to finish.

In order to cure most of the ills of human life, I require not that man should have the wings of the eagle, the swiftness of the stag, the force of the ox, the arms of the lion, the scales of the crocodile or rhinoceros; much less do I demand the sagacity of an angel or cherubim. I am contented to take an increase in one single power or faculty of his soul. Let him be endowed with a greater propensity to industry and labour, a more vigorous spring and activity of mind, a more constant bent to business and application. Let the whole species possess naturally an equal diligence with that which many individuals are able to attain by habit and reflection, and the most beneficial consequences, without any allay of ill, is the immediate and necessary result of this endowment. Almost all the moral as well as natural evils of human life arise from idleness; and were our species, by the original constitution of their frame, exempt from this vice or infirmity, the perfect cultivation of land, the improvement of arts and manufactures, the exact execution of every office and duty, immediately follow; and men at once may fully reach that state of society which is so imperfectly attained by the best regulated government. But as industry is a power, and the most valuable of any, nature seems determined, suitably to her usual maxims, to bestow it on men with a very sparing hand, and rather to punish him severely for his deficiency in it than to reward him for his attainments. She has so contrived his frame that nothing but the most violent necessity can oblige him to labour; and she employs all his other wants to overcome, at least in part, the want of diligence, and to endow him with some share of a faculty of which she has thought fit naturally to bereave him. Here our demands may be allowed very humble, and therefore the more reasonable. If we required the endowments of superior penetration and judgment, of a more delicate taste of beauty, of a nicer sensibility to benevolence and friendship, we might be told that we impiously pretend to break the order of nature, that we want to exalt ourselves into a higher rank of being, that the presents which we require, not being suitable to our state and condition, would only be pernicious to us. But it is hard, I dare to repeat it, it is hard that, being placed in a world so full of wants and necessities, where almost every being and element is either our foe or refuses its assistance . . . we should also have our own temper to struggle with, and should be deprived of that faculty which can alone fence against these multiplied evils.

The *fourth* circumstance whence arises the misery and ill of the universe is the inaccurate workmanship of all the springs and principles of the great machine of nature. It must be acknowledged that there are few parts of the universe which seem not to serve some purpose, and whose removal would not produce a visible defect and disorder in the whole. The parts hang all together, nor can one be touched without affecting the rest, in a greater or less degree. But at the same time, it must be observed that none of these parts or principles, however useful, are so accurately adjusted as to keep precisely within those bounds in which their utility consists; but they are, all of them, apt, on every occasion, to run into the one extreme or the other. One would imagine that this grand production had not received the last hand of the maker —so little finished is every part, and so coarse are the strokes with which it is executed. Thus the winds are requisite to convey the vapours along the surface of the globe, and to assist men in navigation; but how often, rising up to tempests and hurricanes, do they become pernicious? Rains are necessary to nourish all the plants and animals of the earth; but how often are they defective? how often excessive? Heat is requisite to all life and vegetation, but is not always found in the due proportion. On the mixture and secretion of the humours and juices of the body depend the health and prosperity of the animal; but the parts perform not regularly their proper function. What more useful than all the passions of the mind, ambition, vanity, love, anger? But how often do they break their bounds and cause the greatest convulsions in society? There is nothing so advantageous in the universe but what frequently becomes pernicious, by its excess or defect; nor has nature guarded, with the requisite accuracy, against all disorder or confusion. The irregularity is never perhaps so great as to destroy any species, but is often sufficient to involve the individuals in ruin and misery.

On the concurrence, then, of these *four* circumstances does all or the greatest part of natural evil depend. (1) Were all living creatures incapable of pain, or were the world administered by particular volitions, evil never could have found access into the universe; and (2) were animals endowed with a large stock of powers and faculties, beyond what strict necessity requires, or were the several springs and principles of the universe so accurately framed as to preserve always the just temperament and medium, there must have been very little ill in comparison of what we feel at present. What then shall we pronounce on this occasion? Shall we say that these circumstances are not necessary, and that they might easily have been altered in the contrivance of the universe? This decision seems too presumptuous for creatures so blind and ignorant. Let us be more modest in our conclusions. Let us allow that, if the goodness of the Deity (I mean a goodness like the human) could be established on any tolerable reasons *a priori*, these phenomena, however untoward, would not be sufficient to subvert that principle, but might easily, in some unknown manner, be reconcilable to it. But let us still assert that, as this goodness is not antecedently established but must be inferred from the phenomena, there can be no grounds for such an inference while there are so many ills in the universe, and while these ills might so easily have been remedied, as far as human understanding can be allowed to judge on such a subject. I am sceptic enough to allow that the bad appearances, notwithstanding all my reasonings, may be compatible with such attributes as you suppose, but surely they can never prove these attributes. Such a conclusion cannot result from scepticism, but must arise from the phenomena, and from our confidence in the reasonings which we deduce from these phenomena.

Look round this universe. What an immense profusion of beings, animated and organized, sensible and active! You admire this prodigious variety and fecundity. But inspect a little more narrowly these living existences, the only beings worth regarding. How hostile and destructive to each other! How insufficient all of them for their own happiness! How contemptible or odious to the spectator! The whole presents nothing but the idea of a blind nature, impregnated by a great vivifying principle, and pouring forth from her lap, without discernment or parental care, her maimed and abortive children!

Here the Manichaean system occurs as a proper hypothesis to solve the difficulty; and, no doubt, in some respects it is very specious and has more probability than the common hypothesis, by giving a plausible account of the strange mixture of good and ill which appears in life. But if we consider, on the other hand, the perfect uniformity and agreement of the parts of the universe, we shall not discover in it any marks of the combat of a malevolent with a benevolent being. There is indeed an opposition of pains and pleasures in the feelings of sensible creatures; but are not all the operations of nature carried on by an opposition of principles, of hot and cold, moist and dry, light and heavy? The true conclusion is that the original Source of all things is entirely indifferent to all these principles, and has no more regard to good above ill than to heat above cold, or to drought above moisture, or to light above heavy.

There may *four* hypotheses be framed concerning the first causes of the universe: that they are endowed with perfect goodness; that they have perfect malice; that they are opposite and have both goodness and malice; that they have neither goodness nor malice. Mixed phenomena can never prove the two former unmixed principles; and the uniformity and steadiness of general laws seem to oppose the third. The fourth, therefore, seems by far the most probable.

What I have said concerning natural evil will apply to moral with little or no variation; and we have no more reason to infer that the rectitude of the Supreme Being resembles human rectitude than that his benevolence resembles the human. Nay, it will be thought that we have still greater cause to exclude from him moral sentiments, such as we feel them, since moral evil, in the opinion of many, is much more predominant above moral good than natural evil above natural good.

But even though this should not be allowed, and though the virtue which is in mankind should be acknowledged much superior to the vice, yet, so long as there is any vice at all in the universe, it will very much puzzle you anthropomorphites how to account for it. You must assign a cause for it, without having recourse to the first cause. But as every effect must have a cause, and that cause another, you must either carry on the progression *in infinitum* or rest on that original principle, who is the ultimate cause of all things. . . .

Questions

1. What does Hume mean by "evil"?

2. How does Hume show that "the original source of all things" is indifferent to good and evil? What assumptions are involved in his proof?

3. Does Hume's argument that "the original source of all things" is indifferent to good and evil depend on his initial assumptions or on what we can observe of the world? Explain your answer.

4. How do Hume and Leibniz (page 389) differ in their views on God and evil? Can one decide between them? Why or why not? If one can, how does one justify one's choice?

EPILOGUE

The Logical Status of	Alasdair MacIntyre
Religious Belief	(*b. 1923*)

Mr. Alasdair MacIntyre is Lecturer in the Philosophy of Religion at the University of Manchester. His topic here is the justification of religious beliefs. He begins by characterizing the religious attitude with which religious beliefs are held; for he argues that there can be no understanding of religious beliefs apart from the religious attitude. His description of the religious attitude is detailed, and not easily summarized. So we shall only say here that he finds that the religious attitude is not an empirical one. Thus, religious beliefs are not empirical hypotheses to be confirmed or disproved by experiment. But even though they are not empirical hypotheses, it does not follow that religious beliefs are the conclusions of a priori arguments which *must* be accepted once the terms of the argument are understood. Mr. MacIntyre argues that religious beliefs are held by a religious person because they are the pronouncements of a religious authority who is thought to speak as a representative of God. The place of authority in religion is for Mr. MacIntyre the defining characteristic of a theistic religion, and without an appeal to an authority there would be no justification of religious beliefs.

Mr. MacIntyre's account of the justification of religious beliefs raises several questions for the reader. First of all, has Mr. MacIntyre characterized the religious attitude of a theist correctly? What is his evidence for his account of the religious attitude, and has he considered all of the evidence? Second, how does Mr. MacIntyre's account of the justification of religious beliefs compare with the way in which other beliefs, in science and mathematics, for example, are justified? Does he succeed in establishing a case for the autonomy of religious beliefs, which must be, and can only be, justified in their own way? Finally, while Mr. MacIntyre seems to establish a case for religious belief on the grounds that we must either take it or leave it, does he ever answer the question of why we should believe?

This reading is Chapters IV and V of the essay, "The Logical Status of Religious Belief." The original chapter titles are retained.

From *Metaphysical Beliefs: Three Essays,* by Stephen E. Toulmin, Ronald W. Hepburn, and Alasdair MacIntyre, Student Christian Movement Press, Ltd., London, 1957; obtainable in the U.S.A. from Alec R. Allenson, Inc., 635 East Ogden Ave., Naperville, Ill. Reprinted by permission of the publisher.

THE RELIGIOUS ATTITUDE

The description of religious belief that I shall offer will fall into two parts. I shall first attempt to say to what kind of belief the taking up of a religious attitude seems to commit one. Then I shall go on to inquire what kind of justification would be appropriate to such a belief. And in so doing I shall also hope to show what kind of justification of religious beliefs is fundamentally inappropriate.

In a general way the religious attitude has at least two elements to it. The religious believer is committed to the practice of worship in some fairly systematic way. Also he declares that his God acts in the universe. From the myth and ritual of primitive religion to the historical narrations and Eucharistic liturgy of New Testament faith these two elements are found together. But there is a certain tension between them in any theistic faith. For the theist wants to declare in his worship that God is such that nothing adequate can be said about him; but he also wishes to say that God has done this and not that, is like this and not that. How this is so can be best understood by considering how theism emerges from earlier forms of religion. For early man the landscape is full of gods, full that is of actual and potential objects of worship. How he worships it is for the anthropologist to tell us in detail; but before the tree and the spring in some sense of "before" he kneels and says "Thou, O God," then within him the primitive sceptic casts his first doubts. He does not say "Your god does not exist," for to say this to one whose gods have the solidity of trees and streams would be pointless. He says rather "Your god is not a god," suggests that what is worshipped is an inadequate object of worship. So the worshipper purges his divinity of particularity, tries to remove those points in which his god is less than he might be and ascends to a god of all the trees and all the streams, thence to a pantheon of nature and human nature gods (Poseidon and Aphrodite) until he reaches a god who is the first being of the natural universe, whether Zeus or the Prime Mover. At each stage scepticism drives him on, showing him always that his god is less than he might be so long as he remains an object, *a* being, even if the highest. So at last there comes the great break of the Semitic peoples with any God who is an object; God is detached from nature altogether, is placed outside the world. He is neither this nor that, and we can say of him only what he is not. But the sceptic remains dissatisfied: this God may not be an inadequate object, but that is simply because he is not an object at all. The sceptical charge that God does not exist has been made possible. And *prima facie* to rebut it would be to return to an inadequate view of God as an object. But ignoring this point for the moment we are left with a purely negative conception of God. Even apparently positive assertions may conceal a negative content. To say, for example, that God is one, as Aquinas points out, is not to say how many Gods there are; it is to say that God is not among those things that are countable. Whatever we try to say of God turns out to be something that we must deny to be true of deity. So we get the *Mystical Theology* of the pseudo-Dionysius concluding:

> nor is it darkness, nor is it light, nor error nor truth; nor can affirmation or negation apply to it; for while affirmation or negation are applied to those beings that come next to it, we apply not to it affirmation or negation insomuch as it transcends all affirmation by being the perfect and unique cause of all things, and transcends all negation by the pre-eminence of its simple and absolute nature—free from every limitation and beyond them all.

At once we get the paradox that a passage which denies that anything can be said about God uses expressions like "next to," "cause" and "perfect" in speaking of God. The theist both denies that anything adequate can be said about God and yet says a great deal. And in what he says positively we get the core of his religion. He worships and praises God not just because of what God is (or rather is not) but because of what God has done. "We love him because he first loved us." To give a merely phenomenological account of religious attitudes is to miss religion. For the crux of Hebraic religion at least is an attempt to say that a God who is wholly "out of" the world nevertheless acts "in" it.

Yet even although God is believed to act in the world, the worshipper remains systematically reticent about him. This reticence is so fundamental that we must look at the language of worship in somewhat more detail.

In worship we do not talk about God, but to him. We are apt to envisage the relation between religious belief and worship in terms of an intellectualist conception of theory as prior to and directive of practice. Prof. Ryle has shown us how this conception is in general mistaken. Knowing how to perform particular operations does not depend on knowing that particular theoretical principles are to be applied. Similarly we are wrong to conceive of religious practice as the application of religious doctrine. It is not just that as a matter of historical fact the practice of worship precedes the explicit formulation of belief, but that we can worship without being able to say clearly what we believe—Beatrice Webb said her prayers in this way for many years—and that one of the theistic criteria in formulating belief is conformity with the practices and expressions of what are judged to be adequate forms of worship. "The Catholic faith is this, That we worship . . ." not that we believe. In formulating doctrine we are trying to say what we do when we pray. So the language of liturgy is at the heart of the matter.

That this is so may help to bring out why in theism the tradition of negative theology is so insistently reticent about the object of worship. For the language of worship is itself systematically unclear and reticent about the object of worship. There are five characteristic features of such language which co-operate in producing this effect. First, there is the simple fact already noticed that so much of it is vocative. When you speak to someone it is not normally in place to say very much about them. In petitioning God and thanking him we ascribe to him certain power, but the epithets we bestow on him are rarely descriptive and even more rarely precise in their description. This brings us to the second point. A great many of the epithets that we bestow on God are either gerundive or hover uneasily between the gerundive and the descriptive. "Great" and "holy" are obvious examples. "Great art Thou, O God, and greatly to be praised" is the typical utterance here. Third, we habitually in worship use metaphors which express either what we hope from God or our praise of him, rather than what we suppose him to be like: "my rock and my fortress" or "light of light." Fourth, we suggest rather than state the greatness of God by avowing our devotion and by using metaphors which refer not to God at all but to ourselves as worshippers. "Behold I have taken upon me to speak unto the Lord, who am but dust and ashes" is the latter; "We praise Thee, we bless Thee, we worship Thee, we glorify Thee" is the former. And lastly one of the ways of indicating how a particular expression is to be used, one of the ways of making an expression precise, is to say in what kind of situation it may appropriately be used, in what kind of situation it is out of place. But the theist will not allow that there is any situation in which worship is fundamentally inappropriate. Thus there is throughout the language of worship a necessary imprecision about the object of worship. In worship we are concerned with praising God, not with describing him. But of course in worship some assertions are made about God. Of the "divine dark" worshipped in negative theology we say at least that it is dark and that it is divine. As part of theistic worship it is common for liturgical recitals of what God has said and done to have a place. How are we to characterize such assertions?

The first thing to note about them is that they do not occur as individual and isolated propositions each of which raises a separate issue of acceptance or rejection. They always occur as part of a total narration, in which a dramatic wholeness of vision is presented. So in order to understand religious assertions we must attempt to characterize such narrations.

They are commonly denominated myths, and this is the word I propose to use, stressing however that the adoption of the word carries no implication as to the truth-value of these accounts. The first point to be made about myths is the Aristotelian one that they have a beginning, a middle and an end. They are stories, that is, with a plot and a culmination. God figures in them as the predominating character. They may be long or short, refer to many events or to few. As to subject-matter they fall into two classes—those which deal with ostensible happenings outside the history of the human race, such as the creation of the world or the fall of the angels; and those which deal with human happenings, such as the sagas of Abraham and David. How do we understand myths? Exactly as we understand, for example, novels. Every form of utterance that can be used in ordinary discourse may appear in a novel, but, as it were, bracketed. And a great deal of narration may appear in a novel which is ordinary factual narration, about the Jacobites in *Waverley,* for example. But the novel is a total imaginative account, just as the myth is. What makes a novel a novel and not a history is that there occur in them names which are not the names of real people, and the names figure in both the subjects and the predicates of factual assertions. Not that there arises no difficulty about the verifiability of these assertions. We know what it is for Waverley to fall in love, because we know what it is for anyone to fall in love. In myths there occur ordinary factual assertions, about David and Abraham, for example. But it is said in myths that certain things that were done were done by God. How can we construe assertions of this kind? By considering what it would be for these sorts of things to be done by anyone. "God" occurs in myths as the name of an unknown. And it is a logical characteristic of proper names that they can be intelligibly used without our being able to substitute for them a description of what or whom they refer to.[1] We might note at this point that within the Hebrew tradition the word "god" is used in two ways. Sometimes it is used as a description equivalent to "the divine" and in this sense it sometimes means "what is worshipped" and sometimes "what is worthy of worship." But it is also used as a name: so it can be said of God (name) that he is "a great king above all gods" (description). But since the description characterizes by referring to the attitudes of believers, neither name nor description trespass on the reticence of worshipper and negative theologian, even although they figure in positive assertions.

Now a new issue arises. We have spoken of the acceptance or rejection of myths. But with imaginative literature, which is the *genus* in which we have so far placed myths, no such issue arises. Or rather in so far as, for example, an aesthetic issue arises, it is quite different in kind from the issue that is raised by myth, in so far as the myth has religious significance.

The crucial point about myth in a religious sense is that it is concerned with the central situations in human life. Love and death, pain and grief, mar-

---

[1] Discussion of the logical status of proper names has of course been widespread ever since Russell's Theory of Descriptions. And what I say in passing here must appear as an unwarranted *obiter dictum.* But to those acquainted with the philosophical discussions I would only plead that a proper discussion of this topic would have been impossible within the limits of this essay. Those unacquainted with them are referred to the discussion of naming in Bernard Mayo's *The Logic of Personality,* Cape, London, 1952.

riage and birth are as important to myth as they are to poetry—and the connection, of course, is not accidental. Any given myth incorporates an attitude to these themes and to accept a myth is to identify oneself with that attitude and so to make the myth directive of one's behaviour. To accept a sufficiently comprehensive myth is to accept a whole way of living. To talk like this is to lay oneself open to misunderstanding. For one might be taken to mean that a myth provides us with a rule or a code of rules, and if this were so once we had extracted the rules from the myth surely the myth itself might be dispensed with except perhaps as providing an imaginative stimulus to the moral life. So lives of the great capitalists might be used to inculcate the maxim "Cultivate thrift and study the stock market." But myths are in fact directive of the moral life just at those points where rules become no longer relevant. At times of social crisis, at ordinary times when some novel situation arises there may be no rule to tell us what rules are applicable. At times of personal crisis such as bereavement the question of how we are to face this particular death may be obviously unamenable to formulable rules: for the question is how to take death seriously. Rules may always be the subject of revaluation, as in *Crime and Punishment* both Raskolnikov and Sonia reflectively decide to break, the former with the prohibition of murder, the latter with the prohibition of prostitution. But the one is a criminal and the other a saint because of the attitudes manifested in their rule-breaking. Someone might argue that Dostoievsky is representing Sonia as conforming to the fundamental rule to seek the good of others rather than one's own. But, as Plato continually points out, this rule can have as many meanings as there are conceptions of good. Time and again we have to take up attitudes, make decisions and so on where there is no clear rule and sometimes no rule at all. And these are the situations where moral problems are most urgent. For where there is a clear rule there is no problem. And where there is no problem there is no growth for the moral agent. We are morally made and unmade in those decisions where there is no rule to make the decision for us. It is a question then of fundamental attitudes to the human and nonhuman worlds, of those attitudes which receive their definition and their illumination in myths. In this sense of course Dostoievsky is as mythological a writer as the author of Job. A myth offers us a picture, offers us a story: to say that we cannot replace the picture or story by rules is merely one consequence of the vital truism that if you attempt to translate a myth, it ceases to be a myth.

To speak of myths as directive of behaviour is not to speak of anything strange or esoteric. Generations of English nonconformists found the shape of the moral life not in any set of commandments, but in *The Pilgrim's Progess*. At the close of that work Bunyan provides a myth about death. He does not offer us a prediction in picturesque guise about an afterlife; it would be equally irrelevant to try and provide evidence for or evidence against what Bunyan says. But in accepting or rejecting what Bunyan says—and to say "This is 'literature' and I can accept it in an aesthetic fashion without raising any other kind of issue" is one way of rejecting it—we accept or reject a whole way of living. For we accept or reject a role, the role perhaps of Christian or of Christiana, which the myth offers to us. *De te fabula narratur.* And a character of this sort is always represented in myth more schematically than would be possible in a novel because here a role is presented which is the role of all sorts and conditions of men.

All this, however, it may be said, leaves the fundamental issue unraised. For it would be possible to make myths directive of one's behaviour without believing that they told one anything about the universe. But the religious believer commits himself in his use of myth to the view that these stories are in some way or other stories about a real being, God, acting in the world that we are acquainted with in ordinary experience. This particular use of myth stands therefore in need of justification, and the need is accentuated by the content of, for instance, the Hebrew-Christian stories. For they include what the myth alleges to be true statements about real people; so that the myth includes factual assertions. It also includes, for example, moral prescriptions. To accept these stories is to commit oneself at once to such various beliefs as that certain statements make up a piece of accurate history (the Gospels, for example), that a certain moral standpoint is valid (the Ten Commandments or the Sermon on the Mount), that certain parts of the story which cannot be construed literally nonetheless have application and are to be received as valid accounts (the Creation narrative) and so on. And all these are to be accepted together bound in a coherent framework of dramatic narrative. Not only however is it specified that all this shall be accepted; even the mode of acceptance is characterized.

The mode in which a set of religious beliefs has to be accepted is characterized partly by the very form of belief, partly by the content of belief. The form of belief itself imposes two requirements on the acceptance of belief. The content of Hebrew-Christian belief imposes two further requirements. First, if it is to be a belief of the kind we have characterized there must be some single cardinal point in terms of which the acceptance or rejection of the whole can be envisaged. Second the acceptance must be of a kind compatible with the practice of worship. Thus it cannot be in any sense a conditional or provisional acceptance, for this would perhaps make it possible to say "O God, if there is a God, save my soul, if I have one"; but it would not make it possible to worship in the sense already described. Third, the acceptance must be, if it is what the Christian or Hebrew tradition says that is accepted, a matter of free decision. Fourth, the acceptance must be one that can offer some justification of what appears *prima facie* to be nonsense, for example, the giving of imaginative accounts of the creation as in some sense genuine, valid or true accounts.

So the issue of justification is raised. How is religious belief justified, if it is the kind of thing that has been described and if it entails the kind of acceptance that is thus characterized?

THE JUSTIFICATION OF THE
RELIGIOUS ATTITUDE

We can rule out at the start one method of justifying religious belief which has traditionally dominated a great deal of the philosophy of religion. This is the method which disregards the rootedness of religious beliefs in the attitude of worship and attempts to exhibit religious beliefs as explanations of why there is a universe and why the universe is as it is. In other words religious belief is presented as having the logical status of an explanatory hypothesis. What is mistaken in this conception?

The first thing to note is that if it were correct no religious belief would in fact be justified. It does not follow from this that religious beliefs are not hypotheses: but at least if they are they are very bad ones. It is the great merit of Hume's *Dialogues on Natural Religion* to have made this point once and for all. To attempt to account for the nature of the universe, for traces of apparent design, for instance, by inferring an infinite being who designed it is both to make an unwarranted inference and to explain nothing. The inference would be unwarranted in any argument that sought to pass from premises about the universe to a conclusion that there was a God of a certain kind. For either the inference would pose as strict deduction or it would be part of a theoretical explanation. If it were a deduction that was offered, the conclusion would have to be implicit in the premises. We should already have assumed what we sought to infer. For all deductive arguments are circular: they merely make explicit consequences of what has already been said. But *ex hypothesi* premises about the universe would contain no reference, explicit or implicit, to God. Hence they could not validly entail any conclusion about God. Suppose, however, instead that we presented the concept of deity as part of a theoretical explanation. Such a concept would then be justifiable if it were theoretically fruitful, as for example the concept of an electron is. A moment's recollection, however, of the fate of the argument from design at Hume's hands will show us how impossible it is to take up this kind of position. For the traditional argument from design, from Aquinas to Paley or even to Tennant, is precisely an attempt to offer the existence of God as a theoretical hypothesis to explain the order and harmony of the universe. But, as Hume points out, the design in the world, if any, is so multifarious, as indeed is the lack of design and harmony, that a great many rival hypotheses might well be entertained in regard to it with an equal amount of probability. Hume for instance suggests that we might account for the world's imperfections by arguing that it is an early botched attempt at world-making; or that we might account for its order by analogy not with mind, but with the structure of vegetables and suppose the universe a vast vegetable. But where there are possible a number of hypotheses between which there can be no way of deciding we are not in fact dealing with genuine hypotheses. The essence of a genuine hypothesis is that it should suggest observations or experiments which will enable us to decide whether a particular phenomenon is to be explained in one way rather than another. Where the phenomenon in question is the universe there are no observations or experiments to be made over and above those observations which suggest the hypothesis. And these as we have seen can suggest many hypotheses. Which, for the reasons stated, is as good as saying that in this kind of matter there can be no hypotheses.

Thus, if religious beliefs are explanatory hypotheses, there can be no justification whatever for continuing to hold them. But in fact to treat religious beliefs as such is to falsify both the kind of belief they are and the way in which they are characteristically held. To begin with the latter: if religious belief was the kind of thing that could be presented as the conclusion of an argument, we should either have too much certitude or too little for the belief in question to be a religious belief. For if we could produce logically cogent arguments we should produce the kind of certitude that leaves no room for decision; where proof is in place, decision is not. We do not decide to accept Euclid's conclusions; we merely look to the rigour of his arguments. If the existence of God were demonstrable we should be as bereft of the possibility of making a free decision to love God as we should be if every utterance of doubt or unbelief was answered by thunder-bolts from heaven. But this kind of free decision is the essence of the Christian religion. So that to argue for religious belief in this way would be to destroy it. Hume's discovery of the fallacies in such arguments is an essential contribution to theology. So too is his demolishing of the view that belief in God is a hypothesis. For if it were, we should have to hold our beliefs as we hold hypotheses, in a provisional and tentative way. This we noted earlier was alien to the whole spirit of religious belief. Having made our decision, we adhere to belief unconditionally, we commit ourselves as completely as one can ever commit oneself to anything.

Not only, however, does the conception of religious beliefs as hypotheses lead us to misdescribe the religious attitude. It leads us also to misdescribe the content of religious belief. For the climax of all such argument as we have considered has traditionally been to establish "the existence of God." This concept of God's existence seems to me highly misleading. But in order to see exactly why it is misleading we must turn to consider how in fact religious beliefs are justified.

Here we must first recall what we have already noted that there are such things as religions. There may be no shared content in the great religions, but each has its own procedure for deciding whether a given belief or practice is or is not authentic. Each has a criterion by means of which orthodoxy is determined. And in this sense a belief is justified in a particular religion by referring to that rule by means of which it is determined what is and what is not included in the religion.

Such a rule is strictly analogous to the rule by means of which sovereignty is defined in a political society. Political philosophers in posing the question "What is sovereignty?" have usually attempted to answer this question by naming the person or body in whom sovereignty is to be said to reside. But essentially where sovereignty resides in my society is always determined by reference to the rule or rules which state what is to count as law. The rule in Great Britain, for example, is roughly, "What the Queen in Parliament says is law." Such rules, by means of which the sovereign power is defined, are not of course themselves utterances of the Sovereign power. Because they are the ultimate criterion of law, they have no logical justification outside themselves. If Parliament passed an act asserting that what the Queen in Parliament said was law this would do nothing to give the rule of sovereignty more validity than it already possesses. What we mean by an ultimate criterion is precisely that rule which lies at the base of any argument over what the law is, that rule therefore beyond which we cannot go. So it is with the defining rule or rules of a religion. "The Bible and the Bible only is the religion of Protestants," "What the Pope defines *ex cathedra* on matters of faith and morals are dogmas which one is obliged to believe" are examples of such rules. By means of them theologians determine what are and what are not valid doctrines and authentic liturgical practices. As the rule of sovereignty may leave considerable scope for lawyers to disagree, so a rule defining where authority is to be found in a religious society may leave plenty of scope for theologians to disagree. Again, the rule being an ultimate criterion is not to be justified by referring to who has uttered it; that the Bible says that the Bible is authoritative, that the Pope defines his own infallibility *de fide et moribus* are in no sense justifications for accepting the Bible or the Pope as authoritative. That there should be this analogy between political sovereignty and religious authority is not of course accidental. For all political societies were once in a sense religious societies and one has only to read Dante to see the theological background to all discussions of sovereignty. And a political philosopher like Hobbes could be just as aptly labelled a political theologian, more aptly if one considers the tracts of biblical exegesis in *Leviathan.*

Every religion therefore is defined by reference to what it accepts as an authoritative criterion in religious matters. The acceptance or rejection of a religion is thus the acceptance or rejection of such an authority. But now it might be said that one cannot accept on authority what is inherently non-sensical; if someone asserts "Twas brillig and the slithy toves did gyre" and when asked what this means replies that it must be accepted on authority, none of our difficulties have been removed. What puzzles us for example in the acceptance or rejection of the creation narrative, remains as puzzling as ever when we are told that it is accepted because it is allowed in by the fundamental canonical criteria of the Hebrew-Christian tradition.

If someone claimed to be able to tell us which myths and cosmological pictures we must accept; and to be able furthermore to assure us that although we could not know how it was possible for these to represent a true account of these matters nonetheless we could be certain that they did; how could we accept his claims? Only presumably if we accepted all that he said not because of what he said but because it was he that said it. If the authoritative criterion was uttered by someone who was accepted as completely authoritative we should be able to explain how we came to accept a religion as a whole. But what sort of person would this have to be? It would have to be someone who was given complete authority and, that is to say, who was worshipped. We would have to be able to say before him, "My lord and my God." If we were theists believing that God is more than an object in the world, we could only find an authority for theism in one who both accepted allegiance to himself as divine and who declared by his authority that there was more to the divine than himself; who could say both that "He that hath seen me hath seen the Father" and that "The Father is greater than I."

If someone alleges that this is not even a disguised account of the Christian doctrine of the Incarnation, it must be said that this is just to show how essentially this doctrine is bound up with the whole conceptual scheme of Christian theism. And from the logician's point of view the criteria employed in the Christian religion can now be exhibited in a clear schematism. What we say about God we understand in the familiar pictorial senses: we do not derive it from evidence, we recognize that the facts of nature and history do not provide any ground for what we say, yet we say it. Our ground for saying it is that we have the authority of Jesus Christ for saying it: our ground for accepting what he says is what the apostles say about him; our ground for accepting the apostles? Here the argument ends or becomes circular; we either find an ultimate criterion of religious authority, or we refer to the content of what authority says.

Is not all this, it may be protested, so schematic as to miss everything that makes religious belief important to the believer? Certainly, for what makes religion important is its content; whereas what we have been concerned with is the sense in which religious belief might be referred to criteria of meaning and validity, and this is necessarily to exhibit a set of more or less schematic relationships.

At the heart of Christianity we find the concept of authority. But to say this is not to say anything about what is laid down by authority, about the content of religion. We have indeed referred to authority in two senses.[2] In one sense as we have seen the existence of an authoritative rule or set of rules is a necessary condition of there being a determinate religion. And if we supplement reference to such a rule by saying that a religion is always concerned with how men are to live and with what their fundamental attitudes are to be,

---

[2] What I say about authority is liable to misinterpretation in that I may be taken to be smuggling in a theological doctrine under the cover of a logical analysis. I am not here asserting in any way the theological doctrine that a clearly defined authority, such as is notably found in the Church of Rome and is equally notably lacking in the Church of England, is necessary to an effective religion. I am merely asserting that in religious practice there are methods of determining which religious utterances are authentic. These methods operate by referring to criteria. The criteria are thus treated as authoritative. But nothing that I say precludes an appeal to personal religious experience being counted as an appeal to just such a criterion. The rule "What I came to feel (or see or hear) on such and such an occasion is what I judge theological utterance by" is a common enough criterion. Where one is concerned with the origin of a religious tradition (George Fox, Martin Luther or St. Paul) such an appeal to experience is inevitable. For from the original

we produce as near a satisfactory definition of religion as we are likely to get. For by saying that religion is to be thus formally defined without reference to its content we allow for both theism and polytheism, religions of one God like Islam and of no God like primitive Buddhism, all being counted as religions. Whereas any definition in terms of subject-matter and content would be bound to do violence to ordinary usage by ruling out some religion or other. In the second sense of authority, we refer to a person, not to a rule, and to the authoritative witness to that person by others, in this case to Christ by the church. So, if we wish to expand our elucidation of religious belief in the Christian tradition, it must run something as follows.

When a statement about what God has done or said is made it is to be construed, as has been remarked above, in a familiar pictorial sense. So it is when we say "God creates," "God loves" and so on. Part of the meaning of such statements is given ostensively in the Gospel narrative. So we mean by "the love of God" what we see in the Passion narrative. We do not offer evidence for these statements, we offer authority for them. We point to the state of the world as illustrative of doctrine, but never as evidence for it. So Belsen illustrates a world of original sin, but original sin is not a hypothesis to account for happenings like Belsen. We justify a particular religious belief by showing its place in the total religious conception; we justify a religious belief as a whole by referring to authority. We accept authority because we discover some point in the world at which we worship, at which we accept the lordship of something not ourselves. We do not worship authority; but we accept authority as defining the worshipful. So someone may discover the possibility of worship in the life of the Reformed churches and accept the Bible as authoritative; or in the Roman church and accept Papal authority.

It is noteworthy that in our account of religion we have nowhere found a place for a point at which a transition can be made from nonreligious to religious language. One can accept religion in its own terms or reject it; there is no way of justifying it by translating it into other terms. This is the logical correlative of Barthianism in theology. Religion is justified only by referring to a religious acceptance of authority. And this means, if you like, that religion as a whole lacks any justification. But this in no way reflects on the logical standing of religious beliefs. Of science and morals it can also be said that one can justify particular theories or prescriptions, but that one cannot justify

experience the tradition which supplies criteria to later believers is itself defined. I am not of course asserting that those who have pre-eminent religious experiences infer their beliefs from their experiences. If they did their inferences would be invalid (see my paper "Visions" in *New Essays in Philosophical Theology* [Macmillan, N. Y.]). The relationship between experience and subsequent belief and behaviour is a nonlogical one, resembling the relation between an imperative and obedience to it. So it is characteristic of such experiences, whether through feelings, visions or voices, to present imperatives. And the characteristic religious response is "Lord, here am I. Send me." What is learnt by the original experience may be used to discriminate between subsequent experiences, some being rejected as nongenuine because discordant with the original. But it is always open to a man to make his own experience his authority and so become the founder of his own religion.

science as a whole in nonscientific, or morals as a whole in nonmoral, terms. Every field is defined by reference to certain ultimate criteria. That they are ultimate precludes going beyond them.

One concept in particular has been abused in an attempt to justify religion. It is that which appears as the climax of all speculative argument, such as Hume refuted, namely "the existence of God." But this concept of divine existence is of a highly dubious character. Our concept of existence is inexorably linked to our talk about spatio-temporal objects. Even the insight of Frege and Russell that to say that something exists is to say nothing whatsoever about its characteristics presupposes a type of distinction that is appropriately made about objects. So is the mediaeval distinction of essence and existence, the distinction between saying what something is and that it is. When the scholastics came to speak of God they declared that in him essence and existence are not distinct; it would have been clearer to say that the whole concept of existence is inapplicable to God. Prof. J. N. Findlay has argued that because God cannot be thought of both as an adequate object of worship and as *a* particular and therefore limited being we must deny that God exists.[3] Only objects exist and God is not an object. Anselm argued that because God must be conceived of as an adequate object of worship he must be denied nothing and therefore not be denied existence. Put Findlay and Anselm together and we find the one saying that God cannot be said to exist, the other saying that God cannot be said not to exist. The kind of deductive proof that they offer, the kind of proof, that is, which is concerned with the relationship of concepts, only serves to make it clear that the outcome of their arguments is not that God does or does not in fact exist, but that the concepts of existence or nonexistence are equally inapplicable to God. To elucidate the notion of God we have already seen that any nonreligious concept is inappropriate. And to elucidate it *via* the concept of God's existence is to attempt to elucidate it in just such a way. What is wrong with this concept? First, that it suggests that God is a super-object. And second that for anyone who believed, the assertion of God's existence would be as superfluous as would be the assertion of his beloved's existence by a lover; and for anyone who did not believe the concept could make no sense. Either one speaks from within religious language, as it were: in which case "God exists" would be a pointless expression; or one speaks from outside: in which case "God exists" has no determinate meaning. As Kierkegaard puts it: "God does not think, He creates: God does not exist, He is eternal." [4] For a God who existed would not be more than an object; and where an object is concerned one cannot choose to believe or to withhold belief. But with God the necessity of decision is ineluctable and central. This brings us back to the question of the mode of religious belief.

To believe in God resembles not so much believing that something is the case as being engrossed by a passion: Kierkegaard compares the believer to a

---

[3] In "Can God's Existence be Disproved?" reprinted in *New Essays in Philosophical Theology.*

[4] *Concluding Unscientific Postscript,* tr. by Swenson and Lowrie (OUP 1941).

madman; he might equally have compared him to a lover. Those characteristics of the language of worship which we noticed earlier, its tendency to reticence about the object, its highly metaphorical character, its reference to the plight of the worshipper, all these find their parallels in the poetry of love. The inability of the believer to adopt an abstract, neutral, speculative attitude to his belief resembles the lover's lack of objectivity. There is the same total engagement. But if we compare belief to love it must be not so much to romantic love as to that married love which Kierkegaard distinguishes from romantic love by referring to the resolution and decision that underlie it. To characterize that resolution he has to use religious terms and speak of the eternal; and so we find that our analogy has brought us round full circle. Nevertheless both lover and believer commit themselves and both can only say in part to what they commit themselves.

An activity like worship—or love for that matter—is obviously incapable of justification. The appeal to authority is here at the heart of the matter. Critics of religion like Nietzsche, who have attacked religion because it involves an attitude of obedience and humility to authority, have seen far more clearly the nature of what they were attacking than those who have condemned religious belief for illegitimate speculative conclusions.

Finally we must note that all this does not mean that outside the, so to speak, official religions, experiences of awe, intimations of immortality and the like may not occur. Of course they may, but they only form a path to religious belief in the full sense when they lead to an acceptance of authority. If someone asks what religion is or more particularly what the Christian religion is, the only proper answer is to say: "Read the Bible." If a man then asks how he is to accept this, the only possible answer is that he must accept either the Bible itself as authoritative or some other authority such as that of the Church which refers him to the Bible. But of course what will be crucial for his decision will be the content of what he reads. The only apologia for a religion is to describe its content in detail: and then either a man will find himself brought to say "My Lord and my God" or he will not.

Questions

1. What are the two elements which Mr. MacIntyre finds in theistic religious belief? Give an account of the tension between these elements.

2. Name and illustrate the characteristic features of the language of worship which Mr. MacIntyre notices.

3. Why does Mr. MacIntyre say that assertions about God occur in the context of myths? What is his account of the way in which we understand myths? How are myths directive of behavior? To what view of religious myths does a religious believer's use of these myths commit him? Would you say that such a view of myths contradicts the meaning of the word "myth"? Why or why not?

4. How does Mr. MacIntyre characterize the mode in which a set of religious beliefs has to be accepted?

5. What are Mr. MacIntyre's reasons for attacking the view that religious beliefs are explanatory hypotheses?

6. What is Mr. MacIntyre's account of the way in which religious beliefs are justified? What is the nature of a religious authority's authoritativeness? How does a religious authority resemble (or differ from) authorities in other areas of life?

7. Mr. MacIntyre promises to "attempt to say to what kind of belief the taking up of a religious attitude seems to commit one." Support or criticize the view that Mr. MacIntyre does not show *what* one must believe, but rather *how* one holds one's beliefs, if one is religious.

8. What is the point of Mr. MacIntyre's saying, "One can accept religion in its own terms or reject it; there is no way of justifying it by translating it into other terms"? (See page 411.) Do Locke (page 312) and Aquinas (page 328) agree (or disagree) with the views expressed by Mr. MacIntyre? If there is disagreement, how does one decide who has the better case?

9. Is it Mr. MacIntyre's position that one cannot be a Christian believer unless one accepts a religious authority? Why or why not?

10. Does Mr. MacIntyre's account of religious belief make it possible (or impossible) to ask why one should believe? Explain your answer. If it is possible to ask why one should believe, does Mr. MacIntyre offer an answer?

11. Comment on the following remarks:

"If one accepts Mr. MacIntyre's account of the justification of religious beliefs, it is impossible to do two things. It is impossible to give a reason for accepting one religion rather than another, and it is impossible, within a given religion, to offer a reason for accepting one religious belief rather than another. Hence, Mr. MacIntyre has shown both that no reasonable person can be religious and that no religious person can be reasonable."

Suggested Further Reading | Classic Works

Creed, John Martin, and John Sandwith Boys Smith, eds., *Religious Thought in the Eighteenth Century, Illustrated from Writers of the Period,* Cambridge University Press, Cambridge, Eng., 1935.

Dewey, John, *A Common Faith,* Yale University Press, New Haven, 1935.

Dods, Marcus, ed., *The Works of Aurelius Augustine,* Vol. 9, *On Christian Doctrine; The Enchiridion; On Catechising, and On Faith and the Creed,* T. & T. Clark, Edinburgh, 1892.

Gladstone, W. E., ed., *The Works of Joseph Butler,* Vol. 1, *The Analogy of Religion, Natural and Revealed, to the Constitution and Course of Nature,* Oxford University Press, N. Y., 1897.

James, William, *The Varieties of Religious Experience,* many publishers, many editions. (The Gifford Lectures on Natural Religion, delivered at Edinburgh in 1901-1902.)

Kant, Immanuel, *Religion within the Limits of Reason,* many publishers, many editions.

Mill, John Stuart, *Three Essays on Religion: Nature, The Utility of Religion, and Theism,* many publishers, many editions.

Paine, Thomas, *The Age of Reason, Being an Investigation of True and Fabulous Theology,* many publishers, many editions.

Paley, William, *Natural Theology: or, Evidences of the Existence and Attributes of the Deity, Collected from the Appearances of Nature,* many publishers, many editions.

| *Recent Studies*

Barth, Karl, *The Word of God and the Word of Man,* Harper, N. Y., 1957.

Copleston, F. C., *Aquinas,* Penguin Books, Harmondsworth, Middlesex, Eng., 1955.

Flew, Antony, and Alasdair MacIntyre, eds., *New Essays in Philosophical Theology,* Macmillan, N. Y., 1955.

Hick, John, *Faith and Knowledge,* Cornell University Press, Ithaca, 1957.

Kaufmann, Walter, *Critique of Religion and Philosophy,* Harper, N. Y., 1958.

Kimpel, Ben F., *Language and Religion,* Philosophical Library, N. Y., 1957.

Mitchell, Basil, ed., *Faith and Logic,* Allen and Unwin, London, 1957.

Stace, Walter Terence, *Religion and the Modern Mind,* Lippincott, Phila., 1952.

——, *Time and Eternity, An Essay in the Philosophy of Religion,* Princeton University Press, Princeton, 1952.

Tillich, Paul, *Systematic Theology,* University of Chicago Press, Chicago, 1951-1957.

Wisdom, John, "Gods," *Proceedings of the Aristotelian Society,* 1944. Reprinted in *Philosophy and Psycho-Analysis,* by John Wisdom, Blackwell, Oxford, 1957; and in *Logic and Language, First Series,* ed. by Antony Flew, Blackwell, Oxford, 1951.

Chapter Five

THE
PROBLEM
OF

Freedom of the Will

Freedom of Choice and Moral Responsibility

When we examine the grounds of our moral judgments about a person's actions, we find two beliefs always present: (1) the belief that a certain moral standard is applicable to the actions we judge, and (2) the belief that the person acted of his own free will. Our moral judgments rest on good grounds only if, first, we can justify the moral standard which we apply in making our judgments, and second, we can show that the person whom we judge actually did act of his own free will.

The problem of justifying a moral standard we have called "the problem of moral knowledge," and Chapter 6 of this book is devoted to that problem. The problem of showing that a person acted of his own free will and can therefore be held responsible for what he did is the problem of freedom of the will. In order to see what is involved in the belief that a person must act from his own free will if he is to be held responsible for what he does, let us consider the actual conditions which must be satisfied when we hold a person responsible (or when a person holds himself responsible).

Suppose we were told that a person sitting alone on a beach did nothing to help someone who was drowning just off shore. We would certainly condemn the person on moral grounds. But if we then were informed that he was physically disabled and could neither walk nor swim, we would immediately withdraw our moral condemnation. Or, in a second kind of situation, suppose we were told that a person in wartime disclosed military secrets to the enemy. If we then learned that he had betrayed his country only after he was tortured for a number of days, we would excuse his action and would not blame him for what he did. Or, to take a third kind of case, suppose we learned that a man who committed a murder had a form of insanity of such a nature that he was driven by an overwhelming inner compulsion which no amount of will power could control. We would then be doubtful about holding him responsible as a moral agent, and many of us would say that we should not condemn him at all. We retract our moral judgment in the first example because the person we are judging *lacked the ability* to do the right thing in the situation, in the second example because the person was *compelled by an external force or constraint* to do the wrong thing, in the third example because the person was *compelled by an internal force or constraint* to do the wrong thing.

When a person could not have done anything but what he did do, we say that he had no freedom of choice. By this we mean that although the person might have known of alternative actions to the one he finally did, these were not real alternatives either because the person lacked the ability to do them or because he was coerced by an external or internal force to do the act he finally did. In common speech we say of such situations that the person "had no alternative" or "could not have done otherwise." By reflecting on our examples it can now be seen that when a person has no freedom of choice we do not feel justified in doing any of the following things: (1) to praise or blame the person for what he did, (2) to reward or punish him for what he did, (3) to say that he ought to feel pride or guilt about what he did, or (4) to hold him responsible for what he did. We may sum up this argument in the statement: Freedom of choice is a necessary condition for moral responsibility.

Freedom of Choice and the Causes of Choice

A thoughtful person may now raise the question whether it is only freedom of choice which is necessary for moral responsibility. Is there not some further requirement, especially in light of the fact that there are *causes* for a person's choice?

We have seen that a person has freedom of choice when he has the ability to do other acts than the one he chooses to do and he is not under external or internal constraint. We might describe such a situation by saying that the person's act followed from his own free choice. But what made him choose the way he did? If we explain his choice by saying that it resulted from his being the kind of person he was, we might then seek an explanation of why he was that kind of person. An adequate explanation could only be found in a psychological study of his personality development. Such a study would point to certain factors in the person's heredity and environment, especially in the environment of his infancy and early childhood. It would show that there were many causes operating on the person which shaped his personality in such a way that, in the circumstances of a particular situation of choice, the person would be likely to choose to do one kind of act rather than another.

Now the advances being made in psy-chology and its related sciences seem to be giving greater and greater support to the assumption that if we knew *all* the causal factors in one's personality development, and if we knew *all* the circumstances in a situation of choice, we could know exactly how one would choose. And this would hold even in cases where one had freedom of choice as defined above. It is then that the question arises in our minds: Are we really justified in holding a person morally responsible for what he does, even when he has freedom of choice? For if we knew everything about the person's past we would see that he had to become just the kind of person he did become, and given the fact that he was that kind of person at the moment of choice, then we would see that his choice necessarily followed from his being that kind of person. It was, we might say, the only choice that kind of person could have made in the circumstances.

The consequences sometimes drawn from this line of thought are as follows. Granted the person at the moment of choice is able to do any of a number of alternative actions confronting him, and granted that he is not being forced by anyone nor is being constrained by any compulsive desire, nevertheless, he is not really free. His belief that he has a free choice among open possibilities is an illusion because, being the kind of person he is, he cannot choose otherwise than as he finally does choose. Therefore (the conclusion is then drawn) he cannot be held responsible for what he does.

Whether it is legitimate to draw this conclusion is one of the chief questions which constitute the problem of freedom of the will. There is no doubt that people sometimes do draw such a conclusion, and although they might be making a mistake in doing so, it is up to a thinking person to show whether a mistake actually is made and if so, where it lies.

A number of different positions have been taken with regard to the foregoing argument. We shall distinguish three, as representing the sharpest divergence of opinion on the matter. Whether there are possible intermediate positions or combinations among them are points left open for the reader to decide when he reads the selections included in this chapter. There is no agreement among philosophers as to what to call these three views, but perhaps the least misleading names are "mechanistic determinism," "indeterminism," and "nonmechanistic determinism."

MECHANISTIC DETERMINISM. From the point of view of the first position, the argument presented above is perfectly valid. The conclusion does follow from the premises, it is held, because we must accept the principle of determinism, specifically, a mechanistic principle of determinism. The principle of determinism is that everything that happens has a cause. Those who take this first point of view have a mechanistic conception of determinism, according to which the world is a vast machine in which everything that happens is due to the movement of various parts of the machine, these parts being moved by the movement of other parts, and so on. Just as material objects must behave exactly as they do because they are moved by physical forces which completely determine their movement, so human beings must behave just as they do because they are integral parts of the same mechanical universe. Our bodies are material objects which operate strictly in accordance with the laws of physics and chemistry. Our thoughts, our feelings, our "wills" are simply the result of certain physical processes taking place in our nervous systems, the nervous system being necessitated to react by the physical stimuli which impinge upon it.

The whole universe is thus seen as a closed system of causes and effects in which the causes compel the effects to follow. What will happen in the future will happen inevitably as the necessary consequence of what is happening now, and what is happening now must happen that way as the inevitable consequence of what has happened in the past. The future is not open to different possibilities among which we can choose to realize some and not others, since whatever possibilities we do choose to realize were already determined to be the real events of the future by the past causes operating on our choice. Though our choice may not in a given situation be compelled by an external or internal constraint, it is always compelled by causes beyond our control (namely, our heredity and past environment). It follows that a person cannot justifiably be blamed for his act, or be punished for it, or feel guilty about it, or be held responsible for it, since it was the only act he could have done in the circumstances.

INDETERMINISM. The second point of view, which we shall call "indeterminism," upholds man's moral responsibility by denying the principle of determinism. There are two ways in which this has been argued. The first is by asserting that man has a soul as well as a body, and that a person's act of will at the moment of choice is a function of his soul, not his body. This may be called the religious argument for indeterminism, since it is believed that God has created the soul and endowed it with the freedom to choose between good and evil. This God-given freedom means that the soul is not subject to the laws of personality development. The soul is a spiritual (nonmaterial) entity which is not discoverable by empirical observation and does not depend on the body for its existence. By means of an act of will the soul can move the body and so bring about changes in the physical world. This point of view denies determinism because it holds that a person's heredity and environment do not completely determine his actions and choices. A person's heredity and environment may mold his general character, but within the limits of that character his will is free to choose among alternatives confronting him. And this means that at the moment of choice his will is at least partly free from the causes which have operated upon him up to that moment. The fact that man has the capacity to break into the causal chain of events and initiate changes in the physical world implies that the physical world is not a closed system. The future is open to whatever possibilities are realizable through human choices and actions.

The moral implications which the religious indeterminist draws are as follows. Since each person's choices are the direct result of the acts of his own undetermined will, and since it is a person's undetermined soul which alone has the power to make choices, it is the person himself who is morally responsible for the choices he makes. If he does an immoral act, he must accept responsibility for it (provided, of course, that he could have done otherwise and was not

under external or internal constraint). He cannot excuse himself on the ground that his heredity and environment caused him to do it.

A second way of arguing for free will as opposed to determinism is not on the basis of the existence of a soul, but on the basis of our immediate consciousness of freedom which we all experience when we make a choice under the conditions we have called freedom of choice. We know we are not forced by our past to choose one alternative rather than another because careful introspection of our feelings at the moment of choice reveals no causal forces operating on us. We are free to choose because we see the alternatives open to us, and we know from past experience that we have the ability to do any of the alternatives. Freedom of the will is an undeniable fact of the moral life of man. The future has not already been determined by the operation of past causes. What the future will be depends on what happens in the present, and the present includes the choices which human beings now make. If human beings choose one way, for example, there will continue to be wars and crime and poverty in the future. If they choose another way there will eventually be no wars, crime, or poverty. The future is up to us. It all depends on how we choose from moment to moment in the present, and how we choose depends only on the efforts of our own will.

A free choice is not the choice of an undetermined soul, but the choice of our moral self. This self functions within the limits set by our personality development, but these limits allow for some freedom from past causes. Psychology may be able to explain our personality in terms of the past, but it can never explain our moral self. We can shape our moral self by our own efforts. Even though a person may have been raised under conditions which have given him, for example, an aggressive antisocial personality, this does not mean that in a particular situation of choice he must do an aggressive antisocial act. He himself has the freedom to exert his will power and self-control, so that his choice is not determined by the tendencies of his personality. Thus his moral self is the final determiner of what he does (in situations where he has freedom of choice). He is not the helpless creature of his heredity and environment, but a being with the freedom to act according to moral principles. He therefore should properly feel guilt about his own wrongdoing, and it is justifiable to blame (or praise) him, to punish (or reward) him, and to hold him responsible for his actions.

NONMECHANISTIC DETERMINISM. We now turn to a third point of view concerning the necessary conditions for moral responsibility. From this point of view, the position of mechanistic determinism and the position of indeterminism are both unacceptable, the former because it proceeds from an erroneous conception of what the principle of determinism means, the latter because it denies the principle of determinism. We call this third point of view "nonmechanistic determinism." It rejects the indeterminists' claim that we must be to some extent free from past causes if we are to be held morally responsible. It affirms that a nonmechanistic interpretation of determinism provides for all the freedom necessary for moral responsibility. Thus, although it holds that all the actions and choices of a person are

totally determined by past causes in his heredity and environment, it claims that we are justified in holding the person responsible for at least some of his actions and choices. Let us see how this is argued.

According to the nonmechanistic interpretation of determinism, to say that every event has a cause is to say that it is theoretically possible to predict every event from a complete knowledge of preceding events and a complete knowledge of causal laws. The fact that there are causes by which we can explain why something happens does not mean that these causes force (compel, necessitate) the thing to happen. It means only that the event is preceded by certain happenings in a way in which other similar events are preceded by similar happenings. Given sufficient knowledge of these preceding happenings and of the other similar events and their preceding happenings, it is possible to predict with some degree of accuracy the event in question.[1]

From this standpoint, the assertion that all human actions and choices are completely determined by past events means nothing more than that it would be possible to predict such actions and choices if we knew enough about the past. Actually we are constantly making predictions about the actions and choices of people in our daily life. Our past experience with friends and acquaintances is sufficient to give us a reasonable expectation about how they will act when we next meet them. As psychology and the social sciences advance, more

[1] For a more detailed account of this view of determinism, see the selection by David Hume in Chapter 1 (page 98) and the selection by Moritz Schlick in Chapter 2 (page 193).

and more accurate predictions about people's actions and choices will become possible. Nevertheless, we have all been in situations where people have surprised us by doing the unexpected, and in scientific predictions there is still much room for doubt. The question then is whether these failures to predict correctly and this element of doubt are not due to the fact that people's choices are at least in part uncaused, so that even if we knew everything about their personality development, we still could not predict how they were going to choose. According to the determinist, our present inability to predict stems from our ignorance of all the causes (preceding events and causal laws), not from the fact that there is an inherently unpredictable element in human choice. A person's choice may be forever practically unpredictable in the sense that we may always lack sufficient knowledge to make a completely accurate prediction of it. To say that nevertheless the choice is totally determined by past causes is to say that theoretically it is predictable, that is, if we knew all the causes we would be able to predict it with complete accuracy.

The nonmechanistic determinist claims that despite the fact that all human choices are theoretically predictable, we are justified in holding a person responsible for some of his actions. A person can be held responsible for those of his actions which he was not forced (compelled, constrained) to do. Such actions are the ones he chooses to do in situations where he has freedom of choice, that is, where he has the ability to choose among a number of alternatives and is not under external or internal constraint. When determinism is interpreted in a nonmechanistic way, it is possible to believe that

all actions are caused but not all actions are forced or constrained. The possibility of caused but unconstrained actions follows from the idea that causation means predictability, not compulsion.

Whether the nonmechanistic determinist is successful in his attempt to make moral responsibility compatible with determinism is a question the reader must ponder when he reads the selections in this chapter by David Hume (page 442) and P. H. Nowell-Smith (page 463). Both of these selections accept the principle of determinism and, at the same time, claim that we can justifiably hold ourselves and others responsible for what we do. Each selection handles the problem in a different way, but both agree in holding that belief in determinism is perfectly consistent with belief in moral responsibility. For a third way of defending this thesis the reader is referred to the selection in Chapter 6 by Immanuel Kant (page 533). This selection by Kant has been placed in Chapter 6, rather than in the present chapter, because Kant treats the problem of freedom of the will within the framework of a whole theory of moral knowledge. The selection by Kant can be considered as a single great attempt to solve both the problem of freedom of the will and the problem of moral knowledge together.

The Problem of Freedom of the Will

The positions we have discussed in the last three sections are diverging points of view which philosophers have taken on the relations between causation, free will, and moral responsibility. The general problem with which all three positions have been concerned may be analyzed into several groups of questions. One group of questions centers upon causation, another upon freedom, and a third upon the conditions of praise and blame, reward and punishment, pride and guilt, and holding a person responsible. The three groups of questions may be set forth as follows:

1. Are all human actions and choices totally determined by past causes? What does determinism mean when applied to human actions and choices? What does indeterminism mean?

2. Does belief in freedom of the will contradict determinism? In what sense (if any) can a person be said to have free will, if all his actions and choices are totally determined by past causes?

3. Does morality require that we deny determinism? Is there at least one sense of "freedom of the will" (and if so, what sense) which is both consistent with determinism and sufficient for the justification of praise and blame, reward and punishment, pride and guilt, and holding a person responsible?

THE THEOLOGICAL ASPECT OF THE PROBLEM. In the history of Western philosophy the free will problem has also had a theological aspect. The theological question is whether God's omniscience is consistent with his moral goodness and justice. For if God is omniscient (all-knowing), then it would seem that God knows beforehand everything that ever happens in the world. Thus, before a person makes a choice among alternatives confronting him, God already knows which alternative he will choose. How then can the person's choice be free? Does the person really have a choice at all? When God knows beforehand that a certain person is going to choose in a certain way, the person must choose in that way and in no other way, since God's foreknowledge can never

be mistaken and has no gaps in it. But if the person really had no choice, how can God be just in punishing the person for doing a bad action? Indeed, it would appear that God must be extremely unjust to give a person no choice and yet to punish him for what he could not help doing. Thus if God is omniscient it seems he cannot be just. In this chapter the theological aspect of the free will problem is considered in the selection by St. Augustine (page 437).

DETERMINISM AND FATALISM. Much confusion about the problem of freedom of the will can be avoided if we keep in mind the difference between both mechanistic and nonmechanistic determinism on the one hand, and fatalism on the other. Fatalism is the point of view that what happens in the future does not depend on man's choice in the present. If something is fated to happen, then it will happen no matter what human beings now choose to do. The soldier on the battlefield is a fatalist when he believes that a certain bullet "has his name on it," that his death is "a matter of fate" over which he has no control. Because the fatalist is convinced that the event which is fated to happen will happen no matter what choices he makes, he develops an attitude of complete passivity and resignation toward the event. This attitude often becomes generalized into a feeling of futility and helplessness about all of life, so that he comes to regard any effort by anyone to bring about a better world as utterly hopeless, since it is out of our hands whether the future will be better or worse.

Now fatalism in this sense is radically different from nonmechanistic determinism for the following reason. The nonmechanistic determinist recognizes two kinds of future events, those which are not affected by present human choices and those which are, while a fatalist takes a fatalistic attitude toward both kinds of events. He may be fatalistic about crimes and wars as well as about earthquakes, hurricanes, and incurable diseases. If a person were fatalistic about a third world war, for example, he would be certain that it was going to happen and that there was nothing we could do about it. The nonmechanistic determinist would say that whether there will be a third world war depends entirely on the choices human beings make. That there will or that there will not be a third world war, he would say, is something which no one can be certain of, since it is too difficult to predict all the complex and multifarious human choices which would bring about the one eventuality or the other. But the person who believes that a third world war is fated to occur is absolutely certain it will, regardless of the choices people make. Thus the fatalist treats all "fated" events in the same way, disregarding the fact (which his emotions prevent him from acknowledging) that some of them are events of the kind which we know from past experience depend on human choices.

The difference between fatalism and mechanistic determinism is not as easy to recognize as the difference between fatalism and nonmechanistic determinism. (Sometimes the word "fatalism" is used to mean the very same thing as "mechanistic determinism," but, as the following discussion indicates, "fatalism" in such a sense is quite different from "fatalism" in the sense in which it is being used here.) There is a certain emotional similarity between fatalism and mechanistic determinism which should not cause us to overlook the definite conceptual difference between them. The fatalist feels resigned because the future is out of his hands. The mechanistic determinist feels resigned because the past is out of his hands. He realizes that the future will in part be determined by his own choices, but he sees himself making choices determined by the past, like a machine functioning according to the manipulation of outside forces. The future is closed (though what will happen in it is not already known with certainty) because past causes necessitate present choices and present choices necessitate future consequences. But present choices are genuinely effective in the future in the sense that what occurs in the future depends on them. If they were different, the future would be different. They never *can* be different from what they turn out to be, however, because what they turn out to be is the inevitable result of what the past has been. Now the emotional reaction to this conception of one's own choices is often similar to a fatalistic outlook on life, because one feels helpless about what will happen in the future. But the conceptual belief of fatalism is contradictory to that of mechanistic determinism at a crucial point.

The basic tenet of fatalism is that what is fated to happen is not greatly affected, or not affected at all, by human choices; and this is held to be true even of those things which past experience has shown to be greatly affected by human choices. We have seen that if a person were fatalistic about a third world war, he would be sure that it was bound to happen and that there was nothing he or anybody else could do to prevent it. A mechanistic determinist, on the other hand, would say that *if* a third world war occurs then it will be the necessary and inevitable consequence of present and past events, including the choices people made. But he does not say that a third world war is inevitable; for he knows that it will in fact occur only if human beings make certain choices, and he cannot be sure that they will make those choices. All he claims is that whatever choices are made have been necessitated by the environment and heredity of the persons making them, and these causal factors are part of world history. Thus the whole process of world history is, or is not, leading inevitably to a third world war. Whatever will happen will happen inevitably, but we do not know with certainty what will happen because we do not know with certainty how human beings will choose. The fatalist, in contrast, is absolutely certain that those things which are fated to happen will happen, and that they will happen regardless of how human beings choose.

DETERMINISM AND PREDESTINATION. Not only must both senses of determinism be clearly distinguished from fatalism, they also must be distinguished from the doctrine of predestination or foreordination. When people speak of an event as having been "predestined" or "foreordained" to happen, they imply the existence of some purposive agent behind the universe which brought the event about. It is as if the predestined event had been ordered or decreed to happen by an intelligent mind which desired it to happen. In theistic religion this intelligent mind would be God, and the event would be understood as having happened by the will of God. Belief in fatalism does not require belief in predestination, although it is possible for the two to go together. This would occur when the fated event

is viewed as being willed to happen by a purposive agent.

Sometimes predestination takes the form of a belief that everything in history is the outcome of the workings of Fate or Destiny, personified as a being who has written down in one great book the complete account of history before it happens and exactly as the being has willed it to happen. The principal difference between determinism (in both senses) and predestination, then, is that determinism does not imply the existence of a purposive agent behind the world who orders things to happen in the world, while predestination does.

The reader is now invited to become acquainted with some of the ways philosophers have tried to solve the problem of freedom of the will. The reader is advised to keep in mind the differences between mechanistic determinism, nonmechanistic determinism, fatalism, and predestination. He should remember that the problem is concerned with three basic issues: (1) whether and in what sense all human actions and choices are determined, (2) whether and in what sense freedom of the will contradicts determinism, and (3) whether and in what sense morality requires freedom of the will. These issues are investigated in various ways and from various points of view in the reading selections which follow. We have attempted in this chapter to include a sampling of varied opinions on these issues throughout their long history, and, at the same time, to indicate by the order of the selections a historical development of philosophical thought as the issues are gradually clarified and brought under more and more careful examination.

1

Free Will
as Opposed to
Determinism

Nemesius
of Emesa
(c. 390)

Nemesius was the Christian bishop of Emesa, a city which is now called Homs, in Syria. Very little is known of Nemesius other than that he was the author of *A Treatise on the Nature of Man* (written about 390 A.D.), from which the following reading is taken.

In this reading Nemesius begins with an analysis of what it means for a person to make a choice. He then considers the nature of deliberation, and sums up his findings in the statement: ". . . We deliberate only about such things as are indifferently possible." He explains this by dividing all human acts into those which are unavoidable and those which are "open possibilities." Open possibilities are further divided into probable, improbable, and indifferent. The indifferent are those acts, the doing of which is an "even chance" (i.e., neither probable nor improbable). It is the indifferent type of open possibilities about which we deliberate. The reader will notice that this conception of deliberation appears to presuppose "the freedom of indifference," which is usually associated with the doctrine of indeterminism.

That Nemesius thinks of freedom of the will as being inconsistent with determinism becomes clear in his attack upon the idea that "our impulse attends upon inevitable causes." Whether Nemesius denies determinism only in its mechanistic sense or also in its nonmechanistic sense (as defined in the introduction to this chapter) is left to the reader to discover.

The relation between free will and morality is considered by Nemesius toward the end of the selection. He argues that the existence of such things as advice, exhortation, laws, and praise and blame give evidence that we have free will, and he also shows the connection between the idea of sin and the belief that "it lies with us whether we concur with our faults of temperament, or work against them and master them."

The reading is from Chapters XXXIII, XXXIV, XXXV, XXXIX, and XL of *A Treatise on the Nature of Man,* edited and translated from Latin and Greek versions of the text by Professor William Telfer of Cambridge University.

From *Cyril of Jerusalem and Nemesius of Emesa,* edited by William Telfer, The Westminster Press, Phila., 1955. Used by permission.

OF AN ACT OF CHOICE

What, then, is an act of choice? Is it, or is it not, the same thing as a voluntary act? Seeing that everything that is done by choice is also voluntary. The answer is in the negative, for the two things are not convertible as would be the case if choosing and what is voluntary were but one and the same thing, whereas we find that the scope of the term "voluntary" is the wider. For every free choice is voluntary, but not everything that is voluntary is done by free choice. Children, for example, and animals do things voluntarily, but certainly without deliberately choosing to. Anything that we do when angry, provided it is without premeditation, we do voluntarily, but it is certainly not done by an act of choice. Or, to take another example, some dear friend suddenly makes his appearance. We are so willing to see him as even to be delighted, but not because his coming was by our act of choice. Or a man unexpectedly finding a treasure is ready enough to accept it as a godsend, but not as due to his act of choice. From all these examples it may be gathered that to act voluntarily is not the same thing as an act of choice. Can it really be, then, that choosing is the same thing as desiring? Once more we answer in the negative. For we can distinguish three kinds of desiring, lust, anger, and simply wanting a thing. But it is clear that neither anger nor lust is an act of choice, as may be seen from the fact that while men share with irrational animals lust and anger, they do not share with them their faculty of choice. For if while we have anger and lust in common with them, we differ from them when it comes to the faculty of choice, it is clear that the faculty of choice is one thing, but anger and lust are quite another. An intemperate person, in being overcome by his craving and acting accordingly, yet not by an act of choice, points us the same moral. In fact, free choice is at war with lust, over such a man, whereas if free choice and lust were one and the same thing there could not be war between them. Again, when the disciplined man acts as he has deliberately chosen, he does not act according to lust.

Once more, wanting something is not the same as choosing it. This is clear from the fact that not all the things that one may want are properly objects of choice. For we say that we want to keep well, but no one would say that he chose to keep well; no more would one say that wanting to be rich was the same thing as choosing to be rich. Wanting is a right word to use even when what we want is impossible of attainment; choice is the right word only when the thing lies within our power to attain it. So we may rightly say, "I want to be immortal." What we do not say is, "I choose to be immortal."

For wanting applies to the end desired, while choice concerns itself with the means towards the end, the relation being the same as that between what we want, and what we deliberate how to get. For, what we want is the final result, while what we deliberate about is the means for reaching that result. It remains, then, that we make our object of choice only those things that we think we may be able to bring about. We want things of a kind that do not fall within our powers, as, for example, victory for a particular general. It is thus conclusively shown that an act of choice differs at once from anger, from lust, and from merely wanting a thing. Now that it is not the same thing as an opinion, either, is plain, both for like reasons, and also for different ones. For opinion is concerned not only with things that we might possibly do, but may equally have regard to eternal verities. Further, while we call an opinion true or false, we do not apply the adjectives true or false to an act of choice. Again, while opinion may be with regard to universals, choice has only to do with particulars. For choice is of things to be done, and such things are specific.

Neither is deliberation synonymous with an act of choice, as though it were an actual plan. For deliberation is an enquiry as to things that one might do. But when choice has been made of a course, it has been decided upon by process of deliberation. It is plain, then, that deliberation is about things that are still the subject of enquiry, but choice follows only when decision has been reached.

So now that we have stated what an act of choice is not, let us go on to say what it is. It is, then, something that mingles plan, judgement, and desire. It is neither pure desire, nor judgement, nor even plan in isolation, but is a combination of all three. For just as we say that a living creature is composed of soul and body, and that the body by itself is not the living creature, nor the soul by itself, but soul and body together, so likewise do we define an act of choice; that is to say, it is a kind of plan, followed by deliberation, which ends in a decision. It is clear from etymology, however, that an act of choice is not a mere willing of something in the abstract. For an act of choice is a preferring one thing to another. No one prefers a thing, unless after deliberating, or chooses it, except he has passed a judgement. But, as we do not purpose forthwith to translate into deed every possibility that we esteem as good, an act of choice, and the course of action chosen by prior decision of the will, only follow when desire has been roused. Of necessity, therefore, choice and plan concern themselves about the same matters. And from these considerations we may gather that an act of choice is either the desire for some end within our power of attainment, reached after deliberation, or a deliberating about that end, incited by desire. For, when we make our choice, then we desire whatever it is that will has preferred.

But since we said that choice and plan concern themselves about the same matters, we will next make clear what are the things with which planning is concerned, and upon which we deliberate. . . .

WHAT THINGS ARE SUBJECT FOR DELIBERATION

We deliberate about things that depend on our free will and are within the compass of what we can accomplish; things, further, of which the outcome remains uncertain, that is to say, things that could happen in one way, but equally could happen in another way. We say, "dependent on our free will," because deliberation only applies where there is something to be done, and deeds are what are dependent on our free will. For we do not deliberate about points of what is called "theoretical philosophy"; no, nor about God, nor about things that are bound to happen (by which we mean things that are always happening in a particular way, as, for example, the seasonal passage of the year), nor of things that, while they happen always in the same way, happen only at intervals, such as the setting and rising of the sun; nor, again, of things that, though they do not by nature happen always in the same kind of way, yet do so for the most part, such as, that a sixty-year-old man is generally grey, or that a youth of twenty has down on his chin; nor, again, of things that fall out now one way and now another, without any rule, like the occurrence of showers or droughts or hailstorms; nor, again, of things that happen by luck, as we say, on the ground that they are among the less obvious possibilities. It is with this manner of things in mind that we say that subjects for deliberation are either "dependent on our free will" or within the compass of "our agency," seeing that we do not deliberate on behalf of every man, nor as to every kind of matter, but only concerning such as depend upon our free will or lie within the compass of our agency. For example, we do not deliberate how our foes, or people living in distant lands, would best govern themselves; though that is proper matter for their deliberation. Neither, even, do we deliberate about all things that can be done by our agency or lying within the scope of our free will. There must be the further condition that the outcome remains uncertain. For if the outcome is manifest and acknowledged, then the matter is no longer subject for deliberation. Nor is deliberation in place concerning works or practice of science or art; for these (excepting a few arts that are called skilled, such as the art of healing, or of gymnastics, or of navigation) have their fixed rules. We do deliberate about the skilled arts, as well as about whatever else lies within our power, is done by our agency, has its outcome uncertain, and is capable of being done in this way or in that. Further, it has been shown that deliberation is not about the outcome, but about steps leading up to it. For we deliberate not whether to be rich but how and by what means we shall get rich. To put the matter in a nutshell, we deliberate only about such things as are indifferently possible. And it is essential to make this distinction lest we leave anything in the argument lacking in precision.

The powers whereby we are able to achieve anything are called our faculties; for we have a faculty corresponding to everything that we can do. If we have not the appropriate faculty, neither do we accomplish the corresponding deeds. So, then, the deed depends on faculty, and faculty upon our being. For the deed issues from the faculty, and the faculty proceeds from the being, in which, also, it reposes. So, then, as we have said, there are these three things, each in turn derived from the one before, namely, the potential doer, the faculty, and the possible deed. The being is that of the potential doer, the faculty is that which enables us to do the thing, and the possible deed is such as has that nature. Of possible deeds, some are unavoidable, and others open to our choice. Unavoidable things are such as we cannot prevent, or things whose opposites would be impossible. An open possibility is one that can be prevented, or one of which the opposite is possible. For example, it is unavoidable for a living man to breathe, and the opposite to this, namely, to live without breathing, is impossible. On the other hand, an open possibility is that it will rain today, but the opposite is equally possible, that it will not rain today. Again, of open possibilities, some are called probable, some improbable, and some indifferent. That a man of sixty will prove to be grey exemplifies the probable, that one of that age will not be grey, the improbable, and that he will be walking about or will not be walking about, or in general that he will do a particular thing or leave it undone, exemplifies the even chance.

So, then, the only things whereupon we deliberate are the indifferent possibilities. It is an indifferent possibility if we could do either the thing or its opposite. For if we had not that double possibility within our power, to do either the thing or its opposite, we should not deliberate. For no one deliberates where the outcome is assured, or about something impossible. Now if we can take only one of two opposite courses, and the course that we can take is assured, and beyond question, the opposite is impossible.

CONCERNING DESTINY

Those who find in the courses of the stars the cause of everything that happens are not only in conflict with the accepted notions of mankind but are bound to denounce politics as vain. For laws are absurd, courts (in that those they punish are guiltless) are an extravagance, and blame and praise are alike irrational; yes, and prayers are profitless, if everything happens just as it is fated to do. Heaven's providence and man's religion are banished at one stroke; added to which, man is found to be nothing but a plaything of celestial motion, seeing that the moving stars not only move man's bodily members to various actions but the thoughts of his soul as well. In a word, those who assert such things destroy the concept of the possible, at the same moment that they do away with free will. And, thereby, they do nothing less than bring to ruin the whole concept of the universe. Then, too, they make the stars themselves wicked, as now procuring adulteries, and now inciting murders. Or, rather than the stars, it is God their Creator that bears the blame in their place, seeing that he made them such as would pass on to us an impetus to evil deeds which we cannot resist. So the monstrous doctrine of these men not only has such bearing upon human politics, but also denounces God as the cause of the most abominable crimes. Withal, their hypothesis is incapable of proof, and there is no need for us to take any further notice of it, so manifest is its blasphemous and absurd character.

We turn, then, to those who say that things are, at the same time, both in our own power and fated. For, they say, fate contributes something to each thing that is in process; as, for example, in causing water to be cold, each several plant to bear its own appropriate fruit, stones to fall and flames to rise; and, accordingly, fate causes any living creature both to obey its dictates, and also to move of its own accord. When nothing external and fated opposes such movement, then it is perfectly possible for us (they say) to go as we please; we shall accomplish all that we set out to do. The advocates of this doctrine belong to the Stoics, to wit, Chrysippus and Philopator, with many other distinguished members of their school. But the only thing they succeed in proving is that all things happen in accordance with destiny.

For, if they say that, side by side with the working of destiny, we are granted impulses of our own, which are sometimes thwarted by fate but sometimes not, it is clear that everything, including what seems to lie within our own power, falls out as it is destined. Against these teachers, therefore, we repeat our former arguments, and prove their opinion absurd. For, if the same causes persist, there is, as they argue, every necessity that the same things should go on happening, and not in such wise as to give now one result and now another; since it has been assigned to them from all eternity how they should happen. Needs is, then, that the impulse of a living creature circumstanced, in every instance and in all respects, by the same set of causes should be as destined. And if our impulse attends upon inevitable causes, where is there anything left that is in our power? What lies within our power we must be free to do or not to do. There would be such freedom if, the circumstances remaining the same, it were possible for us now to take the initiative, and now to abstain. But if the impulse itself attends upon inevitable causes, it is plain that all to do with impulse itself is fated, even though it be by our agency and in accordance with our own nature, impulse and judgement, that it takes place. For, if initiative were such a thing as might possibly not be fulfilled, then the premiss, as stated, is a false one, namely that, circumstanced by the same causes, the same results must, of necessity, follow. . . .

OF FREE WILL, OR THE POWER OF INITIATIVE

In debating free will, or in other words our power to initiate, the first point to establish is that we possess any such power. For there are many that hold the contrary opinion. That settled, there is the second point, namely, what things they are that lie within our power, and what is the extent of our authority. To begin with the first point, let us first assert that we have free will, and then prove it from facts which even our opponents will concede.

For they say that the cause of anything that happens is either God, or necessity, or fate, or Nature, or fortune, or accident.

Now, whatever God does is creative and providential. What springs from necessity is a motion from cause to effect that follows ever the same course. The working out of destiny is such that all things inevitably reach their destined end (it is indeed identical with that of necessity). The things that Nature works are birth, growth, and decay, and plants and animals. The tricks of fortune are singular and unexpected happenings. For fortune is defined as the coincidence and concurrence of two actions each of which arises from some particular purpose, to produce something quite different from what was intended by either, as when a man digs a ditch and finds a buried treasure. For one man buried the treasure, but not that the other man might find it. Nor did the other man dig for the purpose of finding treasure. The first intended, in his own time, to dig the treasure up again, while the second intended to dig a ditch. What fell out was something different from what either had intended. Finally, the fruits of accident are such things as befall inanimate and irrational things, devoid of nature or of art. To which of these, therefore, shall we attribute those things that happen by human agency (if, that is, we are not to admit that man himself is the cause and origin of his deeds)?

It would be rank blasphemy to ascribe any man's shameful and wicked deeds to God. We cannot ascribe man's deeds to necessity, since they do not follow an invariable pattern. We cannot ascribe them to fate, because fate admits no range of possibilities, but only permits of one inevitable destiny; nor to Nature, artificer of plants and animals; nor to fortune, since the deeds of men are not all singular or unexpected; nor to accident, for accident is the sort of thing that befalls inanimate and irrational things. Surely, there only remains the possibility that man himself, who both does things and makes things, is the initiator of his own works, and possessor of free will.

A further consideration is this; if a man is the initiator of none of his deeds, it is in vain that he deliberates. For what use is taking counsel, if one is master of no single deed? Moreover, it would be a most monstrous thing that the fairest and most honourable attribute of man should turn out to be of no avail. For taking of counsel is with a view to doing something, and the undertaking and doing of something is the occasion for all taking of counsel. And still a further point is this: whatever powers of action we may have, the corresponding particular actions that employ those powers are ours as well. As we possess capabilities needed for various virtues, so surely those virtues themselves are ours to attain. And that those capabilities that can attain to virtue are ours is shown in that excellent saying of Aristotle about the ethical virtues, that "What things we learn by doing them, we also do from having learned them." For, by learning to master pleasures we become temperate, and being temperate, we are masters of our love of pleasure. Or we may put it in another way, and say that anyone will admit that we have the power to rehearse and practise anything. Now rehearsal makes a thing habitual, and habit is second nature. So, if rehearsal is formative of habit, and lies within our initiative, then the attaining of a habit also is within our reach. And if certain habits are within our power, then the corresponding actions, springing from those habits, are in our power also. For deeds proceed from habits. For, surely, it is the habitually upright man that does the righteous deeds, and the wicked man likewise that does the wicked deeds. And surely, too, it lies with us to be just men or wicked, as we will.

Now all our giving of advice and exhortation likewise demonstrates that there are things that lie within our power. For no one on earth would advise a person not to be hungry or thirsty, or not to take wings and fly, since it is not within our power to profit by such advice. It is plain therefore, that things that we can be advised to do, are things that lie within our power. One further and final consideration; laws would be inane if nothing whatever lies within our power. And yet, taught purely by Nature, every race of men observes some laws, which it lays down as knowing itself capable of acting in accordance with them. And the majority of peoples name gods as their lawgivers. For example, Cretans ascribe their laws to Zeus, and Spartans ascribe theirs to Apollo. Surely, then, a knowledge of what is within our power must be naturally distributed throughout mankind. And we must add that conclusions identical with the foregoing are to be drawn from the existence of blame and praise, while all such arguments disprove the thesis that everything is ruled by fate.

OF THE RANGE OF THINGS CONCERNING WHICH WE HAVE FREE WILL

It has been sufficiently demonstrated that there are certain things that lie within our power, and that we are the masters of at least some of our actions. Now let us state what the things are that lie within our power. We say then, in general, that anything we do willingly is a thing that lies within our power. For no deed that does not lie within human power would be said to be done willingly. The things in our power are, in a word, those that bring us blame or praise, or are the subject of advice, or the object of legislation; for so much has been proved already. In a special degree, everything that has to do with the soul lies within our power, together with things concerning which we take counsel. We take counsel about some proposed deed, as having in our power the doing or not doing of it. And counsel is taken in respect of things of even possibility, a possibility being even when we can do either a certain thing or its diametric opposite. Our mind makes the choice which it is to be, and this choice initiates action. These even possibilities are the things that lie in our power, such as, whether to move or stay still, whether to hasten or not, whether or not to grasp at things not indispensable, whether to lie or tell the truth, give or withhold, rejoice over some good that comes to us or take it for granted, or as many such things as there are, where vice or virtue may enter. For, in respect of these things, we have free will.

Among actions of even possibility are the arts. For every art is concerned

with creating something that can either be or not be, of which the initiation
lies with the artist, but not with the thing that may be made. For nothing that
is without beginning, or that must exist, or that is bound to happen is attributed
to an art; neither is anything attributed to art, though having the possibility of
being otherwise than it is, if it contains within itself the cause of its own being,
as is the case with animals and plants. For they are the work of Nature and
not of art. If, then, things attributable to art have their efficient cause external
to themselves, who is the cause of a work of art but the artist himself, who
makes it? For since the making of the work of art lies with the artist, he is
surely the origin and cause of what is made. To be sure, therefore, there lie in
our power both the making of works of art, the virtues, and all activities of
soul and mind.

The man in the street supposes that the doctrine of human free will means
that everything a man does, together with his gifts and attainments, and even
the fortune he enjoys is the fruit of his own choice, and naturally rejects such
a notion. But men of sharper wit actually refute us by adducing a citation
from Scripture that, "A man's ways are not in his own power." "Good people,"
they say, "how can man have free will, seeing that his way is not in his own
hands?" They cite again, "The thoughts of men's hearts are vain," so that we
cannot bring to fruition the thoughts that we conceive. Many such things
they say, not knowing what really is meant by free will. For, of course, we
have not the choice whether to be either rich or poor, or to be always well,
or to enjoy rude health, or to command either what men call a competency,
or a fortune, or aught else that is ruled by providence. But we have the power
to do, determine or promote either good or evil, in all those cases where there
is before us an even balance of possibilities; seeing that an act of choice leads
the way to every deed, and that not the deed only but the choice itself is
subject to judgement. This is proved by what it says in the Gospel, "Everyone
that looketh on a woman to lust after her hath committed adultery with her
already in his heart." Also Job sacrificed to God for the trespasses which his
children committed in thought. For the beginning of sin and of good works
alike is in an act of choice. As for the actual deed, providence sometimes permits it, and sometimes prevents it. So there is the part that we can play, and
the part of providence. What happens must necessarily depend on both together. For if anything were the work of one only, that excludes the other.
The way things happen, then, is by an intermingling of agency; now it will
be by our initiation, and now by decree of providence, and now, again, it will
accord with both at once.

Now providence is in some sense universal, and in some sense is concerned
with particular things and persons. It follows of necessity that the particular
providence must accord with universal providence. Thus, if the atmosphere
is dry, everybody is also dry, although all may not be equally so. And when
the mother does not eat suitably, but gives herself up to gluttony, the consequence is that her children are born with their physical temperament disordered
and their inclinations perverse. It is plain, then, from these considerations, that

it may fall to the lot of some persons to have a difficult temperament, either through sharing the general circumstances of their parents, or from the way their parents chose to feed, or because they themselves have ruined their bodies by gluttony, so that their physical temperaments turned out to be bad, ultimately because of human voluntary action; and providence is not wholly accountable for such situations.

When soul, therefore, yields to physical temperament, and gives way to lust or anger, and is weighed down by poverty or puffed up by wealth, according as fortune apportions them, the evil so constituted is voluntary. For a soul that does not yield to faulty temperament, but corrects and overcomes it, changing it rather than being changed by it, succeeds in establishing for itself wholesome dispositions, by gentle training and a helpful diet. So, from considering those that go about things in the right way, it can be seen that those who do not, sin voluntarily. For it lies with us whether we concur with our faults of temperament, or work against them and master them. And when the man in the street puts up the excuse that his faulty temperament is the cause of his passions, he does not attribute vice to man's choice but to necessity, and caps that by alleging that the acquisition of the virtues does not lie with us either; an assertion which is monstrous!

Questions

1. How does Nemesius distinguish an act of choice from a voluntary action; from desiring something; from wanting something; and from deliberation?

2. Nemesius says that "we deliberate only about such things as are indifferently possible." Explain in detail what he means by this. Give examples.

3. What is Nemesius' criticism of the doctrine that "things are, at the same time, both in our own power and fated"? What does he mean by the word "fated"? State your reasons for accepting, or rejecting, his criticism.

4. "What lies within our power we must be free to do or not to do." What does Nemesius mean by "free" in this statement? Does his conception of being "free" contradict determinism? Why or why not? (For an explanation of determinism, see the introduction to this chapter.)

5. What line of reasoning leads Nemesius to claim that the fact that we give advice and exhortation, that we have laws, and that we praise and blame is evidence against the thesis that everything is ruled by fate? Appraise the validity of this line of reasoning.

6. What things does Nemesius say "lie within our power"? What does he mean by saying this? (You may refer to your answer in Question 4 in answering this.) How is his conception of what lies within our power related to our being held morally responsible for what we do?

2

Free Will and	St. Augustine
God's Foreknowledge	*(354-430)*

St. Augustine (Aurelius Augustinus) was born in Tagaste, North Africa. His studies in philosophy and theology led him to accept Manichaeism, a Persian religion which at that time was a major rival of Christianity. The Manichaeans believed that there is an antagonistic dualism in the world between two principles, one of Darkness (Evil) and the other of Light (Good), and that man's body comes from the former, his soul from the latter. After teaching rhetoric in North Africa and while pursuing his studies in Milan, Augustine gave up Manichaeism and entered upon a period of skepticism. Under the influence of St. Ambrose, Bishop of Milan, Augustine was converted to Christianity. He lived for three years according to monastic rules and was finally ordained a priest. In 396 he became Bishop of Hippo, in Africa, and devoted himself to the development of Christian doctrine. His most important works are: *The Trinity; The City of God; Confessions;* and *On Free Will,* from which this reading is taken.

St. Augustine here offers his celebrated solution to the theological problem concerning freedom of the will. The problem, which is explained in the introduction to this chapter, may be briefly summarized as follows. If God has foreknowledge of everything that happens, then he knows before we make a choice how we are going to choose. Now suppose God knows beforehand that we are going to do an immoral act. It follows that we must do it, since God cannot be mistaken in his foreknowledge. This seems to imply that we could not help but do the act, since we could not make a choice counter to God's foreknowledge. But if we could not help but do the act, we did not have a free choice to do or not to do it, and God should not punish us for doing it. Thus God's foreknowledge appears to be contradictory to his justice in punishing us for our sins.

St. Augustine uses the literary device of a dialogue to present the problem and offer us his solution. The two persons in the dialogue are Evodius and Augustine. Evodius states the problem and Augustine attempts to solve it. The reader will find no difficulty in following the argument at it is presented in this dialogue form.

The reading is from Book III, Sections ii, iii, and iv, of the *De*

Libero Arbitrio (On Free Will), as edited and translated from the Latin by Professor John H. S. Burleigh of the University of Edinburgh.

From *Augustine: Earlier Writings,* by John H. S. Burleigh, The Westminster Press, Phila., 1953. Used by permission.

EVODIUS. I have a deep desire to know how it can be that God knows all things beforehand and that, nevertheless, we do not sin by necessity. Whoever says that anything can happen otherwise than as God has foreknown it is attempting to destroy the divine foreknowledge with the most insensate impiety. If God foreknew that the first man would sin—and that anyone must concede who acknowledges with me that God has foreknowledge of all future events—I do not say that God did not make him, for he made him good, nor that the sin of the creature whom he made good could be prejudicial to God. On the contrary, God showed his goodness in making man, his justice in punishing his sin, and his mercy in delivering him. I do not say, therefore, that God did not make man. But this I say. Since God foreknew that man would sin, that which God foreknew must necessarily come to pass. How then is the will free when there is apparently this unavoidable necessity? . . .

AUGUSTINE. Your trouble is this. You wonder how it can be that these two propositions are not contradictory and incompatible, namely that God has foreknowledge of all future events, and that we sin voluntarily and not by necessity. For if, you say, God foreknows that a man will sin, he must necessarily sin. But if there is necessity there is no voluntary choice in sinning, but rather fixed and unavoidable necessity. You are afraid that by that reasoning the conclusion may be reached either that God's foreknowledge of all future events must be impiously denied, or, if that cannot be denied, that sin is committed not voluntarily but by necessity. Isn't that your difficulty? Ev. Exactly that. Aug. You think, therefore, that all things of which God has foreknowledge happen by necessity and not voluntarily. Ev. Yes. Absolutely. Aug. Try an experiment, and examine yourself a little, and tell me what kind of will you are going to have tomorrow. Will you want to sin or to do right? Ev. I do not know. Aug. Do you think God also does not know? Ev. I could in no wise think that. Aug. If God knows what you are going to will tomorrow, and foresees what all men are going to will in the future, not only those who are at present alive but all who will ever be, much more will he foresee what he is going to do with the just and the impious? Ev. Certainly if I say that God has foreknowledge of my deeds, I should say with even greater confidence that he has foreknowledge of his own acts, and foresees with complete certainty what he is going to do. Aug. Don't you see that you will have to be careful lest someone say to you that, if all things of which God has foreknowledge are done by necessity and not voluntarily, his own future acts will be done not voluntarily but by necessity? Ev. When I said that all future events of which God has foreknowledge happen by necessity, I was having regard only to things which happen within his creation, and not to things which happen in God himself. Indeed, in God nothing happens. Everything is eternal. Aug. God, then, is not active within his creation? Ev. He determined once for all how the order of the universe he created was to go on, and he never changes his mind. Aug. Does he never make anyone happy? Ev. Indeed he does. Aug. He does it precisely at the time when the man in question actually becomes happy. Ev. That is so. Aug. If, then, for example, you yourself are happy one year from now, you will be made happy at that time. Ev. Exactly. Aug. God knows today what he is going to do a year hence? Ev. He eternally had that foreknowledge, but I agree that he has it now, if indeed it is to happen so.

Aug. Now tell me, are you not God's creature? And will not your becoming happy take place within your experience? Ev. Certainly I am God's creature, and if I become happy it will be within my experience. Aug. If God, then, makes you happy, your happiness will come by necessity and not by the exercise of your will? Ev. God's will is my necessity. Aug. Will you then be happy against your will? Ev. If I had the power to be happy, I should be so at once. For I wish to be happy but am not, because not I but God makes me happy. Aug. The truth simply cries out against you. You could not imagine that "having in our power" means anything else than "being able to do what we will." Therefore there is nothing so much in our power as is the will itself. For as soon as we will [*volumus*] immediately will [*voluntas*] is there. We can say rightly that we do not grow old voluntarily but necessarily, or that we do not die voluntarily but from necessity, and so with other similar things. But who but a raving fool would say that it is not voluntarily that we will? Therefore though God knows how we are going to will in the future, it is not proved that we do not voluntarily will anything. When you said that you did not make yourself happy, you said it as if I had denied it. What I say is that when you become happy in the future, it will take place not against your will but in accordance with your willing. Therefore, though God has foreknowledge of your happiness in the future, and though nothing can happen otherwise than as he has foreknown it (for that would mean that there is no foreknowledge), we are not thereby compelled to think that you will not be happy voluntarily. That would be absurd and far from true. God's foreknowledge, which is even today quite certain that you are to be happy at a future date, does not rob you of your will to happiness when you actually attain happiness. Similarly if ever in the future you have a culpable will, it will be none the less your will because God had foreknowledge of it.

Observe, pray, how blind are those who say that if God has foreknowledge of what I am going to will, since nothing can happen otherwise than as he has foreknown it, therefore I must necessarily will what he has foreknown. If so, it must be admitted that I will, not voluntarily but from necessity. Strange folly! Is there, then, no difference between things that happen according to God's foreknowledge where there is no intervention of man's will at all, and things that happen because of a will of which he has foreknowledge? I omit the equally monstrous assertion of the man I mentioned a moment ago, who says I must necessarily so will. By assuming necessity he strives to do away with will altogether. If I must necessarily will, why need I speak of willing at all? But if he puts it in another way, and says that, because he must necessarily so will, his will is not in his own power, he can be countered by the answer you gave me when I asked whether you could become happy against your will. You replied that you would be happy now if the matter were in your power; for you willed to be happy but could not achieve it. And I added that the truth cries out against you; for we cannot say we do not have the power unless we do not have what we will. If we do not have the will, we may think we will but in fact we do not. If we cannot will without willing, those who will have will, and all that is in our power we have by willing. Our will would not be will unless it were in our power. Because it is in our power, it is free. We have nothing that is free which is not in our power, and if we have something it cannot be nothing. Hence it is not necessary to deny that God has foreknowledge of all things, while at the same time our wills are our own. God has foreknowledge of our will, so that of which he has foreknowledge must come to pass. In other words, we shall exercise our wills in the future because he has foreknowledge that we shall do so; and there can be no will or voluntary action unless it be in our power. Hence God has also foreknowledge of our power to will. My power is not taken from me by God's foreknowledge. Indeed, I shall be more certainly in possession of my power because he whose foreknowledge is never mistaken, foreknows that I shall have the power. Ev. Now I no longer deny that whatever God has foreknown must necessarily come to pass, nor that he has foreknowledge of our sins, but in such a way that our wills remain free and within our power.

Aug. What further difficulty do you have? Perhaps you have forgotten what we established in our first disputation, and now wish to deny that we sin voluntarily and under no compulsion from anything superior, inferior or equal to us. Ev. I do not venture to deny that at all. But I must confess I do not yet see how God's foreknowledge of our sins and our freedom of will in sinning can be other than mutually contradictory. We must confess that God is just and knows all things beforehand. But I should like to know with what justice he punishes sins which must necessarily be committed; or how they are not necessarily committed when he knows that they will be committed . . .

Aug. Why do you think our free will is opposed to God's foreknowledge? Is it because it is foreknowledge simply, or because it is God's foreknowledge? Ev. In the main because it is God's foreknowledge. Aug. If you knew in advance that such and such a man would sin, there would be no necessity for him to sin. Ev. Indeed there would, for I should have no real foreknowledge unless I knew for certain what was going to happen. Aug. So it is foreknowledge generally and not God's foreknowledge specially that causes the events foreknown to happen by necessity? There would be no such thing as foreknowledge unless there was certain foreknowledge. Ev. I agree. But why these questions? AUG. Unless I am mistaken, you would not directly compel the man to sin, though you knew beforehand that he was going to sin. Nor does your prescience in itself compel him to sin even though he was certainly going to sin, as we must assume if you have real prescience. So there is no contradiction here. Simply you know beforehand what another is going to do with his own will. Similarly God compels no man to sin, though he sees beforehand those who are going to sin by their own will.

Why then should he not justly punish sins which, though he had foreknowledge of them, he did not compel the sinner to commit? Just as you apply no compulsion to past events by having them in your memory, so God by his foreknowledge does not use compulsion in the case of future events. Just as you remember your past actions, though all that you remember were not actions of your own, so God has foreknowledge of all his own actions, but is not the agent of all that he foreknows. Of evil actions he is not the agent but the just punisher. From this you may understand with what justice God punishes sins, for he has no responsibility for the future actions of men though he knows them beforehand. If he ought not to award punishment to sinners because he knew beforehand that they would sin, he ought not to reward the righteous, because he knew equally that they would be righteous. Let us confess that it belongs to his foreknowledge to allow no future event to escape his knowledge, and that it belongs to his justice to see that no sin goes unpunished by his judgment. For sin is committed voluntarily and not by any compulsion from his foreknowledge.

Questions

1. The first main argument which Augustine gives in reply to Evodius is to show that it is possible to act voluntarily even though all things are foreknown by God. What are the main points of his argument?

2. "Our will would not be will unless it were in our power. Because it is in our power, it is free." What do these two sentences mean? In your answer, give definitions of "will," "being in our power," and "free," as these terms are used by Augustine.

3. The crux of Augustine's solution to the problem lies in his attempt to justify the statement: ". . . It is not necessary to deny that God has foreknowledge of all things, while at the same time our wills are our own." How does he attempt to justify this statement? Why do you think his attempt was or was not successful?

4. How does Augustine reply to Evodius' query: "I should like to know with what justice [God] punishes sins which must necessarily be committed . . ."? Do you find his reply acceptable? Why or why not?

5. Suppose that, instead of there being an omniscient God, there were a group of psychologists in the world who could predict with a high degree of probability (though not with absolute certainty) how some people would act. Would this fact present a serious difficulty about holding those people morally responsible for their acts? Why or why not?

6. In this reading St. Augustine is concerned with the propositions: (a) human behavior is actually foreknown by an omniscient God, and (b) human behavior is compelled or necessitated. Compare each of these propositions with: (c) human behavior is predictable, and (d) human behavior is caused. Which ones (if any) of

these four propositions, in your estimation, contradict the possibility of moral responsibility? State your reasons.

7. Compare St. Augustine's views with Nemesius' analysis of free will in the reading which precedes this one. Would Nemesius be willing to accept St. Augustine's solution to the theological problem of free will? Could St. Augustine's account of God's foreknowledge be made consistent with Nemesius' account of "indifferent possibilities"? Defend your answers.

3

Liberty and Necessity | David Hume
(1711-1776)

[A general introductory note on Hume may be found on page 98.]

In this reading Hume attempts to prove that determinism, if understood properly, does not deny any freedom which is required for religion or morality. Indeed, he concludes that determinism is itself presupposed by religion and morality. His entire argument depends on accepting the "nonmechanistic" view of determinism and rejecting the "mechanistic" view. Although Hume here gives a brief account of the "nonmechanistic" view, a more complete presentation of his theory of determinism is contained in Selection 4 of Chapter 1 (page 98). The reader is advised to consult that selection for a clarification of many of the points made in the discussion of "liberty" (indeterminism) and "necessity" (determinism) in the reading which follows.

Hume distinguishes two meanings of "liberty": (1) "the liberty of spontaneity," by which he means freedom from internal and external constraints upon our will; and (2) "the liberty of indifference," which means freedom from causation or necessity, i.e., indeterminism. In his discussion of liberty Hume also points out that we have a "false sensation or experience" of freedom, which makes us mistakenly believe that we are free from necessity. Hume grants that we have freedom of the will in sense (1), but not in sense (2). He then goes on to show that morality and religion are possible even if "we can never free ourselves from the bonds of necessity." He concludes by arguing that determinism is not only consistent with but is actually required by morality and religion.

This reading is from Book II, Part III, Sections I and II of *A Treatise of Human Nature* (1738-1740).

Of all the immediate effects of pain and pleasure, there is none more remarkable than the *will;* and though, properly speaking, it be not comprehended
among the passions, yet, as the full understanding of its nature and properties
is necessary to the explanation of them, we shall here make it the subject of
our inquiry. I desire it may be observed, that, by the *will,* I mean nothing but
*the internal impression we feel, and are conscious of, when we knowingly give
rise to any new motion of our body, or new perception of our mind.* This impression, like the ones of pride and humility, love and hatred, it is impossible
to define, and needless to describe any further; for which reason we shall cut
off all those definitions and distinctions with which philosophers are wont to
perplex rather than clear up this question; and entering at first upon the subject,
shall examine that long-disputed question concerning *liberty and necessity,*
which occurs so naturally in treating of the will.

It is universally acknowledged that the operations of external bodies are
necessary; and that, in the communication of their motion, in their attraction,
and mutual cohesion, there are not the least traces of indifference or liberty.
Every object is determined by an absolute fate to a certain degree and direction
of its motion, and can no more depart from that precise line in which it moves,
than it can convert itself into an angel, or spirit, or any superior substance.
The actions, therefore, of matter, are to be regarded as instances of necessary
actions; and whatever is, in this respect, on the same footing with matter,
must be acknowledged to be necessary. That we may know whether this be
the case with the actions of the mind, we shall begin with examining matter,
and considering on what the idea of a necessity in its operations are founded,
and why we conclude one body or action to be the infallible cause of another.

It has been observed that in no single instance the ultimate connection of
any objects is discoverable either by our senses or reason, and that we can never
penetrate so far into the essence and construction of bodies, as to perceive the
principle on which their mutual influence depends. It is their constant union
alone with which we are acquainted; and it is from the constant union that
the necessity arises. If objects had not an uniform and regular conjunction with
each other, we should never arrive at any idea of cause and effect; and even
after all, the necessity which enters into that idea, is nothing but a determination of the mind to pass from one object to its usual attendant, and infer the
existence of one from that of the other. Here then are two particulars which
we are to consider as essential to necessity, viz. the constant *union* and the
inference of the mind; and wherever we discover these, we must acknowledge
a necessity. As the actions of matter have no necessity but what is derived from
these circumstances, and it is not by any insight into the essence of bodies we
discover their connection, the absence of this insight, while the union and
inference remain, will never, in any case, remove the necessity. It is the observation of the union which produces the inference; for which reason it might
be thought sufficient, if we prove a constant union in the actions of the mind,
in order to establish the inference along with the necessity of these actions. But
that I may bestow a greater force on my reasoning, I shall examine these par-

ticulars apart, and shall first prove from experience that our actions have a constant union with our motives, tempers, and circumstances, before I consider the inferences we draw from it.

To this end a very slight and general view of the common course of human affairs will be sufficient. There is no light in which we can take them that does not confirm this principle. Whether we consider mankind according to the difference of sexes, ages, governments, conditions, or methods of education; the same uniformity and regular operation of natural principles are discernible. Like causes still produce like effects; in the same manner as in the mutual action of the elements and powers of nature.

There are different trees which regularly produce fruit, whose relish is different from each other; and this regularity will be admitted as an instance of necessity and causes in external bodies. But are the products of Guienne and of Champagne more regularly different than the sentiments, actions, and passions of the two sexes, of which the one are distinguished by their force and maturity, the other by their delicacy and softness?

Are the changes of our body from infancy to old age more regular and certain than those of our mind and conduct? And would a man be more ridiculous, who would expect that an infant of four years old will raise a weight of three hundred pounds, than one who, from a person of the same age, would look for a philosophical reasoning, or a prudent and well concerted action? . . .

The skin, pores, muscles, and nerves of a day-labourer, are different from those of a man of quality: so are his sentiments, actions, and manners. The different stations of life influence the whole fabric, external and internal; and these different stations arise necessarily, because uniformly, from the necessary and uniform principles of human nature. Men cannot live without society, and cannot be associated without government. Government makes a distinction of property, and establishes the different ranks of men. This produces industry, traffic, manufacturers, lawsuits, war, leagues, alliances, voyages, travels, cities, fleets, ports, and all those other actions and objects which cause such a diversity, and at the same time maintain such an uniformity in human life.

Should a traveller, returning from a far country, tell us, that he had seen a climate in the fiftieth degree of northern latitude, where all the fruits ripen and come to perfection in the winter, and decay in the summer, after the same manner as in England they are produced and decay in the contrary seasons, he would find few so credulous as to believe him. I am apt to think a traveller would meet with as little credit, who should inform us of people exactly of the same character with those in Plato's republic on the one hand, or those in Hobbes's *Leviathan* on the other. There is a general course of nature in human actions, as well as in the operations of the sun and the climate. There are also characters peculiar to different nations and particular persons, as well as common to mankind. The knowledge of these characters is founded on the observation of an uniformity in the actions that flow from them; and this uniformity forms the very essence of necessity.

I can imagine only one way of eluding this argument, which is by denying that uniformity of human actions, on which it is founded. As long as actions have a constant union and connection with the situation and temper of the agent, however, we may in words refuse to acknowledge the necessity, we really allow the thing. Now, some may perhaps find a pretext to deny this regular union and connection. For what is more capricious than human actions? What more inconstant than the desires of man? And what creature departs more widely, not only from right reason, but from his own character and disposition? An hour, a moment is sufficient to make him change from one extreme to another, and overturn what cost the greatest pain and labour to establish. Necessity is regular and certain. Human conduct is irregular and uncertain. The one therefore proceeds not from the other.

To this I reply, that in judging of the actions of men we must proceed upon the same maxims, as when we reason concerning external objects. When any phenomena are constantly and invariably conjoined together, they acquire such a connection in the imagination, that it passes from one to the other without any doubt or hesitation. But below this there are many inferior degrees of evidence and probability, nor does one single contrariety of experiment entirely destroy all our reasoning. The mind balances the contrary experiments, and, deducting the inferior from the superior, proceeds with that degree of assurance or evidence, which remains. Even when these contrary experiments are entirely equal, we remove not the notion of causes and necessity; but, supposing that the usual contrariety proceeds from the operation of contrary and concealed causes, we conclude, that the chance or indifference lies only in our judgment on account of our imperfect knowledge, not in the things themselves, which are in every case equally necessary, though, to appearance, not equally constant or certain. No union can be more constant and certain than that of some actions with some motives and characters; and if, in other cases, the union is uncertain, it is no more than what happens in the operations of body; nor can we conclude anything from the one irregularity which will not follow equally from the other.

It is commonly allowed that madmen have no liberty. But, were we to judge by their actions, these have less regularity and constancy than the actions of wise men, and consequently are further removed from necessity. Our way of thinking in this particular is, therefore, absolutely inconsistent; but is a natural consequence of these confused ideas and undefined terms, which we so commonly make use of in our reasonings, especially on the present subject.

We must now show that as the *union* betwixt motives and actions has the same constancy as that in any natural operations, so its influence on the understanding is also the same in *determining* us to infer the existence of one from that of another. If this shall appear, there is no known circumstance that enters into the connection and production of the actions of matter that is not to be found in all the operations of the mind; and consequently we cannot, without a manifest absurdity, attribute necessity to the one, and refuse it to the other.

There is no philosopher, whose judgment is so riveted to this fantastical system of liberty, as not to acknowledge the force of *moral evidence,* and both in speculation and practice proceed upon it as upon a reasonable foundation. Now, moral evidence is nothing but a conclusion concerning the actions of men, derived from the consideration of their motives, temper, and situation. Thus, when we see certain characters or figures described upon paper, we infer that the person who produced them would affirm such facts, the death of Caesar, the success of Augustus, the cruelty of Nero; and, remembering many other concurrent testimonies, we conclude that those facts were once really existent, and that so many men, without any interest, would never conspire to deceive us; especially since they must, in the attempt, expose themselves to the derision of all their contemporaries, when these facts were asserted to be recently and universally known. The same kind of reasoning runs through politics, war, commerce, economy, and indeed mixes itself so entirely in human life, that it is impossible to act or subsist a moment without having recourse to it. A prince, who imposes a tax upon his subjects, expects their compliance. A general, who conducts an army, makes account of a certain degree of courage. A merchant looks for fidelity and skill in his factor or supercargo. A man, who gives orders for his dinner, doubts not of the obedience of his servants. In short, as nothing more nearly interests us than our own actions and those of others, the greatest part of our reasonings is employed in judgments concerning them. Now I assert that whoever reasons after this manner does *ipso facto* believe the actions of the will to arise from necessity, and that he knows not what he means when he denies it.

All those objects, of which we call the one *cause* and the other *effect,* considered in themselves, are as distinct and separate from each other as any two things in nature; nor can we ever, by the most accurate survey of them, infer the existence of the one from that of the other. It is only from experience and the observation of their constant union, that we are able to form this inference; and even after all, the inference is nothing but the effects of custom on the imagination. We must not here be content with saying that the idea of cause and effect arises from objects constantly united; but must affirm that it is the very same with the idea of these objects, and that the *necessary connection* is not discovered by a conclusion of the understanding, but is merely a perception of the mind. Wherever, therefore, we observe the same union, and wherever the union operates in the same manner upon the belief and opinion, we have the idea of cause and necessity, though perhaps we may avoid those expressions. Motion in one body, in all past instances that have fallen under our observation, is followed upon impulse by motion in another. It is impossible for the mind to penetrate further. From this constant union it *forms* the idea of cause and effect, and by its influence *feels* the necessity. As there is the same constancy, and the same influence, in what we call moral evidence, I ask no more. What remains can only be a dispute of words.

And indeed, when we consider how aptly *natural* and *moral* evidence cement together, and form only one chain of argument betwixt them, we shall make no scruple to allow, that they are of the same nature, and derived from the same principles. A prisoner who has neither money nor interest discovers the impossibility of his escape, as well from the obstinacy of the gaoler, as from the walls and bars with which he is surrounded; and in all attempts for his freedom, chooses rather to work upon the stone and iron of the one, than upon the inflexible nature of the other. The same prisoner, when conducted to the scaffold, foresees his death as certainly from the constancy and fidelity of his guards, as from the operation of the axe or wheel. His mind runs along a certain train of ideas: the refusal of the soldiers to consent to his escape; the action of the executioner; the separation of the head and body, bleeding, convulsive motions, and death. Here is a connected chain of natural causes and voluntary actions; but the mind feels no difference betwixt them in passing from one link to another; nor is less certain of the future event than if it were connected with the present impressions of the memory and senses by a train of causes cemented together by what we are pleased to call a *physical necessity*. The same experienced union has the same effect on the mind, whether the united objects be motives, volitions, and actions, or figure and motion. We may change the names of things, but their nature and their operation on the understanding never change.

I dare be positive no one will ever endeavour to refute these reasonings otherwise than by altering my definitions, and assigning a different meaning to the terms of *cause, and effect, and necessity, and liberty, and chance*. According to my definitions, necessity makes an essential part of causation; and consequently liberty, by removing necessity, removes all causes, and is the very same thing with chance. As chance is commonly thought to imply a contradiction, and is at least directly contrary to experience, there are always the same arguments against liberty or free-will. If any one alters the definitions, I cannot pretend to argue with him till I know the meaning he assigns to these terms.

I believe we may assign the three following reasons for the prevalence of the doctrine of liberty, however absurd it may be in one sense, and unintelligible in any other. First, after we have performed any action, though we confess we were influenced by particular views and motives, it is difficult for us to persuade ourselves we were governed by necessity, and that it was utterly impossible for us to have acted otherwise, the idea of necessity seeming to imply something of force, and violence, and constraint, of which we are not sensible. Few are capable of distinguishing betwixt the liberty of *spontaneity,* as it is called in the schools, and the liberty of *indifference;* betwixt that which is opposed to violence, and that which means a negation of necessity and causes. The first is even the most common sense of the word; and as it is only that species of liberty which it concerns us to preserve, our thoughts have been principally turned towards it, and have almost universally confounded it with the other.

Secondly, there is a *false sensation or experience* even of the liberty of indifference, which is regarded as an argument for its real existence. The necessity of any action, whether of matter or of mind, is not properly a quality in the agent, but in any thinking or intelligent being who may consider the action, and consists in the determination of his thought to infer its existence from some preceding objects: as liberty or chance, on the other hand, is nothing but the want of that determination, and a certain looseness, which we feel in passing or not passing from the idea of one to that of the other. Now, we may observe, that though in reflecting on human actions, we seldom feel such a looseness or indifference, yet it very commonly happens that, in performing the actions themselves, we are sensible of something like it: and as all related or resembling objects are readily taken for each other, this has been employed as a demonstrative, or even an intuitive proof of human liberty. We feel that our actions are subject to our will on most occasions, and imagine we feel that the will itself is subject to nothing; because when, by a denial of it, we are provoked to try, we feel that it moves easily every way, and produces an image of itself even on that side on which it did not settle. This image or faint motion, we persuade ourselves, could have been completed into the thing itself; because, should that be denied, we find, upon a second trial, that it can. But these efforts are all in vain; and whatever capricious and irregular actions we may perform, as the desire of showing our liberty is the sole motive of our actions, we can never free ourselves from the bonds of necessity. We may imagine we feel a liberty within ourselves, but a spectator can commonly infer our actions from our motives and character; and even where he cannot, he concludes in general that he might, were he perfectly acquainted with every circumstance of our situation and temper, and the most secret springs of our complexion and disposition. Now, this is the very essence of necessity, according to the foregoing doctrine.

A third reason why the doctrine of liberty has generally been better received in the world than its antagonist, proceeds from *religion,* which has been very unnecessarily interested in this question. There is no method of reasoning more common, and yet none more blamable, than in philosophical debates to endeavour to refute any hypothesis by a pretext of its dangerous consequences to religion and morality. When any opinion leads us into absurdities, it is certainly false; but it is not certain an opinion is false because it is of dangerous consequence. Such topics, therefore, ought entirely to be forborne, as serving nothing to the discovery of truth, but only to make the person of an antagonist odious. This I observe in general, without pretending to draw any advantage from it. I submit myself frankly to an examination of this kind, and dare venture to affirm that the doctrine of necessity, according to my explication of it, is not only innocent, but even advantageous to religion and morality.

I define necessity two ways, conformable to the two definitions of *cause,* of which it makes an essential part. I place it either in the constant union and conjunction of like objects, or in the inference of the mind from the one to the other. Now, necessity, in both these senses, has universally, though tacitly, in the schools, in the pulpit, and in common life, been allowed to belong to the will of man; and no one has ever pretended to deny that we can draw inferences concerning human actions, and that those inferences are founded on the experienced union of like actions with like motives and circumstances. The only particular in which any one can differ from me is, either that perhaps he will refuse to call this necessity; but as long as the meaning is understood, I hope the word can do no harm; or, that he will maintain there is something else in the operations of matter. Now, whether it be so or not is of no consequence to religion, whatever it may be to natural philosophy. I may be mistaken in asserting that we have no idea of any other connection in the actions of body, and shall be glad to be further instructed on that head: but sure I am, I ascribe nothing to the actions of the mind, but what must readily be allowed of. Let no one, therefore, put an invidious construction on my words, by saying simply, that I assert the necessity of human actions, and place them on the same footing with the operations of senseless matter. I do not ascribe to the will that unintelligible necessity, which is supposed to lie in matter. But I ascribe to matter that intelligible quality, call it necessity or not, which the most rigorous orthodoxy does or must allow to belong to the will. I change, therefore, nothing in the received systems, with regard to the will, but only with regard to material objects.

Nay, I shall go further, and assert that this kind of necessity is so essential to religion and morality, that without it there must ensue an absolute subversion of both, and that every other supposition is entirely destructive to all laws, both *divine* and *human*. It is indeed certain, that as all human laws are founded on rewards and punishments, it is supposed as a fundamental principle that these motives have an influence on the mind, and both produce the good and prevent the evil actions. We may give to this influence what name we please; but as it is usually conjoined with the action, common sense requires it should be esteemed a cause, and be looked upon as an instance of that necessity, which I would establish.

This reasoning is equally solid, when applied to *divine* laws, so far as the Deity is considered as a legislator, and is supposed to inflict punishment and bestow rewards with a design to produce obedience. But I also maintain that even where he acts not in his magisterial capacity, but is regarded as the avenger of crimes merely on account of their odiousness and deformity, not only it is impossible, without the necessary connection of cause and effect in human actions, that punishments could be inflicted compatible with justice and moral equity; but also that it could ever enter into the thoughts of any reasonable being to inflict them. The constant and universal object of hatred or anger is a person or creature endowed with thought and consciousness; and when any criminal or injurious actions excite that passion, it is only by their relation to the person or connection with him. But according to the doctrine of liberty or chance, this connection is reduced to nothing, nor are men more accountable for those actions, which are designed and premeditated, than for such as are the most casual and accidental. Actions are, by their very nature, temporary and perishing; and where they proceed not from some cause in the characters and dispositions of the person who performed them, they infix not themselves upon him, and can neither redound to his honour, if good, nor infamy, if evil. The action itself may be blamable; it may be contrary to all the rules of morality and religion: but the person is not responsible for it; and as it proceeded from nothing in him that is durable or constant, and leaves nothing of that nature behind it, it is impossible he can, upon its account, become the object of punishment or vengeance. According to the hypothesis of liberty, therefore, a man is as pure and untainted, after having committed the most horrid crimes, as at the first moment of his birth, nor is his character any way concerned in his actions, since they are derived from it, and the wickedness of the one can never be used as a proof of the depravity of the other. It is only upon the principles of necessity that a person acquires any merit or demerit from his actions, however the common opinion may incline to the contrary.

But so inconsistent are men with themselves, that though they often assert that necessity utterly destroys all merit and demerit either towards mankind or superior powers, yet they continue still to reason upon these very principles of necessity in all their judgments concerning this matter. Men are not blamed for such evil actions as they perform ignorantly and casually, whatever may be their consequences. Why? but because the causes of these actions are only momentary, and terminate in them alone. Men are less blamed for such evil actions as they perform hastily and unpremeditately, than for such as proceed from thought and deliberation. For what reason? but because a hasty temper, though a constant cause in the mind, operates only by intervals, and infects not the whole character. Again, repentance wipes off every crime, especially if attended with an evident reformation of life and manners. How is this to be accounted for? but by asserting that actions render a person criminal, merely as they are proofs of criminal passions or principles in the mind; and when, by any alteration of these principles, they cease to be just proofs, they likewise cease to be criminal. But according to the doctrine of *liberty or chance,* they never were just proofs, and consequently never were criminal.

Here then I turn to my adversary, and desire him to free his own system from these odious consequences before he charges them upon others. Or, if he rather chooses that this question should be decided by fair arguments before philosophers, than by declamations before the people, let him return to what I have advanced to prove that liberty and chance are synonymous; and concerning the nature of moral evidence and the regularity of human actions. Upon a review of these reasonings, I cannot doubt of an entire victory . . .

Questions

1. "Necessity is regular and certain. Human conduct is irregular and uncertain." How does Hume reply to this argument for "liberty" (indeterminism)? Explain why you think his reply is satisfactory or unsatisfactory.

2. Give your reasons for agreeing (or disagreeing) with Hume's view that our inner sensation or feeling of freedom is "false." Why does he think that this feeling provides no evidence against determinism?

3. Is Hume's argument that determinism is required by religion and morality

a good one? If not, where are his errors? If so, why would it ever have been thought that determinism was opposed to religion and morality?

4. Give the line of reasoning which leads Hume to say: "According to the hypothesis of liberty, therefore, a man is as pure and untainted, after having committed the most horrid crimes, as at the first moment of his birth. . . ."

5. If Hume were to read the account of human choice offered by Nemesius of Emesa in the selection beginning on page 427, what specific criticisms do you think he would raise?

4

Science and Free Will | Max Planck
(1858-1947)

Max Planck was born in Kiel, Germany, studied at the Universities of Munich and Berlin, and became Professor of Physics at the University of Berlin. He attained world renown for his quantum theory of energy, published in 1900, which laid the foundation of all modern quantum physics. In 1919 Professor Planck received the Nobel Prize for Physics.

The following reading is a scientist's attempt to solve the problem of freedom of the will. After stating the problem as he sees it, Professor Planck proceeds to show how the principle of universal causation (determinism) is presupposed by the physical sciences, by biology and physiology, and by psychology, the social sciences, and history. He then makes the claim that man has free will and can be held morally responsible for his actions, even though he is subject to the principle of universal causation just as is every other being in the natural world. This claim that man is both free and determined rests on a sharp distinction between man's use of causal explanations to understand nature (science) and man's use of rules to guide his conduct (morality). Man as an intellectual being, trying to understand both the world around him and his own nature, must assume a rigid causal order which has no gaps in it. But man as a moral being, that is, as a practical agent who shapes his own future and the future of others, knows that he is free. This knowledge of his own freedom is "a truth that comes from the immediate dictate of the human consciousness." The dualism between the universal causation of the physical world and the realm of the conscious ego, where man experiences in himself his freedom of the will, is the basic framework in which Professor Planck deals with the free will problem.

This reading is from Chapters IV and V of *Where Is Science Going?* translated from the German by James Murphy.

From *Where Is Science Going?* by Max Planck, translated and edited by James Murphy, George Allen and Unwin, Ltd., London, 1933. Reprinted by permission of the publisher.

This is one of man's oldest riddles. How can the independence of human volition be harmonized with the fact that we are integral parts of a universe which is subject to the rigid order of nature's laws?

At first sight these two aspects of human existence seem to be logically irreconcilable. On the one hand we have the fact that natural phenomena invariably occur according to the rigid sequence of cause and effect. This is an indispensable postulate of all scientific research, not merely in the case of those sciences that deal with the physical aspects of nature, but also in the case of the mental sciences, such as psychology. Moreover, the assumption of an unfailing causal sequence in all happenings is the basis on which our conduct of everyday life is regulated. But, on the other hand, we have our most direct and intimate source of knowledge, which is the human consciousness, telling us that in the last resort our thought and volition are not subject to this causal order. The inner voice of consciousness assures us that at any given moment we are capable of willing this or that alternative. And the corollary of this is that the human being is generally held responsible for his own actions. It is on this assumption that the ethical dignity of man is based.

How can we reconcile that dignity with the principle of causation? Each one of us is an integral part of the world in which we live. If every other event in the universe be a link in the causal chain, which we call the order of nature, how can the act of human volition be looked upon as independent of that order? The principle of causation is either universally applicable or it is not. If not, where do we draw the line, and why should one part of creation be subject to a law that of its nature seems universal, and another part be exempted from that law?

Among all civilized races the profoundest thinkers have tackled this problem and have suggested innumerable solutions. . . .

The protagonists are mainly divided into two schools. One school is interested in the question chiefly from the viewpoint of the advancement of knowledge, holding that the principle of strict causation is an indispensable postulate in scientific research, even including the sphere of mental activity. As a logical consequence of this attitude, they declare that we cannot except human activity in any shape or form from the universal law of causation. The other school is more concerned with the behavior of human beings and with the sense of human dignity, which feels that it would be an unwarrantable degradation if human beings, including even the mentally and ethically highest specimens of the race, were to be considered as inanimate automata in the hands of an iron law of causation. For this school of thinkers the freedom of the will is the highest attribute of man. Therefore we must hold, they say, that the law of causation is excluded from the higher life of the soul, or at least that it does not apply to the conscious mental acts of the higher specimens of humanity.

Between these two schools there is a great number of thinkers who will not go the whole distance in either direction. They feel in a certain sense that both parties are right. They will not deny the logical validity of the one position nor the ethical validity of the other. They recognize that in the mental sciences the principle of causation, as a basis of scientific research, is nowadays being pushed far beyond the borders of inanimate nature and with advantageous results. Therefore they will not deny the play of causality in the mental sphere, though they would like to erect a barrier somewhere within that sphere and entrench the freedom of human volition behind that barrier. . . .

We now come to ask whether and how far science can help us out of the obscure wood wherein philosophy has lost its way. What is the practical attitude adopted by the special sciences in regard to the universal and invariable validity of the law of causation? Does science in its everyday investigations accept the principle of causation as an indispensable postulate? Does it act upon the assumption that there are no loopholes in the causally governed order of nature? Or, while using the principle as a working hypothesis, does scientific practice intimate that there are certain happenings in nature where the law of causation does not function, and that there are regions in the mental sphere where the causal writ does not run? In our endeavor to find a definite answer to those questions we shall have to put them singly to each of the several branches of specialized science. In doing this of course we shall have to be content with quite a summary cross-examination. What has physical science to say to our problem? What has the science of biology to answer? And what have the humanist sciences, such as psychology and history, to say?

Let us begin with the most exact of the natural sciences, namely, physics. In classical dynamics, among which we must include not only mechanics and the theory of gravitation, but also the Maxwell-Lorentz view of electrodynamics, the law of causality has been given a formulation which for exactitude and strictness may be considered almost as ideal, even though it may be somewhat one-sided. It is expressed in a system of mathematical equations through which all happenings in any given physical picture can be absolutely predicted if the time and space conditions are known—that is to say, if the initial state be known and the influences which are brought to bear upon the picture from outside. To put the matter in a more concrete way: according to the law of causation as expressed in the equations of classical dynamics, we can tell where a moving particle or system of particles may be located at any given future moment if we know their location and velocity now and the conditions under which the motion takes place. In this way it was made possible for classical dynamics to reckon beforehand all natural processes in their individual behavior and thus to predict the effect from the cause. The last significant advance which classical dynamics achieved in our day came about through the general relativity theory of Einstein. This theory welded together Newtonian gravitation and Galileo's law of inertia. . . .

Into this harmonized system of classical-relativist physics, however, the quantum hypothesis has recently introduced a certain disturbance, and one cannot yet definitely say what influence the subsequent development of the hypothesis may have on the formulation of fundamental physical laws. Some essential modification seems to be inevitable; but I firmly believe, in company with most physicists, that the quantum hypothesis will eventually find its exact expression in certain equations which will be a more exact formulation of the law of causality.

Besides dynamical laws applied to individual cases, physical science recognizes other laws also, which are called statistical. These latter express to a fairly accurate degree the probability of certain happenings occurring and therefore they allow for exceptions in particular cases. A classical example of this is the conduction of heat. If two bodies of different temperatures be brought into contact with one another then, according to the two laws of thermodynamics, the heat energy will always pass from the warmer to the cooler body. We know to-day from experiment that this law is only a probability; because, especially when the difference of temperatures between two bodies is exceptionally small, it may well happen that at one or other particular point of contact and at one particular moment of time the conduction of heat will take place in the opposite direction—that is to say, from the cooler to the warmer body. The second law of thermodynamics, as in the case of all statistical laws, has an exact significance only for average values arising from a great number of similar happenings and not for each happening itself. If we are to consider the individual happening we can speak only of a definite measure of probability. The case here is quite similar to the case of a nonsymmetrical cube used in playing with dice. Let us suppose that the center of gravity of the cube is not at the center of the body but lies definitely towards one of the sides; then it is likely though by no means certain that when the cube is thrown it will come to rest on that side. The smaller the distance of the center of gravity from the symmetrical center of the cube, the more variable will the result be. Now if we cast the dice sufficiently often and observe what happens in each case, then we can arrive at a law which will tell us that the dice will fall on a certain side so many times out of a thousand, for instance.

Let us return to the example of heat conduction and ask whether the strict validity of the causal law holds for individual cases. The answer is that it does hold; because more thoroughgoing methods of investigation have proved that what we call transfer of heat from one body to another is a very intricate process, unfolding itself through innumerable series of particular processes which are independent of one another and which we call molecular movements. And investigation has further shown that if we presuppose the validity of dynamical laws for each of these particular happenings—that is to say, the law of strict causality—then we can arrive at the causal results through this type of observation. In point of fact, statistical laws are dependent upon the assumption of the strict law of causality functioning in each particular case. And the nonfulfillment of the statistical rule in particular cases is not therefore due to the fact that the law of causality is not fulfilled, but rather to the fact that our observations are not sufficiently delicate and accurate to put the law of causality to a direct test in each case. If it were possible for us to follow the movement of each individual molecule in this very intricate labyrinth of processes, then we should find in each case an exact fulfillment of the dynamical laws.

In speaking of physical science under this aspect we must always distinguish between two different methods of research. One is the macroscopic method, which deals with the object of research in a general and summary manner. The other is the microscopic method, which is more delicate and detailed in its procedure. It is only for the macroscopic observer—that is to say, the man who deals with big quantities in a wholesale way—that chance and probability exist in regard to single elements in the object that he handles. The extent and importance of the chance elements is of course dependent on the measure of knowledge and skill which is brought to bear on the object. On the other hand, for the microscopic investigator only accuracy and strict causality exist. His livelihood depends, as it were, on the quality of each individual item that he deals with in detail. The macroscopic investigator reckons only with mass values and knows only statistical laws. The microscopic investigator reckons with individual values and applies to them dynamical law in its full significance.

Suppose we consider again the example of the dice which I have mentioned already. And suppose we treat it microscopically This means that together with the nature of the dice itself—its nonsymmetrical character and the exact location of its center of gravity—we also take into account its initial position and its initial velocity and the influence of the table on its movement, the resistance of the air and every other peculiarity that may affect it—supposing we could examine all these minutely, then there could be no question of chance; because each time we can reckon the place where the dice would stop and know in what position it would rest.

Without going into any further details, let me say that physical science applies the macroscopic method of research to all happenings where molecules and atoms are concerned. But it naturally strives to refine its treatment towards the microscopic degree of delicacy and always seeks to reduce statistical laws to a dynamic and strictly causal system. Therefore it may be said here that physical science, together with astronomy and chemistry and mineralogy, are all based on the strict and universal validity of the principle of causality.

Let us come now to the science of biology. Here the conditions are very much more intricate, because biology deals with living things and the problem of life has always presented very serious difficulties for scientific research. Of course I cannot speak with special authority in this branch of science. Yet I have no hesitation in saying that even in the most obscure problems, such as the problem of heredity, biology is approaching more and more to the explicit assumption of the universal validity of causal relations. Just as no physicist will in the last resort acknowledge the play of chance in inanimate nature, so no physiologist will admit the play of chance in the absolute sense, although of course the microscopic method of research is very much more difficult to carry out in physiology than in physics. For this latter reason the majority of physiological laws are of a statistical character and are called rules. When an exception occurs in the application of these empirically established rules, this is not attributed to any skip or failure in the causal relation but rather to a want of knowledge and skill in the way that the rule is applied. The science of biology sets its face against permitting exceptions as such to exist. What appear to be exceptions are carefully recorded and collated and are further studied until they are cleared up in the light of causal relations. Very often it happens that this further study of exceptions shows interrelations which were hitherto unthought of, and throws a new light on the rules under which the exceptions were originally found to occur. It very often happens that the universal causal relation is thus corroborated from a new side, and that is the way in which many significant discoveries have been made.

How can we distinguish between what is veritably a causal relation and what is merely a coincidence or external succession of one event following another? The answer is that there is no hard and fast rule for making such a distinction. Science can only accept the universal validity of the law of causation, which enables us definitely to predict effects following a given cause, and in case the predicted effect should not follow then we know that some other facts have come into play which were left out of consideration in our reckoning. . . .

We now come to those sciences which deal with human events. Here the method which the scientist follows can have nothing like the same exactitude as that which he follows in physics. The object of his study is the human mind and its influence on the course of events. The great difficulty here is the meager supply of source materials. While the historian or the sociologist strives to apply purely objective methods to his lines of investigation, he finds himself confronted on all hands with the want of data whereby he might determine the causes that have led to general conditions in the past and lead to the general conditions in the world at the present moment. At the same time, however, he has at least one advantage here which the physicist has not. The historian or the sociologist is dealing with the same kind of activities as he finds in himself. Subjective observation of his own human nature furnishes him with at least a rough means of estimation in dealing with outside personalities or groups of personalities. He can "feel into" them as it were and may thus gain a certain insight into the characteristics of their motives and their thoughts.

Let us ask then what is the attitude of the humanist scientist towards this problem of causation. In the activities of the human mind and in the play of human emotions, and in the outer conduct that results from these, is there everywhere a rigid causal interrelation? And is all conduct in the last resort to be attributed to the causal activity of circumstances, such as past events and present surroundings, leaving no place whatsoever for an absolutely spontaneous action of the human will? Or have we here, in contradistinction to nature, at least a certain degree of freedom or arbitrary volition or chance, whichever name one wishes to choose? From time immemorial this question has been a source of controversy. Those who hold that the human will is absolutely free in its act of volition generally assert that the higher we go in the scale of natural being the less noticeable is the play of necessity and the greater the play of creative freedom, until we finally come to the case of human beings, who enjoy the full autonomy of the will.

Such an opinion cannot be spoken of as correct or incorrect except by putting it to the test of historical and psychological research. And here we have the problem in exactly the same position as in the case of physical science. In other words we cannot know how far the principle of causality is valid except by putting it to the test of outer reality. Of course, a different terminology is used when causal methods are applied in the humanist sciences. In natural science a definite physical picture with given characteristics is the subject of research. In psychology we have a definite individual personality to study. That individual personality has inherited qualities such as bodily conformation, intelligence, imaginative capacity, temperament, personal tastes and so on. Working on this personality we have the physical and psychic influences of the environment, such as climate, food, upbringing, companionship, family life, education, reading, etc. Now the question is whether all these data determine the conduct of this personality in all its particulars and according to definite laws. In other words if we suppose, what is impossible in practice, that we had a thorough and detailed knowledge of all these factors here and now, could we tell with certainty, on the causal basis, how the individual will act a moment hence?

In seeking for a sound and logical and adequate answer to this question we are here in quite a different position from that in which we were when dealing with natural science. Obviously it is extremely difficult to give anything like a definite answer to such a question as that asked above. One may have opinions and make suppositions and assumptions; but these do not furnish logical grounds for an answer. Still I think that it may be said definitely that the direction in which the humanist sciences, such as psychology and history, are developing nowadays furnishes certain grounds for presuming that the question should be answered in the affirmative. The part which force plays in nature, as the cause of motion, has its counterpart in the mental sphere in motive as the cause of conduct. Just as at each and every moment the motion of a material body results necessarily from the combined action of many forces, so human conduct results with the same necessity from the interplay of mutually reinforced or contradicting motives, which partly in the conscious and partially also in the unconscious sphere work their way forward towards the result.

Of course it is perfectly true that many acts which are done by human beings appear to be inexplicable. At times it is an extraordinarily difficult riddle to find anything like reasonable grounds for certain acts, and other acts seem so utterly foolish as to suggest no grounds at all. But consider for a moment the way these acts appear to a trained psychologist and the way they appear to the ordinary man in the street. What is entirely puzzling to the latter is often quite clear to the former. Therefore if we could study the acts of the human being at very close and intimate quarters, we should find that they can be accounted for through causes which lie in the character or in the momentary emotional tension or in the specific external environment. And in those cases where it is extremely difficult and well-nigh impossible to discover these explanatory causes, then we have at least grounds for assuming that if we cannot find any motive as an explanation, we must attribute this not actually to the absence of motive but rather to the unsatisfactory nature of our knowledge of the peculiarities of the situation. Here we have the same case as in the throwing of the unsymmetrical dice. We know that the way in which the dice finally comes to rest is the net result of all the factors active in the throwing of the dice, but in the case of a single throw we cannot detect the functions of strict causality. And so, even though the motive of a certain line of human conduct may often lie utterly hidden, conduct entirely without motive is scientifically just as incompatible with the principles on which mental science is carried on as the assumption of absolute chance in inorganic nature is incompatible with the working principle of physical science.

It is not merely, however, that conduct is conditioned by the motives which lead to it. Each act has also a causal influence on subsequent behavior. And so in the interchange of motive and conduct we have an endless chain of events following one another in the spiritual life, in which every link is bound by a strict causal relation not only with the preceding link but also with the following one.

Attempts have been made to find a way to free these links from the causal chain. Hermann Lotze, in open contradiction to Kant, put forward the suggestion that such a causal chain can have no end, although it has a beginning. In other words, that circumstances occur in which motives appear entirely independently, not caused by any preceding influence, so that the conduct to which these motives lead will be the first link in a new chain. Such an interpretation, Lotze held, must be given especially to the acts of those choice spirits that are called creative geniuses.

Even though we may not question the possibility of such cases happening in the world of reality, yet we may reasonably answer that the thoroughgoing scientific research which has been carried on in the region of psychology would have pointed to such a possibility. But as far as psychological research has gone there are no indications which might furnish a starting-ground for this theory of the so-called free beginning. On the contrary, the deeper scientific research goes into the peculiarities that have characterized even the great spiritual movements of world history, more and more the causal relation emerges into the open. The dependence of each event upon preceding fact and preparatory factors gradually begins to appear under the strong light of scientific investigation, so much so as to warrant the statement that present-day scientific procedure in psychology is founded practically exclusively on the principle of causal inter-relations and the assumption of an active law of causality which permits no exceptions. This means that the postulate of complete determinism is accepted as a necessary condition for the progress of psychological research.

Under these circumstances it is obvious that we cannot erect a definite boundary and say: Thus far but no farther. The principle of causality must be held to extend even to the highest achievements of the human soul. We must admit that the mind of each one of our greatest geniuses—Aristotle, Kant or Leonardo, Goethe or Beethoven, Dante or Shakespeare—even at the moment of its highest flights of thought or in the most profound inner workings of the soul, was subject to the causal fiat and was an instrument in the hands of an almighty law which governs the world.

The average reader may be easily taken aback by such a statement. It may sound derogatory to speak thus of the creative achievements of the highest and noblest of the human race. But on the other hand it must be remembered that we ourselves are only common mortals, and that we could never hope to be in a position to follow out the delicate play of cause and circumstance in the soul of the genius. There is nothing derogatory in saying that they are subject to the law of cause and effect, though it would be derogatory, of course, if this were interpreted in the sense that the ordinary mortal is capable of fol-lowing the workings of that law in the case of supremely gifted souls. Nobody would feel it disrespectful if one were to say that some superhuman intelligence could understand a Goethe or a Shakespeare. The whole point lies in the inadequacy of the observer. Just so the macroscopic physicist is entirely unable to pursue microscopic workings in natural phenomena, yet, as we have seen, this does not mean that the law of causality is not valid for these microscopic happenings. . . .

From all that I have said what conclusion are we to draw in regard to Free Will? In the midst of a world where the principle of causation prevails universally, what room is there for the autonomy of human volition? . . .

. . . Is there something in the nature of man, some inner realm, that science cannot touch? Is it so that when we approach the inner springs of human action science cannot have the last word? Or, to speak more concretely, is there a point at which the causal line of thought ceases and beyond which science cannot go?

This brings us to the kernel of the problem. And I think that the answer will be found automatically suggested by the questions which I have just asked.

The fact is that there is a point, one single point in the immeasurable world of mind and matter, where science and therefore every causal method of re-search is inapplicable, not only on practical grounds but also on logical grounds, and will always remain inapplicable. This point is the individual ego. It is a small point in the universal realm of being; but in itself it is a whole world, embracing our emotional life, our will and our thought. This realm of the ego is at once the source of our deepest suffering and at the same time of our highest happiness. Over this realm no outer power of fate can ever have sway, and we lay aside our own control and responsibility over ourselves only with the laying aside of life itself.

And yet there is a way in which the causal method can be applied within the limits of this inner realm. In principle there is no reason whatsoever why the individual should not make himself the observer of what has happened within himself. In other words, he can look back over the experiences through which he has passed and endeavor to link them up in their causal relations. There is no reason indeed, at least in principle, why he should not scrutinize each experience—by which I mean each decision and line of conduct which he has taken—and study it from the viewpoint of finding out the cause from which it resulted. Of course that is an extremely difficult task; but it is the only soundly scientific way of dealing with our own lives. In order to carry out this plan of action the facts of our own lives which we now place under observation would have to be distanced in the past, so that our present complex of living emotions and inclinations would not enter as factors into the observation. If we could possibly carry out the plan in this detached way, then each experience through which we have passed would make us immeasurably more intelligent than we were before; so intelligent indeed that in relation to our earlier condition we should rise to the level of the superintelligence postulated by Laplace. You remember that Laplace held that if there were a superintelligence standing entirely outside of the facts occurring in the universe, this intelligence would be able to see causal relations in all the happenings of the world of man and nature, even the most intricate and microscopic. It is only by aiming at this sort of distance that the individual could establish the required detachment of the perceiving subject from the object of his research, which [is] an inevitable condition for the application of the causal method in research. The nearer we are to events in time, the more difficult it is to trace their causal structure. And the nearer we are to the events of our own personal experience, the more difficult it is for us to study ourselves in the light of these happenings; for the activities of the observer are here partly the object of research and, in so far as that is so, the causal connection is practically impossible to establish. I am not preaching a moral sermon here or suggesting what ought to be aimed at for the sake of the moral uplift of one's own being. I am only treating the case of individual freedom from the viewpoint of its logical coherence with the principle of causation, and I am saying that *in principle* there is no reason why we should not discover the causal connections in our own personal conduct, but that in practice we never can do so because this would mean that the observing subject would also be the object of research. And that is impossible; for no eye can see itself. But in so far as any man is not entirely to-day that which he was years ago, there is a relative degree to which he might subject his own experiences to causal scrutiny; and I have mentioned this as illustrative of the general principle.

It will occur to many readers to ask if thus in relation to the chain of causality the freedom of the individual will, here and now, is only apparent and results solely from the defects of our own understanding. That way of putting the case is, I am convinced, entirely mistaken. We might illustrate the mistake by saying that it is like the mistake of suggesting that the inability of a runner to outrun his own shadow is due to his lack of speed. The fact that the individual here and now, in regard to his own living present act, cannot be subject to the law of causation is a truth that is based on a perfectly sound logical foundation of an *a priori* kind, such as the axiom that the part is never greater than the whole. The impossibility of the individual contemplating his own activity here and now under the light of the causal principle would hold good even in the case of the superintelligence postulated by Laplace. For, even though this superintelligence might be able to trace the causal structure in the achievements of the most gifted geniuses of the human race, yet that same superintelligence would have to renounce the idea of studying the activities of its own ego at the moment it contemplated the activities of our mortal ego. If there be a Supreme Wisdom whose celestial nature is infinitely elevated above ours, and who can see every convolution in our brains and hear every pulse beat of each human heart, as a matter of course such a Supreme Wisdom sees the succession of cause and effect in everything we do. But this does not in the least invalidate our own sense of responsibility for our own actions. From this standpoint we are on an equal footing with the saints and confessors of the most sublime religions. We cannot possibly study ourselves at the moment or within the environment of any given activity. Here is the place where the freedom of the will comes in and establishes itself, without usurping the right of any rival. . . . I might put the matter in another way and say that the freedom of the ego here and now, and its independence of the causal chain, is a truth that comes from the immediate dictate of the human consciousness.

And what holds good for the present moment of our being holds good also for our own future conduct in which the influences of our present ego plays a part. The road to the future always starts in the present. It is, here and now, part and parcel of the ego. And for that reason the individual can never consider his own future purely and exclusively from the causal standpoint. That is the reason why fancy plays such a part in the construction of the future. It is in actual recognition of this profound fact that people have recourse to the palmist and the clairvoyant to satisfy their individual curiosity about their own future. It is also on this fact that dreams and ideals are based, and here the human being finds one of the richest sources of inspiration.

I might mention here in passing that this practical inapplicability of the law of causation extends beyond the individual. It extends to our relations with our fellow-men. We are too much a part of the life of our fellow beings to be in a position to study them from the viewpoint of motives, which means the causal viewpoint. No ordinary human being can put himself in the position of the superintelligence imagined by Laplace and consider himself capable of tracing all the inner springs of action from which the conduct of his fellow-men originates. On the other hand, however, I would mention here again a phase of the causal application corresponding to that which I have already spoken of in relation to the individual's capacity for scientifically observing his own past experience. To a relative degree it is possible to study the motives on which other people act, just as they are studied by the psychologist. In all such cases there is to a certain degree the requisite distance between the researcher and the object of his research. And therefore to this extent there is no logical incoherence in the idea of a person studying the activities of his fellow beings. Indeed all who wish to influence others do so in everyday life, which is largely the secret of political success. It is the secret of all the power for good which so many people exercise in relation to their fellow beings. Most of us remember from childhood personalities whom we shirked because of some sort of innate feeling of insecurity in their presence, and on the other hand most of us, I imagine, have memories of acquaintances to whose influence we were willingly amenable because we felt a certain reverence towards them. And everybody is more or less familiar with the feeling of withdrawal which comes over one in the presence of a person who is suspected of seeing too clearly into the inner lives of others. All these immediate reactions bear witness to a sort of instinctive recognition that our own lives are in the last analysis subject to causation, though the ego as regards its immediate destiny cannot be subject to that law.

Science thus brings us to the threshold of the ego and there leaves us to ourselves. Here it resigns us to the care of other hands. In the conduct of our own lives the causal principle is of little help; for by the iron law of logical consistency we are excluded from laying the causal foundations of our own future or foreseeing that future as definitely resulting from the present.

But mankind has need of fundamental postulates for the conduct of everyday existence, and this need is far more pressing than the hunger for scientific knowledge. A single deed often has far more significance for a human being than all the wisdom of the world put together. And therefore there must be another source of guidance than mere intellectual equipment. The law of causation is the guiding rule of science; but the Categorical Imperative—that is to say, the dictate of duty—is the guiding rule of life.

Questions

1. In arguing the point that human beings are subject to the same strict determinism as physical objects, Professor Planck takes those human actions which seem to have no causes and compares them with the activity of dice. Thus he concludes that just as we could predict the fall of dice if we knew all the minute causes operating on them as they are thrown and as they hit a surface, so we could predict the actions of human beings if we knew all the minute causes operating in their nervous systems. But this comparison begs the question. For those who assert that human beings have free will are asserting that human behavior is *not* like the fall of dice, but is essentially a different kind of phenomenon. Therefore this argument offered by Professor Planck is invalid.

Is this a sound criticism? Why or why not?

2. What is the "theory of the so-called free beginning"? What is Professor Planck's opinion of it? State why you agree, or disagree, with his opinion.

3. Do the following quotations, which are both from the reading, really contradict each other? Answer by considering their meaning in the light of the whole context of Professor Planck's essay.

> . . . The postulate of complete determinism is accepted as a necessary condition for the purpose of psychological research. . . . The principle of causality must be held to extend even to the highest achievements of the human soul.

> The fact is that there is a point, one single point in the immeasurable world of mind and matter, where science and therefore every causal method of research is inapplicable, not only on practical grounds but also on logical grounds, and will always remain inapplicable. This point is the individual ego.

4. After reading the discussion of "nonmechanistic determinism" in the introduction to this chapter, would you say that Professor Planck does, or does not, believe that human choices and actions are *theoretically* predictable? Defend your answer by reference to Professor Planck's essay.

5. "The fact that the individual here and now, in regard to his own living present act, cannot be subject to the law of causation is a truth that is based on a perfectly sound logical foundation of an *a priori* kind." How does Professor Planck attempt to show this? Is his attempt successful? Why or why not?

6. Compare the following statement with St. Augustine's attempt to solve the theological problem of free will (in the selection beginning on page 437). Where do Professor Planck's views differ from those of St. Augustine on this problem?

> If there be a Supreme Wisdom . . . who can see every convolution in our brains and hear every pulse beat of each human heart, as a matter of course such a Supreme Wisdom sees the succession of cause and effect in everything we do. But this does not in the least invalidate our own sense of responsibility for our own actions.

7. What similarities and what differences do you find between Professor Planck's conception of free will and Immanuel Kant's conception of the autonomy of the will? (See the selection by Kant in Chapter 6, page 533.)

5

Free Will and Moral Responsibility | P. H. Nowell-Smith (*b. 1914*)

P. H. Nowell-Smith is Professor of Philosophy at the University of Leicester, England. He is the author of *Ethics* (1954), a volume in the Pelican Philosophy Series. The reading which follows appeared originally as an article in *Mind,* in 1948. In giving the editors of this book permission to reprint his article, Professor Nowell-Smith requested that there be published with it a short commentary on points in the article which he later came to think of as either wrongly made or not clearly made. In accordance with this request, the editors are pleased to print at the end of the article a commentary which Professor Nowell-Smith wrote in 1958 especially for this book.

The article begins with a presentation of the traditional problem of freedom of the will, and Professor Nowell-Smith states his preference for handling it without resort to any metaphysical conception (such as the appeal to a mechanistic view of the universe, or to the existence of an undetermined soul). His discussion is divided into five sections. In Sections I and II he makes a careful study of the "Libertarian's" (indeterminist's) claim that an action must be uncaused if a person is to be held morally responsible for it. He criticizes this claim by showing that the conditions under which people are ordinarily said to act "freely" and are consequently held responsible do not require that their actions be uncaused. Thus he attempts to show that moral responsibility is not incompatible with determinism. Another way of arguing the same point is to be found in the selection by David Hume (page 442). The reader will find it enlightening to compare these two arguments, and he should try to decide for himself whether either of them really is successful in establishing the point.

After arguing that the Libertarian does not provide a correct analysis of a free and morally responsible action, Professor Nowell-Smith considers what analysis would, first, *explain why* (i.e., for what purposes) we blame or punish one person for doing an action and not another for doing the same action, and second, would *justify* our doing this. In Section III of the article he considers two possible solutions to this problem, the positivist and the intuitionist, and rejects them both. A brief word about the intuitionist solution is perhaps called for here. According to the ethical intuitionist, we directly intuit moral characteristics and moral obligations. Some intuitionists believe that we intuit the quality of right or wrong in an action. (See, for example, the reading by Richard Price in Chapter 6, page 520.) Others say we intuit the relation of "fittingness" between an action and its punishment (or reward). Thus we are said to intuit that we ought to punish (i.e., that it is fitting or proper to punish) one man for an action and not another.

Having rejected the positivist and intuitionist solutions to the problem, Professor Nowell-Smith proceeds to offer his own solution in Sections IV and V. He begins with an analysis of moral judgments. Since moral judgments, according to this analysis, refer to actions which are "fit subjects for praise and blame," he is led to an account of what makes an action a fit subject for praise or blame. In Section V he attempts to show that this account provides both an *explanation* of why we punish or blame people, and a *justification* for our doing so in certain circumstances. In the commentary on his own article, Professor Nowell-Smith makes certain qualifications of his views on punishment and the conditions of "desert" (i.e., the conditions under which a person deserves to be punished).

The reader should examine Professor Nowell-Smith's concepts of freedom, moral judgment, punishment, and desert to see, first, what they mean, and second, whether they offer a satisfactory solution to the problem of freedom of the will.

From "Free Will and Moral Responsibility," by P. H. Nowell-Smith, *Mind*, Vol. 57, No. 225, 1948. Reprinted by permission of the author and the editor of *Mind*.

The traditional problem of free will has been so adequately covered in recent philosophical literature that some excuse must be offered for reopening it; and I do so because, although I believe that the traditional problem has been solved, I believe also that the solution leaves open certain further problems that are both interesting and important. It is to these problems that I propose to devote most of this paper; but, even at the risk of flogging dead horses, I feel bound to say something about the traditional problem itself.

I

The problem arises out of a *prima facie* incompatibility between the freedom of human action and the universality of causal law. It was raised in an acute form when universal determinism was believed to be a necessary presupposition of science; but it was not then new, because the incompatibility, if it exists at all, exists equally between human freedom and the foreknowledge of God. As it appears to the "plain man" the problem may be formulated as follows: "Very often I seem to myself to be acting freely, and this freedom, if it exists, implies that I could have acted otherwise than I did. If this freedom is illusory, I shall need a very convincing argument to prove that it is so, since it appears to be something of which I am immediately aware. Moreover, if there is no freedom, there is no moral responsibility; for it would not be right to praise or blame a man for something that he could not help doing. But, if a man could have acted otherwise than he did, his action must have been uncaused, and universal determinism is therefore untrue."

Broadly, there are two methods of resolving this, as any other, antinomy. We can either assume that the incompatibility is a genuine one at a certain level of thought and try to resolve it at a higher plane in which either or both the terms "freedom" and "necessity" lose their ordinary meaning or we can try to show by an analysis of these terms that no such incompatibility exists. If the latter method is successful, it will show that what is essential in our concept of freedom does not conflict with what is essential in our concept of causal necessity and that the incompatibility arises only because, at some stage in our development of one or both of these concepts, we have been tempted into making a false step. This method seems to me the better (provided always that it is successful), on the ground that it does not resort to any metaphysical conception imported *ad hoc* to solve this problem, which might be objectionable on other grounds. In the first two sections of this paper I shall give a brief outline of the analysis of the problem that I believe to be correct; and for this analysis I claim no originality. The method of presentation will, however, throw into relief the partial nature of the solution and help to indicate the further problems to be discussed in the last three sections.

Freedom, so far from being incompatible with causality, implies it. When I am conscious of being free, I am not directly conscious that my actions are uncaused, because absence of causation is not something of which one could be directly aware. That the plain man and the Libertarian philosopher are right in claiming to know directly the difference between voluntary and involuntary actions, at least in some cases, I have no doubt; but we can never have this direct knowledge that something is uncaused, since this is a general proposition and, like other general propositions, could only be established by reflection on empirical evidence. Fortunately it is not necessary here either to attempt an analysis of causality or to answer the question whether or not it is a necessary presupposition of science. It is now widely recognised that the considerations which lead scientists to suppose that strict determinism is not true are irrelevant to the problem of free will, since these considerations lend no support to the view that the phenomena with which we are concerned are not predictable; and it is to predictability, not to any special theory of the grounds of predictability, that the Libertarian objects. He claims that if our actions are predictable we are "pawns in the hands of fate" and cannot choose what we shall do. If, it is argued, someone can know what I shall do, then I have no choice but to do it.

The fallacy of this argument has often been exposed and the clearest proof that it is mistaken or at least muddled lies in showing that I could not be free to choose what I do *unless* determinism is correct. There are, indeed, grounds for supposing that strict determinism in psychology is not correct; but this, if true, constitutes not an increase but a limitation of our freedom of action. For the simplest actions could not be performed in an indeterministic universe. If I decide, say, to eat a piece of fish, I cannot do so if the fish is liable to turn into a stone or to disintegrate in mid-air or to behave in any other utterly unpredictable manner. It is precisely because physical objects have determinate causal characteristics that we are able to do what we decide to do. To this it is no answer to say that perhaps the behaviour of physical objects is determined while that of volitions is not. For we sometimes cause people to make decisions as well as to act on them. If someone shouts: "Look out! There is a bull," I shall probably run away. My action is caused by my decision to run; but my decision is itself caused by my fear, and that too is caused by what I have heard. Or, again, someone may try to influence my vote by offering me a bribe. If I accept the bribe and vote accordingly, the action is caused by the bribe, my avarice and my sense of obligation to the donor; yet this would certainly be held to be a blameworthy action, and therefore a voluntary one. A genuinely uncaused action could hardly be said to be an action *of* the agent at all; for in referring the action to an agent we are referring it to a cause.

In calling a man "honest" or "brave" we imply that he can be relied on to act honestly or bravely, and this means that we predict such actions from him. This does not mean that we can predict human actions with the same degree of assurance as that with which we predict eclipses. Psychology and the social sciences have not yet succeeded in establishing laws as reliable as those that we have established in some of the natural sciences, and maybe they never will. But any element of unreliability in our predictions of human actions decreases rather than increases the reliability of our moral judgements about them and of our consequent attributions of praise and blame. An expert chess-player has less difficulty in defeating a moderate player than in defeating a novice, because the moves of the moderate player are more predictable; but they could hardly be said to be less voluntary. In calling an action "voluntary" we do not, therefore, mean that it is unpredictable; we mean that no one compelled the agent to act as he did. To say that, on the determinist view, we are "mere pawns in the hands of fate" is to confuse causality with compulsion, to confuse natural laws (descriptions) with social laws (prescriptions) and to think of fate as a malignant deity that continually thwarts our aims. What the protagonist of freedom requires, in short, is not uncaused actions, but actions that are the effects of a peculiar kind of causes. I shall be as brief as possible in saying what these causes are, since this has often been said before. But it is one thing to state the criteria by which we decide whether or not an action is voluntary and another to say why this distinction is important for ethics. The problem which the analysts have not, in my view, sufficiently considered is that of analysing the peculiar relation of "merit" or "fittingness" that is held to exist between voluntary actions and moral responsibility.

II

If someone overpowers me and compels me to fire a gun which causes a death, I should not be held guilty of murder. It would be said that my action was not voluntary; for I could not, had I so wished, have acted otherwise. On the other hand, if I kill someone because I hope to benefit under his will, my action is still caused, namely by my greed; but my action would be held to be voluntary and I should be blamed for it. The criterion here is that, while in the first case the cause is external to me, in the second it is my decision. A similar criterion would be used to distinguish a kleptomaniac from a thief. A kleptomaniac is held to be one who steals without having decided to do so, perhaps even in spite of a decision not to do so. He is not held morally responsible for his action because his action is not held to be voluntary. But in this case it is not true, as it was in the last, that his action is called involuntary because it is caused by some outside force. The cause of kleptomania is obscure; but it is not external compulsion. And, if the cause is not external, how can we say that the kleptomaniac is "compelled"? As used by psychologists, the term "compulsion" is evidently a metaphor, similar to that by which we speak of a man's doing something when "he is not himself." Evidently our moral judgements imply not merely a distinction between voluntary and compelled actions, but a further distinction among actions that are not compelled.

A third example will make it clear that some such distinction must be made. Suppose that a schoolmaster has two pupils A and B, who fail to do a simple sum correctly. A has often done sums of similar difficulty before and done them correctly, while B has always failed. The schoolmaster will, perhaps, threaten A with punishment, but he will give B extra private tuition. On the traditional view his action might be explained as follows: "A has done these sums correctly before; therefore he could have done them correctly on this occasion. His failure is due to carelessness or laziness. On the other hand, B is stupid. He has never done these sums correctly; so I suppose that he *cannot* do them. A's failure is due to a moral delinquency, B's to an intellectual defect. A therefore deserves punishment, but B does not." This is, I think, a fair summary of what the "plain man" thinks about a typical case, and the points to which I wish to draw attention are these:

(*a*) Neither failure is said to be "uncaused."

(*b*) The causes assigned are divided into two classes, moral and intellectual. (Cases of physical deficiency, *e.g.* not being strong or tall enough would go along with the intellectual class, the point being that such deficiencies are nonmoral.)

(*c*) Praise and blame are thought appropriate to moral but not to nonmoral defects.

(*d*) The criterion for deciding whether a defect is moral is "Could the agent have acted otherwise?"

I do not wish to suggest that the reasoning attributed to the plain man in this case is in any way incorrect, only that, particularly in regard to point (*c*) and (*d*) it needs explaining.

It is evident that one of the necessary conditions of moral action is that the agent "could have acted otherwise" and it is to this fact that the Libertarian is drawing attention. His case may be stated as follows: "It is a well-known maxim that 'I ought' implies 'I can.' If I cannot do a certain action, then that action cannot be my duty. On the other hand, 'I ought' as clearly implies 'I need not'; for if I cannot possibly refrain from a certain action, there can be no merit or demerit in doing it. Therefore, in every case of moral choice it is possible for the agent to do the action and also possible for him not to do it; were it not so, there would be no *choice;* for choice is between possibilities. But this implies that the action is uncaused, because a caused action cannot but occur." The fallacy in this argument lies in supposing that, when we say "A could have acted otherwise," we mean that A, being what he was and being placed in the circumstances in which he was placed, could have done something other than what he did. But in fact we never do mean this; and if we believe that voluntary action is uncaused action, that is only because we believe erroneously that uncaused action is a necessary condition of moral responsibility. The Libertarian believes that an action cannot be a moral one if the agent could not have acted otherwise, and he takes no account of possible differences in the causes that might have prevented him from acting otherwise. The Determinist, on the other hand, holds that the objective possibility of alternative actions is an illusion and that, if A in fact did X, then he could not have done any action incompatible with X. But he holds also that differences in the various causes that might have led to X may be of great importance and that it is in fact from the consideration of such differences that we discover the criterion by which we judge an action to be voluntary, and so moral.

We all blame Nero for murdering Agrippina, and the Libertarian holds that this implies that Nero could have abstained from his action. But this last phrase is ambiguous. Even if we admit that it would have been impossible for anyone to predict Nero's action with the degree of assurance with which we predict eclipses, yet an acute observer at Nero's court might have laid longish odds that Nero, being what he was and being placed in the circumstances in which he was placed, would sooner or later murder his mother. To say that Nero might have acted otherwise is to say that he could have decided to act otherwise and that he would have so decided if he had been of a different character. If Nero had been Seneca, for example, he would have preferred suicide to matricide. But what could "If Nero had been Seneca . . ." possibly mean? Unfulfilled conditionals in which both terms are names of individuals constitute, admittedly, a thorny philosophical problem; but it is clear, I think, that if "If Nero had been Seneca . . ." means anything at all, it is a quasi-general proposition which can be analysed either as "If Nero had had the character of Seneca" or "If Seneca had been emperor" or in some similar fashion. None of these analyses are incompatible with the Determinist's contention that, as things stood, Nero could not have abstained. But, adds the Determinist, the cause of his inability to abstain was not external compulsion nor some inexplicable and uncharacteristic quirk. His action was predictable because it was characteristic, and it is for the same reason that he is held to blame.

But the Libertarian's case is not yet fully answered. He might reply: "But, on this analysis, I still cannot blame Nero which in fact I do, and feel that I do justly. If the murder was caused by his character, *he* may not have been to blame. For his character may have been caused by hereditary and environmental factors over which he had no control. Can we justly blame a man if his vicious actions are due to hereditary epilepsy or to the influence of a corrupt and vicious court?" To this the answer is that we can and do. So long as we persist in supposing that, to be moral, an action must be uncaused, we can only push the moral responsibility back in time; and this, so far from solving the problem, merely shows the impossibility of any solution on these lines.

This is made abundantly clear by Aristotle's discussion of the subject, which I shall paraphrase somewhat freely in order to show that it must raise a difficulty which Aristotle does not squarely face. Aristotle says that, if a man plead that he could not help doing X because he was "the sort of man to do X," then he should be blamed for being this sort of man. His character was caused by his earlier actions, Y and Z, that made him the sort of person who would, in the given situation, inevitably do X. But suppose the criminal pleads that at the time of doing Y and Z he did not know that these were vicious actions and did not know that doing vicious actions causes a vicious character? Then, says Aristotle, all we can say in such a case is that not to know that actions create character is the mark of a singularly senseless person. But this is clearly inadequate. For the criminal might proceed: "Very well then, I was a singularly senseless person; I neither knew that Y and Z were vicious actions nor that, if I did them, I would become the sort of person to do X. And, anyhow, at the time of doing Y and Z, I was the sort of person to do Y and Z. These actions were just as much caused as was X. You say that blaming me for doing X is really blaming me for having done Y and Z. Now apply the same argument to Y and Z and see where it leads you. Furthermore my ignorance at the time of doing Y and Z which, according to you, is the real source of the trouble, was not my fault either. My father did not have me properly educated. Blame him, if you must blame somebody; but he will offer the same reply as I have done, and so *ad infinitum.*" This argument carries no conviction; but it admits of no reply, and it is here that the temptation to invoke a metaphysical *deus ex machina* becomes inviting. If we proceed on the assumption that, to be moral, an action must be uncaused, either we shall find a genuinely uncaused action at the beginning of the chain or we shall not. If we do not, then, according to the Libertarian, there can be no moral praise and blame at all (and it was to account for these that Libertarianism was invented); and, if we do, then we must suppose that, while almost all our actions are caused, and therefore amoral, there was in the distant past some one action that was not caused and for which we can justly be praised or blamed. This bizarre theory has in fact been held; but the objections to it are clear. We praise and blame people for what they do now, not for what they might have done as babies, and any theory of moral responsibility must account for this. Secondly the same man is subjected to judgements both of praise and of blame: therefore the subject of these judgements cannot be one solitary act; and, thirdly, even if we were able to discover this one hypothetical infantile act, would it in fact be a fit subject for either praise or blame? If it were genuinely uncaused, it could hardly be either, since it would not be an action *of* the agent.

III

So far we have discovered nothing more startling than the fact that moral actions are the effects of a peculiar kind of causes, namely the voluntary actions of the agent. To sum up this part of the argument, I cannot do better than quote the words of Prof. Ayer: "To say that I could have acted otherwise is to say, first, that I should have acted otherwise, if I had so chosen; secondly, that my action was voluntary in the sense in which the actions say of the kleptomaniac are not; and, thirdly, that nobody compelled me to choose as I did: and these three conditions may very well be fulfilled. When they are fulfilled, I may be said to have acted freely. But this is not to say that it was a matter of chance that I acted as I did, or, in other words, that my action could not be explained. And that my actions should be capable of being explained is all that is required by the postulate of determinism." [1] With this I agree; but it leaves unsolved what is perhaps the most important part of the problem. Granted that we sometimes act "freely" in the sense defined by Ayer, in what sense is it rational or just or moral to praise or blame voluntary actions but not involuntary ones? It is surely not enough to say: "Actions of such-and-such a kind are given the name 'voluntary' and 'are praised and blamed; others are not.'" We need to explain the relation of "fittingness" that is held to obtain between voluntary actions and moral judgement. Suppose that A and B each kill some one. We apply Ayer's tests and decide that A's was a voluntary action and B's not. We hang A, and B is immured in an asylum or regains his liberty. What needs to be explained is (*a*) Why do we do this? and (*b*) Is it morally justifiable?

Before attempting to answer these questions I shall first say something of two alternative solutions, the positivist and the intuitionist. The positivist solution might be on these lines: "Both the questions at the end of the last paragraph are pseudo-questions. We cannot explain why we do things, unless 'explaining' merely means 'discovering efficient causes.' I can discover the efficient causes of human actions, as of other phenomena, by observation; but I cannot discover final causes, because there are no such things and no good has ever come of looking for them. Look at the sterility of the natural sciences before the seventeenth century philosophers substituted explanation in terms of efficient causes for explanation in terms of final ones. Secondly, to ask whether it is moral or rational to act as we do is silly. If you like I will include such action in my definition of 'acting morally or rationally.' What is moral in a given society is what is in accordance with its customs; and to ask whether a custom is moral is to ask whether it is customary, which is ridiculous."

I shall not spend much time in discussing this solution, because the fallacy is, I believe, obvious, and the theory can be refuted without appeal to any dubious intuitions of Natural Law. It is true that in natural science the search for final causes is futile; but this is because such a search rests on the erroneous attribution of human purposes to nature. But in discussing human conduct anthropomorphic ideas are not out of place; it is their transfer to natural phenomena that is illegitimate. Though the right answer to the question "What causes an eclipse of the sun?" cannot be in the form "The sun wants to do so-and-so"; this sort of answer may very well be appropriate when the phenomenon in question is a human action. Not even the positivist denies the existence and causal efficacy of human purposes.

The intuitionist solution cannot so easily be dismissed; in fact it is never

---

[1] "Freedom and Necessity," *Polemic,* No. 5, p. 43.

possible formally to refute someone who claims to be directly aware of something. All that we can do is to show that, in a given case, intuitionism leads to some unplausible conclusion that the intuitionist himself would be reluctant to admit. It is not my intention to show that intuitionism is in general false; indeed, the theory that our knowledge of values is grounded in intuition may very well be true. But moral judgements, as I hope to show in the next section, are not pure value judgements; they are value judgements combined with causal judgements. Whatever else we may be asserting when we call an action right or wrong, we are asserting that it was caused in a certain way; and it is difficult to see how such a causal proposition can be intuited. Furthermore, in default of widespread agreement about intuitions of this relation of fittingness, we are driven to believe that such intuitions, if they occur, are subjective. And there is no such agreement, even among experts. If, as Kant held, the infliction of punishment on a criminal is necessarily a moral act, how is it that Westermarck can say: "The infliction of pain is not an act that the moral consciousness regards with indifference even in the case of a criminal." [2] Again, Ewing, after showing that the retributive theory of punishment cannot be defended except by an appeal to intuition, goes on to say: "Now it seems to me that, instead of being intuitively certain that punishment should be inflicted as an end-in-itself without any consideration of consequences, the intuitive evidence is all the other way." [3] Rashdall, again, holds that the problem must be decided "for each of us by an appeal to his own moral consciousness" [4] and sides, rather tentatively, with the anti-Kantians. This disagreement of experts sheds no light on the truth of the retributive theory of punishment, but it does tend to show that the intuition of fittingness on which that theory relies either does not in fact occur or is at best unreliable and at worst subjective. The intuitionist who claims to be directly aware of the relation of fittingness is, in short, telling us something about his own mind. This may be interesting and important, but it is inconsistent with the proposition that most intuitionists would like to maintain, that such intuitions are objectively true or false. The intuitionist theory cannot be ruled out, but it is a safe rule not to resort to intuitions until driven to do so, because so many alleged intuitions have, in the past, been shown to be not merely not intuited but even false.

IV

The theory that I wish to suggest is that in every so-called moral judgement there are two distinct elements, a value judgement and a moral judgement proper. About value judgements no special theory is implied. In particular, I do not intend to prejudice any of the following issues:

(a) whether value judgements are or are not properly called "judgements" at all,

[2] *Ethical Relativity*, p. 77.
[3] *The Morality of Punishment*, p. 18.
[4] *The Theory of Good and Evil*, pp. 284 ff.

(*b*) whether there is or is not only one type of value (for instance, pleasure), and

(*c*) whether or not value judgements are subjective.

It will, however, follow that, whatever values there may be, there is no such thing as moral value, as such, but that when we attribute moral value to a thing we are saying in a misleading way that the thing has some value or other and is connected with a moral cause.

Whatever our reasons may be, we do in fact regard some states, objects and events as "good" or "valuable" and others as "bad" or "disvaluable"; the former we try to promote, the latter to prevent. Whatever may be the case with value judgements, the strictly moral element in a moral judgement is concerned with an empirical fact and is, therefore, objective. The difference between these two types of judgement can be made clear by an example. Suppose that, for whatever reason, I regard A's life as valuable. (I may hold that all human life is valuable as such, or that A is a good man and that the lives of good men are valuable, or merely that the existence of A is propitious to some scheme in which I am interested.) A may be murdered in cold blood by B or may be run over by C in circumstances over which the latter had no control. In each of these cases I should make the same value judgement, that A's death was "bad." But, while in the first case I should make the further moral judgement that B's action was criminal, in the second I should make no additional moral judgement at all.

The theory can be divided into four parts:

(*a*) Value judgements apply only to events (including their consequences), but not to their causes.

(*b*) Events that are "good" or "bad" constitute moral actions only when they are caused by someone's voluntary decision.

(*c*) "Good" and "bad" events that are also moral actions are fit subjects for praise and blame, while other good and bad events are not.

(*d*) This "fittingness" is a causal relation, discoverable neither by a special "moral sense" nor by intuition nor by *a priori* reasoning, but by reflection on experience.

Of these propositions (*a*) and (*b*) are recommendations to employ a certain terminology in ethical matters; (*c*) is a proposition which will, I think, be generally admitted, provided the suggested terminology is accepted. But it is (*c*) that requires explanation, and the explanation is contained in (*d*). If it is true that praise and blame are means employed to bring about good events and prevent bad ones, they are appropriate not to all good and bad events, but only to those that they can in fact bring about or prevent. Since a moral action is one that can be fittingly praised or blamed, it follows that a moral action is one that can be brought about or prevented by these means. Moral actions are a subclass of good and bad events, and the traditional criterion for deciding whether or not an event belongs to this subclass was, as we saw, "Was the action voluntary, *i.e.* caused by a decision of the agent?" But the application of this criterion involves two difficulties. It is sometimes difficult to decide to what cause an action was due. Is this a case of laziness or a case of stupidity? Was the prisoner in the dock mad or was he avaricious? This is an empirical difficulty and raises no question of principle. But the other difficulty that arises in applying the criterion of voluntariness is to find a rule for deciding what classes of actions are voluntary. If the criterion I have suggested is correct, then we should find that the class of actions generally agreed to be voluntary coincides roughly with the class of actions that are caused by characteristics that can be strengthened or inhibited by praise and blame. And this is what we do in fact find; moral characteristics, as opposed to intellectual and physical ones, are just those that we believe to be alterable in this way. Now the problem of deciding whether or not a characteristic is alterable may be difficult; but the difficulty is an empirical one only, and we know at least how to set about solving it.

This theory implies a utilitarian theory of punishment. Rewards and punishments (for the sake of brevity I shall in future refer only to punishment) are distributed not because certain actions directly "merit" them, but because some useful purpose is believed to be served by inflicting them. It should be noted that the theory that punishment is purposive does not imply that its purposes must always have been those that the Utilitarians had in mind. Furthermore, the fact that some systems of punishment do not in fact produce the intended results, an argument that is often urged against the utilitarian theory, does not tend to show that no result was intended. The performance of Sellenger's Round doubtless does nothing to keep the sun on its course; but that does not prove that it is not intended to do so by the performers. Failure to produce results argues not lack of purpose but lack of skill in the practitioner.

It may be objected that this theory fails to account for the retributive element in punishment and, before elaborating it on the positive side, I shall first suggest a possible explanation both of the fact that the retributive theory is believed and of the fact that its supporters claim to intuit its truth. To do this it is necessary to distinguish between the reasons for which the theory first came to be held and the reasons for which it is held now. An adequate account of the first point would require to be based on a wider knowledge of anthropology than I possess, and I do not claim that the account here suggested is true, even in its broad outlines. Nevertheless it is, I think, plausible to suppose that retributive punishment originally had *some* purpose, even if it was quite different from the one suggested here.

The primitive morality that demands an eye for an eye is by no means incompatible with the theory that punishment is not mere retribution, but is designed to bring about some end; and such practices as the punishment of idiots, animals and even inanimate objects do not prove that their practitioners were intuitionists who claimed to be directly aware that certain actions "ought to be punished," the morality of the punishment being in no way dependent on any supposed advantage to those who inflict it. Such practices are always found in conjunction with a special theological theory as to the nature of the universe. It is held that the Gods require certain sorts of conduct on the part of human beings and that they will visit breaches of the rules with their wrath in the form of plagues, famines and other undesirable events. It is to prevent these that punishment is inflicted; and this explains why it is that what *we* call the morality of the action, which includes the condition that it be voluntary, is not held to affect the morality of punishment, a point which orthodox retributionists have some difficulty in explaining. If the volition of the agent is held to be irrelevant to the operation of God's wrath, it will also be irrelevant to the morality of punishment, since the object of punishment is not to requite a voluntarily committed wrong but to ward off God's anger. Oedipus has committed parricide and incest. He must be punished, not because he did so, still less because he intended to do so, but because the tribe that harbours him will suffer if he is not. Punishment is expiation.

When a society holds theological beliefs other than our own we shall not be surprised to find that its moral ideas differ also. Retributive punishment does not have the object that punishment has with us, and it does not (we believe) achieve the results aimed at. But neither of these facts tends to show that it did not originally have some purpose, and it is a curious fact that the retributive practice tends to become mollified (in the form of purely ritual expiation) and finally abandoned, precisely when the crude theology on which it is based ceases to be believed. Now if retributive practices are due entirely to instinct or to an intuition of fittingness it is hard to see why this should be so. It is apparently a pure coincidence that the intuitive light grows dim precisely when a certain theological theory is abandoned. But if the purposive theory is true it is easy to see why the retributive element should tend to give way before the reformatory and deterrent elements when people abandon the belief that punishment will obviate the failure of crops but conceive (or retain) the belief that it will benefit society by inhibiting certain forms of action. When we abandon the belief that God will visit his wrath on a tribe that harbours an unwitting parricide, we no longer have any motive for punishing him. Consequently we call him innocent. A man is not punishable because he is guilty; he is guilty because he is punishable, that is to say, because some useful result is supposed to accrue from punishing him.

If this is true, we can also explain why it is that modern retributionists, who do not hold the crude theological beliefs with which I have suggested that the practice was originally linked, fall back on an intuition of fittingness. Here, as elsewhere, intuition is invoked to account for a belief that we are quite certain that we hold but for which we have forgotten the original grounds and cannot discover new ones. It often happens that a belief is retained after the theory on which it is based and which alone makes it plausible has been abandoned, and this is particularly liable to happen in ethics for the following reason. Metaphysical and scientific views are changed by the speculation of a few intellectuals, who are regarded by the many as harmless. But morals, as Hume said, excite our passions and produce and prevent action. The moral reformer, therefore, unlike the speculator, is treated as a danger to society; and for this reason morality tends to be more conservative than other branches of thought. Hence there sometimes arises a lack of logical relation between the metaphysical and scientific ideas of a society and its moral code, the latter being partly a survival from older modes of thought. When this process of survival occurs in a society not our own we call it a superstition or a taboo; when it occurs in our own we call it a Moral Law. Now the retributive theory has a logical justification if a certain theological view is accepted. That view having been abandoned, the justification no longer exists and we are forced to fall back on a direct intuition that punishment is fitting.

V

The analysis suggested at the beginning of the last section can now be applied to the examples used earlier in the paper. We saw that, apart from the empirical difficulty of deciding to what class an action belongs, there are two difficulties of principle. One is the problem of determining what classes of actions are voluntary; the other the problem of showing a connexion between being voluntary and being liable to praise or blame. It has, I think, usually been the practice to try to solve the first of these problems first; but this leaves us, as we saw, in the insuperable difficulty of libertarianism and also renders the second problem insoluble. If the theory I have suggested is correct, the second problem should come first and is simply the empirical problem of deciding what characteristics are alterable; and the solution to this problem then provides the criterion for deciding what actions are voluntary. The preliminary analysis of the case of the schoolmaster left unexplained the meaning of the vital sentence, "A could have acted otherwise, while B could not" and also the question "Why is laziness punishable and stupidity not?" It is not enough to say that A's failure was voluntary because he is known to have acted rightly before. Perhaps he was not lazy then but is now. And how do we know that his laziness now is not just as much beyond his control as was his industriousness then and as is B's stupidity now? An analysis made on these lines cannot fail to land us in the difficulty in which Aristotle left us. A will plead that his laziness was caused and therefore involuntary. On the other hand, if, instead of assuming that A ought to be punished because he is morally guilty, we suppose that he ought to be punished for some other reason, the rationale of the schoolmaster's action becomes clear. He knows from experience that, if he adds the fear of punishment to the motives actuating A, then A will tend to get these sums right in future, which is, for him, the end to be achieved. On the other hand, if B is stupid, neither threats nor promises will cause him to do better. When we say that A could have done the sum correctly, had he so chosen, we do not imply that he could, on that occasion, have so chosen. But we do imply that A is such that, under certain circumstances, he will choose to act correctly; and those circumstances can be brought about. Rewards and punishments are means of varying the causal antecedents of actions so that those we desire will occur and those we wish to prevent will not occur. Cleverness and industriousness are both valuable characteristics; the latter is called a "moral" one and the former not, because we know from experience that the former cannot be induced by means of praise and blame, while the latter can. It is surely no accident that the characteristics that we believe to be alterable in this way are precisely those that we call moral; and this also explains why, to be moral, an act must be voluntary. To say that a man could have acted otherwise is to say that he might have been the sort of person who would have acted otherwise; and to attribute his acting as he did to his moral character, as opposed to some amoral defect, is to say that his action was due to one of the characteristics that can be altered by means of rewards and punishments.

It is not necessary to undertake an elaborate analysis of the other examples used. If a man kills someone because he is physically compelled to do so, he will not be prevented from doing so again in similar circumstances by the knowledge that the action will be severely punished. But if his action is due to his own decision, this knowledge may cause him to decide otherwise in future. In the same way the basis for the distinction between the kleptomaniac and the thief is that the latter is held to have decided to steal. Here the cause in both cases lies within the agent and the distinction of internal and external causation did not help us. The fact that one commits a voluntary action and the other does not is important, but by itself it does not account for the differential treatment of the two men. Why are men who steal as a result of a decision said to be worthy of punishment, while those who steal from some other cause are not? The reason is that we believe that the fear of punishment will affect the future behaviour of the thief but not that of the kleptomaniac. If a man steals because he has decided to do so, we can prevent his doing so again by causing him to decide otherwise. If he expects to be punished, then in addition to the motive that tends to make him steal there will be a powerful motive tending to make him refrain. Now the fear of punishment has no such influence on the kleptomaniac; on the other hand, psychoanalysis, by removing the subconscious cause of his tendency to steal, may achieve the desired result. Nor is this merely an interesting but unimportant distinction between kleptomaniacs and thieves; it is the very basis for the distinction. In each case we make the same value judgement, that the abstraction of one's neighbours, goods is undesirable. If we consider the actions of the thief and the kleptomaniac simply as events, without regard to their causes, they are identical and provide no possible basis for differential treatment. Therefore the different moral judgements that we in fact make and the different treatments that we accord cannot be based on the value judgement alone. The moral judgements are concerned with the causes of the actions. But to say that avarice is a reprehensible cause and kleptomania not explains nothing. For we cannot, without appeal to dubious intuitions, assert that of two similar undesirable events one is morally reprehensible and the other not. Nor is it enough to say with the positivists that the fact that we make these distinctions is simply a brute fact about our society and requires no explanation. Some basis must be found for the distinction, and I suggest that it is to be found in the fact that, while potential thieves will be deterred by the prospect of six months' hard labour, potential kleptomaniacs will not.

Generalising from these instances, we can see that the relation that is held to exist between voluntary wrong-doing and punishability is neither an inexplicable sociological fact nor a mysterious relation of "merit" that some of us are able to intuit; it is a relation of cause and effect. If this is so, then, whatever views we may hold about the subjectivity of value judgements, moral judgements, being judgements of cause and effect, are all objective. Many moral philosophers have held subjectivist doctrines about other forms of value, such as pleasure or aesthetic taste, but have been unwilling to allow that moral judgements are subjective, and this in spite of the fact that the arguments leading to subjectivism in aesthetics appear to apply equally to morals. I think that their hesitation has been correct and has not always been due to the irrational considerations, such as the fear that subjectivity in ethics might undermine society, that have sometimes been attributed to them. If the proposed separation of the value element from the moral element in moral judgement be accepted, their unwillingness to accept a purely subjective theory of ethics will have been justified.

AUTHOR'S COMMENTARY

THE MAIN PURPOSE of my article was to analyse the ideas of freedom and desert in terms of the empirical idea of "alterability by rewards and punishments" and thus reduce the number of intuitions required in this area. This attempt led me to conclude that "a man is not punishable because he is guilty; he is guilty because he is punishable, that is to say, because some useful purpose is supposed to accrue from punishing him." The question of freedom is too complicated for discussion in a postscript; something may be said about desert.

1. The idea that a punishment can and should "fit" a crime now seems to me to derive partly from a simple failure to distinguish punishment from damages, the purpose of civil law from the purpose of criminal law. It may be difficult to assess in monetary terms the amount of loss sustained by the plaintiff in a civil suit; but, once this is assessed, it is a simple matter to assess the damages which it is "fitting" for the court to award. For the purpose of the award is, as nearly as possible, to make good the loss. Since a *fine* of $100 awarded by a criminal court has the same effect on the pocket as an award of $100 *damages* in a civil court, we tend to confuse the two and to suppose that the idea of "fittingness" between loss and reparation can be transferred to crime and punishment.

2. The major defect of the article lies in the failure to distinguish *cases* from *rules,* the judge's question, "Should this man in the dock, John Doe, be punished?" from the legislator's question, "Should acts of Type N be prohibited by law and, in consequence, people who do acts of Type N become liable to punishment?" When we say that John Doe deserves to be punished we certainly do not *mean* that it would be useful to punish him; nor would most of

us subscribe to the *moral* view that it is just to punish him if and only if it is useful to do so. Desert is a matter of law. He deserves to be punished at all only if he has broken a law, and the severity of the punishment that he deserves is determined by what the law lays down. Considerations of utility can come in at this point only in so far as the law allows the judge a discretion to bring them in. But the legislator, I should now say, should be guided solely by considerations of utility. It is right to make a law forbidding acts of Type N only if (a) such acts are "bad" in the nonmoral sense referred to in the article and (b) the propensity to do them is one that can be weakened or eliminated by the threat of punishment.

3. In this modified theory the idea of a general fittingness between crime and punishment (as distinct from the fittingness of punishing this man in just this way) still has an important place. Deterring people from a particular type of act is never our sole aim; hence the deterrent effect of a penalty should not be the sole consideration of the legislator. While it still seems to me quite impossible to say that a certain type or degree of punishment is "fitting" to a certain type of crime, a more complex notion of fittingness is possible. Most people would agree that some types of crime are worse than others, whether or not they were prepared to analyse "worse" in terms of degree of disutility. If now we construct a scale of severity of punishment, it seems just that the punishment for a greater crime should be more severe than that for a lesser. This rule embodies a four-term relation of fittingness; it cuts across the principle of deterrence, since it may well occur that a milder penalty would deter people from the greater crime; and it can be accommodated within the framework of a utilitarian account. For a utilitarian will be more concerned to prevent greater crimes than lesser. If the penalty for a lesser crime were made equal to or greater than that for a greater crime—which it well might be if deterrence were our sole criterion—such a system, though tending to decrease the volume of the lesser crime, might increase the volume of the greater. For example, if the penalty for burglary is as great as that for murder, no doubt the number of burglaries will be reduced; but those burglars who are still not deterred will commit murder in order not to be caught. The purely deterrent rule would not then be the most "useful." As in all such matters our decision has to be made after considering the many different consequences of adopting one law rather than another. The admission of an idea of "fittingness" of this complex kind does not seem to me to entail the falsity of my thesis that desert must, *in the end,* be explained in terms of alterability by punishment; but the explanation is a good deal more complicated than I used to think.

Questions

1. Professor Nowell-Smith claims that it is fallacious for the Libertarians to argue that "if our actions are predictable we are 'pawns in the hands of fate' and cannot choose what we shall do." How does he attempt to justify this claim? Give your reasons for agreeing, or disagreeing, with him.

2. If there is not a strict determinism in psychology, Professor Nowell-Smith

says, there is not an increase but a limitation of our freedom of action. What reasons does he give for saying this? Why, in your opinion, are his reasons acceptable, or unacceptable?

3. Professor Nowell-Smith argues that "freedom, so far from being incompatible with causality, implies it." In what respects is his argument similar to, and in what respects is it different from, that of David Hume in the selection in this chapter beginning on page 442?

4. Professor Nowell-Smith asserts that "A could have acted otherwise" does *not* mean "A, being what he was and being placed in the circumstances in which he was placed, could have done something other than what he did." What does he assert that it *does* mean? State why you think he is, or is not, correct in his assertion about what it means.

5. ". . . 'Can we justly blame a man if his vicious actions are due to hereditary epilepsy or to the influence of a corrupt and vicious court?' To this the answer is that we can and do." How does Professor Nowell-Smith defend this answer?

6. Review Section II and the first half of the first paragraph of Section III of the reading. Then state in your own words what it means to act *freely*, according to this portion of the reading.

7. On what grounds does Professor Nowell-Smith reject the positivist explanation of why we hold one person morally responsible and not another?

8. How does Professor Nowell-Smith distinguish moral judgments from value judgments in general? How do you think he would reply to the objection that there are many actions which are "good" or "bad" and are caused by someone's voluntary decision, yet no one would think of calling them "moral" (e.g., an artist's creating a good or bad painting, a historian's writing a good or bad history book, or a chess player's making good or bad moves in a chess game)?

9. According to Professor Nowell-Smith, what is the connection between the fact that an action is voluntary and the fact that it is liable to praise or blame?

10. "A man is not punishable because he is guilty; he is guilty because he is punishable. . . ." What argument does Professor Nowell-Smith give in support of this statement?

11. In order to test your understanding of the reading, complete the following sentence as you think Professor Nowell-Smith has completed it in the reading. Then check your answer with the sentence itself. (It occurs in the first paragraph of Section V.) "Cleverness and industriousness are both valuable characteristics; the latter is called a 'moral' one and the former not, because . . ."

12. How does Professor Nowell-Smith explain why a thief is held morally responsible but not a kleptomaniac? Does his explanation make it possible for us to *justify* holding a thief but not a kleptomaniac responsible? Defend your answer.

13. In his commentary on his article, Professor Nowell-Smith says that "the major defect of the article lies in the failure to distinguish *cases* from *rules*. . . ." Explain what this distinction is, and show its bearing on the problem of justifying punishment.

Suggested Further Reading | *Classic Works*

Aquinas, St. Thomas, *Summa Theologica* (1265-1272), First Part of the Second Part, Questions 6-10, 12-14, 17-20. This material is contained in *The Basic Writings of St. Thomas Aquinas,* Vol. 1, ed. by Anton C. Pegis, Random House, N. Y., 1944, Chap. XI.

Hobbes, Thomas, *Leviathan* (1651), Chap. XXI; *Of Liberty and Necessity* (1654).

James, William, "The Dilemma of Determinism" (1884), reprinted in *Essays in Faith and Morals,* by William James, Longmans, Green, N. Y., 1949.

Mill, John Stuart, *A System of Logic* (1843), Book VI, Chap. 2.

Spinoza, Benedict de, *Ethics* (1678), Parts IV and V. See also *The Philosophy of Spinoza,* ed. by Joseph Ratner, Random House (The Modern Library), N. Y., Chaps. XI, XIV, XV, and XIX.

Introductory Studies

Ayer, A. J., "Freedom and Necessity," *Polemic,* No. 5, 1946. Reprinted in *Philosophical Essays,* by A. J. Ayer, Macmillan, London, 1954.

Campbell, C. A., *Scepticism and Construction,* Allen and Unwin, London, 1931, Chaps. IV and V.

Hobart, R. E., "Free Will as Involving Determination and Inconceivable Without It," *Mind,* Vol. 43, 1934.

Hospers, John, *An Introduction to Philosophical Analysis,* Prentice-Hall, Englewood Cliffs, N. J., 1953, Chap. 4.

Moore, G. E., *Ethics,* Oxford University Press, London, 1912, Chap. VI.

Raab, Francis V., "Free Will and the Ambiguity of 'Could,'" *Philosophical Review,* Vol. 64, 1955.

Wilson, John, "Freedom and Compulsion," *Mind,* Vol. 68, 1958.

Advanced Studies

Campbell, C. A., "Is 'Free Will' a Pseudo-Problem?" *Mind,* Vol. 60, 1951.

———, *On Selfhood and Godhood,* Allen and Unwin, London, 1957, Lecture IX and Appendix B.

Hampshire, S., W. G. Maclagen, and R. M. Hare, "The Freedom of the Will," *Aristotelian Society Supplementary Volume 25,* 1951.

Hook, Sidney, ed., *Determinism and Freedom in the Age of Modern Science,* New York University Press, N. Y., 1958.

Nowell-Smith, P. H., *Ethics,* Penguin Books, Harmondsworth, Middlesex, Eng., 1954, Chaps. 19 and 20.

———, "Determinists and Libertarians," *Mind,* Vol. 63, 1954.

Sellars, Wilfrid, and John Hospers, eds., *Readings in Ethical Theory,* Appleton-Century-Crofts, N. Y., 1952, Sec. VII.

Chapter Six

THE PROBLEM OF
Moral Knowledge

What Is Morality?

All of us possess standards of right and wrong which we acquired in childhood when our parents told us what we ought and ought not to do, when they showed their approval and disapproval, and when they rewarded and punished us. In giving us this moral guidance our parents were committing themselves, whether they were aware of it or not, to certain answers to the fundamental questions of human behavior: How should I live? What sort of person ought I to try to become? What is my duty to others and to myself? What kinds of actions are right and what kinds are wrong? Similarly, we commit ourselves to specific answers to these questions when we bring up our own children. But despite this early moral training which we all receive, we sometimes find ourselves in situations where we are not sure what we ought to do, and in our mature life we may occasionally try to find our own answers to moral questions. To reflect about such questions is to examine the principles on which our practical lives are based. The attempt to find acceptable answers to such questions is the ultimate aim of moral philosophy.

Moral questions are, of course, not the only kind of practical questions. Consider the difference between asking, "How should I live?" and asking, "What should I do in order to increase the profits of my business?" Or to take another example, consider the difference between telling a person who is learning to play baseball what the duties of a catcher are, and telling a person what

his moral duty is. What is the difference? What makes a question or a statement a moral one? Perhaps the best way to answer this is by saying that moral questions are those which we answer by citing moral rules, moral ideals, or moral standards; moral statements are those which, when challenged, we defend the same way. A *moral rule* (sometimes called a moral principle) is a rule which we believe ought to govern the conduct of human beings as human beings, in contrast to the special rules which govern the conduct of human beings as business executives, baseball players, dinner guests, or automobile drivers. The rules of successful business practice, of baseball, of etiquette, and of traffic are none of them moral rules, although they may sometimes prescribe the same actions as are prescribed by moral rules. We would not say that a baseball player was morally obligated to leave the batter's box after striking out, although we would say that he was morally obligated not to throw the game. The act of deliberately losing a baseball game is morally wrong, not because it violates any rule of the game, but because it violates the obligation of all human beings to be honest. A moral rule, then, may be defined as a rule which we expect every human being to follow, simply because he is a human being.

Similarly, a *moral ideal* is a conception of a perfect way of life, rather than a perfect way of swimming, studying, or teaching. Or it is a conception of the good man, rather than of the good swimmer, the good student, or the good teacher. As such, a moral ideal is an ideal which all men ought to try to live up to. *Moral standards* (which may but need not take the form of moral rules or ideals) are the standards by which we decide the goodness or badness of a person's character, or the rightness or wrongness of his action, again simply with respect to his being a human being among other human beings, and not with respect to any special role which he has in practical life.

From these definitions we see that the moral aspect of any rule, ideal, or standard of human conduct is its claim to universal applicability, that is, its claim to apply to all human beings everywhere and at all times. For to say that a moral rule governs the conduct of human beings as human beings is to say that it is a rule which all human beings everywhere and at all times ought to follow. (This is not, however, the same as saying that all human beings everywhere and at all times actually do follow it, or even that they actually believe they ought to follow it.) Thus if we state that the rule, "In ordinary circumstances it is wrong to lie," is a moral rule, we imply that in ordinary circumstances *no* human being ought to lie. The same thing may be said of moral ideals and moral standards. If we point to the life of Abraham Lincoln or of some other historical figure as exemplifying a moral ideal, we are making the implicit value judgment that all human beings ought to try to imitate such a life. And to say, for example, that the standard for determining whether an action is morally right or wrong is whether or not it leads to the general happiness of mankind, is to say that such a standard ought to be adopted universally, and that it is the standard which does distinguish the moral rightness and wrongness of all actions of all men everywhere.

The Problem of Moral Knowledge

The problem of moral knowledge arises when we investigate the possibility of justifying this claim to universality. Suppose a person who asks us a moral question or who challenges our moral judgments is not satisfied with our answer because he is unwilling to accept, as universally binding on all men, the rules, ideals, or standards to which we appeal. Or suppose that we ourselves begin to question the universal applicability of the very rules, ideals, or standards with which we have grown up and which constitute the moral code of our society. At this point we must decide whether we should continue to accept or whether we should reject those rules, ideals, and standards as genuinely moral, i.e., as applicable to all men everywhere. We are forced to examine the basis on which we have previously justified our moral judgments. And this means we must examine the grounds on which our moral knowledge rests. To do this in a clear and systematic way is to do moral philosophy.

The task of moral philosophy is to solve the problem of moral knowledge, that is, to answer the question, "How do we know what rules, ideals, and standards are applicable to all men?" This question demands that we find out, first, whether there is any basis for the justification of moral claims, and second, if there is such a basis, what it consists in. Moral philosophers have disputed about both parts of this problem. Some have denied any basis for justifying moral claims, while others have asserted that there is such a basis. But among the latter there has been fundamental disagreement about what constitutes a valid basis.

The denial of any basis for justifying moral claims is sometimes called *ethical relativism*. According to this point of view there are no rules, ideals, or standards of human conduct that can justifiably be applied to all men everywhere. Within a given society which accepts a certain set of rules, ideals, and standards, these may be applied to the individual members of the society. But there is no justification for applying them to individuals outside the society. Ethical relativism is to be contrasted with the opposite point of view known as *ethical absolutism,* according to which there are rules, ideals, and standards that are genuinely moral, i.e., applicable to all men in all societies.

Ethical Relativism and the Facts of Ethical Relativity

One of the arguments which ethical relativists give in support of their position is based on certain findings in history, psychology, and the social sciences. These findings may be summed up in the following three statements of fact: (1) There exists great variation in the rules, ideals, and standards accepted by different societies at different times in history. (2) Most human beings are ethnocentric, i.e., they believe the rules, ideals, and standards of their own society to be the only true ones. (3) The conscience and moral beliefs of every person come from his social environment. Let us consider these three facts briefly and see how they are claimed to provide a "scientific proof" of ethical relativism.

Through the studies of historians and anthropologists we learn that in some societies slavery has been approved of and in others it has been disapproved of, that some societies have practiced human sacrifice and others have condemned such a practice. We observe that some people have seen nothing wrong in having children work twelve hours a day in coal mines, while others have led reform movements against such "wrongs." We find that in one society public nakedness is considered a very shameful thing, while in another society it is practiced by everyone and considered perfectly proper.

We also find that in each society most people are absolutely sure that their own view of what is right and wrong represents the one true morality. The phenomenon of ethnocentrism is to be observed in the most diverse societies. People everywhere tend to think that their own way of life is superior to all others and that their own moral rules, ideals, and standards are the only acceptable ones. This trait is most pronounced in people who lead provincial lives. We may have noticed complacent, conventional people in our own communities who never have any doubts about their moral beliefs because their lives have brought them into contact only with people who agree with them.

Finally, we learn from psychology that the process by which all people acquire their moral convictions is

the process of "introjection" or incorporation into one's own mind of the precepts and moral attitudes of others, particularly of one's parents or of other persons *in loco parentis* in one's youth. As a result of this process, the attitudes of impressive persons in one's early environment (and to some extent throughout life) become a permanent part of one's own mental structure, become "second nature," as the popular expression has it. Through this process, too, moral standards and conventions become handed on from one generation to another, thus giving permanence and stability to the codes and traditions of society.[1]

Now the ethical relativists take these three facts to mean that the moral judgments of a given society are "relative" to the rules, ideals, and standards accepted by that society, and that those rules, ideals, and standards are themselves "relative" to that society in the sense that they can be applied only in that society. Consequently, the code of one society cannot be judged as better or worse than the code of another. There are no absolute standards of comparison since all standards are "relative" to the society in which they are "introjected" and handed on from one generation to the next. Therefore no code is universally applicable to all men. It follows that the very same kind of action which is right in one society may be wrong in another, that what are vices to us may be virtues to others, and so on. A moral judgment which we believe to be true (e.g., "genocide is wrong") is true only relatively to our own standards. The same judgment will be false relatively to other standards. A person can be said to make a mistake in his moral judgments only in the sense that they do not conform to the accepted code of his society. Thus we must say that for Nazis the judgment that all Jews ought to be exterminated was a correct moral judgment since it conformed to the code of Nazism. In our society, however, the same judgment would be false. To claim that the entire code of Nazism was mistaken, or even to claim that it was morally inferior to another code, is to set up one code as an absolute standard, and this is never justifiable. All standards and ideals come from one social environment or another. Therefore it is nothing but narrow-minded dogmatism to apply one code to all men in all societies. According to the ethical relativist, when we say that a person knows what is right and wrong all we can possibly mean is that the person knows how to apply the particular rules, ideals, and standards of his own society in making moral judgments. We cannot go farther and claim that the person is justified in accepting those rules, ideals, and standards. For ethical relativism, then, there are no grounds for a universal moral code.

Ethical Absolutism

The ethical absolutist, on the other hand, claims that there is one true set of moral rules, ideals, and standards which apply to all men in all societies. According to this view, people can be correct or mistaken not only in their moral judgments, but also in their rules, ideals, and standards, since one moral code may be superior to another.

It is important not to confuse ethical absolutism with ethnocentrism, dogmatism, or intolerance. The ethical absolutist theoretically need not be ethnocentric, dogmatic, or intolerant, although historically he has often been all three. The ethical absolutist may well believe, contrary to ethnocentrism, that the code of his own society is not as advanced, as enlightened, or as justified as that of some other society. Or he may have constructed in his own thought an ideal moral code which he believes is superior

[1] J. C. Flugel, *Man, Morals and Society,* International Universities Press, N. Y., 1945, p. 35. For a more detailed analysis of how we learn moral principles, see the selection by R. M. Hare in this chapter (page 583).

to any existing code, including the one in which he himself was morally educated. But he may hold his belief with some degree of doubt. He may be somewhat uncertain whether one code (either actually existing or mentally constructed) is really better than another. Indeed, to the extent that the ethical absolutist seeks reasons for accepting one code and rejecting another, and to the extent that the reasons which he finds do not yield certainty, he will be undogmatic and skeptical, holding his belief only to some degree of probability. In short, ethical absolutism without ethical dogmatism is the view *that* there are moral truths without certainty as to *what* they are. Finally the ethical absolutist may want to tolerate all sorts of moral beliefs and practices, since he may be in doubt about whether his own are really superior to those of others. He may place a high value on tolerance as a social condition necessary for carrying on the search for the most enlightened moral code. Or he may simply believe in tolerance itself as a true moral virtue and a basic principle of an ideal society. The ethical relativist, on the other hand, though often identified as the supreme advocate of tolerance, cannot in fact claim that tolerance is really a good thing since there are societies which neither practice nor preach tolerance, and in totalitarian societies tolerance is actually an evil. To be consistent the relativist must, therefore, say that tolerance is good only in a democratic type of society, but is bad in a totalitarian society.

The Facts of Ethical Relativity as Compatible with Both Relativism and Absolutism

Is not ethical absolutism clearly false in light of the three facts which the relativist takes as a proof of the relativity of all moral judgments and of all moral codes? The answer is "No," for the following reason. The ethical absolutist can perfectly well accept all three facts without contradicting his own position. We must not confuse *the facts of ethical relativity* with *the theory of ethical relativism*. The fact that people disagree in their moral judgments and codes does not imply that they are all equally justified (or unjustified) in accepting those judgments and codes, or that there is no way to decide which of them are correct and which are mistaken. To show that what one society *believes* to be right another society *believes* to be wrong is by no means to show that what *is* right in one society *is* wrong in another. The relativist's conclusion would follow only under the assumption that an action is right or wrong because it is thought to be right or wrong, and this assumption cannot be taken for granted without further proof. Similarly, the fact that each society maintains that its own moral code is the only true one does not imply that each society is justified in maintaining this. And we must remember that the absolutist himself is not necessarily ethnocentric. Finally, the fact that all moral beliefs come from the social environment has nothing to do with whether or not there are valid grounds for holding them. The grounds which justify a belief are not the same as its psychological causes or origins. We conclude, therefore, that the three facts of ethical relativity are equally compatible with ethical relativism and ethical absolutism.

The real difference between the two ethical theories concerns the possibility of finding grounds on the basis of which, not only moral judgments, but also moral rules, ideals, and standards can be justified. If moral judgments can be justified only on the grounds of rules, ideals, and standards which are themselves without any sort of justification, then ethical relativism is true. On the other hand, if we can justify the acceptance of a set of rules, ideals, and standards as universally binding on all men, then the possibility of ethical absolutism is established. But the full argument for ethical absolutism requires that we state how this can be done, that we state, in other words, how we can obtain genuine knowledge of a universally applicable moral code.

Arguments For and Against Ethical Relativism and Absolutism

Perhaps the strongest argument against ethical absolutism (and for ethical relativism) in recent moral philosophy is based on the idea that moral judgments are not really judgments at all, but are merely "emotive" utterances which express the attitudes of those who utter them. (See the selection by A. J. Ayer in this chapter, page 575.) If one can show that there are no grounds on the basis of which an attitude can ultimately be justified and if, as this view maintains, moral judgments are nothing but expressions of attitudes, it follows that no moral judgment could be said to be true or false in any universal or absolute sense.

Any argument against ethical relativism (and for ethical absolutism) must show how it is possible to obtain genuine moral knowledge, so that we can determine in any given case whether what someone *thinks* is right or wrong is *really* right or wrong, that is, so that we can determine in any given case whether someone's moral judgment is true or false. There have been many different attempts to do this in the history of philosophy, and this chapter contains some of the most important and famous of these attempts. In each case the moral philosopher examines the grounds on which moral knowledge rests and tries to show how these grounds justify the acceptance of a certain rule of conduct, ideal of life, or standard of good behavior, or a certain set of such rules, ideals, and standards, as applicable to all men everywhere. One philosopher finds the grounds of genuine moral knowledge in our knowledge of human nature (Aristotle); another finds such grounds in a special kind of human feeling (Hume); another in a moral intuition (Price); another in pure reason (Kant); and still another in certain consequences of human behavior (Mill). In each case there is a different conception of the ultimate basis of the justification of moral rules, ideals, and standards. It is for the reader to decide for himself which of these conceptions, if any, is correct.

In the reading by R. M. Hare (page 583), we are presented with a new approach to moral philosophy. Mr. Hare studies the way people in everyday life actually use moral statements and the way they actually reason about moral questions. The logical relations among moral concepts and judgments, which are implicit in ordinary moral discourse, are then made explicit and analyzed. Whether this approach to moral philosophy leads to ethical relativism or to ethical absolutism is a matter to be determined by the reader.

The Moral Philosopher and the Moralist

A final remark should be made about the difference between a moral philosopher and a moralist. A moralist is one who tells us what is right and wrong, what our duty is, what ideals we should strive for, what vices we should try to get rid of, and so on. That is, he is primarily concerned with uttering moral judgments and with getting people to become morally good. He may use rational arguments or he may use various other means of persuasion, such as exhortation and inspirational preaching. The moral philosopher, on the other hand, is not primarily concerned with making moral judgments but with examining their meaning and their justifiability. In other words, while the moralist *uses* moral language for moral purposes, the moral philosopher *studies* that language for intellectual purposes. The moral philosopher is trying to *discover truth* (about the meanings of moral concepts and the justification of moral judg-

ments); the moralist is trying to *bring about a better world*. The moralist assumes, in all his activities, that certain rules, ideals, and standards are true. The moral philosopher examines these very assumptions to see whether they are justified. In the selections which follow, the authors will sometimes be found making moral judgments. They will sometimes tell us (as moralists) what they consider to be right and wrong, or what our duty is, in addition to telling us (as moral philosophers) how we can *know* these things. But the main interest in these selections is not the excellence or correctness of their moral content (according to the editors' own moral standards), but the importance of their contribution to the study of moral knowledge. It is as good moral philosophers, not as good moralists, that these particular philosophers were chosen for inclusion in this chapter.

Teleological Naturalism | Aristotle
(384-322 B.C.)

Aristotle was a student in the Academy at Athens, where he was taught by Plato, the founder of the Academy. On the death of Plato in 347 B.C., Aristotle left the Academy and was away from Athens for about thirteen years. He spent part of this time as tutor to the young Alexander of Macedon. When Aristotle returned to Athens he founded his own college, the Lyceum, where he taught until the year before his death.

Aristotle wrote on a wide range of topics, including logic, metaphysics, physics, biology, psychology, politics, dramaturgy, and ethics. His writings have had a great influence over twenty-four centuries of Western intellectual history. The following reading is from *The Nicomachean Ethics,* named for his son, Nicomachus.

In this reading Aristotle attempts to establish our knowledge of what is morally right and wrong on the basis of our knowledge of human nature. The central idea in his ethical theory is that man is a being who seeks certain goals or ends. In order to accomplish these ends, there are certain functions which man must perform in a proper way. Aristotle thinks that if we comprehend clearly what these proper functions are, we will understand the nature of good and evil, virtue and vice. This moral philosophy is called "teleological" because its basic concept is that of *purpose.* It is called "naturalism" because it attempts to derive our moral knowledge solely from our factual knowledge of the nature of man.

This selection includes parts of Books I, II, and X of *The Nicomachean Ethics,* as translated and edited by Professor J. A. K. Thomson. Professor Thomson's explanatory comments are also included, printed in italics.

From *The Ethics of Aristotle,* translated by J. A. K. Thomson, George Allen and Unwin, Ltd., London, 1953. Reprinted by permission of the publisher.

It is thought that every activity, artistic or scientific, in fact every deliberate action or pursuit, has for its object the attainment of some good. We may therefore assent to the view which has been expressed that "the good" is "that at which all things aim." Since modes of action involving the practised hand and the instructed brain are numerous, the number of their ends is proportionately large. For instance, the end of medical science is health; of military science, victory; of economic science, wealth. All skills of that kind which come under a single "faculty"—a skill in making bridles or any other part of a horse's gear comes under the faculty or art of horsemanship, while horsemanship itself and every branch of military practice comes under the art of war, and in like manner other arts and techniques are subordinate to yet others—in all these the ends of the master arts are to be preferred to those of the subordinate skills, for it is the former that provide the motive for pursuing the latter.

Now if there is an end which as moral agents we seek for its own sake, and which is the cause of our seeking all the other ends—if we are not to go on choosing one act for the sake of another, thus landing ourselves in an infinite progression with the result that desire will be frustrated and ineffectual—it is clear that this must be the good, that is the absolutely good. May we not then argue from this that a knowledge of the good is a great advantage to us in the conduct of our lives? Are we not more likely to hit the mark if we have a target? If this be true, we must do our best to get at least a rough idea of what the good really is, and which of the sciences, pure or applied, is concerned with the business of achieving it.

Ethics is a branch of politics. That is to say, it is the duty of the statesman to create for the citizen the best possible opportunity of living the good life. It will be seen that the effect of this injunction is not to degrade morality but to moralize politics. The modern view that "you cannot make men better by act of parliament" would have been repudiated by Aristotle as certainly as by Plato and indeed by ancient philosophers in general.

Now most people would regard the good as the end pursued by that study which has most authority and control over the rest. Need I say that this is the science of politics? It is political science that prescribes what subjects are to be taught in states, which of these the different sections of the population are to learn, and up to what point. We see also that the faculties which obtain most regard come under this science: for example, the art of war, the management of property, the ability to state a case. Since, therefore, politics makes use of the other practical sciences, and lays it down besides what we must do and what we must not do, its end must include theirs. And that end, in politics as well as in ethics, can only be the good for man. For even if the good of the community coincides with that of the individual, the good of the community is clearly a greater and more perfect good both to get and to keep. This is not to deny that the good of the individual is worth while. But what is good for a nation or a city has a higher, a diviner, quality.

Such being the matters we seek to investigate, the investigation may fairly be represented as the study of politics. . . .

Let us resume our consideration of what is the end of political science. For want of a better word we call it "Happiness." People are agreed on the word but not on its meaning.

To resume. Since every activity involving some acquired skill or some moral decision aims at some good, what do we take to be the end of politics—what is the supreme good attainable in our actions? Well, so far as the name goes there is pretty general agreement. "It is happiness," say both intellectuals and the unsophisticated, meaning by "happiness" living well or faring well. But when it comes to saying in what happiness consists, opinions differ, and the account given by the generality of mankind is not at all like that given by the philosophers. The masses take it to be something plain and tangible, like pleasure or money or social standing. Some maintain that it is one of these, some that it is another, and the same man will change his opinion about it more than once. When he has caught an illness he will say that it is health, and when he is hard up he will say that it is money. Conscious that they are out of their depths in such discussions, most people are impressed by anyone who pontificates and says something that is over their heads. Now it would no doubt be a waste of time to examine all these opinions; enough if we consider those which are most in evidence or have something to be said for them. Among these we shall have to discuss the view held by some that, over and above particular goods like those I have just mentioned, there is another which is good in itself and the cause of whatever goodness there is in all these others. . . .

A man's way of life may afford a clue to his genuine views upon the nature of happiness. It is therefore worth our while to glance at the different types of life.

There is a general assumption that the manner of a man's life is a clue to what he on reflection regards as the good—in other words, happiness. Persons of low tastes (always in the majority) hold that it is pleasure. Accordingly they ask for nothing better than the sort of life which consists in having a good time. (I have in mind the three well-known types of life—that just mentioned, that of the man of affairs, that of the philosophic student.) The utter vulgarity of the herd of men comes out in their preference for the sort of existence a cow leads. Their view would hardly get a respectful hearing, were it not that those who occupy great positions sympathize with a monster of sensuality like Sardanapalus.[1] The gentleman, however, and the man of affairs identify the good with honour, which may fairly be described as the end which men pursue in political or public life. Yet honour is surely too superficial a thing to be the good we are seeking. Honour depends more on those who confer than on him who receives it, and we cannot but feel that the good is something personal and almost inseparable from its possessor. Again, why do men seek honour? Surely in order to confirm the favourable opinion they have formed of themselves. It is at all events by intelligent men who know them personally that they seek to be honoured. And for what? For their moral qualities. The inference is clear; public men prefer virtue to honour. It might therefore seem reasonable to suppose that virtue rather than honour is the end pursued in the life of the public servant. But clearly even virtue cannot be quite the end. It is possible, most

[1] [Sardanapalus is usually identified as Assurbanipal, King of Assyria, 668-626 B.C.—Eds.]

people think, to possess virtue while you are asleep, to possess it without acting under its influence during any portion of one's life. Besides, the virtuous man may meet with the most atrocious luck or ill-treatment; and nobody, who was not arguing for argument's sake, would maintain that a man with an existence of that sort was "happy." The third type of life is the "contemplative," and this we shall discuss later.

As for the life of the business man, it does not give him much freedom of action. Besides, wealth obviously is not the good we seek, for the sole purpose it serves is to provide the means of getting something else. So far as that goes, the ends we have already mentioned would have a better title to be considered the good, for they are desired on their own account. But in fact even their claim must be disallowed. We may say that they have furnished the ground for many arguments, and leave the matter at that. . . .

What then is the good? If it is what all men in the last resort aim at, it must be happiness. And that for two reasons: (1) happiness is everything it needs to be, (2) it has everything it needs to have.

We return to the good which is the object of our search. What is it? The question must be asked because good seems to vary with the art or pursuit in which it appears. It is one thing in medicine and another in strategy, and so in the other branches of human skill. We must inquire, then, what is the good which is the end common to all of them. Shall we say it is that for the sake of which everything else is done? In medicine this is health, in military science victory, in architecture a building, and so on—different ends in different arts; every consciously directed activity has an end for the sake of which everything that it does is done. This end may be described as its good. Consequently, if there be some one thing which is the end of all things consciously done, this will be the doable good; or, if there be more than one end, then it will be all of these. Thus the ground on which our argument proceeds is shifted, but the conclusion arrived at is the same.

I must try, however, to make my meaning clearer.

In our actions we aim at more ends than one—that seems to be certain—but, since we choose some (wealth, for example, or flutes and tools or instruments generally) as means to something else, it is clear that not all of them are ends in the full sense of the word, whereas the good, that is the supreme good, is surely such an end. Assuming then that there is some one thing which alone is an end beyond which there are no further ends, we may call *that* the good of which we are in search. If there be more than one such final end, the good will be that end which has the highest degree of finality. An object pursued for its own sake possesses a higher degree of finality than one pursued with an eye to something else. A corollary to that is that a thing which is never chosen as a means to some remoter object has a higher degree of finality than things which are chosen both as ends in themselves and as means to such ends. We may conclude, then, that something which is always chosen for its own sake and never for the sake of something else is without qualification a final end.

Now happiness more than anything else appears to be just such an end, for we always choose it for its own sake and never for the sake of some other thing. It is different with honour, pleasure, intelligence and good qualities generally. We choose them indeed for their own sake in the sense that we should be glad to have them irrespective of any advantage which might accrue from them. But we also choose them for the sake of our happiness in the belief that they will be instrumental in promoting that. On the other hand nobody chooses happiness as a means of achieving them or anything else whatsoever than just happiness.

The same conclusion would seem to follow from another consideration. It is a generally accepted view that the final good is self-sufficient. By "self-sufficient" is meant not what is sufficient for oneself living the life of a solitary but includes parents, wife and children, friends and fellow-citizens in general. For man is a social animal. A self-sufficient thing, then, we take to be one which on its own footing tends to make life desirable and lacking in nothing. And we regard happiness as such a thing. Add to this that we regard it as the most desirable of all things without having it counted in with some other desirable thing. For, if such an addition were possible, clearly we should regard it as more desirable when even the smallest advantage was added to it. For the result would be an increase in the number of advantages, and the larger sum of advantages is preferable to the smaller.

Happiness then, the end to which all our conscious acts are directed, is found to be something final and self-sufficient.

But we desire a clearer definition of happiness. The way to this may be prepared by a discussion of what is meant by the "function" of a man.

But no doubt people will say, "To call happiness the highest good is a truism. We want a more distinct account of what it is." We might arrive at this if we could grasp what is meant by the "function" of a human being. If we take a flutist or a sculptor or any craftsman—in fact any class of men at all who have some special job or profession—we find that his special talent and excellence comes out in that job, and this is his function. The same thing will be true of man simply as man—that is of course if "man" does have a function. But is it likely that joiners and shoemakers have certain functions or specialized activities, while man as such has none but has been left by Nature a function-less being? Seeing that eye and hand and foot and every one of our members has some obvious function, must we not believe that in like manner a human being has a function over and above these particular functions? Then what exactly is it? The mere act of living is not peculiar to man—we find it even in the vegetable kingdom—and what we are looking for is something peculiar to him. We must therefore exclude from our definition the life that manifests itself in mere nurture and growth. A step higher should come the life that is confined to experiencing sensations. But that we see is shared by horses, cows, and the brute creation as a whole. We are left, then, with a life concerning which we can make two statements. First, it belongs to the rational part of man. Secondly, it finds expression in actions. The rational part may be either active or passive: passive in so far as it follows the dictates of reason, active in so far as it possesses and exercises the power of reasoning. A similar distinction can be drawn within the rational life; that is to say, the reasonable element in it may be active or passive. Let us take it that what we are concerned with here is the reasoning power in action, for it will be generally allowed that when we speak of "reasoning" we really mean *exercising* our reasoning faculties. (This seems the more correct use of the word.) Now let us assume for the moment the truth of the following propositions. (*a*) The function of a man is the exercise of his noncorporeal faculties or "soul" in accordance with, or at least not divorced from, a rational principle. (*b*) The function of an individual and of a *good* individual in the same class—a harp player, for example, and a good harp player, and so through the classes—is generically the same, except that we must add superiority in accomplishment to the function, the function of the harp player being merely to play on the harp, while the function of the good harp player is to play on it well. (*c*) The function of man is a certain form of life, namely an activity of the soul exercised in combination with a rational principle or reasonable ground of action. (*d*) The function of a good man is to exert such activity well. (*e*) A function is performed well when performed in accordance with the excellence proper to it. If these assumptions are granted, we conclude that the good for man is "an activity of soul in accordance with goodness" or (on the supposition that there may be more than one form of goodness) "in accordance with the best and most complete form of goodness."

Happiness is more than momentary bliss.

There is another condition of happiness; it cannot be achieved in less than a complete lifetime. One swallow does not make a summer; neither does one fine day. And one day, or indeed any brief period of felicity, does not make a man entirely and perfectly happy. . . .

Our definition of happiness compels us to consider the nature of virtue. But before we can do this we must have some conception of how the human soul is constituted. It will serve our purpose to take over (for what it is worth) the current psychology which divides the soul into "parts."

Happiness, then, being an activity of the soul in conformity with perfect goodness, it follows that we must examine the nature of goodness. When we have done this we should be in a better position to investigate the nature of happiness. There is this, too. The genuine statesman is thought of as a man who has taken peculiar pains to master this problem, desiring as he does to make his fellow-citizens good men obedient to the laws. Now, if the study of moral goodness is a part of political science, our inquiry into its nature will clearly follow the lines laid down in our preliminary observations.

Well, the goodness we have to consider is human goodness. This—I mean human goodness or (if you prefer to put it that way) human happiness—was what we set out to find. By human goodness is meant not fineness of physique but a right condition of the soul, and by happiness a condition of the soul. That being so, it is evident that the statesman ought to have some inkling of psychology, just as the doctor who is to specialize in diseases of the eye must have a general knowledge of physiology. Indeed, such a general background is even more necessary for the statesman in view of the fact that his science is of a higher order than the doctor's. Now the best kind of doctor takes a good deal of trouble to acquire a knowledge of the human body as a whole. Therefore the statesman should also be a psychologist and study the soul with an eye to his profession. Yet he will do so only as far as his own problems make it necessary; to go into greater detail on the subject would hardly be worth the labour spent on it.

Psychology has been studied elsewhere and some of the doctrines stated there may be accepted as adequate for our present purpose and used by us here. The soul is represented as consisting of two parts, a rational and an irrational. As regards the irrational part there is one subdivision of it which appears to be common to all living things, and this we may designate as having a "vegetative" nature, by which I mean that it is the cause of nutrition and growth, since one must assume the existence of some such vital force in all things that assimilate food. Now the excellence peculiar to this power is evidently common to the whole of animated nature and not confined to man. This view is supported by the admitted fact that the vegetative part of us is particularly active in sleep, when the good and the bad are hardest to distinguish. Such a phenomenon would be only natural, for sleep is a cessation of that function on the operation of which depends the goodness or badness of the soul. But enough of this, let us say no more about the nutritive part of the soul, since it forms no portion of goodness in the specifically *human* character.

But there would seem to be another constituent of the soul which, while irrational, contains an element of rationality. It may be observed in the types of men we call "continent" and "incontinent." They have a principle—a rational element in their souls—which we commend, because it encourages them to perform the best actions in the right way. But such natures appear at the same time to contain an irrational element in active opposition to the rational. In paralytic cases it often happens that when the patient wills to move his limbs to the right they swing instead to the left. Exactly the same thing may happen to the soul; the impulses of the incontinent man carry him in the opposite direction from that towards which he was aiming. The only difference is that, where the body is concerned, we see the uncontrolled limb, while the erratic impulse we do not see. Yet this should not prevent us from believing that besides the rational an irrational principle exists running opposite and counter to the other. Yet, as I said, it is not altogether irrational; at all events it submits to direction in the continent man, and may be assumed to be still more amenable to reason in the "temperate" and in the brave man, in whose moral make-up there is nothing which is at variance with reason.

We have, then, this clear result. The irrational part of the soul, like the soul itself, consists of two parts. The first of these is the vegetative, which has nothing rational about it at all. The second is that from which spring the appetites and desire in general; and this does in a way participate in reason, seeing that it is submissive and obedient to it. . . . That the irrational element in us need not be heedless of the rational is proved by the fact that we find admonition, indeed every form of censure and exhortation, not ineffective. It may be, however, that we ought to speak of the appetitive part of the soul as rational, too. In that event it will rather be the rational part that is divided in two, one division rational in the proper sense of the word and in its nature, the other in the derivative sense in which we speak of a child as "listening to reason" in the person of its father.

These distinctions within the soul supply us with a classification of the virtues. Some are called "intellectual," as wisdom, intelligence, prudence. Others are "moral," as liberality and temperance. When we are speaking of a man's *character* we do not describe him as wise or intelligent but as gentle or temperate. Yet we praise a wise man, too, on the ground of his "disposition" or settled habit of acting wisely. The dispositions so praised are what we mean by "virtues."

But first we have to ask what moral virtue or goodness is. It is a confirmed disposition to act rightly, the disposition being itself formed by a continuous series of right actions.

Virtue, then, is of two kinds, intellectual and moral. Of these the intellectual is in the main indebted to teaching for its production and growth, and this calls for time and experience. Moral goodness, on the other hand, is the child of habit, from which it has got its very name, ethics being derived from *ethos,* "habit," by a slight alteration in the quantity of the *e.* This is an indication that none of the moral virtues is implanted in us by Nature, since nothing that Nature creates can be taught by habit to change the direction of its development. For instance a stone, the natural tendency of which is to fall down, could never, however often you threw it up in the air, be trained to go in that direction. No more can you train fire to burn downwards. Nothing in fact, if the law of its being is to behave in one way, can be habituated to behave in another. The moral virtues, then, are produced in us neither *by* Nature nor *against* Nature. Nature, indeed, prepares in us the ground for their reception, but their complete formation is the product of habit.

Consider again these powers or faculties with which Nature endows us. We acquire the ability to use them before we do use them. The senses provide us with a good illustration of this truth. We have not acquired the sense of sight from repeated acts of seeing, or the sense of hearing from repeated acts of hearing. It is the other way round. We had these senses before we used them; we did not acquire them as a result of using them. But the moral virtues we do acquire by first exercising them. The same is true of the arts and crafts in general. The craftsman has to learn how to make things, but he learns in the process of making them. So men become builders by building, harp players by playing the harp. By a similar process we become just by performing just actions, temperate by performing temperate actions, brave by performing brave actions. Look at what happens in political societies—it confirms our view. We find legislators seeking to make good men of their fellows by making good behaviour habitual with them. That is the aim of every lawgiver, and when he is unable to carry it out effectively, he is a failure; nay, success or failure in this is what makes the difference between a good constitution and a bad.

Again, the creation and the destruction of any virtue are effected by identical causes and identical means; and this may be said, too, of every art. It is as a result of playing the harp that harpers become good or bad in their art. The same is true of builders and all other craftsmen. Men will become good builders as a result of building well, and bad builders as a result of building badly. Otherwise what would be the use of having anyone to teach a trade? Craftsmen would all be born either good or bad. Now this holds also of the virtues. It is in the course of our dealings with our fellow-men that we become just or unjust. It is our behaviour in a crisis and our habitual reactions to danger that make us brave or cowardly, as it may be. So with our desires and passions. Some men are made temperate and gentle, others profligate and passionate, the former by conducting themselves in one way, the latter by conducting themselves in another, in situations in which their feelings are involved. We may sum it all up in the generalization, "Like activities produce like dispositions." This makes it our duty to see that our activities have the right character, since the differences of quality in them are repeated in the dispositions that follow in their train. So it is a matter of real importance whether our early education confirms us in one set of habits or another. It would be nearer the truth to say that it makes a very great difference indeed, in fact all the difference in the world. . . .

After this Aristotle proceeds to lay down a proposition or generalization which is cardinal in his system of ethics. Excess or deficiency in his actions impairs the moral quality of the agent.

Let us begin with the following observation. It is in the nature of moral qualities that they can be destroyed by deficiency on the one hand and excess on the other. We can see this in the instances of bodily health and strength. Physical strength is destroyed by too much and also by too little exercise. Similarly health is ruined by eating and drinking either too much or too little, while it is produced, increased, and preserved by taking the right quantity of drink and victuals. Well, it is the same with temperance, courage, and the other virtues. The man who shuns and fears everything and can stand up to nothing becomes a coward. The man who is afraid of nothing at all, but marches up to every danger, becomes foolhardy. In the same way the man who indulges in every pleasure without refraining from a single one becomes incontinent. If, on the other hand, a man behaves like the Boor in comedy and turns his back on every pleasure, he will find his sensibilities becoming blunted. So also temperance and courage are destroyed both by excess and deficiency, and they are kept alive by observance of the mean. . . .

We have now to state the "differentia" of virtue. Virtue is a disposition; but how are we to distinguish it from other dispositions? We may say that it is such a disposition as enables the good man to perform his function well. And he performs it well when he avoids the extremes and chooses the mean in actions and feelings.

It is not, however, enough to give this account of the *genus* of virtue—that it is a disposition; we must describe its *species*. Let us begin, then, with this proposition. Excellence of whatever kind affects that of which it is the excellence in two ways. (1) It produces a good state in it. (2) It enables it to perform its function well. Take eyesight. The goodness of your eye is not only that which makes your eye good, it is also that which makes it function well. Or take the case of a horse. The goodness of a horse makes him a good horse, but it also makes him good at running, carrying a rider, and facing the enemy. Our proposition, then, seems to be true, and it enables us to say that virtue in a man will be the disposition which (*a*) makes him a good man, (*b*) enables him to perform his function well.

Every form of applied knowledge, when it performs its function well, looks to the mean and works to the standard set by that. It is because people feel this that they apply the *cliché,* "You couldn't add anything to it or take anything from it" to an artistic masterpiece, the implication being that too much and too little alike destroy perfection, while the mean preserves it. Now if this be so, and if it be true, as we say, that good craftsmen work to the standard of the mean, then, since goodness like Nature is more exact and of a higher character than any art, it follows that goodness is the quality that hits the mean. By "goodness" I mean goodness of moral character, since it is moral goodness that deals with feelings and actions, and it is in them that we find excess, deficiency, and a mean. It is possible, for example, to experience fear, boldness, desire, anger, pity, and pleasures and pains generally, too much or too little or to the right amount. If we feel them too much or too little, we are wrong. But to have these feelings at the right times on the right occasions towards the right people for the right motive and in the right way is to have them in the right measure, that is, somewhere between the extremes; and this is what characterizes goodness. The same may be said of the mean and extremes in actions. Now it is in the field of actions and feelings that goodness operates; in them we find excess, deficiency, and, between them, the mean, the first two being wrong, the mean right and praised as such. Goodness, then, is a mean condition in the sense that it aims at and hits the mean.

Consider, too, that it is possible to go wrong in more ways than one. (In Pythagorean terminology evil is a form of the Unlimited, good of the Limited.) But there is only one way of being right. That is why going wrong is easy, and going right difficult; it is easy to miss the bull's-eye and difficult to hit it.

Here, then, is another explanation of why the too much and the too little are connected with evil and the mean with good. As the poet says,

Goodness is one, evil is multiform.

We are now in a position to state our definition of virtue with more precision. Observe that the kind of virtue meant here is moral, not intellectual, and that Aristotle must not be taken as saying that the kind of virtue which he regards as the highest and truest is any sort of mean.

We may now define virtue as a disposition of the soul in which, when it has to choose among actions and feelings, it observes the mean relative to us, this being determined by such a rule or principle as would take shape in the mind of a man of sense or practical wisdom. We call it a mean condition as lying between two forms of badness, one being excess and the other deficiency; and also for this reason, that, whereas badness either falls short of or exceeds the right measure in feelings and actions, virtue discovers the mean and deliberately chooses it. Thus, looked at from the point of view of its essence as embodied in its definition, virtue no doubt is a mean; judged by the standard of what is right and best, it is an extreme.

Aristotle enters a caution. Though we have said that virtue observes the mean in actions and passions, we do not say this of all acts and all feelings. Some are essentially evil and, when these are involved, our rule of applying the mean cannot be brought into operation.

But choice of a mean is not possible in every action or every feeling. The very names of some have an immediate connotation of evil. Such are malice, shamelessness, envy among feelings, and among actions adultery, theft, murder. All these and more like them have a bad name as being evil in themselves; it is not merely the excess or deficiency of them that we censure. In their case, then, it is impossible to act rightly; whatever we do is wrong. Nor do circumstances make any difference in the rightness or wrongness of them. When a man commits adultery there is no point in asking whether it is with the right woman or at the right time or in the right way, for to do anything like that is simply wrong. It would amount to claiming that there is a mean and excess and defect in unjust or cowardly or intemperate actions. If such a thing were possible, we should find ourselves with a mean quantity of excess, a mean of deficiency, an excess of excess and a deficiency of deficiency. But just as in temperance and justice there can be no mean or excess or deficiency, because the mean in a sense *is* an extreme, so there can be no mean or excess or deficiency in those vicious actions—however done, they are wrong. Putting the matter into general language, we may say that there is no mean in the extremes, and no extreme in the mean, to be observed by anybody. . . .

A recapitulation of what has been said of Happiness.

We stated that happiness is not a condition—not a state of mind or disposition of character. If it were, it might belong to a man whose whole existence was passed in sleep, while he lived the life of a vegetable, or to the victim of some appalling misfortune. So if we cannot accept this but feel that we must rather insist that happiness is some form of activity; if, moreover, activities may be classified into those which are necessary to some end desirable for the sake of something beyond themselves, and those that are desirable in and for themselves, clearly happiness must be classed among activities desirable in themselves, and not among those desirable as a means to something else. For happiness is not in need of anything—it is self-sufficient. As for activities, they are desirable in themselves when all that is asked of them is their own exercise. Actions which are in conformity with goodness evidently have this character, for the performance of morally good and beautiful actions is desirable on its own account. . . .

Aristotle gives reasons for thinking that Happiness in its highest and best manifestation is found in cultivating the "contemplative" life.

But if happiness is an activity in accordance with virtue, it is reasonable to assume that it will be in accordance with the highest virtue; and this can only be the virtue of the best part of us. Whether this be the intellect or something else—whatever it is that is held to have a natural right to govern and guide us, and to have an insight into what is noble and divine, either as being itself also divine or more divine than any other part of us—it is the activity of this part in accordance with the virtue proper to it that will be perfect happiness. Now this activity has a speculative or contemplative character. This is a conclusion which may be accepted as in harmony with the truth. For "contemplation" is the highest form of activity, since the intellect is the highest thing in us and the objects which come within its range are the highest that can be known. But it is also the most continuous activity, for we can think about intellectual problems more continuously than we can keep up any sort of physical action. Again, we feel sure that a modicum of pleasure must be one of the ingredients of happiness. Now it is admitted that activity along the lines of "wisdom" is the pleasantest of all the good activities. At all events it is thought that philosophy ("the pursuit of wisdom") has pleasures marvellous in purity and duration, and it stands to reason that those who have knowledge pass their time more pleasantly than those who are engaged in its pursuit. Again, self-sufficiency will be found to belong in an exceptional degree to the exercise of the speculative intellect. The wise man, as much as the just man and everyone else, must have the necessaries of life. But, given an adequate supply of these, the just man also needs people with and towards whom he can put his justice into operation; and we can use similar language about the temperate man, the brave man, and so on. But the wise man can do more. He can speculate all by himself, and the wiser he is the better he can do it. Doubtless it helps to have fellow-workers, but for all that he is the most self-sufficing of men. Finally it may well be thought that the activity of contemplation is the only one that is praised on its own account, because nothing comes of it beyond the act of contemplation, whereas from practical activities we count on gaining something more or less over and above the mere action. Again, it is commonly believed that, to have happiness, one must have leisure; we occupy ourselves in order that we may have leisure, just as we make war for the sake of peace. Now the practical virtues find opportunity for their exercise in politics and in war, but these are occupations which are supposed to leave no room for leisure. Certainly it is true of the trade of war, for no one deliberately chooses to make war for the sake of making it or tries to bring about a war. A man would be regarded as a bloodthirsty monster if he were to make war on a friendly state just to produce battles and slaughter. The business of the politician also makes leisure impossible. Besides the activity itelf, politics aims at securing positions of power and honour or the happiness of the politician himself or his fellow-citizens—a happiness obviously distinct from that which we are seeking.

We are now in a position to suggest the truth of the following statements. (*a*) Political and military activities, while pre-eminent among good activities in beauty and grandeur, are incompatible with leisure, and are not chosen for their own sake but with a view to some remoter end, whereas the activity of the intellect is felt to excel in the serious use of leisure, taking as it does the form of contemplation, and not to aim at any end beyond itself, and to own a pleasure peculiar to itself, thereby enhancing its activity. (*b*) In this activity we easily recognize self-sufficiency, the possibility of leisure and such freedom from fatigue as is humanly possible, together with all the other blessings of pure happiness. Now if these statements are received as true, it will follow that it is this intellectual activity which forms perfect happiness for a man— provided of course that it ensures a complete span of life, for nothing incomplete can be an element in happiness.

Yes, but such a life will be too high for *human* attainment. It will not be lived by us in our merely human capacity but in virtue of something divine within us, and so far as this divine particle is superior to man's composite nature, to that extent will its activity be superior to that of the other forms of excellence. If the intellect is divine compared with man, the life of the intellect must be divine compared with the life of a human creature. And we ought not to listen to those who counsel us *O man, think as man should* and *O mortal, remember your mortality.* Rather ought we, so far as in us lies, to put on immortality and to leave nothing unattempted in the effort to live in conformity with the highest thing within us. Small in bulk it may be, yet in power and preciousness it transcends all the rest. We may in fact believe that this is the true self of the individual, being the sovran and better part of him. It would be strange, then, if a man should choose to live not his own life but another's. Moreover, the rule, as I stated it a little before, will apply here—the rule that what is best and pleasantest for each creature is that which intimately belongs to it. Applying it, we shall conclude that the life of the intellect is the best and pleasantest for man, because the intellect more than anything else *is* the man. Thus it will be the happiest life as well.

The moral as distinct from the intellectual life will, though only in a secondary degree, be happy too. For the moral activities are human *par excel-*

lence. When we display courage or justice or any other virtue it is in our dealings with our fellow men, when we are careful to observe what is due to each in all contracts and exchange of services, indeed in our actions and feelings of every kind, all of which are manifestly human experiences. Some of these, we think, are actually the products of our bodily constitution—goodness of character is felt to have in many ways an intimate connexion with the passions. Prudence, too, is bound up with moral goodness, and goodness with prudence, because the first principles from which prudence starts are given by the moral virtues, for which the right standard is set by prudence. But these virtues, thus closely linked with the passions, go to form the composite being called man. Now the virtues of our composite nature are essentially human. Therefore the life that is lived in the performance of these virtues, and the happiness that ensues from such a life, must also be purely human. But the happiness of the intellectual life is something quite distinct from this. We must leave it at that, for a detailed discussion would go beyond the scope of the question before us. It would further appear that such happiness stands in need of external accessories to but a small extent or less than the happiness founded on moral goodness. The necessaries of life are required by both, and in equal measure. Granted; in this respect the difference between them may be small. But there will be a vast difference in what they require for the exercise of their powers. Thus the liberal man will need money to practise his liberality, as will indeed the just man to meet his obligations. The brave man will need strength if he is to do something brave, and the temperate man the opportunity of being intemperate. (Otherwise how can he, or the possessor of any other virtue, prove that he possesses the virtue?) Another question is whether it is the purpose of an action or the action itself that is the most decisive factor in producing moral goodness on the assumption generally made that goodness depends on both. Well, the perfect character will obviously need both for its formation. But many extraneous things are needed for the performance of virtuous actions, and the greater and finer the actions, the more numerous will be these accessories. On the other hand the student of intellectual problems has no need of all these paraphernalia; perhaps they are rather a hindrance to his thinking. Yet after all he is a man and a member of society and, in so far as he is that, he will choose to act on moral grounds. And this means that he will have need of external goods to permit him to live on the human level.

That perfect happiness is a speculative activity will further appear from the following considerations. The gods in our conception of them enjoy the most complete blessedness and felicity. But what kind of actions can we rightly attribute to them? If we say "just actions," how absurd it will be to picture them as making contracts and restoring deposits and all that sort of thing! Shall we say "brave actions" then? Can you imagine the gods seeking glory by facing dangers and alarms? And what of liberal actions? Whom are they to be liberal to? What an odd idea that the gods actually possess coined money or something like it! Then there are temperate actions. But what could temperate actions mean in their case? What a piece of vulgarity to commend the gods for not having flagitious desires! And if we go through the whole list we shall find that all forms of virtuous activity must be paltry for the gods and unworthy of them. Nevertheless men have always thought of them as at least living beings and, if living, then doing something, for we cannot suppose that they are always asleep, like Endymion. But if from a living being there is taken away action, not to mention creation or production, what is left him but contemplation? We must conclude then that the activity of God, which is blessed above all others, must take the form of contemplation. And from this it follows that among human activities that which is most akin to God's will bring us the greatest happiness. What also goes to show the truth of this is the fact that the lower animals cannot partake of happiness, for they are utterly incapable of contemplation. The life of the gods is altogether happy, that of man is happy so far as it includes something that resembles the divine activity; but none of the other animals can be properly described as happy, because they are in no way capable of speculation or contemplation. Happiness then covers the same ground as contemplation and those who have the greatest power of contemplation are the happiest, not accidentally but as an essential element of their contemplation. For contemplation is itself beyond price. We conclude that happiness is a form of contemplation. . . .

Such then is our theory of ethics. But theory is not practice and has no effect on the practice of the average man.

Assuming then that we have adequately discussed, at least in outline, the subjects of happiness and the different forms of goodness, may we consider the task we set before us as now complete? Or would it not be better to say that in the science of conduct the end, as we have so often had occasion to say, is not to obtain a theoretical acquaintance with the different points at issue, but rather to put our theories into practice? If that be true, it is not enough to *know* about goodness; we must endeavour to possess and use it, and in some way to see to it that we become good. Now if discourses on the theory of ethics were enough in themselves to make men good,

Many and great the rewards they would win,

as Theognis has it. And they would deserve them, and all we should have to do would be to provide ourselves with such discourses. But the plain truth is that, while theories may very powerfully stimulate and encourage generous youth, and may inspire a character naturally noble and sincerely loving the beauty of goodness with a passion for virtue, they are unable to push the many in the direction of lofty principles. For it is the nature of the many to yield to the suggestions of fear rather than honour, and to abstain from evil not because of the disgrace but the penalties entailed by not abstaining. Living under the dictates of passion, they chase the pleasures fit for such natures and the means of gratifying them, and they shun the pains which are the opposite of these pleasures. But the honourable and the truly delightful—of that they have no conception, having never tasted genuine pleasure. What theory, what homily can ever reform people like that? To uproot by argument habits long embedded in the character is a difficult, perhaps an impossible, task. We may, I take it, regard ourselves as fortunate if we can get some portion of goodness by acquiring for ourselves all the recognized means of becoming good.

To become good we must have a suitable nature rightly directed by habit and education.

Now some thinkers hold that goodness comes by nature, others that we acquire it by habit, others that we are made good by teaching. The bounty of nature is clearly beyond our control; it is bestowed by some divine dispensation on those who are in the true sense of the word "fortunate." As for arguments and teaching, it is to be feared they are not efficacious in all instances. Like a piece of land, which has to be prepared for the seed that is to grow there, the mind of the pupil has to be prepared for the inculcation of good habits, if it is to like and dislike the things it ought. The man who is passion's slave will not listen to or understand the logic of anyone who tries to dissuade him from going on as he is doing. When a man is in that state, what chance have you of changing his mind by argumentation? In fact one may venture on the broad statement that passion is not amenable to reason but only to force. We must then have a character to work upon which has a natural bias towards virtue, loving the noble and hating the base.

Education in goodness is best undertaken by the state.

Yet it is far from easy to obtain a right training in goodness from youth upwards, unless one has been brought up under right laws. To live a hard and sober life is not an attractive prospect for most, especially when they are young. For this reason the nurture and the pursuits of young persons should be regulated by law, for hard conditions and sober living will cease to be painful when they have become habitual. Of course, it is not enough to receive the right nurture and supervision in youth. We must also practise what we have learnt and make a habit of it when we are grown up. So we shall need laws for the regulation of adult behaviour as well, for the whole indeed of our lives; for people are by and large readier to submit to punishment and compulsion than moved by arguments and ideals. Hence some believe that, while lawgivers are under an obligation to encourage and inspire the citizens in the pursuit of virtue for its beauty, not doubting that those who have been well brought up will respond, they are also bound to inflict chastisement and penalties on the disobedient and ill-conditioned, and to deport the hopeless cases altogether. They take the line that, while the good man no doubt, living as he does with some kind of moral standard, will listen to reason, the degraded, who are all for pleasure, must be chastised by pain like beasts of burden. This is also the reason they give for maintaining that the punishment for transgressors should take the form of those pains which come nearest to being the opposite of their darling pleasures.

Be that as it may, I repeat that, if a man is to turn out well, he must have been properly educated and trained, and must thereafter persevere in good habits of life and do no wrong either with or against his will. This result can be produced only by submitting one's life to the guidance of intelligence in some form and a right system with truth in it. Now a father has not got the power to enforce obedience to his authority, nor indeed, broadly speaking, has any individual, unless he happens to be a king or something equivalent. But law, emanating as a rule from a certain wisdom and intelligence, does have the power of compulsion. We dislike people who thwart our inclinations, even if they are entirely justified in doing so, but we do not grumble at the law when it orders what is right. Yet Sparta, with perhaps one or two other places, is the only state in which the lawgiver seems to have been at pains to regulate the nurture and day-to-day life of the community. In the majority of states the problem has not been faced, and every man does as he likes with his life in the manner of the Cyclops in Homer, "laying down the law for children and wife."

Questions

1. When Aristotle says that the good of the community is greater and more perfect than the good of the individual, does he imply that the community can justifiably sacrifice the individual's good in order to further its own good? Defend your answer by giving a general account of Aristotle's views on the relation between ethics and politics.

2. Aristotle defines the good as "an end beyond which are no further ends." Such an end is whatever a person desires for its own sake rather than for the sake of something else. It follows that whatever a person desires for its own sake is good, and there is no sense in saying that a person can desire what is in fact evil.

How might Aristotle reply to this argument?

3. Explain what Aristotle means by happiness. How is it to be distinguished from pleasure?

4. Aristotle attempts to define the good for man (happiness) in terms of the peculiar function of man, which he identifies as the activity of reasoning. But there are other functions peculiar to man, such as his ability to blush or to be ashamed, and his ability to use his thumb in handling things. Clearly the fact that something is peculiar to man does not mean that it defines the good for man. For how do we know that the good for man does not lie in those functions which man has in common with animals?

Is this a good criticism of Aristotle's position? Why or why not?

5. What is the basis for Aristotle's distinction between moral virtues and intellectual virtues? Why does he discuss intellectual virtues in a book on ethics?

6. Many people would say that the life of Jesus exemplifies moral goodness at its highest level. Yet Jesus certainly carried to great extremes his inward purity, his refusal to compromise his ideals, his honesty, and his love of humanity. Does the life of Jesus provide evidence against Aristotle's conception of virtue as a mean?

7. Try to give some examples of what Aristotle calls "contemplation." What does he think is being contemplated by a person during an act of contemplation?

8. Since our highest virtue according to Aristotle is contemplation, then a man who spends his life in contemplation leads a better life than a man who spends his life in alleviating the sufferings of others.

State why you think this conclusion does, or does not, follow from Aristotle's point of view.

9. Aristotle's whole ethical system is based on knowledge of human nature. If we know the nature of man, he is saying, then we can derive from that knowledge the knowledge of good and evil. Do you think that knowledge of man's nature is *sufficient* for obtaining moral knowledge? Is it *necessary, but not sufficient*? Is it *neither necessary nor sufficient*? Is it *totally irrelevant* to obtaining moral knowledge? Defend your answer.

2

The Moral Sense

David Hume
(1711-1776)

[A general introductory note on Hume may be found on page 98.]

Hume believes that we obtain moral knowledge through what he calls "the moral sense." In order to understand what he means by this, it is necessary to begin with his discussion of human motivation. According to Hume neither our reason itself nor the knowledge which we gain by the use of our reason can directly determine our actions. Only "passion" (which includes for Hume what we now call emotions, attitudes, desires, wishes, and needs) can act as a motivating force on our behavior. Reason can tell us what the probable consequences of our actions will be, and can thus indirectly cause us to act one way rather than another, depending on whether we like or dislike the consequences of which it informs us. Reason also has the power to correct mistaken suppositions on the basis of which we act, and to tell us what means will most likely bring about an end we have already chosen. By itself, however, reason is powerless to determine the choice of an end. The conclusion which Hume draws from his study of motivation is that passion can neither be in conflict nor in harmony with reason.

Hume next proceeds to argue that, since reason cannot directly influence our actions, it cannot be a source of moral knowledge. From what source, then, do we get our moral knowledge? Hume's answer is: From the moral sense. The reader will discover for himself the full meaning of this answer when he becomes acquainted with Hume's own argument in the reading which follows.

The reading is taken from Book II, Part II, Section III, and Book III, Part I, Sections I and II of *A Treatise of Human Nature* (1738-1740), and from Section IX of *An Enquiry Concerning the Principles of Morals* (1751). Hume's own section headings are used.

The "Conclusion" is from pages 92 through 95 of Hume: *An Inquiry Concerning the Principles of Morals* (The Library of Liberal Arts No. 62, N. Y., 1957). Reprinted by permission of the publishers, The Liberal Arts Press, Inc.

OF THE INFLUENCING MOTIVES OF THE WILL

Nothing is more usual in philosophy, and even in common life, than to talk of the combat of passion and reason, to give the preference to reason, and assert that men are only so far virtuous as they conform themselves to its dictates. Every rational creature, it is said, is obliged to regulate his actions by reason; and if any other motive or principle challenge the direction of his conduct, he ought to oppose it, till it be entirely subdued, or at least brought to a conformity with that superior principle. On this method of thinking the greatest part of moral philosophy, ancient and modern, seems to be founded; nor is there an ampler field, as well for metaphysical arguments, as popular declamations, than this supposed preëminence of reason above passion. The eternity, invariableness, and divine origin of the former have been displayed to the best advantage; the blindness, inconstancy, and deceitfulness of the latter have been as strongly insisted on. In order to show the fallacy of all this philosophy, I shall endeavour to prove *first,* that reason alone can never be a motive to any action of the will; and *secondly,* that it can never oppose passion in the direction of the will.

The understanding exerts itself after two different ways, as it judges from demonstration or probability; as it regards the abstract relations of our ideas, or those relations of objects of which experience only gives us information. I believe it scarce will be asserted that the first species of reasoning alone is ever the cause of any action. As its proper province is the world of ideas, and as the will always places us in that of realities, demonstration and volition seem upon that account to be totally removed from each other. Mathematics, indeed, are useful in all mechanical operations, and arithmetic in almost every art and profession: but it is not of themselves they have any influence. Mechanics are the art of regulating the motions of bodies *to some designed end or purpose;* and the reason why we employ arithmetic in fixing the proportions of numbers is only that we may discover the proportions of their influence and operation. A merchant is desirous of knowing the sum total of his accounts with any person: why? but that he may learn what sum will have the same *effects* in paying his debt, and going to market, as all the particular articles taken together. Abstract or demonstrative reasoning, therefore, never influences any of our actions, but only as it directs our judgment concerning causes and effects; which leads us to the second operation of the understanding.

It is obvious that when we have the prospect of pain or pleasure from any object, we feel a consequent emotion of aversion or propensity, and are carried to avoid or embrace what will give us this uneasiness or satisfaction. It is also obvious that this emotion rests not here, but, making us cast our view on every side, comprehends whatever objects are connected with its original one by the relation of cause and effect. Here then reasoning takes place to discover this relation; and according as our reasoning varies, our actions receive a subsequent variation. But it is evident, in this case, that the impulse arises not from reason, but is only directed by it. It is from the prospect of pain or pleasure that the aversion or propensity arises towards any object: and these emotions extend themselves to the causes and effects of that object, as they are pointed out to us by reason and experience. It can never in the least concern us to know that such objects are causes and such others effects, if both the causes and effects be indifferent to us. Where the objects themselves do not affect us, their connection can never give them any influence; and it is plain that, as reason is nothing but the discovery of this connection, it cannot be by its means that the objects are able to affect us.

Since reason alone can never produce any action, or give rise to volition, I infer, that the same faculty is as incapable of preventing volition, or of disputing the preference with any passion or emotion. This consequence is necessary. It is impossible reason could have the latter effect of preventing volition, but by giving an impulse in a contrary direction to our passions; and that impulse, had it operated alone, would have been ample to produce volition. Nothing can oppose or retard the impulse of passion, but a contrary impulse; and if this contrary impulse ever arises from reason, that latter faculty must have an original influence on the will, and must be able to cause, as well as hinder, any act of volition. But if reason has no original influence, it is impossible it can withstand any principle which has such an efficacy, or ever keep the mind in suspense a moment. Thus, it appears, that the principle which opposes our passion cannot be the same with reason, and is only called so in an improper sense. We speak not strictly and philosophically, when we talk of the combat of passion and of reason. Reason is, and ought only to be, the slave of the passions, and can never pretend to any other office than to serve and obey them. As this opinion may appear somewhat extraordinary, it may not be improper to confirm it by some other considerations.

A passion is an original existence, or, if you will, modification of existence, and contains not any representative quality, which renders it a copy of any other existence or modification. When I am angry, I am actually possessed with the passion, and in that emotion have no more a reference to any other object, than when I am thirsty, or sick, or more than five feet high. It is impossible, therefore, that this passion can be opposed by, or be contradictory to truth and reason; since this contradiction consists in the disagreement of ideas, considered as copies, with those objects which they represent.

What may at first occur on this head is that as nothing can be contrary to truth or reason, except what has a reference to it, and as the judgments of our understanding only have this reference, it must follow that passions can be contrary to reason only, so far as they are *accompanied* with some judgment or opinion. According to this principle, which is so obvious and natural, it is only in two senses that any affection can be called unreasonable. First, When a passion, such as hope or fear, grief or joy, despair or security, is founded on the supposition of the existence of objects, which really do not exist. Secondly, When in exerting any passion in action, we choose means insufficient for the designed end, and deceive ourselves in our judgment of causes and effects. Where a passion is neither founded on false suppositions, nor chooses means insufficient for the end, the understanding can neither justify nor condemn it. It is not contrary to reason to prefer the destruction of the whole world to the scratching of my finger. It is not contrary to reason for me to choose my total ruin, to prevent the least uneasiness of an Indian, or person wholly unknown to me. It is as little contrary to reason to prefer even my own acknowledged lesser good to my greater, and have a more ardent affection for the former than the latter. A trivial good may, from certain circumstances, produce a desire superior to what arises from the greatest and most valuable enjoyment; nor is there anything more extraordinary in this, than in mechanics to see one pound weight raise up a hundred by the advantage of its situation. In short, a passion must be accompanied with some false judgment, in order to its being unreasonable; and even then it is not the passion, properly speaking, which is unreasonable, but the judgment.

The consequences are evident. Since a passion can never, in any sense, be called unreasonable, but when founded on a false supposition, or when it chooses means insufficient for the designed end, it is impossible that reason and passion can ever oppose each other, or dispute for the government of the will and actions. The moment we perceive the falsehood of any supposition, or the insufficiency of any means, our passions yield to our reason without any opposition. I may desire any fruit as of an excellent relish; but whenever you convince me of my mistake, my longing ceases. I may will the performance of certain actions as means of obtaining any desired good; but as my willing of these actions is only secondary, and founded on the supposition that they are causes of the proposed effect; as soon as I discover the falsehood of that supposition, they must become indifferent to me.

It is natural for one, that does not examine objects with a strict philosophic eye, to imagine that those actions of the mind are entirely the same, which produce not a different sensation, and are not immediately distinguishable to the feeling and perception. Reason, for instance, exerts itself without producing any sensible emotions; and except in the more sublime disquisitions of philosophy, or in the frivolous subtilties of the schools, scarce ever conveys any pleasure or uneasiness. Hence it proceeds that every action of the mind, which operates with the same calmness and tranquillity, is confounded with reason by all those who judge of things from the first view and appearance. Now it is certain there are certain calm desires and tendencies, which, though they be real passions, produce little emotion in the mind, and are more known by their effects than by the immediate feeling or sensation. These desires are of two kinds; either certain instincts originally implanted in our natures, such as benevolence and resentment, the love of life, and kindness to children; or the general appetite to good, and aversion to evil, considered merely as such. When any of these passions are calm, and cause no disorder in the soul, they are very readily taken for the determinations of reason, and are supposed to proceed from the same faculty with that which judges of truth and falsehood. Their nature and principles have been supposed the same, because their sensations are not evidently different.

Beside these calm passions, which often determine the will, there are certain violent emotions of the same kind, which have likewise a great influence on that faculty. When I receive any injury from another, I often feel a violent passion of resentment, which makes me desire his evil and punishment, independent of all considerations of pleasure and advantage to myself. When I am immediately threatened with any grievous ill, my fears, apprehensions, and aversions rise to a great height, and produce a sensible emotion.

The common error of metaphysicians has lain in ascribing the direction of the will entirely to one of these principles, and supposing the other to have no influence. Men often act knowingly against their interest; for which reason, the view of the greatest possible good does not always influence them. Men often counteract a violent passion in prosecution of their interests and designs; it is not, therefore, the present uneasiness alone which determines them. In general we may observe that both these principles operate on the will; and where they are contrary, that either of them prevails, according to the *general* character or *present* disposition of the person. What we call strength of mind implies the prevalence of the calm passions above the violent; though we may easily observe, there is no man so constantly possessed of this virtue as never on any occasion to yield to the solicitations of passion and desire. From these variations of temper proceeds the great difficulty of deciding concerning the actions and resolutions of men, where there is any contrariety of motives and passions.

MORAL DISTINCTIONS NOT DERIVED FROM REASON

. . . It has been observed that nothing is ever present to the mind but its perceptions; and that all the actions of seeing, hearing, judging, loving, hating, and thinking, fall under this denomination. The mind can never exert itself in any action which we may not comprehend under the term of *perception;* and consequently that term is no less applicable to those judgments by which we distinguish moral good and evil, than to every other operation of the mind. To approve of one character, to condemn another, are only so many different perceptions.

Now, as perceptions resolve themselves into two kinds, viz. *impressions* and *ideas,* this distinction gives rise to a question, with which we shall open up our present inquiry concerning morals, *whether it is by means of our ideas or* impressions *we distinguish betwixt vice and virtue, and pronounce an action blamable or praiseworthy?* This will immediately cut off all loose discourses and declamations, and reduce us to something precise and exact on the present subject.

Those who affirm that virtue is nothing but a conformity to reason; that there are eternal fitnesses and unfitnesses of things, which are the same to every rational being that considers them; that the immutable measure of right and wrong impose an obligation, not only on human creatures, but also on the Deity himself: all these systems concur in the opinion that morality, like truth, is discerned merely by ideas, and by their juxtaposition and comparison. In order, therefore, to judge of these systems, we need only consider whether it be possible from reason alone, to distinguish betwixt moral good and evil, or whether there must concur some other principles to enable us to make that distinction.

If morality had naturally no influence on human passions and actions, it were in vain to take such pains to inculcate it; and nothing would be more fruitless than that multitude of rules and precepts with which all moralists abound. Philosophy is commonly divided into *speculative* and *practical;* and as morality is always comprehended under the latter division, it is supposed to influence our passions and actions, and to go beyond the calm and indolent judgments of the understanding. And this is confirmed by common experience, which informs us that men are often governed by their duties, and are deterred from some actions by the opinion of injustice, and impelled to others by that of obligation.

Since morals, therefore, have an influence on the actions and affections, it follows that they cannot be derived from reason; and that because reason alone, as we have already proved, can never have any such influence. Morals excite passions, and produce or prevent actions. Reason of itself is utterly impotent in this particular. The rules of morality, therefore, are not conclusions of our reason. . . .

But to make these general reflections more clear and convincing, we may illustrate them by some particular instances, wherein this character of moral good or evil is the most universally acknowledged. Of all crimes that human creatures are capable of committing, the most horrid and unnatural is ingratitude, especially when it is committed against parents, and appears in the more flagrant instances of wounds and death. This is acknowledged by all mankind, philosophers as well as the people: the question only arises among philosophers, whether the guilt or moral deformity of this action be discovered by demonstrative reasoning, or be felt by an internal sense, and by means of some sentiment, which the reflecting on such an action naturally occasions. This question will soon be decided against the former opinion, if we can show the same relations in other objects, without the notion of any guilt or iniquity attending them.

Reason or science is nothing but the comparing of ideas, and the discovery of their relations; and if the same relations have different characters, it must evidently follow, that those characters are not discovered merely by reason. To put the affair, therefore, to this trial, let us choose any inanimate object, such as an oak or elm; and let us suppose, that, by the dropping of its seed, it produces a sapling below it, which, springing up by degrees, at last overtops and destroys the parent tree: I ask, if, in this instance, there be wanting any relation which is discoverable in parricide or ingratitude? Is not the one tree the cause of the other's existence; and the latter the cause of the destruction of the former, in the same manner as when a child murders his parent? It is not sufficient to reply, that a choice or will is wanting. For in the case of parricide, a will does not give rise to any *different* relations, but is only the cause from which the action is derived; and consequently produces the *same* relations, that in the oak or elm arise from some other principles. It is a will or choice that determines a man to kill his parent: and they are the laws of matter and motion that determine a sapling to destroy the oak from which it sprung. Here then the same relations have different causes; but still the relations are the same: and as their discovery is not in both cases attended with a notion of immorality, it follows, that that notion does not arise from such a discovery.

But to choose an instance still more resembling; I would fain ask any one, why incest in the human species is criminal, and why the very same action, and the same relations in animals, have not the smallest moral turpitude and deformity? If it be answered, that this action is innocent in animals, because they have not reason sufficient to discover its turpitude; but that man, being endowed with that faculty, which *ought* to restrain him to his duty, the same action instantly becomes criminal to him. Should this be said, I would reply, that this is evidently arguing in a circle. For, before reason can perceive this turpitude, the turpitude must exist; and consequently is independent of the decisions of our reason, and is their object more properly than their effect. According to this system, then, every animal that has sense and appetite and will, that is, every animal must be susceptible of all the same virtues and vices, for which we ascribe praise and blame to human creatures. All the difference is that our superior reason may serve to discover the vice or virtue, and by that means may augment the blame or praise: but still this discovery supposes a separate being in these moral distinctions, and a being which depends only on the will and appetite, and which, both in thought and reality, may be distinguished from reason. Animals are susceptible of the same relations with respect to each other as the human species, and therefore would also be susceptible of the same morality, if the essence of morality consisted in these relations. Their want of a sufficient degree of reason may hinder them from perceiving the duties and obligations of morality, but can never hinder these duties from existing; since they must antecedently exist, in order to their being perceived. Reason must find them, and can never produce them. This argument deserves to be weighed, as being, in my opinion, entirely decisive.

Nor does this reasoning only prove, that morality consists not in any rela-tions that are the objects of science; but if examined, will prove with equal certainty that it consists not in any *matter of fact,* which can be discovered by the understanding. This is the *second* part of our argument; and if it can be made evident, we may conclude that morality is not an object of reason. But can there be any difficulty in proving that vice and virtue are not matters of fact, whose existence we can infer by reason? Take any action allowed to be vicious; wilful murder, for instance. Examine it in all lights, and see if you can find that matter of fact, or real existence, which you call *vice.* In whichever way you take it, you find only certain passions, motives, volitions, and thoughts. There is no other matter of fact in the case. The vice entirely escapes you, as long as you consider the object. You never can find it, till you turn your reflec-tion into your own breast, and find a sentiment of disapprobation, which arises in you, towards this action. Here is a matter of fact; but it is the object of feeling, not of reason. It lies in yourself, not in the object. So that when you pronounce any action or character to be vicious, you mean nothing, but that from the constitution of your nature you have a feeling or sentiment of blame from the contemplation of it. Vice and virtue, therefore, may be compared to sounds, colours, heat, and cold, which, according to modern philosophy, are not qualities in objects, but perceptions in the mind: and this discovery in morals, like that other in physics, is to be regarded as a considerable advancement of the speculative sciences; though, like that too, it has little or no influence on practice. Nothing can be more real, or concern us more, than our own senti-ments of pleasure and uneasiness; and if these be favourable to virtue, and unfavourable to vice, no more can be requisite to the regulation of our conduct and behaviour.

I cannot forbear adding to these reasonings an observation, which may, perhaps, be found of some importance. In every system of morality which I have hitherto met with, I have always remarked that the author proceeds for some time in the ordinary way of reasoning, and establishes the being of a God, or makes observations concerning human affairs; when of a sudden I am sur-prised to find, that instead of the usual copulations of propositions, *is,* and *is not,* I meet with no proposition that is not connected with an *ought,* or an *ought not.* This change is imperceptible; but is, however, of the last consequence. For as this *ought,* or *ought not,* expresses some new relation or affirmation, it is neces-sary that it should be observed and explained; and at the same time that a reason should be given for what seems altogether inconceivable, how this new relation can be a deduction from others, which are entirely different from it. But as authors do not commonly use this precaution, I shall presume to recom-mend it to the readers; and am persuaded, that this small attention would sub-vert all the vulgar systems of morality, and let us see that the distinction of vice and virtue is not founded merely on the relations of objects, nor is perceived by reason.

MORAL DISTINCTIONS DERIVED
FROM A MORAL SENSE

Thus the course of the argument leads us to conclude that since vice and virtue are not discoverable merely by reason, or the comparison of ideas, it must be by means of some impression or sentiment they occasion that we are able to mark the difference betwixt them. Our decisions concerning moral rectitude and depravity are evidently perceptions; and as all perceptions are either impressions or ideas, the exclusion of the one is a convincing argument for the other. Morality, therefore, is more properly felt than judged of; though this feeling or sentiment is commonly so soft and gentle that we are apt to confound it with an idea, according to our common custom of taking all things for the same which have any near resemblance to each other.

The next question is, of what nature are these impressions, and after what manner do they operate upon us? Here we cannot remain long in suspense, but must pronounce the impression arising from virtue to be agreeable, and that proceeding from vice to be uneasy. Every moment's experience must convince us of this. There is no spectacle so fair and beautiful as a noble and generous action; nor any which gives us more abhorrence than one that is cruel and treacherous. No enjoyment equals the satisfaction we receive from the company of those we love and esteem; as the greatest of all punishments is to be obliged to pass our lives with those we hate or contemn. A very play or romance may afford us instances of this pleasure which virtue conveys to us; and pain, which arises from vice.

Now, since the distinguishing impressions by which moral good or evil is known are nothing but *particular* pains or pleasures, it follows that, in all inquiries concerning these moral distinctions, it will be sufficient to show the principles which make us feel a satisfaction or uneasiness from the survey of any character, in order to satisfy us why the character is laudable or blamable. An action, or sentiment, or character, is virtuous or vicious; why? because its view causes a pleasure or uneasiness of a particular kind. In giving a reason, therefore, for the pleasure or uneasiness, we sufficiently explain the vice or virtue. To have the sense of virtue is nothing but to *feel* a satisfaction of a particular kind from the contemplation of a character. The very *feeling* constitutes our praise or admiration. We go no further; nor do we inquire into the cause of the satisfaction. We do not infer a character to be virtuous, because it pleases; but in feeling that it pleases after such a particular manner, we in effect feel that it is virtuous. The case is the same as in our judgments concerning all kinds of beauty, and tastes, and sensations. Our approbation is implied in the immediate pleasure they convey to us.

I have objected to the system which establishes eternal rational measures of right and wrong, that it is impossible to show, in the actions of reasonable creatures, any relations which are not found in external objects; and therefore, if morality always attended these relations, it were possible for inanimate matter to become virtuous or vicious. Now it may, in like manner, be objected to the present system, that if virtue and vice be determined by pleasure and pain, these qualities must, in every case, arise from the sensations; and consequently any object, whether animate or inanimate, rational or irrational, might become morally good or evil, provided it can excite a satisfaction or uneasiness. But though this objection seems to be the very same, it has by no means the same force in the one case as in the other. For it is evident that, under the term *pleasure,* we comprehend sensations, which are very different from each other, and which have only such a distant resemblance as is requisite to make them be expressed by the same abstract term. A good composition of music and a bottle of good wine equally produce pleasure; and, what is more, their goodness is determined merely by the pleasure. But shall we say, upon that account, that the wine is harmonious, or the music of a good flavour? In like manner, an inanimate object, and the character or sentiments of any person, may, both of them, give satisfaction; but, as the satisfaction is different, this keeps our sentiments concerning them from being confounded, and makes us ascribe virtue to the one and not to the other. Nor is every sentiment of pleasure or pain, which arises from characters and actions, of that *peculiar* kind which makes us praise or condemn. The good qualities of an enemy are hurtful to us, but may still command our esteem and respect. It is only when a character is considered in general, without reference to our particular interest, that it causes such a feeling or sentiment as denominates it morally good or evil. It is true, those sentiments from interest and morals are apt to be confounded, and naturally run into one another. It seldom happens that we do not think an enemy vicious, and can distinguish betwixt his opposition to our interest and real villainy or baseness. But this hinders not but that the sentiments are in themselves distinct; and a man of temper and judgment may preserve himself from these illusions. In like manner, though it is certain a musical voice is nothing but one that naturally gives a *particular* kind of pleasure; yet it is difficult for a man to be sensible that the voice of an enemy is agreeable, or to allow it to be musical. But a person of a fine ear, who has the command of himself, can separate these feelings, and give praise to what deserves it. . . .

CONCLUSION

It is sufficient for our present purpose, if it be allowed, what surely, without the greatest absurdity, cannot be disputed, that there is some benevolence, however small, infused into our bosom; some spark of friendship for humankind; some particle of the dove kneaded into our frame, along with the elements of the wolf and serpent. Let these generous sentiments be supposed ever so weak, let them be insufficient to move even a hand or finger of our body, they must still direct the determinations of our mind and, where everything else is equal, produce a cool preference of what is useful and serviceable to mankind above what is pernicious and dangerous. A *moral distinction,* therefore, immediately arises; a general sentiment of blame and approbation; a tendency, however faint, to the objects of the one, and a proportionable aversion to those of the other. Nor will those reasoners who so earnestly maintain the predominant selfishness of humankind be anywise scandalized at hearing of the weak sentiments of virtue implanted in our nature. On the contrary, they are found as ready to maintain the one tenet as the other; and their spirit of satire (for such it appears, rather than of corruption) naturally gives rise to both opinions, which have, indeed, a great and almost an indissoluble connection together.

Avarice, ambition, vanity, and all passions vulgarly, though improperly, comprised under the denomination of *self-love* are here excluded from our theory concerning the origin of morals, not because they are too weak, but because they have not a proper direction for that purpose. The notion of morals implies some sentiment common to all mankind, which recommends the same object to general approbation and makes every man, or most men, agree in the same opinion or decision concerning it. It also implies some sentiment so universal and comprehensive as to extend to all mankind, and render the actions and conduct, even of the persons the most remote, an object of applause or censure, according as they agree or disagree with that rule of right which is established. These two requisite circumstances belong alone to the sentiment of humanity here insisted on. The other passions produce, in every breast, many strong sentiments of desire and aversion, affection and hatred, but these neither are felt so much in common nor are so comprehensive as to be the foundation of any general system and established theory of blame or approbation.

When a man denominates another his *enemy,* his *rival,* his *antagonist,* his *adversary,* he is understood to speak the language of self-love and to express sentiments peculiar to himself and arising from his particular circumstances and situation. But when he bestows on any man the epithets of *vicious* or *odious* or *depraved,* he then speaks another language and expresses sentiments in which he expects all his audience are to concur with him. He must here, therefore, depart from his private and particular situation and must choose a point of view common to him with others: he must move some universal principle of the human frame and touch a string to which all mankind have an accord and symphony. If he means, therefore, to express that this man possesses qualities whose tendency is pernicious to society, he has chosen this common point of view and has touched the principle of humanity in which every man, in some degree, concurs. While the human heart is compounded of the same elements as at present, it will never be wholly indifferent to public good, nor entirely unaffected with the tendency of characters and manners. And though this affection of humanity may not generally be esteemed so strong as vanity or ambition, yet being common to all men, it can alone be the foundation of morals or of any general system of blame or praise. One man's ambition is not another's ambition, nor will the same event or object satisfy both; but the humanity of one man is the humanity of everyone; and the same object touches this passion in all human creatures.

But the sentiments which arise from humanity are not only the same in all human creatures and produce the same approbation or censure, but they also comprehend all human creatures; nor is there anyone whose conduct or character is not, by their means, an object, to everyone, of censure or approbation. On the contrary, those other passions, commonly denominated selfish, both produce different sentiments in each individual, according to his particular situation, and also contemplate the greater part of mankind with the utmost indifference and unconcern. Whoever has a high regard and esteem for me, flatters my vanity; whoever expresses contempt, mortifies and displeases me. But as my name is known but to a small part of mankind, there are few who come within the sphere of this passion, or excite, on its account, either my affection or disgust. But if you represent a tyrannical, insolent, or barbarous behavior, in any country or in any age of the world, I soon carry my eye to the pernicious tendency of such a conduct and feel the sentiment of repugnance and displeasure toward it. No character can be so remote as to be, in this light, wholly indifferent to me. What is beneficial to society or to the person himself must still be preferred. And every quality or action of every human being must by this means be ranked under some class or denomination expressive of general censure or applause.

What more, therefore, can we ask to distinguish the sentiments dependent on humanity from those connected with any other passion, or to satisfy us why the former are the origin of morals, not the latter? Whatever conduct gains my approbation, by touching my humanity, procures also the applause of all mankind by affecting the same principle in them; but what serves my avarice or ambition pleases these passions in me alone and affects not the avarice and ambition of the rest of mankind. There is no circumstance of conduct in any man, provided it have a beneficial tendency, that is not agreeable to my humanity, however remote the person; but every man, so far removed as neither to cross nor serve my avarice and ambition, is regarded as wholly indifferent by those passions. The distinction, therefore, between these species of sentiment being so great and evident, language must soon be molded upon it and must invent a peculiar set of terms in order to express those universal sentiments of censure or approbation which arise from humanity, or from views of general usefulness and its contrary. *Virtue* and *vice* become then known: morals are recognized; certain general ideas are framed of human conduct and behavior; such measures are expected from men in such situations: this action is determined to be conformable to our abstract rule; that other, contrary. And by such universal principles are the particular sentiments of self-love frequently controlled and limited.

Questions

1. How does Hume attempt to show that "reason alone can never produce any action, or give rise to volition . . ."?

2. What is Hume's argument that from reason alone we cannot derive the distinction between good and evil? Explain in your own words the point of his arguments concerning ingratitude and incest.

3. Why, according to Hume, are vice and virtue not objective matters of fact?

4. "The *ought* cannot be derived solely from the *is*." In the light of Hume's

moral philosophy, state what you would take this sentence to mean, and then explain why Hume would or would not accept it.

5. Does Hume, like Aristotle, attempt to base our knowledge of right and wrong on our knowledge of man's nature? If so, how do the two philosophers differ in their ways of arguing? If not, on what does Hume attempt to base our knowledge of right and wrong? (Aristotle's views are to be found in the preceding selection of this chapter, beginning on page 491.)

6. From Hume's point of view, why is not a good composition of music or a bottle of good wine *morally* good? Can Hume's method for distinguishing moral goodness from other kinds of goodness be used to distinguish correctly between moral goodness and prudence (knowing how to achieve one's own ends)? Explain and defend your answer.

7. Hume's moral philosophy has been attacked on the following grounds:

"According to Hume's position, what makes murder wrong is the fact that people disapprove of murder. This implies that if people came to approve of murder, it would no longer be wrong but would thereby become right. But such a consequence outrages the moral feelings of all decent people, and therefore Hume's theory must be false."

What do you think of this argument?

8. Would it be possible for a person who accepted Hume's theory to be an ethical absolutist, or must he be an ethical relativist? (For the meaning of "ethical absolutist" and "ethical relativist," see the introduction to this chapter.)

9. What line of reasoning leads Hume to make the shocking statement: "It is not contrary to reason to prefer the destruction of the whole world to the scratching of my finger"?

10. Professor C. D. Broad has said:

> . . . The logical consequence of Hume's theory is . . . that . . . disputes on moral questions . . . *could* be settled, and that the way to settle them is to collect statistics of how people in fact do feel. And to me this kind of answer seems utterly irrelevant to this kind of question. If I am right in this, Hume's theory must be false.[1]

Is this a good argument against Hume?

3

Ethical Intuitionism | Richard Price
| (1723-1791)

Richard Price was born in Wales, the son of a dissenting minister. During the time of the American Revolutionary War he became famous for two pamphlets which he wrote in defense of American independence. Throughout his life he published various essays on social

[1] C. D. Broad, *Five Types of Ethical Theory*, Routledge and Kegan Paul, London, 1930, p. 115.

and political problems, but his major contribution to philosophy was *A Review of the Principal Questions in Morals* (1758).

Price begins his ethical treatise with a discussion of the moral sense theory as it was propounded by Francis Hutcheson, a British philosopher of the eighteenth century. According to Hutcheson's theory, which is essentially the same as that of David Hume (Selection 2 of this chapter), moral rightness and wrongness are not objective properties of actions but are the result of subjective feelings, which are aroused in us when we perceive actions which we call right and wrong. The problem which Price is considering, then, is "whether *right* and *wrong* are real characters of *actions,* or only qualities of our *minds.*" Price's own answer is that right and wrong are objective properties of actions which we know by means of our understanding (reason, intellect). This position is sometimes called "ethical intuitionism" because moral knowledge is viewed as a direct awareness or intuition of objective moral qualities. Its fundamental principle is that morality is not something created by or dependent on human minds, but is something which exists in the world for human minds to discover and recognize.

This selection is taken from Sections I, II, and III of Chapter I of *A Review of the Principal Questions in Morals,* as edited by D. Daiches Raphael. Price's own section headings are used.

From *A Review of the Principal Questions in Morals,* by Richard Price, ed. by D. Daiches Raphael, The Clarendon Press, Oxford, 1948. Reprinted by permission of the publisher.

THE QUESTIONS STATED CONCERNING THE FOUNDATION OF MORALS

Some actions we all feel ourselves irresistibly determined to approve, and others to disapprove. Some actions we cannot but think *right,* and others *wrong,* and of all actions we are led to form some opinion, as either *fit* to be performed or *unfit;* or neither fit nor unfit to be performed; that is, *indifferent.* What the power within us is, which thus determines, is the question to be considered.

A late very distinguished writer, Dr. *Hutcheson,* deduces our moral ideas from a *moral sense;* meaning by this *sense,* a power within us, different from reason, which renders certain actions pleasing and others displeasing to us. As we are so made that certain impressions on our bodily organs shall excite certain ideas in our minds, and that certain outward forms, when presented to us, shall be the necessary occasions of pleasure or pain. In like manner, according to Dr. *Hutcheson,* we are so made that certain affections and actions of moral agents shall be the necessary occasions of agreeable or disagreeable sensations in us, and procure our love or dislike of them. He has indeed well shewn that we have a faculty determining us *immediately* to approve or disapprove actions, abstracted from all views of private advantage; and that the highest pleasures of life depend upon this faculty. Had he proceeded no farther, and intended nothing more by the *moral sense,* than our *moral faculty* in general, little room would have been left for any objections: But then he would have meant by it nothing *new,* and he could not have been considered as the *discoverer* of it. From the term *sense,* which he applies to it, from his rejection of all the arguments that have been used to prove it to be an intellectual power, and from the whole of his language on this subject; it is evident, he considered it as the effect of a *positive constitution* of our minds, or as an *implanted* and *arbitrary* principle by which a *relish* is given us for certain moral objects and forms and aversion to others, similar to the relishes and aversions created by any of our other senses. In other words, our ideas of morality, if this account is right, have the same origin with our ideas of the sensible qualities of bodies, the harmony of sounds, or the beauties of painting or sculpture; that is, the mere good pleasure of our Maker adapting the mind and its organs in a particular manner to certain objects. Virtue (as those who embrace this scheme say) is an affair of taste. Moral right and wrong signify nothing *in the objects themselves* to which they are applied, any more than agreeable and harsh; sweet and bitter; pleasant and painful; but only *certain effects in us.* Our perception of *right,* or moral good, in actions, is that agreeable *emotion,* or feeling, which certain actions produce in us; and of *wrong,* or moral evil, the contrary. They are particular modifications of our minds, or impressions which they are made to receive from the contemplation of certain actions, which the contrary actions *might* have occasioned, had the Author of nature so pleased; and which to suppose to belong to these actions themselves is as absurd as to ascribe the pleasure or uneasiness, which the observation of a particular form gives us, to the form itself. 'Tis therefore, by this account, improper to say of an action, that it *is right,* in much the same sense that it is improper to say of an object of taste, that it is *sweet;* or of *pain,* that it is *in* fire.

The present enquiry therefore is: Whether this be a true account of virtue or not; whether it *has* or has *not* a foundation in the *nature* of its object; whether *right* and *wrong* are real characters of *actions,* or only qualities of our *minds;* whether, in short, they denote what actions *are,* or only *sensations* derived from the particular frame and structure of our natures.

I am persuaded, all attentive persons, who have not before considered this question, will wonder that it should be a subject of dispute, and think I am going to undertake a very needless work. I have given the naked and just state of it. And it is worth our attention, as we go along, that it is the *only* question about the foundation of morals, which can rationally and properly be made a subject of debate. For, granting that we have perceptions of *moral right* and *wrong,* they must denote either what the actions, to which we apply them, *are,* or only our *feelings;* and the *power* of perceiving them must be either that power whose object is truth, or some *implanted power* or *sense.* If the former is true, then is *morality* equally unchangeable with *all truth:* If, on the contrary,

the latter is true, then is it that only which, according to the different constitutions of the *senses* of beings, it *appears* to be to them?

As to the schemes which found morality on self-love, on positive laws and
compacts, or the Divine will; they must either mean that moral good and evil
are only other words for *advantageous* and *disadvantageous, willed* and *forbidden.* Or they relate to a very different question; that is, not to the question,
what is the nature and true *account* of virtue; but, what is the *subject-matter*
of it.

As far as the former may be the intention of the schemes I have mentioned,
they afford little room for controversy. Right and wrong when applied to actions
which are commanded or forbidden by the will of God, or that produce good
or harm, do not signify merely, that such actions are commanded or forbidden,
or that they are useful or hurtful, but a *sentiment* [1] concerning them and our
consequent approbation or disapprobation of the performance of them. Were
not this true, it would be palpably absurd in any case to ask whether it is *right*
to obey a command, or *wrong* to disobey it; and the propositions, *obeying a
command is right,* or *producing happiness is right,* would be most trifling, as
expressing no more than that obeying a command is obeying a command, or
producing happiness is producing happiness. Besides, on the supposition that
right and wrong denote only the relations of actions to will and law, or to
happiness and misery, there could be no dispute about the faculty that perceives
right and wrong, since it must be owned by all that these relations are objects
of the investigations of *reason.*

Happiness requires something in its own nature, or in ours, to give it influence, and to determine our desire of it and approbation of pursuing it. In
like manner, all laws, will, and compacts suppose *antecedent right* to give them
effect; and, instead of being the *constituents* of right, they owe their whole force
and obligation to it.

Having premised these observations, the question now returns—What is
the power within us that perceives the distinctions of *right* and *wrong?*

My answer is: The UNDERSTANDING.

In order to prove this, it is necessary to enter into a particular enquiry into
the origin of our ideas in general, and the distinct provinces of the *understanding* and of *sense.*

OF THE ORIGIN OF OUR IDEAS IN GENERAL

SENSATION and REFLECTION have been commonly reckoned the sources of all
our ideas: and Mr. *Locke* has taken no small pains to prove this. How much
soever, on the whole, I admire his excellent *Essay,* I cannot think him sufficiently clear or explicit on this subject. It is hard to determine exactly what
he meant by *sensation* and *reflection.* If by the former we understand, the
effects arising from the impressions made on our minds by external objects;

---

[1] [Price uses the word "sentiment" to mean opinion, not feeling.—D. D. Raphael]

and by the latter, the notice the mind takes of its own operations; it will be impossible to derive some of the most important of our ideas from them. This is the explanation Mr. *Locke* gives of them in the beginning of his *Essay*. But it seems probable that what he chiefly meant was that all our ideas are either derived *immediately* from these two sources, or ultimately *grounded* upon ideas so derived; or, in other words, that they furnish us with all the subjects, materials, and occasions of knowledge, comparison, and internal perception. This, however, by no means renders them, in any proper sense, the sources of all our ideas: Nor indeed does it appear, notwithstanding all he has said of the operations of the mind about its ideas, that he thought we had any faculty different from sensation and reflection which could give rise to any *simple ideas;* or that was capable of more than compounding, dividing, abstracting, or enlarging ideas previously in the mind. But be this as it may, what I am going to observe, will, I believe, be found true.

The power, I assert, that *understands,* or the faculty within us that discerns *truth,* and that compares all the objects of thought, and *judges* of them, is a spring of new ideas.[2]

As, perhaps, this has not been enough attended to, and as the question to be discussed is, whether our *moral ideas* are derived from the *understanding* or from a *sense;* it will be necessary to state distinctly the different natures and provinces of sense and reason.

To this purpose we may observe, first, that the power which judges of the perceptions of the senses, and contradicts their decisions; which discovers the nature of the sensible qualities of objects, enquires into their causes, and distinguishes between what is real and what is not real in them, must be a power within us which is superior to sense.

Again, it is plain that one sense cannot judge of the objects of another; the eye, for instance, of harmony, or the ear of colours. The faculty, therefore, which views and compares the objects of *all* the senses, cannot be sense. When, for instance, we consider sound and colour together, we observe in them *essence, number, identity, diversity,* etc., and determine their reality to consist, not in being properties of *external substances,* but in being modifications of *our souls.* The power which takes cognizance of all this, and gives rise to these notions, must be a power capable of subjecting all things alike to its inspection, and of acquainting itself with necessary truth and existence.

[2] The reader is desired to remember that by *ideas,* I mean here almost constantly *simple ideas,* or original and uncompounded perceptions of the mind. That our ideas of right and wrong are of this sort will be particularly observed hereafter. It may also be right to take notice that I all along speak of the understanding, in the most confined and proper sense of it. What gives occasion for observing this is the division which has been made by some writers, of all the powers of the soul into understanding and will; the former comprehending under it all the powers of external and internal sensation, as well as those of judging and reasoning; and the latter, all the affections of the mind, as well as the power of acting and determining.

There may be further some occasion for observing that the two acts of the understanding being intuition and deduction, I have in view the former. 'Tis plain, on the contrary, that those writers, who argue against referring our moral ideas to reason, have generally the latter only in view.

Sense consists in the obtruding of certain impressions upon us, independently of our wills; but it cannot perceive what they are, or whence they are derived. It lies prostrate under its object, and is only a capacity in the soul of having its own state altered by the influence of particular causes. It must therefore remain a stranger to the objects and causes affecting it.

Were not *sense* and *knowledge* entirely different, we should rest satisfied with sensible impressions, such as light, colours, and sounds, and enquire no farther about them, at least when the impressions are strong and vigorous: Whereas, on the contrary, we necessarily desire some farther acquaintance with them, and can never be satisfied till we have subjected them to the survey of reason. Sense presents *particular* forms to the mind; but cannot rise to any *general* ideas. It is the intellect that examines and compares the presented forms, that rises above individuals to universal and abstract ideas; and thus looks downward upon objects, takes in at one view an infinity of particulars, and is capable of discovering general truths. Sense sees only the *outside* of things; reason acquaints itself with their *natures*. Sensation is only a mode of feeling in the mind; but knowledge implies an active and vital energy of the mind. Feeling pain, for example, is the effect of sense; but the understanding is employed when pain itself is made an object of the mind's reflexion, or held up before it, in order to discover its nature and causes. Mere sense can perceive nothing in the most exquisite work of art, suppose a plant or the body of an animal, but what is painted in the eye or what might be described on paper. It is the intellect that must perceive in it order and proportion; variety and regularity; design, connection, art, and power; aptitudes, dependencies, correspondencies, and adjustment of parts so as to subserve an end, and compose one perfect whole; things which can never be represented on a sensible organ, and the ideas of which cannot be passively communicated, or stamped on the mind by the operation of external objects. Sense cannot perceive any of the modes of thinking beings; these can be discovered only by the mind's survey of itself.

In a word, it appears that *sense* and *understanding* are faculties of the soul totally different: The one being conversant only about *particulars;* the other about *universals:* The one not *discerning,* but *suffering;* the other not *suffering,* but *discerning;* and signifying the soul's *Power* of surveying and examining all things, in order to judge of them; which *Power,* perhaps, can hardly be better defined, than by calling it, in *Plato's* language, the power in the soul to which belongs the apprehension of TRUTH.

OF THE ORIGIN OF OUR IDEAS OF
MORAL RIGHT AND WRONG

Let us now return to our first enquiry, and apply the foregoing observations to our ideas of *right* and *wrong* in particular.

'Tis a very necessary previous observation, that our ideas of *right* and *wrong* are simple ideas, and must therefore be ascribed to some power of *im-*

mediate perception in the human mind. He that doubts this need only try to give definitions of them, which shall amount to more than synonymous expressions. Most of the confusion in which the question concerning the foundation of morals has been involved has proceeded from inattention to this remark. There are, undoubtedly, some actions that are *ultimately* approved, and for justifying which no reason can be assigned; as there are some ends, which are *ultimately* desired, and for chusing which no reason can be given. Were not this true, there would be an infinite progression of reasons and ends, and therefore nothing could be at all approved or desired.

Supposing, then, that we have a power *immediately* perceiving right and wrong: the point I am now to endeavour to prove, is that this power is the *Understanding,* agreeably to the assertion at the end of the *first* section. I cannot but flatter myself, that the main obstacle to the acknowledgment of this has been already removed, by the observations made in the preceding section, to shew that the understanding is a power of immediate perception, which gives rise to new original ideas; nor do I think it possible that there should have been many disputes on this subject had this been properly considered.

But, in order more explicitly and distinctly to evince what I have asserted (in the only way the nature of the question seems capable of) let me.

First, Observe that it implies no absurdity, but evidently *may* be true. It is undeniable that many of our ideas are derived from our INTUITION of truth, or the discernment of the natures of things by the understanding. This therefore *may* be the source of our moral ideas. It is at least *possible* that *right* and *wrong* may denote what we *understand* and *know* concerning certain objects, in like manner with proportion and disproportion, connexion and repugnancy, contingency and necessity. I will add that nothing has been offered which has any tendency to prove the contrary. All that can appear, from the objections and reasonings of the Author [3] of the *Enquiry into the original of our ideas of beauty and virtue,* is only what has been already observed, and what does not in the least affect the point in debate: Namely, that the words *right* and *wrong, fit* and *unfit,* express simple and undeniable ideas. But that the power perceiving them is properly a *sense* and not *reason;* that these ideas denote nothing *true* of actions, nothing in the *nature* of actions; this, he has left entirely without proof. He appears, indeed, to have taken for granted that if virtue and vice are *immediately* perceived, they must be perceptions of an *implanted* sense. But no conclusion could have been more hasty. For will any one take upon him to say that all powers of immediate perception must be arbitrary and implanted; or that there can be no simple ideas denoting any thing besides the qualities and passions of the mind? In short: Whatever some writers have said to the contrary, it is certainly a point not yet decided, that virtue is wholly factitious, and to be *felt* not *understood.*

As there are some propositions, which, when attended to, necessarily determine all minds to *believe* them: And as there are some ends, whose natures are such, that, when perceived, all beings immediately and necessarily *desire* them:

---

[3] [*Hutcheson.*—D. D. Raphael]

So it is very credible that, in like manner, there are some actions whose natures are such, that, when observed, all rational beings immediately and necessarily *approve* them.

I do not at all care what follows from Mr. *Hume's* assertion, that all our ideas are either *impressions, or copies of impressions;* or from Mr. *Locke's* assertion that they are all *deducible from* SENSATION *and* REFLECTION. The first of these assertions is, I think, destitute of all proof; supposes, when applied in this as well as many other cases, the point in question; and, when pursued to its consequences, ends in the destruction of all truth and the subversion of our intellectual faculties. The other wants much explication to render it consistent with any tolerable account of the original of our moral ideas: Nor does there seem to be any thing necessary to convince a person, that all our ideas are not deducible from sensation and reflexion, except taken in a very large and comprehensive sense, besides considering how Mr. *Locke* derives from them our *moral ideas.* He places them among our ideas of relations, and represents *rectitude* as signifying the conformity of actions to some rules or laws; which rules or laws, he says, are either the *will of God,* the *decrees of the magistrate,* or the *fashion of the country:* From whence it follows, that it is an absurdity to apply *rectitude* to rules and laws themselves; to suppose the *divine* will to be directed by it; or to consider it as *itself* a rule and law. But, it is undoubted, that this great man would have detested these consequences; and, indeed, it is sufficiently evident that he was strangely embarrassed in his notions on this, as well as some other subjects. But,

Secondly, I know of no better way of determining this point, than by referring those who doubt it to common sense, and putting them upon considering the nature of their own perceptions. Could we suppose a person, who, when he perceived an external object, was at a loss to determine whether he perceived it by means of his organs of sight or touch; what better method could be taken to satisfy him? There is no possibility of doubting in any such cases. And it seems not more difficult to determine in the present case.

Were the question, what that perception is, which we have of number, diversity, causation or proportion; and whether our ideas of them signify truth and reality perceived by the understanding, or impressions made by the objects to which we ascribe them, on our minds; were, I say, this the question, would it not be sufficient to appeal to every man's consciousness? These perceptions seem to me to have no greater pretence to be denominated perceptions of the understanding, than *right* and *wrong.*

It is true, some impressions of pleasure or pain, satisfaction or disgust, generally attend our perceptions of virtue and vice. But these are merely their effects and concomitants, and not the perceptions themselves, which ought no more to be confounded with them, than a particular truth (like that for which *Pythagoras* offered a Hecatomb) ought to be confounded with the pleasure that may attend the discovery of it. Some emotion or other accompanies, perhaps, all our perceptions; but more remarkably our perceptions of right and wrong. And this is what has led to the mistake of making them to signify nothing but impressions, which error some have extended to all objects of knowledge; and thus have been led into an extravagant and monstrous scepticism.

But to return; let any one compare the ideas arising from our *powers of sensation,* with those arising from our *intuition of the natures of things,* and enquire which of them his ideas of right and wrong most resemble. On the issue of such a comparison may we safely rest this question. It is scarcely conceivable that any one can impartially attend to the nature of his own perceptions, and determine that, when he thinks gratitude or beneficence to be *right,* he perceives nothing *true* of them, and *understands* nothing, but only receives an impression from a *sense.* Was it possible for a person to question whether his idea of *equality* was gained from sense or intelligence, he might soon be convinced, by considering whether he is not sure that certain lines or figures are *really* equal, and that their equality must be perceived by all minds, as soon as the objects themselves are perceived. In the same manner may we satisfy ourselves concerning the origin of the idea of *right:* For have we not a like consciousness, that we discern the one, as well as the other, *in* certain objects? Upon what possible grounds can we pronounce the one to be *sense,* and the other *reason?* Would not a Being purely intelligent, having happiness within his reach, *approve* of securing it for himself? Would not he *think* this right; and would it not *be* right? When we contemplate the happiness of a species, or of a world, and pronounce concerning the actions of reasonable beings which promote it, that they are *right;* is this judging erroneously? Or is it no determination of judgment at all, but a species of mental taste? Are not such actions *really right?* Or is every apprehension of rectitude in them false and delusive, just as the like apprehension is concerning the effects of external and internal sensation, when taken to belong to the causes producing them?

It seems, beyond contradiction, certain that every being must *desire* happiness for himself; and can those natures of things, from which the *desire* of happiness and *aversion* to misery necessarily arise, leave, at the same time, a rational nature totally indifferent as to any *approbation* of actions procuring the one, or preventing the other? Is there nothing that any *understanding* can perceive to be amiss in a creature's bringing upon himself, or others, calamities and ruin? Is there nothing truly wrong in the absolute and eternal misery of an innocent being?—"It *appears* wrong to us."—And what reason can you have for doubting, whether it appears what *it is?* Should a being, after being flattered with hopes of bliss, and having his expectations raised by encouragements and promises, find himself, without reason, plunged into irretrievable torments; would he not *justly* complain? Would he want a *sense* to cause the idea of *wrong* to arise in his mind? Can goodness, gratitude, and veracity, appear to any mind under the same characters, with cruelty, ingratitude, and treachery? Darkness may as soon appear to be light.

It would, I doubt, be to little purpose to plead further here, the natural and universal apprehensions of mankind, that our ideas of right and wrong belong to the understanding, and denote real characters of actions; because it will be easy to reply that they have a like opinion of the *sensible qualities* of bodies; and that nothing is more common than for men to mistake their own sensations for the properties of the objects producing them, or to apply, to the object itself, what they find always accompanying it, whenever observed. Let it therefore be observed,

Thirdly, That if right and wrong denote effects of sensation, it must imply the greatest absurdity to suppose them applicable to actions: That is, the ideas of *right* and *wrong,* and of *action,* must in this case be incompatible; as much so, as the idea of pleasure and a regular form, or of pain and the collisions of bodies. All sensations, as such, are modes of consciousness, or feelings of a sentient being, which must be of a nature totally different from the particular causes which produce them. A *coloured body,* if we speak accurately, is the same absurdity with a *square sound.* We need no experiments to prove that heat, cold, colours, tastes, etc., are not real qualities of bodies; because the ideas of matter and of these qualities, are incompatible. But is there indeed any such incompatibility between *actions* and *right?* Or any such absurdity in affirming the one of the other? Are the ideas of them as different as the idea of a sensation, and its cause?

On the contrary; the more we enquire, the more indisputable, I imagine, it will appear to us that we express necessary truth, when we say of some actions, they are right; and of others, they are wrong. Some of the most careful enquirers think thus, and find it out of their power not to be persuaded that these are real distinctions belonging to the natures of actions. Can it be so difficult to distinguish between the ideas of sensibility and reason; between the *intuitions of truth* and the *passions of the mind?* Is that a scheme of morals we can be very fond of, which makes our perceptions of moral good and evil in actions and manners to be all vision and fancy? Who can help seeing that right and wrong are as absolutely unintelligible, and void of sense and meaning, when supposed to signify nothing true of actions, no essential, inherent difference between them; as the perceptions of the external and internal senses are, when thought to be properties of the objects that produce them?

How strange would it be to maintain that there is no possibility of *mistaking* with respect to right and wrong; that the apprehensions of all beings, on this subject, are alike just, since all sensation must be alike *true* sensation? Is there a greater absurdity, than to suppose that the *moral rectitude* of an action is nothing absolute and unvarying; but capable, like all the modifications of pleasure and pain, of being intended and remitted, of increasing and lessening, of rising and sinking with the force and liveliness of our feelings? Would it be less ridiculous to suppose this of the relations between given quantities, of the equality of numbers, or the figure of bodies?

In the last place, let it be considered that all actions, undoubtedly, have a *nature.* That is, *some character* certainly belongs to them, and somewhat there is to be *truly* affirmed of them. This may be that some of them are right, others wrong. But if this is not allowed; if no actions are, *in themselves,* either right or wrong, or any thing of a moral and obligatory nature, which can be an object to the understanding; it follows that, in themselves, they *are* all indifferent. This is what is essentially true of them, and this is what all understandings, that perceive right, must perceive them to be. But are we not conscious that we perceive the contrary? And have we not as much reason to believe the contrary, as to believe or trust at all our own discernment?

In other words, every thing having a *nature* or *essence,* from whence such and such truths concerning it necessarily result, and which it is the proper province of the understanding to perceive; it follows that nothing whatever can be exempted from its inspection and sentence, and that of every thought, sentiment, and subject, it is the natural and ultimate judge. *Actions,* therefore, *ends* and *events* are within its province. Of these, as well as all other objects, it belongs to it to judge. What is this judgment? One would think it impossible for any person, without some hesitation and reluctance, to reply that the judgment he forms of them is this: that they are all essentially *indifferent,* and that there is no one thing fitter to be done than another. If this is judging truly, how obvious is it to infer that it signifies not what we do; and that the determination to think otherwise is an imposition upon rational creatures? Why then should they not labour to suppress in themselves this determination, and to extirpate from their natures all the delusive ideas of morality, worth, and virtue? What though the ruin of the world should follow? There would be nothing *really* wrong in this.

A rational agent void of all moral judgment, incapable of perceiving a difference, in respect of fitness and unfitness to be performed, between actions, and acting from blind propensions without any sentiments concerning what he does, is not possible to be imagined. And, do what we will, we shall find it out of our power, in earnest to persuade ourselves, that reason can have no concern in judging of and directing our conduct; or to exclude from our minds all notions of right and wrong in actions.

But what deserves particular consideration here is this. If all actions and all dispositions of beings are in *themselves indifferent,* the all-perfect understanding of the Deity, without doubt, perceives this; and therefore he cannot *approve,* or *disapprove* of any of his own actions, or of the actions of his creatures: The end he pursues, and the manner in which he treats his creatures must appear to him what it *is—indifferent.* What foundation then is left for his moral perfections? How can we conceive him to pursue universal happiness as his end, when, at the same time, we suppose nothing *in* the nature of that end to engage the choice of any being? Is it no diminution of his perfect character, to suppose him guided by mere unintelligent inclination, without any direction from reason, or any *moral approbation?*

In short, it seems sufficient to overthrow any scheme, that such consequences, as the following, should arise from it: That no one being can judge one end to be better than another, or believe a real moral difference between actions, without giving his assent to an impossibility; without mistaking the *affections of his own mind* for *truth,* and *sensation* for *knowledge.* That there being nothing intrinsically proper or improper, just or unjust; there is nothing *obligatory;* but all beings enjoy, from the reasons of things and the nature of actions, liberty to act as they will.

The following important corollary arises from these arguments:

That morality is *eternal and immutable.*

Right and wrong, it appears, denote what actions *are.* Now whatever any thing *is,* that it is, not by will, or decree, or power, but by *nature and necessity.* Whatever a triangle or circle is, that it is unchangeably and eternally. It depends upon no will or power, whether the three angles of a triangle and two right ones shall be *equal;* whether the periphery of a circle and its diameter shall be *incommensurable;* or whether matter shall be *divisible, moveable, passive,* and *inert.* Every object of the understanding has an indivisible and invariable essence; from whence arise its properties, and numberless truths concerning it. Omnipotence does not consist in a power to alter the nature of things, and to destroy necessary truth (for this is contradictory, and would infer the destruction of all wisdom, and knowledge) but in an absolute command over all *particular, external* existences, to create or destroy them, or produce any possible changes among them. The natures of things, then, being immutable, whatever we suppose the natures of actions to be, they must be immutably. If they are indifferent, this indifference is itself immutable, and there neither is nor can be any one thing that, *in reality,* we *ought* to do rather than another. The same is to be said of right and wrong, of moral good and evil, as far as they express *real characters* of actions. They must immutably and necessarily belong to those actions of which they are *truly* affirmed.

No will, therefore, can render *any thing* good and obligatory, which was not so antecedently, and from eternity; or any action right, that is not so in itself; meaning by *action,* not the bare external effect produced, but the ultimate principle of conduct, or the determination of a reasonable being, considered as arising from the perception of some motives and reasons and intended for some end. According to this sense of the word *action,* whenever the principle from which we act is different, the action is different, though the external effects produced, may be the same. If we attend to this, the meaning and truth of what I have just observed, will be easily seen. Put the case of any action, the performance of which is *indifferent,* or attended with no circumstances of the agent that render it better or fitter to be done than omitted. Is it not plain that, *while all things continue the same,* it is as impossible for any will or power to make acting obligatory here, as it is for them to make two equal things unequal without producing any change in either? It is true, the doing of any indifferent thing may become obligatory, in consequence of a command from a being possessed of rightful authority over us: But it is obvious that, in this case, the command produces a change in the circumstances of the agent, and that what, in consequence of it, becomes obligatory, is not the same with what *before* was indifferent. The external effect, that is, the *matter of the action* is indeed the same; but nothing is plainer than that actions, in this sense the same, may in a moral view be totally different according to the ends aimed at by them, and the principles of morality under which they fall.

When an action, otherwise indifferent, becomes obligatory, by being made the subject of a *promise;* we are not to imagine that our own will or breath alters the nature of things by making what is indifferent not so. But what was indifferent *before* the promise is still so; and it cannot be supposed that, *after* the promise, it becomes obligatory, without a contradiction. All that the promise does is to alter the connexion of a particular effect; or to cause that to be an *instance* of right conduct which was not so before. There are no effects producible by us, which may not, in this manner, fall under different principles of morality; acquire connexions sometimes with happiness, and sometimes with misery; and thus stand in different relations to the eternal rules of duty.

The objection, therefore, to what is here asserted, taken from the effects of positive laws and promises, has no weight. It appears that when an obligation to particular indifferent actions arises from the command of the Deity, or positive laws, it is by no means to be inferred from hence, that obligation is the creature of will, or that the nature of what is indifferent is changed: Nothing then becoming obligatory, which was not so from eternity; that is, *obeying the divine will, and just authority.* And had there been nothing right in this, had there been no reason from the natures of things for obeying God's will; it is certain, it could have induced no obligation, nor at all influenced an intellectual nature as such. Will and laws signify nothing, abstracted from something previous to them, in the character of the lawgiver and the relations of beings to one another, to give them force and render disobedience a crime. If mere will ever obliged, what reason can be given why the will of one being should oblige, and of another not; why it should not oblige alike to every thing it requires; and why there should be any difference between *power* and *authority?* It is truth and reason, then, that, in all cases, oblige, and not mere will. So far, we see, is it from being possible that any will or laws should *create* right; that they can have no effect, but in virtue of natural and antecedent right.

Thus, then, is morality fixed on an immovable *basis,* and appears not to be, in any sense, *factitious;* or the *arbitrary production* of any power human or divine; but *equally everlasting* and *necessary* with all *truth* and *reason.* And this we find to be as evident, as that right and wrong signify a *reality* in what is so denominated.

Questions

1. What is meant by saying that morality is a matter of taste? What view of moral knowledge would lead to such a statement?

2. Why does it follow from the moral sense theory, according to Price, that it is "improper to say of an action, that it *is right"?*

3. What are Price's reasons for claiming that "This action is right" cannot mean the same thing as "God wills that we do this action"?

4. Explain in your own words what Price means by saying: ". . . All laws, will, and compacts suppose *antecedent right* to give them effect; and, instead of being the *constituents* of right, they owe their whole force and obligation to it."

5. What does Price mean by "the understanding"? What role does "the understanding" play in obtaining moral knowledge, according to Price?

6. Why, in your opinion, is the following criticism of Price justified or unjustified?

"Price confuses the psychological origins of our moral ideas with the grounds of moral knowledge. Actually, he only tells us where our moral ideas come from. He does not show us how we can decide whether our moral ideas are true or false."

7. In his ethical theory, Price is trying to account for the fact that we all do think actions are *really* right or wrong, and that this seems to imply something more than that such actions merely *appear* right or wrong to us. In what way does this approach to the problem of moral knowledge influence Price's solution to the problem? What other ways of approaching the problem are possible? (Refer to other selections in this chapter, if you wish, in answering this question.)

8. After reading the selection by Hume beginning on page 508, state how Price and Hume are opposed to one another in their moral philosophies. Discuss the possibility or impossibility of reconciling the two positions.

9. The disagreement between Price and Hume is sometimes called the dispute between ethical *objectivism* and ethical *subjectivism*. How is this dispute different from, and how is it similar to, the dispute between ethical *absolutism* and ethical *relativism,* as those terms were defined in the introduction to this chapter?

10. How might Price reply to the following objection against ethical intuitionism?

"Suppose two individuals have conflicting ethical intuitions, so that one intuits an action to be really right and the other intuits the same action to be really wrong. Ethical intuitionism provides no way of determining which intuition is true and which false. Therefore it leads to a denial of genuine moral knowledge, which is the very thing it was intended to establish."

4

A Priori Ethics | Immanuel Kant
(1724-1804)

[A general introductory note on Kant may be found on page 116.]

This reading consists of the major portion of Kant's *Fundamental Principles of the Metaphysic of Morals.* In this book Kant is trying to make explicit the moral concepts which are implicit in the ethical outlook of ordinary people in everyday life. The entire book is basically a study, in Kant's words, of "the common idea of duty and of moral laws." Kant is not trying to impose on us his own moral opinions, nor is he making a special theory of his own about moral knowledge which he wishes others to adopt. Instead of trying to get us to think about moral matters in a way different from the way we have always thought about them, his object is to make clear to us the logical foundations underlying the way in which we actually do think about moral matters in our practical life. He is trying to answer the question: What is it that, upon careful reflection, all of us really believe to be the essence of our moral duty?

Kant's fundamental thesis is that moral knowledge is a priori, that is, it is knowledge which rests solely on grounds of pure reason. He attempts to prove this by a detailed analysis of the meaning of moral duty. He begins by considering what it means for a person to have moral worth. A person has moral worth, according to Kant, when he has a good will, and a good will is the disposition to do our duty just because it is our duty. In other words, a person has a good will when his actions are motivated, not by his desires or "inclinations," but only by his duty. The intentions of the person, not the consequences of his actions, are the only thing relevant to his moral worth.

To act from duty, however, requires that we know what our duty is, and Kant claims that the nature of our duty can be derived from pure reason alone. The key to his argument lies in his conception of moral law; for duty is simply obedience to the moral law, and, therefore, if we understand what the moral law is, we know what our duty is. Kant believes that if a law is to be a moral law, it must be both universal and necessary. It must apply without exception not only to all men but to all rational beings, so that if there should exist somewhere in the universe beings who have nothing in common with men but the capacity to reason, the same moral law which commands men will also command them, and their moral duty will be identical with that of men. Now, according to Kant, the only kind of law which would have these characteristics would be a law *which commands nothing but obedience to law as such*. Our moral duty, therefore, is to act in accordance with the conception of law itself, in short, to act lawfully. And this means to act in accordance with a universal rule or principle which applies impartially to all rational beings in the universe. Thus each person is to act in the way that he would be willing as a rational being to have everyone else act. As Kant puts it: Each person is to act so that he can will that the maxim of his action become a universal law. It follows that what is right or wrong for one person is right or wrong for everyone—indeed, for all rational beings—in all places and at all times. The moral law, then, being a universal concept which applies to the world but is independent of all contingencies in the world, can only rest on grounds of pure reason.

What it means to try to put this ethical theory into practice the reader will discover for himself when he becomes acquainted with Kant's full argument. It should be remarked that Kant gives a number of examples to illustrate his meaning, and the careful reader will raise the question whether Kant's examples are always consistent with his theory.

The general result for moral knowledge implied by Kant's theory is a total separation, an impassable gulf, between science and ethics, between our knowledge of what is and our knowledge of what ought to be, between the realm of facts and the realm of values. Kant was emphatic in asserting that empirical knowledge of the natural world is completely irrelevant to our knowledge of what is right and wrong. In his own words, his central purpose was "to construct a pure moral philosophy, perfectly cleared of everything which is only empirical, and which belongs to anthropology." (Kant's use of "anthropology," the science of man, covers what would now be called psychology and the social sciences.) This is what Kant meant by a "metaphysic of morals": an account of moral principles which shows them to be derivable from pure reason alone.

This selection is taken from T. K. Abbott's translation of the *Fundamental Principles of the Metaphysic of Morals.* It contains all the essential steps in Kant's argument, and his own section headings are used.

From Kant: *Fundamental Principles of the Metaphysic of Morals,* translated by Thomas K. Abbott with an introduction by Marvin Fox (The Library of Liberal Arts No. 16, N. Y., 1949). Reprinted by permission of the publishers, The Liberal Arts Press, Inc.

PREFACE

As my concern here is with moral philosophy, I limit the question suggested to this: whether it is not of the utmost necessity to construct a pure moral philosophy, perfectly cleared of everything which is only empirical, and which belongs to anthropology? For that such a philosophy must be possible is evident from the common idea of duty and of the moral laws. Everyone must admit that if a law is to have moral force, that is, to be the basis of an obligation, it must carry with it absolute necessity; that, for example, the precept, "Thou shalt not lie," is not valid for men alone, as if other rational beings had no need to observe it; and so with all the other moral laws properly so called; that, therefore, the basis of obligation must not be sought in the nature of man, or in the circumstances in the world in which he is placed, but *a priori* simply in the conceptions of pure reason; and although any other precept which is founded on principles of mere experience may be in certain respects universal, yet in as far as it rests even in the least degree on an empirical basis, perhaps only as to a motive, such a precept, while it may be a practical rule, can never be called a moral law.

Thus not only are moral laws with their principles essentially distinguished from every other kind of practical knowledge in which there is anything empirical, but all moral philosophy rests wholly on its pure part. When applied to man, it does not borrow the least thing from the knowledge of man himself (anthropology), but gives laws *a priori* to him as a rational being. No doubt these laws require a judgment sharpened by experience, in order, on the one hand, to distinguish in what cases they are applicable, and, on the other, to procure for them access to the will of the man, and effectual influence on conduct; since man is acted on by so many inclinations that, though capable of the idea of a practical pure reason, he is not so easily able to make it effective *in concreto* in his life.

A metaphysic of morals is therefore indispensably necessary, not merely for speculative reasons, in order to investigate the sources of the practical principles which are to be found *a priori* in our reason, but also because morals themselves are liable to all sorts of corruption as long as we are without that clue and supreme canon by which to estimate them correctly. For in order that an action should be morally good, it is not enough that it *conform* to the moral law, but it must also be done *for the sake of the law,* otherwise that conformity is only very contingent and uncertain; since a principle which is not moral, although it may now and then produce actions conformable to the law, will also often produce actions which contradict it. Now it is only in a pure philosophy that we can look for the moral law in its purity and genuineness (and, in a practical matter, this is of the utmost consequence): we must, therefore, begin with pure philosophy (metaphysic), and without it there cannot be any moral philosophy at all. That which mingles these pure principles with the empirical does not deserve the name of philosophy (for what distinguishes philosophy from common rational knowledge is that it treats in separate sciences what the latter only comprehends confusedly); much less does it deserve that of moral philosophy, since by this confusion it even spoils the purity of morals themselves and counteracts its own end.

TRANSITION FROM THE COMMON RATIONAL KNOWLEDGE OF MORALITY TO THE PHILOSOPHICAL

Nothing can possibly be conceived in the world, or even out of it, which can be called good without qualification, except a *good will*. Intelligence, wit, judgment, and the other *talents* of the mind, however they may be named, or courage, resolution, perseverance, as qualities of temperament, are undoubtedly good and desirable in many respects; but these gifts of nature may also become extremely bad and mischievous if the will which is to make use of them, and which, therefore, constitutes what is called *character,* is not good. It is the same with the *gifts of fortune.* Power, riches, honor, even health, and the general well-being and contentment with one's condition which is called *happiness,* inspire pride, and often presumption, if there is not a good will to correct the influence of these on the mind, and with this also to rectify the whole principle of acting, and adapt it to its end. The sight of a being who is not adorned with a single feature of a pure and good will, enjoying unbroken prosperity, can never give pleasure to an impartial rational spectator. Thus a good will appears to constitute the indispensable condition even of being worthy of happiness.

There are even some qualities which are of service to this good will itself, and may facilitate its action, yet which have no intrinsic unconditional value, but always presuppose a good will, and this qualifies the esteem that we justly have for them, and does not permit us to regard them as absolutely good. Moderation in the affections and passions, self-control, and calm deliberation are not only good in many respects, but even seem to constitute part of the intrinsic worth of the person; but they are far from deserving to be called good without qualification, although they have been so unconditionally praised by the ancients. For without the principles of a good will, they may become extremely bad; and the coolness of a villain not only makes him far more dangerous, but also directly makes him more abominable in our eyes than he would have been without it.

A good will is good not because of what it performs or effects, not by its aptness for the attainment of some proposed end, but simply by virtue of the volition—that is, it is good in itself, and considered by itself is to be esteemed much higher than all that can be brought about by it in favor of any inclination, nay, even of the sum-total of all inclinations. Even if it should happen that, owing to special disfavor of fortune, or the niggardly provision of a step-motherly nature, this will should wholly lack power to accomplish its purpose, if with its greatest efforts it should yet achieve nothing, and there should remain only the good will (not, to be sure, a mere wish, but the summoning of all means in our power), then, like a jewel, it would still shine by its own light, as a thing which has its whole value in itself. Its usefulness or fruitlessness can neither add to nor take away anything from this value. It would be, as it were, only the setting to enable us to handle it the more conveniently in common commerce, or to attract to it the attention of those who are not yet connoisseurs, but not to recommend it to true connoisseurs, or to determine its value.

There is, however, something so strange in this idea of the absolute value of the mere will, in which no account is taken of its utility, that notwithstanding the thorough assent of even common reason to the idea, yet a suspicion must arise that it may perhaps really be the product of mere high-flown fancy, and that we may have misunderstood the purpose of nature in assigning reason as the governor of our will. Therefore we will examine this idea from this point of view.

In the physical constitution of an organized being, that is, a being adapted suitably to the purposes of life, we assume it as a fundamental principle that no organ for any purpose will be found but what is also the fittest and best adapted for that purpose. Now in a being which has reason and a will, if the proper object of nature were its *conservation,* its *welfare,* in a word, its *happiness,* then nature would have hit upon a very bad arrangement in selecting the reason of the creature to carry out this purpose. For all the actions which the creature has to perform with a view to this purpose, and the whole rule of its conduct, would be far more surely prescribed to it by instinct, and that end would have been attained thereby much more certainly than it ever can be by reason. Should reason have been communicated to this favored creature over and above, it must only have served it to contemplate the happy constitution of its nature, to admire it, to congratulate itself thereon, and to feel thankful for it to the beneficent cause, but not that it should subject its desires to that weak and delusive guidance, and meddle bunglingly with the purpose of nature. In a word, nature would have taken care that reason should not break forth into *practical exercise,* nor have the presumption, with its weak insight, to think out for itself the plan of happiness and of the means of attaining it. Nature would not only have taken on herself the choice of the ends but also of the means, and with wise foresight would have entrusted both to instinct.

And, in fact, we find that the more a cultivated reason applies itself with deliberate purpose to the enjoyment of life and happiness, so much the more does the man fail of true satisfaction. And from this circumstance there arises in many, if they are candid enough to confess it, a certain degree of *misology,* that is, hatred of reason, especially in the case of those who are most experienced in the use of it, because after calculating all the advantages they derive—I do not say from the invention of all the arts of common luxury, but even from the sciences (which seem to them to be after all only a luxury of the understanding)—they find that they have, in fact, only brought more trouble on their shoulders rather than gained in happiness; and they end by envying rather than despising the more common stamp of men who keep closer to the guidance of mere instinct, and do not allow their reason much influence on their conduct. And this we must admit, that the judgment of those who would very much lower the lofty eulogies of the advantages which reason gives us in regard to the happiness and satisfaction of life, or who would even reduce them below zero, is by no means morose or ungrateful to the goodness with which the world is governed, but that there lies at the root of these judgments the idea that our existence has a different and far nobler end, for which, and not for happiness, reason is properly intended, and which must, therefore, be regarded as the supreme condition to which the private ends of man must, for the most part, be postponed.

For as reason is not competent to guide the will with certainty in regard to its objects and the satisfaction of all our wants (which it to some extent even multiplies), this being an end to which an implanted instinct would have led with much greater certainty; and since, nevertheless, reason is imparted to us as a practical faculty, that is, as one which is to have influence on the *will,* therefore, admitting that nature generally in the distribution of her capacities has adapted the means to the end, its true destination must be to produce a *will*, not merely good as a *means* to something else, but *good in itself*, for which reason was absolutely necessary. This will then, though not indeed the sole and complete good, must be the supreme good and the condition of every other, even of the desire of happiness. Under these circumstances, there is nothing inconsistent with the wisdom of nature in the fact that the cultivation of the reason, which is requisite for the first and unconditional purpose, does in many ways interfere, at least in this life, with the attainment of the second, which is always conditional—namely, happiness. Nay, it may even reduce it to nothing, without nature thereby failing of her purpose. For reason recognizes the establishment of a good will as its highest practical destination, and in attaining this purpose is capable only of a satisfaction of its own proper kind, namely, that from the attainment of an end, which end again is determined by reason only, notwithstanding that this may involve many a disappointment to the ends of inclination.

We have then to develop the notion of a will which deserves to be highly esteemed for itself, and is good without a view to anything further, a notion which exists already in the sound natural understanding, requiring rather to be cleared up than to be taught, and which in estimating the value of our actions always takes the first place and constitutes the condition of all the rest. In order to do this, we will take the notion of duty, which includes that of a good will, although implying certain subjective restrictions and hindrances. These, however, far from concealing it or rendering it unrecognizable, rather bring it out by contrast and make it shine forth so much the brighter.

I omit here all actions which are already recognized as inconsistent with duty, although they may be useful for this or that purpose, for with these the question whether they are done *from duty* cannot arise at all, since they even conflict with it. I also set aside those actions which really conform to duty, but to which men have *no* direct *inclination*, performing them because they are impelled thereto by some other inclination. For in this case we can readily distinguish whether the action which agrees with duty is done *from duty* or from a selfish view. It is much harder to make this distinction when the action accords with duty, and the subject has besides a *direct* inclination to it. For example, it is always a matter of duty that a dealer should not overcharge an inexperienced purchaser; and wherever there is much commerce the prudent tradesman does not overcharge, but keeps a fixed price for everyone, so that a child buys of him as well as any other. Men are thus *honestly* served; but this is not enough to make us believe that the tradesman has so acted from duty and from principles of honesty; his own advantage required it; it is out of the question in this case to suppose that he might besides have a direct inclination in favor of the buyers, so that, as it were, from love he should give no advantage to one over another. Accordingly the action was done neither from duty nor from direct inclination, but merely with a selfish view.

On the other hand, it is a duty to maintain one's life; and, in addition, everyone has also a direct inclination to do so. But on this account the often anxious care which most men take for it has no intrinsic worth, and their maxim has no moral import. They preserve their life *as duty requires,* no doubt, but not *because duty requires.* On the other hand, if adversity and hopeless sorrow have completely taken away the relish for life, if the unfortunate one, strong in mind, indignant at his fate rather than desponding or dejected, wishes for death, and yet preserves his life without loving it—not from inclination or fear, but from duty—then his maxim has a moral worth.

To be beneficent when we can is a duty; and besides this, there are many minds so sympathetically constituted that, without any other motive of vanity or self-interest, they find a pleasure in spreading joy around them, and can take delight in the satisfaction of others so far as it is their own work. But I maintain that in such a case an action of this kind, however proper, however amiable it may be, has nevertheless no true moral worth, but is on a level with other inclinations, for example, the inclination to honor, which, if it is happily directed to that which is in fact of public utility and accordant with duty, and consequently honorable, deserves praise and encouragement, but not esteem. For the maxim lacks the moral import, namely, that such actions be done *from duty,* not from inclination. Put the case that the mind of that philanthropist was clouded by sorrow of his own, extinguishing all sympathy with the lot of others, and that while he still has the power to benefit others in distress, he is not touched by their trouble because he is absorbed with his own; and now suppose that he tears himself out of this dead insensibility and performs the action without any inclination to it, but simply from duty, then first has his action its genuine moral worth. Further still, if nature has put little sympathy in the heart of this or that man, if he, supposed to be an upright man, is by temperament cold and indifferent to the sufferings of others, perhaps because in respect of his own he is provided with the special gift of patience and fortitude, and supposes, or even requires, that others should have the same—and such a man would certainly not be the meanest product of nature—but if nature had not specially framed him for a philanthropist, would he not still find in himself a source from whence to give himself a far higher worth than that of a good-natured temperament could be? Unquestionably. It is just in this that the moral worth of the character is brought out which is incomparably the highest of all, namely, that he is beneficent, not from inclination, but from duty.

To secure one's own happiness is a duty, at least indirectly; for discontent with one's condition, under a pressure of many anxieties and amidst unsatisfied wants, might easily become a great *temptation to transgression of duty.* But here again, without looking to duty, all men have already the strongest and most intimate inclination to happiness, because it is just in this idea that all inclinations are combined in one total. But the precept of happiness is often of such a sort that it greatly interferes with some inclinations, and yet a man cannot form any definite and certain conception of the sum of satisfaction of all of them which is called happiness. It is not then to be wondered at that a single inclination, definite both as to what it promises and as to the time within which it can be gratified, is often able to overcome such a fluctuating idea, and that a gouty patient, for instance, can choose to enjoy what he likes, and to suffer what he may, since, according to his calculation, on this occasion at least, he has [only][1] not sacrificed the enjoyment of the present moment to a possibly mistaken expectation of a happiness which is supposed to be found in health. But even in this case, if the general desire for happiness did not influence his will, and supposing that in his particular case health was not a necessary element in this calculation, there yet remains in this, as in all other cases, this law—namely, that he should promote his happiness not from inclination but from duty, and by this would his conduct first acquire true moral worth.

It is in this manner, undoubtedly, that we are to understand those passages of Scripture also in which we are commanded to love our neighbor, even our enemy. For love, as an affection, cannot be commanded, but beneficence for duty's sake may, even though we are not impelled to it by any inclination—nay, are even repelled by a natural and unconquerable aversion. This is *practical* love, and not *pathological*—a love which is seated in the will, and not in the propensions of sense—in principles of action and not of tender sympathy; and it is this love alone which can be commanded.

The second[2] proposition is: That an action done from duty derives its moral worth, *not from the purpose* which is to be attained by it, but from the maxim by which it is determined, and therefore does not depend on the realization of the object of the action, but merely on the *principle of volition* by which the action has taken place, without regard to any object of desire. It is clear from what precedes that the purposes which we may have in view in our actions, or their effects regarded as ends and springs of the will, cannot give to actions any unconditional or moral worth. In what, then, can their worth lie if it is not to consist in the will and in reference to its expected effect? It cannot lie anywhere but in the *principle of the will* without regard to the ends which can be attained by the action. For the will stands between its *a priori* principle, which is formal, and its *a posteriori* spring, which is material, as between two roads, and as it must be determined by something, it follows that it must be determined by the formal principle of volition when an action is done from duty, in which case every material principle has been withdrawn from it.

The third proposition, which is a consequence of the two preceding, I would express thus: *Duty is the necessity of acting from respect for the law.* I may have *inclination* for an object as the effect of my proposed action, but I cannot have *respect* for it just for this reason that it is an effect and not an energy of will. Similarly, I cannot have respect for inclination, whether my own or another's; I can at most, if my own, approve it; if another's, sometimes even love it, that is, look on it as favorable to my own interest. It is only what is connected with my will as a principle, by no means as an effect—what does not subserve my inclination, but overpowers it, or at least in case of choice

---

[1] [Brackets in text indicate T. K. Abbott's notes.—Eds.]

[2] [The first proposition was that to have moral worth an action must be done from duty.—T. K. Abbott]

excludes it from its calculation—in other words, simply the law of itself, which can be an object of respect, and hence a command. Now an action done from duty must wholly exclude the influence of inclination, and with it every object of the will, so that nothing remains which can determine the will except objectively the *law,* and subjectively *pure respect* for this practical law, and consequently the maxim [3] that I should follow this law even to the thwarting of all my inclinations.

Thus the moral worth of an action does not lie in the effect expected from it, nor in any principle of action which requires to borrow its motive from this expected effect. For all these effects—agreeableness of one's condition, and even the promotion of the happiness of others—could have been also brought about by other causes, so that for this there would have been no need of the will of a rational being; whereas it is in this alone that the supreme and unconditional good can be found. The pre-eminent good which we call moral can therefore consist in nothing else than *the conception of law* in itself, *which certainly is only possible in a rational being,* in so far as this conception, and not the expected effect, determines the will. This is a good which is already present in the person who acts accordingly, and we have not to wait for it to appear first in the result.

But what sort of law can that be the conception of which must determine the will, even without paying any regard to the effect expected from it, in order that this will may be called good absolutely and without qualification? As I have deprived the will of every impulse which could arise to it from obedience to any law, there remains nothing but the universal conformity of its actions to law in general, which alone is to serve the will as a principle, that is, I am never to act otherwise than so *that I could also will that my maxim should become a universal law.* Here, now, it is the simple conformity to law in general, without assuming any particular law applicable to certain actions, that serves the will as its principle, and must so serve it if duty is not to be a vain delusion and a chimerical notion. The common reason of men in its practical judgments perfectly coincides with this, and always has in view the principle here suggested. Let the question be, for example: May I when in distress make a promise with the intention not to keep it? I readily distinguish here between the two significations which the question may have: whether it is prudent or whether it is right to make a false promise? The former may undoubtedly often be the case. I see clearly indeed that it is not enough to extricate myself from a present difficulty by means of this subterfuge, but it must be well considered whether there may not hereafter spring from this lie much greater inconvenience than that from which I now free myself, and as, with all my supposed *cunning,* the consequences cannot be so easily foreseen but that credit once lost may be much more injurious to me than any mischief which I seek to avoid at present, it should be considered whether it would not be more

---

[3] A *maxim* is the subjective principle of volition. The objective principle (*i.e.,* that which would also serve subjectively as a practical principle to all rational beings if reason had full power over the faculty of desire) is the practical *law.*

prudent to act herein according to a universal maxim, and to make it a habit to promise nothing except with the intention of keeping it. But it is soon clear to me that such a maxim will still only be based on the fear of consequences. Now it is a wholly different thing to be truthful from duty, and to be so from apprehension of injurious consequences. In the first case, the very notion of the action already implies a law for me; in the second case, I must first look about elsewhere to see what results may be combined with it which would affect myself. For to deviate from the principle of duty is beyond all doubt wicked; but to be unfaithful to my maxim of prudence may often be very advantageous to me, although to abide by it is certainly safer. The shortest way, however, and an unerring one, to discover the answer to this question whether a lying promise is consistent with duty, is to ask myself, Should I be content that my maxim (to extricate myself from difficulty by a false promise) should hold good as a universal law, for myself as well as for others; and should I be able to say to myself, "Every one may make a deceitful promise when he finds himself in a difficulty from which he cannot otherwise extricate himself"? Then I presently become aware that, while I can will the lie, I can by no means will that lying should be a universal law. For with such a law there would be no promises at all, since it would be in vain to allege my intention in regard to my future actions to those who would not believe this allegation, or if they over-hastily did so, would pay me back in my own coin. Hence my maxim, as soon as it should be made a universal law, would necessarily destroy itself.

I do not, therefore, need any far-reaching penetration to discern what I have to do in order that my will may be morally good. Inexperienced in the course of the world, incapable of being prepared for all its contingencies, I only ask myself: Canst thou also will that thy maxim should be a universal law? If not, then it must be rejected, and that not because of a disadvantage accruing from it to myself or even to others, but because it cannot enter as a principle into a possible universal legislation, and reason extorts from me immediate respect for such legislation. I do not indeed as yet *discern* on what this respect is based (this the philosopher may inquire), but at least I understand this—that it is an estimation of the worth which far outweighs all worth of what is recommended by inclination, and that the necessity of acting from *pure* respect for the practical law is what constitutes duty, to which every other motive must give place because it is the condition of a will being good *in itself,* and the worth of such a will is above everything.

Thus, then, without quitting the moral knowledge of common human reason, we have arrived at its principle. And although, no doubt, common men do not conceive it in such an abstract and universal form, yet they always have it really before their eyes and use it as the standard of their decision. Here it would be easy to show how, with this compass in hand, men are well able to distinguish, in every case that occurs, what is good, what bad, conformable to duty or inconsistent with it, if, without in the least teaching them anything new, we only, like Socrates, direct their attention to the principle they themselves employ; and that, therefore, we do not need science and philosophy to know what we should do to be honest and good, yea, even wise and virtuous. Indeed we might well have conjectured beforehand that the knowledge of what every man is bound to do, and therefore also to know, would be within the reach of every man, even the commonest. . . .

TRANSITION FROM POPULAR MORAL PHILOSOPHY TO THE METAPHYSIC OF MORALS

If we have hitherto drawn our notion of duty from the common use of our practical reason, it is by no means to be inferred that we have treated it as an empirical notion. On the contrary, if we attend to the experience of men's conduct, we meet frequent and, as we ourselves allow, just complaints that one cannot find a single certain example of the disposition to act from pure duty. Although many things are done in *conformity* with what *duty* prescribes, it is nevertheless always doubtful whether they are done strictly *from duty,* so as to have a moral worth. Hence there have at all times been philosophers who have altogether denied that this disposition actually exists at all in human actions, and have ascribed everything to a more or less refined self-love. Not that they have on that account questioned the soundness of the conception of morality; on the contrary, they spoke with sincere regret of the frailty and corruption of human nature, which, though noble enough to take as its rule an idea so worthy of respect, is yet too weak to follow it; and employs reason, which ought to give it the law only for the purpose of providing for the interest of the inclinations, whether singly or at the best in the greatest possible harmony with one another.

In fact, it is absolutely impossible to make out by experience with complete centainty a single case in which the maxim of an action, however right in itself, rested simply on moral grounds and on the conception of duty. Sometimes it happens that with the sharpest self-examination we can find nothing beside the moral principle of duty which could have been powerful enough to move us to this or that action and to so great a sacrifice; yet we cannot from this infer with certainty that it was not really some secret impulse of self-love, under the false appearance of duty, that was the actual determining cause of the will. We like then to flatter ourselves by falsely taking credit for a more noble motive; whereas in fact we can never, even by the strictest examination, get completely behind the secret springs of action, since, when the question is of moral worth, it is not with the actions which we see that we are concerned, but with those inward principles of them which we do not see.

Moreover, we cannot better serve the wishes of those who ridicule all morality as a mere chimera of human imagination overstepping itself from vanity, than by conceding to them that notions of duty must be drawn only from experience (as from indolence, people are ready to think is also the case with all other notions); for this is to prepare for them a certain triumph. I am willing to admit out of love of humanity that even most of our actions are correct, but if we look closer at them we everywhere come upon the dear self which is always prominent, and it is this they have in view, and not the strict command of duty, which would often require self-denial. Without being an enemy of virtue, a cool observer, one that does not mistake the wish for good, however lively, for its reality, may sometimes doubt whether true virtue is actually found anywhere in the world, and this especially as years increase and the judgment is partly made wiser by experience, and partly also more acute in observation. This being so, nothing can secure us from falling away altogether from our ideas of duty, or maintain in the soul a well-grounded respect for its law, but the clear conviction that although there should never have been actions which really sprang from such pure sources, yet whether this or that takes place is not at all the question; but that reason of itself, independent of all experience, ordains what ought to take place, that accordingly actions of which perhaps the world has hitherto never given an example, the feasibility even of which might be very much doubted by one who founds everything on experience, are nevertheless inflexibly commanded by reason; that, for example, even though there might never yet have been a sincere friend, yet not a whit the less is pure sincerity in friendship required of every man, because, prior to all experience, this duty is involved as duty in the idea of a reason determining the will by *a priori* principles.

When we add further that, unless we deny that the notion of morality has any truth or reference to any possible object, we must admit that its law must be valid, not merely for men, but for all *rational creatures generally,* not merely under certain contingent conditions or with exceptions, but *with absolute necessity,* then it is clear that no experience could enable us to infer even the possibility of such apodictic laws. For with what right could we bring into unbounded respect as a universal precept for every rational nature that which perhaps holds only under the contingent conditions of humanity? Or how could laws of the determination of *our* will be regarded as laws of the determination of the will of rational beings generally, and for us only as such, if they were merely empirical and did not take their origin wholly *a priori* from pure but practical reason?

Nor could anything be more fatal to morality than that we should wish to derive it from examples. For every example of it that is set before me must be first itself tested by principles of morality, whether it is worthy to serve as an original example, that is, as a pattern, but by no means can it authoritatively furnish the conception of morality. Even the Holy One of the Gospels must first be compared with our ideal of moral perfection before we can recognize Him as such; and so He says of Himself, "Why call ye Me [whom you see] good; none is good [the model of good] but God only [whom ye do not see]?" But whence have we the conception of God as the supreme good? Simply from the *idea* of moral perfection, which reason frames *a priori* and connects inseparably with the notion of a free will. Imitation finds no place at all in morality, and examples serve only for encouragement, that is, they put beyond doubt the feasibility of what the law commands; they make visible that which the practical rule expresses more generally, but they can never authorize us to set aside the true original which lies in reason, and to guide ourselves by examples. . . .

From what has been said, it is clear that all moral conceptions have their seat and origin completely *a priori* in the reason, and that, moreover, in the commonest reason just as truly as in that which is in the highest degree speculative; that they cannot be obtained by abstraction from any empirical, and therefore merely contingent, knowledge; that it is just this purity of their origin that makes them worthy to serve as our supreme practical principle, and that just in proportion as we add anything empirical, we detract from their genuine influence and from the absolute value of actions; that it is not only of the greatest necessity, in a purely speculative point of view, but is also of the greatest practical importance, to derive these notions and laws from pure reason, to present them pure and unmixed, and even to determine the compass of this practical or pure rational knowledge, that is, to determine the whole faculty of pure practical reason; and, in doing so, we must not make its principles dependent on the particular nature of human reason, though in speculative philosophy this may be permitted, or may even at times be necessary; but since moral laws ought to hold good for every rational creature, we must derive them from the general concept of a rational being. In this way, although for its *application* to man morality has need of anthropology, yet, in the first instance, we must treat it independently as pure philosophy, that is, as metaphysic, complete in itself (a thing which in such distinct branches of science is easily done); knowing well that, unless we are in possession of this, it would not only be vain to determine the moral element of duty in right actions for purposes of speculative criticism, but it would be impossible to base morals on their genuine principles, even for common practical purposes, especially of moral instruction, so as to produce pure moral dispositions, and to engraft them on men's minds to the promotion of the greatest possible good in the world.

But in order that in this study we may not merely advance by the natural steps from the common moral judgment (in this case very worthy of respect) to the philosophical, as has been already done, but also from a popular philosophy, which goes no further than it can reach by groping with the help of examples, to metaphysic (which does not allow itself to be checked by anything empirical and, as it must measure the whole extent of this kind of rational knowledge, goes as far as ideal conceptions, where even examples fail us), we must follow and clearly describe the practical faculty of reason, from the general rules of its determination to the point where the notion of duty springs from it.

Everything in nature works according to laws. Rational beings alone have the faculty of acting according *to the conception* of laws—that is, according to principles, that is, have a *will*. Since the deduction of actions from principles requires *reason,* the will is nothing but practical reason. If reason infallibly determines the will, then the actions of such a being which are recognized as objectively necessary are subjectively necessary also, that is, the will is a faculty to choose *that only* which reason independent of inclination recognizes as practically necessary, that is, as good. But if reason of itself does not sufficiently determine the will, if the latter is subject also to subjective conditions (particular impulses) which do not always coincide with the objective conditions, in a word, if the will does not *in itself* completely accord with reason (which is actually the case with men), then the actions which objectively are recognized as necessary are subjectively contingent, and the determination of such a will according to objective laws is *obligation,* that is to say, the relation of the objective laws to a will that is not thoroughly good is conceived as the determination of the will of a rational being by principles of reason, but which the will from its nature does not of necessity follow.

The conception of an objective principle, in so far as it is obligatory for a will, is called a command (of reason), and the formula of the command is called an Imperative.

All imperatives are expressed by the word *ought* [or *shall*], and thereby indicate the relation of an objective law of reason to a will which from its subjective constitution is not necessarily determined by it (an obligation). They say that something would be good to do or to forbear, but they say it to a will which does not always do a thing because it is conceived to be good to do it. That is practically *good,* however, which determines the will by means of the conceptions of reason, and consequently not from subjective causes, but objectively, that is, on principles which are valid for every rational being as such. It is distinguished from the *pleasant* as that which influences the will only by means of sensation from merely subjective causes, valid only for the sense of this or that one, and not as a principle of reason which holds for every one.

A perfectly good will would therefore be equally subject to objective laws (viz., laws of good), but could not be conceived as *obliged* thereby to act lawfully, because of itself from its subjective constitution it can only be determined by the conception of good. Therefore no imperatives hold for the Divine will, or in general for a *holy* will; *ought* is here out of place because the volition is already of itself necessarily in unison with the law. Therefore imperatives are only formulae to express the relation of objective laws of all volition to the subjective imperfection of the will of this or that rational being, for example, the human will.

Now all *imperatives* command either *hypothetically* or *categorically.* The former represent the practical necessity of a possible action as means to something else that is willed (or at least which one might possibly will). The categorical imperative would be that which represented an action as necessary of itself without reference to another end, that is, as objectively necessary.

Since every practical law represents a possible action as good, and on this account, for a subject who is practically determinable by reason as necessary, all imperatives are formulae determining an action which is necessary according to the principle of a will good in some respects. If now the action is good only as a means *to something else,* then the imperative is *hypothetical;* if it is conceived as good *in itself* and consequently as being necessarily the principle of a will which of itself conforms to reason, then it is *categorical.*

Thus the imperative declares what action possible by me would be good, and presents the practical rule in relation to a will which does not forthwith perform an action simply because it is good, whether because the subject does not always know that it is good, or because, even if it know this, yet its maxims might be opposed to the objective principles of practical reason.

Accordingly the hypothetical imperative only says that the action is good for some purpose, *possible* or *actual.* In the first case it is a *problematical,* in the second an *assertorial* practical principle. The categorical imperative which declares an action to be objectively necessary in itself without reference to any purpose, that is, without any other end, is valid as an *apodictic* (practical) principle.

Whatever is possible only by the power of some rational being may also be conceived as a possible purpose of some will; and therefore the principles of action as regards the means necessary to attain some possible purpose are in fact infinitely numerous. All sciences have a practical part consisting of problems expressing that some end is possible for us, and of imperatives directing how it may be attained. These may, therefore, be called in general imperatives of *skill.* Here there is no question whether the end is rational and good, but only what one must do in order to attain it. The precepts for the physician to make his patient thoroughly healthy, and for a poisoner to ensure certain death, are of equal value in this respect, that each serves to effect its purpose perfectly. Since in early youth it cannot be known what ends are likely to occur to us in the course of life, parents seek to have their children taught a *great many things,* and provide for their *skill* in the use of means for all sorts of arbitrary ends, of none of which can they determine whether it may not perhaps hereafter be an object to their pupil, but which it is at all events *possible* that he might aim at; and this anxiety is so great that they commonly neglect to form and correct their judgment on the value of the things which may be chosen as ends.

There is *one* end, however, which may be assumed to be actually such to all rational beings (so far as imperatives apply to them, viz., as dependent beings), and, therefore, one purpose which they not merely *may* have, but which we may with certainty assume that they all actually *have* by a natural necessity, and this is *happiness.* The hypothetical imperative which expresses the practical necessity of an action as means to the advancement of happiness is *assertorial.* We are not to present it as necessary for an uncertain and merely possible purpose, but for a purpose which we may presuppose with certainty and *a priori* in every man, because it belongs to his being. Now skill in the choice of means to his own greatest well-being may be called *prudence,* in the narrowest sense. And thus the imperative which refers to the choice of means to one's own happiness, that is, the precept of prudence, is still always *hypothetical;* the action is not commanded absolutely, but only as means to another purpose.

Finally, there is an imperative which commands a certain conduct immediately, without having as its condition any other purpose to be attained by it. This imperative is *categorical*. It concerns not the matter of the action, or its intended result, but its form and the principle of which it is itself a result; and what is essentially good in it consists in the mental disposition, let the consequence be what it may. This imperative may be called that of *morality*. . . .

. . . In the case of this categorical imperative or law of morality, the difficulty (of discerning its possibility) is a very profound one. It is an *a priori* synthetical practical proposition;[4] and as there is so much difficulty in discerning the possibility of speculative propositions of this kind, it may readily be supposed that the difficulty will be no less with the practical.

In this problem we will first inquire whether the mere conception of a categorical imperative may not perhaps supply us also with the formula of it, containing the proposition which alone can be a categorical imperative; for even if we know the tenor of such an absolute command, yet how it is possible will require further special and laborious study, which we postpone to the last section.

When I conceive a hypothetical imperative, in general I do not know beforehand what it will contain until I am given the condition. But when I conceive a categorical imperative, I know at once what it contains. For as the imperative contains besides the law only the necessity that the maxims[5] shall conform to this law, while the law contains no conditions restricting it, there remains nothing but the general statement that the maxim of the action should conform to a universal law, and it is this conformity alone that the imperative properly represents as necessary.

There is therefore but one categorical imperative, namely, this: *Act only on that maxim whereby thou canst at the same time will that it should become a universal law*.

Now if all imperatives of duty can be deduced from this one imperative as from their principle, then, although it should remain undecided whether what is called duty is not merely a vain notion, yet at least we shall be able to show what we understand by it and what this notion means.

Since the universality of the law according to which effects are produced constitutes what is properly called *nature* in the most general sense (as to

---

[4] I connect the act with the will without presupposing any condition resulting from any inclination, but *a priori*, and therefore necessarily (though only objectively, that is, assuming the idea of a reason possessing full power over all subjective motives). This is accordingly a practical proposition which does not deduce the willing of an action by mere analysis from another already presupposed (for we have not such a perfect will), but connects it immediately with the conception of the will of a rational being, as something not contained in it.

[5] A "maxim" is a subjective principle of action, and must be distinguished from the *objective principle*, namely, practical law. The former contains the practical rule set by reason according to the conditions of the subject (often its ignorance or its inclinations), so that it is the principle on which the subject *acts;* but the law is the objective principle valid for every rational being, and is the principle on which it *ought to act*—that is an imperative.

form)—that is, the existence of things so far as it is determined by general laws—the imperative of duty may be expressed thus: *Act as if the maxim of thy action were to become by thy will a universal law of nature.*

We will now enumerate a few duties, adopting the usual division of them into duties to ourselves and to others, and into perfect and imperfect duties.

1. A man reduced to despair by a series of misfortunes feels wearied of life, but is still so far in possession of his reason that he can ask himself whether it would not be contrary to his duty to himself to take his own life. Now he inquires whether the maxim of his action could become a universal law of nature. His maxim is: From self-love I adopt it as a principle to shorten my life when its longer duration is likely to bring more evil than satisfaction. It is asked then simply whether this principle founded on self-love can become a universal law of nature. Now we see at once that a system of nature of which it should be a law to destroy life by means of the very feeling whose special nature it is to impel to the improvement of life would contradict itself, and therefore could not exist as a system of nature; hence that maxim cannot possibly exist as a universal law of nature, and consequently would be wholly inconsistent with the supreme principle of all duty.

2. Another finds himself forced by necessity to borrow money. He knows that he will not be able to repay it, but sees also that nothing will be lent to him unless he promises stoutly to repay it in a definite time. He desires to make this promise, but he has still so much conscience as to ask himself: Is it not unlawful and inconsistent with duty to get out of a difficulty in this way? Suppose, however, that he resolves to do so, then the maxim of his action would be expressed thus: When I think myself in want of money, I will borrow money and promise to repay it, although I know that I never can do so. Now this principle of self-love or of one's own advantage may perhaps be consistent with my whole future welfare; but the question now is, Is it right? I change then the suggestion of self-love into a universal law, and state the question thus: How would it be if my maxim were a universal law? Then I see at once that it could never hold as a universal law of nature, but would necessarily contradict itself. For supposing it to be a universal law that everyone when he thinks himself in a difficulty should be able to promise whatever he pleases, with the purpose of not keeping his promise, the promise itself would become impossible, as well as the end that one might have in view in it, since no one would consider that anything was promised to him, but would ridicule all such statements as vain pretenses.

3. A third finds in himself a talent which with the help of some culture might make him a useful man in many respects. But he finds himself in comfortable circumstances and prefers to indulge in pleasure rather than to take pains in enlarging and improving his happy natural capacities. He asks, however, whether his maxim of neglect of his natural gifts, besides agreeing with his inclination to indulgence, agrees also with what is called duty. He sees then that a system of nature could indeed subsist with such a universal law, although men (like the South Sea islanders) should let their talents rest and resolve to

devote their lives merely to idleness, amusement, and propagation of their species—in a word, to enjoyment; but he cannot possibly *will* that this should be a universal law of nature, or be implanted in us as such by a natural instinct. For, as a rational being, he necessarily wills that his faculties be developed, since they serve him, and have been given him, for all sorts of possible purposes.

4. A fourth, who is in prosperity, while he sees that others have to contend with great wretchedness and that he could help them, thinks: What concern is it of mine? Let everyone be as happy as Heaven pleases, or as he can make himself; I will take nothing from him nor even envy him, only I do not wish to contribute anything to his welfare or to his assistance in distress! Now no doubt, if such a mode of thinking were a universal law, the human race might very well subsist, and doubtless even better than in a state in which everyone talks of sympathy and good-will, or even takes care occasionally to put it into practice, but, on the other side, also cheats when he can, betrays the rights of men, or otherwise violates them. But although it is possible that a universal law of nature might exist in accordance with that maxim, it is impossible to *will* that such a principle should have the universal validity of a law of nature. For a will which resolved this would contradict itself, inasmuch as many cases might occur in which one would have need of the love and sympathy of others, and in which, by such a law of nature, sprung from his own will, he would deprive himself of all hope of the aid he desires.

These are a few of the many actual duties, or at least what we regard as such, which obviously fall into two classes on the one principle that we have laid down. We must be *able to will* that a maxim of our action should be a universal law. This is the canon of the moral appreciation of the action generally. Some actions are of such a character that their maxim cannot without contradiction be even *conceived* as a universal law of nature, far from it being possible that we should *will* that it *should* be so. In others, this intrinsic impossibility is not found, but still it is impossible to *will* that their maxim should be raised to the universality of a law of nature, since such a will would contradict itself. It is easily seen that the former violate strict or rigorous (inflexible) duty; the latter only laxer (meritorious) duty. Thus it has been completely shown by these examples how all duties depend as regards the nature of the obligation (not the object of the action) on the same principle.

If now we attend to ourselves on occasion of any transgression of duty, we shall find that we in fact do not will that our maxim should be a universal law, for that is impossible for us; on the contrary, we will that the opposite should remain a universal law, only we assume the liberty of making an *exception* in our own favor or (just for this time only) in favor of our inclination. Consequently, if we considered all cases from one and the same point of view, namely, that of reason, we should find a contradiction in our own will, namely, that a certain principle should be objectively necessary as a universal law, and yet subjectively should not be universal, but admit of exceptions. As, however, we at one moment regard our action from the point of view of a will wholly conformed to reason, and then again look at the same action from the point of view of a will affected by inclination, there is not really any contradiction, but an antagonism of inclination to the precept of reason, whereby the universality of the principle is changed into a mere generality, so that the practical principle of reason shall meet the maxim half way. Now, although this cannot be justified in our own impartial judgment, yet it proves that we do really recognize the validity of the categorical imperative and (with all respect for it) only allow ourselves a few exceptions which we think unimportant and forced from us.

We have thus established at least this much—that if duty is a conception which is to have any import and real legislative authority for our actions, it can only be expressed in categorical, and not at all in hypothetical, imperatives. We have also, which is of great importance, exhibited clearly and definitely for every practical application the content of the categorical imperative, which must contain the principle of all duty if there is such a thing at all. We have not yet, however, advanced so far as to prove *a priori* that there actually is such an imperative, that there is a practical law which commands absolutely of itself and without any other impulse, and that the following of this law is duty. . . .

The will is conceived as a faculty of determining oneself to action *in accordance with the conception of certain laws*. And such a faculty can be found only in rational beings. Now that which serves the will as the objective ground of its self-determination is the *end,* and if this is assigned by reason alone, it must hold for all rational beings. On the other hand, that which merely contains the ground of possibility of the action of which the effect is the end, this is called the *means.* The subjective ground of the desire is the *spring,* the objective ground of the volition is the *motive*; hence the distinction between subjective ends which rest on springs, and objective ends which depend on motives valid for every rational being. Practical principles are *formal* when they abstract from all subjective ends; they are *material* when they assume these, and therefore particular, springs of action. The ends which a rational being proposes to himself at pleasure as *effects* of his actions (material ends) are all only relative, for it is only their relation to the particular desires of the subject that gives them their worth, which therefore cannot furnish principles universal and necessary for all rational beings and for every volition, that is to say, practical laws. Hence all these relative ends can give rise only to hypothetical imperatives.

Supposing, however, that there were something *whose existence* has *in itself* an absolute worth, something which, being *an end in itself,* could be a source of definite laws, then in this and this alone would lie the source of a possible categorical imperative, that is, a practical law..

Now I say: man and generally any rational being *exists* as an end in himself, *not merely as a means* to be arbitrarily used by this or that will, but in all his actions, whether they concern himself or other rational beings, must be always regarded at the same time as an end. All objects of the inclinations have only a conditional worth; for if the inclinations and the wants founded on them did not exist, then their object would be without value. But the inclinations themselves, being sources of want, are so far from having an absolute worth for which they should be desired that, on the contrary, it must be the universal wish of every rational being to be wholly free from them. Thus the worth of any object which is *to be acquired* by our action is always conditional. Beings, whose existence depends not on our will but on nature's, have nevertheless, if they are rational beings, only a relative value as means, and are therefore called *things;* rational beings, on the contrary, are called *persons,* because their very nature points them out as ends in themselves, that is, as something which must not be used merely as means, and so far therefore restricts freedom of action (and is an object of respect). These, therefore, are not merely subjective ends whose existence has a worth *for us* as an effect of our action, but *objective ends,* that is, things whose existence is an end in itself—an end, moreover, for which no other can be substituted, which they should subserve *merely* as means, for otherwise nothing whatever would possess *absolute worth;* but if all worth were conditioned and therefore contingent, then there would be no supreme practical principle of reason whatever.

If then there is a supreme practical principle or, in respect of the human will, a categorical imperative, it must be one which, being drawn from the conception of that which is necessarily an end for everyone because it is *an end in itself,* constitutes an *objective* principle of will, and can therefore serve as a universal practical law. The foundation of this principle is: *rational nature exists as an end in itself.* Man necessarily conceives his own existence as being so; so far then this is a *subjective* principle of human actions. But every other rational being regards its existence similarly, just on the same rational principle that holds for me; so that it is at the same time an objective principle from which as a supreme practical law all laws of the will must be capable of being deduced. Accordingly the practical imperative will be as follows: *So act as to treat humanity, whether in thine own person or in that of any other, in every case as an end withal, never as means only.* We will now inquire whether this can be practically carried out.

To abide by the previous examples:

First, under the head of necessary duty to oneself: He who contemplates suicide should ask himself whether his action can be consistent with the idea of humanity *as an end in itself.* If he destroys himself in order to escape from painful circumstances, he uses a person merely as *a mean* to maintain a tolerable condition up to the end of life. But a man is not a thing, that is to say, something which can be used merely as means, but must in all his actions be always considered as an end in himself. I cannot, therefore, dispose in any way of a man in my own person so as to mutilate him, to damage or kill him. (It belongs to ethics proper to define this principle more precisely, so as to avoid all misunderstanding, for example, as to the amputation of the limbs in order to preserve myself; as to exposing my life to danger with a view to preserve it, etc. This question is therefore omitted here.)

Secondly, as regards necessary duties, or those of strict obligation, towards others: He who is thinking of making a lying promise to others will see at once that he would be using another man *merely as a mean,* without the latter containing at the same time the end in himself. For he whom I propose by such a promise to use for my own purposes cannot possibly assent to my mode of acting towards him, and therefore cannot himself contain the end of this action. This violation of the principle of humanity in other men is more obvious if we take in examples of attacks on the freedom and property of others. For then it is clear that he who transgresses the rights of men intends to use the person of others merely as means, without considering that as rational beings they ought always to be esteemed also as ends, that is, as beings who must be capable of containing in themselves the end of the very same action.

Thirdly, as regards contingent (meritorious) duties to oneself: It is not enough that the action does not violate humanity in our own person as an end in itself; it must also *harmonize with* it. Now there are in humanity capacities of greater perfection which belong to the end that nature has in view in regard to humanity in ourselves as the subject; to neglect these might perhaps be consistent with the *maintenance* of humanity as an end in itself, but not with the *advancement* of this end.

Fourthly, as regards meritorious duties towards others: The natural end which all men have is their own happiness. Now humanity might indeed subsist although no one should contribute anything to the happiness of others, provided he did not intentionally withdraw anything from it; but after all, this would only harmonize negatively, not positively, with *humanity as an end in itself,* if everyone does not also endeavor, as far as in him lies, to forward the ends of others. For the ends of any subject which is an end in himself ought as far as possible to be *my* ends also, if that conception is to have its *full* effect with me.

This principle that humanity and generally every rational nature is *an end in itself* (which is the supreme limiting condition of every man's freedom of action) is not borrowed from experience, *first,* because it is universal, applying as it does to all rational beings whatever, and experience is not capable of determining anything about them; *secondly,* because it does not present humanity as an end to men (subjectively), that is, as an object which men do of themselves actually adopt as an end; but as an objective end which must as a law constitute the supreme limiting condition of all our subjective ends, let them be what we will; it must therefore spring from pure reason. In fact the objective principle of all practical legislation lies (according to the first principle) in *the rule* and its form of universality which makes it capable of being a law (say, for example, a law of nature); but the *subjective* principle is in the *end;* now by the second principle, the subject of all ends is each rational being inasmuch as it is an end in itself. Hence follows the third practical principle of the will, which is the ultimate condition of its harmony with the universal practical reason, viz., the idea of *the will of every rational being as a universally legislative will.*

On this principle all maxims are rejected which are inconsistent with the will being itself universal legislator. Thus the will is not subject to the law, but so subject that it must be regarded *as itself giving the law,* and on this ground only subject to the law (of which it can regard itself as the author). . . .

Looking back now on all previous attempts to discover the principle of morality, we need not wonder why they all failed. It was seen that man was bound to laws by duty, but it was not observed that the laws to which he is subject are *only those of his own giving,* though at the same time they are *universal,* and that he is only bound to act in conformity with his own will— a will, however, which is designed by nature to give universal laws. For when one has conceived man only as subject to a law (no matter what), then this law required some interest, either by way of attraction or constraint, since it did not originate as a law from *his own* will, but this will was according to a law obliged by *something else* to act in a certain manner. Now by this necessary consequence all the labor spent in finding a supreme principle of *duty* was irrevocably lost. For men never elicited duty, but only a necessity of acting from a certain interest. Whether this interest was private or otherwise, in any case the imperative must be conditional, and could not by any means be capable of being a moral command. I will therefore call this the principle of *Autonomy* of the will, in contrast with every other which I accordingly reckon as *Heteronomy.*

The conception of every rational being as one which must consider itself as giving in all the maxims of its will universal laws, so as to judge itself and its actions from this point of view—this conception leads to another which depends on it and is very fruitful, namely, that of a *kingdom of ends.*

By a "kingdom" I understand the union of different rational beings in a system by common laws. Now since it is by laws that ends are determined as regards their universal validity, hence, if we abstract from the personal differences of rational beings, and likewise from all the content of their private ends, we shall be able to conceive all ends combined in a systematic whole (including both rational beings as ends in themselves, and also the special ends which each may propose to himself), that is to say, we can conceive a kingdom of ends, which on the preceding principles is possible.

For all rational beings come under the *law* that each of them must treat itself and all others *never merely as means,* but in every case *at the same time as ends in themselves.* Hence results a systematic union of rational beings by common objective laws, that is, a kingdom which may be called a kingdom of ends, since what these laws have in view is just the relation of these beings to one another as ends and means. It is certainly only an ideal.

A rational being belongs as a *member* to the kingdom of ends when, although giving universal laws in it, he is also himself subject to these laws. He belongs to it *as sovereign* when, while giving laws, he is not subject to the will of any other.

A rational being must always regard himself as giving laws either as member or as sovereign in a kingdom of ends which is rendered possible by the freedom of will. He cannot, however, maintain the latter position merely by the maxims of his will, but only in case he is a completely independent being without wants and with unrestricted power adequate to his will.

Morality consists then in the reference of all action to the legislation which alone can render a kingdom of ends possible. This legislation must be capable of existing in every rational being, and of emanating from his will, so that the principle of this will is never to act on any maxim which could not without contradiction be also a universal law, and accordingly always so to act *that the will could at the same time regard itself as giving in its maxims universal laws.* If now the maxims of rational beings are not by their own nature coincident with this objective principle, then the necessity of acting on it is called practical necessitation, that is, *duty.* Duty does not apply to the sovereign in the kingdom of ends, but it does to every member of it and to all in the same degree. . . .

TRANSITION FROM THE METAPHYSIC OF MORALS TO THE CRITIQUE OF PURE PRACTICAL REASON

The Concept of Freedom Is the Key that Explains the Autonomy of the Will

The *will* is a kind of causality belonging to living beings in so far as they are rational, and *freedom* would be this property of such causality that it can be efficient, independently on foreign causes *determining* it; just as *physical necessity* is the property that the causality of all irrational beings has of being determined to activity by the influence of foreign causes.

The preceding definition of freedom is *negative,* and therefore unfruitful for the discovery of its essence; but it leads to a *positive* conception which is so much the more full and fruitful. Since the conception of causality involves that of laws, according to which, by something that we call cause, something else, namely, the effect, must be produced; hence, although freedom is not a property of the will depending on physical laws, yet it is not for that reason lawless; on the contrary, it must be a causality acting according to immutable laws, but of a peculiar kind; otherwise a free will would be an absurdity. Physical necessity is a heteronomy of the efficient causes, for every effect is possible only according to this law—that something else determines the efficient cause to exert its causality. What else then can freedom of the will be but autonomy, that is, the property of the will to be a law to itself? But the proposition: The will is in every action a law to itself, only expresses the principle to act on no other maxim than that which can also have as an object itself as a universal law. Now this is precisely the formula of the categorical imperative and is the principle of morality, so that a free will and a will subject to moral laws are one and the same. . . .

How Is a Categorical Imperative Possible?

Every rational being reckons himself *qua* intelligence as belonging to the world of understanding, and it is simply as an efficient cause belonging to that world that he calls his causality a *will.* On the other side, he is also conscious of himself as a part of the world of sense in which his actions, which are mere appearances [phenomena] of that causality, are displayed; we cannot, however, discern how they are possible from this causality which we do not know; but instead of that, these actions as belonging to the sensible world must be viewed as determined by other phenomena, namely, desires and inclinations. If therefore I were only a member of the world of understanding, then all my actions would perfectly conform to the principle of autonomy of the pure will; if I were only a part of the world of sense, they would necessarily be assumed to conform wholly to the natural law of desires and inclinations, in other words, to the heteronomy of nature. (The former would rest on morality as the supreme principle, the latter on happiness.) Since, however, *the world of understanding contains the foundation of the world of sense, and consequently of its laws also,* and accordingly gives the law to my will (which belongs wholly to the world of understanding) directly, and must be conceived as doing so, it follows that, although on the one side I must regard myself as a being belonging to the world of sense, yet, on the other side, I must recognize myself, as an intelligence, as subject to the law of the world of understanding, that is, to reason, which contains this law in the idea of freedom, and therefore as subject to the autonomy of the will; consequently I must regard the laws of the world of understanding as imperatives for me, and the actions which conform to them as duties.

And thus what makes categorical imperatives possible is this—that the idea of freedom makes me a member of an intelligible world, in consequence of which, if I were nothing else, all my actions *would* always conform to the autonomy of the will; but as I at the same time intuit myself as a member of the world of sense, they *ought* so to conform, and this *categorical* "ought" implies a synthetic *a priori* proposition, inasmuch as besides my will as affected by sensible desires there is added further the idea of the same will, but as belonging to the world of the understanding, pure and practical of itself, which contains the supreme condition according to reason of the former will; precisely as to the intuitions of sense there are added concepts of the understand.ng which of themselves signify nothing but regular form in general, and in this way synthetic *a priori* propositions become possible, on which all knowledge of physical nature rests.

The practical use of common human reason confirms this reasoning. There is no one, not even the most consummate villain, provided only that he is otherwise accustomed to the use of reason, who, when we set before him examples of honesty of purpose, of steadfastness in following good maxims, of sympathy and general benevolence (even combined with great sacrifices of advantages and comfort), does not wish that he might also possess these qualities. Only on account of his inclinations and impulses he cannot attain this in himself, but at the same time he wishes to be free from such inclinations which are burdensome to himself. He proves by this that he transfers himself in thought with a will free from the impulses of the sensibility into an order of things wholly different from that of his desires in the field of the sensibility; since he cannot expect to obtain by that wish any gratification of his desires, nor any position which would satisfy any of his actual or supposable inclinations (for this would destroy the pre-eminence of the very idea which wrests that wish from him), he can only expect a greater intrinsic worth of his own person. This better person, however, he imagines himself to be when he transfers himself to the point of view of a member of the world of the understanding, to which he is involuntarily forced by the idea of freedom, that is, of independence on *determining* causes of the world of sense; and from this point of view he is conscious of a good will, which by his own confession constitutes the law for the bad will that he possesses as a member of the world of sense—a law whose authority he recognizes while transgressing it. What he morally "ought" is then what he necessarily "would" as a member of the world of the understanding, and is conceived by him as an "ought" only inasmuch as he likewise considers himself as a member of the world of sense.

Questions

1. What reasons does Kant give for saying that for an action to be morally good, it must not only conform to the moral law but also must be done for the sake of the law?

2. What does Kant mean by saying that only a good will can be called good without qualification? What arguments does he give in support of this view? How valid do you think his arguments are?

3. What would you say is the difference between our desires and our will, in Kant's sense of "will"? What does he mean by saying, ". . . the will is nothing but practical reason"?

4. Kant distinguishes: (a) actions inconsistent with duty, (b) actions consistent with duty, but not done from duty, and (c) actions consistent with duty and done from duty. Give an example of each and explain why Kant considers this distinction important for morals.

5. When Kant says that the actions of people who take delight in helping others have "no true moral worth," does he mean that our moral duty is to help others, not out of love for them, but only with a kind of cold determination and grim disposition to be morally upright? Defend your answer by specific references to the text of the reading.

6. According to Kant, is our own personal happiness always opposed to our moral duty? Why or why not?

7. What are Kant's three propositions of morality? He claims that the third proposition is a consequence of the first two. Give a careful appraisal of the justifiability of that claim.

8. Not conformity to any particular law, but "simple conformity to law in general" defines our moral duty. What does Kant mean by "simple conformity to law in general"? To clarify your answer give some examples, but do not give the same examples that Kant does.

9. Kant says that although common men do not conceive the moral law (Act only so that you can will that your maxim become a universal law.) in such an abstract and universal form, "yet they always have it really before their eyes and use it as the standard of their decision." Does Kant give any argument in defense of this assertion? If so, what is it, and is it in your opinion sound? If not, what argument do you think could be made for it, or against it?

10. Suppose someone objected to Kant's theory, saying that it was too idealistic, that is, it would be impossible to put into practice. What would Kant be likely to say in reply?

11. According to Kant, why must the moral law be valid "not merely for men, but for all *rational creatures generally,* not merely under certain contingent conditions or with exceptions, but *with absolute necessity"*?

12. Explain clearly the difference between a hypothetical and a categorical imperative. Show how this distinction is used by Kant in describing three kinds of imperatives: imperatives of skill, of prudence, and of morality. Give examples.

13. The categorical imperative is "an *a priori* synthetical practical proposition." State what this means in your own words. (You may refer to the selection by Kant in Chapter 1, beginning on page 116, for an explanation of the terms "a priori" and "synthetical.")

14. Analyze the four examples Kant gives of "duties to ourselves and to others" and "perfect and imperfect duties," in order to determine whether any of these examples fail to exemplify what they are supposed to exemplify.

15. Summarize the steps in Kant's line of reasoning to show that the "practical imperative" (So act to treat humanity, whether in thine own person or in that of any other, in every case as an end withal, never as means only.) means essentially the same thing as the "categorical imperative" (So act that the maxim of thine action can become a universal law.).

16. Explain what Kant means by a "kingdom of ends." How is this concept connected with the concept of the moral law?

17. What does Kant mean by the "autonomy of the will"? If you have read selections from Chapter 5, "The Problem of Freedom of the Will," state why you think that Kant has succeeded, or has not succeeded, in providing either a partial or a whole solution to the problem of freedom of the will.

18. Study Kant's entire theory to see whether there are any traces of empirical arguments (arguments based on what we learn from experience) in it. Point out any places where Kant has failed to remain within the boundaries of a priori reasoning.

19. Is the following statement a fair criticism? Defend your answer.

"Kant's theory rests upon a fundamental logical error. He tries to deduce from the general concept of moral duty what our duty is, and this is the same mistake as trying to deduce from an analysis of the meaning of the word 'vote' how a person ought to vote."

20. Construct a reply which Kant might make to the statement that his whole theory is merely an elaborate psychological "rationalization" of his Pietistic upbringing. (Kant's parents were members of a Protestant sect known as Pietism, whose moral code tended to condemn personal pleasures.) Is such a statement at all relevant to the truth of what Kant has to say about morality? Why or why not?

21. Suppose it were claimed that Kant's entire moral philosophy is simply an argument to the effect that we should all obey the Golden Rule: Do unto others as you would have them do unto you. Is it true that the Golden Rule follows from Kant's conception of moral duty? If it does, is this *all* Kant's theory amounts to? Defend your answers.

22. In the introduction to this selection, it was said that the general result of Kant's theory is that there is a total separation, an impassable gulf, between science and ethics, between our knowledge of what is and our knowledge of what ought to be, between the realm of facts and the realm of values. Outline the main reasons for which you now think this is, or is not, so.

23. Compare the moral philosophy of Richard Price, given in the preceding selection (page 520), with that of Kant. What elements do both theories have in common? At what points do they differ?

5

Utilitarianism

John Stuart Mill
(1806-1873)

John Stuart Mill was the son of a famous British economist and social philosopher, James Mill. Through his philosophical writings, the son established a greater name than his father's. In 1843 he published *A System of Logic, Ratiocinative and Inductive,* a major work in its field. His other important works include the *Essay on Liberty* (1859); *An Examination of Sir William Hamilton's Philosophy* (1865); and his chief study in moral philosophy, *Utilitarianism* (1863). Mill had a strong social conscience and became a leader of liberalism and social reform in Victorian England, putting into practice many of the principles he had set forth in his moral philosophy.

In the first part of this reading, Mill is trying to clarify the meaning of the utilitarian standard of morality. In particular he is defending it against certain distortions of meaning which it suffered at the hands of both its opponents and its popularizers. In the second part, Mill attempts to show that utilitarianism is a true ethical system. Here he is directly concerned with the central problem of moral philosophy: the justification of a moral standard. Mill not only tries to justify utilitarianism, he also discusses the difficulties involved in any attempt to "prove" an ethical system. In this discussion he critically examines the ultimate grounds of moral knowledge.

This selection comes from Chapters II and IV of *Utilitarianism*. Mill's own chapter titles are used.

From Mill: *Utilitarianism* (The Library of Liberal Arts No. 1, N. Y., 1957). Reprinted by permission of the publishers, The Liberal Arts Press, Inc.

WHAT UTILITARIANISM IS

A passing remark is all that needs be given to the ignorant blunder of supposing that those who stand up for utility as the test of right and wrong use the term in that restricted and merely colloquial sense in which utility is opposed to pleasure. An apology is due to the philosophical opponents of utili-

tarianism for even the momentary appearance of confounding them with anyone capable of so absurd a misconception; which is the more extraordinary,
inasmuch as the contrary accusation, of referring everything to pleasure, and
that, too, in its grossest form, is another of the common charges against utilitarianism: and, as has been pointedly remarked by an able writer, the same
sort of persons, and often the very same persons, denounce the theory "as
impracticably dry when the word 'utility' precedes the word 'pleasure,' and as
too practically voluptuous when the word 'pleasure' precedes the word 'utility.'"
Those who know anything about the matter are aware that every writer, from
Epicurus to Bentham, who maintained the theory of utility meant by it, not
something to be contradistinguished from pleasure, but pleasure itself, together
with exemption from pain; and instead of opposing the useful to the agreeable
or the ornamental, have always declared that the useful means these, among
other things. Yet the common herd, including the herd of writers, not only in
newspapers and periodicals, but in books of weight and pretension, are perpetually falling into this shallow mistake. Having caught up the word "utilitarian," while knowing nothing whatever about it but its sound, they habitually
express by it the rejection or the neglect of pleasure in some of its forms: of
beauty, of ornament, or of amusement. Nor is the term thus ignorantly mis-
applied solely in disparagement, but occasionally in compliment, as though it
implied superiority to frivolity and the mere pleasures of the moment. And this
perverted use is the only one in which the word is popularly known, and the
one from which the new generation are acquiring their sole notion of its meaning. Those who introduced the word, but who had for many years discontinued
it as a distinctive appellation, may well feel themselves called upon to resume
it if by doing so they can hope to contribute anything toward rescuing it from
this utter degradation.

The creed which accepts as the foundation of morals "utility" or the "greatest happiness principle" holds that actions are right in proportion as they tend
to promote happiness; wrong as they tend to produce the reverse of happiness.
By happiness is intended pleasure and the absence of pain; by unhappiness,
pain and the privation of pleasure. To give a clear view of the moral standard
set up by the theory, much more requires to be said; in particular, what things
it includes in the ideas of pain and pleasure, and to what extent this is left an
open question. But these supplementary explanations do not affect the theory
of life on which this theory of morality is grounded—namely, that pleasure and
freedom from pain are the only things desirable as ends; and that all desirable
things (which are as numerous in the utilitarian as in any other scheme) are
desirable either for pleasure inherent in themselves or as means to the promotion of pleasure and the prevention of pain.

Now such a theory of life excites in many minds, and among them in some
of the most estimable in feeling and purpose, inveterate dislike. To suppose
that life has (as they express it) no higher end than pleasure—no better and
nobler object of desire and pursuit—they designate as utterly mean and grovel-
ing, as a doctrine worthy only of swine, to whom the followers of Epicurus

were, at a very early period, contemptuously likened; and modern holders of the doctrine are occasionally made the subject of equally polite comparisons by its German, French, and English assailants.

When thus attacked, the Epicureans have always answered that it is not they, but their accusers, who represent human nature in a degrading light, since the accusation supposes human beings to be capable of no pleasures except those of which swine are capable. If this supposition were true, the charge could not be gainsaid, but would then be no longer an imputation; for if the sources of pleasure were precisely the same to human beings and to swine, the rule of life which is good enough for the one would be good enough for the other. The comparison of the Epicurean life to that of beasts is felt as degrading, precisely because a beast's pleasures do not satisfy a human being's conceptions of happiness. Human beings have faculties more elevated than the animal appetites and, when once made conscious of them, do not regard anything as happiness which does not include their gratification. I do not, indeed, consider the Epicureans to have been by any means faultless in drawing out their scheme of consequences from the utilitarian principle. To do this in any sufficient manner, many Stoic, as well as Christian, elements require to be included. But there is no known Epicurean theory of life which does not assign to the pleasures of the intellect, of the feelings and imagination, and of the moral sentiments a much higher value as pleasures than to those of mere sensation. It must be admitted, however, that utilitarian writers in general have placed the superiority of mental over bodily pleasures chiefly in the greater permanency, safety, uncostliness, etc., of the former—that is, in their circumstantial advantages rather than in their intrinsic nature. And on all these points utilitarians have fully proved their case; but they might have taken the other and, as it may be called, higher ground with entire consistency. It is quite compatible with the principle of utility to recognize the fact that some kinds of pleasure are more desirable and more valuable than others. It would be absurd that, while in estimating all other things quality is considered as well as quantity, the estimation of pleasure should be supposed to depend on quantity alone.

If I am asked what I mean by difference of quality in pleasures, or what makes one pleasure more valuable than another, merely as a pleasure, except its being greater in amount, there is but one possible answer. Of two pleasures, if there be one to which all or almost all who have experience of both give a decided preference, irrespective of any feeling of moral obligation to prefer it, that is the more desirable pleasure. If one of the two is, by those who are competently acquainted with both, placed so far above the other that they prefer it, even though knowing it to be attended with a greater amount of discontent, and would not resign it for any quantity of the other pleasure which their nature is capable of, we are justified in ascribing to the preferred enjoyment a superiority in quality so far outweighing quantity as to render it, in comparison, of small account.

Now it is an unquestionable fact that those who are equally acquainted with and equally capable of appreciating and enjoying both do give a most marked preference to the manner of existence which employs their higher faculties. Few human creatures would consent to be changed into any of the lower animals for a promise of the fullest allowance of a beast's pleasures; no intelligent human being would consent to be a fool, no instructed person would be an ignoramus, no person of feeling and conscience would be selfish and base, even though they should be persuaded that the fool, the dunce, or the rascal is better satisfied with his lot than they are with theirs. They would not resign what they possess more than he for the most complete satisfaction of all the desires which they have in common with him. If they ever fancy they would, it is only in cases of unhappiness so extreme that to escape from it they would exchange their lot for almost any other, however undesirable in their own eyes. A being of higher faculties requires more to make him happy, is capable probably of more acute suffering, and certainly accessible to it at more points, than one of an inferior type; but in spite of these liabilities, he can never really wish to sink into what he feels to be a lower grade of existence. We may give what explanation we please of this unwillingness; we may attribute it to pride, a name which is given indiscriminately to some of the most and to some of the least estimable feelings of which mankind are capable; we may refer it to the love of liberty and personal independence, an appeal to which was with the Stoics one of the most effective means for the inculcation of it; to the love of power or to the love of excitement, both of which do really enter into and contribute to it; but its most appropriate appellation is a sense of dignity, which all human beings possess in one form or other, and in some, though by no means in exact, proportion to their higher faculties, and which is so essential a part of the happiness of those in whom it is strong that nothing which conflicts with it could be otherwise than momentarily an object of desire to them. Whoever supposes that this preference takes place at a sacrifice of happiness—that the superior being, in anything like equal circumstances, is not happier than the inferior—confounds the two very different ideas of happiness and content. It is indisputable that the being whose capacities of enjoyment are low has the greatest chance of having them fully satisfied; and a highly endowed being will always feel that any happiness which he can look for, as the world is constituted, is imperfect. But he can learn to bear its imperfections, if they are at all bearable; and they will not make him envy the being who is indeed unconscious of the imperfections, but only because he feels not at all the good which those imperfections qualify. It is better to be a human being dissatisfied than a pig satisfied; better to be Socrates dissatisfied than a fool satisfied. And if the fool, or the pig, are of a different opinion, it is because they only know their own side of the question. The other party to the comparison knows both sides.

It may be objected that many who are capable of the higher pleasures occasionally, under the influence of temptation, postpone them to the lower. But this is quite compatible with a full appreciation of the intrinsic superiority of the higher. Men often, from infirmity of character, make their election for the nearer good, though they know it to be the less valuable; and this no less when the choice is between two bodily pleasures than when it is between bodily and mental. They pursue sensual indulgences to the injury of health, though perfectly aware that health is the greater good. It may be further objected that many who begin with youthful enthusiasm for everything noble, as they advance in years, sink into indolence and selfishness. But I do not believe that those who undergo this very common change voluntarily choose the lower description of pleasures in preference to the higher. I believe that, before they devote themselves exclusively to the one, they have already become incapable of the other. Capacity for the nobler feelings is in most natures a very tender plant, easily killed, not only by hostile influences, but by mere want of sustenance; and in the majority of young persons it speedily dies away if the occupations to which their position in life has devoted them, and the society into which it has thrown them, are not favorable to keeping that higher capacity in exercise. Men lose their high aspirations as they lose their intellectual tastes, because they have not time or opportunity for indulging them; and they addict themselves to inferior pleasures, not because they deliberately prefer them, but because they are either the only ones to which they have access or the only ones which they are any longer capable of enjoying. It may be questioned whether anyone who has remained equally susceptible to both classes of pleasures ever knowingly and calmly preferred the lower, though many, in all ages, have broken down in an ineffectual attempt to combine both.

From this verdict of the only competent judges, I apprehend there can be no appeal. On a question which is the best worth having of two pleasures, or which of two modes of existence is the most grateful to the feelings, apart from its moral attributes and from its consequences, the judgment of those who are qualified by knowledge of both, or, if they differ, that of the majority among them, must be admitted as final. And there needs be the less hesitation to accept this judgment respecting the quality of pleasures, since there is no other tribunal to be referred to even on the question of quantity. What means are there of determining which is the acutest of two pains, or the intensest of two pleasurable sensations, except the general suffrage of those who are familiar with both? Neither pains nor pleasures are homogeneous, and pain is always heterogeneous with pleasure. What is there to decide whether a particular pleasure is worth purchasing at the cost of a particular pain, except the feelings and judgment of the experienced? When, therefore, those feelings and judgment declare the pleasures derived from the higher faculties to be preferable *in kind,* apart from the question of intensity, to those of which the animal nature, disjoined from the higher faculties, is susceptible, they are entitled on this subject to the same regard.

I have dwelt on this point as being a necessary part of a perfectly just conception of utility or happiness considered as the directive rule of human conduct. But it is by no means an indispensable condition to the acceptance of the utilitarian standard; for that standard is not the agent's own greatest happiness, but the greatest amount of happiness altogether; and if it may possibly be doubted whether a noble character is always the happier for its nobleness, there can be no doubt that it makes other people happier, and that the world in general is immensely a gainer by it. Utilitarianism, therefore, could only attain its end by the general cultivation of nobleness of character, even if each individual were only benefited by the nobleness of others, and his own, so far as happiness is concerned, were a sheer deduction from the benefit. But the bare enunciation of such an absurdity as this last renders refutation superfluous.

According to the greatest happiness principle, as above explained, the ultimate end, with reference to and for the sake of which all other things are desirable—whether we are considering our own good or that of other people—is an existence exempt as far as possible from pain, and as rich as possible in enjoyments, both in point of quantity and quality; the test of quality and the rule for measuring it against quantity being the preference felt by those who, in their opportunities of experience, to which must be added their habits of self-consciousness and self-observation, are best furnished with the means of comparison. This, being according to the utilitarian opinion the end of human action, is necessarily also the standard of morality, which may accordingly be defined "the rules and precepts for human conduct," by the observance of which an existence such as has been described might be, to the greatest extent possible, secured to all mankind; and not to them only, but, so far as the nature of things admits, to the whole sentient creation.

. . . The utilitarian morality does recognize in human beings the power of sacrificing their own greatest good for the good of others. It only refuses to admit that the sacrifice is itself a good. A sacrifice which does not increase or tend to increase the sum total of happiness, it considers as wasted. The only self-renunciation which it applauds is devotion to the happiness, or to some of the means of happiness, of others, either of mankind collectively or of individuals within the limits imposed by the collective interests of mankind.

I must again repeat what the assailants of utilitarianism seldom have the justice to acknowledge, that the happiness which forms the utilitarian standard of what is right in conduct is not the agent's own happiness but that of all concerned. As between his own happiness and that of others, utilitarianism requires him to be as strictly impartial as a disinterested and benevolent spectator. In the golden rule of Jesus of Nazareth, we read the complete spirit of the ethics of utility. "To do as you would be done by," and "to love your neighbor as yourself," constitute the ideal perfection of utilitarian morality. As the means of making the nearest approach to this ideal, utility would enjoin, first, that laws and social arrangements should place the happiness or (as, speaking practically, it may be called) the interest of every individual as nearly as possible in harmony with the interest of the whole; and, secondly, that education and opinion, which have so vast a power over human character, should so use that power as to establish in the mind of every individual an indissoluble association between his own happiness and the good of the whole, especially between his own happiness and the practice of such modes of conduct, negative and positive, as regard for the universal happiness prescribes; so that not only he may be unable to conceive the possibility of happiness to himself, consistently with conduct opposed to the general good, but also that a direct impulse to promote the general good may be in every individual one of the habitual motives of action, and the sentiments connected therewith may fill a large and prominent place in every human being's sentient existence. If the impugners of the utilitarian morality represented it to their own minds in this its true character, I know not what recommendation possessed by any other morality they could possibly affirm to be wanting to it; what more beautiful or more exalted developments of human nature any other ethical system can be supposed to foster, or what springs of action, not accessible to the utilitarian, such systems rely on for giving effect to their mandates.

The objectors to utilitarianism cannot always be charged with representing it in a discreditable light. On the contrary, those among them who entertain anything like a just idea of its disinterested character sometimes find fault with its standard as being too high for humanity. They say it is exacting too much to require that people shall always act from the inducement of promoting the general interests of society. But this is to mistake the very meaning of a standard of morals and confound the rule of action with the motive of it. It is the business of ethics to tell us what are our duties, or by what test we may know them; but no system of ethics requires that the sole motive of all we do shall be a feeling of duty; on the contrary, ninety-nine hundredths of all our actions are done from other motives, and rightly so done if the rule of duty does not condemn them. It is the more unjust to utilitarianism that this particular misapprehension should be made a ground of objection to it, inasmuch as utilitarian moralists have gone beyond almost all others in affirming that the motive has nothing to do with the morality of the action, though much with the worth of the agent. He who saves a fellow creature from drowning does what is morally right, whether his motive be duty or the hope of being paid for his trouble; he who betrays the friend that trusts him is guilty of a crime, even if his object be to serve another friend to whom he is under greater obligations.[1] But to speak only of actions done from the motive of duty, and in direct obedience to principle: it is a misapprehension of the utilitarian mode of thought to conceive it as implying that people should fix their minds upon so wide a generality as the world, or society at large. The great majority of good actions are intended not for the benefit of the world, but for that of individuals,

---

[1] An opponent, whose intellectual and moral fairness it is a pleasure to acknowledge (the Rev. J. Llewellyn Davies), has objected to this passage, saying, "Surely the rightness or wrongness of saving a man from drowning does depend very much upon the motive with which it is done. Suppose that a tyrant, when his enemy jumped into the sea to escape from him, saved him from drowning simply in order that he might inflict upon him more exquisite tortures, would it tend to clearness to speak of that rescue as 'a morally right action'? Or suppose again, according to one of the stock illustrations of ethical inquiries, that a man betrayed a trust received from a friend, because the discharge of it would fatally injure that friend himself or someone belonging to him, would utilitarianism compel one to call the betrayal 'a crime' as much as if it had been done from the meanest motive?"

I submit that he who saves another from drowning in order to kill him by torture afterwards does not differ only in motive from him who does the same thing from duty or benevolence; the act itself is different. The rescue of the man is, in the case supposed, only

of which the good of the world is made up; and the thoughts of the most virtuous man need not on these occasions travel beyond the particular persons concerned, except so far as is necessary to assure himself that in benefiting them he is not violating the rights, that is, the legitimate and authorized expectations, of anyone else. The multiplication of happiness is, according to the utilitarian ethics, the object of virtue: the occasions on which any person (except one in a thousand) has it in his power to do this on an extended scale—in other words, to be a public benefactor—are but exceptional; and on these occasions alone is he called on to consider public utility; in every other case, private utility, the interest or happiness of some few persons, is all he has to attend to. Those alone the influence of whose actions extends to society in general need concern themselves habitually about so large an object. In the case of abstinences indeed—of things which people forbear to do from moral considerations, though the consequences in the particular case might be beneficial—it would be unworthy of an intelligent agent not to be consciously aware that the action is of a class which, if practiced generally, would be generally injurious, and that this is the ground of the obligation to abstain from it. The amount of regard for the public interest implied in this recognition is no greater than is demanded by every system of morals, for they all enjoin to abstain from whatever is manifestly pernicious to society. . . .

It may not be superfluous to notice a few more of the common misapprehensions of utilitarian ethics, even those which are so obvious and gross that it might appear impossible for any person of candor and intelligence to fall into them; since persons, even of considerable mental endowment, often give themselves so little trouble to understand the bearings of any opinion against which they entertain a prejudice, and men are in general so little conscious of this voluntary ignorance as a defect that the vulgarest misunderstandings of ethical doctrines are continually met with in the deliberate writings of persons of the greatest pretensions both to high principle and to philosophy. We not uncommonly hear the doctrine of utility inveighed against as a *godless* doctrine. If it be necessary to say anything at all against so mere an assumption, we may say that the question depends upon what idea we have formed of the moral character of the Deity. If it be a true belief that God desires, above all things, the happiness of his creatures, and that this was his purpose in their creation, utility is not only not a godless doctrine, but more profoundly religious than

the necessary first step of an act far more atrocious than leaving him to drown would have been. Had Mr. Davies said, "The rightness or wrongness of saving a man from drowning does depend very much" not upon the motive, but "upon the *intention*," no utilitarian would have differed from him. Mr. Davies, by an oversight too common not to be quite venial, has in this case confounded the very different ideas of Motive and Intention. There is no point which utilitarian thinkers (and Bentham pre-eminently) have taken more pains to illustrate than this. The morality of the action depends entirely upon the intention—that is, upon what the agent *wills to do*. But the motive, that is, the feeling which makes him will so to do, if it makes no difference in the act, makes none in the morality: though it makes a great difference in our moral estimation of the agent, especially if it indicates a good or a bad habitual *disposition*—a bent of character from which useful, or from which hurtful actions are likely to arise.

any other. If it be meant that utilitarianism does not recognize the revealed will of God as the supreme law of morals, I answer that a utilitarian who believes in the perfect goodness and wisdom of *God* necessarily believes that whatever God has thought fit to reveal on the subject of morals must fulfill the requirements of utility in a supreme degree. But others besides utilitarians have been of the opinion that the Christian revelation was intended, and is fitted, to inform the hearts and minds of mankind with a spirit which should enable them to find for themselves what is right, and incline them to do it when found, rather than to tell them, except in a very general way, what it is; and that we need a doctrine of ethics, carefully followed out, to *interpret* to us the will of God. Whether this opinion is correct or not, it is superfluous here to discuss; since whatever aid religion, either natural or revealed, can afford to ethical investigation is as open to the utilitarian moralist as to any other. He can use it as the testimony of God to the usefulness or hurtfulness of any given course of action by as good a right as others can use it for the indication of a transcendental law having no connection with usefulness or with happiness.

Again, utility is often summarily stigmatized as an immoral doctrine by giving it the name of "expediency," and taking advantage of the popular use of that term to contrast it with principle. But the expedient, in the sense in which it is opposed to the right, generally means that which is expedient for the particular interest of the agent himself; as when a minister sacrifices the interests of his country to keep himself in place. When it means anything better than this, it means that which is expedient for some immediate object, some temporary purpose, but which violates a rule whose observance is expedient in a much higher degree. The expedient, in this sense, instead of being the same thing with the useful, is a branch of the hurtful. Thus it would often be expedient, for the purpose of getting over some momentary embarrassment, or attaining some object immediately useful to ourselves or others, to tell a lie. But inasmuch as the cultivation in ourselves of a sensitive feeling on the subject of veracity is one of the most useful, and the enfeeblement of that feeling one of the most hurtful, things to which our conduct can be instrumental; and inasmuch as any, even unintentional, deviation from truth does that much toward weakening the trustworthiness of human assertion, which is not only the principal support of all present social well-being, but the insufficiency of which does more than any one thing that can be named to keep back civilization, virtue, everything on which human happiness on the largest scale depends—we feel that the violation, for a present advantage, of a rule of such transcendent expediency is not expedient, and that he who, for the sake of convenience to himself or to some other individual, does what depends on him to deprive mankind of the good, and inflict upon them the evil, involved in the greater or less reliance which they can place in each other's word, acts the part of one of their worst enemies. Yet that even this rule, sacred as it is, admits of possible exceptions is acknowledged by all moralists; the chief of which is when the withholding of some fact (as of information from a malefactor, or of bad news from a person dangerously ill) would save an individual (especially an individual other than oneself) from great and unmerited evil, and when the withholding can only be effected by denial. But in order that the exception may not extend itself beyond the need, and may have the least possible effect in weakening reliance on veracity, it ought to be recognized and, if possible, its limits defined; and, if the principle of utility is good for anything, it must be good for weighing these conflicting utilities against one another and marking out the region within which one or the other preponderates. . . .

OF WHAT SORT OF PROOF THE PRINCIPLE OF UTILITY IS SUSCEPTIBLE

... Questions of ultimate ends do not admit of proof, in the ordinary acceptation of the term. To be incapable of proof by reasoning is common to all first principles, to the first premises of our knowledge, as well as to those of our conduct. But the former, being matters of fact, may be the subject of a direct appeal to the faculties which judge of fact—namely, our senses and our internal consciousness. Can an appeal be made to the same faculties on questions of practical ends? Or by what other faculty is cognizance taken of them?

Questions about ends are, in other words, questions what things are desirable. The utilitarian doctrine is that happiness is desirable, and the only thing desirable, as an end; all other things being only desirable as means to that end. What ought to be required of this doctrine, what conditions is it requisite that the doctrine should fulfill—to make good its claim to be believed?

The only proof capable of being given that an object is visible is that people actually see it. The only proof that a sound is audible is that people hear it; and so of the other sources of our experience. In like manner, I apprehend, the sole evidence it is possible to produce that anything is desirable is that people do actually desire it. If the end which the utilitarian doctrine proposes to itself were not, in theory and in practice, acknowledged to be an end, nothing could ever convince any person that it was so. No reason can be given why the general happiness is desirable, except that each person, so far as he believes it to be attainable, desires his own happiness. This, however, being a fact, we have not only all the proof which the case admits of, but all which it is possible to require, that happiness is a good, that each person's happiness is a good to that person, and the general happiness, therefore, a good to the aggregate of all persons. Happiness has made out its title as *one* of the ends of conduct and, consequently, one of the criteria of morality.

But it has not, by this alone, proved itself to be the sole criterion. To do that, it would seem, by the same rule, necessary to show, not only that people desire happiness, but that they never desire anything else. Now it is palpable that they do desire things which, in common language, are decidedly distinguished from happiness. They desire, for example, virtue and the absence of vice no less really than pleasure and the absence of pain. The desire of virtue is not as universal, but it is as authentic a fact as the desire of happiness. And hence the opponents of the utilitarian standard deem that they have a right to infer that there are other ends of human action besides happiness, and that happiness is not the standard of approbation and disapprobation.

But does the utilitarian doctrine deny that people desire virtue, or maintain that virtue is not a thing to be desired? The very reverse. It maintains not only that virtue is to be desired, but that it is to be desired disinterestedly, for itself. Whatever may be the opinion of utilitarian moralists as to the original conditions by which virtue is made virtue, however they may believe (as they do) that actions and dispositions are only virtuous because they promote another end than virtue, yet this being granted, and it having been decided, from considerations of this description, what *is* virtuous, they not only place virtue at the very head of the things which are good as means to the ultimate end, but they also recognize as a psychological fact the possibility of its being, to the individual, a good in itself, without looking to any end beyond it; and hold that the mind is not in a right state, not in a state conformable to utility, not in the state most conducive to the general happiness, unless it does love virtue in this manner—as a thing desirable in itself, even although, in the individual instance, it should not produce those other desirable consequences which it tends to produce, and on account of which it is held to be virtue. This opinion is not, in the smallest degree, a departure from the happiness principle. The ingredients of happiness are very various, and each of them is desirable in itself, and not merely when considered as swelling an aggregate. The principle of utility does not mean that any given pleasure, as music, for instance, or any given exemption from pain, as for example health, is to be looked upon as means to a collective something termed happiness, and to be desired on that account. They are desired and desirable in and for themselves; besides being means, they are a part of the end. Virtue, according to the utilitarian doctrine, is not naturally and originally part of the end, but it is capable of becoming so; and in those who live it disinterestedly it has become so, and is desired and cherished, not as a means to happiness, but as a part of their happiness.

To illustrate this further, we may remember that virtue is not the only thing originally a means, and which if it were not a means to anything else would be and remain indifferent, but which by association with what it is a means to comes to be desired for itself, and that too with the utmost intensity. What, for example, shall we say of the love of money? There is nothing originally more desirable about money than about any heap of glittering pebbles. Its worth is solely that of the things which it will buy; the desires for other things than itself, which it is a means of gratifying. Yet the love of money is not only one of the strongest moving forces of human life, but money is, in many cases, desired in and for itself; the desire to possess it is often stronger than the desire to use it, and goes on increasing when all the desires which point to ends beyond it, to be compassed by it, are falling off. It may, then, be said truly that money is desired not for the sake of an end, but as part of the end. From being a means to happiness, it has come to be itself a principal ingredient of the individual's conception of happiness. The same may be said of the majority of the great objects of human life: power, for example, or fame, except that to each of these there is a certain amount of immediate pleasure annexed, which has at least the semblance of being naturally inherent in them—a thing which cannot be said of money. Still, however, the strongest natural attraction, both of power and of fame, is the immense aid they give to the attainment of our other wishes; and it is the strong association thus generated between them and all our objects of desire which gives to the direct desire of them the intensity it often assumes, so as in some characters to surpass in strength all other desires. In these cases the means have become a part of the end, and a more important part of it than any of the things which they are means to. What was once desired as an instrument for the attainment of happiness has come to be desired for its own sake. In being desired for its own sake it is, however, desired as *part* of happiness. The person is made, or thinks he would be made, happy by its mere possession; and is made unhappy by failure to obtain it. The desire of it is not a different thing from the desire of happiness any more than the love of music or the desire of health. They are included in happiness. They are some of the elements of which the desire of happiness is made up. Happiness is not an abstract idea but a concrete whole; and these are some of its parts. And the utilitarian standard sanctions and approves their being so. Life would be a poor thing, very ill provided with sources of happiness, if there were not this provision of nature by which things originally indifferent, but conducive to, or otherwise associated with, the satisfaction of our primitive desires, become in themselves sources of pleasure more valuable than the primitive pleasures, both in permanency, in the space of human existence that they are capable of covering, and even in intensity.

Virtue, according to the utilitarian conception, is a good of this description. There was no original desire of it, or motive to it, save its conduciveness to pleasure, and especially to protection from pain. But through the association thus formed it may be felt a good in itself, and desired as such with as great intensity as any other good; and with this difference between it and the love of money, of power, or of fame—that all of these may, and often do, render the individual noxious to the other members of the society to which he belongs, whereas there is nothing which makes him so much a blessing to them as the cultivation of the disinterested love of virtue. And consequently, the utilitarian standard, while it tolerates and approves those other acquired desires, up to the point beyond which they would be more injurious to the general happiness than promotive of it, enjoins and requires the cultivation of the love of virtue up to the greatest strength possible, as being above all things important to the general happiness.

It results from the preceding considerations that there is in reality nothing desired except happiness. Whatever is desired otherwise than as a means to some end beyond itself, and ultimately to happiness, is desired as itself a part of happiness, and is not desired for itself until it has become so. Those who desire virtue for its own sake desire it either because the consciousness of it is a pleasure, or because the consciousness of being without it is a pain, or for both reasons united; as in truth the pleasure and pain seldom exist separately, but almost always together—the same person feeling pleasure in the degree of virtue attained, and pain in not having attained more. If one of these gave him no pleasure, and the other no pain, he would not love or desire virtue, or would desire it only for the other benefits which it might produce to himself or to persons whom he cared for.

We have now, then, an answer to the question, of what sort of proof the principle of utility is susceptible. If the opinion which I have now stated is psychologically true—if human nature is so constituted as to desire nothing which is not either a part of happiness or a means of happiness—we can have no other proof, and we require no other, that these are the only things desirable. If so, happiness is the sole end of human action, and the promotion of it the test by which to judge of all human conduct; from whence it necessarily follows that it must be the criterion of morality, since a part is included in the whole.

And now to decide whether this is really so, whether mankind do desire nothing for itself but that which is a pleasure to them, or of which the absence is a pain, we have evidently arrived at a question of fact and experience, dependent, like all similar questions, upon evidence. It can only be determined by practiced self-consciousness and self-observation, assisted by observation of others. I believe that these sources of evidence, impartially consulted, will declare that desiring a thing and finding it pleasant, aversion to it and thinking of it as painful, are phenomena entirely inseparable or, rather, two parts of the same phenomenon—in strictness of language, two different modes of naming the same psychological fact; that to think of an object as desirable (unless for the sake of its consequences) and to think of it as pleasant are one and the same thing; and that to desire anything except in proportion as the idea of it is pleasant is a physical and metaphysical impossibility.

So obvious does this appear to me that I expect it will hardly be disputed; and the objection made will be, not that desire can possibly be directed to anything ultimately except pleasure and exemption from pain, but that the will is a different thing from desire; that a person of confirmed virtue or any other person whose purposes are fixed carries out his purposes without any thought of the pleasure he has in contemplating them or expects to derive from their fulfillment, and persists in acting on them, even though these pleasures are much diminished by changes in his character or decay of his passive sensibilities, or are outweighed by the pains which the pursuit of the purposes may bring upon him. All this I fully admit and have stated it elsewhere as positively and emphatically as anyone. Will, the active phenomenon, is a different thing from desire, the state of passive sensibility, and, though originally an offshoot from it, may in time take root and detach itself from the parent stock, so much so that in the case of a habitual purpose, instead of willing the thing because we desire it, we often desire it only because we will it. This, however, is but an instance of that familiar fact, the power of habit, and is nowise confined to the case of virtuous actions. Many indifferent things which men originally did from a motive of some sort they continue to do from habit. Sometimes this is done unconsciously, the consciousness coming only after the action; at other times with conscious volition, but volition which has become habitual and is put in operation by the force of habit, in opposition perhaps to the deliberate preference, as often happens with those who have contracted habits of vicious or hurtful indulgence. Third and last comes the case in which the habitual act of will in the individual instance is not in contradiction to the general intention prevailing at other times, but in fulfillment of it, as in the case of the person of confirmed virtue and of all who pursue deliberately and consistently any determinate end. The distinction between will and desire thus understood is an authentic and highly important psychological fact; but the fact consists solely in this—that will, like all other parts of our constitution, is amenable to habit, and that we may will from habit what we no longer desire for itself, or desire only because we will it. It is not the less true that will, in the beginning, is entirely produced by desire, including in that term the repelling influence of pain as well as the attractive one of pleasure. Let us take into consideration no longer the person who has a confirmed will to do right, but him in whom that virtuous will is still feeble, conquerable by temptation, and not to be fully relied on; by what means can it be strengthened? How can the will to be virtuous, where it does not exist in sufficient force, be implanted or awakened? Only by making the person *desire* virtue—by making him think of it in a pleasurable light, or of its absence in a painful one. It is by associating the doing right with pleasure, or the wrong with pain, or by eliciting and impressing and bringing home to the person's experience the pleasure naturally involved in the one or the pain in the other, that it is possible to call forth that will to be virtuous which, when confirmed, acts without any thought of either pleasure or pain. Will is the child of desire, and passes out of the dominion of its parent only to come under that of habit. That which is the result of habit affords no presumption of being intrinsically good; and there would be no reason for wishing that the purpose of virtue should become independent of pleasure and pain were it not that the influence of the pleasurable and painful associations which prompt to virtue is not sufficiently to be depended on for unerring constancy of action until it has acquired the support of habit. Both in feeling and in conduct, habit is the only thing which imparts certainty; and it is because of the importance to others of being able to rely absolutely on one's feelings and conduct, and to oneself of being able to rely on one's own, that the will to do right ought to be cultivated into this habitual independence. In other words, this state of the will is a means to good, not intrinsically a good; and does not contradict the doctrine that nothing is a good to human beings but in so far as it is either itself pleasurable or a means of attaining pleasure or averting pain.

But if this doctrine be true, the principle of utility is proved. Whether it is so or not must now be left to the consideration of the thoughtful reader.

Questions

1. "An act is right if it is useful." "An act is right if it brings pleasure." Mill says that the principle of utilitarianism is not identical with either of these statements, but in a sense combines them both. Explain in what sense it is a combination of both statements.

2. Mill distinguishes quality of pleasure from quantity of pleasure. What does he mean by this difference? Elucidate your answer by means of examples. Suppose an action brought about a great quantity of low quality pleasure, and another action brought about a small quantity of high quality pleasure. How would Mill decide which action was the better?

3. "Human beings have faculties more elevated than the animal appetites. . . ." What standard is Mill using here to determine the degree of "elevation" of our faculties? Is this standard derivable from the "greatest happiness principle"? Why or why not?

4. What would Mill be likely to reply to the following objection?
"You say: 'Better to be a human being dissatisfied than a pig satisfied.' But by your own test of competent acquaintance with both experiences as the method for deciding which is the better, you have no grounds for making that statement, for you have never been a pig."

5. Does Mill ever provide a satisfactory answer to the fundamental question: Why should I seek the greatest happiness for all if my doing so interferes with my own happiness? Defend your answer.

6. ". . . The motive has nothing to do with the morality of the action, though much with the worth of the agent." From the point of view of utilitarianism, what is meant by "the morality of the action" as distinct from "the worth of the agent"? Is there any connection between the two? Explain by means of examples.

7. State why you think Mill does, or does not, adequately reply to the objection that "utilitarianism does not recognize the revealed will of God as the supreme law of morals. . . ."

8. After reading the selection by Kant in this chapter (page 533), analyze the different grounds on which Mill and Kant, respectively, would base the moral judgment, "It is wrong to lie." Would there ever be an action which Kant would approve of and Mill disapprove of, or an action which Kant would disapprove of and Mill approve of? If so, give examples and explain why they would disagree in each case. If not, explain in detail why not.

9. It is now widely accepted among philosophers that there is a glaring error in the following argument. Where is it?
"The only proof capable of being given that an object is visible is that people actually see it. The only proof that a sound is audible is that people hear it; and so of the other sources of our experience. In like manner, I apprehend, the sole evidence it is possible to produce that anything is desirable is that people do actually desire it."

10. What differences and what similarities do you find between Mill's conception of happiness and Aristotle's? (See the selection beginning on page 491.)

11. From the point of view of Kant's ethical theory (see the reading beginning on page 533), the promotion of happiness has nothing to do with deciding what is morally right and wrong. For Mill, on the other hand, the promotion of happiness is itself the "criterion of morality." Is there any possible way to determine which of these views is justified? If so, briefly outline the way. If not, show clearly why not.

6

The Emotive Theory | A. J. Ayer
(*b. 1910*)

[A general introductory note on A. J. Ayer may be found on page 277.]

In this reading Professor Ayer is concerned with the question whether moral statements are empirically verifiable. The reader is advised to consult the selection by Professor Ayer on page 277, in order to understand the general position from which he approaches the problem of moral knowledge.

Professor Ayer begins by rejecting two types of moral philosophy: naturalism and non-naturalism (or intuitionism). Naturalism is the view that moral statements are empirically verifiable, that is, moral knowledge is simply knowledge of a certain set of empirical facts. The moral philosophies of Aristotle (page 491), of Hume (page 508), and of Mill (page 560) may all be considered different forms of naturalism. Non-naturalism, on the other hand, is the view that moral statements are not empirically verifiable, but are nevertheless genuinely true or false. The theories of Price (page 520) and of Kant (page 533) may be considered two different versions of this point of view. It should be noted that Professor Ayer calls non-naturalism the "absolutist view," but this term is not used in the same way as the term "ethical absolutism" is used in the introduction to this chapter.

After giving his arguments against both naturalism and non-naturalism, Professor Ayer sets forth his own position, which has come to be known as "the emotive theory." According to this theory, moral statements do not express propositions, which can be true or false. They express emotions or attitudes, which can be neither true nor false. Since truth and falsity do not apply to moral statements, there is consequently no such thing as moral knowledge. The general principle of "radical empiricism," which Professor Ayer is trying to defend throughout his book, *Language, Truth and Logic,* is thus preserved: All statements which are "synthetic," i.e., which express propositions conveying information about the world, are empirically verifiable. All other statements are either (1) "analytic," i.e., they express propositions which are true or false a priori and do not describe anything in the world, or (2) "emotive," i.e., utterances which express no propositions at all and therefore cannot be true or false. Moral statements, Ayer claims, belong in the latter category.

This selection is taken from Chapter VI of *Language, Truth and Logic.*

From *Language, Truth and Logic,* by Alfred Jules Ayer, reprinted through permission by the author and by Dover Publications, Inc., New York 10, N. Y. ($1.25, paperbound).

The ordinary system of ethics, as elaborated in the works of ethical philosophers, is very far from being a homogeneous whole. Not only is it apt to contain pieces of metaphysics, and analyses of nonethical concepts: its actual ethical contents are themselves of very different kinds. We may divide them, indeed, into four main classes. There are, first of all, propositions which express definitions of ethical terms, or judgements about the legitimacy or possibility of certain definitions. Secondly, there are propositions describing the phenomena of moral experience, and their causes. Thirdly, there are exhortations to moral virtue. And, lastly, there are actual ethical judgements. It is unfortunately the case that the distinction between these four classes, plain as it is, is commonly ignored by ethical philosophers; with the result that it is often very difficult to tell from their works what it is that they are seeking to discover or prove.

In fact, it is easy to see that only the first of our four classes, namely that which comprises the propositions relating to the definitions of ethical terms, can be said to constitute ethical philosophy. The propositions which describe the phenomena of moral experience, and their causes, must be assigned to the science of psychology, or sociology. The exhortations to moral virtue are not propositions at all, but ejaculations or commands which are designed to provoke the reader to action of a certain sort. Accordingly, they do not belong to any branch of philosophy or science. As for the expressions of ethical judgements, we have not yet determined how they should be classified. But inasmuch as they are certainly neither definitions nor comments upon definitions, nor quotations, we may say decisively that they do not belong to ethical philosophy. A strictly philosophical treatise on ethics should therefore make no ethical pronouncements. But it should, by giving an analysis of ethical terms, show what is the category to which all such pronouncements belong. And this is what we are now about to do.

A question which is often discussed by ethical philosophers is whether it is possible to find definitions which would reduce all ethical terms to one or two fundamental terms. But this question, though it undeniably belongs to ethical philosophy, is not relevant to our present enquiry. We are not now concerned to discover which term, within the sphere of ethical terms, is to be taken as fundamental; whether, for example, "good" can be defined in terms of "right" or "right" in terms of "good," or both in terms of "value." What we are interested in is the possibility of reducing the whole sphere of ethical terms to nonethical terms. We are enquiring whether statements of ethical value can be translated into statements of empirical fact.

That they can be so translated is the contention of those ethical philosophers who are commonly called subjectivists, and of those who are known as utilitarians. For the utilitarian defines the rightness of actions, and the goodness of ends, in terms of the pleasure, or happiness, or satisfaction, to which they give rise; the subjectivist, in terms of the feelings of approval which a certain person, or group of people, has towards them. Each of these types of definition makes moral judgements into a subclass of psychological or sociological judgements; and for this reason they are very attractive to us. For, if either was correct, it would follow that ethical assertions were not generically different from the factual assertions which are ordinarily contrasted with them; and the account which we have already given of empirical hypotheses would apply to them also.

objections to Subjectivist

Nevertheless we shall not adopt either a subjectivist or a utilitarian analysis of ethical terms. We reject the subjectivist view that to call an action right, or a thing good, is to say that it is generally approved of, because it is not self-contradictory to assert that some actions which are generally approved of are not right, or that some things which are generally approved of are not good. And we reject the alternative subjectivist view that a man who asserts that a certain action is right, or that a certain thing is good, is saying that he himself approves of it, on the ground that a man who confessed that he sometimes approved of what was bad or wrong would not be contradicting himself. And a similar argument is fatal to utilitarianism. We cannot agree that to call an *Utilitarianism* action right is to say that of all the actions possible in the circumstances it would cause, or be likely to cause, the greatest happiness, or the greatest balance of pleasure over pain, or the greatest balance of satisfied over unsatisfied desire, because we find that it is not self-contradictory to say that it is sometimes wrong to perform the action which would actually or probably cause the greatest happiness, or the greatest balance of pleasure over pain, or of satisfied over unsatisfied desire. And since it is not self-contradictory to say that some pleasant things are not good, or that some bad things are desired, it cannot be the case that the sentence "x is good" is equivalent to "x is pleasant," or to "x is desired." And to every other variant of utilitarianism with which I am acquainted the same objection can be made. And therefore we should, I think, conclude that the validity of ethical judgements it not determined by the felicific tendencies of actions, any more than by the nature of people's feelings; but that it must be regarded as "absolute" or "intrinsic," and not empirically calculable.

If we say this, we are not, of course, denying that it is possible to invent a language in which all ethical symbols are definable in nonethical terms, or even that it is desirable to invent such a language and adopt it in place of our own; what we are denying is that the suggested reduction of ethical to nonethical statements is consistent with the conventions of our actual language. That is, we reject utilitarianism and subjectivism, not as proposals to replace our existing ethical notions by new ones, but as analyses of our existing ethical notions. Our contention is simply that, in our language, sentences which contain normative ethical symbols are not equivalent to sentences which express psychological propositions, or indeed empirical propositions of any kind.

It is advisable here to make it plain that it is only normative ethical symbols, and not descriptive ethical symbols, that are held by us to be indefinable in factual terms. There is a danger of confusing these two types of symbols, because they are commonly constituted by signs of the same sensible form. Thus a complex sign of the form "x is wrong" may constitute a sentence which expresses a moral judgement concerning a certain type of conduct, or it may constitute a sentence which states that a certain type of conduct is repugnant to the moral sense of a particular society. In the latter case, the symbol "wrong" is a descriptive ethical symbol, and the sentence in which it occurs expresses an ordinary sociological proposition; in the former case, the symbol "wrong" is a normative ethical symbol, and the sentence in which it occurs does not, we maintain, express an empirical proposition at all. It is only with normative ethics that we are at present concerned; so that whenever ethical symbols are used in the course of this argument without qualification, they are always to be interpreted as symbols of the normative type.

In admitting that normative ethical concepts are irreducible to empirical concepts, we seem to be leaving the way clear for the "absolutist" view of ethics—that is, the view that statements of value are not controlled by observation, as ordinary empirical propositions are, but only by a mysterious "intellectual intuition." A feature of this theory, which is seldom recognized by its advocates, is that it makes statements of value unverifiable. For it is notorious that what seems intuitively certain to one person may seem doubtful, or even false, to another. So that unless it is possible to provide some criterion by which one may decide between conflicting intuitions, a mere appeal to intuition is worthless as a test of a proposition's validity. But in the case of moral judgements, no such criterion can be given. Some moralists claim to settle the matter by saying that they "know" that their own moral judgements are correct. But such an assertion is of purely psychological interest, and has not the slightest tendency to prove the validity of any moral judgement. For dissentient moralists may equally well "know" that their ethical views are correct. And, as far as subjective certainty goes, there will be nothing to choose between them. When such differences of opinion arise in connection with an ordinary empirical proposition, one may attempt to resolve them by referring to, or actually carrying out, some relevant empirical test. But with regard to ethical statements, there is, on the "absolutist" or "intuitionist" theory, no relevant empirical test. We are therefore justified in saying that on this theory ethical statements are held to be unverifiable. They are, of course, also held to be genuine synthetic propositions.

Considering the use which we have made of the principle that a synthetic proposition is significant only if it is empirically verifiable, it is clear that the acceptance of an "absolutist" theory of ethics would undermine the whole of our main argument. And as we have already rejected the "naturalistic" theories which are commonly supposed to provide the only alternative to "absolutism" in ethics, we seem to have reached a difficult position. We shall meet the diffi- culty by showing that the correct treatment of ethical statements is afforded by a third theory, which is wholly compatible with our radical empiricism.

We begin by admitting that the fundamental ethical concepts are un- analysable, inasmuch as there is no criterion by which one can test the validity of the judgements in which they occur. So far we are in agreement with the absolutists. But, unlike the absolutists, we are able to give an explanation of this fact about ethical concepts. We say that the reason why they are unanalys- able is that they are mere pseudo-concepts. The presence of an ethical symbol in a proposition adds nothing to its factual content. Thus if I say to someone, "You acted wrongly in stealing that money," I am not stating anything more than if I had simply said, "You stole that money." In adding that this action is wrong I am not making any further statement about it. I am simply evincing my moral disapproval of it. It is as if I had said, "You stole that money," in a peculiar tone of horror, or written it with the addition of some special exclama- tion marks. The tone, or the exclamation marks, adds nothing to the literal meaning of the sentence. It merely serves to show that the expression of it is attended by certain feelings in the speaker.

If now I generalise my previous statement and say, "Stealing money is wrong," I produce a sentence which has no factual meaning—that is, expresses no proposition which can be either true or false. It is as if I had written "Steal- ing money!!" where the shape and thickness of the exclamation marks show, by a suitable convention, that a special sort of moral disapproval is the feeling which is being expressed. It is clear that there is nothing said here which can be true or false. Another man may disagree with me about the wrongness of stealing, in the sense that he may not have the same feelings about stealing as I have, and he may quarrel with me on account of my moral sentiments. But he cannot, strictly speaking, contradict me. For in saying that a certain type of action is right or wrong, I am not making any factual statement, not even a statement about my own state of mind. I am merely expressing certain moral sentiments. And the man who is ostensibly contradicting me is merely express- ing his moral sentiments. So that there is plainly no sense in asking which of us is in the right. For neither of us is asserting a genuine proposition.

What we have just been saying about the symbol "wrong" applies to all normative ethical symbols. Sometimes they occur in sentences which record ordinary empirical facts besides expressing ethical feeling about those facts: sometimes they occur in sentences which simply express ethical feeling about a certain type of action, or situation, without making any statement of fact. But in every case in which one would commonly be said to be making an ethical judgement, the function of the relevant ethical word is purely "emotive." It is used to express feeling about certain objects, but not to make any assertion about them.

It is worth mentioning that ethical terms do not serve only to express feeling. They are calculated also to arouse feeling, and so to stimulate action. Indeed some of them are used in such a way as to give the sentences in which they occur the effect of commands. Thus the sentence "It is your duty to tell the truth" may be regarded both as the expression of a certain sort of ethical feeling about truthfulness and as the expression of the command "Tell the truth." The sentence "You ought to tell the truth" also involves the command "Tell the truth," but here the tone of the command is less emphatic. In the sentence "It is good to tell the truth" the command has become little more than a suggestion. And thus the "meaning" of the word "good," in its ethical usage, is differentiated from that of the word "duty" or the word "ought." In fact we may define the meaning of the various ethical words in terms both of the different feelings they are ordinarily taken to express, and also the different responses which they are calculated to provoke.

We can now see why it is impossible to find a criterion for determining the validity of ethical judgements. It is not because they have an "absolute" validity which is mysteriously independent of ordinary sense-experience, but because they have no objective validity whatsoever. If a sentence makes no statement at all, there is obviously no sense in asking whether what it says is true or false. And we have seen that sentences which simply express moral judgements do not say anything. They are pure expressions of feeling and as such do not come under the category of truth and falsehood. They are unverifiable for the same reason as a cry of pain or a word of command is unverifiable—because they do not express genuine propositions.

Thus, although our theory of ethics might fairly be said to be radically subjectivist, it differs in a very important respect from the orthodox subjectivist theory. For the orthodox subjectivist does not deny, as we do, that the sentences of a moralizer express genuine propositions. All he denies is that they express propositions of a unique nonempirical character. His own view is that they express propositions about the speaker's feelings. If this were so, ethical judgements clearly would be capable of being true or false. They would be true if the speaker had the relevant feelings, and false if he had not. And this is a matter which is, in principle, empirically verifiable. Furthermore they could be significantly contradicted. For if I say, "Tolerance is a virtue," and someone answers, "You don't approve of it," he would, on the ordinary subjectivist theory, be contradicting me. On our theory, he would not be contradicting me, because, in saying that tolerance was a virtue, I should not be making any statement about my own feelings or about anything else. I should simply be evincing my feelings, which is not at all the same thing as saying that I have them.

The distinction between the expression of feeling and the assertion of feeling is complicated by the fact that the assertion that one has a certain feeling often accompanies the expression of that feeling, and is then, indeed, a factor in the expression of that feeling. Thus I may simultaneously express boredom and say that I am bored, and in that case my utterance of the words, "I am bored," is one of the circumstances which make it true to say that I am expressing or evincing boredom. But I can express boredom without actually saying that I am bored. I can express it by my tone and gestures, while making a statement about something wholly unconnected with it, or by an ejaculation, or without uttering any words at all. So that even if the assertion that one has a certain feeling always involves the expression of that feeling, the expression of a feeling assuredly does not always involve the assertion that one has it. And this is the important point to grasp in considering the distinction between our theory and the ordinary subjectivist theory. For whereas the subjectivist holds that ethical statements actually assert the existence of certain feelings, we hold that ethical statements are expressions and excitants of feeling which do not necessarily involve any assertions.

We have already remarked that the main objection to the ordinary subjectivist theory is that the validity of ethical judgements is not determined by the nature of their author's feelings. And this is an objection which our theory escapes. For it does not imply that the existence of any feelings is a necessary and sufficient condition of the validity of an ethical judgement. It implies, on the contrary, that ethical judgements have no validity.

There is, however, a celebrated argument against subjectivist theories which our theory does not escape. It has been pointed out by Moore that if ethical statements were simply statements about the speaker's feelings, it would be impossible to argue about questions of value. To take a typical example: if a man said that thrift was a virtue, and another replied that it was a vice, they would not, on this theory, be disputing with one another. One would be saying that he approved of thrift, and the other that *he* didn't; and there is no reason why both these statements should not be true. Now Moore held it to be obvious that we do dispute about questions of value, and accordingly concluded that the particular form of subjectivism which he was discussing was false.

It is plain that the conclusion that it is impossible to dispute about questions of value follows from our theory also. For as we hold that such sentences as "Thrift is a virtue" and "Thrift is a vice" do not express propositions at all, we clearly cannot hold that they express incompatible propositions. We must therefore admit that if Moore's argument really refutes the ordinary subjectivist theory, it also refutes ours. But, in fact, we deny that it does refute even the ordinary subjectivist theory. For we hold that one really never does dispute about questions of value.

This may seem, at first sight, to be a very paradoxical assertion. For we certainly do engage in disputes which are ordinarily regarded as disputes about questions of value. But, in all such cases, we find, if we consider the matter closely, that the dispute is not really about a question of value, but about a question of fact. When someone disagrees with us about the moral value of a certain action or type of action, we do admittedly resort to argument in order to win him over to our way of thinking. But we do not attempt to show by our arguments that he has the "wrong" ethical feeling towards a situation whose nature he has correctly apprehended. What we attempt to show is that he is mistaken about the facts of the case. We argue that he has misconceived the agent's motive: or that he has misjudged the effects of the action, or its probable effects in view of the agent's knowledge; or that he has failed to take into account the special circumstances in which the agent was placed. Or else we employ more general arguments about the effects which actions of a certain type tend to produce, or the qualities which are usually manifested in their performance. We do this in the hope that we have only to get our opponent to agree with us about the nature of the empirical facts for him to adopt the same moral attitude towards them as we do. And as the people with whom we argue have generally received the same moral education as ourselves, and live in the same social order, our expectation is usually justified. But if our opponent happens to have undergone a different process of moral "conditioning" from ourselves, so that, even when he acknowledges all the facts, he still disagrees with us about the moral value of the actions under discussion, then we abandon the attempt to convince him by argument. We say that it is impossible to argue with him because he has a distorted or undeveloped moral sense; which signifies merely that he employs a different set of values from our own. We feel that our own system of values is superior, and therefore speak in such derogatory terms of his. But we cannot bring forward any arguments to show that our system is superior: For our judgement that it is so is itself a judgement of value, and accordingly outside the scope of argument. It is because argument fails us when we come to deal with pure questions of value, as distinct from questions of fact, that we finally resort to mere abuse.

In short, we find that argument is possible on moral questions only if some system of values is presupposed. If our opponent concurs with us in expressing moral disapproval of all actions of a given type *t*, then we may get him to condemn a particular action A, by bringing forward arguments to show that A is of type *t*. For the question whether A does or does not belong to that type is a plain question of fact. Given that a man has certain moral principles, we argue that he must, in order to be consistent, react morally to certain things in a certain way. What we do not and cannot argue about is the validity of these moral principles. We merely praise or condemn them in the light of our own feelings.

Questions

1. According to Professor Ayer, both subjectivists and utilitarians translate moral statements into statements of empirical fact. How does he attempt to show this? Taking Hume as an example of a subjectivist and Mill as an example of a utilitarian, show that Professor Ayer's argument does, or does not, hold for the views of these two philosophers. (For Hume's and Mill's views, see the selections in this chapter beginning on pages 508 and 560, respectively.)

2. On what grounds does Professor Ayer reject the subjectivist and utilitarian analyses of ethical terms? Appraise the validity of his argument.

3. What objection does Professor Ayer raise against ethical intuitionism? How might Price, as an ethical intuitionist, defend himself against Professor Ayer's

attack? (For Price's theory, see the selection in this chapter beginning on page 520.)

4. On what basis does Professor Ayer claim that a person who says, "You acted wrongly in stealing that money," is not stating anything more than if he had said, "You stole that money"? Many people have been shocked by this claim and have called it outrageously immoral. Others have said it is obviously untrue. Do you think it is immoral? Do you think it is obviously untrue? Defend your answers.

5. Sometimes the emotive theory of ethics is called "the imperative theory" because the sentence "It is your duty to tell the truth" is said to be the expression of the command "Tell the truth." The imperative theory has been attacked on the grounds that it cannot account for the fact that, while the command "Tell the truth" has a moral statement corresponding to it, the commands "Shut the door," "Smoke Camels," "Throw a pass on the next play" do not. Thus, the argument runs, the imperative theory cannot explain the difference between moral and nonmoral commands. Could Professor Ayer satisfactorily answer this objection? If so, how?

6. A criticism which many have raised against the emotive theory is that when one person says, "Euthanasia is wrong," and another says, "Euthanasia is not wrong," they are contradicting one another. That is, if what one is saying is true, what the other is saying must be false. But according to Professor Ayer's theory, there is no contradiction in such a situation. Give your reasons for deciding that Professor Ayer does, or does not, successfully reply to this criticism.

7. Explain by means of examples the difference between the expression of a feeling and the assertion of a feeling. Of what importance is this distinction in understanding the emotive theory of ethics?

8. A philosopher has attacked Ayer's position by saying that if it were true, then a murderer could remove the wrongness of his deed by crying, "Hurrah for murder!"

Is this a good criticism?

9. Compare carefully Ayer's view of moral statements with Hume's theory of the moral sense. How do the two views differ? (Compare Question 8 above with Question 7 on Hume, page 520.)

10. Are all disputes about values really disputes about facts, as Ayer claims? When we say that a person has a "distorted or undeveloped moral sense," is it true that we mean "merely that he employs a different set of values from our own"?

11. Why does Ayer's theory imply ethical relativism? (For the meaning of "ethical relativism," see the introduction to this chapter.)

7

Moral Reasoning | R. M. Hare
(b. 1919)

Richard Mervyn Hare is a Fellow of Balliol College, Oxford. Besides *The Language of Morals* (1952), he has published a number of articles in leading philosophical journals.

In this reading, which is taken from *The Language of Morals,*

Mr. Hare approaches the second-order problems of moral philosophy by way of the study of moral language. In order to answer the question, "What are the grounds on which moral knowledge rests?" he examines the way in which people in everyday life use words and sentences when they arrive at moral decisions, justify moral judgments, and learn moral principles. Mr. Hare is concerned with the psychology of moral reasoning only as it enlightens us about the logic of moral reasoning. That is to say, his basic purpose is not to describe the actual process by which people are morally educated and by which they morally educate others, but to clarify the logical nature of the grounds on which our claim to moral knowledge rests. In this way he attempts to work out a solution to the problem of moral knowledge which is based on the meanings of moral words and the relations between moral statements as they arise out of the practical situations of everyday life.

The reading is from Chapter 4 of *The Language of Morals.*

From *The Language of Morals,* by R. M. Hare, The Clarendon Press, Oxford, 1952. Reprinted by permission of the publisher.

Without principles, most kinds of teaching are impossible, for what is taught is in most cases a principle. In particular, when we learn *to do* something, what we learn is always a principle. Even to learn or be taught a fact (like the names of the five rivers of the Punjab) is to learn how to answer a question; it is to learn the principle "When asked 'What are the names of the five rivers of the Punjab?' answer 'The Jhelum, the Chenab, etc.'" By this I do not of course mean that to learn to do anything is to learn to recite by rote some universal imperative sentence. This would involve us in a vicious regress; for learning to recite is a kind of learning, and must have its principles; but in that case we should have to learn to recite the principles of reciting. The point is rather this, that to learn to do anything is never to learn to do an individual act; it is always to learn to do acts of a certain kind in a certain kind of situation; and this is to learn a principle. Thus, in learning to drive, I learn, not to change gear *now,* but to change gear when my engine makes a certain kind of noise. If this were not so, instruction would be of no use at all; for if all an instructor could do were to tell us to change gear *now*, he would have to sit beside us for the rest of our lives in order to tell us just when, on each occasion, to change gear.

Thus without principles we could not learn anything whatever from our elders. This would mean that every generation would have to start from scratch and teach itself. But even if each generation were able to teach itself, it could not do so without principles; for self-teaching, like all other teaching, is the teaching of principles. This may be seen by [an] artificial example. Let us suppose that [a man] made all his choices on some principle, but always forgot, as soon as he had made the choice, what the principle had been. He would have, accordingly, each time he made a decision, to go over all the effects of the alternative actions. This would be so time-consuming that he would not have the leisure to make many decisions in the course of his life. He would spend his whole time deciding matters like whether to step off with the right or the left foot, and would never reach what we should call the more important decisions. But if he could remember the principles on which he acted, he would be in a much better position; he could *learn* how to act in certain kinds of circumstance; he could learn to single out quickly the relevant aspects of a situation, including the effects of the various possible actions, and so choose quickly, and in many cases habitually. Thus his powers of considered decision would be set free for more momentous decisions. When the cabinet-maker has learnt how to make a dovetail without thinking much about it, he will have time to think about such things as the proportions and aesthetic appearance of the finished product. And it is the same with our conduct in the moral sphere; when the performance of the lesser duties has become a matter of habit, we have time to think about the greater.

There is a limit in practice to the amount that can be taught to someone by someone else. Beyond this point, self-teaching is necessary. The limit is set by the variety of conditions which may be met with in doing whatever is being taught; and this variety is greater in some cases than in others. A sergeant can teach a recruit almost all there is to be known about fixing bayonets on parade, because one occasion of fixing bayonets on parade is much like another; but a driving instructor cannot do more than begin to teach his pupil the art of driving, because the conditions to be met with in driving are so various. In most cases, teaching cannot consist in getting the learner to perform faultlessly a fixed drill. One of the things that has to be included in any but the most elementary kinds of instruction is the opportunity for the learner to make decisions for himself, and in so doing to examine, and even modify to suit particular types of case, the principles which are being taught. The principles that are taught us initially are of a provisional kind. Our training, after the initial stages, consists in taking these principles, and making them less provisional; we do this by using them continually in our own decisions, and sometimes making exceptions to them; some of the exceptions are made because our instructor points out to us that certain cases are instances of classes of exceptions to the principle; and some of the exceptions we decide on for ourselves. . . .

We may illustrate this process of modifying principles from the example already used, that of learning to drive. I am told, for instance, always to draw into the side of the road when I stop the car; but later I am told that this does not apply when I stop before turning into a sideroad to the offside—for then I must stop near the middle of the road until it is possible for me to turn. Still later I learn that in this manoeuvre it is not necessary to stop at all if it is an uncontrolled junction and I can see that there is no traffic which I should obstruct by turning. When I have picked up all these modifications to the rule, and the similar modifications to all the other rules, and practice them habitually as so modified, then I am said to be a good driver, because my car is always in the right place on the road, travelling at the right speed, and so on. The good driver is, among other things, one whose actions are so exactly governed by principles which have become a habit with him, that he normally does not have to *think* just what to do. But road conditions are exceedingly various, and therefore it is unwise to let all one's driving become a matter of habit. One can never be certain that one's principles of driving are perfect—indeed, one can be very sure that they are not; and therefore the good driver not only drives well from habit, but constantly attends to his driving habits, to see whether they might not be improved; he never stops learning.

It is hardly necessary to point out that principles of driving, like other principles, are normally not inculcated by their verbal repetition, but by example, demonstration, and other practical means. We learn to drive, not by precept, but by being shown how to do particular bits of driving; the precepts are usually only explanatory or mnemonic of what we are being shown. Thereafter, we try to do the particular manoeuvres ourselves, and are criticized for failures, commended when we do them well, and so gradually get the hang of the various principles of good driving. For although our instruction is far from being purely verbal, nevertheless what we are being taught are principles. The fact that the derivation of particular acts (or commands to do them) from principles is normally done nonverbally does not show that it is not a logical process, any more than the inference:

The clock has just struck seven times
The clock strikes seven times at seven o'clock only
∴ It is just after seven o'clock

is shown to be nonlogical because it is never made explicitly in words.

Drivers often know just what to do in a certain situation without being able to enunciate in words the principle on which they act. This is a very common state of affairs with all kinds of principles. Trappers know just where to set their traps, but often cannot explain just why they have put a trap in a particular place. We all know how to use words to convey our meaning; but if a logician presses us for the exact definition of a word we have used, or the exact rules for its use, we are often at a loss. This does not mean that the setting of traps or the use of words or the driving of cars does not proceed according to principles. One may know how, without being able to say how —though if a skill is to be taught, it is easier if we *can* say how.

We must not think that, if we can decide between one course and another without further thought (it seems self-evident to us, which we should do), this necessarily implies that we have some mysterious intuitive faculty which tells us what to do. A driver does not know when to change gear by intuition; he knows it because he has learnt and not forgotten; what he knows is a principle, though he cannot formulate the principle in words. The same is true of moral decisions which are sometimes called "intuitive." We have moral "intuitions" because we have learnt how to behave, and have different ones according to how we have learnt to behave.

It would be a mistake to say that all that had to be done to a man to make him into a good driver was to tell him, or otherwise inculcate into him, a lot of general principles. This would be to leave out the factor of decision. Very soon after he begins to learn, he will be faced with situations to deal with which the provisional principles so far taught him require modification; and he will then have to decide what to do. He will very soon discover which decisions were right and which wrong, partly because his instructor tells him, and partly because having seen the effects of the decisions he determines in future not to bring about such effects. On no account must we commit the mistake of supposing that decisions and principles occupy two separate spheres and do not meet at any point. All decisions except those, if any, that are completely arbitrary are to some extent decisions of principle. We are always setting precedents for ourselves. It is not a case of the principle settling everything down to a certain point, and decision dealing with everything below that point. Rather, decision and principles interact throughout the whole field. Suppose that we have a principle to act in a certain way in certain circumstances. Suppose then that we find ourselves in circumstances which fall under the principle, but which have certain other peculiar features, not met before, which make us ask "Is the principle really intended to cover cases like this, or is it incompletely specified—is there here a case belonging to a class which should be treated as exceptional?" Our answer to this question will be a decision, but a decision of principle, as is shown by the use of the value-word "should." If we decide that this should be an exception, we thereby modify the principle by laying down an exception to it.

Suppose, for example, that in learning to drive I have been taught always to signal before I slow down or stop, but have not yet been taught what to do when stopping in an emergency; if a child leaps in front of my car, I do not signal, but keep both hands on the steering-wheel; and thereafter I accept the former principle with this exception, that in cases of emergency it is better to steer than to signal. I have, even on the spur of the moment, made a decision of principle. To understand what happens in cases like this is to understand a great deal about the making of value-judgements.

I do not wish to seem to be pressing too far my comparison, in respect of the way in which they are learnt, between principles of driving and principles of conduct. It is necessary also to bear in mind some distinctions. In the first place, the expression "good driver" is itself ambiguous in that it is not immediately clear what standard is being applied. It might be simply a standard of expertness; we might call a person a good driver if he were able to do just what he wanted with his car; we might say "Although a very good driver, he is most inconsiderate to other road users." On the other hand, we sometimes expect a good driver to have moral qualities as well; we do not, according to this criterion, call a man a good driver if he drives expertly, but without the slightest heed for the convenience or safety of other people. The line between these two standards of good driving is not easy to draw in practice. There is also a third standard, according to which a driver is said to be good if he conforms to the accepted principles of good driving as laid down, for example, in the *Highway Code*. Since the *Highway Code* is compiled with a definite purpose in view, this standard coincides to a great extent with the second.

Secondly, there are two ways of looking at driving instruction:

(1) We establish at the beginning certain ends, for example the avoidance of collisions, and instruction consists in teaching what practices are conducive to those ends. According to this way of looking at them, the principles of good driving are hypothetical imperatives.

(2) We teach at first simple rules of thumb, and the learner only gradually comes to see what the ends are, at which the instruction is aimed.

It must not be thought that either (1) or (2) by itself gives a complete account of our procedure. Which method we adopt depends to a great extent on the maturity and intelligence of the learner. In teaching African soldiers to drive, we might incline more to the second method; if I had to teach my two-year-old son to drive, I should have to adopt the same methods as I now adopt for teaching him to refrain from interfering with the controls when I am driving myself. With a highly intelligent learner, on the other hand, we may adopt a method which has more of (1) in it than of (2).

It must not be thought, however, that method (2) is ever entirely without a place even in the case of the most rational of learners. It may be that the desirability of avoiding collisions is at once understood and accepted even by comparatively stupid learners; but there are a great many more ends than this which a good driver has to aim at. He has to avoid causing many kinds of avoidable inconvenience both to himself and to others; he has to learn not to do things which result in damage to his vehicle, and so on. It is of no use to establish at the beginning a general end, "the avoidance of avoidable inconvenience"; for "inconvenience" is a value-word, and until he has had experience of driving, the learner will not know what sorts of situation are to count as avoidable inconvenience. The general end or principle is vacuous until by our detailed instruction we have given it content. Therefore it is always necessary to start, to some extent, by teaching our learner *what* to do, and leaving it for him to find out later *why*. We may therefore say that although moral principles, which are normally taught us when we are immature, are taught largely by method (2), and principles of driving preponderantly by method (1), there is not an absolute division between the two sorts of principle in this respect. What I have just said about first learning *what* to do, and about the initial vacuity of the general end, is borrowed from Aristotle. The one fundamental distinction between principles of driving and principles of conduct is that the latter are, in Aristotle's term, "architectonic" of the former; for the ends of good driving (safety, the avoidance of inconvenience to others, the preservation of property, and so on) are justified ultimately, if justification is sought, by appeal to moral considerations.

It would be folly, however, to say that there is only one way of learning a skill or any other body of principles, or of justifying a particular decision made in the practice of it. There are many ways, and I have tried to make the above account sufficiently general to cover all of them. It is sometimes said by writers on morals that we have to justify an act by reference to its effects, and that we tell which effects are to be sought, which avoided, by reference to some principle. Such a theory is that of the utilitarians, who bid us look at the effects, and examine these in the light of the principle of utility, to see which effects would maximize pleasure. Sometimes, on the other hand, it is said that an act is justified directly by reference to the principles which it observes, and these principles in their turn by reference to the effects of always observing them. Sometimes it is said that we should observe principles and ignore the effects— though for the reasons given above "effects" cannot be here intended in the sense in which I have been using it. What is wrong with these theories is not what they say, but their assumption that they are telling us the only way to justify actions, or decide what actions to do. We do, indeed, justify and decide on actions in all these ways; for example, sometimes, if asked why we did A, we say, "Because it was a case falling under principle P," and if asked to justify P in turn, we go into the effects of observing it and of not observing it. But sometimes, when asked the same question "Why did you do A?" we say "Because if I hadn't, E would have happened," and if asked what was wrong about E happening, we appeal to some principle.

The truth is that, if asked to justify as completely as possible any decision, we have to bring in both effects—to give content to the decision—and principles, and the effects in general of observing those principles, and so on, until we have satisfied our inquirer. Thus a complete justification of a decision would consist of a complete account of its effects, together with a complete account of the principles which it observed, and the effects of observing those principles —for, of course, it is the effects (what obeying them in fact consists in) which give content to the principles too. Thus, if pressed to justify a decision completely, we have to give a complete specification of the way of life of which it is a part. This complete specification it is impossible in practice to give; the nearest attempts are those given by the great religions, especially those which can point to historical persons who carried out the way of life in practice. Suppose, however, that we can give it. If the inquirer still goes on asking "But why *should* I live like that?" then there is no further answer to give him, because we have already, *ex hypothesi,* said everything that could be included in this further answer. We can only ask him to make up his own mind which way he ought to live; for in the end everything rests upon such a decision of principle. He has to decide whether to accept that way of life or not; if he accepts it, then we can proceed to justify the decisions that are based upon it; if he does not accept it, then let him accept some other, and try to live by it. The sting is in the last clause. To describe such ultimate decisions as arbitrary, because *ex hypothesi* everything which could be used to justify them has already been included in the decision, would be like saying that a complete description of the universe was utterly unfounded, because no further fact could be called upon in corroboration of it. This is not how we use the words "arbitrary" and "unfounded." Far from being arbitrary, such a decision would be the most well-founded of decisions, because it would be based upon a consideration of everything upon which it could possibly be founded.

It will be noticed how, in talking of decisions of principle, I have inevitably started talking value-language. Thus we decide that the principle *should* be modified, or that it is *better* to steer than to signal. . . . To make a value-judgement is to make a decision of principle. To ask whether I ought to do A in these circumstances is (to borrow Kantian language with a small though important modification) to ask whether or not I will that doing A in such circumstances should become a universal law. . . . The same question could be put in other words by asking "What attitude shall I adopt and recommend towards doing A in such circumstances?"; for "attitude," if it means anything, means a principle of action.

As Kant points out in the important passage on the Autonomy of the Will, we have to make our own decisions of principle. Other people cannot make them for us unless we have first decided to take their advice or obey their orders. There is an interesting analogy here with the position of the scientist, who also has to rely on his own observations. It might be said that there is a difference here between decisions and observations, to the detriment of the former, in that an observation, once made, is public property, whereas decisions have to be made by the agent himself on each occasion. But the difference is only apparent. A scientist would not have become a scientist unless he had convinced himself that the observations of other scientists were in general reliable. He did this by making some observations of his own. When we learnt elementary chemistry at school, we had some theoretical periods and some practical. In the theoretical periods we studied books; in the practical periods we made experiments, and found, if we were lucky, that the results tallied with what the books said. This showed us that what the books said was not all nonsense; so that even if, by reason of disturbing factors ignored by us, our experiments came out wrong, we were inclined to trust the books and acknowledge that we had made a mistake. We were confirmed in this assumption by the fact that we often discovered later what the mistake had been. If our observations, however carefully we did them, were always at variance with the textbooks, we should not be tempted to make science our profession. Thus the confidence of the scientist in other people's observations is ultimately based, among other things, on his own observations and his own judgements about what is reliable. He has in the end to rely on himself.

The case of the moral agent is not dissimilar. When in our early days we are given our elementary moral instruction, there are some things that we are told, and some things that we do. If, when we did as we were told, the total effects of our so doing, when they happened, were always such as we would not have chosen, had we known, then we should seek better advice, or, if prevented from so doing, either work out our own salvation or become moral defectives. If we are in general given what we subsequently come to see to have been good advice, we decide in general to follow the advice and adopt the principles of those who have given us this good advice in the past. This is what happens to any child who is well brought up. Just as the scientist does not try to rewrite all that is in the textbooks, but takes that for granted and sticks to his own particular researches, so this fortunate child will take over bodily the principles of his elders and adapt them in detail, by his own decisions, to suit his own circumstances from time to time. This is how in a well-ordered society morality remains stable, and at the same time gets adapted to changing circumstances.

There are, however, many ways in which this happy state of affairs can deteriorate. Let us consider a process that seems to occur quite often in history; it occurred in Greece during the fifth and fourth centuries, and it has occurred in our own time. Suppose that the people of a certain generation—I will call it the first generation—have got very settled principles, inherited from their fathers. Suppose that they have become so settled as to be second nature, so that generally speaking people act on the principles without thinking, and their power of making considered decisions of principle becomes atrophied. They act always by the book, and come to no harm, because the state of the world in their time remains much the same as that for which the principles were thought out. But their sons, the second generation, as they grow up, find that conditions have changed (e.g. through a protracted war or an industrial revolution), and that the principles in which they have been brought up are no longer adequate. Since, in their education, much stress has been laid on observing principles, and very little on making the decisions on which these principles are ultimately based, their morality has no roots, and becomes completely unstable. Books on "The Whole Duty of Man" are no longer written or read. Often, when they do what it says in such books, they subsequently find cause to regret their decisions; and there are too many cases of this kind for any confidence in the old principles, as a body, to remain. No doubt there are among these old principles certain very general ones, which will remain acceptable unless human nature and the state of the world undergo a most fundamental change; but the second generation, not having been brought up to make decisions of principle, but to do what it says in the book, will not, most of them, be able to make those crucial decisions which would determine which principles to keep, which to modify, and which to abandon. Some people will have been so steeped in the old principles that they just follow them come what may; and these will on the whole be more fortunate than the others, for it is better to have some principles, even if they sometimes lead to decisions which we regret, than to be morally adrift. The bulk of the second generation, and still more perhaps of the third, will not know which of the principles to keep and which to reject; and so they will come more and more to live from day to day—not a bad thing, because it trains their powers of decision, but it is an unpleasant and dangerous state to be in. A few among them, the rebels, will shout from the housetops that some or all of the old moral principles are worthless; some of these rebels will advocate new principles of their own; some will have nothing to offer. Though they increase the confusion, these rebels perform the useful function of making people decide between their rival principles; and if they not only advocate new principles, but sincerely try to live by them, they are conducting a moral experiment which may be of the utmost value to man (in which case they go down in history as great moral teachers), or may, on the other hand, prove disastrous both to them and to their disciples.

It may take several generations for this disease to play itself out. Morality regains its vigour when ordinary people have learnt afresh to decide for themselves what principles to live by, and more especially what principles to teach their children. Since the world, though subject to vast material changes, changes only very slowly in matters that are fundamental from the moral point of view, the principles which win the acceptance of the mass of people are not likely to differ enormously from those which their fathers came to distrust. The moral principles of Aristotle resemble those of Aeschylus more than they differ from them, and we ourselves shall perhaps come back to something recognizably like the morality of our grandfathers. But there will be some changes; some of the principles advocated by the rebels will have been adopted. That is how morality progresses—or retrogresses. The process is reflected by very subtle changes in the uses of value-words; the impossibility of translating Aristotle's catalogue of virtues into modern English may serve as an example, and the disappearance without trace of the word "righteous" may serve as another.

The question "How shall I bring up my children?" which we have mentioned, is one to the logic of which, since ancient times, few philosophers have given much attention. A child's moral upbringing has an effect upon him which will remain largely untouched by anything that happens to him thereafter. If he has had a stable upbringing, whether on good principles or on bad ones, it will be extremely difficult for him to abandon those principles in later life—difficult but not impossible. They will have for him the force of an objective moral law; and his behaviour will seem to give much evidence in support of intuitionist ethical theories, provided that it is not compared with the behaviour of those who stick just as firmly to quite different principles. But nevertheless, unless our education has been so thorough as to transform us into automata, we can come to doubt or even reject these principles; that is what makes human beings, whose moral systems change, different from ants, whose moral system does not. Therefore, even if for me the question "What shall I do in such and such a situation?" is almost invariably answered without ambiguity by the moral intuition which my upbringing has given me, I may, if I ask myself "How shall I bring up my children?" pause before giving an answer. It is here that the most fundamental moral decisions of all arise; and it is here, if only moral philosophers would pay attention to them, that the most characteristic uses of moral words are to be found. Shall I bring up my children *exactly* as I was brought up, so that they have the same intuitions about morals as I have? Or have circumstances altered, so that the moral character of the father will not provide a suitable equipment for the children? Perhaps I shall try to bring them up like their father, and shall fail; perhaps their new environment will be too strong for me, and they will come to repudiate my principles. Or I may have become so bewildered by the strange new world that, although I still act from force of habit on the principles that I have learnt, I simply do not know what principles to impart to my children, if, indeed, one in my condition can impart any settled principles at all. On all these questions, I have to make up my mind; only the most hide-bound father will try to bring up his children, without thinking, in exactly the way that he himself was brought up; and even he will usually fail disastrously.

Many of the dark places of ethics become clearer when we consider this dilemma in which parents are liable to find themselves. We have already noticed that, although principles have in the end to rest upon decisions of principle, decisions as such cannot be taught; only principles can be taught. It is the powerlessness of the parent to make for his son those many decisions of principle which the son during his future career will make, that gives moral language its characteristic shape. The only instrument which the parent possesses is moral education—the teaching of principles by example and precept, backed up by chastisement and other more up-to-date psychological methods. Shall he use these means, and to what extent? Certain generations of parents have had no doubts about this question. They have used them to the full; and the result has been to turn their children into good intuitionists, able to cling to the rails, but bad at steering round corners. At other times parents—and who shall blame them?—suffer from lack of confidence; they are not sure enough what they themselves think, to be ready to impart to their children a stable way of life. The children of such a generation are likely to grow up opportunists, well able to make individual decisions, but without the settled body of principles which is the most priceless heritage that any generation can leave to its successors. For, though principles are in the end built upon decisions of principle, the building is the work of many generations, and the man who has to start from the beginning is to be pitied; he will not be likely, unless he is a genius, to achieve many conclusions of importance, any more than the average boy, turned loose without instruction upon a desert island, or even in a laboratory, would be likely to make any of the major scientific discoveries.

The dilemma between these two extreme courses in education is plainly a false one. Why it is a false one is apparent, if we recall what was said earlier about the dynamic relation between decisions and principles. It is very like learning to drive. It would be foolish, in teaching someone to drive, to try to inculcate into him such fixed and comprehensive principles that he would never have to make an independent decision. It would be equally foolish to go to the other extreme and leave it to him to find his own way of driving. What we do, if we are sensible, is to give him a solid basis of principles, but at the same time ample opportunity of making the decisions upon which these principles are based, and by which they are modified, improved, adapted to changed circumstances, or even abandoned if they become entirely unsuited to a new environment. To teach only the principles, without giving the opportunity of subjecting them to the learner's own decisions of principle, is like teaching [science] [1] exclusively from the textbooks without entering the laboratory. On the other hand, to abandon one's child or one's driving-pupil to his own self-expression is like putting a boy into a laboratory and saying "Get on with it." The boy may enjoy himself or kill himself, but will probably not learn much science.

The moral words, of which we may take "ought" as an example, reflect in their logical behaviour this double nature of moral instruction—as well they may, for it is in moral instruction that they are most typically used. The sentences in which they appear are normally the expression of decisions of principle—and it is easy to let the decisions get separated, in our discussion of the subject, from the principles. This is the source of the controversy between the "objectivists," as intuitionists sometimes call themselves, and the "subjectivists," as they often call their opponents. The former lay stress on the fixed principles that are handed down by the father, the latter on the new decisions which have to be made by the son. The objectivist says "Of course you know what you ought to do; look at what your conscience tells you, and if in doubt go by the consciences of the vast majority of men." He is able to say this, because our consciences are the product of the principles which our early training has indelibly planted in us, and in one society these principles do not differ much from one person to another. The subjectivist, on the other hand, says "But surely, when it comes to the point—when I have listened to what other people say, and given due weight to my own intuitions, the legacy of my upbringing— I have in the end to decide for myself what I ought to do. To deny this is to be a conventionalist; for both common moral notions and my own intuitions are the legacy of tradition, and—apart from the fact that there are so many different traditions in the world—traditions cannot be started without someone doing what I now feel called upon to do, decide. If I refuse to make my own decisions, I am, in merely copying my fathers, showing myself a lesser man than they; for whereas they must have initiated, I shall be merely accepting." This plea of the subjectivist is quite justified. It is the plea of the adolescent who wants to be adult. To become morally adult is to reconcile these two apparently conflicting positions by learning to make decisions of principle; it is to learn to use "ought"-sentences in the realization that they can only be verified by reference to a standard or set of principles which we have by our own decision accepted and made our own. This is what our present generation is so painfully trying to do.

Questions

1. ". . . . Without principles we could not learn anything whatever from our elders." Why not, according to Mr. Hare? In your answer make clear what is meant by a "principle."

2. Mr. Hare claims that when we say we have "moral intuitions," all we really mean is that we have learned how we ought to act in a given situation without

[1] [This word is inserted at the request of Mr. Hare. It was erroneously omitted from the text as originally printed.—Eds.]

having to think about it. Is this a good reason for rejecting the ethical intuitionist's view of moral knowledge? Why or why not? (The ethical intuitionist's view is set forth in the reading by Price beginning on page 520.)

3. Mr. Hare asserts that to give a complete justification of any decision we can only specify the total way of life of which it is a part, and then let the person make up his own mind what way of life he wants to live. Does this imply that morality is merely a matter of personal taste, concerning which we cannot argue? Defend your answer.

4. Why does Mr. Hare think that an ultimate decision to adopt one way of life rather than another is not "arbitrary"? State your reasons for agreeing, or disagreeing, with him.

5. Defend or attack the claim that Mr. Hare has discovered a consistent way to combine the utilitarian outlook in ethics with the Kantian outlook. (For the utilitarian outlook, see the reading by Mill beginning on page 560. For the Kantian outlook, see the reading beginning on page 533.)

6. Why are the learning of principles and the making of decisions *both* important in moral education, according to Mr. Hare?

7. ". . . The world, though subject to vast material changes, changes only very slowly in matters that are fundamental from the moral point of view. . . ." Give your reasons for accepting, or for doubting, this statement.

8. Why does Mr. Hare think that the study of the way children are brought up is important for understanding the nature of moral reasoning?

9. At the end of the reading, Mr. Hare offers an explanation of the subjectivist-objectivist dispute in moral philosophy. How plausible is his explanation, in your opinion? What would a subjectivist such as Hume be likely to say about this explanation? (For Hume's position, see the reading beginning on page 508.) What would an objectivist such as Price be likely to say about it? (For Price's position, see the reading beginning on page 520.)

10. After reading the account of moral statements given by Professor A. J. Ayer in the selection which immediately precedes this one (page 575), what criticisms do you think he might raise against Mr. Hare's view of the justification of moral decisions and the learning of moral principles? How might Mr. Hare reply to these criticisms?

11. Referring to the meanings of "ethical relativism" and "ethical absolutism" explained in the introduction to this chapter, would you say that Mr. Hare's views lead to ethical relativism, to ethical absolutism, or to neither? Why?

Suggested Further Reading | Classic Works

Bentham, Jeremy, *An Introduction to the Principles of Morals and Legislation* (1789).
Bradley, F. H., *Ethical Studies* (1876).
Butler, Joseph, *Sermons Upon Human Nature* (1726).
Green, T. H., *Prolegomena to Ethics* (1883).
Moore, G. E., *Principia Ethica* (1903).
Plato, *Republic; Protagoras; Gorgias; Philebus.*
Sidgwick, Henry, *The Methods of Ethics* (1874).
Smith, Adam, *The Theory of Moral Sentiments* (1759).
Spinoza, Benedict de, *Ethics* (1678).

| Introductory Studies

Baier, K., *The Moral Point of View,* Cornell University Press, Ithaca, 1958.

Broad, C. D., *Five Types of Ethical Theory,* Routledge and Kegan Paul, London, 1930.

Dewey, John, *Reconstruction in Philosophy,* Holt, N. Y., 1920, Chap. VII.

——, *The Quest for Certainty,* Allen and Unwin, London, 1930, Chap. X.

Ewing, A. C., *The Definition of Good,* Macmillan, N. Y., 1947.

Parker, Dewitt H., *The Philosophy of Value,* University of Michigan Press, Ann Arbor, 1957.

Perry, Ralph Barton, *General Theory of Value,* Longmans, Green, N. Y., 1926.

——, *Realms of Value,* Harvard University Press, Cambridge, Mass., 1954.

Schlick, Moritz, *Problems of Ethics,* tr. by David Rynin, Prentice-Hall, Englewood Cliffs, N. J., 1939.

Stace, W. T., *The Concept of Morals,* Macmillan, N. Y., 1937.

Toulmin, Stephen E., *An Examination of the Place of Reason in Ethics,* Cambridge University Press, Cambridge, Eng., 1950.

| Advanced Studies

Dewey, John, *Theory of Valuation,* Vol. 2, No. 4, *International Encyclopedia of Unified Science,* University of Chicago Press, Chicago, 1939.

Edel, Abraham, *Ethical Judgment,* Free Press, Glencoe, Ill., 1955.

Edwards, Paul, *The Logic of Moral Discourse,* Free Press, Glencoe, Ill., 1955.

Hartmann, Nicolai, *Ethics,* tr. by Stanton Coit, Macmillan, N. Y., 1932, 3 vols.

Ladd, John, *The Structure of a Moral Code,* Harvard University Press, Cambridge, Mass., 1957, Parts I and II.

Nowell-Smith, P. H., *Ethics,* Penguin Books, Harmondsworth, Middlesex, Eng., 1954.

Rice, Philip Blair, *On the Knowledge of Good and Evil,* Random House, N. Y., 1955.

Sellars, Wilfrid, and John Hospers, eds., *Readings in Ethical Theory,* Appleton-Century-Crofts, N. Y., 1952.

Stevenson, Charles L., *Ethics and Language,* Yale University Press, New Haven, 1944.

| Periodicals

Many excellent articles on the problem of moral knowledge are to be found in recent and current issues of the following periodicals: *Analysis; Aristotelian Society Supplementary Volumes; Ethics; Journal of Philosophy; Mind; Philosophical Quarterly; Philosophical Review; Philosophy; Philosophy and Phenomenological Research;* and *Proceedings of the Aristotelian Society.*

Chapter Seven

THE PROBLEM OF

Political Principles

Political Principles in Decisions of Everyday Life

Whenever we make a value judgment concerning the justice or injustice of laws, or concerning the rights of citizens, we appeal to some political principle as the basis for our judgment. The political principle functions as the standard according to which we condemn (or commend) what it is we are judging. Thus, if we heard that Congress was considering a law which would require that no book could be published in the United States unless it had been passed by a board of censors, we would call such a law a violation of our rights. We would condemn it on the basis of a political principle, in this case the principle of freedom of the press. If we knew of a country where the law does not allow women to vote, most of us would condemn the law as unjust, or at least judge that country to be less just than our own. The principle we would appeal to in this case would be that the right to vote should not be denied on account of sex.

As citizens of a state (i.e., a politically organized community) each of us is confronted with decisions involving the appeal to political principles. When we decide to vote for one candidate rather than another, to join a political organization and participate in its activities, or to write a letter to our congressman advocating that a certain law be passed or not be passed, we are implicitly referring to some set of political principles. These principles are the ultimate grounds on which our decisions rest, even though we may never have examined them critically or may not even be aware of them. Of course our political decisions are not always arrived at in a rational manner.

We may decide on the basis of mere whim or caprice, or on the basis of blind emotion and irrational needs (such as hero worship, patriotic fervor, desire for revenge, and the need for a scapegoat). But if our decisions are in some measure a matter of reason rather than emotion, they must finally be derived from political principles. This is true even when we decide to "do nothing." For the decision to "do nothing" is a decision not to try to change the course of events, and in so far as this decision is based on reason, it rests on the assumption that, according to one's principles, there are no particular wrongs or injustices in the present situation which require political action to remedy them.

We have so far discussed how political principles function as the basis for decisions. Sometimes, however, our political principles are themselves brought into question, and we must decide whether to continue to accept them or to reject them and adopt a new set of principles. Such a challenge may occur in either our practical life or our intellectual life. In our practical life the challenge can take two forms. If all or most of our political principles are embodied in the laws and social policies of our own country, those principles are challenged whenever our country comes under attack from outside, whether by actual military aggression or by all the various pressures that can be brought to bear on a country short of war. We are then confronted with the momentous question: Are my political principles so sound that I am justified in defending them even if such defense means the death or injury of other human beings? And our principles can be shown to be sufficiently sound to justify this only if they can be shown to be truer or more valid than the principles of the enemy.

The other practical situation in which our political principles are challenged occurs when a law or social policy of our society is in conflict with our principles. We are then confronted with the necessity of examining our principles to see whether they can be upheld on rational grounds even when they demand action in opposition to our own society. Such action may consist in violent revolution or in the peaceful and orderly attempt to change laws; it may consist in passive resistance to a law or the organizing of a reform movement. But whatever the action be, the fact that it is in fundamental opposition to the *status quo* places a demand, both on the individual and on the society, to examine the validity of the political principles involved on either side.

The need to show that our political principles are justified occurs in practical life, then, whenever our principles allow us to be in harmony with our society but the society itself is under attack, or whenever our principles do not allow us to be in harmony with our society. Intellectually, our political principles are challenged whenever we discuss them openly with someone who disagrees with them, and whenever we think critically about them ourselves. The question, "Why do you believe in such-and-such principles?" may be asked us by others or by ourselves. In either case we are forced to scrutinize the grounds on which our principles rest to see if they are good grounds. If upon doing this we find that they are not good grounds, we may change our political principles and this, in turn, may change our decisions in practical life.

Three Functions of Political Principles

So far we have considered the functions which political principles perform in the decisions of the citizens of a state. In the history of political thought, however, political principles have had two other functions. One is to serve as standards on the basis of which legislators justify their decisions about what social policies to enact into law. The other is to serve as standards on the basis of which the authority of the state itself is justified. Thus political principles function as guides to the *citizen's* political decisions, to the *legislator's* decisions, and to the decisions of *those who inquire into the foundation of any political authority* (including the authority of legislators to legislate). We may then say that political principles are those principles appealed to in answering three questions: (1) The citizen's question: What ought I to do as a responsible member of a society governed by laws which I am forced to obey? (2) The legislator's question: What policies ought to be made and how ought they to be carried out? (3) The question of the political theorist (also the question of the founder of a state, or the maker of a constitution): What is the basis of legitimate authority? It should be noted that each of these is a value question. The value standards which are required for answering them are political principles. What these political principles themselves are based on is a matter which it is the task of political philosophy to inquire into.

Two Meanings of "Political Philosophy"

The term "political philosophy" has two closely connected but different meanings. On the one hand, it means the set of political principles accepted by any person or group, together with the reasons (if any) which are given to justify the set of principles. In this sense, everyone (citizen, legislator, or founder of a state) who makes political decisions on the grounds of some principle has a political philosophy. In the second sense of the term, "political philosophy" refers more to an activity or process than to a set of standards or principles. In this sense political philosophy is the second-order activity of examining and critically evaluating the grounds on which political principles rest. Its aim is to understand and clarify the meaning of the basic concepts (such as "freedom," "equality," "justice," and "rights") used in stating political principles, to determine the precise nature of the grounds on which a person's or group's political principles are alleged to rest, and to come to some conclusion about the legitimacy or validity of those grounds. This is called a "second-order" activity because it consists in making statements about the meaning and truth of other statements, namely, the statements of political principles and of the reasons given to support them. Political principles themselves (and hence political philosophy in its *first* sense) are first-order statements. They are about such things as freedom, equality, justice, and the rights of man. Political philosophy in its second sense is not about such things, but about the political principles which are about such things. It operates on a second level of discourse: discourse about the discourse about such things as freedom, equality, justice, and the rights of man.

What is the relation between these two senses of "political philosophy"?

The answer to this question may be made clear by supposing that someone were to ask us to formulate in so many words our political principles, and then to state why we believe them to be true. Perhaps we would first refer to certain famous phrases like "The right to life, liberty, and the pursuit of happiness," "Government by consent of the governed," and "Equal justice under law." But how clearly would we understand these words? Or perhaps we would refer to our country's Constitution and Bill of Rights. But that kind of answer would not differ from the reasoning of a person in a totalitarian dictatorship who referred to his country's legal principles to justify his political standards. Could we really give good reasons to support our belief in democratic rule and the freedoms set forth in the Bill of Rights? It is the attempt to get clear in our own minds just what it is we believe about the rights of man, about freedom, equality, and justice, and to discover whether we are really justified in holding these beliefs, which gives rise to political philosophy in the second sense.

Once we have begun to philosophize in this way we are asking second-order questions about political principles. But one of the chief purposes of doing this is to arrive at a first-order discourse in which we can state our political principles clearly, relate them to one another in an orderly and consistent system, and show their acceptability on rational grounds. In short, the only way to a clear, consistent, and justifiable political philosophy in the first sense is by means of the pursuit of political philosophy in the second sense.

The difference between political philosophy in both of these senses and political science is now easy to see. The political philosopher is concerned with the evaluation of political practices and the justification of political principles; the political scientist is concerned with accurately describing the various political practices and principles of different societies, and with explaining their origin and operation. A political scientist can describe the rights which people have in a given society, when those rights are defined in terms of the laws and customs of the society. But he cannot, as a political scientist, state that people have certain rights which the laws and customs ought to recognize. Similarly, he can state that such-and-such persons have the authority to perform such-and-such functions in a given political system. Within the system he can determine whether any authority is *legal*. But he cannot, as a political scientist, decide whether that authority is *legitimate* or *justified*. He can show the effects of having a certain kind of government upon the economy, upon the religious and educational institutions, and upon other aspects of community life, but he cannot show that one kind of government is better than another, and he cannot show why there should be any government at all (i.e., he cannot, as a political scientist, disprove the political philosophy of anarchy). The same individual, of course, may be both a political scientist and a political philosopher. But his two roles should never be confused.

The Problem of Political Principles

The main questions which constitute the problem of political principles are: What do the key concepts used in political principles mean? How can political principles be arranged in a consistent system? and, How can political principles be justified? These are all questions on the second level of discourse and, consequently, can only be answered by political philosophy in the second sense. The readings in this chapter have been chosen as representing some of the different ways philosophers have dealt with these questions. The reader will notice, however, that most of the philosophers do not remain strictly on the second level of discourse. They not only investigate the meaning and truth of political principles, they also propound their own principles and express value judgments which are based on their principles. Thus political philosophy has traditionally included both the first-order advocacy of political principles and the second-order investigation of their grounds. Let us take a few of the questions with which political philosophers have been concerned and see how the two levels of discourse are involved in answering them.

Some philosophers have directed their attention to the questions: What is the foundation of legitimate authority? What is the basis of our obligation to obey the law? Why does the state (or sovereign) have a rightful claim to the citizen's allegiance? Examples of attempts to answer these questions are to be found in the selections by Locke (page 613) and Rousseau (page 624) in this chapter. These questions have been answered by some philosophers as first-order questions about political authority, political obligation, and political allegiance, that is, as questions which could be answered merely by stating a set of political principles. But other philosophers have seen the necessity of examining the logical grounds of the principles they would offer in answering the questions. For only by way of such an examination could the demand be fully met to *justify* political authority, obligation, and allegiance.

Another question which political philosophers have been concerned with is: What is the true end of government? (Sometimes phrased: What is the purpose of the State?) The question is not meant to be interpreted as asking what were the actual purposes people had in mind when, at different moments in history, they instituted their governments. It is intended to ask for the *true* purpose of government, that is, the purpose any government ought to serve, or the purpose it would serve if it were a just government. Thus the question demands the stating of political principles, such as standards of justice or the public good. When philosophers offer such principles in answering this question, they realize that they must justify them, and accordingly endeavor to do so. They are then obliged to consider the second-order question: What reasons can be accepted as validating grounds for political principles concerning the proper ends of government?

A third question which has concerned many political philosophers is: Where do our human (or natural) rights come from? This question arises when the distinction is made between legal rights and human, or natural, rights. The latter are rights which we claim to possess independently of the laws of a state, and which we believe ought to be recognized by those laws. The former are rights which are sanctioned by the laws of a state (i.e., the laws prohibit one citizen from denying the exercise of

rights to another). Historically, the distinction has been assumed whenever people have urged that the law of the land conform to the inherent ("unalienable") rights of man. As soon as the distinction is made, however, the philosopher wants to know where people get their alleged natural rights, which must come from some extralegal or supralegal source. In investigating this source, the philosopher is examining the grounds on which people rest their claims to these rights. Thus the question, "Where do our human rights come from?" involves the question, "What reasons can be given to justify our claim to human rights?" In this way the question is seen to have a second-order aspect, namely, an inquiry into the logical basis of those political principles which consist in our claims to human rights.

Political Philosophy and Social Philosophy

A few remarks should be added about the difference between "political philosophy" as we have been using that term and "social philosophy." Although the latter term is used in many different ways, one of its common meanings is that it is an inquiry similar to, but broader in scope than, political philosophy. In this sense social philosophy is concerned with the principles which determine the right, proper, or ideal relations among all persons and groups in a society, while political philosophy is concerned only with those relations which define the structure of executive, judicial, and legislative authority in the society. Thus social principles include political principles but extend beyond them. They include those standards which are appealed to whenever someone criticizes or appraises an aspect of cultural life, whether it has to do with political institutions or religious institutions, with economic affairs or with etiquette and manners, with technological influences or family life, with the educational system or with the way people spend their leisure time.

Just as political philosophy has a first-order and a second-order aspect, so does social philosophy. The first-order aspect of social philosophy is the expounding and advocating of a set of social principles or values as the basis for all social criticism. The second-order aspect of social philosophy is the critical examination of the grounds on which social principles rest and the attempt to find good grounds for them.

In this chapter we are concerned primarily with that part of social philosophy which deals with the political structure and functions of a society. The reader will be introduced to philosophical thinking about a limited area of man's social experience, but if he learns how to do this kind of thinking well, he will be prepared for an intelligent consideration of the broader problems of social criticism.

Political Philosophy and Moral Philosophy

The difference between political philosophy and moral philosophy (or ethics) is not like the difference described above between political philosophy and social philosophy. The reason for this is that moral philosophy sometimes functions as a "higher" discipline than political philosophy. By this is meant that political principles are sometimes thought to be derivable from, or entailed by, moral principles (moral rules, ideals, or standards). The problem of second-order political philosophy then becomes secondary to the problem of moral knowledge (the subject of Chapter 6). Once a solution to the latter is reached, a solution to the former automatically follows.

Not all political philosophies, however, accept this view of the relation between political principles and moral principles. The reader who has already studied Chapter 6, "The Problem of Moral Knowledge," should attempt to decide, when reading each of the selections which follow, what the philosopher's views are concerning the relation between politics and morals.

1

Nature, Law and Justice | Cicero (106-43 B.C.)

Marcus Tullius Cicero, the Roman orator, politician, and lawyer, was also a lifelong student of philosophy. He studied under the Greek philosophers of his time, and although he has never been considered an original philosophical thinker, he did write on a wide range of philosophical subjects. His method was to draw freely on Greek sources, some of which he translated directly into Latin, others of which he adapted to his own thinking. The reading which follows is from his *De Legibus* (*Laws*), a book in which Cicero has given us a coherent statement of the social implications of the concepts of nature and law propounded by the Stoic philosophers. These concepts had great influence on the Roman Law of Cicero's time, and have continued to influence legal, political, and moral philosophy down to our own day.

In the *De Legibus* Cicero's thesis is that no law of a state is self-justifying. The fact that a law is the command of a state is not a sufficient reason for obeying it, since a person can always ask, "But is what is commanded right?" The laws of a state can only be justified by some idea of a moral order which lies behind them and to which they conform. For Cicero this moral order is to be found in Nature. Thus the laws of an ideal state must be enacted in accordance with Nature. The reader must determine what Cicero means by "Nature" and discover why he believes it to be the source of moral order. Then the reader may consider possible grounds for accepting or rejecting Cicero's use of Nature as a standard for judging the laws of a state.

This reading is from Books I and II of the *De Legibus*. The *De Legibus* is written in the form of a dialogue, the speakers being Marcus Tullius Cicero himself, his brother Quintus, and his friend and publisher, Titus Pomponius Atticus. The translation from the Latin is by Clinton Walker Keyes.

Reprinted by permission of the publishers from the Loeb Classical Library volume translated by C. W. Keyes, *Cicero: De Re Publica, De Legibus*, Cambridge, Mass.: Harvard University Press.

MARCUS. I shall seek the root of Justice in Nature, under whose guidance our whole discussion must be conducted.

ATTICUS. Quite right. Surely with her as our guide, it will be impossible for us to go astray.

MAR. Do you grant us, then, Pomponius (for I am aware of what Quintus thinks), that it is by the might of the immortal gods, or by their nature, reason, power, mind, will, or any other term which may make my meaning clearer, that all Nature is governed? For if you do not admit it, we must begin our argument with this problem before taking up anything else.

ATT. Surely I will grant it, if you insist upon it. . . .

MAR. I will not make the argument long. Your admission leads us to this: that animal which we call man, endowed with foresight and quick intelligence, complex, keen, possessing memory, full of reason and prudence, has been given a certain distinguished status by the supreme God who created him; for he is the only one among so many different kinds and varieties of living beings who has a share in reason and thought, while all the rest are deprived of it. But what is more divine, I will not say in man only, but in all heaven and earth, than reason? And reason, when it is full grown and perfected, is rightly called wisdom. Therefore, since there is nothing better than reason, and since it exists both in man and God, the first common possession of man and God is reason. But those who have reason in common must also have right reason in common. And since right reason is Law, we must believe that men have Law also in common with the gods. Further, those who share Law must also share Justice; and those who share these are to be regarded as members of the same commonwealth. If indeed they obey the same authorities and powers, this is true in a far greater degree; but as a matter of fact they do obey this celestial system, the divine mind, and the God of transcendent power. Hence we must now conceive of this whole universe as one commonwealth of which both gods and men are members.

And just as in States distinctions in legal status are made on account of the blood relationships of families, so in the universe the same thing holds true, but on a scale much vaster and more splendid, so that men are grouped with Gods on the basis of blood relationship and descent. For when the nature of man is examined, the theory is usually advanced (and in all probability it is correct) that through constant changes and revolutions in the heavens, a time came which was suitable for sowing the seed of the human race. And when this seed was scattered and sown over the earth, it was granted the divine gift of the soul. For while the other elements of which man consists were derived from what is mortal, and are therefore fragile and perishable, the soul was generated in us by God. Hence we are justified in saying that there is a blood relationship between ourselves and the celestial beings; or we may call it a common ancestry or origin. Therefore among all the varieties of living beings, there is no creature except man which has any knowledge of God, and among men themselves there is no race either so highly civilized or so savage as not to know that it must believe in a god, even if it does not know in what sort of god it ought to believe. Thus it is clear that man recognizes God because, in a way, he remembers and recognizes the source from which he sprang.

Moreover, virtue exists in man and God alike, but in no other creature besides; virtue, however, is nothing else than Nature perfected and developed to its highest point; therefore there is a likeness between man and God. As this is true, what relationship could be closer or clearer than this one? For this reason, Nature has lavishly yielded such a wealth of things adapted to man's convenience and use that what she produces seems intended as a gift to us, and not brought forth by chance; and this is true, not only of what the fertile earth bountifully bestows in the form of grain and fruit, but also of the animals; for it is clear that some of them have been created to be man's slaves, some to supply him with their products, and others to serve as his food. Moreover innumerable arts have been discovered through the teachings of Nature; for it is by a skilful imitation of her that reason has acquired the necessities of life. Nature has likewise not only equipped man himself with nimbleness of thought, but has also given him the senses, to be, as it were, his attendants and messengers; she has laid bare the obscure and none too [obvious][1] meanings of a great many things, to serve as the foundations of knowledge, as we may call them; and she has granted us a bodily form which is convenient and well suited to the human mind. For while she has bent the other creatures down toward their food, she has made man alone erect, and has challenged him to look up toward heaven, as being, so to speak, akin to him, and his first home. . . .

The points which are now being briefly touched upon are certainly important; but out of all the material of the philosophers' discussions, surely there comes nothing more valuable than the full realization that we are born for Justice, and that right is based, not upon men's opinions, but upon Nature. This fact will immediately be plain if you once get a clear conception of man's fellowship and union with his fellow-men. For no single thing is so like another, so exactly its counterpart, as all of us are to one another. Nay, if bad habits and false beliefs did not twist the weaker minds and turn them in whatever direction they are inclined, no one would be so like his own self as all men would be like all others. And so, however we may define man, a single definition will apply to all. This is a sufficient proof that there is no difference in kind between man and man; for if there were, one definition could not be applicable to all men; and indeed reason, which alone raises us above the level of the beasts and enables us to draw inferences, to prove and disprove, to discuss and solve problems, and to come to conclusions, is certainly common to us all, and, though varying in what it learns, at least in the capacity to learn it is invariable.

[1] [Brackets indicate gaps in Cicero's text. The words within brackets are interpolations by editors of Cicero.—Eds.]

For the same things are invariably perceived by the senses, and those things which stimulate the senses stimulate them in the same way in all men; and those rudimentary beginnings of intelligence to which I have referred, which are imprinted on our minds, are imprinted on all minds alike; and speech, the mind's interpreter, though differing in the choice of words, agrees in the sentiments expressed. In fact, there is no human being of any race who, if he finds a guide, cannot attain to virtue.

The similarity of the human race is clearly marked in its evil tendencies as well as in its goodness. For pleasure also attracts all men; and even though it is an enticement to vice, yet it has some likeness to what is naturally good. For it delights us by its lightness and agreeableness; and for this reason, by an error of thought, it is embraced as something wholesome. It is through a similar misconception that we shun death as though it were a dissolution of nature, and cling to life because it keeps us in the sphere in which we were born; and that we look upon pain as one of the greatest of evils, not only because of its cruelty, but also because it seems to lead to the destruction of nature. In the same way, on account of the similarity between moral worth and renown, those who are publicly honoured are considered happy, while those who do not attain fame are thought miserable. Troubles, joys, desires, and fears haunt the minds of all men without distinction, and even if different men have different beliefs, that does not prove, for example, that it is not the same quality of superstition that besets those races which worship dogs and cats as gods, as that which torments other races. But what nation does not love courtesy, kindliness, gratitude, and remembrance of favours bestowed? What people does not hate and despise the haughty, the wicked, the cruel, and the ungrateful? Inasmuch as these considerations prove to us that the whole human race is bound together in unity, it follows, finally, that knowledge of the principles of right living is what makes men better.

The next point, then, is that we are so constituted by Nature as to share the sense of Justice with one another and to pass it on to all men. And in this whole discussion I want it understood that what I shall call Nature is [that which is implanted in us by Nature]; that, however, the corruption caused by bad habits is so great that the sparks of fire, so to speak, which Nature has kindled in us are extinguished by this corruption, and the vices which are their opposites spring up and are established. But if the judgments of men were in agreement with Nature, so that, as the poet says, they considered "nothing alien to them which concerns mankind," then Justice would be equally observed by all. For those creatures who have received the gift of reason from Nature have also received right reason, and therefore they have also received the gift of Law, which is right reason applied to command and prohibition. And if they have received Law, they have received Justice also. Now all men have received reason; therefore all men have received Justice. Consequently Socrates was right when he cursed, as he often did, the man who first separated utility from Justice; for this separation, he complained, is the source of all mischief. . . .

Now all this is to make it more easily understood that Justice is inherent in Nature.

QUINTUS. You certainly need to say very little more on that head, for from what you have already said, Atticus is convinced, and certainly I am, that Nature is the source of Justice.

ATT. How can I help being convinced, when it has just been proved to us, first, that we have been provided and equipped with what we may call the gifts of the gods; next, that there is only one principle by which men may live with one another, and that this is the same for all, and possessed equally by all; and, finally, that all men are bound together by a certain natural feeling of kindliness and good-will, and also by a partnership in Justice? Now that we have admitted the truth of these conclusions, and rightly, I think, how can we separate Law and Justice from Nature? . . .

MAR. But the most foolish notion of all is the belief that everything is just which is found in the customs or laws of nations. Would that be true, even if these laws had been enacted by tyrants? If the well-known Thirty had desired to enact a set of laws at Athens, or if the Athenians without exception were delighted by the tyrants' laws, that would not entitle such laws to be regarded as just, would it? No more, in my opinion, should that law be considered just which a Roman interrex proposed, to the effect that a dictator might put to death with impunity any citizen he wished, even without a trial. For Justice is one; it binds all human society, and is based on one Law, which is right reason applied to command and prohibition. Whoever knows not this Law, whether it has been recorded in writing anywhere or not, is without Justice.

But if Justice is conformity to written laws and national customs, and if, as the same persons claim, everything is to be tested by the standard of utility, then anyone who thinks it will be profitable to him will, if he is able, disregard and violate the laws. It follows that Justice does not exist at all, if it does not exist in Nature, and if that form of it which is based on utility can be overthrown by that very utility itself. And if Nature is not to be considered the foundation of Justice, that will mean the destruction [of the virtues on which human society depends]. For where then will there be a place for generosity, or love of country, or loyalty, or the inclination to be of service to others or to show gratitude for favours received? For these virtues originate in our natural inclination to love our fellow-men, and this is the foundation of Justice. Otherwise not merely consideration for men but also rites and pious observances in honour of the gods are done away with; for I think that these ought to be maintained, not through fear, but on account of the close relationship which exists between man and God. But if the principles of Justice were founded on the decrees of peoples, the edicts of princes, or the decisions of judges, then Justice would sanction robbery and adultery and forgery of wills, in case these acts were approved by the votes or decrees of the populace. But if so great a power belongs to the decisions and decrees of fools that the laws of Nature can be changed by their votes, then why do they not ordain that what is bad and baneful shall be considered good and salutary? Or, if a law can make Justice out of Injustice, can it not also make good out of bad? But in fact we can perceive the difference between good laws and bad by referring them to no other standard than Nature; indeed, it is not merely Justice and Injustice which are distinguished by Nature, but also and without exception things which are honourable and dishonourable. For since an intelligence common to us all makes things known to us and formulates them in our minds, honourable actions are ascribed by us to virtue, and dishonourable actions to vice; and only a madman would conclude that these judgments are matters of opinion, and not fixed by Nature. For even what we, by a misuse of the term, call the virtue of a tree or of a horse, is not a matter of opinion, but is based on Nature. And if that is true, honourable and dishonourable actions must also be distinguished by Nature. For if virtue in general is to be tested by opinion, then its several parts must also be so tested; who, therefore, would judge a man of prudence and, if I may say so, hard common sense, not by his own character but by some external circumstance? For virtue is reason completely developed; and this certainly is natural; therefore everything honourable is likewise natural. For just as truth and falsehood, the logical and illogical, are judged by themselves and not by anything else, so the steadfast and continuous use of reason in the conduct of life, which is virtue, and also inconstancy, which is vice, [are judged] by their own nature.

[Or, when a farmer judges the quality of a tree by nature,] shall we not use the same standard in regard to the characters of young men? Then shall we judge character by Nature, and judge virtue and vice, which result from character, by some other standard? But if we adopt the same standard for them, must we not refer the honourable and the base to Nature also? Whatever good thing is praiseworthy must have within itself something which deserves praise, for goodness itself is good by reason not of opinion but of Nature. For, if this were not true, men would also be happy by reason of opinion; and what statement could be more absurd than that? Wherefore since both good and evil are judged by Nature and are natural principles, surely honourable and base actions must also be distinguished in a similar way and referred to the standard of Nature. But we are confused by the variety of men's beliefs and by their disagreements, and because this same variation is not found in the senses, we think that Nature has made these accurate, and say that those things about which different people have different opinions and the same people not always identical opinions are unreal. However, this is far from being the case. For our senses are not perverted by parent, nurse, teacher, poet, or the stage, nor led astray by popular feeling; but against our minds all sorts of plots are constantly being laid, either by those whom I have just mentioned, who, taking possession of them while still tender and unformed, colour and bend them as they wish, or else by that enemy which lurks deep within us, entwined in our every sense—that counterfeit of good, which is, however, the mother of all evils—pleasure. Corrupted by her allurements, we fail to discern clearly what things are by Nature good, because the same seductiveness and itching does not attend them.

To close now our discussion of this whole subject, the conclusion, which stands clearly before our eyes from what has already been said, is this: Justice and all things honourable are to be sought for their own sake. And indeed all good men love fairness in itself and Justice in itself, and it is unnatural for a good man to make such a mistake as to love what does not deserve love for itself alone. . . .

. . . It is certainly true that, since Law ought to be a reformer of vice and an incentive to virtue, the guiding principles of life may be derived from it. It is therefore true that wisdom is the mother of all good things; and from the Greek expression meaning "the love of wisdom" philosophy has taken its name. And philosophy is the richest, the most bounteous, and the most exalted gift of the immortal gods to humanity. For she alone has taught us, in addition to all other wisdom, that most difficult of all things—to know ourselves. This precept is so important and significant that the credit for it is given, not to any human being, but to the god of Delphi. For he who knows himself will realize, in the first place, that he has a divine element within him, and will think of his own inner nature as a kind of consecrated image of God; and so he will always act and think in a way worthy of so great a gift of the gods, and, when he has examined and thoroughly tested himself, he will understand how nobly equipped by Nature he entered life, and what manifold means he possesses for the attainment and acquisition of wisdom. For from the very first he began to form in his mind and spirit shadowy concepts, as it were, of all sorts, and when these have been illuminated under the guidance of wisdom, he perceives that he will be a good man, and, for that very reason, happy. For when the mind, having attained to a knowledge and perception of the virtues, has abandoned its subservience to the body and its indulgence of it, has put down pleasure as if it were a taint of dishonour, has escaped from all fear of death or pain, has entered into a partnership of love with its own, recognizing as its own all who are joined to it by Nature; when it has taken up the worship of the gods and pure religion, has sharpened the vision both of the eye and of the mind so that they can choose the good and reject the opposite—a virtue which is called prudence because it foresees—then what greater degree of happiness can be described or imagined? And further, when it has examined the heavens, the earth, the seas, the nature of the universe, and understands whence all these things came and whither they must return, when and how they are destined to perish, what part of them is mortal and transient and what is divine and eternal; and when it almost lays hold of the ruler and governor of the universe, and when it realizes that it is not shut in by [narrow] walls as a resident of some fixed spot, but is a citizen of the whole universe, as it were of a single city—then in the midst of this universal grandeur, and with such a view and comprehension of nature, ye immortal gods, how well it will know itself, according to the precept of the Pythian Apollo! . . .

II

MAR. Once more, then, let us look at the character and nature of Law, for fear that, though it must be the standard to which we refer everything, we may now and then be led astray by an incorrect use of terms, and forget the rational principles on which our laws must be based.

I find that it has been the opinion of the wisest men that Law is not a product of human thought, nor is it any enactment of peoples, but something eternal which rules the whole universe by its wisdom in command and prohibition. Thus they have been accustomed to say that Law is the primal and ultimate mind of God, whose reason directs all things either by compulsion or restraint. Wherefore that Law which the gods have given to the human race has been justly praised; for it is the reason and mind of a wise lawgiver applied to command and prohibition.

QUIN. You have touched upon this subject several times before. But please make the character of this heavenly Law clear to us, so that the waves of habit may not carry us away and sweep us into the common mode of speech on such subjects.

MAR. Ever since we were children, Quintus, we have learned to call, "If one summon another to court," and other rules of the same kind, laws. But we must come to the true understanding of the matter, which is as follows: this and other commands and prohibitions of nations have the power to summon to righteousness and away from wrong-doing; but this power is not merely older than the existence of nations and States, it is coeval with that God who guards and rules heaven and earth. For the divine mind cannot exist without reason, and divine reason cannot but have this power to establish right and wrong. . . . For reason did exist, derived from the Nature of the universe, urging men to right conduct and diverting them from wrong-doing, and this reason did not first become Law when it was written down, but when it first came into existence; and it came into existence simultaneously with the divine mind. Wherefore the true and primal Law, applied to command and prohibition, is the right reason of supreme Jupiter.

QUIN. I agree with you, brother, that what is right and true is also eternal, and does not begin or end with written statutes.

MAR. Therefore, just as that divine mind is the supreme Law, so, when [reason] is perfected in man [that also is Law; and this perfected reason exists] in the mind of the wise man; but those rules which, in varying forms and for the need of the moment, have been formulated for the guidance of nations, bear the title of laws rather by favour than because they are really such. For every law which really deserves that name is truly praiseworthy, as they prove by approximately the following arguments. It is agreed, of course, that laws were invented for the safety of citizens, the preservation of States, and the tranquillity and happiness of human life, and that those who first put statutes of this kind in force convinced their people that it was their intention to write down and put into effect such rules as, once accepted and adopted, would make possible for them an honourable and happy life; and when such rules were drawn up and put in force, it is clear that men called them "laws." From this point of view it can be readily understood that those who formulated wicked and unjust statutes for nations, thereby breaking their promises and agreements, put into effect anything but "laws." It may thus be clear that in the very definition of the term "law" there inheres the idea and principle of choosing what is just and true. I ask you then, Quintus, according to the custom of the philosophers: if there is a certain thing, the lack of which in a State compels us to consider it no State at all, must we consider this thing a good?

QUIN. One of the greatest goods, certainly.

MAR. And if a State lacks Law, must it for that reason be considered no State at all?

QUIN. It cannot be denied.

MAR. Then Law must necessarily be considered one of the greatest goods.

QUIN. I agree with you entirely.

MAR. What of the many deadly, the many pestilential statutes which nations put in force? These no more deserve to be called laws than the rules a band of robbers might pass in their assembly. For if ignorant and unskilful men have prescribed deadly poisons instead of healing drugs, these cannot possibly be called physicians' prescriptions; neither in a nation can a statute of any sort be called a law, even though the nation, in spite of its being a ruinous regulation, has accepted it. Therefore Law is the distinction between things just and unjust, made in agreement with that primal and most ancient of all things, Nature; and in conformity to Nature's standard are framed those human laws which inflict punishment upon the wicked but defend and protect the good.

Questions

1. State in your own words the relation between God, man, and Nature which Marcus (Cicero) expounds in the first part of the reading. What reasons does Marcus give in support of his views?

2. What is the relation between Nature and Justice, according to Cicero? What is meant by the terms "Nature" and "Justice"?

3. What is Cicero's argument that a law cannot make Justice out of Injustice? Examine the grounds of his argument and state your reasons for accepting or rejecting it.

4. Does the fact that men disagree about what is good and evil disprove Cicero's views on Justice? Why or why not? In your answer take into consideration what Marcus (Cicero) says about such disagreements.

5. How does one tell, according to Cicero, whether the laws of a state conform to the Law of Nature?

6. Construct a reply which Cicero would be likely to give to the following argument by John Stuart Mill, and then state why you believe the reply you have constructed does, or does not, successfully answer Mill's criticism.

It has never been settled by any accredited doctrine, what particular departments of the order of nature shall be reputed to be designed for our moral instruction and guidance; and accordingly each person's individual predilections, or momentary convenience, have decided to what parts of the divine government the practical conclusions that he was desirous of establishing should be recommended to approval as being analogous. One such recommendation must be as fallacious as another, for it is impossible to decide that certain of the Creator's works are more truly expressions of his character than the rest; and the only selection that does not lead to immoral results is the selection of those which most conduce to the general good, in other words, of those which point to an end, which if the entire scheme is the expression of a single omnipotent and consistent will, is evidently not the end intended by it.[1]

2

Civil Government	John Locke
	(1632-1704)

[A general introductory note on Locke may be found on page 70.]

In his *Second Treatise on Civil Government,* which he titled, "An Essay Concerning the True Original, Extent and End of Civil Government," Locke attempts to understand the nature and grounds of political authority. In the following reading, which is taken from this *Treatise,* Locke is concerned with two questions. He wants to know what the concept of a state, or political society, means, and he wants to determine the grounds on which political authority can be justified. Both questions he endeavors to answer by contrasting the essential conditions of human life in political societies with what can be supposed to be the essential conditions of human life outside of political societies, or, as Locke puts it, in the state of nature. After setting forth the essential conditions of human life in the state of nature, Locke analyzes the concept of political society in terms of a hypothetical "original compact," an act whereby a group of men terminate their existence in the state of nature and form a political community. The account of the original compact is not intended to be a description of an actual historical event, but is rather a way of elucidating concretely the concept of a political society. It also serves as the basis of political authority, since the compact entails an obligation or duty on the part of a citizen to obey the law.

Locke continues his study of the grounds of political authority by

[1] John Stuart Mill, "Nature," in *Three Essays on Religion,* many publishers, many editions.

asking: What is the end (or purpose) of government? Although he attempts to answer this by stating the purposes for which men would leave the state of nature and form a political society, this again is not intended to be a historical account of the purposes men had in mind when they originally instituted their governments on earth. Locke is writing an essay in philosophy, not in history or anthropology. In the last section of the reading, Locke considers the conditions under which it is right to dissolve a government, that is, to have political authority taken away from a legislature or a ruler and given to the citizens. This kind of dissolution is not to be confused with the dissolution of a whole political society, where the citizens terminate their political association and revert to the state of nature. The reading ends with the concluding paragraphs of Locke's *Treatise*, where he discusses the obligations of the ruler to the ruled and the grounds on which these obligations rest.

The reading is from Chapters II, VIII, IX, and XIX of the *Second Treatise on Civil Government*, first published in 1690. Locke's own chapter titles are used.

OF THE STATE OF NATURE

To understand political power aright, and derive it from its original, we must consider, what state all men are naturally in, and that is, a state of perfect freedom to order their actions, and dispose of their possessions and persons, as they think fit, within the bounds of the law of nature, without asking leave, or depending upon the will of any other man.

A state also of equality, wherein all the power and jurisdiction is reciprocal, no one having more than another; there being nothing more evident, than that creatures of the same species and rank, promiscuously born to all the same advantages of nature, and the use of the same faculties, should also be equal one amongst another without subordination or subjection, unless the lord and master of them all should, by any manifest declaration of his will, set one above another, and confer on him, by an evident and clear appointment, an undoubted right to dominion and sovereignty.

This equality of men by nature, the judicious Hooker [1] looks upon as so evident in itself, and beyond all question, that he makes it the foundation of that obligation to mutual love amongst men, on which he builds the duties they owe one another, and from whence he derives the great maxims of justice and charity. His words are:

"The like natural inducement hath brought men to know that it is no less their duty, to love others than themselves; for seeing those things which are

[1] [Richard Hooker (1553-1600), English theologian and author of *Ecclesiastical Polity.*—Eds.]

equal, must needs all have one measure; if I cannot but wish to receive good, even as much at every man's hands, as any man can wish unto his own soul, how should I look to have any part of my desire herein satisfied, unless myself be careful to satisfy the like desire, which is undoubtedly in other men. We all being of one and the same nature; to have any thing offered them repugnant to this desire, must needs in all respects grieve them as much as me; so that if I do harm, I must look to suffer, there being no reason that others should shew greater measure of love to me, than they have by me shewed unto them; my desire therefore to be loved of my equals in nature, as much as possible may be, imposeth upon me a natural duty of bearing toward them fully the like affection; from which relation of equality between ourselves and them that are as ourselves, what several rules and canons natural reason hath drawn, for direction of life, no man is ignorant." *Eccl. Pol.*, lib. i.

But though this be a state of liberty, yet it is not a state of licence: though man in that state have an uncontrollable liberty to dispose of his person or possessions, yet he has not liberty to destroy himself, or so much as any creature in his possession, but where some nobler use than its bare preservation calls for it. The state of nature has a law of nature to govern it, which obliges every one, and reason, which is that law, teaches all mankind, who will but consult it, that being all equal and independent, no one ought to harm another in his life, health, liberty, or possessions: for men being all the workmanship of one omnipotent, and infinitely wise maker; all the servants of one sovereign master, sent into the world by his order, and about his business; they are his property, whose workmanship they are, made to last during his, not one another's pleasure: and being furnished with like faculties, sharing all in one community of nature, there cannot be supposed any such subordination among us, that may authorize us to destroy one another, as if we were made for one another's uses, as the inferior ranks of creatures are for ours. Every one, as he is bound to preserve himself, and not to quit his station wilfully, so by the like reason, when his own preservation comes not in competition, ought he as much as he can to preserve the rest of mankind, and not unless it be to do justice on an offender, take away, or impair the life, or what tends to the preservation of the life, the liberty, health, limb or goods of another.

And that all men may be restrained from invading others rights, and from doing hurt to one another, and the law of nature be observed, which willeth the peace and preservation of all mankind, the execution of the law of nature is, in that state, put into every man's hands, whereby every one has a right to punish the transgressors of that law to such a degree, as may hinder its violation. For the law of nature would, as all other laws that concern men in this world, be in vain, if there were nobody that in the state of nature had a power to execute that law, and thereby preserve the innocent and restrain offenders. And if any one in the state of nature may punish another for any evil he has done, every one may do so: for in that state of perfect equality where naturally there is no superiority or jurisdiction of one over another, what any may do in prosecution of that law, every one must needs have a right to do.

And thus, in the state of nature, one man comes by a power over another; but yet no absolute or arbitrary power, to use a criminal, when he has got him in his hands, according to the passionate heats, or boundless extravagancy of his own will; but only to retribute to him, so far as calm reason and conscience dictates, what is proportionate to his transgression, which is so much as may serve for reparation and restraint: for these two are the only reasons why one man may lawfully do harm to another, which is that we call punishment. In transgressing the law of nature, the offender declares himself to live by another rule than that of reason and common equity, which is that measure God has set to the actions of men for their mutual security, and so he becomes dangerous to mankind, the tie, which is to secure them from injury and violence, being slighted and broken by him, which being a trespass against the whole species, and the peace and safety of it, provided for by the law of nature, every man upon this score, by the right he hath to preserve mankind in general, may restrain, or where it is necessary, destroy things noxious to them, and so may bring such evil on any one, who hath transgressed that law, as may make him repent the doing of it, and thereby deter him, and, by his example others, from doing the like mischief. And in this case, and upon this ground, every man hath a right to punish the offender, and be executioner of the law of nature.

I doubt not but this will seem a very strange doctrine to some men; but before they condemn it, I desire them to resolve me, by what right any prince or state can put to death, or punish an alien, for any crime he commits in their country. 'Tis certain their laws, by virtue of any sanction they receive from the promulgated will of the legislative, reach not a stranger: they speak not to him, nor, if they did, is he bound to hearken to them. The legislative authority, by which they are in force over the subjects of that commonwealth, hath no power over him. Those who have the supreme power of making laws in England, France or Holland, are to an Indian, but like the rest of the world, men without authority: and therefore, if by the law of nature every man hath not a power to punish offences against it, as he soberly judges the case to require, I see not how the magistrates of any community can punish an alien of another country; since, in reference to him, they can have no more power than what every man naturally may have over another. . . .

OF THE BEGINNING OF POLITICAL SOCIETIES

Men being, as has been said, by nature all free, equal, and independent, no one can be put out of his estate and subjected to the political power of another without his own consent, which is done by agreeing with other men, to join and unite into a community for their comfortable, safe, and peaceable living, one amongst another, in a secure enjoyment of their properties, and a greater security against any that are not of it. This any number of men may do, because it injures not the freedom of the rest; they are left, as they were, in the liberty of the state of nature. When any number of men have so consented to make one community or government, they are thereby presently incorporated, and make one body politic, wherein the majority have a right to act and conclude the rest.

For, when any number of men have, by the consent of every individual, made a community, they have thereby made that community one body, with a power to act as one body, which is only by the will and determination of the majority. For that which acts any community, being only the consent of the individuals of it, and it being one body, must move one way, it is necessary the body should move that way whither the greater force carries it, which is the consent of the majority, or else it is impossible it should act or continue one body, one community, which the consent of every individual that united into it agreed that it should; and so everyone is bound by that consent to be concluded by the majority. And therefore we see that in assemblies empowered to act by positive laws where no number is set by that positive law which empowers them, the act of the majority passes for the act of the whole, and of course determines as having, by the law of nature and reason, the power of the whole.

And thus every man, by consenting with others to make one body politic under one government, puts himself under an obligation to everyone of that society to submit to the determination of the majority, and to be concluded by it; or else this original compact, whereby he with others incorporates into one society, would signify nothing, and be no compact if he be left free and under no other ties than he was in before in the state of nature. For what appearance would there be of any compact? What new engagement if he were no farther tied by any decrees of the society than he himself thought fit and did actually consent to? This would be still as great a liberty as he himself had before his compact, or anyone else in the state of nature hath, who may submit himself and consent to any acts of it if he thinks fit.

For if the consent of the majority shall not in reason be received as the act of the whole, and conclude every individual, nothing but the consent of every individual can make any thing to be the act of the whole, which, considering the infirmities of health and avocations of business, which in a number though much less than that of a commonwealth, will necessarily keep many away from the public assembly; and the variety of opinions and contrariety of interests which unavoidably happen in all collections of men, 'tis next impossible ever to be had. And, therefore, if coming into society be upon such terms, it will be only like Cato's coming into the theatre, *tantum ut exiret*. Such a constitution as this would make the mighty *Leviathan* of a shorter duration than the feeblest creatures, and not let it outlast the day it was born in, which cannot be supposed till we can think that rational creatures should desire and constitute societies only to be dissolved. For where the majority cannot conclude the rest, there they cannot act as one body, and consequently will be immediately dissolved again.

Whosoever, therefore, out of a state of nature unite into a community, must be understood to give up all the power necessary to the ends for which they unite into society to the majority of the community, unless they expressly agreed in any number greater than the majority. And this is done by barely agreeing to unite into one political society, which is all the compact that is, or needs be, between the individuals that enter into or make up a commonwealth. And thus, that which begins and actually constitutes any political society is nothing but the consent of any number of freemen capable of a majority, to unite and incorporate into such a society. And this is that, and that only, which did or could give beginning to any lawful government in the world. . . .

OF THE ENDS OF POLITICAL SOCIETY AND GOVERNMENT

If man in the state of nature be so free as has been said, if he be absolute lord of his own person and possessions, equal to the greatest and subject to no body, why will he part with his freedom? Why will he give up this empire, and subject himself to the dominion and control of any other power? To which 'tis obvious to answer, that though in the state of nature he hath such a right, yet the enjoyment of it is very uncertain and constantly exposed to the invasion of others; for all being kings as much as he, every man his equal, and the greater part no strict observers of equity and justice, the enjoyment of the property he has in this state is very unsafe, very unsecure. This makes him willing to quit this condition which, however free, is full of fears and continual dangers; and 'tis not without reason that he seeks out and is willing to join in society with others who are already united, or have a mind to unite for the mutual preservation of their lives, liberties, and estates, which I call by the general name, property.

The great and chief end, therefore, of men's uniting into commonwealths, and putting themselves under government, is the preservation of their property; to which in the state of nature there are many things wanting.

First, There wants an established, settled, known law, received and allowed by common consent to be the standard of right and wrong, and the common measure to decide all controversies between them. For though the law of nature be plain and intelligible to all rational creatures, yet men, being biased by their interest, as well as ignorant for want of study of it, are not apt to allow of it as a law binding to them in the application of it to their particular cases.

Secondly, In the state of nature there wants a known and indifferent judge, with authority to determine all differences according to the established law. For everyone in that state being both judge and executioner of the law of nature, men being partial to themselves, passion and revenge is very apt to carry them too far, and with too much heat in their own cases, as well as negligence and unconcernedness, make them too remiss in other men's.

Thirdly, In the state of nature there often wants power to back and support the sentence when right, and to give it due execution. They, who by any injustice offended, will seldom fail where they are able by force to make good their injustice. Such resistance many times makes the punishment dangerous, and frequently destructive to those who attempt it.

Thus mankind, notwithstanding all the privileges of the state of nature, being but in an ill condition while they remain in it, are quickly driven into society. Hence it comes to pass, that we seldom find any number of men live any time together in this state. The inconveniences that they are therein exposed to by the irregular and uncertain exercise of the power every man has of punishing the transgressions of others, make them take sanctuary under the established laws of government, and therein seek the preservation of their property. 'Tis this makes them so willingly give up every one his single power of punishing to be exercised by such alone as shall be appointed to it amongst them, and by such rules as the community, or those authorized by them to that purpose, shall agree on. And in this we have the original right and rise of both the legislative and executive power as well as of the governments and societies themselves.

For in the state of Nature to omit the liberty he has of innocent delights, a man has two powers.

The first is to do whatsoever he thinks fit for the preservation of himself and others within the permission of the law of nature; by which law, common to them all, he and all the rest of mankind are one community, make up one society distinct from all other creatures; and were it not for the corruption and viciousness of degenerate men, there would be no need of any other, no necessity that men should separate from this great and natural community, and associate into less combinations.

The other power a man has in the state of nature is the power to punish the crimes committed against that law. Both these he gives up when he joins in a private, if I may so call it, or particular political society, and incorporates into any commonwealth separate from the rest of mankind.

The *first* power, *viz.* of doing whatsoever he thought fit for the preservation of himself and the rest of mankind, he gives up to be regulated by laws made by the society, so far forth as the preservation of himself and the rest of that society shall require; which laws of the society in many things confine the liberty he had by the law of nature.

Secondly, The power of punishing he wholly gives up, and engages his natural force (which he might before employ in the execution of the law of nature, by his own single authority, as he thought fit) to assist the executive power of the society as the law thereof shall require. For being now in a new state, wherein he is to enjoy many conveniences from the labour, assistance, and society of others in the same community, as well as protection from its whole strength, he is to part also with as much of his natural liberty, in providing for himself, as the good, prosperity, and safety of the society shall require, which is not only necessary but just, since the other members of the society do the like.

But though men when they enter into society give up the equality, liberty, and executive power they had in the state of nature into the hands of the society, to be so far disposed of by the legislative as the good of the society shall require, yet it being only with an intention in everyone the better to preserve himself, his liberty and property (for no rational creature can be supposed to change his condition with an intention to be worse), the power of the society or legislative constituted by them can never be supposed to extend farther than the common good, but is obliged to secure everyone's property by providing against those three defects above-mentioned that made the state of nature so unsafe and uneasy. And so, whoever has the legislative or supreme power of any commonwealth, is bound to govern by established standing laws, promulgated and known to the people, and not by extemporary decrees, by indifferent and upright judges, who are to decide controversies by those laws; and to employ the force of the community at home only in the execution of such laws, or abroad to prevent or redress foreign injuries and secure the community from inroads and invasion. And all this to be directed to no other end but the peace, safety, and public good of the people. . . .

OF THE DISSOLUTION OF GOVERNMENT

He that will with any clearness speak of the dissolution of government, ought in the first place to distinguish between the dissolution of the society and the dissolution of the government. That which makes the community, and brings men out of the loose state of nature into one politic society, is the agreement which every one has with the rest to incorporate and act as one body, and so be one distinct commonwealth. The usual, and almost only way whereby this union is dissolved, is the inroad of foreign force making a conquest upon them. For in that case (not being able to maintain and support themselves as one entire and independent body) the union belonging to that body which consisted therein, must necessarily cease, and so every one return to the state he was in before, with a liberty to shift for himself and provide for his own safety, as he thinks fit, in some other society. Whenever the society is dissolved, 'tis certain the government of that society cannot remain. Thus conquerors' swords often cut up governments by the roots, and mangle societies to pieces, separating the subdued or scattered multitude from the protection of and dependence on that society which ought to have preserved them from violence. The world is too well instructed in, and too forward to allow of this way of dissolving of governments, to need any more to be said of it; and there wants not much argument to prove that where the society is dissolved, the government cannot remain; that being as impossible as for the frame of an house to subsist when the materials of it are scattered and dissipated by a whirlwind, or jumbled into a confused heap by an earthquake.

Besides this overturning from without, governments are dissolved from within,

First, When the legislative is altered, civil society being a state of peace amongst those who are of it, from whom the state of war is excluded by the umpirage which they have provided in their legislative for the ending all differences that may arise amongst any of them. 'Tis in their legislative that the members of a commonwealth are united and combined together into one coherent living body. This is the soul that gives form, life, and unity to the commonwealth. From hence the several members have their mutual influence, sympathy, and connexion. And therefore when the legislative is broken, or dissolved, dissolution and death follow. For the essence and union of the society consisting in having one will, the legislative, when once established by the majority, has the declaring and, as it were, keeping of that will. The constitution of the legislative is the first and fundamental act of society, whereby provision is made for the continuation of their union under the direction of persons and bonds of laws, made by persons authorized thereunto, by the consent and appointment of the people, without which no one man, or number of men, amongst them can have authority of making laws that shall be binding to the rest. When any one, or more, shall take upon them to make laws whom the people have not appointed so to do, they make laws without authority, which the people are not therefore bound to obey; by which means they come again to be out of subjection, and may constitute to themselves a new legislative, as they think best, being in full liberty to resist the force of those who, without authority, would impose any thing upon them. Every one is at the disposure of his own will, when those who had, by the delegation of the society, the declaring of the public will, are excluded from it, and others usurp the place who have no such authority or delegation. . . .

There is secondly another way whereby governments are dissolved, and that is, when the legislative, or the prince, either of them act contrary to their trust.

The legislative acts against the trust reposed in them when they endeavour to invade the property of the subject, and to make themselves, or any part of the community, masters or arbitrary disposers of the lives, liberties, or fortunes of the people.

The reason why men enter into society is the preservation of their property; and the end why they choose and authorize a legislative is that there may be laws made, and rules set, as guards and fences to the properties of all the members of the society, to limit the power and moderate the dominion of every part and member of the society. For since it can never be supposed to be the will of the society that the legislative should have a power to destroy that which every one designs to secure by entering into society, and for which the people submitted themselves to legislators of their own making: whenever the legislators endeavour to take away and destroy the property of the people, or to reduce them to slavery under arbitrary power, they put themselves into a state of war with the people, who are thereupon absolved from any farther obedience, and are left to the common refuge which God hath provided for all men against force and violence. Whensoever therefore the legislative shall transgress this fundamental rule of society, and either by ambition, fear, folly, or corruption, endeavour to grasp themselves, or put into the hands of any other, an absolute power over the lives, liberties, and estates of the people, by this breach of trust they forfeit the power the people had put into their hands for quite contrary ends, and it devolves to the people; who have a right to resume their original liberty, and by the establishment of a new legislative (such as they shall think fit), provide for their own safety and security, which is the end for which they are in society. What I have said here concerning the legislative in general holds true also concerning the supreme executor, who having a double trust put in him, both to have a part in the legislative and the supreme execution of the law, acts against both, when he goes about to set up his own arbitrary will as the law of the society. . . .

Here 'tis like the common question will be made, Who shall be judge whether the prince or legislative act contrary to their trust? This, perhaps, ill-affected and factious men may spread amongst the people, when the prince only makes use of his due prerogative. To this I reply, The people shall be judge; for who shall be judge whether his trustee or deputy acts well and according to the trust reposed in him, but he who deputes him and must, by having deputed him, have still a power to discard him when he fails in his trust? If this be reasonable in particular cases of private men, why should it be otherwise in that of the greatest moment, where the welfare of millions is concerned and also where the evil, if not prevented, is greater, and the redress very difficult, dear, and dangerous?

But, farther, this question (Who shall be judge?) cannot mean that there is no judge at all. For where there is no judicature on earth to decide controversies amongst men, God in heaven is judge. He alone, 'tis true, is judge of the right. But every man is judge for himself, as in all other cases so in this, whether another hath put himself into a state of war with him, and whether he should appeal to the supreme Judge, as *Jephtha* did.

If a controversy arise betwixt a prince and some of the people in a matter where the law is silent or doubtful, and the thing be of great consequence, I should think the proper umpire, in such a case, should be the body of the people. For in such cases where the prince hath a trust reposed in him, and is dispensed from the common, ordinary rules of the law; there, if any men find themselves aggrieved, and think the prince acts contrary to, or beyond that trust, who so proper to judge as the body of the people (who at first lodged that trust in him) how far they meant it should extend? But if the prince, or whoever they be in the administration, decline that way of determination, the appeal then lies nowhere but to Heaven. Force between either persons who have no known superior on earth, or which permits no appeal to a judge on earth, being properly a state of war, wherein the appeal lies only to Heaven; and in that state the injured party must judge for himself when he will think fit to make use of that appeal and put himself upon it.

To conclude, The power that every individual gave the society when he entered into it, can never revert to the individuals again, as long as the society lasts, but will always remain in the community; because without this there can be no community, no commonwealth, which is contrary to the original agreement; so also when the society hath placed the legislative in any assembly of men, to continue in them and their successors, with direction and authority for providing such successors, the legislative can never revert to the people whilst that government lasts; because, having provided a legislative with power to continue for ever, they have given up their political power to the legislative, and cannot resume it. But if they have set limits to the duration of their legislative, and made this supreme power in any person or assembly only temporary; or else when, by the miscarriages of those in authority, it is forfeited; upon the forfeiture of their rulers, or at the determination of the time set, it reverts to the society, and the people have a right to act as supreme, and continue the legislative in themselves or place it in a new form, or new hands, as they think good.

Questions

1. The state of nature, according to Locke, is a state of freedom and of equality. What do "freedom" and "equality" mean in this context? How does their meaning differ from the kind of freedom and equality which would be realized in an ideally democratic political society?

2. Even in the state of nature men have obligations to one another, according to Locke. On what are these obligations based? Since there are no civil laws in the state of nature, does Locke mean that there is a moral law higher than, and independent of, civil law? Defend your answer by reference to the text.

3. What similarities and what differences do you find between Locke's view of the relation of the state of nature to political society and Cicero's view of the relation of the Law of Nature to the laws of states? (For Cicero's view, see the selection beginning on page 604.)

4. What is Locke's argument concerning majority rule? From Locke's point of view, would it ever be right for a government to oppose the will of the majority? In your answer, consider a case in which a majority wanted to take away the property of a minority.

5. "If man in the state of nature be so free as has been said, if he be absolute lord of his own person and possessions, equal to the greatest and subject to no body, why will he part with his freedom?" In your own words, what is Locke's answer?

6. What does Locke mean by "property"? What is his argument to show that the chief end of government is the preservation of property?

7. How does Locke answer the challenge of the despot: that he who is in supreme power has the authority to rule and no one else has a right to place a limitation on his rule? Would a benevolent despot (i.e., one who always ruled for the public good) have legitimate authority to rule, according to Locke?

8. Explain the distinction between dissolving a government and dissolving a political society. Show why this is, or is not, the same as dissolving a political association from without and dissolving it from within.

9. In Locke's theory of government, what are the obligations of a ruler (whether legislative or executive) to the ruled? Do the ruled have any obligations to the ruler? To one another? In your answer state the *grounds* of these political obligations.

10. What is the role of "the appeal to Heaven" in Locke's political philosophy? Does his use of this concept mean that if a just God does not exist, there is no basis for political obligation? Why or why not?

3

The Social Contract

Jean Jacques Rousseau

(1712-1778)

Jean Jacques Rousseau was born of French parents in Geneva. He was given little formal education, but he traveled widely, read much, and was acquainted with many of the intellectual leaders of his time, including David Hume and Denis Diderot. His chief works are *On the Origin of Inequality Among Men* (1755); *The Social Contract* (1762); *Emile* (1762); and *Confessions* (published posthumously).

The idea of a social contract, that is, a voluntary agreement among men to obey certain rules or keep certain promises, has been used by political philosophers for a number of different purposes. The English philosopher, Thomas Hobbes (1588-1679), used the idea to explain the origin of states. This view was criticized by David Hume in an essay, "Of the Original Contract" (1748), in which Hume pointed out that history shows the origin of most states to be a matter of conquest or violent revolution, a new rule being imposed on people by force. In the seventeenth century, John Locke used the idea of an "original compact" to elucidate the concept of a political society and to determine the grounds of legitimate political authority. (See the selection by Locke in this chapter, beginning on page 613.) Rousseau uses the idea of a social contract to provide a foundation for legitimate authority, and also to construct an ideal political community.

As a first step in the study of Rousseau, the reader must be clear about the terms of the social contract, that is, about what people promise one another when they make the contract. Next, the reader should notice carefully how Rousseau uses the words "Sovereign" and "general will," and especially how he distinguishes the will of the majority and the will of all from the general will. Once these concepts are grasped, the main arguments of Rousseau's political philosophy are easier to follow.

It should be noted that the moral philosophy of Immanuel Kant (Chapter 6, page 533) is a development of Rousseau's political philosophy. Some help in understanding Rousseau's doctrine of the general will may be gained by considering the place of the categorical imperative in Kant's moral philosophy.

Rousseau's *Social Contract* was first published in 1762. This selection is drawn from all four books of that work and aims at giving a complete account of the way in which Rousseau believes the ideal political community must be organized. The translation from the French is the work of an anonymous translator, published in London in 1791. It has been revised and edited by Professor Charles Frankel. Rousseau's chapter titles are used.

From *The Social Contract,* by Jean Jacques Rousseau, Hafner Library of Classics, Hafner Publishing Co., N. Y. Reprinted by permission of the publisher.

My design in this treatise is to enquire whether, taking men such as they are, and laws such as they may be made, it is not possible to establish some just and certain rule for the administration of the civil order. In the course of my research I shall endeavour to unite what right permits with what interest prescribes, that justice and utility may not be separated. . . .

Man is born free, and yet we see him everywhere in chains. Those who believe themselves the masters of others cease not to be even greater slaves than the people they govern. How this happens I am ignorant; but, if I am asked what renders it justifiable, I believe it may be in my power to resolve the question.

If I were only to consider force, and the effects of it, I should say, "When a people is constrained to obey, and does obey, it does well; but as soon as it can throw off its yoke, and does throw it off, it does better: for a people may certainly use, for the recovery of their liberty, the same right that was employed to deprive them of it: it was either justifiably recovered, or unjustifiably torn from them." But the social order is a sacred right which serves for the basis of all others. Yet this right comes not from nature; it is therefore founded on conventions. The question is, what those conventions are. . . .

OF THE RIGHT OF THE STRONGEST

The strongest are still never sufficiently strong to ensure them continual mastership, unless they find means of transforming force into right, and obedience into duty. Hence the right of the strongest—a right which seems ironical in appearance, but is really established as a principle. But shall we never have an explanation of this term? Force is a physical power; I do not see what morality can result from its effects. To yield to force is an act of necessity, not of inclination; or it is at best only an act of prudence. In what sense then can it be a duty?

Let us suppose for a moment the existence of this pretended right. I see nothing that can arise from it but inexplicable nonsense. For, if we admit that force constitutes right, the effect changes with the cause: all force which overcomes the first succeeds to its right. As soon as men can disobey with impunity, they can do so justifiably; and because the strongest is always in the right, strength is the only thing men should seek to acquire. But what sort of right is that which perishes with the force that gave it existence? If it is necessary to obey by force, there can be no occasion to obey from duty; and when force is no more, all obligation ceases with it. We see, therefore, that this word "right" adds nothing to force, but is indeed an unmeaning term.

If in saying, "Let us obey the powerful," they mean to say, "Let us yield to force," the precept is good, but it is superfluous, for it never is or can be violated. All power, we are told, comes from God. I grant it does; but all diseases likewise come from the same hand, and yet who ever forbade us to call in a physician? If a robber surprises me in a corner of a wood, is it necessary that I should not only give him my purse when forced to do so, but am I in conscience obliged to give it to him, though I should be in a position to escape? For the fact is, the pistol which he holds is also a power.

We must grant, therefore, that force does not constitute right, and that obedience is only due to legitimate powers. Thus everything goes back to my first question.

THAT WE MUST ALWAYS GO BACK TO A FIRST CONVENTION

Had I granted all which I have refuted, the favourers of despotism would not have found their cause advanced by it. There will always be a great difference between subduing a multitude and governing a society. When unorganized men are successively subjugated by one individual, whatever number there may be of them, they appear to me only as a master and slaves; I cannot regard them as a people and their chief; they are, if you please, an *aggregation,* but they are not as yet an *association;* for there is neither public property, nor a political body, among them. A man may have enslaved half the world, and yet continue only a private individual; his interest is separate from that of others, and confined to himself alone. When such a man falls, his empire remains unconnected and without any bond of union, as an oak dissolves and becomes a mass of ashes when consumed by fire.

"A people," says Grotius,[1] "can give themselves to a king." According to Grotius, then, they are a people before they give themselves to a king. The donation itself is a civil act, and supposes a public consultation. It would therefore be better before we examine the act by which they elected a king, to enquire into that by which they became a people; for that act, being necessarily anterior to the other, is the true foundation of society.

[1] [Hugo Groot (Grotius, 1583-1645), Dutch political philosopher and author of *De Jure Belli et Pacis* (*Concerning the Right of War and Peace*).—Eds.]

In fact, if there was no prior convention, where would be—unless the election was unanimous—the obligation which should bind the minority to submit to the choice of the majority? And whence would a hundred men, who wish to submit to a master, derive the right of binding by their votes ten other men who were not disposed to acknowledge any chief? The law which gives the majority of votes the power of deciding for the whole body can only be established by a convention, and proves that there must have been unanimity at one time at least.

OF THE SOCIAL COMPACT

I will suppose that men in the state of nature are arrived at that crisis when the strength of each individual is insufficient to overcome the resistance of the obstacles to his preservation. This primitive state can therefore subsist no longer; and the human race would perish unless it changed its manner of life.

As men cannot create for themselves new forces, but merely unite and direct those which already exist, the only means they can employ for their preservation is to form by aggregation an assemblage of forces that may be able to overcome the resistance, to be put in motion as one body, and to act in concert.

This assemblage of forces must be produced by the concurrence of many; but as the force and the liberty of each man are the chief instruments of his preservation, how can he engage them elsewhere without danger to himself, and without neglecting the care which is due himself? This difficulty, which leads directly to my subject, may be expressed in these words:

"Where shall we find a form of association which will defend and protect with the whole common force the person and the property of each associate, and by which every person, while uniting himself with all, shall obey only himself and remain as free as before?" Such is the fundamental problem of which the Social Contract gives the solution.

The articles of this contract are so unalterably fixed by the nature of the act that the least modification renders them vain and of no effect; so that they are the same everywhere, and are everywhere tacitly understood and admitted, even though they may never have been formally announced; until, the social compact being violated, each individual is restored to his original rights, and resumes his native liberty, while losing the conventional liberty for which he renounced it.

The articles of the social contract will, when clearly understood, be found reducible to this single point: the total alienation of each associate, and all his rights, to the whole community; for, in the first place, as every individual gives himself up entirely, the condition of every person is alike; and being so, it would not be to the interest of any one to render that condition offensive to others.

Nay, more than this, the alienation being made without any reserve, the union is as complete as it can be, and no associate has any further claim to anything: for if any individual retained rights not enjoyed in general by all, as there would be no common superior to decide between him and the public, each person being in some points his own judge, would soon pretend to be so in everything; and thus would the state of nature be continued and the association necessarily become tyrannical or be annihilated.

Finally, each person gives himself to all, and so not to any one individual; and as there is no one associate over whom the same right is not acquired which is ceded to him by others, each gains an equivalent for what he loses, and finds his force increased for preserving that which he possesses.

If, therefore, we exclude from the social compact all that is not essential, we shall find it reduced to the following terms:

Each of us places in common his person and all his power under the supreme direction of the general will; and as one body we all receive each member as an indivisible part of the whole.

From that moment, instead of as many separate persons as there are contracting parties, this act of association produces a moral and collective body, composed of as many members as there are votes in the assembly, which from this act receives its unity, its common self, its life, and its will. This public person, which is thus formed by the union of all other persons, took formerly the name of "city," [2] and now takes that of "republic" or "body politic." It is called by its members "State" when it is passive, "Sovereign" when in activity, and, whenever it is compared with other bodies of a similar kind, it is denominated "power." The associates take collectively the name of "people," and separately, that of "citizens," as participating in the sovereign authority, and of "subjects," because they are subjected to the laws of the State. But these terms are frequently confounded and used one for the other; and it is enough that a man understands how to distinguish them when they are employed in all their precision.

OF THE SOVEREIGN

It appears from this formula that the act of association contains a reciprocal engagement between the public and individuals, and that each individual, contracting, as it were, with himself, is engaged under a double character; that is, as a member of the Sovereign engaging with individuals, and as a member of the State engaged with the Sovereign. But we cannot apply here the maxim of

---

[2] The true sense of this word is almost entirely lost among the moderns: the name of "city" is now generally used to signify a town, and that of "citizen" applied to a burgess. Men do not seem to know that *houses* make a "town," but that *citizens* make a "city." The Carthaginians once paid dearly for a mistake of this kind. I have never seen it mentioned that the title of *cives* was ever given to the subjects of any prince, not even to the Macedonians formerly, or to the English at present, although they are nearer liberty than any other people. The French alone use the name of "citizen" familiarly to all, because they have no true idea of it, as appears from their dictionaries; and without knowing its meaning they are in danger of falling into the crime of lèse majesté, by usurping a title to which they have no just claim. . . .

civil right, that no person is bound by any engagement which he makes with himself; for there is a material difference between an obligation to oneself individually, and an obligation to a collective body of which oneself constitutes a part.

It is necessary to observe here that public deliberation, which can bind all the subjects to the Sovereign, in consequence of the double character under which the members of that body appear, cannot, for the opposite reason, bind the Sovereign to itself; and consequently that it is against the nature of the body politic for the sovereign power to impose on itself any law which it cannot break. Being able to consider itself as acting under one character only, it is in the situation of an individual forming a contract with himself; and we see therefore that there neither is nor can be any kind of fundamental law obligatory for the body of the people, not even the social contract itself. But this does not mean that this body could not very well engage itself to others in any manner which would not derogate from the contract; for, with respect to what is external to it, it becomes a simple being, an individual. But the body politic, or the Sovereign, which derives its existence from the sacredness of the contract, can never bind itself, even towards outsiders, in anything that would derogate from the original act, such as alienating any portion of itself, or submitting to another Sovereign. To violate the contract by which it exists would be to annihilate itself; and that which is nothing can produce nothing.

As soon as this multitude is united in one body, you cannot offend one of its members without attacking the body; much less can you offend the body without incurring the resentment of all the members. Thus duty and interest equally oblige the two contracting parties to lend aid to each other; and the same men must endeavour to unite under this double character all the advantages which attend it.

Further, the Sovereign, being formed only of the individuals who compose it, neither has, nor can have, any interest contrary to theirs; consequently, the sovereign power need give no guarantee to its subjects, because it is impossible that the body should seek to injure all its members; and we shall see presently that it can do no injury to any individual in particular. The Sovereign, by its nature, is always everything it ought to be.

But this is not so with the relation of subjects towards the Sovereign, which, notwithstanding the common interest, has nothing to make them responsible for the performance of their engagements if some means is not found of ensuring their fidelity.

In fact, each individual may, as a man, have a private will, dissimilar or contrary to the general will which he has as a citizen. His own private interest may dictate to him very differently from the common interest; his absolute and naturally independent existence may make him regard what he owes to the common cause as a gratuitous contribution, the omission of which would be less injurious to others than the payment would be burdensome to himself; and considering the moral person which constitutes the State as a creature of the imagination, because it is not a man, he may wish to enjoy the rights of a citizen without being disposed to fulfil the duties of a subject. Such an injustice would in its progress cause the ruin of the body politic.

In order, therefore, to prevent the social compact from becoming an empty formula, it tacitly comprehends the engagement, which alone can give effect to the others—that whoever refuses to obey the general will shall be compelled to it by the whole body: this in fact only forces him to be free; for this is the condition which, by giving each citizen to his country, guarantees his absolute personal independence, a condition which gives motion and effect to the political machine. This alone renders all civil engagements justifiable, and without it they would be absurd, tyrannical, and subject to the most enormous abuses.

OF THE CIVIL STATE

The passing from the state of nature to the civil state produces in man a very remarkable change, by substituting justice for instinct in his conduct, and giving to his actions a moral character which they lacked before. It is then only that the voice of duty succeeds to physical impulse, and a sense of what is right, to the incitements of appetite. Man, who had till then regarded none but himself, perceives that he must act on other principles, and learns to consult his reason before he listens to his inclinations. Although he is deprived in this new state of many advantages which he enjoyed from nature, he gains in return others so great, his faculties so unfold themselves by being exercised, his ideas are so extended, his sentiments so exalted, and his whole mind so enlarged and refined, that if, by abusing his new condition, he did not sometimes degrade it even below that from which he emerged, he ought to bless continually the happy moment that snatched him forever from it, and transformed him from a circumscribed and stupid animal to an intelligent being and a man.

In order to draw a balance between the advantages and disadvantages attending his new situation, let us state them in such a manner that they may be easily compared. Man loses by the social contract his *natural* liberty, and an unlimited right to all which tempts him, and which he can obtain; in return he acquires *civil* liberty, and proprietorship of all he possesses. That we may not be deceived in the value of these compensations, we must distinguish natural liberty, which knows no bounds but the power of the individual, from civil liberty, which is limited by the general will; and between possession, which is only the effect of force or of the right of the first occupant, from property, which must be founded on a positive title. In addition we might add to the other acquisitions of the civil state that of moral liberty, which alone renders a man master of himself; for it is *slavery* to be under the impulse of mere appetite, and *freedom* to obey a law which we prescribe for ourselves. But I have already said too much on this head, and the philosophical sense of the word "liberty" is not at present my subject.

THAT SOVEREIGNTY IS INALIENABLE

The first and most important consequence of the principles already established is that the general will alone can direct the forces of the State agreeably to the end of its institution, which is the common good; for if the clashing of private interests has rendered the establishing of societies necessary, the agreement of the same interests has made such establishments possible. It is what is common in these different interests that forms the social bond; and if there was not some point in which they all unanimously centered, no society could exist. It is on the basis of this common interest alone that society must be governed.

I say, therefore, that sovereignty, being only the exercise of the general will, can never alienate itself, and that the Sovereign, which is only a collective being, cannot be represented but by itself: the *power* may well be transmitted but not the *will*.

Indeed, if it is not impossible that a private will should accord on some point with the general will, it is at least impossible that such agreement should be regular and lasting; for the private will is inclined by its nature to partiality, and the general will to impartiality. It is even more impossible to guarantee the continuance of this agreement, even if we were to see it always exist; because that existence must be owing not to art but to chance. The Sovereign may indeed say: "My will at present actually agrees with the will of such and such a man, or at least with what he declares to be his will"; but it cannot say, "Our wills shall likewise agree tomorrow"; since it would be absurd for the will to bind itself for the future, and since it does not belong to any will to consent to what might be injurious to the being from whom the will proceeds. If, therefore, the people promise unconditionally to obey, the act of making such a promise dissolves their existence, and they lose their quality of a people; for at the moment that there is a master, there is no longer a Sovereign, and from that moment the body politic is destroyed.

I do not say that the commands of chiefs cannot pass for general wills, so long as the Sovereign, being free to oppose them, does not do so. In such cases we must presume from their silence that the people yield their consent. But I shall explain this more at large presently.

THAT SOVEREIGNTY IS INDIVISIBLE

For the same reason that sovereignty is inalienable, it is indivisible. For the will is general [3] or it is not; it is either the will of the whole body of the people, or only of a part. In the first case, this declared will is an act of sovereignty

[3] To make the will general, it is not always necessary that it should be unanimous; but it is indispensably necessary that every vote should be counted: any formal exclusion destroys generality.

and constitutes law; in the second, it is but a private will or an act of magistracy, and is at most but a decree. . . .

WHETHER THE GENERAL WILL CAN ERR

It follows from what has been said that the general will is always right and tends always to the public advantage; but it does not follow that the deliberations of the people have always the same rectitude. Our will always seeks our own good, but we do not always perceive what it is. The people are never corrupted, but they are often deceived, and only then do they seem to will what is bad.

There is frequently much difference between the *will of all* and the *general will*. The latter regards only the common interest; the former regards private interest, and is indeed but a sum of private wills: but remove from these same wills the pluses and minuses that cancel each other, and then the general will remains as the sum of the differences.[4]

If, when the people, sufficiently informed, deliberated, there was to be no communication among them, from the grand total of trifling differences the general will would always result, and their resolutions be always good. But when cabals and partial associations are formed at the expense of the great association, the will of each such association, though *general* with regard to its members, is *private* with regard to the State: it can then be said no longer that there are as many voters as men, but only as many as there are associations. By this means the differences being less numerous, they produce a result less general. Finally, when one of these associations becomes so large that it prevails over all the rest, you have no longer the sum of many opinions dissenting in a small degree from each other, but one great dictating dissentient; from that moment there is no longer a general will, and the predominating opinion is only an individual one.

It is therefore of the utmost importance for obtaining the expression of the general will, that no partial society should be formed in the State, and that every citizen should speak his opinion entirely from himself:[5] such was the unique and sublime system of the great Lycurgus. When there are partial societies, it is politic to multiply their number, that they may be all kept on an equality. This method was pursued by Solon, Numa, and Servius. These are

[4] "Each interest," says the Marquis d'A. [d'Argenson], "has its different principles. The agreement of two private interests is formed by opposition to a third." He might have added that the agreement of all interests is produced by opposition to that of each. If there were no different interests, we should scarcely perceive the common interest, which never finds any opposer; everything would go on regularly of itself, and politics be no longer an art.

[5] "Divisions," says Machiavelli, "sometimes injure and sometimes serve a republic. The injury is done by cabals and factions, the service by a party which maintains itself without cabals or factions. Since, therefore, it is impossible for the founder of a republic to provide against enmities, he must make the best provision he can against factions." (*History of Florence,* Bk. VII.)

the only precautions that can be taken to make the general will always intelligent, and prevent the people from being deceived.

OF THE LIMITS OF THE SOVEREIGN POWER

If the state or city is only a moral person, the existence of which consists in the union of its members, and if its most important care is that of preserving itself, there is a necessity for its possessing a universally compulsive power, for moving and disposing each part in the manner most convenient to the whole. As nature gives to every man absolute command over all his members, the social compact gives to the body politic absolute command over the members of which it is formed; and it is this power, when directed by the general will, that bears, as I have said before, the name of "sovereignty."

But, besides the public person, we have to consider the private persons who compose it, and whose lives and liberty are naturally independent of it. The point here is to distinguish properly between the respective rights of the citizens and the Sovereign,[6] and between the duties which the former have to fulfil in quality of subjects, and the natural rights which they ought to enjoy in quality of men.

It is granted that all which an individual alienates by the social compact is only that part of his power, his property, and his liberty, the use of which is important to the community; but we must also grant that the Sovereign is the only judge of what is important to the community.

All the services which a citizen can render to the State ought to be rendered as soon as the Sovereign demands them; but the Sovereign cannot, on its side, impose any burden on the subject useless to the community; it cannot even have the inclination to do so; for, under the law of reason, nothing is done without a cause, any more than under the law of nature.

The engagements which bind us to the social body are only obligatory because they are mutual; and their nature is such that in fulfilling them we cannot labour for others without labouring at the same time for ourselves. Wherefore is the general will always right, and wherefore do all the wills invariably seek the happiness of every individual among them, if it is not that there is no person who does not appropriate the word "each" to himself, and who does not think of himself when he is voting for all? This proves that the equality of right, and the idea of justice which it inspires, is derived from the preference which each gives to himself, and consequently from the nature of man; that the general will, to be truly such, ought to be so in its object, as well as its essence: that it ought to come from all, if we are to apply it to all; and that it loses its natural rectitude when it tends towards any one individual and determinate object, be-

[6] Attentive readers, be not too hasty, I beg of you, to accuse me of contradicting myself. I could not avoid doing so terminologically, on account of the poverty of the language; but have patience until I explain my meaning.

cause then, judging of what is external to us, we have no true principle of equity to guide us.

In fact, as soon as it is a matter of an individual fact or right, on any point which has not been previously regulated by a general convention, the affair becomes contentious. It is a process wherein the persons interested are one of the parties, and the public the other, but where I do not see any law that must be followed, or any judge who ought to decide. It would be ridiculous in such a case to bring the question to an express decision of the general will, which could only be the conclusion of one party, and consequently, which would be, with respect to the other party, but an external and private will, hurried on that occasion into injustice, and subject to error. Thus, in the same manner as a private will cannot represent the general will, the general will, in its turn, changes its nature if its object is private, and cannot, as the general will, pronounce either on a man or a fact. When the people of Athens, for example, nominated or cashiered their chiefs, decreed honours to one, imposed punishments on another, and, by the multitude of their private decrees, exercised indiscriminately all the acts of government, the people, properly speaking, had then no longer a general will; they acted no longer as Sovereign but as magistrate. This will appear contradictory to common ideas; but I must have time to unfold mine.

We should perceive by this that the generality of the will depends less on the number of voters than on the common interest which unites them; for, in this institution, each necessarily submits to the conditions which he imposes on others—an admirable union of interest and justice, which gives to the common deliberations a character of equity that vanishes in the discussion of all private affairs for want of a common interest to combine and identify the ruling of the judge with that of the party.

By whatever path we return to our principle, we always arrive at the same conclusion—that is, that the social compact establishes among citizens such an equality that they are all engaged under the same conditions, and should all enjoy the same rights. Thus, by the nature of the compact all acts of sovereignty, that is to say, all authentic acts of the general will, oblige or favour all citizens alike in such a manner as evinces that the Sovereign knows no person but the body of the nation, and does not make any distinction among the individuals who compose it. What, therefore, is properly an act of sovereignty? It is not a convention between a superior and an inferior, but a convention of the body with each of its members—a justifiable convention because it has the social contract for its basis; equitable, because it is common to all; beneficial, because it can have no other object but the general good; and solid, because it is guaranteed by the public force and the supreme power. While subjects are under the governance of such conventions only, they obey no one but only their own will: and to enquire how far the respective rights of the Sovereign and citizens extend is to ask how far the citizens can engage with themselves, each towards all, and all towards each.

We see by this that the sovereign power, all absolute, all sacred, all inviolable as it is, neither will, nor can, exceed the bounds of general conventions, and that every man may fully dispose of what is left to him of his property and his liberty by these conventions; so that the Sovereign never has any right to lay a greater charge on one subject than on another, because then the affair would become personal, and in such cases the power of the Sovereign is no longer competent. . . .

OF THE LEGISLATOR

The legislator [7] is in every sense a most extraordinary man in the State. If he must be so from his genius, he is no less so from his employment, which is neither magistracy nor sovereignty. This employment, which constitutes the republic, enters not into its constitution; it is a particular and superior function, which has nothing in common with human empire; because, if he who commands men must not preside over the laws, he who presides over the laws must not have the command over men: otherwise his laws, employed as the ministers of his passions, would frequently merely perpetuate his injustices; and it would be impossible to prevent private aims from defiling the sanctity of his work. . . .

He who compiles the laws, therefore, has not, nor ought he to have, any right to legislate, and the people cannot, even if they should be inclined, deprive themselves of that incommunicable right, because, according to the fundamental compact, it is only the general will that can compel individuals, and it can never be known whether a private will is conformable to the general will until it has been submitted to the free vote of the people. I have affirmed this already, but a repetition may not be useless. . . .

OF THE PEOPLE

What people, then, are in a proper state to receive laws? Those who are already united by some original bond of origin, interest, or convention, but who have not yet had any established system of laws; those in whom neither customs nor superstitions have taken root; those who are not afraid of being borne down by sudden invasion, but who, without entering into the quarrels of their neighbours, can by themselves resist each of them, or be assisted by the one to subdue the other; those whose members may be all known to each other, and among whom there is no necessity for laying a heavier burden on a man than he is able to bear; those who may do without other peoples, and whom other peoples do without; those who are neither rich nor poor, but have enough to support themselves; and, finally, those who unite the stability of an established state with the docility of a new people. The arduous work of legislation is made difficult less by what it is necessary to establish than by what it is necessary to

[7] [By "the legislator" Rousseau here means the one who compiles or drafts what is proposed as the law of the land, not the one who decides that this shall be the law of the land.—Eds.]

destroy; and what makes legislators succeed too seldom is the impossibility of finding the simplicity of nature united with those establishments which are necessary for society. But as we very rarely see all the requisite circumstances combine together, so we seldom find any State well constructed. . . .

HOW THE SOVEREIGN AUTHORITY IS MAINTAINED

The sovereign, having no other force but the legislative power, acts only by the laws; and the laws being only the authentic acts of the general will, the Sovereign can never act but when the people are assembled. . . .

It is not sufficient for an assembly of the people to have once fixed the constitution of the State by sanctioning a body of laws, it is not enough that they should have established a perpetual government, or have provided rules, once for all, for the election of magistrates. In addition to extraordinary assemblies which unforeseen events can require, there must be regular and periodic assemblies which nothing can abolish or prorogue, so that on the stated day the people shall be legally convoked, without anything else being needed for their formal convocation. . . .

At the moment that the people are legally assembled as a sovereign body, all the jurisdiction of government ceases, the executive power is suspended, and the person of the least citizen is as sacred as that of the highest magistrate, because where the person represented may be found, there is no longer a need for a representative. . . .

OF DEPUTIES OR REPRESENTATIVES

As soon as men cease to consider public service as the principal duty of citizens, and rather choose to serve with their purse than with their persons, we may pronounce the State to be on the very verge of ruin. Are the citizens called upon to march out to war? They pay soldiers for the purpose, and remain at home. Are they summoned to council? They nominate deputies, and stay at home. And thus, in consequence of idleness and money, they have soldiers to enslave their country, and representatives to sell it. . . .

The better a State is constituted, the more do public affairs intrude upon private affairs in the minds of the citizens. Private concerns even become considerably fewer, because each individual shares so largely in the common happiness that he has not so much occasion to seek for it in private resources. In a well-conducted city, each member flies with joy to the assemblies; under a bad government, no one is disposed to bend his way thither, because no one is interested in proceedings where he foresees that the general will will not prevail, and in the end every man turns his attention to his own domestic affairs. Good laws lead on to better, and bad ones seldom fail to generate still worse. When once you hear some one say, when speaking of the affairs of the State, "What is it to me?" you may give over the State for lost.

It was the decline of patriotism, the activity of private interest, the immense extent of States, the increase of conquests, and the abuses of government, that suggested the expedient of having deputies or representatives of the people in the assemblies of the nation. . . .

Sovereignty cannot be represented for the same reason that it cannot be alienated; its essence is the general will, and that will must speak for itself, or it does not exist: it is either itself or not itself: there is no intermediate possibility. The deputies of the people, therefore, are not and cannot be their representatives; they can only be their commissioners, and as such are not qualified to conclude anything definitively. No act of theirs can be a law, unless it has been ratified by the people in person; and without that ratification nothing is a law. The people of England deceive themselves when they fancy they are free; they are so, in fact, only during the election of members of parliament: for, as soon as a new one is elected, they are again in chains, and are nothing. And thus, by the use they make of their brief moments of liberty, they deserve to lose it. . . .

THAT THE GENERAL WILL CANNOT BE DESTROYED

So long as several men unite and consider themselves as one body, they have but one will, which is to promote the common safety and general well-being. While this union continues, all the springs of the State will be vigorous and simple, the maxims by which they are regulated will be clear and comprehensible; and there will be no jarring, opposing interests; the common good will then be everywhere evident, and nothing will be necessary but a sound understanding to perceive it. For peace, union, and equality are enemies of political subtleties. Men of integrity and simplicity are difficult to deceive because of their very simplicity: lures and refined pretexts do not impose upon them, and they have not even cunning enough to be dupes. When we see, among the happiest people in the world, groups of peasants directing affairs of State under an oak, and always acting wisely, can we help but despise the refinements of those nations which render themselves illustrious and miserable by so much art and mystery?

A State thus governed requires but very few laws; and whenever it becomes necessary to promulgate new ones, the necessity is perceived universally. He who proposes them only says what all have already felt, and neither faction nor eloquence is required to obtain the passage of a measure which each person has already resolved to adopt, as soon as he is sure that the others will act with him. . . .

But when the social bond once begins to relax and the State to grow weak, when private interests begin to take the lead, and smaller societies have an influence on the greater, the common interest changes and finds many opposers: there is no longer unanimity of opinion; the general will is no longer the will of all; everything is contested; and the best advice is never adopted without much dispute and opposition.

Finally, when a State upon the brink of ruin supports only a vain illusory form and the social bond no longer unites the hearts of the people, and when the sacred name of public good is made use of to cover the basest interest, then the general will is silenced; and every one, being directed by secret motives, no more gives an opinion as a citizen than if the State had never existed; decrees which have no other object but private interest are then passed, to which the name of laws is falsely given.

But does it follow that the general will is annihilated or corrupted? No: it will remain always constant, unalterable, and pure; but it is rendered subordinate to other wills, which domineer over it. In this state of affairs, though each individual detaches his interest from the common interest, yet he finds it impossible to separate them entirely; but his part of the common will appears trifling to him when balanced against some private advantage which he has in view. This particular object only excepted, he is in every point as solicitous as any other member to promote the general welfare on his own account. Even by selling his vote for money he does not destroy his own general will, he only eludes it. The fault which such a man commits is that of changing the state of the question, and answering something else than what he was asked: instead of saying by his vote, "It is advantageous to the State," he says, "It is advantageous to such a man, or to such a party, that such a motion should pass." Thus the law for regulating public assemblies is not so much intended to maintain there the general will as to enforce the full and clear repetition of the question on which that will is to determine.

OF SUFFRAGE

It is evident from what has been said in the preceding chapter that the manner of conducting general affairs is the best criterion by which to judge of the morality and health of the body politic. In proportion to the degree of concord which reigns in the assemblies, that is, the nearer opinion approaches unanimity, the more the general will predominates; while tumults, dissensions, and long debates declare the ascendancy of private interests and the declining situation of the State. . . .

From these various considerations, maxims may be drawn for regulating the manner of counting the votes and determining the opinion of a public assembly, which must vary according as the general will is more or less easy to ascertain and the State more or less in decline.

There is one law only which, by its nature, requires unanimous consent; I mean the social compact: for civil association is the most voluntary of all acts; every man being born free and master of himself, no person can under any pretense whatever subject him without his consent. To affirm that the son of a slave is born a slave is to pronounce that he is not born a man.

Should there be any men who oppose the social compact, their opposition will not invalidate it, but only hinder their being included: they are foreigners among citizens. When the State is instituted, residence constitutes consent; to inhabit a territory is to submit to the sovereignty.[8]

Except in this original contract, a majority of votes is sufficient to bind all the others. This is a consequence of the contract itself. But it may be asked how a man can be free and yet forced to conform to the will of others. How are the opposers free when they are in submission to laws to which they have never consented?

I answer that the question is not fairly stated. The citizen consents to all the laws, to those which are passed in spite of his opposition, and even to those which sentence him to punishment if he violates any one of them. The constant will of all the members of the State is the general will; it is by that they are citizens and free.[9] When any law is proposed in the assembly of the people, the question is not precisely to enquire whether they approve the proposition or reject it, but if it is conformable or not to the general will, which is their will. Each citizen, in giving his suffrage, states his mind on that question; and the general will is found by counting the votes. When, therefore, the motion which I opposed carries, it only proves to me that I was mistaken, and that what I believed to be the general will was not so. If my particular opinion had prevailed, I should have done what I was not willing to do, and, consequently, I should not have been in a state of freedom.

This is indeed supposing that all the characteristics which mark the general will still reside in the most votes: when that ceases to be the case, whatever measures may be adopted, it means the end of liberty.

. . . Though the difference of one single vote will destroy equality, and one opposing voice prevent unanimity, yet there are several grades of unequal division between equality and unanimity, and in each of them the number may be fixed according to the situation and occasions of the body politic.

Two general rules may suffice for regulating these proportions: one is that the more serious and important the deliberations are, the nearer the number of votes which pass them should approach unanimity; the other is that the greater necessity there is for expediting the affair, the smaller may be the majority: and on motions which require to be determined on the spot, a majority of one may be deemed sufficient. The first of these maxims seems most applicable to laws,

---

[8] This must always be understood of a man in a free State; because elsewhere his family, his property, or the want of an asylum to fly to, and also necessity or force, may detain an inhabitant against his will; and then his sojourn does not suppose his consent, either to the contract or to the violation of the contract.

[9] At Genoa we see inscribed over the gates of their prisons and on the chains affixed to their galley slaves the word "Libertas." This application of it is noble as well as just. In fact, it is only the bad people in every State that hinder the citizens from being free. Any country where all such men were chained to the oar would be the seat of perfect liberty.

and the second to practical business. Be that as it may, it is by combining these two rules that the number of voices proper to form the majority on different occasions must be established.

Questions

1. "Man is born free, and yet we see him everywhere in chains. . . . How this happens I am ignorant; but, if I am asked what renders it justifiable, I believe it may be in my power to resolve the question." Thus it appears that Rousseau intends to show that it is right (justifiable) for man to be in chains rather than free!

Is this interpretation correct? What does being "free" and being "in chains" mean in this context? By saying that man is *born* free, does Rousseau mean that babies at the moment of birth are more free than adults? If not, what does he mean by this?

2. What is Rousseau's argument against the doctrine that might makes right? State why you find his argument valid or invalid.

3. Rousseau distinguishes the act whereby a people elect their rulers and the act whereby they become a people. What is the meaning of this distinction, and what role does it play in Rousseau's political theory?

4. What does Rousseau say is the purpose for which men form a social contract?

5. What are the terms of the social contract, according to Rousseau? Explain them as clearly as you can in your own words.

6. Rousseau claims that the terms of the social contract are "everywhere tacitly understood and admitted." How would Rousseau reply to someone who said to him, "I have never signed any such contract, nor have I ever made a verbal agreement of the sort you describe. Therefore, its terms are not binding on me"?

7. From Rousseau's point of view, is it ever *possible* for anyone to break the social contract? Is it ever *justifiable* for anyone to break it? Defend your answers by reference to the text.

8. "The Sovereign, by its nature, is always everything it ought to be." Give Rousseau's argument in support of this statement, and show clearly why it does *not* mean that a ruler can do no wrong.

9. Compare, in detail, Rousseau's account of the transition from man in the state of nature to man in political society with Locke's account of the same thing. (For Locke's account, see the selection beginning on page 613.)

10. Explain what Rousseau means by the difference between a private will and the general will, and the difference between the general will and the will of all.

11. Why, and in what specific sense, do all men have equal rights in Rousseau's ideal state?

12. Considering Rousseau's conceptions of sovereignty and the general will, state the case *for* one of the following theses and *against* the other:

"Rousseau provides the justification for absolute and unconditional totalitarianism."

"Rousseau provides the justification for a democratic, liberal, open society."

13. What is Rousseau's argument against government by representatives? Must one accept this argument if one accepts what Rousseau says about the social contract? Why or why not?

14. In the last section of the reading, Rousseau considers the problem of "how a man can be free and yet forced to conform to the will of others." State why you think his solution to this problem is, or is not, a satisfactory one.

4

Natural Rights | Margaret Macdonald
(1903-1956)

The late Margaret Macdonald, one of the leading practitioners of British philosophical analysis, was Reader in Philosophy at the University of London. For a number of years she was editor of the British journal, *Analysis*. She wrote many philosophical articles and edited a collection of essays, *Philosophy and Analysis* (1955).

In the article which is here reprinted in its entirety, Miss Macdonald examines the meaning and justification of statements about natural rights. Her essay remains throughout on the second level of philosophical discourse. She does not herself make statements about natural rights, but only makes statements about such statements. The two questions which concern her are: What does the claim that men have natural rights mean? and, How can a claim to natural rights be justified?

Miss Macdonald analyzes the meaning of the claim that men have natural rights in terms of three basic types of propositions: (1) tautological or analytical propositions, (2) empirical or contingent propositions, and (3) assertions (or expressions) of value. Propositions of type (1) correspond to Hume's "relations of ideas," and propositions of type (2) to Hume's "matters of fact." (This distinction is made by Hume in the reading beginning on page 98.) Propositions about natural rights are then shown to be a "curious hybrid of types (1) and (2)." The argument here turns on a careful analysis of the appeals to human nature as "rational," and to "natural law" as governing human relations independently of the laws of particular societies which people make in claiming to have natural rights. Propositions of type (3) are also seen to be involved, since man's rational nature and natural law are used as standards by which to judge social relations and the laws of particular societies.

In the section of her article titled "The Social Contract," Miss Macdonald considers how the doctrine of natural rights came to be connected with the theory of the social contract. Here she makes reference to the political philosophy of John Locke (see the selection beginning on page 613) and of the Founding Fathers of the United States. This discussion raises the question of how a pure tautology (that man has natural rights was said to follow from the definition of "man" as a rational being, and thus to say a man has natural rights is simply to say he is a man) can give rise to a value standard and a whole political movement having vast social consequences. In the section on "Rights and Reason," Miss Macdonald pursues this question and comes to the conclusion that when people assert their natural rights they are really expressing what they believe to be the fundamental conditions of a good society.

The last section of the essay, "Propositions and Decisions," is a study of the third type of proposition, namely, assertions (or expressions) of value. Here Miss Macdonald presents her own views of the nature and justification of value statements. Since statements about natural rights, she maintains, are at bottom value statements, she must consider the nature and justification of value statements in general to complete her account of natural rights.

This article was originally published in the *Proceedings of the Aristotelian Society* for 1947-1948.

From "Natural Rights," by Margaret Macdonald, *Proceedings of The Aristotelian Society,* 1947-1948. Reprinted by permission of Miss Macdonald's literary executors and The Aristotelian Society.

Doctrines of natural law and natural rights have a long and impressive history from the Stoics and Roman jurists to the Atlantic Charter and Roosevelt's Four Freedoms.[1] That men are entitled to make certain claims by virtue simply of their common humanity has been equally passionately defended and vehemently denied. Punctured by the cool scepticism of Hume; routed by the contempt of Bentham for "nonsense upon stilts"; submerged by idealist and Marxist philosophers in the destiny of the totalitarian state; the claim to "natural rights" has never been quite defeated. It tends in some form to be renewed in every crisis in human affairs, when the plain citizen tries to make, or expects his leaders to make, articulate his obscure, but firmly held, conviction that he is not a mere pawn in any political game, nor the property of any government or ruler, but the living and protesting individual for whose sake all political games are played and all governments instituted. As one of Cromwell's soldiers expressed it to that dictator: "Really, sir, I think that the poorest he that is in England hath a life to live as the greatest he." [2]

It could, perhaps, be proved hedonistically that life for most ordinary citizens is more *comfortable* in a democratic than a totalitarian state. But would an appeal for effort, on this ground, have been sanctioned between 1939-45? However true, it would have been rejected as inefficient because *uninspired.* Who could be moved to endure "blood and toil, tears and sweat" for the sake of a

---

[1] Freedom of Speech and Worship; Freedom from Want and Fear of all persons everywhere.

[2] *Clarke Papers,* vol. 1, p. 301.

little extra comfort? What, then, supplied the required inspiration? An appeal to the instinct of national self-preservation? But societies have been known to collapse inexplicably almost without waiting to be physically defeated. No doubt there are several answers, but at least one, I suggest, was an appeal to the values of freedom and equality among men. An appeal to safeguard and restore, where necessary, the Rights of Man, those ultimate points at which authority and social differences vanish, leaving the solitary individual with his essential human nature, according to one political theory, or a mere social fiction, according to another.

All this sounds very obscure. And the doctrine of natural law and of the natural rights of men is very obscure—which justifies the impatience of its opponents. It seems a strange law which is unwritten, has never been enacted, and may be unobserved without penalty, and peculiar rights which are possessed antecedently to all specific claims within an organized society. Surely, it will be said, the whole story now has only historical interest as an example of social mythology? Nothing is so dead as dead ideology. All this may be true,[3] but nevertheless the doctrine is puzzling. For if it is sheer nonsense why did it have psychological, political and legal effects? Men do not reflect and act upon collections of meaningless symbols or nonsense rhymes.

There seems no doubt that the assertions of certain Greek philosophers about the "natural" equality of men and their consequent right to freedom caused intelligent contemporaries to become uneasy about the institution of slavery;[4] that doctrines of the primal Rights of Man were significantly connected with the French and American Revolutions. It even seems probable that the Communist Manifesto owed much of its success not to its "scientific" analysis of capitalist society, but to its denouncement of a wage slavery degrading to human nature and its appeal to all workers to assert their equal brotherhood. A major crime of capitalist society for Marx and Engels was that it had destroyed all ties between men other than naked self-interest and had "resolved personal worth into exchange value." Only after the proletarian revolution would *human* history begin and men treat each other as equal human beings, not as exploiter and exploited. The object of the transfer of class power is to end class power and to reveal or restore some essential human nature at present disguised by distorting social relationships.

So even if the theory were dead, the puzzle of its effects would remain, and suggest that it had been introduced to solve a genuine problem of political and social philosophy. And it is interesting, therefore, to inquire what the problem was; whether it has found an alternative solution, or is bogus and insoluble.

Why should people have supposed, and, as I believe, continue to suppose, in obscure fashion, that they have "natural" rights, or rights as human beings, independently of the laws and governments of any existing society? It is, surely,

[3] It is not quite true, for the doctrines of natural law and consequent natural rights flourish in Catholic social philosophy. See, e.g. *The Rights of Man and Natural Law* by Jacques Maritain [Geoffrey Bles, Ltd., London], 1944.

[4] Cf. *The Open Society* by K. Popper [Routledge and Kegan Paul, Ltd., London, 1945]; vol. 1, esp. pp. 58-59.

partly at least, because no existing social compulsion or relationship is self-justifying. Men may always ask why they should or should not endure it and expect a convincing answer. And, ultimately, it would seem, they may challenge the dictates of all existing governments and the pressures of every society if they find them equally oppressive, i.e. if they deny what the individual considers his fundamental "right." But since, *ex hypothesi,* this "right" is denied by every existing law and authority, it must be a right possessed independently of them and derived from another source. If, e.g. the laws of every existing society condemn a human being to be a slave, he, or another on his behalf, may yet hold that he has a "right" to be free. What sort of proposition is this and how is such a claim to be justified? This seems to be one most important problem which the doctrine of natural rights tried to solve.

NATURAL LAW, NATURAL LAWS AND NATURAL RIGHTS

There are an indefinite number of different types of propositions and other forms of human utterance. I will, for my present purpose, notice three. (1) Tautological or analytic propositions which state rules for the uses of symbols or which follow from such rules within a linguistic or logical system. (2) Empirical or contingent propositions which state matter of fact and existence. Propositions which describe what does or may occur in the world and not the symbolic techniques employed in such description. (3) Assertions or expressions of value. With the help of this classification it may be possible to show that some of the difficulties of the doctrine of natural rights have been due to an attempt to interpret propositions about natural rights as a curious hybrid of types (1) and (2) of the above classification.

For in the theory which conceived of natural rights as guaranteed by a "natural" law, the position seems to have been considered in the following terms. The "rights" of a slave, e.g. derive from the laws in any society which govern his artificial status as a slave. Yet he has a right to be free. But in virtue of what status and law? Only it seems by his status of being a man like other men. This, however, is a natural status as opposed to one determined by social convention. Every man is human "by nature"; no human being is "by nature" a slave of another human being. There must then be an essential human nature which determines this status and a law governing the relations of human beings as such, independently of the laws of all particular societies concerning their artificial relationships. But essential human nature or human "essence" is constituted by those properties expressed in the definition of "human being." And what is expressed or entailed by a definition is a necessary or analytic proposition. Thus by a logical fusion of the characteristics of two different types of proposition, statements about natural rights tended in this theory to be represented as statements of a necessary natural fact.

But not even statements of actual fact, necessary or contingent. For another element intervened. Though the slave had an actual "right" to be free, he was not free, because no existing law admitted his right. Because laws were imperfect, he was not free though he "ought" to be. And this introduces into the situation a further complication. By nature a man must be that which yet he is not. Or, it follows from the definition of "human being" that every human being is, or must be, free—or possess any other "natural" right though his freedom is ideal and not real. But the ideal as well as the actual is natural fact.

Thus the Roman lawyers, who gave the earliest authoritative statements of the doctrine of natural law, conceived of natural law as an ideal or standard, not yet completely exemplified in any existing legal code, but also as a standard fixed by nature to be discovered and gradually applied by men. And the good lawyer kept his eye on this standard as the good gardener keeps his eye fixed on the prize rose which he is hoping to reproduce among his own blooms next summer. For the lawyer, said Ulpian, is not merely the interpreter of existing laws but also the priest or guardian of justice, which is the "fixed and abiding disposition to give every man his right." [5] This standard was not determined by men, but by nature, or, sometimes, by God. It was fact and not fancy.

The institution of slavery showed that no existing code was perfectly just. Thus natural *law* is only imperfectly realized in positive *laws*. And it is significant that the lawyers and later political theorists who adopted this distinction talked only of natural *law* and *the* Law of Nature, never of natural laws and laws of nature. But what is most characteristic of legal codes and systems is that they consist of many laws, regulating the different relations of men as debtor and creditor, property owner and thief, employer and employee, husband and wife, etc. But natural law was not conceived of as consisting of ideal regulations corresponding to all positive laws. Indeed, if completely realized, some positive laws would be abolished, e.g. those relating to slave owner and slave. Natural law was not formulated in natural *laws*. It was neither written nor customary and might even be unknown. But it applies, nevertheless, to all men everywhere whether they are debtors or creditors, masters or servants, bond or free. But how is it discovered?

It seems probable that the concept of natural law influenced the later conception of natural or scientific laws obtained by the observation of natural events. For natural law applies impartially to all men in all circumstances, as the law of gravitation applies to all bodies. But the law of gravitation is obtained by deduction from the observation of bodies in sense perception. Are the Law of Nature and the Rights which it implies known by similar observation of the nature of man? The law of gravitation, like all other laws of nature, states a uniformity exemplified in the actual movements of natural bodies. But no existing society may observe the Law of Nature or guarantee natural rights. These cannot, therefore, have been learned from observation of the actual practice of existing societies.

"Man is born free," said Rousseau, "and everywhere he is in chains." What sort of proposition is this? Did Rousseau observe ten or ten million babies immediately after birth and record when the infant limbs were manacled? The

[5] Sabine: *History of Political Theory* [G. C. Harrap and Co., Ltd., London, 1948], p. 170.

law of nature applies to all men equally, said Cicero. For if we had not been corrupted by bad habits and customs "no one would be so like his own self as all men would be like others."[6] But since everyone everywhere has been subjected to customs and laws of varying degrees of imperfection, where and when did Cicero observe our uncorrupted nature? How can facts about nature be discovered which have never been observed or confirmed by observation?

The answer lies in the peculiar status given to reason in the theory. Propositions about natural law and natural rights are not generalizations from experience nor deductions from observed facts subsequently confirmed by experience. Yet they are not totally disconnected from natural fact. For they are known as entailed by the intrinsic or essential nature of man. Thus they are known by reason. But they are entailed by the proposition that an essential property of men is that they have reason. The standard of natural law is set by reason and is known because men have reason. But that men have reason, i.e. are able to deduce the ideal from the actual, is a natural fact. And it is by having this specific, and natural, characteristic of being rational that men resemble each other and differ from the brutes. Reason is the great leveller or elevator. According to Sir Frederick Pollock, "Natural law was conceived to be an ultimate principle of fitness with regard to the nature of man as a rational and social being which is, or ought to be, the justification of every form of positive law."[7] "There is, in fact," said Cicero, "a true law—namely right reason—which is in accordance with nature, applies to all men and is unchangeable and eternal."[8] And for Grotius, too, "The law of nature is a dictate of right reason."[9]

Let it be admitted that all or most human beings are intelligent or rational. And that what is known by reason is certainly true. But, also, what can be known by unaided reason is what *must* be true, and perhaps what *ought* to be but never what *is* true of matter of fact. And statements which are logically certain are tautological or analytic and are neither verified nor falsified by what exists. Statements about what ought to be are of a peculiar type which will be discussed later, but it is certain that they say nothing about what *is*. Because it is confused on these distinctions, the theory of natural law and natural rights constantly confounds reason with right and both with matter of fact and existence. The fact that men do reason is thought to be somehow a natural or empirical confirmation of what is logically deduced by reason as a standard by which to judge the imperfections of what exists.

THE SOCIAL CONTRACT

Though the Roman lawyers conceded that a man might be entitled by natural law to that which he was denied by every positive law, they do not seem to have related this to any particular doctrine of legal and political authority. But in the seventeenth century the doctrines of natural law and natural

---

[6] *Laws,* Bk. 1, 10, 28-9 (trans. C. W. Keyes).
[7] The History of the Law of Nature; *Essays in the Law* [Macmillan, London], 1922.
[8] *Republic,* Bk. 3, p. 22 (trans. Sabine and Smith).
[9] Bk. 1, ch. 1, sec. x, 1.

rights were directly connected with the contract theory of the State. Because he is rational, Locke emphasized, man is subject to the law of nature even before the establishment of civil society. And he never ceases to be so subject. By right of the law of nature men lived in a state of freedom, equality and the possession of property "that with which a man hath mixed his labour." True, this picture differs from that of Hobbes whose "natural man" is constantly at war, possesses only the right to preserve his life, if he can, but usually finds it short and nasty. Nevertheless, even Hobbes's unpleasant savages have sufficient sense, or reason, to enable them to escape their "natural" predicament. Locke's natural individualists are peaceful property owners who nevertheless sometimes dispute and want an impartial arbitrator. Civil society is formed by compact that natural rights may be better preserved. Man did not enter society, said Paine, to become *worse* than he was before by surrendering his natural rights but only to have them better secured. His natural rights are the foundation of all his civil rights. It was essential for the social contract theorists to deny that all rights are the gift of civil society, since existing societies denied certain rights which they affirmed. In order to claim them, therefore, it was supposed that they had been enjoyed or were such as would be enjoyed by rational creatures in a "natural" as opposed to an established society. The Declaration of the French Revolutionary Assembly enunciated the Rights of Man and of citizens; the two being distinct.

His "natural" rights attach, by virtue of his reason, to every man much as do his arms and legs. He carries them about with him from one society to another. He cannot lose them without losing himself. "Men are born free and equal," said the French Assembly, "in respect of their *natural* and *imprescriptible* rights of liberty, property, security and resistance of oppression." [10] The framers of the American Declaration of Independence declare as self-evident truths that all men are created equal, that they are endowed by their creator with certain inalienable rights, among which are Life, Liberty and the Pursuit of Happiness and that governments are instituted to secure these rights.[11] The free people of Virginia proclaimed [12] that the rights with which men enter society they cannot by any compact deprive themselves or their posterity.

These were self-evident truths about a state which men might have left or not yet attained but which was "natural" to them as opposed to accidental or conventional. A person is accidentally a native of England, France, America; a Red Indian, Negro or Jew. His social environment is determined by accident of birth. He may change his family by adoption and his citizenship by naturalization. And he is accidentally, or conventionally, a doctor, soldier, employer, etc. These conventionalities determine his civic and legal rights in a particular society. But he is not accidentally human. Humanity is his essence or nature. There is no essence of "being Greek" or "being English"; of "being a creditor"

[10] Declaration of the Rights of Man and of Citizens, by the National Assembly of France, 1791.

[11] Declaration of Independence of the United States of America, July 4, 1776.

[12] The Virginia Declaration of Rights, June 12, 1776.

or "being an old age pensioner" all of which properties, however, might be the basis of civil rights. The nature of man determines his "natural" rights. And since, though not accidental, it also seemed to be a matter of fact that men exist and are rational, rights claimed on account of this fact seemed also to be natural and to follow from the essence of man, even though they might be denied. But the essence of man is expressed in the definition of the word "man." So that the statement "Men have natural rights" is equivalent to the propositional function "x is human entails x has natural rights" which is a tautology. Again the ambiguity inherent in the theory between what is necessary and what is natural is revealed. It is hard to believe that a barren tautology generated the ardours of that time in which it was good to be alive and to be young was "very heaven." [13] But what is meant by the nature or essence of man by "being rational" or "having reason"?

RIGHTS AND REASON

" 'Man' equals 'rational animal' [definition]" is the fossil preserved in logic textbooks since Aristotle. It was never accompanied by any adequate account of the meaning of "rational" which was, however, generally assumed to include the capacity to abstract and generalize by the use of symbols in speech and writing; to formulate and understand general propositions and laws; and to perceive necessary or logical connections between propositions. It is true that Aristotle himself used the term "reason" more widely to include the practical intelligence manifested in various skills and the appropriate behaviour of the well-trained character in various moral situations. But usually reason is conceived to be the capacity by which men understand abstractions. This was certainly Kant's view. To be rational is to be able to think abstractly. And the most characteristic activities of men, including living in societies, are due to this capacity to use reason. It is peculiar to men and shared by no other animal. Hence the basis of the equality of men for the exponents of natural law, and of their intrinsic worth for Kant is the fact that they all have reason. Men share all other characteristics with the brutes and might themselves have them in varying degrees, but reason was alike in all men; it was man's defining characteristic. Hence it is the foundation, too, of his natural rights, as a human being.

It is probable that other animals do not abstract and generalize for they do not use symbols. But neither is it true that all men do this with equal skill. Reason, in this sense, is no less or no more invariable among human beings than sense perception, and the rights of man might as well depend upon eyesight as upon rationality. But if the term reason is to be used more widely to include nonverbal manifestations of intelligence, knowing-how as well as knowing-that,[14] then intelligence does not set an unbridgeable gulf between men and

---

[13] Wordsworth in *The French Revolution.*

[14] See Presidential Address to the Aristotelian Society by Professor G. Ryle, 1945, and *The Concept of Mind* [Hutchinson and Co., Ltd., London], 1949, ch. II.

other living creatures. For in many activities, those, e.g. of hunting, building, fighting, and even social organization, other creatures display skill, adaptability of means to ends, and other characteristics which are evidence of intelligence in men. And as for social life, ants use tools, domesticate other insects, and live a highly organized social life. Bees and wasps manage their affairs by a complicated system of government. Moreover, many of the most characteristic human activities depend very little on abstract thought or use of symbols, e.g. cooking, sewing, knitting, carpentry. And at a higher level the excellence of pictures, sculptures, symphonies, is not due to their expression of abstract thought. But where in this variety are we to find the constant factor by which to determine human rights? What passport will admit to the Kingdom of Ends?

What may be agreed is that only at a certain level of intellectual development do men claim natural rights. Savages do not dream of life, liberty and the pursuit of happiness. For they do not question what is customary. Neither do the very depressed and downtrodden. It was not the slaves who acclaimed their right to be free but the philosophers and lawyers. Marx and Engels were not themselves wage slaves of the industrial system. It is generally agreed that the doctrines of natural rights, natural law and the social contract, are individualistic. To claim rights as an individual independently of society, a man must have reached a level of self-consciousness which enables him to isolate himself in thought from his social environment. This presupposes a considerable capacity for abstraction. To this extent natural rights, or the ability to claim natural rights, depends on reason. But it does not follow from this that reason alone constitutes the specific nature of man or that the worth of human beings is determined solely by their I.Q.'s. Reason is only one human excellence.

But the Aristotelian dream of fixed natures pursuing common ends dies hard. It reappears in M. Maritain's account of the Rights of Man cited earlier. He says, e.g.:

> . . . there is a human nature and this human nature is the same in all men . . . and possessed of a nature, constituted in a given determinate fashion, man obviously possesses ends which correspond to his natural constitution and which are the same for all—as all pianos, for instance, whatever their particular type and in whatever spot they may be, have as their end the production of certain attuned sounds. If they do not produce these sounds, they must be attuned or discarded as worthless . . . since man has intelligence and can determine his ends, it is up to him to put himself in tune with the ends necessarily demanded by his nature.[15]

And men's rights depend upon this common nature and end by which they are subject to the natural or "unwritten" law. But this seems to me a complete mistake. Human beings are not like exactly similar bottles of whisky each marked "for export only" or some device indicating a common destination or end. Men do not share a fixed nature, nor, therefore, are there any ends which they must necessarily pursue in fulfillment of such nature. There is no definition

[15] *Loc. cit.*, p. 35.

of "man." There is a more or less vague set of properties which characterize in varying degrees and proportions those creatures which are called "human." These determine for each individual human being what he *can* do but not what he *must* do. If he has an I.Q. of 85 his intellectual activities will be limited; if he is physically weak he cannot become a heavyweight boxer. If a woman has neither good looks nor acting ability she is unlikely to succeed as a film star. But what people may do with their capacities is extremely varied, and there is no one thing which they must do in order to be human. It would be nonsense to say: "I am not going to be an actress, a school teacher, a postman, a soldier, a taxpayer, but simply a human being." For what is the alternative? A man may choose whether he will become a civil servant or a schoolmaster; a conservative or a socialist, but he cannot choose whether he will be a man or a dog. There is certainly a sense in which it is often said that in the air-raid shelter or in the battle people forgot that they were officers or privates, assistant secretaries or typists, rich or poor, and remembered only that they were all human beings, i.e. all liable to die without regard to status. But that is always true. They did not remember that they were something *in addition* to being the particular human being they each were and which they might be without being any particular individual. And, as individuals, when the "All Clear" sounded, each returned to pursue his or her own ends, not the purpose of the human race. Certainly, many human beings may co-operate in a joint enterprise to achieve a particular end which each chooses. But that cannot be generalized into the spectacle of all human beings pursuing one end. There is no end set for the human race by an abstraction called "human nature." There are only ends which individuals choose, or are forced by circumstances to accept. There are none which they *must* accept. Men are not created for a purpose as a piano is built to produce certain sounds. Or if they are we have no idea of the purpose.

It is the emphasis on the individual sufferer from bad social conditions which constitutes the appeal of the social contract theory and the "natural" origin of human rights. But it does not follow that the theory is true as a statement of verifiable fact about the actual constitution of the world. The statements of the Law of Nature are not statements of the laws of nature, not even of the laws of an "ideal" nature. For nature provides no standards or ideals. All that exists, exists at the same level, or is of the same logical type. There are not, by nature, prize roses, works of art, oppressed or unoppressed citizens. Standards are determined by human choice, not set by nature independently of men. Natural events cannot tell us what we ought to do until we have made certain decisions, when knowledge of natural fact will enable the most efficient means to be chosen to carry out those decisions. Natural events themselves have no value, and human beings as natural existents have no value either, whether on account of possessing intelligence or having two feet.

One of the major criticisms of the doctrine of natural rights is that the list of natural rights varies with each exponent. For Hobbes, man's only natural right is self-preservation. More "liberal" theorists add to life and security, liberty, the pursuit of happiness and sometimes property. Modern socialists would probably include the right to "work or adequate maintenance." M. Maritain enumerates a list of nine natural rights which include besides the rights to life, liberty, and property of the older formulations, the right to pursue a religious vocation, the right to marry and raise a family, and, finally, the right of every human being to be treated as a person and not as a thing.[16] It is evident that these "rights" are of very different types which would need to be distinguished in a complete discussion of the problem. My aim in this paper, however, is only to try to understand what can be meant by the assertion that there are some rights to which human beings are entitled independently of their varying social relationships. And it seems difficult to account for the wide variations in the lists of these "rights" if they have all been deduced from a fixed human nature or essence, subject to an absolutely uniform "natural law." Nor is the disagreement one which can be settled by more careful empirical observation of human beings and their legal systems. The doctrine seems to try to operate by an analogy which it is logically impossible to apply.

The word "right" has a variety of uses in ordinary language, which include the distinction between "legal right" and "moral right." "A has a legal right against B" entails B has a duty to A which will be enforced by the courts. A has a claim against B recognized by an existing law. No person has a legal right which he cannot claim from some other (legal) person and which the law will not enforce. That A has a moral right against B likewise entails that B has a duty to A. But it is not necessarily a duty which can be legally enforced. A has a right to be told the truth by B and B has a corresponding duty to tell A the truth. But no one, except in special circumstances recognized by law, can force B to tell the truth, or penalize him, except by censure, if he does not. No one can, in general, claim to be told the truth, by right, under penalty. But a creditor can claim repayment of a debt or sue his debtor.

When the lawyers said that a slave had a right in natural law to be free, they thought of a legal right not provided for by any existing statute, enactment or custom and to whose universal infringement no penalties attached. But this, surely, is the vanishing point of law and of legal right. It indicates that there just wasn't a law or legal right by which a slave might demand his freedom. But perhaps there was a moral right and a moral obligation. The slave ought to be free and maybe it was the duty of every slaveholder to free his slaves and of legislators to enact laws forbidding slavery. But until this happened there was no law which forbade a man to keep slaves. Consequently, there is no point in saying there was "really" a natural law which forbade this. For the natural law was impotent. Statements about natural law were neither statements of natural fact nor legal practice.

So, does it follow that a "natural" right is just a "moral" right? Kant said, in effect, that to treat another human being as a person of intrinsic worth, an end in himself, is just to treat him in accordance with the moral law applicable to all rational beings on account of their having reason. But this is not quite the sense in which the term "natural rights" has been historically used. Declara-

---

[16] *Loc. cit.,* p. 60.

tions of the Rights of Man did not include his right to be told the truth, to have promises kept which had been made to him, to receive gratitude from those he had benefited, etc. The common thread among the variety of natural rights is their *political* character. Despite their rugged individualism, no exponent of the Rights of Man desired to enjoy them, in solitude, on a desert island. They were among the articles of the original Social Contract; clauses in Constitutions, the inspiration of social and governmental reforms. But "Keep promises"; "Tell the truth"; "Be grateful" are not inscribed on banners carried by aggrieved demonstrators or circulated among the members of an oppressed party. Whether or not morality can exist without society, it is certain that politics cannot. Why then were "natural rights" conceived to exist independently of organized society and hence of political controversies? I suggest that they were so considered in order to emphasize their basic or fundamental character. For words like freedom, equality, security, represented for the defenders of natural rights what they considered to be the fundamental moral and social values which should be or should continue to be realized in any society fit for intelligent and responsible citizens.

When the contract theorists talked of the rights as human beings which men had enjoyed in the state of nature, they seemed to be asserting unverifiable and nonsensical propositions since there is no evidence of a state of nature in which men lived before the establishment of civil societies. But they were not simply talking nonsense. They were, in effect, saying "In any society and under every form of government men ought to be able to think and express their thoughts freely, to live their lives without arbitrary molestation with their persons and goods. They ought to be treated as equal in value, though not necessarily of equal capacity or merit. They ought to be assured of the exclusive use of at least some material objects other than their own bodies; they ought not to be governed without some form of consent. And that the application of these rights to the particular conditions of a society, or their suspension, if necessary, should be agreed with them." The exponents of the natural Rights of Man were trying to express what they deemed to be the fundamental conditions of *human* social life and government. And it is by the observance of some such conditions, I suggest, that human societies are distinguished from ant hills and beehives.

This, however, has frequently been denied by utilitarian, idealist and Marxist philosophers who, though differing in other respects, agree in holding that the rights of an individual must be determined only by the needs and conveniences of society as a whole. Surely, they say, there can be no "natural" right to life in any society when a man may be executed as a criminal or killed as a conscripted soldier. And very little right to liberty exists when external danger threatens the state. "The person with rights and duties," says the evolutionist utilitarian Ritchie, "is the product of society and the rights of the individual must, therefore, be judged from the point of view of society as a whole and not the society from the point of view of the individual." [17] It is

---

[17] Ritchie: *Natural Rights* [Macmillan, London], p. 101.

the duty of the individual to preserve society for his descendants. For individuals perish but England remains. But the plain man may well ask why he must preserve a society for his descendants if it neither is, nor shows any prospect of being, worth living in. Will his descendants thank him for this consideration? All that seems to follow from Ritchie's view is that at any time the members of a society may agree to sacrifice some goods in order to achieve a certain result. And the result will include the restoration of basic rights. Does the ordinary citizen consider that he has no right to life and liberty because he agrees to (or does not protest against) the suspension of those rights in an emergency? He would be very unlikely to approve of such suspension if he thought the result would be the massacre or enslavement of himself, his contemporaries and possibly his children and descendants at the arbitrary will of a ruler or government. To suspend, or even to forfeit rights, as a criminal does, also temporarily, is not to deny rights. Nor is it to deny that such practices must be justified to the individuals required to submit to them. Though it may be much more useful to society that a man should remain a slave and even that he may be happier in that condition, it is not possible to prove to him that he has no right to be free, however much society wants his slavery. In short, "natural rights" are the conditions of a good society. But what those conditions are is not given by nature or mystically bound up with the essence of man and his inevitable goal, but is determined by human decisions.

PROPOSITIONS AND DECISIONS

Assertions about natural rights, then, are assertions of what ought to be as the result of human choice. They fall within class 3 of the division stated on page 644, as being ethical assertions or expressions of value. And these assertions or expressions include all those which result from human choice and preference, in art and personal relations, e.g. as well as in morals and politics. Such utterances in which human beings express choices determined by evaluation of better and worse have been variously interpreted, and it is, indeed, difficult to introduce a discussion of the topic without assuming an interpretation. I have tried, e.g. to avoid the use of the words "proposition" and "statement" in referring to these utterances since these words emphasize a relation between what is asserted and a fact by which it is verified or falsified. And this leads either to the attempts of the natural law and natural rights theories to find a "natural" fact which justifies these assertions or to a search for nonsensible entities called "Values" as the reference of ethical terms. Yet, of course, it is, in some sense, true that "No one ought to be ill-treated because he is a Jew, a Negro or not able to count above ten." Alternatively, to talk of "expressions of value" sounds as though such utterances are sophisticated ways of cheering and cursing. Just as the blow becomes sublimated into the sarcastic retort so our smiles of delight at unselfish action and howls of woe at parricide become intellectualized into apparent judgments about good and evil, right and wrong, without, however, losing their fundamentally emotive character.[18] On this view, value judgments do not state what is true or false, but are expressions of feeling, sometimes combined with commands to do or forbear. But whatever its emotional causes and effects, an articulate utterance does not seem to be simply a substitute for a smile or a tear. It *says* something. But I cannot hope in a necessarily brief discussion to do justice to the enormous variety of value utterances. So I will plunge, and say that value utterances are more like records of *decisions* than propositions.[19] To assert that "Freedom is better than slavery" or "All men are of equal worth" is not to state a fact but to *choose a side*. It announces *This is where I stand*.

I mentioned earlier that in the late war propaganda appeals to defend our comforts and privileges would have been rejected as uninspiring but that appeals to defend the rights of all men to freedom and equality obtained the required response, at least in all but the depraved and cynical. I now suggest that they did so because they accorded with our decisions about these ultimate social values. For whether or not we were more or less comfortable as a result, we should not choose to act only upon orders about which we had not in some way been consulted; to suppress the truth; to imprison without trial or to permit human individuals or classes of individuals to be treated as of no human value.

Two questions suggest themselves on this view. Firstly, if ethical judgments, and particularly the ethical judgments which concern the fundamental structure of society are value decisions, who makes these decisions and when? Is this not, as much as the natural law theory, the use of an analogy without application? I did safeguard myself to some extent by saying that these assertions are "more like" decisions than they are like propositions. They are unlike propositions because they are neither tautologies nor statements of verifiable fact. But it is also true that if asked when we decided in favour of free speech or democratic government or many of our social values we could not give a date. It is, therefore, suggested that we no more record a decision by a value assertion than we signed a Social Contract. Nevertheless, I think the analogy does emphasize important differences between value and other assertions. For, if intelligent, we do choose our politics as we choose our friends or our favoured poems, novels, pictures, symphonies, and as we do not choose to accept Pythagoras's theorem or the law of gravitation. And when challenged we affirm our decision or stand by our choice. We say, "I did not realize how much I valued free speech until I went to Germany in 1936," indicating that a choice had been made, but so easily that it had seemed scarcely necessary to record its occurrence.

For, indeed, the fundamental values of a society are not always recorded in explicit decisions by its members, even its rulers, but are expressed in the life of the society and constitute its quality. They are conveyed by its "tone"

---

[18] Cf. A. J. Ayer: *Language, Truth and Logic* [V. Gollancz, Ltd., London, 1946], ch. 6. [See our Chapter 6, Selection 6.—Eds.]

[19] Dr. K. R. Popper makes a similar distinction in an interesting discussion of value judgments in *The Open Society*, vol. 1, ch. 5.

and atmosphere as well as its laws and Statutory Rules and Orders. The members of a society whose values are freedom and equality behave differently, walk, speak, fight differently from the members of a slave society. Plato expressed this nastily in the Republic [20] when he said that in a democracy even the horses and asses behaved with a gait expressive of remarkable freedom and dignity, and like everyone else became "gorged with freedom." Suspicion, fear and servility are absent, or, at least, inconspicuous in such a society. And no one who visited Germany after 1933 needs to be reminded of the change of atmosphere.

Decisions concerning the worth of societies and social institutions are not made by an *élite,* by rulers or a governing class but, explicitly or by acceptance, by those who live and work in the society and operate its institutions. But these decisions may be changed by the effective propaganda of a minority who have reached other decisions of whose value they desire to convince the majority. Perhaps, ultimately, men get the societies and governments which they choose, even if not those which they deserve, for they may deserve better than passion, indolence or ignorance permits them to choose.

This leads to a second question. Upon what grounds or for what reasons are decisions reached? Consider the expression of the doctrine of equality; that all human beings are of equal worth, intrinsic value, or are ends in themselves. Is there an answer to the question, Why? On what *evidence* is this assertion based? How can such a decision be maintained despite the obvious differences between human beings? The answer of the natural law theorists and of Kant was that the "natural" fact that all men have reason proves that they are of intrinsic worth, and are thus entitled to the Rights of Man. It is not clear, however, whether imbeciles and lunatics forfeit human rights. No one can deny that they are human beings. A person who becomes insane does not thereby become a mere animal. But if statements about the possession by anything of a natural characteristic is related to a decision of worth as evidence for a conclusion, then it would be illogical to retain the decision when the characteristics were absent or had changed. It is irrational to continue to believe a proposition when evidence shows that it is false. I affirm that no natural characteristic constitutes a *reason* for the assertion that all human beings are of equal worth. Or, alternatively, that *all* the characteristics of *any* human being are equally reasons for this assertion. But this amounts to saying that the decision of equal worth is affirmed of all human beings *whatever their particular characteristics*. It does not follow that they are of equal *merit* and that their treatment should not vary accordingly, in ways compatible with their intrinsic value. But even a criminal, though he has lost merit and may deserve punishment, does not become worthless. He cannot be cast out of humanity.

I am aware that this view needs much more elaboration, and especially illustration than can be given in very limited space. I can, therefore, indicate only in a general way the type of value assertions and the manner in which they are related to each other and to other assertions. They are not related as

[20] Book 8.

evidence strengthening a conclusion. For decisions are not true or false and are not deduced from premises. Do we, then, decide without reason? Are decisions determined by chance or whim? Surely, it will be said, the facts have some relevance to what is decided? To say that decisions are made without reason looks like saying that we choose by tossing a coin; opening the *Works of Shakespeare* or *The Bible* at random and reading the first sentence; or shutting our eyes and sticking a pin into the list of starters to pick the Derby winner. These seem very irrational methods of choice. Nevertheless, we do sometimes choose by a not very dissimilar procedure. If two candidates for a post are of exactly equal merit, the selectors may well end by plumping for one or the other. This, it may be said, was justified because there was "nothing to choose between them," not that the decision bore no relation to their merits. But there are some choices into which merit hardly enters. Those involving personal relations, for instance. It would seem absurd to try to prove that our affections were not misplaced by listing the characteristics of our friends. To one who asked for such "proof" we should reply, with Montaigne: [21]

> If a man urge me to tell him wherefore I loved him, I feel it cannot be expressed but by answering, because it was he, because it was myself. . . . It is not one especial consideration, nor two, nor three, nor four, nor a thousand. It is I wot not what kind of quintessence of all this commixture which seized my will.

Yet it is also correct to say that our decisions about worth are not merely arbitrary, and intelligent choices are not random. They cannot be proved correct by evidence. Nor, I suggest, do we try to prove them. What we do is to support and defend our decisions. The relation of the record of a decision to the considerations which support it is not that of proof to conclusion. It is much more like the defence of his client by a good counsel.

Consider an analogous situation in art. Suppose one were trying to defend a view that Keats is a greater poet than Crabbe. [22] One would compare passages from each writer, showing the richness and complexity of the imagery and movement of Keats's verse and the monotonous rhythm, moral platitudes and poverty-stricken images of Crabbe. One would aid the effect by reading passages aloud for their comparable musical effects; would dwell on single lines and passages which show the differences between the evocative language of Keats and the conventional "poetic diction" of Crabbe. The "Season of mists and mellow fruitfulness" of the one and the "finny tribes," etc., of the other. One might eventually resort to the remarks of the best critics on both writers. In short, one would employ every device to "present" Keats, to build up a convincing advocacy of his poetry. And the resistance of Crabbe's defender might collapse, and he would declare the case won with the verdict "Keats is the better poet." But nothing would have been *proved*. Crabbe's supporter might still disagree. He would dwell on Crabbe's "sincerity"; his genuine sympathy

---

[21] *Essays* (trans. John Florio), *Of Friendship.*

[22] [George Crabbe (1754-1832), English poet who wrote *The Village, The Parish Register,* and so on.—Eds.]

with the poor and excuse his poetic limitations as due to a bad tradition for which he was not responsible. He might add that Crabbe was one of Jane Austen's favourite poets. And if he so persisted he would not be *wrong,* i.e. he would not be believing falsely that Crabbe was a better poet than Keats but much more persuasion would be needed to induce him to alter his decision.

Compare with this the correct attitude to the proof of a scientific law. If the empirical evidence is conclusive, then a person who rejects the conclusion is either stupid or biased. He is certainly believing a false proposition. We do not "defend" the law of gravitation but all instructed persons accept the proof of the law.

On the other hand, we do not refer to Mill's proof but to his "magnificent defence" of civil liberty. For a successful defence involves much more than statement of facts. The facts of the case are known to both the prosecuting and defending counsel. The question is, should the accused be condemned or acquitted? The skilful lawyer uses these facts, but he uses them differently from the scientist. He marshals them so as to emphasize those which favour his client. He interprets those which appear unfavourable in terms of legal decisions in similar cases which would benefit the accused. He chooses language which does not merely state, but impress: he uses voice, gesture, facial expression, all the devices of eloquence and style in order to influence the decision of the jury in favour of his client. His client may still lose, but he would admit that he has a better chance of winning if he briefs a good counsel.

But, it may be asked, is this a recommendation to take fraudulent advocacy as our model for defending the rights of man? Not at all. Lawyers and art critics are not frauds, but neither are they scientists. They are more like artists who use material with results which impress and convince but do not *prove*. There is no conceivable method of *proving* that Keats is a better poet than Crabbe or that freedom is better than slavery. For assertions of value cannot be subjected to demonstrative or inductive methods. It is for this reason that such assertions have been regarded as simple expressions of feeling or emotion like cries of pain and anger. But we do not defend or support a cry of pain or shout of joy though it may be related to a cause. If our value choices are defensible their defence requires other methods.

The lawyer says: "I agree that my client was on the premises; I deny that his being there in those circumstances constitutes a *trespass*. This may be confirmed from *Gower* v. *Flint* where this ruling was given in similar circumstances." The critic says: "You agree that Keats's imagery is *rich* and *complex;* his language *original* and *powerful:* that Crabbe, on the contrary, is *frigid* and *conventional* in language; *meagre* in imagery, etc., etc." The lawyer supports his plea from previous decisions. The critic likewise appeals not to physical or psychological facts about the occurrences of marks on paper, internal pictures, etc., but to previous decisions *evaluating* these and other occurrences. Rich and powerful poetry is good; frigid and meagre versifying is bad. If we stand by our previous decisions it does not follow that we *must* on account of them make a further decision now, but they are certainly relevant. Incorporated into a system of skilful advocacy they may win a favourable verdict. But, on the other hand, we may reject our former decisions. Elaborate imagery, lyrical quality, are dismissed as *barbarous* or *sentimental;* our choice is now for the *plain* and *elegant* statement. Such a complete change in systems of evaluation seems to occur in different ages. The eighteenth century listened to Shakespeare, but gave the palm to Pope. The Victorians saw Georgian houses but chose sham Gothic. So we may present the authoritarian with an attractive picture of a free and democratic society, and if he already values independence, experimentation, mutual trust, he may agree that these values are realized in such a society. But he may call independence, insolence; experimentation, rash meddling; and the picture will fail in its effect.

There are no certainties in the field of values. For there are no true or false beliefs about values, but only better or worse decisions and choices. And to encourage the better decisions we need to employ devices which are artistic rather than scientific. For our aim is not intellectual assent, but practical effects. These are not, of course, absolutely separate, for intellectual assent to a proposition or theory is followed by using it. But values, I think, concern only behaviour. They are not known, but accepted and acted upon.

Intellectuals often complain that political propaganda, e.g. is not conducted as if it were scientific argument. But if moral values are not capable of scientific proof it would be irrational to treat them as if they were. The result of a confusion of logical types is to leave the field of nonscientific persuasion and conviction to propagandists of the type of the late Dr. Goebbels.

Questions

1. If the statement that men have natural rights is a "curious hybrid" of a tautological proposition and an empirical proposition, what aspect of the meaning of the statement is tautological, and what aspect is empirical?

2. What would you say is the meaning of the term "natural law" as it is used in the reading? Would Cicero accept the meaning you have given to the term? Why or why not? (For the view of Cicero, see the selection beginning on page 604.)

3. According to Miss Macdonald, what is the connection between natural rights and the social contract?

4. "Men do not share a fixed nature, nor, therefore, are there any ends which they must necessarily pursue in fulfillment of such nature." What argument does Miss Macdonald give in support of this statement? What conclusions does she draw from it with regard to natural rights and natural law?

5. What line of reasoning leads Miss Macdonald to claim that the appeal to natural rights is really the advocating of certain fundamental moral and social values?

6. People make a claim to natural rights, Miss Macdonald suggests, "because no existing social compulsion or relationship is self-justifying." What is meant by this phrase? How could the claim to natural rights be used to justify an existing social compulsion or relationship?

7. What does Miss Macdonald mean by saying that "value utterances are more like records of *decisions* than propositions"? What evidence does she give for the truth of this statement?

8. If value assertions are expressions of decisions, and if the claim that men have natural rights is a value assertion, then that claim is the expression of a decision.

How does Miss Macdonald answer the question: Who makes such a decision, and when?

9. What argument does Miss Macdonald give to show that "no natural characteristic constitutes a *reason* for the assertion that all human beings are of equal worth"? Give your own critical appraisal of this argument.

10. Miss Macdonald attempts to clarify the justification of value assertions by comparing it with two kinds of reasoning: a lawyer's defense of his client and an aesthetic argument concerning the relative merits of two poets. Explain the two kinds of reasoning, and show how they would apply to value assertions in which people claim to have natural rights.

11. ". . . There are no true or false beliefs about values, but only better or worse decisions and choices." State why you agree, or disagree, with this position.

Suggested Further Reading | Classic Works

Aristotle, *Politics; Nicomachean Ethics.*
Bentham, Jeremy, *An Introduction to the Principles of Morals and Legislation* (1789).
Burke, Edmund, *Reflections on the Revolution in France* (1790).
Hamilton, Alexander, John Jay, and James Madison, *The Federalist* (1787-1788).
Hobbes, Thomas, *Leviathan* (1651).
Jefferson, Thomas, *Collected Papers.* Good selections are to be found in *Thomas Jefferson on Democracy,* ed. by Saul K. Padover, Mentor Books, N. Y., and *The Political Writings of Thomas Jefferson,* ed. by Edward Dumbauld, Liberal Arts Press, N. Y.
Machiavelli, Niccolo, *Discourses* (1516-1519); *The Prince* (1532).
Mill, James, *An Essay on Government* (1816).
Mill, John Stuart, *On Liberty* (1859); *Considerations on Representative Government* (1861).
Paine, Thomas, *The Rights of Man* (1791-1792).
Plato, *Republic; Laws; The Statesman.*

| Introductory Studies

Gough, J. W., *The Social Contract,* 2nd ed., Clarendon Press, Oxford, 1957.
Laski, Harold J., *Authority in the Modern State,* Yale University Press, New Haven, 1927.
———, *Liberty in the Modern State,* Harper, N. Y., 1930.
———, *The State in Theory and Practice,* Viking, N. Y., 1935.
Perry, Ralph Barton, *Puritanism and Democracy,* Vanguard, N. Y., 1944.
———, *Realms of Value,* Harvard University Press, Cambridge, Mass., 1954, Chaps. XI-XIV.
Stace, W. T., *The Destiny of Western Man,* Reynal and Hitchcock, N. Y., 1942.
Weldon, T. D., *The Vocabulary of Politics,* Penguin Books, Harmondsworth, Middlesex, Eng., 1953.

| Advanced Studies

Brown, Stuart M., Jr., "Inalienable Rights," *Philosophical Review,* Vol. 64, 1955.
Cameron, J. M., and T. D. Weldon, "The Justification of Political Attitudes," *Aristotelian Society Supplementary Volume 29,* 1955.

Carritt, E. F., *Ethical and Political Thinking*, Clarendon Press, Oxford, 1947.

Cohen, J., and H. L. A. Hart, "Theory and Justification in Jurisprudence," *Aristotelian Society Supplementary Volume 29*, 1955.

Frankena, William K., "Natural and Inalienable Rights," *Philosophical Review*, Vol. 64, 1955.

Hart, H. L. A., "The Ascription of Responsibility and Rights," *Proceedings of the Aristotelian Society*, 1948-49; reprinted in *Logic and Language, First Series*, ed. by Antony Flew, Blackwell, Oxford, 1951.

———, "Are There Any Natural Rights?" *Philosophical Review*, Vol. 64, 1955.

Laslett, Peter, ed., *Philosophy, Politics and Society*, Macmillan, N. Y., 1956.

Macdonald, Margaret, "The Language of Political Theory," *Proceedings of the Aristotelian Society*, 1940-41; reprinted in *Logic and Language, First Series*, ed. by Antony Flew, Blackwell, Oxford, 1951.

Plamenatz, J., W. D. Lamont, and H. B. Acton, "Rights," *Aristotelian Society Supplementary Volume 24*, 1950.

Rawls, John, "Justice as Fairness," *Philosophical Review*, Vol. 67, 1958.

Rhees, R., T. D. Weldon, and P. H. Nowell-Smith, "Science and Politics," *Aristotelian Society Supplementary Volume 23*, 1949.

THE
PROBLEM
OF

Philosophy of History

Philosophy of History

One of the most perplexing questions which a person can ask himself is, "Why was I put in this world?" The use of "put" in the question implies that there is some agency in charge of the world and thus responsible for the questioner's position in it. The questioner's task, then, is to gain some knowledge of that agency and its plans for the world, so that he will know how he fits into those plans.

The context in which many people would answer the question, "Why was I put in this world?" is a religious one. God is the agent who is in charge of the world, and a person can know his place in the world when he knows God's plan for the world. God's plan is an important feature of both Judaism and Christianity, and we may turn to these religions for illustrations of such a plan. The clue to a Jew's place in God's plan is to be found in God's covenant with Abraham:

When Abram was ninety-nine, the Eternal appeared to Abram and said, "I am God Almighty; live ever mindful of my presence, and so be blameless; I will make my compact with you and multiply your descendants greatly." Abram fell on his face; and God continued, "As for me, my compact is made with you, and you shall be the father of many a nation; no longer shall your name be Abram, but Abraham (Many-father), for I have appointed you to be the father of many a nation; I will make you most fruitful, I will make nations out of you, and kings shall spring from you. And I will ratify my compact for all time, between me and yourself and your descendants from generation to generation, engaging to be a God to you and to your descendants after you. Also, I will give you and your descendants after you the land where you are residing, the whole of the land of Canaan, as a possession for all time; and I will be their God." [1]

In Judaism the fulfillment of God's plan is the settling of his worshipers in the land of Canaan. In Christianity this old, geographical goal of the Jews is transferred into the spiritual realm, and Christianity is to culminate in the union of the community of worshipers with God. The achievement of this goal is movingly described in The Revelation of St. John the Divine. The use of the phrase "the new Jerusalem" in the following passage is the touchstone of Christianity's link with the covenant between God and Abraham:

Then I saw the new heaven and the new earth, for the first heaven and the first earth had passed away; and the sea is no more. And I saw the holy City, the new Jerusalem, descending from God out of heaven, all ready like a bride arrayed for her husband. And I heard a loud voice out of the throne crying,

"Lo, God's dwelling-place is with men,
with men will he dwell;
they shall be his people,
and God will himself be with them:
he shall wipe every tear from their eyes,
and death shall be no more—
no more wailing, no more crying, no more pain,
for the former things have passed away."

Then he who was seated on the throne said, "Lo, I make all things new." And he said, "Write this: 'these words are trustworthy and genuine.'" Then he

[1] Genesis, XVII:1-8. From *The Bible: A New Translation*, by James Moffatt. Copyright 1922, 1935, and 1950, Harper & Brothers, N. Y. Used by permission.

said, "All is over! I am the alpha and the omega, the beginning and the end. I will let the thirsty drink of the fountain of the water of Life without price. The conqueror shall obtain this, and I will be his God, and he shall be my son. . . ." [2]

A person's acceptance of a religious answer to the question, "Why was I put in this world?" hinges, of course, on his accepting the religion in which the answer is to be found; and his acceptance of the religion must finally be a matter of faith in the revelations on which the religion is based. But just as there is an enterprise closely connected with religion called "natural theology," whose practitioners have tried to show that God's existence can be proved by reasonable arguments,[3] so there is another enterprise closely connected with religion called "philosophy of history," whose practitioners have tried to show that God's plan for the world can be proved by reasonable arguments. In philosophy of history, however, the identity of God may be lost in the word "history," as when the Marxist philosopher of history Friedrich Engels writes, "To carry through his world-emancipating act is the *historical* mission of the modern proletariat." But the religious origins of philosophy of history cannot be denied. The "new Jerusalem," its supernatural perfection sometimes reduced to a naturally attainable perfection, can be discovered in the goal of history described in every philosophy of history.

[2] The Revelation of St. John, XXI:1-7. From *The Bible: A New Translation,* by James Moffatt. Copyright 1922, 1935, and 1950, Harper & Brothers, N. Y. Used by permission.

[3] The relation between religion and natural theology is explored at length in Chapter 4, "The Problem of Knowledge of God."

A philosophy of history, then, is an exposition of the plan or pattern which lies behind human affairs, and which is being unfolded in the course of human history. It should be noticed that in this sense of the phrase both Judaism and Christianity have philosophies of history; but in this chapter we shall not consider philosophies of history whose basis is revelation.

Philosophers of history are not agreed about the method by which the plan of history is to be discovered. Hence, there are many philosophies of history; but all share certain general characteristics. They are all designed to answer the question, "Why was I put in this world?" They answer it by telling a person that his importance lies in his being a member of a certain group (the human species, or a particular class, or a particular nation are typical examples), and that his group is an instrument of history destined to fulfill the goal of history. The goal of history is variously described. The perfection of the human species, the achievement of a classless society, and the government of the world by a particular nation are typical examples of goals which philosophers have discovered for history. Thus, from a philosophy of history, a person learns that he has been put in this world to make his contribution to the achievement of the goal of history.

When we first ask the question, "Why was I put in this world?" and seek to understand our place in the whole scheme of things, a strong element of despair is likely to haunt us. The despair has at least two sources: our realization of the comparatively short span of the life of an individual on earth, and our realization of the comparatively limited powers of any one individual. We may be overcome with a feeling of our own insignificance. It may seem hopeless to think we can achieve some impressive purpose in our lifetime. But how encouraging it is when we are shown that our short life and puny powers are part of some greater entity, the human species, for example, and that our life and efforts, insignificant in themselves, can have meaning in the larger context of the perfection of the human species, or some other goal of history. What is more, since it is a characteristic of philosophies of history to describe the achievement of the goal of history as inevitable, we may have the pleasure of knowing what the culmination of human history must be, even though we may not be living to witness it. In contrast with the point of view described above, it follows that if one is neither appalled by the shortness of human life nor distressed by the limitations of individual effort, and if one could be satisfied to pursue one's *own* purposes undaunted by the prospect of failure which seems to threaten us in the nature of things, then one is probably not in the market for a philosophy of history.

In this chapter, however, we shall be interested in the logical, rather than the psychological, basis of philosophies of history. Our question will be, "What grounds are there for accepting (or rejecting) a philosophy of history?" To illuminate this question we shall comment briefly on the methods which have been proposed in the Kantian and the Marxist philosophies of history, as ways of discovering the plan of history.

Method in Philosophy of History

This chapter contains four readings: "The Idea of a Universal History on a Cosmopolitical Plan" by Immanuel Kant; "Criticism of Kant's Philosophy of History" by Mr. W. H. Walsh; "The Marxist Philosophy of History" by Friedrich Engels; and "History: The Class Struggle or Socialized Intelligence?" by John Dewey.

We have already said that a philosophy of history is an exposition of the plan or pattern which lies behind human affairs, and which is being unfolded in the course of human history. The readings by Kant and Engels are philosophies of history in this first sense. But "philosophy of history" also means the critical examination of methods which have been used for discovering the plan of history. The readings in this chapter by Walsh and Dewey are critical examinations of the methods of Kant and of the Marxists, respectively. In addition to these two senses of "philosophy of history," there is a third which must also be mentioned. In contrast with philosophy of history as the exposition of a plan which lies *behind* human affairs, the phrase "philosophy of history" may also be used as a name for predictions of what the future will be like based on a study of the past, without trying to read into history some goal which *must* be achieved in the course of human affairs. The selection by Dewey, as well as containing a statement of his criticism of Marxism, is also a sketch of Dewey's own philosophy of history, in the third meaning of that phrase.

In this chapter our chief aim is to introduce the reader to philosophy of history as the exposition of the plan or pattern which lies behind human affairs, and which is being unfolded in the course of human history. Our examples of this sort of philosophy of history are, as we have said, the selections by Kant and Engels. For Kant, the goal of history will be fulfilled when the human species is brought to perfection; for so he understands the ideal of nature as expressed in human history. For Engels, the goal of history will be fulfilled when the working class (the proletariat) has achieved the classless society; for so he understands the material implications of human history.

The problem for the reader is to discover which of these two philosophies of history tells us what the true goal of history is (if either does). One of the clues to the correctness of a philosophy of history lies in the method by which it was produced. It should be clear from a philosopher's method why his philosophy of history is correct and any other philosophy of history untenable. We have already mentioned, however, that there is no agreement among philosophers about a method for discovering the principles of a philosophy of history; and two different methods are illustrated by the essays of Kant and Engels.

Kant says that the course of history is "to a certain degree . . . determined *a priori*." It is difficult to know what Kant meant by this remark; and the difficulties are explored by Mr. Walsh in his efforts to determine the logical status of the principles of Kant's philosophy of history. Presumably, however, the principles which Kant has discovered are principles which are in some way given to history and cannot be inferred from the course of historical events. Our question then is, "How did Kant acquire his knowledge of these principles?" Until we have an answer to this question we cannot be sure that Kant has discovered the plan of history.

Engels expounds the Marxist philosophy of history; his method of discovering the plan of history is to infer the goal of history from what has happened in the past. Engels' method then at least has the advantage of looking scientific. But before Engels can satisfy us, we must ask several questions about his philosophy of history. We are familiar with the natural scientist's maxim that the future will resemble the past, but can we infer from the past that the future (i.e., history) has a goal? We must also ask whether Engels has been exhaustive or only selective in his examination of the past. Dewey is particularly critical of the Marxist philosophy of history on this score. Finally, we must ask whether Engels would allow that the Marxist philosophy of history might be disproved. This last question is the most crucial which can be asked of any philosophy of history (in the first sense of the term), for it calls into question the very possibility of discovering *the* philosophy of history. For if a philosophy of history may be disproved, history's achievement of its goal is not inevitable; and philosophy of history can have no legitimate appeal as knowledge of the way in which human history *must* culminate. On the other hand, if a philosophy of history cannot be disproved, then it is nothing more than a set of conceptions, either so unrelated to actual events or related in such a highly selective way, that we cannot learn from it what the future *must* be.

Nothing of what has been said above must be taken as discouraging the study of the past as a clue to the future, provided one does not mistake one's predictions for inevitabilities. Indeed, in his essay Dewey advocates such a study of the past as the intelligent alternative to "philosophy of history" in its first sense, which the Marxists adopt. We may, in other words, study the past to discover not what *must* happen but what *might* happen. Consequently, we may plan on the basis of our knowledge either to alter, if we can, or to accept, if we must, what is to happen.

The reader's task is to try to decide which view of the philosophy of history is more acceptable. He must choose between what we have called the first sense of "philosophy of history," the attempt to discover the inevitable goal of history, and what we have called the third sense of the term, the attempt to understand what might happen in history on the basis of an empirical study of the past. We have also distinguished another sense of "philosophy of history" (the second sense), the critical examination of the methods which have been used in constructing philosophies of history in the first sense. Part of the reader's task is to make such a critical examination himself. By so doing he will be aided in coming to a reasonable decision as to what particular philosophy of history in the first sense to accept for himself, or whether to reject them all in favor of philosophy of history in the third sense.

1

The Idea of a Universal History on a Cosmopolitical Plan

Immanuel Kant
(1724-1804)

[A general introductory note on Kant may be found on page 116.]

This essay by Kant enables the reader to meet, in a small compass, all the characteristics of a prophetic philosophy of history. A belief in a force that shapes human history, a belief in a plan that is imposed on history, a belief in the goal of human society as the fulfilling of the plan are all illustrated here. The reader's immediate task is to learn what Kant believes the plan of history to be. Then he may turn to these questions: How does Kant know that he has discovered the plan of human history? and, How could Kant tell that someone else is mistaken if that person claims to have discovered another plan of history? When the reader has considered these questions for himself, he may turn to Mr. W. H. Walsh's "Criticism" (page 679) for assistance in the further examination of Kant's philosophy of history.

Because of the similarities between Kant's account of the role of nature in human history and theological accounts of the role of God in the world, Kant's essay raises certain other questions which are dealt with in different ways in other parts of this book. Thus, the reader may want to look up the problem of proving God's existence (pages 339 ff.) when he considers the question of how Kant might show that nature governs human history. In addition the reader might like to examine the selections on the problem of miracles (pages 370 ff.) and the problem of God and evil (pages 389 ff.), where some of the questions which interest Kant are considered from a more definitely theological point of view.

This essay was first published in 1784. The translation from the German is by Thomas De Quincey.

Appeared originally in the *London Magazine* for October 1824; reprinted by De Quincey in 1859 in Vol. 13 of his Collective Edition of his writings.

Whatsoever difference there may be in our notions of the *freedom of the will* metaphysically considered, it is evident that the manifestations of this will, viz. human actions, are as much under the control of universal laws of nature as any other physical phenomena. It is the province of History to narrate these manifestations; and, let their causes be ever so secret, we know that History, simply by taking its station at a distance and contemplating the agency of the human will upon a large scale, aims at unfolding to our view a regular stream of tendency in the great succession of events—so that the very same course of incidents which, taken separately and individually, would have seemed perplexed, incoherent, and lawless, yet viewed in their connexion and as the actions of the human *species* and not of independent beings, never fail to discover a steady and continuous, though slow, development of certain great predispositions in our nature. Thus, for instance, deaths, births, and marriages, considering how much they are separately dependent on the freedom of the human will, should seem to be subject to no law according to which any calculation could be made beforehand of their amount: and yet the yearly registers of these events in great countries prove that they go on with as much conformity to the laws of nature as the oscillations of the weather. These, again, are events which in detail are so far irregular that we cannot predict them individually; and yet, taken as a whole series, we find that they never fail to support the growth of plants, the currents of rivers, and other arrangements of nature, in a uniform and uninterrupted course. Individual men, and even nations, are little aware that, whilst they are severally pursuing their own peculiar and often contradictory purposes, they are unconsciously following the guidance of a great natural purpose which is wholly unnoticed by themselves, and are thus promoting and making efforts for a great process which, even if they perceived it, they would little regard.

Considering that men, taken collectively as a body, do not proceed, like brute animals, under the law of an instinct, nor yet again, like rational cosmopolites, under the law of a preconcerted plan, one might imagine that no systematic history of their actions (such, for instance, as the history of bees or beavers) could be possible. At the sight of the actions of man displayed on the great stage of the world, it is impossible to escape a certain degree of disgust: with all the occasional indications of wisdom scattered here and there, we cannot but perceive the whole sum of these actions to be a web of folly, childish vanity, and often even of the idlest wickedness and spirit of destruction. Hence, at last, one is puzzled to know what judgment to form of our species, so conceited of its high advantages. In such a perplexity there is no resource for the philosopher but this—that, finding it impossible to presume in the human race any *rational* purpose of its own, he must endeavour to detect some *natural* purpose in such a senseless current of human actions; by means of which a history of creatures that pursue no plan of their own may yet admit a systematic form as the history of creatures that are blindly pursuing a plan of nature. Let us now see whether we can succeed in finding out a clue to such a history, leaving it to nature to produce a man capable of executing it—just as she produced a Kepler who unexpectedly brought the eccentric courses of the planets under determinate laws, and afterwards a Newton who explained these laws out of a universal ground in Nature:

PROPOSITION THE FIRST

All tendencies of any creature to which it is predisposed by Nature are destined in the end to develop themselves perfectly and agreeably to their final purpose.

External as well as internal (or anatomical) examination confirms this remark in all animals. An organ which is not to be used, a natural arrangement that misses its purpose, would be a contradiction in physics. Once departing from this fundamental proposition, we have a Nature no longer tied to laws, but objectless and working at random; and a cheerless reign of Chance steps into the place of Reason.

PROPOSITION THE SECOND

In Man, as the sole rational creature upon earth, those tendencies which have the use of his reason for their object are destined to obtain their perfect development in the species only, and not in the individual.

Reason in a creature is a faculty for extending the rules and purposes of the exercise of all its powers far beyond natural instinct; and it is illimitable in its plans. It works, however, not instinctively, but tentatively, by means of practice, through progress and regress, in order to ascend gradually from one degree of illumination to another. On this account, either it would be necessary for each man to live an inordinate length of time in order to learn how to make a perfect use of his natural tendencies; or else, supposing the actual case that Nature has limited his term of life, she must then require an incalculable series of generations (each delivering its quota of knowledge to its immediate successor) in order to ripen the germs which she has laid in our species to that degree of development which corresponds with her final purpose. And the period of this mature development must exist at least in idea to Man as the object of his efforts: because otherwise his own natural predispositions must of necessity be regarded as objectless; and this would at once take away all *practical* principles, and would expose Nature, the wisdom of whose arrangements must in all other cases be assumed as a fundamental postulate, to the suspicion of capricious dealing in the case of Man only.

PROPOSITION THE THIRD

It is the will of Nature that Man should owe to himself alone everything which transcends the mere mechanic constitution of his animal existence, and that he should be susceptible of no other happiness or perfection than what he has created for himself, instinct apart, through his own reason.

Nature does nothing superfluously, and in the use of means to her ends does not play the prodigal. Having given to Man reason, and freedom of the will grounded upon reason, she had hereby sufficiently made known the purpose which governed her in the choice of the furniture and appointments, intellectual and physical, with which she has accoutred him. Thus provided, he had no need for the guidance of instinct, or for knowledge and forethought created to his hand; for these he was to be indebted to himself. The means of providing for his own shelter from the elements, for his own security, and the whole superstructure of delights which add comfort and embellishment to life, were to be the work of his own hands. So far indeed has she pushed this principle that she seems to have been frugal even to niggardliness in the dispensation of her animal endowments to Man, and to have calculated her allowance to the nicest rigour of the demand in the very earliest stage of his existence: as if it had been her intention hereby to proclaim that the highest degree of power, of intellectual perfection, and of happiness to which he should ever toil upwards from a condition utterly savage, must all be wrung and extorted from the difficulties and thwartings of his situation, and the merit therefore be exclusively his own; thus implying that she had at heart his own rational self-estimation rather than his convenience or comfort. She has indeed beset Man with difficulties; and in no way could she have so clearly made known that her purpose with Man was not that he might live in pleasure, but that by a strenuous wrestling with those difficulties he might make himself worthy of living in pleasure. Undoubtedly it seems surprising on this view of the case that the earlier generations appear to exist only for the sake of the latter, viz. for the sake of forwarding that edifice of man's grandeur in which only the latest generations are to dwell, though all have undesignedly taken part in raising it. Mysterious as this appears, it is, however, at the same time necessary, if we once assume a race of rational animals as destined by means of this characteristic reason to a perfect development of their tendencies, and subject to mortality in the individual, but immortal in the species.

PROPOSITION THE FOURTH

The means which Nature employs to bring about the development of all the tendencies she has laid in Man is the antagonism of these tendencies in the social state—no farther, however, than to that point at which this antagonism becomes the cause of social arrangements founded in law.

By antagonism of this kind I mean the *unsocial sociality* of man—that is, a tendency to enter the social state, combined with a perpetual resistance to that tendency which is continually threatening to dissolve it. Man has gregarious inclinations, feeling himself in the social state more than Man, by means of the development thus given to his natural tendencies. But he has also strong antigregarious inclinations, prompting him to insulate himself, which arise out of the unsocial desire (existing concurrently with his social propensities) to force all things into compliance with his own humour—a propensity to which he naturally anticipates resistance from his consciousness of a similar spirit of resistance to others existing in himself. Now, this resistance it is which awakens all the powers of Man, drives him to master his propensity to indolence, and, in the shape of ambition, love of honour, or avarice, impels him to procure distinction for himself amongst his fellows. In this way arise the first steps from the savage state to the state of culture, which consists peculiarly in the social worth of Man. Talents of every kind are now unfolded, taste formed, and by gradual increase of light a preparation is made for such a mode of thinking as is capable of converting the rude natural tendency to moral distinctions into determinate practical principles, and finally of exalting a social concert that had been *pathologically* extorted from the mere necessities of situation into a *moral* union founded on the reasonable choice. But for these antisocial propensities, so unamiable in themselves, which give birth to that resistance which every man meets with in his own self-interested pretensions, an Arcadian life would arise, of perfect harmony and mutual love, such as must suffocate and stifle all talents in their very germs. Men, as gentle as the sheep they fed, would communicate to their existence no higher value than belongs to mere animal life, and would leave the vacuum of creation, which exists in reference to the final purpose of man's nature as a rational nature, unfilled. Thanks, therefore, to Nature for the enmity, for the jealous spirit of envious competition, for the insatiable thirst after wealth and power! These wanting, all the admirable tendencies in man's nature would remain for ever undeveloped. Man, for his own sake as an individual, wishes for concord; but Nature knows better what is good for Man as a species; and she ordains discord. He would live in ease and passive content: but Nature wills that he shall precipitate himself out of this luxury of indolence into labours and hardships, in order that he may devise remedies against them, and thus raise himself above them by an intellectual conquest, not sink below them by an unambitious evasion. The impulses which she has with this view laid in his moral constitution, the sources of that antisociality and universal antagonism from which so many evils arise, but which again stimulate a fresh reaction of the faculties, and by consequence more and more aid the development of the primitive tendencies, all tend to betray the adjusting hand of a wise Creator, not that of an Evil Spirit that has bungled in the execution of his own designs, or has malevolently sought to perplex them with evil.

PROPOSITION THE FIFTH

The highest problem for the Human Species, to the solution of which it is irresistibly urged by natural impulses, is the establishment of a universal Civil Society founded on the empire of political justice.

Since it is only in the social state that the final purpose of Nature with regard to Man (viz. the development of all his tendencies) can be accomplished

—and in such a social state as combines with the utmost possible freedom and consequent antagonism of its members the most rigorous determination of the boundaries of this freedom, in order that the freedom of such individual may coexist with the freedom of others—and since it is the will of Nature that this as well as all other objects of his destination should be the work of men's own efforts: on these accounts a society in which freedom under laws is united with the greatest possible degree of irresistible power—*i.e.* a perfect civil constitution—is the highest problem of Nature for Man: because it is only by the solution of this problem that Nature can accomplish the rest of her purposes with our species. Into this state of restraint Man, who is otherwise so much enamoured of lawless freedom, is compelled to enter by necessity—and that the greatest of all necessity, viz. a necessity self-imposed; his natural inclinations making it impossible for Man to preserve a state of perfect liberty for any length of time in the neighbourhood of his fellows. But, under the restraint of a civil community, these very inclinations lead to the best effects: just as trees in a forest, for the very reason that each endeavours to rob the other of air and sun, compel each other to shoot upwards in quest of both, and thus attain a fine erect growth—whereas those which stand aloof from each other under no mutual restraint, and throw out their boughs at pleasure, become crippled and distorted. All the gifts of art and cultivation which adorn the human race —in short, the most beautiful forms of social order—are the fruits of the antisocial principle, which is compelled to discipline itself, and by means won from the very resistance of Man's situation in this world to give perfect development to all the germs of Nature.

PROPOSITION THE SIXTH

This problem is at the same time the most difficult of all, and the one which is latest solved by Man.

The difficulty which is involved in the bare idea of such a problem is this: Man is an animal that, so long as he lives amongst others of his species, stands in need of a master. For he inevitably abuses his freedom in regard to his equals; and, although, as a reasonable creature, he wishes for a law that may set bounds to the liberty of all, yet do his self-interested animal propensities seduce him into making an exception in his own favour whensoever he dares. He requires a master, therefore, to curb his will, and to compel him into submission to a universal will which may secure the possibility of universal freedom. Now, where is he to find this master? Of necessity, amongst the human species. But, as a human being, this master will also be an animal that requires a master. Lodged in one or many, it is impossible that the supreme and irresponsible power can be certainly prevented from abusing its authority. Hence it is that this problem is the most difficult of any; nay, its perfect solution is impossible: out of wood so crooked and perverse as that which man is made of, nothing absolutely straight can ever be wrought. An approximation to this idea is therefore all which Nature enjoins us. That it is also the last of all problems to which the human species addresses itself is clear from this—that it presupposes *just notions* of the nature of a good constitution, great *experience,* and above all a *will* favourably disposed to the adoption of such a constitution: three elements that can hardly, and not until after many fruitless trials, be expected to concur.

PROPOSITION THE SEVENTH

The problem of the establishment of a perfect Constitution of Society depends upon the problem of a system of International Relations adjusted to law, and apart from this latter problem cannot be solved.

To what purpose is labour bestowed upon a civil constitution adjusted to law for individual men, *i.e.* upon the creation of a Commonwealth? The same antisocial impulse which first drove men to such a creation is again the cause that every commonwealth, in its external relations—*i.e.* as a state in reference to other states—occupies the same ground of lawless and uncontrolled liberty; consequently each must anticipate from the other the very same evils which compelled individuals to enter the social state. Nature accordingly avails herself of the spirit of enmity in Man, as existing even in the great national corporations of that animal, for the purpose of attaining through the inevitable antagonism of this spirit a state of rest and security: *i.e.* by wars, by the immoderate exhaustion of incessant preparations for war, and by the pressure of evil consequences which war at last entails upon any nation even through the midst of peace, she drives nations to all sorts of experiments and expedients; and finally, after infinite devastations, ruin, and universal exhaustion of energy, to one which reason should have suggested without the cost of so sad an experience—viz. to quit the barbarous condition of lawless power, and to enter into a federal league of nations, in which even the weakest member looks for its rights and for protection not to its own power, or its own adjudication, but to this great confederation (*Foedus Amphictyonum*), to the united power, and the adjudication of the collective will. Visionary as this idea may seem, and as such laughed at in the Abbé de St. Pierre and in Rousseau (possibly because they deemed it too near to its accomplishment), it is notwithstanding the inevitable resource and mode of escape under that pressure of evil which nations reciprocally inflict; and, hard as it may be to realize such an idea, states must of necessity be driven at last to the very same resolution to which the savage man of nature was driven with equal reluctance—viz. to sacrifice brutal liberty, and to seek peace and security in a civil constitution founded upon law. All wars therefore are so many tentative essays (not in the intention of Man, but in the intention of Nature) to bring about new relations of states, and by revolutions and dismemberments to form new political bodies. These again, either from internal defects or external attacks, cannot support themselves, but must undergo similar revolutions; until at last, partly by the best possible arrangement of civil government within, and partly by common concert and legal compact without, a condition is attained which, like a well-ordered commonwealth, can maintain itself in the way of an automaton.

Now, whether (in the first place) it is to be anticipated from an epicurean concourse of efficient causes that states, like atoms, by accidental shocking together, should go through all sorts of new combinations to be again dissolved by the fortuitous impulse of fresh shocks, until at length by pure accident some combination emerges capable of supporting itself (a case of luck that could hardly be looked for); or whether (in the second place) we should rather assume that Nature is in this instance pursuing her regular course of raising our species gradually from the lower steps of animal existence to the very highest of a human existence, and *that* not by any direct interposition in our favour, but through man's own spontaneous and artificial efforts (spontaneous, but yet extorted from him by his situation), and in this apparently wild arrangement of things is developing with perfect regularity the original tendencies she has implanted; or whether (in the third place) it is more reasonable to believe that out of all this action and reaction of the human species upon itself nothing in the shape of a wise result will ever issue—that it will continue to be as it has been, and therefore that it cannot be known beforehand, but that the discord which is so natural to our species will finally prepare for us a hell of evils under the most moral condition of society, such as may swallow up this very moral condition itself and all previous advance in culture by a reflux of the original barbaric spirit of desolation (a fate, by the way, against which it is impossible to be secured under the government of blind chance, with which liberty uncontrolled by law is identical, unless by underlaying this chance with a secret nexus of wisdom): to all this the answer turns upon the following question: Whether it be reasonable to assume a final purpose of all natural processes and arrangements in the parts, and yet a want of purpose in the whole? What therefore the objectless condition of savage life effected in the end—viz. that it checked the development of the natural tendencies in the human species, but then, by the very evils it thus caused, drove man into a state where those tendencies could unfold and mature themselves, namely, the state of civilisation—that same service is performed for states by the barbaric freedom in which they are now existing—viz. that, by causing the dedication of all national energies and resources to war, by the desolations of war, and still more by causing the necessity of standing continually in a state of preparation for war, it checks the full development of the natural tendencies in its progress, but, on the other hand, by these very evils and their consequences, it compels our species at last to discover some law of counterbalance to the principle of antagonism between nations, and, in order to give effect to this law, to introduce a federation of states, and consequently a cosmopolitical condition of security (or police) corresponding to that municipal security which arises out of internal police. This federation will itself not be exempt from danger—else the powers of the human race would go to sleep; it will be sufficient that it contain a principle for restoring the equilibrium between its own action and reaction, and thus checking the two functions from destroying each other. Before this last step is taken, human nature—then about half-way advanced in its progress—is in the deepest abyss of evils under the deceitful semblance of external prosperity; and Rousseau was not so much in the wrong when he preferred the condition of the savage to that of the civilized man at the point where he has reached, but is hesitating to take, the final step of his ascent. We are at this time in a high degree of *culture* as to arts and sciences. We are *civilized* to superfluity in what regards the graces and decorums of life. But to entitle us to consider ourselves *moralized* much is still wanting. Yet the idea of morality belongs even to that of *culture;* but the use of this idea, as it comes forward in mere *civilisation,* is restrained to its influence on manners, as seen in the principle of honour, in respectability of deportment, etc. Nothing indeed of a true moral influence can be expected so long as states direct all their energies to idle plans of aggrandizement by force, and thus incessantly check the slow motions by which the intellect of the species is unfolding and forming itself, to say nothing of their shrinking from all *positive* aid to those motions. But all good that is not engrafted upon moral good is mere show and hollow speciousness—the dust and ashes of mortality. And in this delusive condition will the human race linger, until it shall have toiled upwards in the way I have mentioned from its present chaotic abyss of political relations.

PROPOSITION THE EIGHTH

The History of the Human Species as a whole may be regarded as the unravelling of a hidden Plan of Nature for accomplishing a perfect State of Civil Constitution for society in its internal relations (and, as the condition of that, by the last proposition, in its external relations also) as the sole state of society in which the tendencies of human nature can be all and fully developed.

This proposition is an inference from the preceding. A question arises upon it—whether experience has yet observed any traces of such an unravelling in History? I answer, some little: for the whole period (to speak astronomically) of this unravelling is probably too vast to admit of our collecting even the form of its orbit or the relation of the parts to the whole from the small fraction of it which Man has yet left behind him; just as little as it is possible from the astronomical observations hitherto made to determine the course which our sun together with his whole system of planets pursues amongst the heavenly host; although upon universal grounds derived from the systematic frame of the universe, as well as upon the little stock of observation as yet accumulated, enough is known to warrant us in asserting that there *is* such a course. Meantime our human nature obliges us to take an interest even in the remotest epoch to which our species is destined, provided we can anticipate it with certainty. So much the less can *we* be indifferent to it, inasmuch as it appears within our power by intellectual arrangements to contribute something towards the acceleration of the species in its advance to this great epoch. On this account the faintest traces of any approximation in such a direction become of importance to us. At present all states are so artificially interconnected that no one can possibly become stationary in its internal culture without retrograding in power and influence with respect to all the rest; and thus, if not the progress, yet the nondeclension, of this purpose of Nature is sufficiently secured through the ambition of nations. Moreover, civil liberty cannot at this day any longer be so arrested in its progress but that all the sources of livelihood, and more immediately trade, must betray a close sympathy with it, and sicken as *that* sickens; and hence a decay of the state in its external relations. Gradually, too, this liberty extends itself. If the citizen be hindered from pursuing his interest in any way most agreeable to himself provided only it can coexist with the liberty of others, in that case the vivacious life of general business is palsied, and in connexion with that again the powers of the whole. Hence it arises that all personal restriction, whether as to commission or omission, is more and more withdrawn; religious liberty is established; and thus, by little and little, with occasional interruptions, arises *Illumination:* a blessing which the human race must win even from the self-interested purposes of its rulers, if they comprehend what is for their own advantage. Now, this Illumination, and with it a certain degree of cordial interest which the enlightened man cannot forbear taking in all the good which he perfectly comprehends, must by degrees mount upwards even to the throne, and exert an influence on the principles of government. At present, for example, our governments have no money disposable for national education, because the estimates for the next war have absorbed the whole by anticipation. The first act, therefore, by which the state will express its interest in the advancing spirit of the age will be by withdrawing its opposition at least to the feeble and tardy exertions of the people in this direction. Finally, war itself becomes gradually not only so artificial a process, so uncertain in its issue, but also in the after-pains of inextinguishable national debts (a contrivance of modern times) so anxious and burthensome, and, at the same time, the influence which any convulsions of one state exert upon every other state is so remarkable in our quarter of the globe—linked as it is in all parts by the systematic intercourse of trade—that at length those governments which have no immediate participation in the war, under a sense of their own danger, offer themselves as mediators, though as yet without any authentic sanction of law, and thus prepare all things from afar for the formation of a great primary state-body, or Cosmopolitic Areopagus, such as is wholly unprecedented in all preceding ages. Although this body at present exists only in rude outline, yet already a stirring is beginning to be perceptible in all its limbs, each of which is interested in the maintenance of the whole. Even now there is enough to justify a hope that, after many revolutions and remodellings of states, the supreme purpose of Nature will be accomplished in the establishment of a Cosmopolitic State, as the bosom in which all the original tendencies of the human species are to be developed.

PROPOSITION THE NINTH

A philosophical attempt to compose a Universal History,[1] in the sense of a Cosmopolitical History, upon a plan tending to unfold the purpose of Nature in a perfect Civil Union of the Human Species (instead of the present imperfect union), is to be regarded as possible and as capable even of helping forward this very purpose of Nature.

At first sight it is certainly a strange, and apparently an extravagant, project, to propose a History of Man founded on any idea of the course which human affairs would take if adjusted to certain reasonable ends. On such a plan it may be thought that nothing better than a romance could be the result. Yet, if we assume that Nature proceeds not without plan and final purpose even in the motions of human free-will, this idea may possibly turn out very useful; and, although we are too short-sighted to look through the secret mechanism of her arrangements, this idea may yet serve as a clue for connecting into something like *systematic* unity the great abstract of human actions that else seem a chaotic and incoherent *aggregate*. For, if we take our beginning from the Grecian History, as the depository, or at least the collateral voucher, for all elder or synchronous History; if we pursue down to our own times its influence upon the formation and malformation of the Roman People as a political body that swallowed up the Grecian state, and the influence of Rome upon the Barbarians by whom Rome itself was destroyed; and if to all this we add, by way of episode, the political history of every other people so far as it has come to our knowledge through the records of the two enlightened nations above mentioned; we shall then discover a regular gradation of improvement in civil polity as it has grown up in our quarter of the globe, which quarter is in all probability destined to give laws to all the rest. If further we direct an exclusive attention to the civil constitution, with its laws and the external relations of the state, in so far as both, by means of the good which they contained, served for a period to raise and to dignify other nations, and with them the arts and sciences—yet again by their defects served also to precipitate them into ruin, but so that always some germ of illumination survived which, being more and more developed by every revolution, prepared continually a still higher step of improvement—in that case, I believe that a clue will be discovered not only for the unravelling of the intricate web of human affairs, and for the guidance of future statesmen in the art of political prophecy (a benefit which has been extracted from History even whilst it was regarded as an incoherent result from a lawless freedom of will), but also such a clue as will open a consolatory prospect into futurity, in which at a remote distance we shall

[1] [The reader must remember what Kant means by a *Universal History*. In the common sense, as the history of the whole world in its separate divisions, such a history exists already in many shapes that perhaps could not be essentially improved. But in Kant's sense, as a history of the whole *as* a whole, no essay has been made towards it.—Tr.]

discover the human species seated upon an eminence won by infinite toil, where all the germs are unfolded which Nature has implanted, and its destination upon this earth accomplished. Such a justification of Nature, or rather of Providence, is no mean motive for choosing this cosmopolitical station for the survey of History. For what does it avail to praise and to draw forth to view the magnificence and wisdom of the creation in the irrational kingdom of Nature, if that part in the great stage of the supreme wisdom which contains the object of all this mighty display—viz. the history of the human species—is to remain an eternal objection to it, the bare sight of which obliges us to turn away our eyes with displeasure, and (from the despair which it raises of ever discovering in it a perfect and rational purpose) finally leads us to look for such a purpose only in another world?

My object in this essay would be wholly misinterpreted if it were supposed that, under the idea of a Cosmopolitical History which to a certain degree has its course determined *a priori,* I had any wish to discourage the cultivation of *empirical* History in the ordinary sense. On the contrary, the philosopher must be well versed in History who could execute the plan I have sketched, which is indeed a most extensive survey of History, only taken from a new station. However, the extreme, and, simply considered, praiseworthy, circumstantiality with which the history of every nation is written in our times, must naturally suggest a question of some embarrassment. In what way will our remote posterity be able to cope with the enormous accumulation of historical records which a few centuries will bequeath to them? There is no doubt that they will estimate the historical details of times far removed from their own, the original monuments of which will long have perished, simply by the value of that which will then concern themselves—viz. by the good or evil performed by nations and their governments in a *cosmopolitical* view. To direct the eye upon this point as connected with the ambition of rulers and their servants, in order to guide them to the only means of bequeathing an honourable record of themselves to distant ages, may furnish some small motive (over and above the great one of justifying Providence) for attempting a Philosophic History on the plan I have here explained.

Questions

1. What does Kant mean by a "universal" or "cosmopolitical history"? What does Kant mean by "Nature"?

2. What does Kant mean by a "law of Nature"? How does Kant believe that individual men *follow* laws of nature? How do acting "under the law of instinct," acting "under the law of a preconcerted plan," and "blindly pursuing a plan of Nature" differ from one another?

3. Give a brief account of the "plan of Nature" for the human species, which Kant has discovered. Why does Kant believe that the value of an individual is to be found only in his being a part of the whole human species?

4. What does Kant mean when he says that "a Cosmopolitical History . . . to a certain degree has its course determined *a priori*"?

5. Judging by Kant's example, how does one go about discovering a "plan of Nature"? What is the logical status of Kant's propositions? Are his propositions statements of matters of fact, which could be confirmed (or disproved) by experience? Or, are his propositions rather like theorems in a "geometry" of history? Or, are his propositions rather like revelations in a religion? What difference does the logical status of Kant's propositions make in both the way we regard their truth or falsity, and the way we might use them to govern our lives?

6. In what respects do Kant's views on the "plan of Nature" resemble those of Leibniz on God's relation to the world (page 389)? Do Kant's views admit (or escape) the sort of criticism which Hume levels against the view that a superior being is responsible for the course of human affairs? (See page 393.)

2

Criticism of Kant's Philosophy of History

W. H. Walsh
(b. 1913)

Mr. W. H. Walsh is a Fellow and Tutor of Merton College, Oxford, and a University Lecturer in Philosophy. In this essay he argues that what Kant says about history is not very helpful to anyone who wants to understand it. His method is to attack the logic of Kant's principles of the philosophy of history. He shows that these principles do not describe the course of history, as Kant supposes they do; and failing in this, they do not explain history in the sense that Kant hopes that it can be explained. In his analysis of the logic of Kant's principles, Mr. Walsh makes use of Leibniz's division of true propositions into truths of fact and truths of reason. This classification of propositions is similar to Hume's distinction between matter-of-fact statements and relation-of-idea statements. Thus, the reader may find an acquaintance with Hume (page 105) helpful here.

This selection is the whole of Chapter VI, Section 3, from *An Introduction to Philosophy of History.*

From *An Introduction to Philosophy of History,* by W. H. Walsh, Hutchinson's University Library, London, 1951. Reprinted by permission.

I shall begin with the external character of Kant's approach to history. I refer to the fact that there is on his theory a complete gulf between the activity of the historian discovering facts about the past and that of the philosopher devising a point of view from which sense can be made of them. The philosopher, it appears, can produce a rationale of history without taking any account of the detailed course of historical change. His standpoint is reached by the combination of a number of *a priori* principles (such as that Nature does nothing in vain) with certain broad generalizations about human behavior, generalizations which may be confirmed by a scrutiny of historical records but are not necessarily arrived at by processes of historical research. And the comment we must make on this is that though Kant puts his standpoint forward as one from which some future historian may attempt a satisfactory universal history, it is by no means clear that the project will have any appeal to working historians. For if we are assured in advance of experience (and in some sense we are assured, though the point, as we shall see, is a difficult one) that history does and must conform to a certain pattern, what incentive is there to undertake the laborious task of tracing that pattern empirically?

Two possible ways of meeting this difficulty must now be considered.

First, it might be urged that the *a priori* knowledge Kant is ascribing to the philosopher of history is on his own account very limited in scope, and so far from constituting a bar to positive historical enquiry ought rather to act as a stimulus to it. The argument for its so doing would depend for its plausibility on appeal to a parallel case—that of the philosophy of nature. In the *Critique of Pure Reason* and elsewhere Kant tried to show that there were certain propositions of a very general kind which philosophers could assert about nature independently of experience, and argued that the knowledge of these propositions was a positive encouragement to empirical enquiry (for instance, the conviction that nature is orderly stimulated Kepler to further investigations in the face of discouraging results). Similarly, it might be said, knowledge of the proposition that there is a certain pattern in the historical process should encourage historians to pursue their studies, much as the conviction that there is a way out of a maze encourages the lost to go on looking for it.

But this line of defence fails when we observe that the parallel adduced is not strictly accurate. The "universal laws of nature," of which Kant claims in the *Critique of Pure Reason* that we have *a priori* knowledge and of which the general law of causality is the best-known instance, are one and all formal principles: they are of use in enabling us to anticipate, not the details, but only the general form of experience. By knowing the principle that every event has a cause, for instance, we know nothing about the causal connections between particular events; we know only that it is reasonable to look for causes whenever we meet with natural events. To put the point another way, from the proposition that all events have causes nothing follows about the particular causal relations we shall meet with in nature. But the principle taken for granted by the Kantian philosopher of history is in this respect quite different; for when we are assured of that principle, as Kant thinks we are, we are assured not merely that there is *a* pattern in history but further that it is a pattern *of a certain kind*. In other words, the principle assumed in Kant's philosophy of history is a material principle, and it is just because of this that its relation to the assertions of working historians is of importance.

We are therefore driven back on the alternative line of defence, to which I shall make a somewhat devious approach.

It is a common practice among philosophers today to follow Leibniz in dividing true propositions into truths of fact and truths of reason. Truths of fact are validated or confuted by reference to particular experiences; truths of reason, about the nature and number of which there is much controversy, are agreed to be valid irrespective of what in particular occurs. Now the question might be asked into which class we should put the principle of the Kantian philosopher of history.[1] The answer is not easy to find. For on the one hand we must say that the principle looks like a factual truth, since, as we have just seen, it concerns not the form but, in a wide sense, the matter of experience. On the other hand it seems reasonably clear that Kant did not envisage the possibility that it was open to confutation by experience, but regarded it as resting on *a priori* grounds; and in this respect it looks like a truth of reason.

What this suggests is that the status of Kant's principle, and our supposed knowledge of it, require more careful investigation than we have hitherto given to them. And when we compare what he has to say about history with some of his other doctrines (notably those in the appendix to the Dialectic in the *Critique of Pure Reason* and those in the *Critique of Judgment*) we see that he is in fact assigning a special standing to the principle he has sought to establish. He regards it, in fact, neither as an empirical proposition nor as a necessary truth in the sense in which the general law of causality is for him a necessary truth, but rather as what he calls in the first *Critique* a regulative or heuristic principle, useful in the prosecution of empirical research but not itself susceptible of any kind of proof. And for that reason it is not, in the strict sense, "known" to anyone. The only propositions which, on Kant's view, we can be said to know are, on the one hand, propositions concerning matters of fact, on the other propositions such as the "universal laws of nature" mentioned above; and the principle with which we are concerned falls into neither class. It is a principle of whose truth we can have subjective but not objective certainty; we can be assured of it, thanks to its being closely involved in moral practice,[2] but more than that we cannot claim.

Recognition of these subtleties puts Kant's case in a different light; yet even so the position is not wholly clear. We are now being invited to believe that the principle which guides the philosophical historian is a heuristic principle, which would assign it the same status as, for example, the principle of teleology, to which, Kant thought, working biologists must make appeal. When we adopt that principle we direct our scientific studies on the assumption that nature is working purposively, at any rate in regard to some of her products; and this is (or may be) an important step on the road to scientific discovery.

---

[1] ["The History of the Human Species as a whole may be regarded as the unravelling of a hidden Plan of Nature for accomplishing a perfect State of Civil Constitution for society . . . as the sole state of society in which the tendencies of human nature can be all and fully developed." Kant's Proposition the Eighth, see page 675.—Eds.]

[2] See the section of the *Critique of Pure Reason* entitled "On Opinion, Knowledge and Belief" (B848/A820).

If this parallel can be justified—if we can show that there is a precise analogy between what the historian gets and what the biologist gets from philosophy—then Kant's contention is at any rate a respectable one. Unfortunately here again the parallel suggested does not seem to be exact.

The trouble is that Kant is claiming that philosophers can provide working historians not merely with a general principle (as they can provide working biologists with the general principle of teleology) but with a special principle of a particular kind. If I am warranted in assuming the teleological principle in nature I am warranted in expecting that I shall meet in nature with examples of purposive behaviour; and I plan my researches accordingly. What I have done is to accept teleology as a methodological postulate or working assumption. But an assumption of that kind does not lead me to anticipate finding any particular sort of purposive pattern in nature. By contrast, if I accept the Kantian principle of historical interpretation I am able to say, without reference to experience, not only that history has a plot, but also, in general terms, what that plot is. As we saw before, it is not only the form of experience that Kant's principle enables me to anticipate, but, to an important extent, its matter too; and this it is which makes everyday historians suspicious of the Kantian account.

It is useless in this connection to point out that, if we follow Kant strictly, we cannot be said to "know" in advance of experience the general plot to which history may be expected to conform. We do indeed lack scientific knowledge of it, just as we do of other principles of the heuristic kind; but this has no bearing on the situation. For the fact remains that on Kant's view we are well assured of the principle in question. We may not be able to prove it, but that does not mean that it is open to doubt.

I conclude that though the Kantian doctrine is a great deal more complex and more subtle than might appear at first sight, it is nevertheless one which historians would find difficult to characterize as other than arbitrary. The problem for a theory of this type is to give an account of the relation of the *a priori* to the empirical elements in philosophical history, to avoid the easily proffered reproach that the philosophical historian is merely making the facts up, or selecting them, to suit his own wishes. It does not seem to me that Kant has an adequate answer to this problem, though he was acutely aware of the general problem of which it is a specification. Nor is it comforting to observe that parallel difficulties are to be found in regard to Hegel's philosophy of history.

In the above remarks I have concentrated exclusively on the epistemological side of Kant's theory of history. I should add at this point that there are critics such as Mr. Carritt,[3] who have attacked Kant's views on moral grounds as well, urging that history cannot have a moral point if it demands (as Kant seems to be saying) so many innocent victims in the accomplishment of its goal. But this is a charge which I shall not discuss, since in my view Kant's theory falls to the ground independently of whether it can be met successfully or not.

[3] See his *Morals and Politics.*

Questions

1. What does Mr. Walsh mean by "the external character of Kant's approach to history"?

2. Why does Mr. Walsh argue that the propositions of Kant's philosophy of history are neither (a) a priori principles, like "Every event has a cause," nor (b) truths of fact, nor (c) truths of reason, nor (d) regulative or heuristic principles?

3. How does Mr. Walsh's analysis of the logical character of Kant's principles show them to be useless to someone who wants to understand the course of history?

4. Mr. Walsh takes Kant at his word and regards him as an adviser to historians. What, however, is the prospect of regarding him as recommending a social ideal under the persuasive guise of an historical inevitability? Thus, when Kant says that the plan of nature is for the human species to be formed into an international society, might he really be recommending the formation of an international society as a *good* goal for mankind? What would be Kant's grounds for urging such an ideal? How could someone defend the accepting (or rejecting) of Kant's ideal? (Though simple to state, this last question is not easy to answer. It has the advantage, however, of calling the reader's attention to the connection between Kant's philosophy of history and his account of moral knowledge [page 533].)

3

The Marxist Philosophy of History | Friedrich Engels (*1820-1895*)

In 1844, Friedrich Engels became the friend of the now famous economist and political philosopher, Karl Marx (1818-1883). Their friendship and their collaboration in research and writing lasted until Marx's death. The following selection by Engels is a classic statement of the Marxist philosophy of history, written by the man who was Marx's closest associate, and who regarded himself as speaking for Marx. In his second preface (1885) to *Herr Eugen Dühring's Revolution in Science,* the book from which this account of the Marxist philosophy of history is taken, Engels acknowledges his debt to Marx for ". . . the genesis and development of the mode of outlook expounded in this book . . . ," and adds ". . . it was of course self-understood between us that this exposition of mine should not be issued without his knowledge. I read the manuscript to him before it was printed. . . ."

Marx's view of history owes much to the philosophy of G. W. F. Hegel (1770-1831). Hegel's philosophy is a remarkable combination and development of certain themes drawn from the philosophies of

Kant, Aristotle, and Plato, and the Christian religion. Described briefly, and much too baldly, Hegel views history as a conflict between Spirit, which is trying to impose its form (idea) on the World, and the World (matter), which resists the impositions of Spirit. Spirit is bound to succeed finally, but its success can only be achieved little by little. Spirit clashes with the World and imposes a little of its form on the World. This success encourages Spirit to a new clash, and the World becomes a little more spiritualized. This clash of the antitheses, Spirit and the World, is the most important example of Hegel's dialectic. The dialectic is the mechanism by which anything comes into and goes out of existence. Whatever exists is the product of the clash of opposites, but the product of these clashing opposites is short-lived; for the new entity which their union creates calls forth its own opposite with which it must clash in order to continue the dialectical growth of the World. For Hegel, if we could understand the form which Spirit ultimately wishes to impose on the World, we should know the goal of history.

Marx was enormously impressed by Hegel's philosophy of history, but he subjected it to what might be called a dialectical transformation, or as he put it himself, he stood Hegel's philosophy on its head. Marx rejects the idea that a supramundane spirit, or intelligence, is endeavoring to transform the world; he upends the picture by arguing that the only intelligence to be reckoned with is that of the minds of individual human beings, and that the individual's mind is conditioned by the world in which he lives. The material conditions, or more exactly the economic arrangements, of the world shape the minds of the people who live under them. There is a dialectic at work for Marx, too; for the historical goal of the world is to produce the working class (the proletariat) which is to be the foundation of a classless society, a goal that is to be achieved only by the destruction of certain preliminary but historically necessary classes, such as the capitalist class (the bourgeoisie). This is the famous materialist philosophy of history. The ideal society will be achieved when the goal of history is achieved; and, for Marx, any society now in existence can do no better than to take the goal of history as its own, making its achievement as easy as possible. Such is the Marxist philosophy of history in brief outline. We leave the reader to discover the details for himself. For a criticism of the Marxist philosophy of history on historical lines, the reader may turn to the selection by John Dewey (page 698). In addition the reader should consider whether the Marxist philosophy of history is open to the sort of logical criticism which Mr. W. H. Walsh levels against Kant (page 679).

This reading is the whole of Chapter II, "Theoretical Socialism," from Part III of *Herr Eugen Dühring's Revolution in Science*. The book was first published in 1878. The translation from the German is by Emile Burns.

From *Anti-Dühring,* by Friedrich Engels, International Publishers, N. Y., 1939. Reprinted by permission of the publisher.

The materialist conception of history starts from the principle that production, and with production the exchange of its products, is the basis of every social order; that in every society which has appeared in history the distribution of the products, and with it the division of society into classes or estates, is determined by what is produced and how it is produced, and how the product is exchanged. According to this conception, the ultimate causes of all social changes and political revolutions are to be sought, not in the minds of men, in their increasing insight into eternal truth and justice, but in changes in the mode of production and exchange; they are to be sought not in the *philosophy* but in the *economics* of the epoch concerned. The growing realisation that existing social institutions are irrational and unjust, that reason has become nonsense and good deeds a scourge is only a sign that changes have been taking place quietly in the methods of production and forms of exchange with which the social order, adapted to previous economic conditions, is no longer in accord. This also involves that the means through which the abuses that have been revealed can be got rid of must likewise be present, in more or less developed form, in the altered conditions of productions. These means are not to be *invented* by the mind, but *discovered* by means of the mind in the existing material facts of production.

Where then, on this basis, does modern socialism stand?

The existing social order, as is now fairly generally admitted, is the creation of the present ruling class, the bourgeoisie. The mode of production peculiar to the bourgeoisie—called, since Marx, the capitalist mode of production—was incompatible with the local privileges and privileges of birth as well as with the reciprocal personal ties of the feudal system; the bourgeoisie shattered the feudal system, and on its ruins established the bourgeois social order, the realm of free competition, freedom of movement, equal rights for commodity owners, and all the other bourgeois glories. The capitalist mode of production could now develop freely. From the time when steam and the new tool-making machinery had begun to transform the former manufacture into large-scale industry, the productive forces evolved under bourgeois direction developed at a pace that was previously unknown and to an unprecedented degree. But just as manufacture, and the handicraft industry which had been further developed under its influence, had previously come into conflict with the feudal fetters of the guilds, so large-scale industry, as it develops more fully, comes into conflict with the barriers within which the capitalist mode of production holds it confined. The new forces of production have already outgrown the bourgeois form of using them; and this conflict between productive forces and mode of production is not a conflict which has risen in men's heads, as for example the conflict between original sin and divine justice; but it exists in the facts, objectively, outside of us, independently of the will or purpose even of the men who brought it about. Modern socialism is nothing but the reflex in thought of this actual conflict, its ideal reflection in the minds first of the class which is directly suffering under it—the working class.

In what, then, does this conflict consist?

Previous to capitalist production, that is to say, in the Middle Ages, small-scale production was general, on the basis of the private ownership by the workers of their means of production; the agricultural industry of the small peasant, freeman or serf, and the handicraft industry of the towns. The instruments of labour—land, agricultural implements, the workshop and tools—were the instruments of labour of individuals, intended only for individual use, and therefore necessarily puny, dwarfish, restricted. But just because of this they belonged, as a rule, to the producer himself. To concentrate and enlarge these scattered, limited means of production, to transform them into the mighty levers of production of the present day, was precisely the historic role of the capitalist mode of production and of its representative, the bourgeoisie. In Part IV of *Capital* Marx gives a detailed account of how, since the fifteenth century, this process has developed historically through the three stages of simple co-operation, manufacture and large-scale industry. But as Marx also points out, the bourgeoisie was unable to transform those limited means of production into mighty productive forces except by transforming them from individual means of production into *social* means of production, which could be used only *by a body of men as a whole.* The spinning wheel, the hand loom and the blacksmith's hammer were replaced by the spinning machine, the mechanical loom and the steam hammer; and the factory, making the co-operation of hundreds and thousands of workers necessary, took the place of the individual workroom. And, like the means of production, production itself changed from a series of individual operations into a series of social acts, and the products from the products of individuals into social products. The yarn, the cloth and the metal goods which now came from the factory were the common product of many workers through whose hands it had to pass successively before it was ready. No individual can say of such products: I made it, that is *my* product.

But where the natural spontaneous division of labour within society is the basic form of production, it imprints upon the products the form of *commodities,* the mutual exchange, purchase and sale of which enables the individual producers to satisfy their manifold needs. And this was the case during the Middle Ages. The peasant, for example, sold agricultural products to the artisan and purchased from him in exchange the products of his craft. Into this society of individual producers, producers of commodities, the new mode of production thrust itself, setting up, in the midst of the spontaneous *planless* division of labour which then existed throughout society, the *planned* division of labour organised in the individual factory; alongside of *individual* production, *social* production made its appearance. The products of both were sold on the same market, and consequently at prices which were at least approximately the same. But the planned organization was stronger than the natural division of labour; the factories in which labour was socially organised produced their commodities more cheaply than the separate small producers. Individual production was vanquished on one field after another; social production revolutionised the whole former mode of production. But, this, its revolutionary character, was so little understood that, on the contrary, it was introduced as a means of stimulating and accelerating the production of commodities. In its origin, it was directly linked with certain levers of commodity production and exchange which were already in existence: merchant's capital, handicraft, wage labour. Inasmuch as it itself came into being as a new form of commodity production, the forms of appropriation characteristic of commodity production remained in full force also for it.

In commodity production as it had developed in the Middle Ages, the question could never arise of who should be the owner of the product of labour. The individual producer had produced it, as a rule, from raw material which belonged to him and was often produced by himself, with his own instruments of labour, and by his own manual labour or that of his family. There was no need whatever for the product to be appropriated by him; it belonged to him as an absolute matter of course. His ownership of the product was therefore based *upon his own labour*. Even where outside help was used, it was as a rule subsidiary, and in many cases received other compensation in addition to wages; the guild apprentice and journeyman worked less for the sake of their board and wages than to train themselves to become master craftsmen. Then came the concentration of the means of production in large workshops and manufactories, their transformation into means of production that were in fact social. But the social means of production and the social products were treated as if they were still, as they had been before, the means of production and the products of individuals. Hitherto, the owner of the instruments of labour had appropriated the product because it was as a rule his own product, the auxiliary labour of other persons being the exception; now, the owner of the instruments of labour continued to appropriate the product, although it was no longer *his* product, but exclusively the product of *other's labour*. Thus, therefore, the products, now socially produced, were not appropriated by those who had really set the means of production in motion and really produced the products, but by the *capitalists*. Means of production and production itself had in essence become social. But they were subjected to a form of appropriation which has as its presupposition private production by individuals, with each individual owning his own product and bringing it on to the market. The mode of production is subjected to this form of appropriation, although it removes the presuppositions on which the latter was based.[1] In this contradic-

---

[1] There is no need here to explain that although the form of appropriation remains the same, the *character* of the appropriation is revolutionised by the process described above, **to no** less a degree than production. My appropriation of my own product and my appro-

tion, which gives the new mode of production its capitalist character, *the whole conflict of today is already present in germ.* The more the new mode of production gained the ascendancy on all decisive fields of production and in all countries of decisive economic importance, supplanting individual production except for insignificant relics, the *more glaring necessarily became the incompatibility of social production with capitalist appropriation.*

The first capitalists found, as we have said, the form of wage labour already in existence; but wage labour as the exception, as an auxiliary occupation, as a supplementary, as a transitory phase. The agricultural labourer who occasionally went to work as a day labourer had a few acres of his own land, from which if necessary he could get his livelihood. The regulations of the guilds ensured that the journeyman of today became the master craftsman of tomorrow. But as soon as the means of production had become social and were concentrated in the hands of capitalists, this situation changed. Both the means of production and the products of the small, individual producer lost more and more of their value; there was nothing left for him to do but to go to the capitalist, and work for wages. Wage labour, hitherto an exception and subsidiary, became the rule and the basic form of all production; hitherto an auxiliary occupation, it now became the labourer's exclusive activity. The occasional wage worker became the wage worker for life. The number of lifelong wage workers was also increased to a colossal extent by the simultaneous disintegration of the feudal system, the dispersal of the retainers of the feudal lords, the eviction of peasants from their homesteads, etc. The separation between the means of production concentrated in the hands of the capitalists, on the one side, and the producers now possessing nothing but their labour power, on the other, was made complete. *The contradiction between social production and capitalist appropriation became manifest as the antagonism between proletariat and bourgeoisie.*

We saw that the capitalist mode of production thrust itself into a society of commodity producers, individual producers, whose social cohesion resulted from the exchange of their products. But every society based on commodity production has the peculiarity that in it the producers have lost control of their own social relationships. Each produces for himself, with the means of production which happen to be at his disposal and in order to satisfy his individual needs through the medium of exchange. No one knows how much of the article he produces is coming onto the market, or how much demand there is for it; no one knows whether his individual product will meet a real need, whether he will cover his costs or even be able to sell it at all. Anarchy reigns in social production. But commodity production, like all other forms of production, has its own laws, which are inherent in and inseparable from it; and these laws assert themselves

priation of another person's product are certainly two very different forms of appropriation. It may be noted in passing that wage labour, in which the whole capitalist mode of production is already present in embryo form, is a very old institution; in isolated and scattered form it developed alongside slavery for centuries. But the germ could only develop into the capitalist mode of production when the necessary historical conditions had come into existence.

in spite of anarchy, in and through anarchy. These laws are manifested in the sole form of social relationship which continues to exist, in exchange, and enforce themselves on the individual producers as compulsory laws of competition. At first therefore, they are unknown even to these producers, and have to be discovered by them gradually only through long experience. They assert themselves therefore apart from the producers and against the producers, as the natural laws of their form of production, working blindly. The product dominates the producers.

In mediaeval society, especially in the earlier centuries, production was essentially for the producer's own use; for the most part its aim was to satisfy only the needs of the producer and his family. Where, as in the countryside, personal relations of dependence existed, it also contributed towards satisfying the needs of the feudal lord. No exchange was involved, and consequently the products did not assume the character of commodities. The peasant family produced almost everything it required—utensils and clothing as well as food. It was only when it succeeded in producing a surplus beyond its own needs and the payments in kind due to the feudal lord—it was only at this stage that it also began to produce commodities; these surplus products, thrown into social exchange, offered for sale, became commodities. The town artisans, it is true, had to produce for exchange from the very beginning. But even they supplied the greatest part of their own needs themselves; they had gardens and small fields; they sent their cattle out into the communal woodland, which also provided them with timber and firewood; the women spun flax, wool, etc. Production for the purpose of exchange, the production of commodities, was only in its infancy. Hence, restricted exchange, restricted market, stable methods of production, local isolation from the outside world, and local unity within: the Mark in the countryside, the guild in the town.

With the extension of commodity production, however, and especially with the emergence of the capitalist mode of production, the laws of commodity production, previously latent, also began to operate more openly and more potently. The old bonds were loosened, the old dividing barriers broken through, the producers more and more transformed into independent, isolated commodity producers. The anarchy of social production became obvious, and was carried to further and further extremes. But the chief means through which the capitalist mode of production accentuated this anarchy in social production was the direct opposite of anarchy: the increasing organisation of production on a social basis in each individual productive establishment. This was the lever with which it put an end to the former peaceful stability. In whatever branch of industry it was introduced, it could suffer no older method of production to exist alongside it; where it laid hold of a handicraft, that handicraft was wiped out. The field of labour became a field of battle. The great geographical discoveries and the colonisation which followed on them multiplied markets and hastened on the transformation of handicraft into manufacture. The struggle broke out not only between the individual local producers; the local struggles developed into national struggles, the trade wars of the seven-

teenth and eighteenth centuries. Finally, large-scale industry and the creation
of the world market have made the struggle universal and at the same time
given it an unparalleled intensity. Between individual capitalists, as between
whole industries and whole countries, advantages in natural or artificial conditions of production decide life or death. The vanquished are relentlessly cast
aside. It is the Darwinian struggle for individual existence, transferred from
Nature to society with intensified fury. The standpoint of the animal in Nature
appears as the last word in human development. The contradiction between
social production and capitalist appropriation reproduces itself as *the antithesis
between the organisation of production in the individual factory and the anarchy
of production in society as a whole.*

The capitalist mode of production moves in these two forms of manifestation of the contradiction immanent in it from its very nature, without hope of
escaping from that "vicious circle" which Fourier long ago discovered in it.
But what Fourier in his day was as yet unable to see is that this circle is
gradually narrowing; that the motion is rather in the form of a spiral and
must meet its end, like the motion of the planets, by collision with the centre.
It is the driving force of the social anarchy of production which transforms the
immense majority of men more and more into proletarians, and it is in turn
the proletarian masses who will ultimately put an end to the anarchy of production. It is the driving force of the social anarchy of production which
transforms the infinite perfectibility of the machine in large-scale industry into
a compulsory commandment for each individual industrial capitalist to make
his machinery more and more perfect, under penalty of ruin. But the perfecting
of machinery means rendering human labour superfluous. If the introduction
and increase of machinery meant the displacement of millions of hand workers
by a few machine workers, the improvement of machinery means the displacement of larger and larger numbers of the machine workers themselves, and
ultimately the creation of a mass of available wage workers exceeding the
average requirements of capital for labour—a complete industrial reserve
army—a reserve that would be available at periods when industry was working
at high pressure, but would be thrown out onto the streets by the crash inevitably following the boom; a reserve that would at all times be like a leaden weight
on the feet of the working class in their fight for existence against capital, a
regulator to keep wages down to the low level which suits the needs of capital.
Thus it comes about that machinery, to use Marx's phrase, becomes the most
powerful weapon in the war of capital against the working class, that the
instruments of labour constantly tear the means of subsistence out of the
hands of the labourer, that the very product of the labourer is turned into an
instrument for his subjection. Thus it comes about that the economising of
the instruments of labour becomes from the outset a simultaneous and absolutely
reckless waste of labour power and robbery of the normal conditions necessary
for the labour function; that machinery, "the most powerful instrument for
shortening labour time, becomes the most unfailing means for placing every

moment of the labourer's time and that of his family at the disposal of the capitalist for the purpose of expanding the value of his capital." [2]

Thus it comes about that the excessive labour of some becomes the necessary condition for the lack of employment of others, and that large-scale industry, which hunts all over the world for new consumers, restricts the consumption of the masses at home to a starvation minimum and thereby undermines its own internal market. "The law that always equilibrates the relative surplus population, or industrial reserve army, to the extent and energy of accumulation, this law rivets the labourer to capital more firmly than the wedges of Vulcan did Prometheus to the rock. It establishes an accumulation of misery, corresponding with accumulation of capital. Accumulation of wealth at one pole is, therefore, at the same time accumulation of misery, agony of toil, slavery, ignorance, brutality, mental degradation, at the opposite pole, *i.e.*, on the side of the class that *produces its own products in the form of capital.*" [3]

And to expect any other distribution of the products from the capitalist mode of production is like expecting the electrodes of a battery, while they are in contact with the battery, not to decompose water, not to develop oxygen at the positive pole and hydrogen at the negative.

We have seen how the perfectibility of modern machinery, pushed to an extreme point, through the medium of the anarchy of production in society is transformed into a compulsory commandment for the individual industrial capitalist constantly to improve his machinery, constantly to increase its productive power. The mere possibility of extending his field of production is transformed for him into a similar compulsory commandment. The enormous expanding power of large-scale industry, compared with which the expanding power of gases is mere child's play, now appears to us as a *necessity* for both qualitative and quantitative expansion that laughs at all counteracting pressure. Such counteracting pressure comes from consumption, sale, markets for the products of large-scale industry. But the capacity of the market to expand, both extensively and intensively, is controlled directly by quite other and far less effective laws. The expansion of the market cannot keep pace with the expansion of production. The collision becomes inevitable, and as it can yield no solution so long as it does not burst the capitalist mode of production itself, it becomes periodic. Capitalist production brings into being a new "vicious circle."

And in fact, since 1825, when the first general crisis broke out, the whole industrial and commercial world, the production and exchange of all civilised peoples and of their more or less barbarian dependent people have been dislocated practically once in every ten years. Trade comes to a standstill, the markets are glutted, the products lie in great masses, unsalable, ready money disappears, credit vanishes, the factories are idle, the working masses go short of the means of subsistence because they have produced too much of them, bank-

[2] *Capital,* Vol. I, p. 445 (Kerr edition).
[3] *Capital,* Vol. I, p. 709 (Kerr edition).

ruptcy follows upon bankruptcy, forced sale upon forced sale. The stagnation lasts for years, both productive forces and products are squandered and destroyed on a large scale, until the accumulated masses of commodities are at last disposed of at a more or less considerable depreciation, until production and exchange gradually begin to move again. By degrees the pace quickens; it becomes a trot; the industrial trot passes into a gallop, and the gallop in turn passes into the headlong onrush of a complete industrial, commercial, credit and speculative steeplechase, only to land again in the end, after the most breakneck jumps—in the ditch of a crash. And so on again and again. We have now experienced it five times since 1825, and at this moment (1877) we are experiencing it for the sixth time. And the character of these crises is so clearly marked that Fourier hit them all off when he described the first as *crise pléthorique,* a crisis of superabundance.

In these crises, the contradiction between social production and capitalist appropriation comes to a violent explosion. The circulation of commodities is for the moment reduced to nothing; the means of circulation, money, becomes an obstacle to circulation; all the laws of commodity production and commodity circulation are turned upside down. The economic collision has reached its culminating point: *the mode of production rebels against the mode of exchange; the productive forces rebel against the mode of production, which they have outgrown.*

The fact that the social organisation of production within the factory has developed to the point at which it has become incompatible with the anarchy of production in society which exists alongside it and above it—this fact is made palpable to the capitalists themselves by the violent concentration of capitals which take place during crises through the ruin of many big and even more small capitalists. The whole mechanism of the capitalist mode of production breaks down under the pressure of the productive forces which it itself created. It is no longer able to transform the whole of this mass of means of production into capital; they lie idle, and for this very reason the industrial reserve army must also lie idle. Means of production, means of subsistence, available labourers, all the elements of production and of general wealth are there in abundance. But "abundance becomes the source of distress and want" (Fourier), because it is precisely abundance that prevents the conversion of the means of production and subsistence into capital. For in capitalist society the means of production cannot begin to function unless they have first been converted into capital, into means for the exploitation of human labour power. The necessity for the means of production and subsistence to take on the form of capital stands like a ghost between them and the workers. It alone prevents the coming together of the material and personal levers of production; it alone forbids the means of production to function, the workers to work and to live. Thus on the one hand the capitalist mode of production stands convicted of its own incapacity any longer to control these productive forces. And on the other hand these productive forces themselves press forward with increasing force to put an end to the contradiction, to rid themselves of their character as capital, *to the actual recognition of their character as social productive forces.*

It is this pressure of the productive forces, in their mighty upgrowth, against their character as capital, increasingly compelling the recognition of their social character, which forces the capitalist class itself more and more to treat them as social productive forces, in so far as this is at all possible within the framework of capitalist relations. Both the period of industrial boom, with its unlimited credit inflation, and the crisis itself through the collapse of great capitalist establishments, urge forward towards that form of the socialisation of huge masses of means of production which we find in the various kinds of joint-stock companies. Many of these means of production are from the outset so colossal that, like the railways, they exclude all other forms of capitalist exploitation. At a certain stage of development even this form no longer suffices; the official representative of capitalist society, the state, is constrained to take over their management. This necessity of conversion into state property makes itself evident first in the big institutions for communication: the postal service, telegraphs and railways.

If the crises revealed the incapacity of the bourgeoisie any longer to control the modern productive forces, the conversion of the great organisations for production and communication into joint-stock companies and state property shows that for this purpose the bourgeoisie can be dispensed with. All the social functions of the capitalists are now carried out by salaried employees. The capitalist has no longer any social activity save the pocketing of revenues, the clipping of coupons and gambling on the Stock Exchange, where the different capitalists fleece each other of their capital. Just as at first the capitalist mode of production displaced the workers, so now it displaces the capitalists, relegating them, just as it did the workers, to the superfluous population, even if in the first instance not to the industrial reserve army.

But neither the conversion into joint-stock companies nor into state property deprives the productive forces of their character as capital. In the case of joint-stock companies this is obvious. And the modern state, too, is only the organisation with which bourgeois society provides itself in order to maintain the general external conditions of the capitalist mode of production against encroachments either by the workers or by individual capitalists. The modern state, whatever its form, is an essentially capitalist machine; it is the state of the capitalists, the ideal collective body of all capitalists. The more productive forces it takes over as its property, the more it becomes the real collective body of all the capitalists, the more citizens it exploits. The workers remain wage-earners, proletarians. The capitalist relationship is not abolished; it is rather pushed to an extreme. But at this extreme it is transformed into its opposite. State ownership of the productive forces is not the solution of the conflict, but it contains within itself the formal means, the key to the solution.

This solution can only consist in the recognition in practice of the social nature of the modern productive forces, in bringing, therefore, the mode of production, appropriation and exchange into accord with the social character of the means of production. And this can only be brought about by society, openly and without deviation, taking possession of the productive forces which have outgrown all control other than that of society itself. Thereby the social character of the means of production and of the products—which today operates against the producers themselves, periodically breaking through the mode of production and exchange and enforcing itself only as a blind law of Nature, violently and destructively—is quite consciously asserted by the producers, and is transformed from a cause of disorder and periodic collapse into the most powerful lever of production itself.

The forces operating in society work exactly like the forces operating in Nature: blindly, violently, destructively, so long as we do not understand them and fail to take them into account. But when once we have recognised them and understood how they work, their direction and their effects, the gradual subjection of them to our will and the use of them for the attainment of our aims depends entirely upon ourselves. And this is quite especially true of the mighty productive forces of the present day. So long as we obstinately refuse to understand their nature and their character—and the capitalist mode of production and its defenders set themselves against any such attempt—so long do these forces operate in spite of us, against us, and so long do they control us, as we have shown in detail. But once their nature is grasped, in the hands of the producers working in association they can be transformed from demoniac masters into willing servants. It is the difference between the destructive force of electricity in the lightning of a thunderstorm and the tamed electricity of the telegraph and the arc light; the difference between a conflagration and fire in the service of man. This treatment of the productive forces of the present day, on the basis of their real nature at last recognised by society, opens the way to the replacement of the anarchy of social production by a socially planned regulation of production in accordance with the needs both of society as a whole and of each individual. The capitalist mode of appropriation, in which the product enslaves first the producer, and then also the appropriator, will thereby be replaced by the mode of appropriation of the products based on the nature of the modern means of production themselves: on the one hand direct social appropriation as a means to the maintenance and extension of production, and on the other hand direct individual appropriation as a means to life and pleasure.

By more and more transforming the great majority of the population into proletarians, the capitalist mode of production brings into being the force which, under penalty of its own destruction, is compelled to carry out this revolution. By more and more driving towards the conversion of the vast socialised means of production into state property, it itself points the way for the carrying through of this revolution. *The proletariat seizes the state power, and transforms the means of production in the first instance into state property.* But in doing this, it puts an end to itself as the proletariat, it puts an end to all class differences and class antagonisms, it puts an end also to the state as the state. Former society, moving in class antagonisms, had need of the state, that is, an organisation of the exploiting class at each period for the maintenance of its external conditions of production; that is, therefore, for the forcible holding down of the exploited class in the conditions of oppression (slavery, villeinage or serfdom, wage labour) determined by the existing mode of production. The state was the official representative of society as a whole, its embodiment in a visible corporation; but it was this only in so far as it was the state of that class which itself, in its epoch, represented society as a whole; in ancient times, the state of the slave-owning citizens; in the Middle Ages, of the feudal nobility; in our epoch, of the bourgeoisie. When ultimately it becomes really representative of society as a whole, it makes itself superfluous. As soon as there is no longer any class of society to be held in subjection; as soon as, along with class domination and the struggle for individual existence based on the former anarchy of production, the collisions and excesses arising from these have also been abolished, there is nothing more to be repressed which would make a special repressive force, a state, necessary. The first act in which the state really comes forward as the representative of society as a whole—the taking possession of the means of production in the name of society—is at the same time its last independent act as a state. The interference of the state power in social relations becomes superfluous in one sphere after another, and then ceases of itself. The government of persons is replaced by the administration of things and the direction of the processes of production. The state is not "abolished," *it withers away*. It is from this standpoint that we must appraise the phrase "free people's state"—both its justification at times for agitational purposes, and its ultimate scientific inadequacy—and also the demand of the so-called anarchists that the state should be abolished overnight.

Since the emergence in history of the capitalist mode of production, the taking over of all means of production by society has often been dreamed of by individuals as well as by whole sects, more or less vaguely and as an ideal of the future. But it could only become possible, it could only become a historical necessity, when the material conditions for its realisation had come into existence. Like every other social advance, it becomes realisable not through the perception that the existence of classes is in contradiction with justice, equality, etc., not through the mere will to abolish these classes, but through certain new economic conditions. The division of society into an exploiting and an exploited class, a ruling and an oppressed class, was the necessary outcome of the low development of production hitherto. So long as the sum of social labour yielded a product which only slightly exceeded what was necessary for the bare existence of all; so long, therefore, as all or almost all the time of the great majority of the members of society was absorbed in labour, so long was society necessarily divided into classes. Alongside of this great majority exclusively absorbed in labour there developed a class, freed from direct productive labour, which managed the general business of society: the direction of labour, affairs of state, justice, science, art, and so forth. It is therefore the law of the division of labour which lies at the root of the division into classes. But this does not mean that this division into classes was not established by violence and robbery, by deception and fraud, or that the ruling class, once in the saddle, has ever failed to strengthen its domination at the cost of the working class and to convert its social management into the exploitation of the masses.

But if, on these grounds, the division into classes has a certain historical justification, it has this only for a given period of time, for given social conditions. It was based on the insufficiency of production; it will be swept away by the full development of the modern productive forces. And in fact the abolition of social classes has as its presupposition a stage of historical development at which the existence not merely of some particular ruling class or other but of any ruling class at all, that is to say, of class difference itself, has become an anachronism, is out of date. It therefore presupposes that the development of production has reached a level at which the appropriation of means of production and of products, and with these, of political supremacy, the monopoly of education and intellectual leadership by a special class of society, has become not only superfluous but also economically, politically and intellectually a hindrance to development.

This point has now been reached. Their political and intellectual bankruptcy is hardly still a secret to the bourgeoisie themselves, and their economic bankruptcy recurs regularly every ten years. In each crisis society is smothered under the weight of its own productive forces and products of which it can make no use, and stands helpless in face of the absurd contradiction that the producers have nothing to consume because there are no consumers. The expanding force of the means of production bursts asunder the bonds imposed upon them by the capitalist mode of production. Their release from these bonds is the sole condition necessary for an unbroken and constantly more rapidly progressing development of the productive forces, and therewith of a practically limitless growth of production itself. Nor is this all. The appropriation by society of the means of production puts an end not only to the artificial restraints on production which exist today, but also to the positive waste and destruction of productive forces and products which is now the inevitable accompaniment of production and reaches its zenith in crises. Further, it sets free for society as a whole a mass of means of production and products by putting an end to the senseless luxury and extravagance of the present ruling class and its political representatives. The possibility of securing for every member of society, through social production, an existence which is not only fully sufficient from a material standpoint and becoming richer from day to day, but also guarantees to them the completely unrestricted development and exercise of their physical and mental faculties—this possibility now exists for the first time, but it *does exist.*

The seizure of the means of production by society puts an end to commodity production, and therewith to the domination of the product over the producer. Anarchy in social production is replaced by conscious organisation on a planned basis. The struggle for individual existence comes to an end. And at this point, in a certain sense, man finally cuts himself off from the animal world, leaves the conditions of animal existence behind him and enters conditions which are really human. The conditions of existence forming man's environment, which up to now have dominated man, at this point pass under the dominion and control of man, who now for the first time becomes the real conscious master of Nature, because and in so far as he has become master of his own social organisation. The laws of his own social activity, which have hitherto confronted him as external, dominating laws of Nature, will then be applied by man with complete understanding, and hence will be dominated by man. Men's own social organisation which has hitherto stood in opposition to them as if arbitrarily decreed by Nature and history, will then become the voluntary act of men themselves. The objective, external forces, which have hitherto dominated history, will then pass under the control of men themselves. It is only from this point that men, with full consciousness, will fashion their own history; it is only from this point that the social causes set in motion by men will have, predominantly and in constantly increasing measure, the effects willed by men. It is humanity's leap from the realm of necessity into the realm of freedom.

To carry through his world-emancipating act is the historical mission of the modern proletariat. And it is the task of scientific socialism, the theoretical expression of the proletarian movement, to establish the historical conditions and, with these, the nature of this act, and thus to bring to the consciousness of the now oppressed class the conditions and nature of the act which it is its destiny to accomplish.

Questions

1. What is the Marxist philosophy of history? How much of what Engels says is a description of what has happened, and how much is a prediction of what will happen?

2. Engels' statement, "The proletariat seizes the state power, and transforms the means of production in the first instance into state property" (page 694) is meant to be a prediction. What are the grounds for his prediction? How does one tell whether they are good grounds?

3. Could a Marxist ever be shown to be mistaken about the goal of history which he has discovered? Why or why not? How would a Marxist show that it is *impossible* for capitalists, for example, to take steps (not necessarily violent ones) to bring about a classless society?

4. How long should one wait for the historical goal predicted by a philosophy of history to be achieved? From the philosophies of history which you have read (the Kantian, page 667; and the Marxist) does it ever appear that enough time could have elapsed for one to say that a philosophy of history's prediction has been refuted because it has not come about? Why or why not?

5. Engels' first principle is, "Production, and with production the exchange of its products, is the basis of every social order." In the light of Mr. W. H. Walsh's examination of Kant's philosophy of history (page 679), how would you classify this principle? Is it (a) an a priori principle like "Every event has a cause," (b) a truth of fact, (c) a truth of reason, or (d) a regulative or heuristic principle?

How does your conclusion about its classification affect the way in which it can be used in the study of history? (The reader should subject other of the Marxist principles to a similar examination.)

4

History: The Class Struggle or Socialized Intelligence?

John Dewey
(1859-1952)

For the American philosopher John Dewey, the central philosophical problem was the nature of human intelligence. But he was interested in intelligence not simply as an object of study. He also wanted to foster the growth of intelligent human beings, and he wanted them to be able to use their intelligence freely for the benefit of society as a whole. Dewey's interest in intelligence bore practical fruit in his work in organizing and directing the Laboratory School at the University of Chicago. His interest in the education of children was lifelong, and his educational theories exert a major influence on American elementary and secondary schools today. Education, however, was only one of many social problems which interested Dewey. He believed that most social problems could be solved by the application of intelligence, and this belief led him to associate intelligence with democracy and liberalism. For he thought that only in a democratic society could intelligence be used freely to attack social problems, and a liberal democracy would be one in which the use of intelligence is unhindered by either private interest or social custom.

In this selection Dewey attacks the Marxist philosophy of history, which explains historical change as the result of class conflict; he argues that the course of history is better explained by the growing influence of the products of human intelligence, particularly science and technology. As a preface to his view of history, we offer two brief statements by Dewey about intelligence. In these statements he gives an account of intelligence and its value as a social asset, and he defines liberalism as the freeing of intelligence for the betterment of society.

Liberalism and Intelligence

I

We are always dependent upon the experience that has accumulated in the past, and yet there are always new forces coming in, new needs arising, that demand, if the new forces are to operate and the new needs to be satisfied, a reconstruction of the patterns of old experience. The old and the new have forever to be integrated with each other, so that the values of old experience may become the servants and instruments of new desires and aims. We are always possessed by habits and customs, and this fact signifies that we are always influenced by the inertia and the momentum of forces temporally outgrown but nevertheless still present with us as a part of our being. Human life gets set in patterns, institutional and moral. But change is also with us and demands the constant remaking of old habits and old ways of thinking, desiring, and acting. The effective ratio between the old and the stabilizing and the new and disturbing is very different at different times. Sometimes whole communities seem to be dominated by custom, and changes are produced only by irruptions and invasions from outside. Sometimes, as at present, change is so varied and accelerated that customs seem to be dissolving before our very eyes. But be the ratio little or great, there is always an adjustment to be made, and as soon as the need for it becomes conscious, liberalism has a function and a meaning. It is not that liberalism creates the need, but that the necessity for adjustment defines the office of liberalism.

For the only adjustment that does not have to be made over again, and perhaps even under more unfavorable circumstances than when it was first attempted, is that effected through intelligence as a method. In its large sense, this remaking of the old through union with the new is precisely what intelligence is. It is conversion of past experience into knowledge and projection of that knowledge in ideas and purposes that anticipate what may come to be in the future and that indicate how to realize what is desired. Every problem that arises, personal or collective, simple or complex, is solved only by selecting material from the store of knowledge amassed in past experience and by bringing into play habits already formed. But the knowledge and the habits have to be modified to meet the new conditions that have arisen. In collective problems, the habits that are involved are traditions and institutions. The standing danger is either that they will be acted upon implicitly, without reconstruction to meet new conditions, or else that there will be an impatient and blind rush forward, directed only by some dogma rigidly adhered to. The office of intelligence in every problem that either a person or a community meets is to effect a working connection between old habits, customs, institutions, beliefs, and new conditions. What I have called the mediating function of liberalism is all one with the work of intelligence. This fact is the root, whether it be consciously realized or not, of the emphasis placed by liberalism upon the role of freed intelligence as the method of directing social action.[1]

II

Liberalism has to assume the responsibility for making it clear that intelligence is a social asset and is clothed with a function as public as is its origin, in the concrete, in social coöperation. It was Comte who, in reaction against the purely individualistic ideas that seemed to him to underlie the French Revolution, said that in mathematics, physics, and astronomy there is no right of private conscience. If we remove the statement from the context of actual scientific procedure, it is dangerous because it is false. The individual inquirer has not only the right but the duty to criticize the ideas, theories, and "laws" that are current in science. But if we take the statement in the

[1] John Dewey, *Liberalism and Social Action,* Putnam, N. Y., 1935, pp. 49-50.

context of scientific method, it indicates that he carries on this criticism in virtue of a socially generated body of knowledge and by means of methods that are not of private origin and possession. He uses a method that retains public validity even when innovations are introduced in its use and application.

Henry George, speaking of ships that ply the ocean with a velocity of five or six hundred miles a day, remarked, "There is nothing whatever to show that the men who today build and navigate and use such ships are one whit superior in any physical or mental quality to their ancestors, whose best vessel was a coracle of wicker and hide. The enormous improvement which these ships show is not an improvement of human nature; it is an improvement of society—it is due to a wider and fuller union of individual efforts in accomplishment of common ends." This single instance, duly pondered, gives a better idea of the nature of intelligence and its social office than would a volume of abstract dissertation. Consider merely two of the factors that enter in and their social consequences. Consider what is involved in the production of steel, from the first use of fire and then the crude smelting of ore, to the processes that now effect the mass production of steel. Consider also the development of the power of guiding ships across trackless wastes from the day when they hugged the shore, steering by visible sun and stars, to the appliances that now enable a sure course to be taken. It would require a heavy tome to describe the advances in science, in mathematics, astronomy, physics, chemistry, that have made these two things possible. The record would be an account of a vast multitude of coöperative efforts, in which one individual uses the results provided for him by a countless number of other individuals, and uses them so as to add to the common and public store. A survey of such facts brings home the actual social character of intelligence as it actually develops and makes its way. Survey of the consequences upon the ways of living of individuals and upon the terms on which men associate together, due to the new method of transportation, would take us to the wheat farmer of the prairies, the cattle raiser of the plains, the cotton grower of the South; into a multitude of mills and factories, and to the counting-room of banks, and what would be seen in this country would be repeated in every country of the globe.[2]

In studying the following selection, the reader has a double task. He must find out both why Dewey believes the Marxist philosophy of history to be untenable, and what Dewey's own view of the course of history is. The success of Dewey's refutation of Marx turns on the acceptability of Dewey's own view of history; so the reader must assure himself that Dewey is safe from both the sort of logical criticism which Mr. W. H. Walsh levels against Kant's philosophy of history (page 679), and the sort of historical criticism which Dewey himself levels against the Marxist philosophy of history.

This selection is drawn from Chapter III, "Renascent Liberalism" in *Liberalism and Social Action*. The book was first published in 1935,

[2] John Dewey, *op. cit.,* pp. 67-69.

We hear a great deal in these days about class conflict. The past history of man is held up to us as almost exclusively a record of struggles between classes, ending in the victory of a class that had been oppressed and the transfer of power to it. It is difficult to avoid reading the past in terms of the contemporary scene. Indeed, fundamentally it is impossible to avoid this course. With a certain proviso, it is highly important that we are compelled to follow this path. For the past as past is gone, save for esthetic enjoyment and refreshment, while the present is with us. Knowledge of the past is significant only as it deepens and extends our understanding of the present. Yet there is a proviso. We must grasp the things that are most important in the present when we turn to the past and not allow ourselves to be misled by secondary phenomena no matter how intense and immediately urgent they are. Viewed from this standpoint, the rise of scientific method and of technology based upon it is the genuinely active force in producing the vast complex of changes the world is now undergoing, not the class struggle whose spirit and method are opposed to science. If we lay hold upon the causal force exercised by this embodiment of intelligence we shall know where to turn for the means of directing further change.

When I say that scientific method and technology have been the active force in producing the revolutionary transformations society is undergoing, I do not imply no other forces have been at work to arrest, deflect and corrupt their operation. Rather this fact is positively implied. At this point, indeed, is located the conflict that underlies the confusions and uncertainties of the present scene. The conflict is between institutions and habits originating in the prescientific and pretechnological age and the new forces generated by science and technology. The application of science, to a considerable degree, even its own growth, has been conditioned by the system to which the name of capitalism is given, a rough designation of a complex of political and legal arrangements centering about a particular mode of economic relations. . . .

Because of conditions that were set by the legal institutions and the moral ideas existing when the scientific and industrial revolutions came into being, the chief usufruct of the latter has been appropriated by a relatively small class. Industrial entrepreneurs have reaped out of all proportion to what they sowed. By obtaining private ownership of the means of production and exchange they deflected a considerable share of the results of increased productivity to their private pockets. This appropriation was not the fruit of criminal conspiracy or of sinister intent. It was sanctioned not only by legal institutions of age-long standing but by the entire prevailing moral code. The institution of private property long antedated feudal times. It is the institution with which men have lived, with few exceptions, since the dawn of civilization. Its existence has deeply impressed itself upon mankind's moral conceptions. Moreover, the new industrial forces tended to break down many of the rigid class barriers that had been in force, and to give to millions a new outlook and inspire a new hope; especially in this country with no feudal background and no fixed class system.

Since the legal institutions and the patterns of mind characteristic of ages of civilization still endure, there exists the conflict that brings confusion into every phase of present life. The problem of bringing into being a new social orientation and organization is, when reduced to its ultimates, the problem of using the new resources of production, made possible by the advance of physical science, for social ends, for what Bentham called the greatest good of the greatest number. Institutional relationships fixed in the prescientific age stand in the way of accomplishing this great transformation. Lag in mental and moral patterns provides the bulwark of the older institutions; in expressing the past they still express present beliefs, outlooks and purposes. Here is the place where the problem of liberalism centers today.

The argument drawn from past history that radical change must be effected by means of class struggle, culminating in open war, fails to discriminate between the two forces, one active, the other resistant and deflecting, that have produced the social scene in which we live. The active force is, as I have said, scientific method and technological application. The opposite force is that of older institutions and the habits that have grown up around them. Instead of discrimination between forces and distribution of their consequences, we find the two things lumped together. The compound is labeled the capitalistic or the bourgeois class, and to this class as a class is imputed all the important features of present industrialized society—much as the defenders of the régime of economic liberty exercised for private property are accustomed to attribute every improvement made in the last century and a half to the same capitalistic régime. Thus in orthodox communist literature, from the Communist Manifesto of 1848 to the present day, we are told that the bourgeoisie, the name for a distinctive class, has done this and that. It has, so it is said, given a cosmopolitan character to production and consumption; has destroyed the national basis of industry; has agglomerated population in urban centers; has transferred power from the country to the city, in the process of creating colossal productive force, its chief achievement. In addition, it has created crises of ever renewed intensity; has created imperialism of a new type in frantic effort to control raw materials and markets. Finally, it has created a new class, the proletariat, and has created it as a class having a common interest opposed to that of the bourgeoisie, and is giving an irresistible stimulus to its organization, first as a class and then as a political power. According to the economic version of the Hegelian dialectic, the bourgeois class is thus creating its own complete and polar opposite, and this in time will end the old power and rule. The class struggle of veiled civil war will finally burst into open revolution and the result will be either the common ruin of the contending parties or a revolutionary reconstitution of society at large through a transfer of power from one class to another.

The position thus sketched unites vast sweep with great simplicity. I am concerned with it here only as far as it emphasizes the idea of a struggle between classes, culminating in open and violent warfare as being the method for production of radical social change. For, be it noted, the issue is not whether some amount of violence will accompany the effectuation of radical change of institutions. The question is whether force or intelligence is to be the method upon which we consistently rely and to whose promotion we devote our energies. Insistence that the use of violent force is *inevitable* limits the use of available intelligence, for wherever the inevitable reigns intelligence cannot be used. Commitment to inevitability is always the fruit of dogma; intelligence does not pretend to *know* save as a result of experimentation, the opposite of preconceived dogma. Moreover, acceptance in advance of the inevitability of violence tends to produce the use of violence in cases where peaceful methods might otherwise avail. The curious fact is that while it is generally admitted that this and that particular social problem, say of the family, or railroads or banking, must be solved, if at all, by the method of intelligence, yet there is supposed to be some one all-inclusive social problem which can be solved only by the use of violence. This fact would be inexplicable were it not a conclusion from dogma as its premise.

It is frequently asserted that the method of experimental intelligence can be applied to physical facts because physical nature does not present conflicts of class interests, while it is inapplicable to society because the latter is so deeply marked by incompatible interests. It is then assumed that the "experimentalist" is one who has chosen to ignore the uncomfortable fact of conflicting interests. Of course, there *are* conflicting interests; otherwise there would be no social problems. The problem under discussion is precisely *how* conflicting claims are to be settled in the interest of the widest possible contribution to the interests of all—or at least of the great majority. The method of democracy—inasfar as it is that of organized intelligence—is to bring these conflicts out into the open where their special claims can be seen and appraised, where they can be discussed and judged in the light of more inclusive interests than are represented by either of them separately. There is, for example, a clash of interests between munition manufacturers and most of the rest of the population. The more the respective claims of the two are publicly and scientifically weighed, the more likely it is that the public interest will be disclosed and be made effective. There is an undoubted objective clash of interests between finance-capitalism that controls the means of production and whose profit is served by maintaining relative scarcity, and idle workers and hungry consumers. But what generates violent strife is failure to bring the conflict into the light of intelligence where the conflicting interests can be adjudicated in behalf of the interest of the great majority. Those most committed to the dogma of inevitable force recognize the need for intelligently discovering and expressing the dominant social interest up to a certain point and then draw back. The "experimentalist" is one who would see to it that the method depended upon by all in some degree in every democratic community be followed through to completion.

In spite of the existence of class conflicts, amounting at times to veiled civil war, any one habituated to the use of the method of science will view with considerable suspicion the erection of actual human beings into fixed entities called classes, having no overlapping interests and so internally unified and externally separated that they are made the protagonists of history—itself hypothetical. Such an idea of classes is a survival of a rigid logic that once prevailed in the sciences of nature, but that no longer has any place there. This conversion of abstractions into entities smells more of a dialectic of concepts than of a realistic examination of facts, even though it makes more of an emotional appeal to many than do the results of the latter. To say that all past historic social progress has been the result of coöperation and not of conflict would be also an exaggeration. But exaggeration against exaggeration, it is the more reasonable of the two. And it is no exaggeration to say that the measure of civilization is the degree in which the method of coöperative intelligence replaces the method of brute conflict.

But the point I am especially concerned with just here is the indiscriminate lumping together as a single force of two different things—the results of scientific technology and of a legal system of property relations. It is science and technology that have had the revolutionary social effect while the legal system has been the relatively static element. According to the Marxians themselves, the economic foundations of society consist of two things, the forces of production on one side and, on the other side, the social relations of production, that is, the legal property system under which the former operates. The latter lags behind, and "revolutions" are produced by the power of the forces of production to change the system of institutional relations. But what are the modern forces of production save those of scientific technology? And what is scientific technology save a large-scale demonstration of organized intelligence in action?

It is quite true that what is happening socially is the result of the combination of the two factors, one dynamic, the other relatively static. If we choose to call the combination by the name of capitalism, then it is true, or a truism, that capitalism is the "cause" of all the important social changes that have occurred—an argument that the representatives of capitalism are eager to put forward whenever the increase of productivity is in question. But if we want to *understand,* and not just to paste labels, unfavorable or favorable as the case may be, we shall certainly begin and end with discrimination. Colossal increase in productivity, the bringing of men together in cities and large factories, the elimination of distance, the accumulation of capital, fixed and liquid—these things would have come about, at a certain stage, no matter what the established institutional system. They are the consequence of the new means of technological production. Certain other things have happened because of inherited institutions and the habits of belief and character that accompany and support them. If we begin at this point, we shall see that the release of productivity is the product of coöperatively organized intelligence, and shall also see that the institutional framework is precisely that which is not subjected as yet, in any considerable measure, to the impact of inventive and constructive intelligence. That coercion and oppression on a large scale exist, no honest person can deny. But these things are not the product of science and technology but of the perpetuation of old institutions and patterns untouched by scientific method. The inference to be drawn is clear.

The argument, drawn from history, that great social changes have been effected only by violent means, needs considerable qualification, in view of the vast scope of changes that are taking place without the use of violence. But even if it be admitted to hold of the past, the conclusion that violence is the method now to be depended upon does not follow—unless one is committed to a dogmatic philosophy of history. The radical who insists that the future method of change must be like that of the past has much in common with the hidebound reactionary who holds to the past as an ultimate fact. Both overlook the *fact that history in being a process of change generates change not only in details but also in the method of directing social change*. It is true that the social order is largely conditioned by the use of coercive force, bursting at times into open violence. But what is also true is that mankind now has in its possession a new method, that of coöperative and experimental science which expresses the method of intelligence. I should be meeting dogmatism with dogmatism if I asserted that the existence of this historically new factor completely invalidates all arguments drawn from the effect of force in the past. But it is within the bounds of reason to assert that the presence of this social factor demands that the present situation be analyzed on its own terms, and not be rigidly subsumed under fixed conceptions drawn from the past.

Any analysis made in terms of the present situation will not fail to note one fact that militates powerfully against arguments drawn from past use of violence. Modern warfare is destructive beyond anything known in older times. This increased destructiveness is due primarily, of course, to the fact that science has raised to a new pitch of destructive power all the agencies of armed hostility. But it is also due to the much greater interdependence of all the elements of society. The bonds that hold modern communities and states together are as delicate as they are numerous. The self-sufficiency and independence of a local community, characteristic of more primitive societies, have disappeared in every highly industrialized country. The gulf that once separated the civilian population from the military has virtually gone. War involves paralysis of all normal social activities, and not merely the meeting of armed forces in the field. The Communist Manifesto presented two alternatives: *either* the revolutionary change and transfer of power to the proletariat, *or* the common ruin of the contending parties. Today, the civil war that would be adequate to effect transfer of power and a reconstitution of society at large, as understood by official Communists, would seem to present but one possible consequence: the ruin of all parties and the destruction of civilized life. This fact alone is enough to lead us to consider the potentialities of the method of intelligence.

The argument for putting chief dependence upon violence as the method of effecting radical change is, moreover, usually put in a way that proves altogether too much for its own case. It is said that the dominant economic class has all the agencies of power in its hands, directly, the army, militia and police; indirectly, the courts, schools, press and radio. I shall not stop to analyze this statement. But if one admits it to be valid, the conclusion to be drawn is surely the folly of resorting to a use of force against force that is so well intrenched. The positive conclusion that emerges is that conditions that would promise success in the case of use of force are such as to make possible great change without any great recourse to such a method.[1]

Those who uphold the necessity of dependence upon violence usually much oversimplify the case by setting up a disjunction they regard as self-evident. They say that the sole alternative is putting our trust in parliamentary procedures as they now exist. This isolation of lawmaking from other social forces and agencies that are constantly operative is wholly unrealistic. Legislatures and congresses do not exist in a vacuum—not even the judges on the bench live in completely secluded soundproof chambers. The assumption that it is possible for the constitution and activities of lawmaking bodies to persist unchanged while society itself is undergoing great change is an exercise in verbal formal logic.

It is true that in this country, because of the interpretations made by courts of a written constitution, our political institutions are unusually inflexible. It is also true, as well as even more important (because it is a factor in causing this rigidity) that our institutions, democratic in form, tend to favor in substance a privileged plutocracy. Nevertheless, it is sheer defeatism to assume in advance of actual trial that democratic political institutions are incapable either of further development or of constructive social application. Even as they now exist, the forms of representative government are potentially capable of expressing the public will when that assumes anything like unification. And there is nothing inherent in them that forbids their supplementation by political agencies that represent definitely economic social interests, like those of producers and consumers.

The final argument in behalf of the use of intelligence is that as are the means used so are the actual ends achieved—that is, the consequences. I know of no greater fallacy than the claim of those who hold to the dogma of the necessity of brute force that this use will be the method of calling genuine democracy into existence—of which they profess themselves the simon-pure adherents. It requires an unusually credulous faith in the Hegelian dialectic of opposites to think that all of a sudden the use of force by a class will be

---

[1] It should be noted that Marx himself was not completely committed to the dogma of the inevitability of force as the means of effecting revolutionary changes in the system of "social relations." For at one time he contemplated that the change might occur in Great Britain and the United States, and possibly in Holland, by peaceful means.

transmuted into a democratic classless society. Force breeds counterforce; the Newtonian law of action and reaction still holds in physics, and violence is physical. To profess democracy as an ultimate ideal and the suppression of democracy as a means to the ideal may be possible in a country that has never known even rudimentary democracy, but when professed in a country that has anything of a genuine democratic spirit in its traditions, it signifies desire for possession and retention of power by a class, whether that class be called Fascist or Proletarian. . . .

Questions

1. How does Dewey's statement of the communist (Marxist) philosophy of history compare with Engels' statement of the Marxist philosophy of history? If there are any differences, how do you account for them?

2. How does Dewey criticize the communist view of the "bourgeois class" as a causal factor in history? According to Dewey, what important elements in history have communists failed to notice in constructing their philosophy of history? How might a communist reply to Dewey?

3. What is Dewey's own view of the course of history? Could he be said to have a philosophy of history? Why or why not?

4. How do you think that a communist might criticize Dewey's view of the course of history? For instance, could a communist maintain successfully that intelligence, as Dewey understands it, can only be socially effective when it is exercised by the working class (proletariat)? Why or why not?

5. What is the logical status of Dewey's principle that ". . . Scientific method and technology have been the active force in producing the revolutionary transformations society is undergoing." In the light of Mr. W. H. Walsh's examination of Kant's philosophy of history (page 679), would you classify the above principle as (a) an a priori principle like "Every event has a cause," (b) a truth of fact, (c) a truth of reason, or (d) a regulative or heuristic principle?

How does your conclusion about its classification affect the way in which it can be used in the study of history?

6. It has been said that history has no purpose; only human beings have purposes. Does this point of view make Marxist (and Kantian) philosophy of history impossible? Why or why not? How does Dewey's account of the course of history fare when judged from this point of view?

Suggested Further Reading | *Philosophies of History*

Beard, Charles A., and Mary R. Beard, *The American Spirit, A Study of the Idea of Civilization in the United States,* Macmillan, N. Y., 1942.

Buckle, Henry T., *History of Civilization in England,* Vol. 1, 3 vols., 1857-1861; especially Chaps. I-V.

Hegel, G. W. F., *The Philosophy of History,* rev. ed., Colonial Press, N. Y., 1900.

Lenin, V. I., *Selected Works,* Vol. 11, *The Theoretical Principles of Marxism,* International Publishers, N. Y., 1935-1938.

———, *State and Revolution,* Martin Lawrence, Ltd., London, 1933.

Marx, Karl, *Communist Manifesto,* H. Regnery Co., Chicago, 1955.

Toynbee, Arnold J., *A Study of History,* abridgement of Vols. 1-10 by D. C. Somervell, Oxford University Press, N. Y., 1947-1957.

| *Critical Studies*

Berlin, Isaiah, *Historical Inevitability,* Oxford University Press, N. Y., 1954.

———, *Karl Marx, His Life and Environment,* 2nd ed., Oxford University Press, N. Y., 1948.

Cohen, Morris R., *Meaning of Human History,* Open Court, La Salle, Ill., 1947.

Collingwood, R. G., *The Idea of History,* Oxford University Press, N. Y., 1946.

Gardiner, Patrick, *The Nature of Historical Explanation,* Oxford University Press, N. Y., 1952.

Löwith, Karl, *Meaning in History, The Theological Implications of the Philosophy of History,* University of Chicago Press, Chicago, 1949.

Popper, K. R., *The Open Society and Its Enemies,* rev. ed., Princeton University Press, Princeton, 1955.

White, Morton, *Social Thought in America, The Revolt Against Formalism,* Viking, N. Y., 1949.

Index